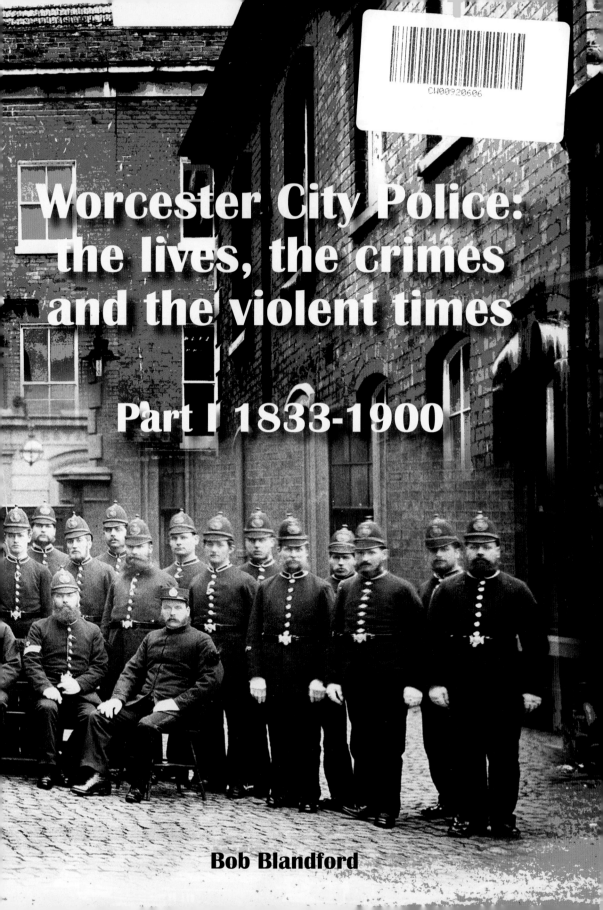

# Worcester City Police: the lives, the crimes and the violent times

## Part I 1833-1900

**Bob Blandford**

**The Whole Picture Publishing Company Ltd.,
Addison Road, Beechwood Park, Worcester WR3 8EA**

© 2016 Bob Blandford and The Whole Picture Publishing Company Ltd
*http://www.the-whole-picture-publishing.co.uk*

ISBN 978-0-9927418-2-2

9 780992 741822 >

Written, produced and designed by Bob Blandford and published by
The Whole Picture Publishing Company Limited.
All rights reserved

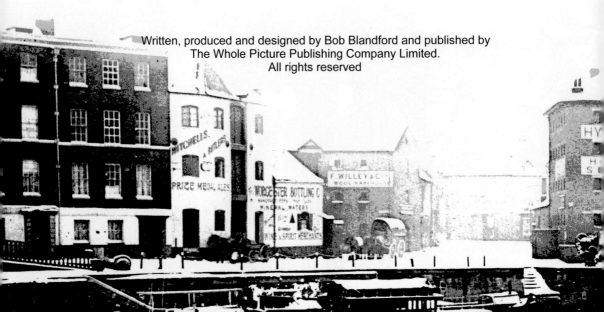

# The
# SPIKE

## The story of Worcester City Police

### Bob Blandford

FIRKINS &COMP

MERCHANTS

OFFICES
9 FORECATES SEVERN IRON WAREHOUSE

SAUCE

# Contents

**Note:** *Images of original documents used throughout this book are from the Worcester City Collection (b496.5 BA9630) held by Worcestershire Archive and Archaeology Service at the Hive, and reproduced with the kind permission of Worcester City Council and WAAS.  Grateful thanks to both authorities and their staff*

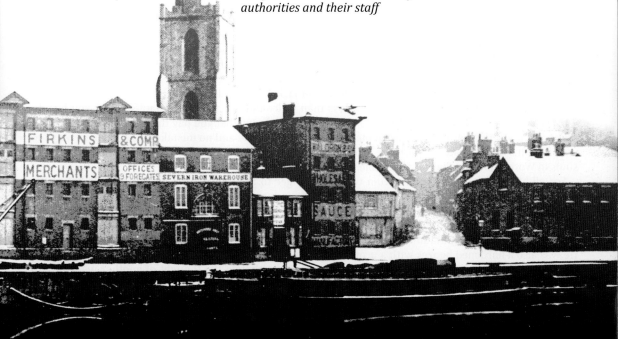

# 1:
# Butcher Tom

## Dateline: Saturday, March 2nd 1833

Butcher Tom had been caught. Again.

Served him right for getting drunk in the Woolpack and bragging about his latest criminal jaunt that had netted him and his thieving mate Martin Smith a dozen pairs of wooden clogs and boots, the rightful property of down-to-earth, honest-to-goodness cobbler and bootmaker William Brooks of nearby Broad Street. Of all the miserable luck...

Martin Smith had been seen coming out of the shop by a snooping kid who'd followed him through Dolday and then run off to alert one of the Watchmen. Sadly for them, *this* Watchman had taken notice: any other day they'd have got away with it.

Butcher Tom, not long turned 20, had been christened Thomas Evans, but had won his nickname, alongside something of a hard-case reputation in the city, for a catalogue of violence-fuelled petty thefts and minor disorders which had seen him hauled before the justices several times already and had earned him more than one back-breaking spell in the city gaol pummelling rocks into a fine powder. He'd never questioned *why*, or even wondered *if,* the punishment fitted the crime, nor did he give a toss anyway: he just did his bit regardless, just the same as every man-jack inmate did.

When you're a guest at William Griffiths' less than welcoming Friar Street establishment, you just do what you're told to do until ordered not to – the alternative being that you pay the penalty with your own blood and tears. Guv'nor Griffiths 'isself made certain-sure of that, and no mistake – as Tom knew only too well from his own sweated experience, verified daily in the talk of the city's 168 pubs, one for every 95 souls in Worcester. Now he was in trouble. Again.

For all his tender years, Butcher Tom was no stranger to the unforgiving rat-ridden cells below the Court-room in the Guildhall for this, the first Assizes session of that year of our Lord 1833, Mr Sergeant Ludlow presiding upstairs in judicial splendour, awaiting the opportunity to decide his, as well as several others', fate in the name of their Most Gracious Majesty, King William IV.

Fatally for Tom, his reputation was as a show-off and, in the parlance of the day, 'a very bad character'. He was also a hardened boozer with a propensity for noisy outbursts when in drink – 'carousings', as the *Worcester Herald* reported on the occasion of his arrest – although the thought of another week or two breaking rocks held no particular terror for him.

He was young and fit – too fit for his own good sometimes – and he'd done it before and survived.

*First blood for the New Police...*
*The Journal (foreground) got it right. The Herald (inset) didn't!*

... But for this caution, he no doubt would have been robbed.

NIGHTLY PATROL.—About 120 of the most respectable inhabitants of All Saints' parish have enrolled themselves as a nightly patrol. They commenced patrolling on Wednesday night, and the good effects of their public-spirited conduct have already become manifest. About half-past nine on the first night, as the party on duty were going their rounds, they found a female engaged in a scuffle with a man whom she had hold of, while two other men were endeavouring to disengage him from her grasp; as soon as the patrol came up, the three men made off, but one named Edward Stephens was captured. As the woman said she had been robbed, Stephens was detained until Monday, but she did not appear, and he was consequently discharged.—On Thursday night the patrol, with the watchmen, captured two notorious characters, named Martin Smith and Thomas Evans, the latter better known by the nickname of "Butcher Tom." On Friday morning they were taken before the Magistrates, … Smith charged with stealing, … clogs, &c. stolen from the shop of Mr. … d-street; which robbery we recently … to understand that the patrol … to the state of … against … company. … such as are foun… every one … This alone would … every … acquainted with pol… to the assured outrage and robber… of … at unseasonable ho… even- the patrol is for four … continue during ing, when they are … believe that the remainder of the night … the impression some thieves have already left … their calling an that the active measures now ta… unprofitable one.

In our last page we have inserted a …

BEER SHOP.—In our last page …

… from her … *imprisonment.*
… stealing three pieces of … furniture, from the house of … *months' imprisonment.*
… EVANS, Thomas, alias *Butcher Bob,* … clogs and boots from the shop of Mr. … *Seven years' transportation.* Both … characters.
…victed of having stolen gloves in h… to Mr. P. Birch.—*Seven years'* … was another indictment against him …
…ER, alias BASSETT, 15, con… a bundle containing … len.—*Eight m…*

On the other hand, the possibility of a month or two on The Crank, the formidable giant treadmill housed in the gaunt stockade not known for nothing as The Punishment House and demanding the forced labours of the unfortunates sentenced to a term of 'hard', filled him with marginally more dread.

The prospect of joining those damned souls who had no choice but to keep on treading in silence for up to ten Godforsaken hours a day, six days a week – the Sabbath being given over to prayer and solitary reflection even for the wicked – was bad, but he'd survive it despite the terrifying tales he'd heard... eighteen men and women, twelve on the wheel, six off, each waiting their time to climb on in relay at the sound of the gaoler's whistle... the wheel revolving twice in a minute, every miserable soul ordered to 24 minutes' hard graft before the whistle orders him or her off in his/her turn, and there to gain his/her breath for just two sweated minutes before stepping on again.

The expectation at Worcester was some 13,000 treads in ten hours or God help them.

Tom had so far been spared the horrors of 'the everlasting staircase', but he *had* seen the scars some of the toughened old prison-house lags still bore after they'd become so exhausted they simply couldn't summon the energy to take one more step and just fell off, permitting the wheel to take its own unforgiving revenge. Solid oak, The Crank was no respecter of those whose back-breaking labours kept it in perpetually revolving motion: bones shattered and legs lost, hacked off to halt the spread of deadly infection were by no means rare, nor were those who'd been turned half-mad by the sound of creaking timbers or the piercing shrill of a whistle. Some of the injuries he'd seen had made him think that the lucky ones were those that had been struck with the apoplexy and died where they fell, in full sight of the others they'd earlier sweated alongside on the wheel.

But that was for the old 'uns, not for a fine, fit Worcester lad like him. He'd do his turn, walk away and then get on with his life – which, up to then had consisted of a litany of everyday hassles that had won him his cock o' the town reputation that he wore with pride.

So the last caper was bigger than the others in his past? No matter: his fate couldn't be anywhere near so final as that that had befallen two highway robbers sharing a surname but actually unrelated – James and Joseph Carter, hanged side-by-side at the County Gaol in Salt Lane just three days earlier, and still the major topic of conversation in Worcester's drinking houses and snatched whispers in the Guv'nor's Friar Street bridewell.

Even so, he was deeply conscious that at that moment, his prospects

*The City Gaol, house of correction 1724 - 1867. After it closed, the buildings were used to house 35 deserving poor and were later demolished by their new owner William Laslett to make way for the Almshouses that to this day still carry his name*

*(Top, right)*
*Worcester Herald March 1833: getting it wrong!*

for the foreseeable future were not especially blessed, and while he trusted that the Carters' capital fate was not to be the realistic outcome of his and Martin Smith's latest spree – after all, Marty Smith was the thief, he was only there on account of receiving the pitiful haul, although in the eyes of the justices, the offences were one and the same – the next worst fate would be the loss of the next ten or fourteen years sacrificed in a penal colony felling trees and making roads in the far-off New World, wherever that was.

But then, that wouldn't be a fair trade-off for the latest escapade, would it...? *Would it?* Where would be the justice in that? No, even at its most unimaginable worst it'd be a month – perhaps two if the Beak was in a bad mood – on the Wheel, and there'd be an end to it.

He and Martin the habitual thief had spent the freezing night in the old familiar territory of the City Gaol, kicked awake with no brek'ast and trundled through the streets at dawn, out of the sight of decent folks and shackled together with five other adult males, a 15-year old lad named Henry Jones already destined for a

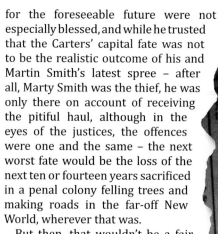

...will have to work for others one of... ...eight years will be one series of the most labori... ...and without the slightest intermission. The punish... ...ment is too little for you, but it is the only one left to me after your lives are spared." His Lordship then directed that the three prisoners should be *transported for life.*

### CITY CALENDAR.

BEFORE MR. SERGEANT LUDLOW.

NEAL, Charles, aged 50, convicted of stealing a parcel from the Kington and Worcester Mail Coach, containing a 5*l.* note and some papers, the property of Mr. T. Devereux, Attorney, Bromyard.—There was another indictment against him.— Neal was the driver of the coach from which the parcel was stolen.—*Seven years' transportation.*

BERRY, Benjamin, 20, convicted of stealing a till from the shop of Mrs. Bradford, Cross—*seven year's transportation.* —Berry has long been known as a bad character.

MILLER, James, 30, convicted of stealing two haunches of mutton and a piece of beef, from the shop of Mr. Payne, Bridge-street.—*Twelve months' imprisonment.*

EVANS, Mary, 29, for stealing money from her master, Jas. Taylor, of Losemore,—*Six months' imprisonment.*

WILLIS, John, 22, convicted of stealing three pieces of drugget and a piece of check furniture, from the house of Mr. Pierpoint.—*Nine months' imprisonment.*

SMITH, Martin, 20, and EVANS, Thomas, alias *Butcher Bob,* 20, convicted of stealing clogs and boots from the shop of Mr. Brooks, Broad-street.—*Seven years' transportation.* Both the prisoners are very bad characters.

STAPLES, John, 31, convicted of having stolen gloves in his possession, belonging to Mr. P. Birch.—*Seven years' transportation.*—There was another indictment against him for the same offence.

JONES, Henry, alias FISHER, alias BASSETT, 15, convicted of stealing, in the Market House, a bundle containing gloves and money, the property of Eliz. Allen.—*Eight months' imprisonment.*

### NISI PRIUS COURT.

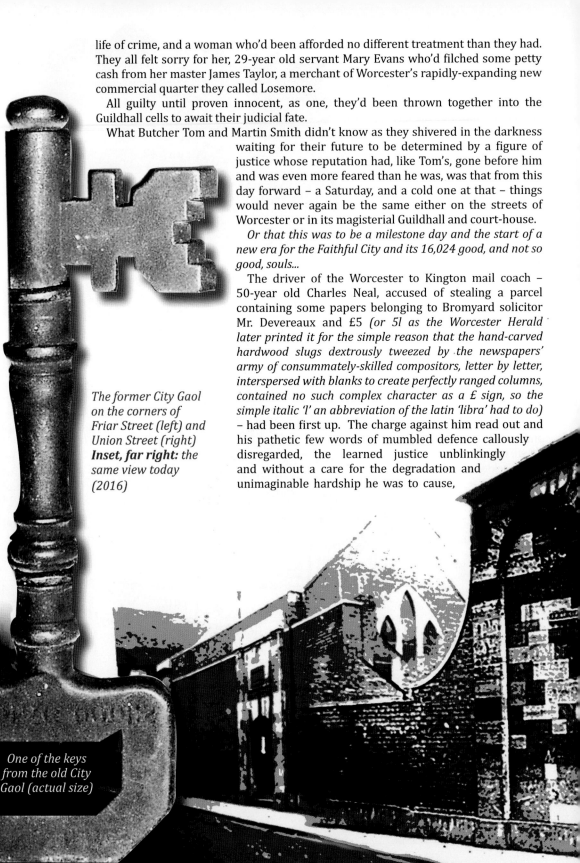

life of crime, and a woman who'd been afforded no different treatment than they had. They all felt sorry for her, 29-year old servant Mary Evans who'd filched some petty cash from her master James Taylor, a merchant of Worcester's rapidly-expanding new commercial quarter they called Losemore.

All guilty until proven innocent, as one, they'd been thrown together into the Guildhall cells to await their judicial fate.

What Butcher Tom and Martin Smith didn't know as they shivered in the darkness waiting for their future to be determined by a figure of justice whose reputation had, like Tom's, gone before him and was even more feared than he was, was that from this day forward – a Saturday, and a cold one at that – things would never again be the same either on the streets of Worcester or in its magisterial Guildhall and court-house.

*Or that this was to be a milestone day and the start of a new era for the Faithful City and its 16,024 good, and not so good, souls...*

The driver of the Worcester to Kington mail coach – 50-year old Charles Neal, accused of stealing a parcel containing some papers belonging to Bromyard solicitor Mr. Devereaux and £5 *(or 5l as the Worcester Herald later printed it for the simple reason that the hand-carved hardwood slugs dextrously tweezed by the newspapers' army of consummately-skilled compositors, letter by letter, interspersed with blanks to create perfectly ranged columns, contained no such complex character as a £ sign, so the simple italic 'l' an abbreviation of the latin 'libra' had to do)* – had been first up. The charge against him read out and his pathetic few words of mumbled defence callously disregarded, the learned justice unblinkingly and without a care for the degradation and unimaginable hardship he was to cause,

*The former City Gaol on the corners of Friar Street (left) and Union Street (right)* **Inset, far right:** *the same view today (2016)*

*One of the keys from the old City Gaol (actual size)*

sent him down with the almost unbelievably vicious sentence of seven years' transportation to the penal colony in the new world of Australia.

Called next was a contemporary of Tom's and Martin's, 20-year old Benjamin Berry, accused of stealing a till from the shop of Mrs Bradford on the Cross. Devoid of any deep deliberation save a look at his watch, Mr. Sergeant Ludlow passed the same sentence – seven years' transportation to the same New South Wales colony, duly entered by court clerk Henry Mears in the Sentence Log.

30-year old James Miller was next called, hauled up the well-trod steps to the hushed court, the clanking of his leg irons and wrist restraints adding an audible backdrop to the buzz of the hallowed court-room. His crime? Filching two haunches of mutton and a piece of beef from Mr Payne's shop in Bridge Street. Sentence: twelve months' 'hard'.

The Crank was to have one more body to keep it in perpetual motion. Or to break.

A weeping Mary Evans of Losemore was called next. Sentence: six months' imprisonment at Guv'nor Griffiths' lodging-house. She wept even louder when the full weight of her sentence and the loss of half a year's liberty sank in.

John Willis aged 22 was the fifth to feel the ire of Mr Sergeant Ludlow that cold March morning. His fate? Nine months' imprisonment for stealing three pieces of drugget floor covering and a piece of check furniture. That they were from the Sansome Walk house of well-respected and almost legendary Worcester solicitor and surgeon Richard Pierpoint served only to add an extra dimension to the severity of the sentence.

John Staples aged 31, a known thug already with an extensive criminal record, now accused of stealing a pair of gloves, the rightful property of Mr Philip Birch Esq., was next sentenced. His fate? Another one sentenced that day to seven years' hard labour digging ditches and felling trees in the wild, far-off colonies with no guarantee of a return to hearth and home. Like, ever.

Cocky 15 year-old Henry Jones, alias Henry Fisher, alias Henry Bassett was next and if he hadn't already got the makings of a hardened criminal, the events of the next few minutes and the sentence of eight months in the close enforced association of three dozen of Worcester's leering scum and low-life in the not so tender mercies of the Guv'nor would ensure that he very quickly would.

Finally, it was Butcher Tom's and Martin Smith's turn. After the pitch-black of the cell, the frozen daylight that violated the courtroom was blinding. Sitting in lofty majesty and eyeing them with evident distaste, Mr. Sergeant Ludlow relished the fact that these two thugs were the last of an event-filled day that, thanks to him, had already seen the lives of seven specimens of low-life and criminality from Worcester's dark underbelly shattered – with providence, beyond repair.

Breaking two more would be of not the slightest hardship to him, and the sooner the better.

Justice not only had to be done, but also to be seen to be done, and Mr. Sergeant Ludlow was not the man to be found soft or lacking on either score.

**But there was something else too...**

Eyeing the proceedings from the well of the court were four unusually intent men, increasingly familiar around town of late, but never before seen together, least of all in somewhere quite so public as the Guildhall. The four were **Henry Sharpe, George Williams, James Douglas** and **John Leary**.

Up to a few days earlier there had been a fifth, named **Michael Fannon**, but despite repeated warnings, he'd been stripped of his duties and sent on his way for drunkenness. So, for the time being, they were a depleted band – although Butcher Tom was already better acquainted with them than he might have liked, for these were the first officers of the City's 'new' police force and the day's courtroom proceedings were the first wholly devoted to dealing with cases brought by this new and so far untried body of law enforcers.

The fall-out from the unfortunate Fannon affair had cast a dark cloud over the fledgling police force that was still only a matter of weeks old, so this day was almost as grand a trial for the remaining four, and none more so than their leader, 32-year old Nottinghamshire ex-soldier and ex-London copper and hard-man, Inspector **Henry Sharpe**.

It's likely that the four officials exchanged brief and no doubt expectant glances with Butcher Tom and Martin Smith, shackled together in the dock, flanked by two of the mayor's most determined no-nonsense officers and blinking against the thin March daylight as they awaited the passing of their sentences.

The double verdict came despite virtually unheard pleas of mitigation – and when it did, it was every bit as bad as it could possibly be, just as it had been with several others that morning: *immediate removal to a prison hulk in Woolwich to await the next convict transportation to Australia for a term of hard labour of no less than seven long, long years.*

**Seven years' transportation!**

It hit them like a bolt of lightning: first shock, then numbness as the full dread of their sentences sunk in... in short, that the next seven miserable years of their lives were already accounted for, promised nothing but strain, pain, grief and hopelessness, and for all they would be likely to benefit from them, might just as well be written-off.

*Only one way in and one way out of the cells under the Guildhall – and this is it... This is where Butcher Tom and Martin Smith spent the moments before and immediately after each being sentenced to seven years' toiling in a penal colony in New South Wales*

Worse... that by the time they'd again be able to walk anywhere without the shackle of a restraining chain or the risk of a sharp stick against their backs – or just to walk out into the sunshiny air or regain any form of free-spirit liberty and run, jump or roll-over in the grass – they'd both be broken, and perhaps prematurely old, Tom a man of twenty-seven, probably nearer thirty by the time he'd see England and the flower of its maidenhood again.

No, a whole year on the wheel would be preferable, but....

*It was too late.  His fate was sealed.*

By contrast, across the court-room, the smiles on the hardened faces of their accusers and captors already indicated in no uncertain terms that, just as they'd planned, the justices were on their side, that they personally were off the rack at least for the time being, and that from here on in they were to be as one in the crackdown of crime in Worcester where the previous few years had witnessed an unparalleled increase in lawlessness and behaviour most unbecoming the otherwise pretty and genteel Faithful City.

**Henry Sharpe** in particular had good reason to feel pleased. 1833 had not begun well, but if the new force he headed was ever going to be accepted – and it was far from a foregone conclusion that it would, as he and his three remaining co-collaborators were only too well aware – it was going to have to prove its worth and then be judged on its own merits.  As things stood, it was going to be a tall order.  But at least, the day's proceedings thus far had afforded a promising start to the lately-withering prospect of survival.

With Butcher Tom and Martin Smith, silent and stunned into disbelief, now dragged back down to the cell to face their unpleasant fate and the day's proceedings effectively concluded, it had been a rewarding day for the New Police of Worcester City – which, if the gentlemen of the press, notably the *Worcester Herald* and the *Worcester Journal*, did their job properly, would present it as having scored its first batch of victories in the city's long-awaited, if largely impotent fight-back against the massed legions of outrage, crime and escalating disorder.

The press did not materially fail them. Despite the *Herald*'s reporter uncharacteristically mis-transcribing his notes and referring to Butcher Tom as Butcher *Bob* – an error not repeated by the longer-established, although not so well-subscribed *Journal* – by the time the report of the day's judicial proceedings had been brought before Worcester's reading public the following Thursday for *Journal* readers, two days later for the *Herald*'s subscribers, there was no doubt about it: via the New Police, Mayor John Pearkes Lavender and his Commissioners and the entire town Corporation had publicly declared war on the lawless and the growing ranks of persistent nuisances, drunks, thugs, petty thieves, rustlers, chancers, con-artists, hard-cases, mobsters, plunderers, hassle-mongers, pimps, prostitutes and the out-and-out criminal classes that had been dragging the City's fair name through the murkiest mire for just too long.

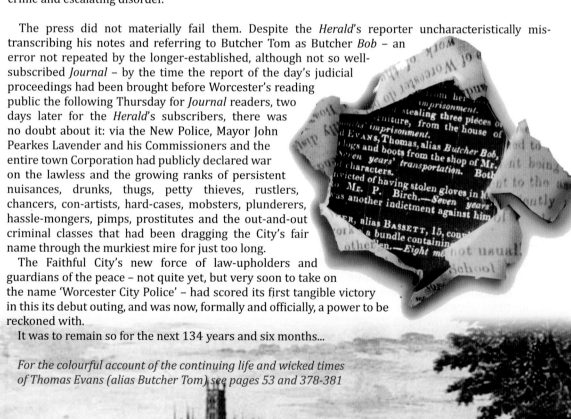

The Faithful City's new force of law-upholders and guardians of the peace – not quite yet, but very soon to take on the name 'Worcester City Police' – had scored its first tangible victory in this its debut outing, and was now, formally and officially, a power to be reckoned with.

It was to remain so for the next 134 years and six months...

*For the colourful account of the continuing life and wicked times of Thomas Evans (alias Butcher Tom) see pages 53 and 378-381*

# 2:
# The City, law and disorder
# up to 1823

Beyond the Garden of Eden, there's no such thing as a totally ordered society.

Where there's people, there's disorder. When laws fail, society fails. Civilisation is only possible when society acts within a framework of laws supported by an organised system of enforcement, and no community can exist without either. The alternatives are divisiveness and anarchy.

Attractive though the notion might be, an entirely crime-free community is an unattainable dream that has *never* existed and never *will* exist except in some utopian myth-land. It certainly never existed in Worcester. If it did, this book would not have happened, and right now you would be looking at your upturned palms and wondering quite why.

Though Worcester's 'New Police' (*not yet officially Worcester City Police: that term was to be coined two years later*) came into being in January 1833 and this book picks up the tale from ten years before, that's not to say that the Faithful City was un-policed up to then. In fact, the social history of Worcester **is** the history of its policing: like the continuing story of Worcester and its pubs, the two cannot be divorced, and despite times when Worcester made Dodge City look like some sleepy backwater on a wet Monday night, they remain one and the same.

It's even fair to say that with a few notable exceptions, the story of policing in Worcester right up to the present day could – and but for some ill-judged exceptions, *should* – be taken as the very model of how policing ought to be done, and while it never the once amounted to a tale of complete triumph of good over bad, there's much about the way Worcester countered the forces of lawlessness and disorder to justify some pride in a job well done.

While a comprehensive outline of the evolution of what was to become a model local police force might

*Fiat justitia ruat cœlum*

*One of the city's four heraldic maces, symbol of the Mayor's authority – dating from the 1760s*

provide a convenient backdrop to the creation of Worcester City Police, it's largely irrelevant and scarcely makes for a riveting read: half a millennium's activity whittles-down to a dry list of Acts and dates that parallel the general history of policing and peace-keeping in Britain as a whole – and anyway, has been covered in far more depth in countless works specifically dedicated to just that subject alone.

*Even so, in as few words as it's possible to get away with, the bare bones of the matter at least merit a brief glance...*

For perhaps a thousand years after Christianity had reached England, fear of being cast into Hell to live-out eternity in conflagration and Godless damnation was sufficient to keep the majority on the straight and narrow. But when superstition, fear and the dread of ultimately justifying your life before a vengeful Maker failed, stronger measures were demanded: on one hand the Church proved a formidable, unforgiving and sadistic adversary for those that overstepped its bounds, while on the other, the secular nobles on whose land the masses' entire existence depended and for whom an unblemished peace and the docility of the population at large was in their best interests, exacted a hefty toll on those that chose the alternative route, whether by choice or circumstance.

If law and order came at a price demanding a sadistic disregard for human life, the justification claimed by those that wielded the figurative big stick went along the lines of '*what do the victims matter so long as those that remain learn from it?*'

And so, in essence, it remained – the law-*makers* and the law-*givers* versus the massed ranks of actual and potential law-*breakers*, little of any substance altering the status quo for the better part of a thousand years. What changes there were up to the next milestone – or millstone, depending on what side of the criminal fence you stood on – merely amounted to the organisations actively charged with maintaining the peace, and the rank and personalities of those administering the penalties for disturbing it.

With the cost of transgression and stepping out of line likely to be the loss of liberty and even life, crime and disorder was not to be recommended. The capital charges of murder, rape, arson, treason, witchcraft and sorcery aside, punishment for theft, robbery, assault, drunkenness, vice, civil disorder and breach of the peace may well have been out of all proportion to the crimes, but at least it served as a powerful deterrent and chief reason to follow the straight-and-narrow – a principle that all night-walkers, felons, malefactors, vagrants, thieves, vagabonds, ne'ers-do-well, plotters and all disorderly and general nuisances, malcontents and failures to toe-the-line did well to heed.

Come the dawn of the nineteenth century, the solid, well-tried and dependable hierarchy of good citizens having a collective responsibility to hunt down and bring to justice their less than worthy ne'er-do-well brethren had stood the nation well in the years since its inception – and to its eternal credit, still does. This had been the chief outcome of the key **Statute of Winchester (1285)** making the whole community answerable for all incursions on the collective peace, and giving individuals aged between 12 and 60 the bounden duty '...to keep *watch (note italics)* from the sun setting to the sun rising'.

## Statute of Winchester (1285) and Justice of the Peace Act (1361)

The Ages may have been Dark, but the move was a shining initiative that had placed the onus of law and order at the very heart of those likely to gain or lose the most from it. It was from this surprisingly early date too, that a title that was to play a key role in the development of modern policing first came into common parlance: 'watchman'. From the 1300s onwards, the responsible person thus appointed found himself hierarchically answerable to a court-appointed *constable* – another term with ancient origins, stemming from the Roman 'comes stabuli' *(attendant [or count] of the stables)*.

The essential backbone of modern policing was made complete with the **Justice of the Peace Act *1361***, providing for the appointment of 'three or four of the most worthy [persons... in every County in England] to restrain Offenders and Rioters and to arrest, take and chastise them according to the Law and Customs of the Realm', and for centuries to come, the chain of responsibility thus created went on to serve the nation as a whole in perfectly good stead.

If illustration of the effectiveness and permanence of English jurisprudence is required, it was to be another three hundred years before the next milestone was to appear – and while up to then there had been little to separate Worcester from the rest of the Kingdom at large, the next leap forward was a largely local addition to the Statute Book, although its framework was unique only in certain elements...

This was James Ist's **Charter of the City of Worcester 1622** substituting a mayor, one Thomas Hurdman, for the former Bailiffs, giving him and his successors powers as Chief Presiding Officer, confirming the role of Sheriff alongside six Aldermen and a Recorder with powers for justice, and creating Worcester as both a City and a County in itself, an island within, yet entirely remote from and separate to, Worcestershire.

Under its terms, 'The Mayor, Recorder, and Aldermen of the City to be Justices, during the time they shall be in office, for the preservation of the peace, and to chastise and punish offenders, according to the Statutes, for offences committed within the City. They are also to adjust and rectify abuses in weights and measures or in selling victuals contrary to the Statutes and to punish forestallers, regraters, extortioners &c, within the City'.

One further development ought to be included in this simplified outline of the ancestry of Worcester City Police – and thankfully it was brief, if exceedingly brutal, but it left its mark for generations to come. This was the unwelcome re-appearance of martial law following the Civil War. Less than enchanted with the City that had not only openly proclaimed its allegiance to the Royalist cause and resisted to the very last its puritanical alternative, Lord Protector Oliver Cromwell bore down heavily on its treacherous citizens, exacting an arguably heavier toll on human life and property than any other city in the land. Worcester, the City that had witnessed the first and last bloody exchanges of the Civil War, was never to forgive him for it: just seventy years on, his stylised effigy was placed, pinned by his ears, over the doorway of the seat of justice, the Guildhall.

### Not called 'The Faithful City' for nothing

As if to ram home the city's allegiances in a traditional Worcester gesture of two-finger defiance to those that disagreed, its main entrance was – and still is – aggressively flanked by the watchful images of Cromwell's despised adversaries, Charles I and his royal heir, Charles II. The former holds the symbol representing the church, while his exiled, later restored son holds the symbols of legal government. ***Not for nothing did Worcester win its proud title 'The Faithful City'.***

At the 1660 Restoration of the monarchy and a return to the former values, the Mayor, Aldermen and Recorder re-assumed their former roles as Justices of the Peace – and yet again, the solid effectiveness and permanence of the system is underlined as by the time the city was preparing to take law and order to a higher level with a formalised network of officers paid out of the public purse, the Magistracy still followed the familiar bottom-to-top Watchmen>Constables>JPs>Judges>Crown order that had largely ensured effective legal stability for several centuries and still, with only the smallest amendments, does.

The city's parishes had long held a loose option of hiring watchmen – dubbed 'Charlies' and even 'Dogberries' even from the 1700s – for patrolling at night, although not all took advantage of it. As was to be the deciding factor set then and still in painful evidence, it all came down to £sd and whether the freemen a) thought them necessary, and b) were prepared to shell-out for them.

Worcester being Worcester, very often the latter proved to be the case. The better-heeled St Nicholas ward was one of the exceptions: years on, the *Worcester Herald* reported the discovery of the churchwardens' accounts for February 16th 1786 and a bill for £3 3s for 'a large deal watch box for watchmen with oak quarters and oak boards for the bottom and two deal seats inside and deal roof to ditto, finding the oak, the deal, the nails and workmanship to ditto'. 3s 6d was later charged for painting it. The parish also picked up the 12/3d bill for the watchman's great-coat with 'trimings, sleeve lineing and pockets, $1^1/_2$ dozen buttons at 1/2d and three small ditto at 7d and a shalloon'. Whatever a shalloon is unclear, but it cost 6d.

The bill for one month's night watch was '£1 4s, ditto for candles 3s 2d., and mending ye watch box 1/-' Seven years later, the St Nicholas watchman's wage had been upped to 6s 9d and Richard Hill, later appointed beadle of the church, was the hard put-upon office-holder. In a night assault by some roughs who at that time were the terror of the inhabitants but with a particular penchant for harassing the already hard-pressed Charlies, Richard Hill received a concussion of the brain, but after lying unconscious for some time, he recovered and was rewarded by a promotion to the old beadledom.

Fast-forward to 1820, switch the focus to 52.19123°N 2.22231°W and, but for the names of the personalities, precious little had altered...

The city was still governed by a Mayor (*The Right Worshipful Elias Isaac Esq*), Recorder (*The Right Honourable George, Earl of Coventry*), six aldermen chosen out of 24 principal citizens who also acted as magistrates (*the Worshipfuls Humphrey Chamberlain Esq., Thomas Farley Esq., Richard Nash Esq., Thomas Carden Esq., William Morton Esq., and John Blew Esq.*); a Sheriff (*Worshipful Francis Hooper, Gent.*); and two annually-elected Chamberlains (*Henry Clifton, Gent and William Wanklin, Gent*).

Under them served a Town Clerk (*Benjamin Johnson Esq*), two coroners (*John Platt and Nathaniel Mence, both gents*) and 48 Common Council men who composed the Corporate Body. They were attended by a Sword Bearer (*Mr John Shuck*), and four Serjeants at Mace (*Messrs John Crane, William Allen, William Powell and William Whittall*).

Unnamed, sadly, are the thirteen Constables, four musicians and four beadles that made up the City's Corporation.

In the intervening half millennium between Edward Ist and the reigning monarch George IV, there had been hardly anything exceptional about Worcester's judicial (and/or 'policing') system save the misdemeanours, the locations, the circumstances, and the names of the villains and no-gooders that committed them, or the upright and generally law-abiding citizens that hounded them and sometimes even brought them to book.

According to Lewis' contemporary **General and Commercial Directory,** Worcester was '...large, populous and handsome, about four miles in circumference, its general appearance exhibit(ing) undoubted proofs of the opulence of its merchants, tradesmen and inhabitants'. Its population hovered around 15,000, of which half was directly involved in the city's foremost industry, gloving.

The Guildhall that had served as the City's (and County's) seat of justice since 1723 remained, according to Lewis' 1820 directory: '...among the public buildings in this City, most worthy of remark. The hall on the first floor is spacious and lofty: to the West, there are two courts of justice, wherein are held the assizes and sessions for the County and City'. The northern of the two – to the right as you enter via the same steps that have existed since its unveiling, and to this day still called 'The Court Room' – was where the Assize cases and Nisi Prius (*ie unless already heard by a lower court*) hearings were held, the former presided-over by Government-appointed judges, the latter by local magistrates.

The southernmost, to the left and now the Mayor's Parlour, was the scene of the Magistrates' (and later Police) court, held for determining cases of a pettier nature. To add to the confusion, up to the completion of the Shirehall in 1838, County court cases were also heard here both for the City and County of Worcester, and for the entirely separate County of Worcester*shire*.

All of which is very stately, correct and fitting description of Worcester from what amounted to a guide book and Yellow Pages of its day.

What Lewis had drawn a veil over, however, were the changing times and the dark areas now tainting the city's painterly image: over the previous few years, violence had become an everyday affair, the streets were becoming dangerously unsafe, everyone was a potential victim and the mood was turning sombre.

Any one of several factors could have sparked-off this new and clearly noticeable increase in crime, but the fatal combination of three killer issues made the outcome all-but unavoidable.

In no particular order of importance they can be summed up as:

i) *a marked reduction in demand for agricultural labour through the increased use of mechanisation, thus reducing whole families into destitution (and prostitution) with no other means of supporting themselves*
ii) *an unprecedented increase in population drawn to the city by the lure of increased prospects from sweated labour in the factories; and*
iii) *newly-re-vamped poor laws and game laws that had turned some practices that had been traditionally ignored or overlooked into statutory crimes.*

So far, so bad... but add to that the coinciding influx of hundreds of wild untamed navvies – Irish labourers, aimless drifters, military deserters and a gaggle of fit, feisty, hungry young men lured by the promise of good wages from the construction, improvement and constant maintenance of the canal, and later the railways – and the scene is set for some lively, and not always friendly, action.

Throw-in the addition of coarsened canal- and river-going boatmen, sometimes hardened ex-sailors, mooring overnight in the basins with cargoes of coal and other materials from the Black Country, and just to add flavour, a growing militarism that had led to the compulsory imposition of fighting soldiers billeted on unwelcoming property owners, and the resulting mish-mash was to turn a city where policing was little more than a half-hearted notion into one that gave pointed new meaning to the term 'Wild West'.

*Their effect was as predictable as day following night – an immediate and inevitable escalation in crime and disorder, and growing calls for a vastly-improved system of policing.*

## 1800: forces of law and order unable to cope with escalating crimes

The vestry-appointed constables and volunteer watchmen were neither available in adequate numbers nor possessed with anything like the required professional skills to cope with the changing times; for the most part, the poorly-paid role of snooper, sneak, tell-tale and whipping-boy appealed only to the self-seeking, the old, and the easily bribed, devoid of the proper character or sufficiently well supported or financed to be even remotely effective. The streets remained un-policed and largely unregulated by day, and crimes only came to the attention of the justices by the public's, or on the rarest occasions, the watchman's referral to one or other of the parish-appointed constables whose role was more of an administrative nature and rarely-seen middle-man.

The underlying issues were not specifically local but, being more exposed to their effects than most others, Worcester was hit hard.

The powers-that-were responded by doling-out gaol sentences with as callous a disregard for human dignity and suffering as the mediaeval barons and nobles had, and once the courts had concluded their business, the city was already finding itself hard-pressed to accommodate those it had found unfit to restore to the streets and liberty.

With day-time policing all but negligible and the parish-appointed Specials on the streets seen as fair game to the coarsened navvies, boatmen, squaddies and sailors drawn to the growing number of public- and beer-houses where ale was strong, cheap and readily available, small wonder the Houses of Correction were full to overflowing.

Worse, the prisons – of which by 1813 the City had two, the Bridewell in Friar Street and the new County Gaol in Salt Lane *(later, Castle Street)* – had become little more than training schools to turn those convicted for petty misdemeanours into skilled, hardened criminals well versed in '*...the knowledge and practice of every species of criminality. No description can convey an adequate idea of the state of a place where it is difficult to say which is the most prevalent, misery or vice; where one part of the inhabitants are entirely destitute, and the other part utterly depraved*' wrote a prison visitor to the City gaol.

Up to a few years earlier, the old Castle replacing earlier versions dating from 1113 – at least two of which had been destroyed by fire – had been the main house of correction. Standing on grounds bordering the cathedral at the bottom of what's now Severn Street *(originally High Timber Street on account of the stockade fencing surrounding it)* the wooden structures had been re-built in stone between 1621 and 1650 and then subjected to complete repair and reform between 1788 and 1784 to the point that '*...few prisons in the kingdom afford a more striking example of attention to every useful improvement that could be introduced for the general benefit and service of its inhabitants*'.

At huge cost, eighteen new cells had been added, each 10ft by 7ins and 12 feet high, covered by arches with apertures and ventilation passing through the centre of them '*...and cells for solitary confinement, or the examination of prisoners before trial. Its walls are ten feet high; it has an oak floor and is furnished with barrack bedsteads*'. There were also separate buildings for women felons and debtors.

At the summer Assizes of 1788, the Grand Jury of the County had expressed complete satisfaction with the improvements to the castle as it had proved '*...peculiarly gratifying to them to find that every substantial benefit had been derived from the improvements thus made in the old, as could possibly have been procured by erecting a new prison, and that a very heavy expence (sic) had therefore been saved to the tenantry of the county, by adopting the judicious plan of reform they had pursued*'.

On the other hand, in a pamphlet entitled 'An Account of the Present State of the Prisons and Houses of Correction in the Oxford Circuit', prison philanthropist John Howard commenting on Worcester, observed that:

> '*... in each of the cells the felons lie together on the floors. These cells were dirty and the apertures for air were all stopt through the inattention of the gaoler. The late keeper and his wife who succeeded him, both died of the gaol fever. The gaoler is a butcher who lives some miles distant and his son, a young man, has the charge of this large prison. Salary £150 in lieu of the tap. The number of prisoners at the time of my visit was – debtors 23; felons &c 31; convicts 16*'

Despite the completion of a new Penitentiary House in 1795, it was 'as you were' just 24 years later when the Castle was found to have been radically less than secure: in 1807, the entire line-up of felons due to be hauled up for the Assizes before Chief Baron MacDonald that day had all done a timely runner and were still at large!

Worcester and its insecure penal capabilities were viewed as a national disgrace – with the result that a complete re-think of its holding provision was ordered. The outcome could hardly be deemed surprising: that the castle and the prison it contained were ordered to be demolished. In its place – although not on the same site – was to be a completely new County Prison: the very heavy 'expence' the County had been spared in 1795 now amounted to a staggering £19,000.

Demolition of the old castle took years longer than originally expected: even by 1824 some of its foundations still remained – although, according to a visitor's letter to the *Worcester Herald* that year: '...leaving the cathedral, I went to view the remains of Worcester Castle, every trace of which will soon be removed, and most likely its site in a short time will be occupied by dwelling-houses; even the Castle Hill which we are told was the Donjon is vanishing before the spade and the pick-axe – those relentless enemies of antiquity'. [**Note:** *Castle Hill is clearly evident at the far right of the image of the City, below*].

By general consent, not least according to the justices, the cost of the new Gaol, completed in 1813 and designed to take the form of a castle, was money well spent: '...it is surrounded by a brick wall 15 feet high, which encloses about three acres of ground, the different wards are well arranged for the different classes

of criminals, and separate ones are appropriated for the male and female debtors'.

*Yet within five years of the new County Gaol being opened, it had already been deemed insecure and described as debasing all who were confined with its walls.*

It was, by any standards, a formidable looking building – so formidable in fact, that its very presence led to a re-naming of the ancient thoroughfare of Salt Lane which it now overshadowed. Henceforward – and still to this day – it was known as Castle Street.

It had initially been reserved for felons whose crimes had been committed outside the city although it was also used as an overflow when the City Gaol was at its capacity and also as a stronghold for Worcester's prisoners awaiting trial for more serious crimes. Ten years after its construction, a rumour had been put about that it had been built on insecure foundations which were giving way in several places, and there were fears that the prize new prison would have to be demolished and re-built.

According to the City's top-selling newspaper of the day, the weekly *Worcester Herald*: '...it was with pain that we heard this report and we made every enquiry upon the subject but were unable, till the present week, to obtain any authentic particulars. At length, however, we have ascertained that the state of the Gaol has undergone considerable discussion, and the Magistrates are of the opinion that it is, in its present state, nearly conformable to the spirit (*of the General Gaol Act 1823*) and may, at a very little expense, be rendered conformable to the letter of the Act'.

The report went on add that every part of the buildings had been minutely inspected and found to be largely sound with the exception of the Hospital ward, the top half of which had had to be demolished and rebuilt, and a crack in the arch of No5 solitary cell.

The Gaol needed to be austere, impregnable and capable of instilling fear into the soul of everyone who looked upon it. Besides, hangings of those sentenced to pay the ultimate penalty were carried out here. Murder, highway robbery and other crimes demanding the death sentence – typically theft of property in excess of 7l although leniency was often applied in such cases which also required ratification from Parliament – were fairly uncommon occurrences in the city: less so in the County.

Not that the new County Gaol's governor and clerk Benjamin Lovett Stable, or its turnkeys and executioners made such a distinction. They treated all condemned men the same. Women too, come to that.

Striking more fear into the hearts of the city dwellers at the time was Worcester City and County Gaol in Friar Street. Besides, **this** bridewell had its notorious treadwheel.

Lewis tells us that it was '...formerly a house of grey friars; it is the most entire of any ancient religious house in Worcester; it was granted to the Citizens by Henry VIII after the dissolution of monasteries in 1539 and purchased for £541'. It had been a prison from 1724, but that it was no more secure than the old Castle is attested-to by a whole raft of reports relating tales of felons escaping: one, a noted city locksmith named John Bradshaw, had found his escape such an easy affair that he'd also managed to leg it over the wall carrying a stash of the governor's silver!

The 1820s was a key decade for prisons and prison reform, following publication of papers indicating that the state of most of the gaols under corporate jurisdiction, including those in Worcester, were in very disgraceful condition and were in dire need of some kind of legal regulation. At least, there had been some cleaning-up of conditions in the years to 1822 – notably, the total segregation of men and women '...so as to prevent them from seeing, conversing or holding intercourse with each other', and new rules introduced whereby women could only be attended-to by female officers.

At least the sexes were not only now segregated, but were also confined in separate buildings or parts of the prison. They were also divided into distinct classes – the gaolers urged to take care that debtors, felons, convicts, prisoners awaiting trial, vagrants and witnesses were all kept separate from each other. Also at Worcester, idle detention and time left to ponder on the wisdom or otherwise of one's life-course to date was not an option. In return for their upkeep, all prisoners at the City Gaol were expected to be employed in the household work of the building and some other tasks that might be unpicking ships' tarred ropes (oakum) or breaking stones into a fine powder.

Prayers were said daily and Divine Service on Sunday was compulsory – Church of England only. Prisoners were also supposed to be given schooling in reading and writing, but that was optional and not rigidly enforced.

New regulations stemming from the time also meant that the use of irons within the prison confines was also being phased-out, and debtors were allowed to receive assistance from friends before their trial, but not pending payment of the debt if convicted.

Calls had also been made for all prisoners to have their own separate bed, soap, towel, paper and comb but quite how successful they had been is not clear although can probably be guessed. In what precious few idle moments were granted them, gaming for money or goods was banned while any prisoner could be punished by solitary confinement and a diet of bread and water at the whim of the Gaoler, with other more dire punishments if approved by the justices.

As well as provision for around 40 male and female prisoners – a figure regularly tripled and more so, particularly in later years – the Friar Street bridewell was also home to Gaoler-in Chief 'Guv'nor' William Griffiths, born 1799 and his wife Mary who was also Matron and as such, Superintendent of the female complement. They conducted daily inspection of all their charges and were required to keep a daily record of punishments and occurrences with particular note of the 'compellance of the prisoners to perform their hard labours', especially the time spent on the Gaol's notorious and most feared form of punishment, the tread-wheel.

## The Crank – Worcester's notorious treadwheel

Not everyone was in favour of the Wheel – the sweated labour mechanism used for grinding corn and known by those sentenced to gruelling periods employed in its perpetual motion as 'the everlasting staircase' or in the hushest of tones as 'The Crank'. It's not recorded when the wheel was introduced at Worcester City Gaol, but it's likely to have been a permanent feature in the promotion of prison discipline as well as a useful source of income for most of its existence.

It's believed that prisoners on the Worcester Wheel paced some 13,000 treads during a 10-hour day during summertime, two-thirds that during the winter months. The wheels at Lewes, Ipswich, St Albans and Cambridge gaols were considered less punishing – Lewes the softest of all at an expected summertime rate of 6,600 treads in a day; the wheel at Durham was considered on a par with Worcester, and wheels at Brixton, Guildford and Reading considered heavier-going. The most notorious wheel of all was at Warwick, with a crippling summer rate of some 17,000 treads in ten hours.

Men and women alike were sentenced to long hard spells at the wheel and in some prisons – although, to Guv'nor Griffiths's credit, not believed to be Worcester – all prisoners, even those on petty charges and on remand were also often ordered to spells at the wheel. By the time of the construction of the new County Gaol however, opinions were deeply divided whether or not the form of punishment was as useful in reforming prisoners as its supporters claimed, and initially local Magistrates had voted against its introduction on the grounds of expense and on medical objections, preferring the penalty of solitary confinement and reduced rations.

For the first four years of its existence, the new Worcester County gaol had existed *without* the deterrent of a tread-wheel and prisoners ordered to confinement there considered themselves to have got a cushy number. But getting off light was a situation that could not be seen to be tolerated, least of all at a time of escalating disorder, and the issue was settled by Home Secretary Robert Peel who waded into the argument with the observation that '...from what (he) could learn, wherever the tread-wheel had been introduced, it had uniformly contributed to the general health of the prisoners so exercised'.

It was a damning statement that stunned the local magistracy into action and moves were instantly put in hand for plans and estimates for the construction of a second working Worcester wheel.

The initial designs were rejected and its 1700l cost considered excessive, but by mid 1825, the *Herald* reported that '...the Tread Mill in the County Gaol has been completed in such a manner as promised to answer every object of its erection'.

It was not before time. Even several years earlier it had become painfully evident that the state of the nation's morals as a whole, and Worcester's in particular had never sunk so low, while law and order – for years a key feature of the generally law-abiding Faithful City – was in melt-down and leading the city into anarchy: the old powers-that-were had lost their grip and something needed to be done to halt the serious decline before Worcester found itself drowning in a pit of vice, squalor, violence, disorder and overcrowded gaols.

With typical lassitude, Worcester proved slow to respond, but once it did, the result was far-reaching – a document that, more than any other single initiative, paved the way for the creation of Worcester City Police...

# 3:

# The Watch years

## 1823 - 1833

It's questionable that King George IV cared or even knew very much at all about events unfolding in the Faithful City – unlike his father George III who had a particular fondness for Worcester and would have made the city his capital in the event of London falling to Napoleon and the French. But regardless, for the sake of a quiet life and no doubt on the advice of his ministers, on the otherwise unremarkable Friday that was May 30th 1823 he gave his official assent to a new initiative geared to forging an improved new future for the city.

This was the **'Worcester Improvement *(Paving and Lighting)* Act 1823'** and its introduction sums it up as 'An Act for better supplying the City of Worcester and the Liberties thereof with water; and for more effectively Paving, Lighting, *Watching* (note those italics again!) and otherwise improving the said City'.

It was, frankly, well overdue.

As a document in itself it's knotted-up in legalese and makes tedious reading, but such was the City's need and the depth of what it was making provision for, that it needed to be: some paragraphs stretch to over 1,000 words without the respite of punctuation – typically, one covering the relationship of Commissioners and landlords rolls-out at a solid slab of 1136 words – and it took the *Worcester Journal* four pages of broadsheet stretched over four editions to précis it, the final instalment appearing on September 11th 1823.

After repealing all former Acts relative to the city, it proceeds to appoint as Commissioners '...all Justices of the Peace for the city, not residing at a greater distance than three miles from the city, and all persons occupying premises of the annual rent or value of £20 and in possession of rents, &c. to the yearly value of £60 or possessed of a personal estate of the clear value of £1000'. Seven Commissioners 'competent to act' were demanded; there was a £50 penalty for taking the oath without being qualified, and their first meeting was pegged for March 23rd 1824.

Accounting for far and away the bulk of the copious wordage was the Commissioners' role in what today would be termed compulsory purchase and slum clearance – notably what had become generally degrading no-go areas behind Broad Street and around All Saints Church – while other key elements included: levying rates and recourse to apply to the Quarter Sessions for those considering themselves aggrieved by the outcome; house owners to pay the expences (sic) of laying water pipes and keeping them in repair; provision of lamps for lighting the parishes and extra-parochial places in the city with penalties for breaking the lamps plus the cost of repairing the damage; all streets and lanes to be named and the

...think most expedient, and...
thereof as the said Commissioners...
to lay into the said streets, lanes, ways...
or places.

*Power to employ Watchmen.*—And...
that it shall be lawful for the said Com...
they are hereby authorised and em...
to time, ... and as they shall think ... as they
ploy such ... many watchmen & night con... ployed for
shall jud... edient and necessary, to be ...and such
the good ... ... bles from ... ...
watchme... ppoint othe... ... ... watch-
move an... how many of ...
and also ... hall attend ... and now
men and ... what stations they sh... be
they sh... r what number of hours they shall watch,
placed, ... they shall go their rounds, and also ... in
and ho... what wages or othe... ances shall be
and de... r their services : and the said Common a-
paid to ... empowered to make such further orders, and
ers are ... rom time to time, for the better government
regulat... of the said watchmen and night cons ables,
and d... of their services shall require.
as the ... *empowered to act as Constables*—And be it
*Wat*... ed, that the said watchmen and night con-
furthe... exert themselves in the prevention of fires,
stable... urders, burglaries, robberies, and other out-
and a... ders, and breaches of the peace ; and they
rages, ... required & empowered to apprehend all night
are be... elons, malefactors, vagrants, and disturbers o
walk... all disorderly and suspected persons, wh...
... isbehaving or wandering within the sa...
shall be found ... hem in the watch-house, or other p...
city, and to lodg... rity, to be there detained until t...
son or place of se... carried before some Justice o...
can conveniently ... city, to be examined and dealt
Peace for the s... city, and all such watchmen and night
... and all such watchmen and night
stables shall be sworn in as constables before any Ju...
of the Peace for the said city, and act as such while i...
execution of the powers and authorities of this act...
...spectively invested with such...

names conspicuously painted; houses and shops to be numbered; preventing nuisances and obstructions; offensive substances (*ie from slaughter-houses and privies*) only to be removed between 10pm and 7am, extended to 8am between Michaelmas and Lady Day; penalties on wagons parking in the street; and Commissioners' power to appoint Treasurer, Clerk and other officers.

### Watchmen to be employed by City rather than parishes

Almost tucked away and barely distinguishable from the reams of jargon-filled paras, clauses, sub-sections and codicils relating to what could be taken to be the far more pressing issues of streets and lighting, references to what was to pave the way for Worcester City Police could almost be overlooked – so comparatively small was the proportion of space devoted to the appointment of Watchmen only now being brought directly under the umbrella of the City as a corporate whole.

In a landmark ruling, the Act laid down that the Commissioners could appoint '... as many Watchmen and Night Constables as (they) shall judge expedient, and also fix and determine what wages and other allowances shall be paid to them for their services: such watchmen to be sworn in as Constables before a Justice of the Peace'.

They were to be paid 12/6d a week with an extra shilling allowance in winter for candles; they operated out of the City Gaol on the corners of Friar Street and Union Street, and their hours were 9.45pm to 4am in summer, and 5am in winter. They were also uniformed – notably their distinctive tall top hat, reinforced with leather and a cane strengthening ring at the sides and on the crown.

If there's a grey area in the Act, it's the thin and often unclear distinction between the roles of constable and watchman: distinguishing between one and the other is a difficult task that the press and even the justices regularly mistook to be one and the same. Small wonder really, considering this – taken from the Act:

*'...all such watchmen and night constables shall be sworn in as constables before any Justice of the Peace for the said city, and act as such while in the execution of the powers and authorities of this act; and they are hereby respectively invested with such and the same powers, authorities, privileges and protections as constables are invested with, and entitled to by law'.*

Er, pardon?

Where there **was** clarity, however, was in reference to their organisation – including the precise number of '...said watchmen and night constables (who) shall attend nightly, and how they shall be armed, and at what stations they shall be placed, and for what number of hours they shall watch, and how often they shall go to their rounds, and also to fix and determine what wages or other allowances shall be paid to them for their services'.

Their job-spec was also outlined, and they were also expected to '... exert themselves in the prevention of fires, and also of murders, burglaries, robberies, and other outrages, disorders and breaches of the peace; and they are hereby required & empowered to apprehend all night walkers, felons, malefactors, vagrants and disturbers of the peace, and all disorderly and suspected persons, who shall be found misbehaving or wandering within the said city, and to lodge them in the watch-house, or other prison or place of security, to be detained until they can conveniently be carried before some Justice of the Peace for the said city, to be examined and dealt with according to the law'.

Conduct and behaviour while in office and penalties for neglect of duty also came under the Act's spotlight. For neglect of duty they could expect to be fined between 5s and 40s according to the severity of each case '... and be it further enacted, that if such watchmen, or any of them, shall not perform and keep the lawful orders, rules and regulations of the said Commissioners, or shall in any manner neglect their duty, or misbehave

*Last survivor of the Worcester Watchmen's staves, now preserved in the Guildhall and a reminder of the hard treatment to be expected in the event of deviance from the straight and narrow*

*(Worcester City Council)*

themselves, every person so offending shall forfeit and pay for every such neglect or offence any sum not exceeding forty shillings, nor less than five shillings; and if the said Commissioners think proper, be immediately discharged from his office'.

Rules and regulations regarding the watchmen's relationships with the keepers of what to the Commissioners were becoming increasingly disorderly dens of vice and impropriety, the inns and public houses springing up in increasing numbers throughout the city, are also clear and unequivocal: '...if any victualler, or keeper of any public house, wine vaults or liquor shop, shall knowingly harbour, entertain, or suffer to remain, in his or her public house or premises, any watchman so to be appointed during any part of his time appointed for his being on duty, every such victualler or keeper, or other person so offending, shall, for every offence, forfeit and pay any sum not exceeding five pounds, nor less than twenty shillings'.

*And that was pretty much that...*

Yet, for all its brevity and buttoned-up wordage on the law-and-order front, it was to prove to be a key piece of legislation and an important step forward for Worcester – although it had noticeably stopped short of establishing a fully-formed local professional police force, funded by purely local taxation. Even if it hadn't, Worcester would still not have been the first: Glasgow had beaten everybody else to that particular goal, having steam-rollered The Glasgow Police Act through Parliament some twenty-three years earlier (1800), thus paving the way for the formation of the City of Glasgow Police, generally considered to be the first of its kind in Britain: Newcastle-upon-Tyne and Liverpool weren't far behind.

Even so, this was a promising start, geared to addressing the changing circumstances of the times with its stark back-drop of increasing industrialisation and exploding population – the combined impact of which had ignited the flames of an unwelcome escalation in crime, anti-social behaviour and general lawnessnesss. Better still, it positioned Worcester well ahead of most of Britain's remaining towns and cities in establishing a form of official constabulary – in addition to which, it also left the way clear for the formation of a future permanent police force and was, as such, tailored to stand the city in good stead for as long as was required before the next stage.

The Commissioners wasted little time in doing what civic administrators even up to now are particularly adept at doing – knuckling-down to the arduous task of arranging meetings, although it wasn't until their second get-together that they decided that the Watch was of sufficient importance to merit their time. At that belated, although still crucial meeting, they decided that the number of watchmen would be limited to eight, and that the city would be divided into four quadrants, largely following the lines of the main streets in a cruciform pattern – north-south High Street and east-west Broad Street and the bridge.

The ratio gave the city one watchman to 1,875 people: at the same time, the ratio in London was around 1:100. In a curious ruling on the same day, they also ordered that no stallion horses be permitted to be publicly shown except outside the County Gaol!

Though the watchmen are not named, contemporary evidence from other sources suggests that quickly recruited were: **Thomas Watkins (St Helens), Thomas Fox, John Williams, Thomas Jolley, Thomas Hill, Leonard Darke, Thomas Davis and James Mason** who was later appointed Constable of All Saints.

Three later additions recruited over the next few years to replace men who'd vacated their roles for reasons unknown, were **William Hale, John Ball and** *(first name unknown)* **Hardwick**, later Constable of St Clements. At the same time, the existing parish-appointed constables included **George Hale (*Constable of St Nicholas*) John Nicholls, Joseph Orchard** (later, or possibly at the same time, a high-profile Mayor's Officer, as was **Thomas Tilt), William Griffiths** (23 and son of the Governor the Gaol, whose role he was to accede to before long), **Timothy Saunders**, and three more whose first names are not known: **Bowkett, Garland and Penn**.

The new watchmen were officially Night Watchmen, they were armed with a lantern, staff and a rattle, and for the most part, their duties were in support of the constables, their nightly lot largely taken up with dealing with absconding militiamen who were instantly ordered back to their Regiment, beggars, boisterous youths, drunks and general nuisances found 'knocking on the shutters' and breaking the peace, and belligerent prostitutes found walking the streets and prepared to kick up any amount of fuss if their nightly activities were in any way tampered with.

Another section of the community accounting for much of the time of the already hard-pressed law enforcers was vagrants. This year had also seen the introduction of the new Vagrant Act that had particular relevance to the city, shining brightly – literally, since 1818 when the city was first lit by gas – in the midst of hundreds of square miles of darkened fields and untamed countryside and a magnet for rich pickings by beggars and thieves.

A key provision of the Act laid down that '...every person wandering abroad and placing himself or herself in any public place, street &c to beg or gather alms, or causing or procuring or encouraging any child or children to do so' would be deemed idle and disorderly and liable to be picked up the Watchmen. A first offence meant a night in the Watch-house with an order to leave the city at dawn in the hope that they never returned. If they failed to heed the warning, punishment for the second and subsequent offences was harsh: 14 days' solitary and an order to pay for 'lodgings' and if he or she couldn't afford the price of the charge, thereafter ordered to one calendar month on the tread-wheel.

Among some of the harsher provisions, was that the constables (*and watchmen*) would personally incur a penalty of 20s if they allowed gipsies, or other vagabonds, to encamp on the waste grounds of the respective parishes.

It was, essentially, just a start and the seeds of an embryo police force had been sown, but as the saying went then – as it still does – the road to hell is paved with good intentions. And so it proved to be...

For all their promise and new professional status, memories of Worcester's old, tired and corrupt 'Charlies' died hard and city folk were slow to accept them in the spirit in which they were intended. Worse, the new officers were regarded as snoopers and kill-joys by the majority of the people they were employed to protect, and quickly proved unpopular – individually and as an official body. Almost as soon as they took to the streets, a group of local yobs calling themselves 'The Lambs' began making their lives even more wretched with what the *Herald* termed 'nocturnal sprees'. One of their japes was a deliberate campaign of wilful damage to the new lamps, those in the Barbourne area proving particularly vulnerable, and before long the Lambs' larks took an even more sinister turn. As the *Herald* reported just weeks after the watchmen had first begun patrolling: '...since the recent establishment of watchmen in this city, they have, by their vigilance, become exceedingly obnoxious to those nocturnal disturbers denominated "The Lambs", and several petty attempts have been made by those fellows to annoy them in the discharge of their duty'. To which the reporter had appended the warning that the Magistrates remained determined to punish repeated action 'with the utmost rigour'.

The fact is that even with the support of thirteen constables, the force was simply inadequate and no match for the increasingly lawless Worcester masses – least of all on drunken Saturday nights. This, from the *Herald* just weeks after their formal adoption, is a typical and far from isolated incident:

> '*On Saturday night, at about eleven, the watchman was called into the Dog and Duck, in Nicholas-street, by the landlord, to quell a disturbance made by three men, whom he took into custody, but upon their promising to behave quietly he allowed to depart. Between twelve and one, a number of boatmen and others, armed with large sticks &c., and headed by the same [three] fellows, returned, swearing they would knock the watchmen's brains out; and when they arrived in the Corn Market commenced a general attack on every person they could see, and several, who were summoned to aid the civil power, were considerably injured'.*

Quelling the riot and getting the ringleaders to the Watch-house proved a troublesome task that escalated into an almighty free-for-all, but with the help of men who'd come out of the pubs to watch – 'summoned to aid the civil power' as the terminology of the day had it – they managed to get their attackers to the Friar Street nick for charging. It resulted in hefty sentences for the three ringleaders, William Boughton, William Heming, both described as boatmen, and labourer George Cresswell, with warrants out for several others including a waterman Joseph Hughes who was additionally charged with being drunk and 'indecently exposing his person'.

The *Herald* called the whole affair 'sickening and an atrocious outrage'.

Not unnaturally and entirely understandably given the precarious nature of the job, the incident quickly resulted in the watchmen departing from their agreed work-pattern as instead of patrolling their own patch, they paired-up for safety and jointly patrolled their two parishes – a highly controversial and unofficial move scarcely geared towards serving the best interests of crime-fighting, but at least giving the unfortunate officers a measure more protection than if they'd attempted the task solo. Occasionally things got so tough that they teamed up to patrol in threes. Not that that changed things overmuch: the practice was highlighted several times as the newspapers reported increasing accounts of not *one*, but *three* watchmen being attacked and assaulted, **Thomas Watkins, John Williams** and **Thomas Jolley** being a regular trio.

District C – taking in St Andrews parish and some of the worst slums and sink-holes around the old Copenhagen Slip and the brothels and low tenements of Grope *(later re-named Group so as not to offend sensitive ears)* Lane, was a particularly troublesome hotspot.

The powers-that-were had been counting on the very sight of a watchman with his lanthorn being sufficient to deter potential ne'ers-do-well from venturing out at night: sadly, that rarely proved to be the case and in more cases than not, their presence tended to arouse the opposite sentiment to the one intended.

Far more effective as a graphic deterrent to stepping outside the law, were the public executions that still drew huge crowds to the County Gaol to gawp on the sadistic ritual. In mid-1823, James Davis (22) found guilty of sheep-stealing, and burglar Josiah Rutter (24) were publicly hung before '...an unusually large concourse of spectators witness(ing) the awful spectacle. The caps being pulled over their faces, the fatal bolt was drawn and the world closed upon the wretched men forever' (*Worcester Journal*).

Another draw-back to the Watchmen's overall effectiveness was their being limited to clearing the city's streets at night only: day-time was another area and out of their, although not the constables', remit, leaving the Commissioners wondering whether to extend their activities and at what cost.

One area of activity that was popular with the masses but outlawed by the justices who ordered the constables (*by day*) and watchmen (*by night*) to come down heavily on the transgressors – a hopeless task given the number, and the nature, of people involved – was organised 'mills', or bare-knuckle fighting.

The time-honoured way for Worcester gentlemen to settle any argument, by the 1820s organised brawls that were frankly little more than street fighting with loose rules, had become a regular event on Pitchcroft and elsewhere, drawing massive crowds for sometimes as many as a dozen bouts that only halted when one of of the pugilists was too bloodied to defend himself or was, more likely, out cold. The city had been a centre for organised bouts of professional pugilism for some time and had staged some of top national events attracting names like Spring and Langan who'd battled for 48 rounds for the championship of England here, but that was a different affair to two amateurs slugging it out to an unruly crowd – and worse, being staged-managed by professionals with a keen eye on the lucrative sideline offered to, and by, the betting fraternity, consequently attracting punters and spectators in their hundreds. As such, the justices viewed the events as breaches of the peace.

In one set-to recorded by the *Journal* in October this year, a Worcester waterman named Jordan completely hammered one of his own kind from Gloucester by name of Wheeler over ten bruising rounds in which the local lad had come away with just one 'slight blow on the mouth'. Wheeler was out for the count and had been carted off to the Infirmary, but a

[ City of Worcester. ]

# THE

# Conftables' Oath.

YOU fhall be good and true to our Sovereign Lord King GEORGE, to his Heirs and Succeffors, Kings and Queens of Great-Britain, and to the Mayor of this City for the Time being; alfo you fhall well and truly occupy and execute the Office of a Conftable for this Year next enfuing; all Affrays, Bloodfheds, and Mifrules, in that mean time to be done within the faid City, or Liberties of the fame that may come to your Knowledge, you fhall well and truly prefent, fo often as you fhall be thereunto reafonably required on his Majefty's Behalf or the Office of the Mayor of the faid City. You fhall by your Power put under Arreft, and bring to Ward, all Traitors, Felons, Petty Pickers, Sufpected Perfons, and Breakers of his Majefty's Peace, that you know of; and all that commonly ufe Gaming, Diceing, Carding, to arreft them, or at leaft to prefent them, when you fhall be thereunto required. You fhall, at your Seffions or Leet, prefent all and every Offence done contrary to the Statutes of the Firft of King James, the Fourth of King James, and the One and twentieth of King James, to reftrain the inordinate haunting and tipling in Inns, Alehoufes, and other Victualling houfes: And for the repreffing of Drunkennefs, you fhall be affiftant to Mr. Mayor, Mr. Aldermen, and all other Officers, in the due executing of their Offices. And all Warrants to you to be directed, from Mr. Mayor, Mr. Recorder, and Mr. Aldermen, you fhall endeavour yourfelves, to your Power, truly to execute and ferve them. And the Watches of your Wards you fhall truly fummons, and fee them to be obferved and kept, when the Time of the Year fhall come, according to the Laws; and all other Things truly to do and execute that belongeth to the Office of a Conftable.

## So Help You GOD.

dispute that had arisen between the pairs' seconds sparked-off another unscheduled bout that stretched to 22 rounds, and this time the Worcester man named as Williams and described as a local bruiser, was carried off having come out a poor second *(in terms of the contest – not, necessarily in fulfilling the role that had landed him there!)*

Acting under orders and attempting to disperse the mob and deliver the main participants to the gaol left the city's pitiful compliment of law enforcers on nothing less than what might today be termed a hiding to nothing – so much so that their reputation by the end of their second year amounted to little more than being viewed with suspicion, a burden on the rates, to a man susceptible to a back-hander in both senses of the term, and as a force, only partially effective. Crucially, their presence had done precious little to halt the escalation in crime, a situation not missed on the justices at the Assize sessions at the end of the year. Its chairman Thomas Bund wailed to the Grand Jury that he found it '...lamentable to see so many prisoners in the calendar; we must all deplore the great, and lately peculiar increase of crime, and it is incumbent on us to do all that lies within our power to discourage vice and give encouragement to industry, sobriety, and particularly religion'. *They could only hope for a more encouraging year to follow...*

1824

As if their workload wasn't already crippling, the watchmen were now being ordered to give special attention to areas not necessarily viewed as crime quite so much as an unwelcome nuisance. In particular was the all-too prevalent issue of street-walking. Never anything new, its shocking upturn during the previous few years was likely a matter of brutal survival for the majority of women and girls, some as young as 11, now drawn to it because of the increasingly harsh economic conditions. Alternatively, with the streets now busy with hundreds of unprincipled navvies, boatmen and squaddies, often drunk and with cash in their pockets, the good-time girls had sensed some rich pickings to be had.

Whatever the cause, prostitution in Worcester was on a marked up, it was becoming glaringly more noticeable, the women were becoming disgracefully blatant and possessive of their territory and their clients, more people were complaining, and the justices wanted it curtailed.

Early on in the year, the city had come out in a particularly bad light compared to Hereford where a vice and morals clean-up operation had 'given very general satisfaction' and there were now calls for the same in Worcester. In a letter to the editor of the *Worcester Journal* in July, a visitor to the city praised virtually every aspect of the Faithful City, with just one crucial aspect marring his fulsome description:

> *'...I admire your city, and should, therefore, like to see it divested of aught that renders it unworthy of admiration. With this view, suffer me while I say a word respecting those unhappy women who not only infest your streets at night, but present themselves in the day-time, tricked out in all the finery they can procure (and) offending the feelings of every one who has any regard to modesty... it is dangerous to suffer abandoned women to pass unmolested though your streets, to exhibit themselves in the eyes of those of their own sex, who are acquiring a livelihood by servitude or the labour of their hand.'*

While the flurry of letters to the press largely concerned higher-class street-walkers, the scale of vice among the lower classes received little public exposure even though it was beginning to create deepening concern as in its wake, the associated evils of drunkenness, street crime and other anti-social offences continued their sharp upwards trend, and as usual, in the frontline were the numerically, not to mention psychologically, inadequate watchmen, not all of whom were immune to the offer of a payment in kind as inducement to turn a deaf 'un.

Under increasing pressure to clean up not only their own act, but also the city's rapidly-tarnishing reputation, magistrates again turned their attention to the easy-target of the growing number of pubs in the city – at the time numbering around 160 and increasingly, and not without justification, viewed as festering dens of vice and lawlessness.

In a *Herald* notice proclaiming the Brewster Sessions due to take place on September 23rd this year, magistrates made it clear that from here on in, theirs was going to be hard line and that '...persons having anything to alledge (sic) against the orderly conduct of such (Public) Houses, may appear and make their Complaints to the Magistrates; and it is also to be particularly observed, that no publican who keeps a Nine-Pin Alley, suffers Cards or gaming of any Kind in his House, will have a Licence granted him; and that their Houses must not be open after Ten o'Clock at Night in the Winter, and Eleven o'Clock in the Summer. Persons applying for Licences for keeping Dram Shops or retailing Spiritous Liquors, will be granted them on condition only, that they are not sold [on] any part of the day on Sunday'.

What's more, the justices were adamant that the city's morals would be cleaned up and restored to past glories, vowing to clamp down hard on victuallers overstepping the bounds of their licence. Adding their weight to increasing calls for closure of the city's drinking establishments – *in toto* for preference – Worcester was also rapidly becoming viewed as a centre for the growing number of Temperance houses whose firebrand orators put more pressure on the already creaking forces of moral turpitude.

## Watchmen's lot not a happy one

Clearly, there was rarely a dull minute for the hard-pressed watchmen, and danger lurked around every corner. One Friday night in September this year, **Tommy Davis** watchman in the volatile parish of All Saints, went in search of a madman seen firing a pistol near the bridge. He tackled the man – or, as the *Herald* innocently put it 'remonstrated with him on the impropriety of his conduct' – which caused the young thug to wrest Davis' staff from his hand '...and beat him so severely about his head, that he was carried home insensible; his life was at first despaired of, but he is now much better. The fellow is well known; but has not yet been taken'.

who were engaged in the attack.
About one o'clock on Saturday morning, Davis, the watchman of All Saints, observed a young man firing a pistol near the Bridge: Davis remonstrated with him on the impropriety of his conduct, which so incensed him that he wrested Davis' staff from his hand, and beat him so severely about the head, that he was carried home insensible; his life was at first despaired of, but he is now much better. The fellow is well known; but has not yet been taken.
Committed to Worcester County Gaol.—By B. John-

Just a week on, the faithful and dependable, if regularly bashed-about **Tommy Davis** was back at his post – and again in the thick of it, as the *Herald* again reports: '...we are sorry to find that a band of disorderly persons seem again disposed to disturb our streets at night; late on Saturday night, two separate attacks were made by a considerable body of men upon the watchman of All Saints, who, however, with the assistance of some respectable inhabitants, succeeded into taking into custody three persons, – Wm Hales, John Pitt and (*first name not listed, but later revealed as Henry*) Barton; the two former were on Monday morning held to bail, and the latter is committed for trial at the Sessions; Hales received a severe blow on the head from one of the Constables, whose spirited conduct on the occasion was most praiseworthy; informations have been laid against the other two persons engaged in the attack'.

The following Monday morning, Henry Barton was sentenced at the Worcester City Sessions to four months imprisonment for the assault. He appeared in the court soaked from head to foot as en route to the Guildhall for his trial he'd feigned a fit and had a bucket of water thrown over him: the fit instantly passed.

At the same session, known Worcester characters Henry Baylis and John Staples were each sentenced to three months' imprisonment for an attack on **George Hale**, Constable of St. Nicholas. The magistrates heard that while conveying some female prisoners from the Guildhall to the newly-built County Gaol, the gaol's female turnkey Charlotte Briggs was attacked in Foregate Street by Margaret Wood – an attack witnessed by the constable who took her into custody, prompting Baylis and Staples to attempt to rescue her thereby allowing her an opportunity to run away (*although she was later re-captured and sentenced to* *a month's imprisonment for the assault on Mrs Briggs).*

Meanwhile, John Staples' life of crime was already well-established and nine feloniously-active years later, he was to re-emerge accused of stealing a pair of gloves, the property of Mr Philip Birch Esq. He was tried at the same City Assizes as Thomas Evans, alias Butcher Tom, and received the same sentence – seven years' transportation with no guarantee of a return to hearth and home. He was sent along with Thomas Evans and Martin Smith to the prison hulk 'Discovery' moored at Woolwich and later shipped out to Australia on the ***Fairlie***, the same convict ship as Butcher Tom, to complete his sentence creating roads in the wild, far-off colonies. (*See pages 378-381*).

This year also saw even the well-run workhouse rocked with scandal after a high-profile case came before the shocked City magistrates. Its Superintendent of Wool Spinning, 38-year old Griffith Jones found himself sharing the Crank at the City gaol with some of his former charges after being sentenced to six months' hard for stealing wool, the property of brushmaker Josiah Smith of High Street.

It's rare the press singled-out any of the watchmen for special treatment – assuming that heroics and attention to duty was all in a day's work – and it was to be well into the next fateful year before the reporters realised that here were some heroes in the making and some cracking tales with which to regale their readers.

## 1825

After the city's first watchman 'hero' **Tommy Davis** had come to prominence, another to rise to some public recognition during the course of this year was a constable and Mayor's Officer – the ever-dependable **Joe Orchard** who, the *Herald* reported, had been assaulted by James Day one Saturday night early on in the year: Day was committed to the City Gaol for the offence. Orchard's official role – whether constable, mayor's officer or even New Police-man in later years, was constantly a source of confusion, but there was none where his abilities as a law enforcement officer were concerned. Throughout, he displayed remarkable qualities and a rare attention to duty, often at risk to his own life.

Later this year, a second Watchman also came to the press' – and thus, the public's – attention. This was **Tommy Watkins**, Watchman of St Helens, who had earlier come in for some praise from the *Herald* after he'd interrupted some horse thieves attempting to steal a horse valued at 30l from a stable in Fish Street.

Perhaps even more so than **Joe Orchard** at the time, watchman **Watkins** appears not only to be among the most active, but also the most set-upon, with the 'sheets' reporting a steady stream of blow-by-blow accounts of some quite vicious assaults. If he'd known how bad it was to become within a few years, it's likely he'd have walked away and returned to his previous profession... *(See 1826 and the Book of the Watch, p34, and reports of his death, following another violent incident, July 1830)*

The County receipts, published on November 24th this year and presented to the Michaelmas sessions broke down the running costs of the County Gaol and the City Bridewell for the year. The costs of apprehending and carrying prisoners and others to and between the two houses of correction was £151 10s 4d.; use of 'waggon and horses to convey prisoners for trial £7; removing prisoners for transportation £143 14s; special constables attending the race course £5 15s; salary to the (*County*) Gaoler £150; salary to the Keeper of the (*City*) Bridewell £125; ditto clerk and four turnkeys £252; Matron for one year £30; Chaplain £120; apothecary £80 who also received an additional 8 guineas (£8 8s) for attending eight inquests into prisoners who'd died while still incarcerated; woman waiting upon prisoners £13; baker for the year £31 4s; gardener for the year £4 7s 6d.; and uniforms for the prisoners £175 6s 3d.

The cost of two Watchmen for the Bridewell was a very modest £36 8s.

To offset those charges, wages earned by prisoners in manufacturing goods and grinding corn on the treadwheel amounted to £276 0s 10 $\frac{1}{4}$d

There seems to have been some differences of opinion between Guv'nor Griffiths and the Watchmen at the outset of this year and in January, for reasons unknown, the Guv'nor had taken the seemingly unilateral decision not to allow the admission of prisoners at night – a move scarcely calculated to make the Watchmen's role any easier. No amount of persuasion or cajoling would persuade him to change his mind and the City Commissioners were left with little alternative but to build a purpose-designed Watch-house in the grounds of, but separate to, the City Gaol.

It was completed by April at a cost of £138 9s 6d and was to be the Watchmen's home for the next twelve turbulent years.

This was to prove a lean year for news on the policing front – the year's one highlight being the City Corporation's decision to grant the Freedom of the City to ex-Home Secretary Robert Peel, a move suggested by one of the Corporation's rising stars, Henry Clifton who was destined to become Mayor in future years (*1831-2, succeeding Worcester Journal proprietor, editor and publisher Harvey Berrow Tymbs*).

In mid-May, the *Herald* reported:

*'At a Chamber meeting of the Mayor and Corporation of this city, on Friday, the following Resolution was, on the motion of Henry Clifton, Esq. unanimously agreed to: – "That the freedom of this ancient and loyal city be presented to the Right Hon. Robert Peel, late Secretary of State for the Home Department, in testimony of the high sense the Body Corporate entertain in his consummate abilities and inflexible integrity as a Statesman, and his invariable fidelity and attachment to the Constitution in Church and State'*

It was to be more than a year before there was any further progress on the issue, but that's not to say that the combined forces of law and order were idle or lacking in any sense of duty: it was just a matter of 'business as usual' with more of the familiar old pattern of goodies v baddies emerging, the goodies not always coming off best.

### The Book of the Watch 1826-30

The actual Book of the Watch covering the period from July 11th 1826 – May 13th 1830 is preserved in the original archives section in the Hive and a priceless volume it is too: it shows that during the second half of 1826 alone, poor old **Tommy Watkins** was assaulted on July 11th, twice on July 13th, and again on 14th, 16th 26th July and on November 26th.

The still remarkably well-preserved volume, sadly the only one appearing to have survived, not only permits a fascinating illustration of just how disorderly life had become in Worcester around this time, but also the variety and incidence of misdemeanours that had become the everyday lot of the Watch: the first entry dated July 11th 1826 reads 'Charlotte Anne Griffiths, charged by **Thomas Watkins**, Watchman, with disorderly conduct in the street at 12 o'clock at night. Ordered to two months on the treadwheel' *(see the original report, p361)*.

*Courtesy: Worcester CiCo/WAAS*

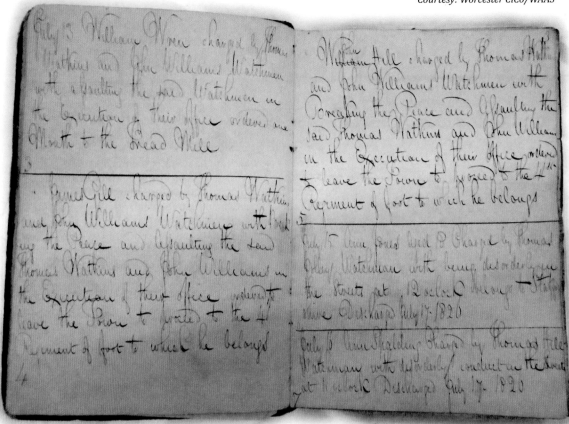

Charlotte Anne Griffiths sounds a thorough bad'un. As well as appearing in the first entry in the book, she also re-appears in one of the last: on April 25th 1830, aged 28 she was charged by Watchman **Thomas Hill** with being in the Streets at 12 o'clock at Night and having two persons with her to make a disturbance and to assault on a young man of the Name of Short ('Remanded till next Monday')

For July 13th just two days later, there's four entries – three involving **Tommy Watkins.** The first reads: 'Thomas Janner, charged by **Thomas Fox**, Watchman with breaking the Peace (at) 1 oclock in the Morning. Native of Devon Labourer ordered one Month to the Tread Mill'.

The second 'William Wren, charged by **Thomas Watkins and John Williams**, Watchmen, with assaulting said Watchmen in the execution of their office. Ordered one month on the treadwheel'.

The third: 'James Gill charged by **Thomas Watkins and John Williams** Watchmen with Breaking the Peace and Assaulting the said **Thomas Watkins and John Williams** in the Execution of their office ordered to leave the Town and proceed to the 41st Regiment of Foot to which he belongs'.

And the fourth a carbon copy of the third, this time William, crossed out to read John, Hill.

***Other entries in the fascinating slice of Worcester's history and a colourful illustration of the Watchmen's daily grind of the time, include:***
- Mary Evins 30, charged by watchman **Leonard Dark** with being drunk in the streets at a late hour
- Sarah Coley aged 21, charged by watchman **Thomas Davis** with being disorderly in the streets
- Sarah Powell 16, charged by the same watchman with the same offence the next day (*August 26th*)
- Alfred Stevens aged 14 charged by Henry Bushell, Printer, of stealing from his warehouse Ivory Balls. Seven days imprisonment
- Emanuel Onslow 22, charged with knocking on the shutters and breaking the peace at a late hour in the Night (*with William Wood, 20, and John Street 23. October 18th 1826*). Discharged after a reprimand, **Emanuel Onslow** was to go on to a stellar career with the New, and later Worcester City police, which, while of no long duration saw him rise through the ranks to Sergeant.
- Jane Young charged by Watchman **Williams** with being drunk and disorderly in the streets at 2am

on January 25th 1827 and described as having been '...in prison many times, a notorious character' to which magistrate Thomas Carden himself appended, dated and signed a post-script: 'A notorious abandoned prostitute. Let her be kept to hard labour for one month' (*see below*)

- The same session saw Thomas Carden append similar post-scripts to Mary Ann Darke and Mary Ann Taylor, both charged by Watchman **Thomas Hill** with being in the streets, fighting and breaking the peace, Darke being noted as 'a very old offender'. Carden wrote 'Mary Ann Taylor came to Worcester only yesterday. Allowed her liberty on leaving the Town immediately. Mary Ann Davis, an old offender, one month's confinement to hard labour'
- John Florence aged 21 charged by **Orchard** with being disorderly in the streets and being indecent in exposing his person (*July 21st*)
- Samuel Bradley 21 Waterman, Jonathan Cole 24, spinner, William Harber 18 glover, Sarah Coley 20 single woman and Mary Fuller 19 ditto all charged by Mr Slade churchwarden of Saint Martins with being assembled in a house of ill-fame in Watercourse Alley on June 7th 1829 and there breaking the peace the whole of the night till half-past three o'clock on Sunday morning'. Samuel Bradley further charged with striking Watchman Davis several blows in the face for which he was fined 20/- and 5/6d expenses and Sarah Coley one month's hard labour. The others were discharged
- John Hugh 24 charged by Hill Watchman to assist in bringing Lloyd to the Watch House which he refused and also endeavoured to stir up the mob to attack the Watchmen in the execution of their duty

WCiCo/WAAS

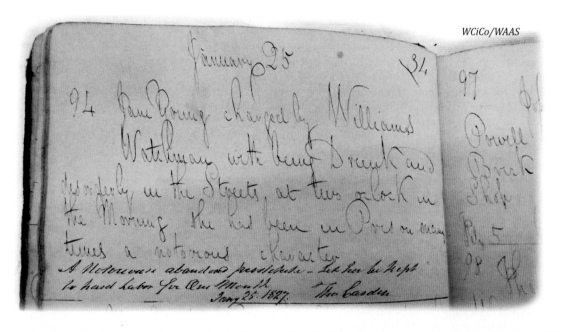

Occasionally, fines were shown as having been paid to the Watchman – as on July 27th 1827 when a 34-year old glover named Samuel Smith was charged by Watchman **Williams** 'for endeavouring to create a tumult in the streets at one o'clock on Sunday morning'. In what looks like magistrate Thomas Best's hand was the note 'Pay 2/- to the Watchman and discharged'.

For all its outward signs of affluence and prosperity, Worcester was not an excessively happy city by the beginning of this year. Agriculture was in depression, the glove trade that provided employment for far and away the greater part of Worcester's working population and their families was in difficulties like never before, and unemployment and discontent were rife.

Increasing numbers of families were in dire poverty and, faced with little choice they could either place themselves in the hands of the parish, or they could turn to crime. Both options attracted new converts on a scale unprecedented, but with a depressing sense of déjà-vu, men who'd sweated all day to earn an honest crust now began to feel themselves hard done by when they realised that hand-outs were being made to shirkers for sitting at home while doing little or nothing towards their families' upkeep.

An (unidentified) *Herald* journalist wrote that in his day the time had been that men had considered themselves disgraced by asking for relief '...*but that feeling is now long gone by and the independent spirit has all-but been destroyed. It has had a bad moral effect*'. Sounds rather familiar....

Accordingly, the majority of men that were in work now regarded themselves as under-paid and made increasing demands on the parishes to have their wages made up from the rates levied for the relief of the poor. Another observer remarked '...men are employed on the roads at a very low rate. They consider it a matter of right to be paid from the poors' rate. When the unemployed poor are put by the parish to work on the roads, they become lazy; they know that whether they sit on the wheelbarrow all the day or work hard, the result on Saturday night would be the same' – a sly reference to the fact that on the parish, they could expect to receive between 8d and 10d a day, sufficient for bread and vittles for the family or alternatively, and just as commonly, half a gallon of ale for himself.

One of the least welcome off-shoots of the economic situation had been a marked new increase in poaching as a way of survival. But what might have begun as setting snares to catch a few hares and rabbits to feed a hungry family was now turning into widespread rustling involving hen-roosts, pigeon coops, pig-sties, and eventually whole fields of sheep and even cattle. A worrying upwards trend was also the marked upturn in the use of violence used by the poachers to protect themselves from the increasingly unwelcome attention of the gamekeepers and, inevitably the constables and watchmen duly called in to take charge – and then when they started getting too close, the use of firearms. The trend was to be remarked on in the course of scores of trials henceforth: murder and manslaughter trials involving poachers, gamekeepers and constables became surprisingly common in the County, although inevitably less so in the city.

## Prisons population up by more than a fifth

Barely surprising then, that this year witnessed a large increase in prison population – in Worcester up by more than a fifth – and it'd be tempting to attribute it to the increased effectiveness and vigilance of the watchmen: the fact is that it's just as likely to be the result of the harsh economic conditions in combination with the introduction of the Poor Laws and the Vagrants Act, and another sign of the justices' desperation in tackling the issues at hand.

Times were hard – desperately hard, leading to even more pressure on the already overburdened prisons now buckling under the weight of having to find room for a new class of felons: debtors. In an early 'Shock, Horror'-style report that was never out of vogue but was to reach its height more than a century later, the *Times* reported early this year that '...the sum total of these poor creatures is 3820; of whom 2866 are imprisoned in England only; in Scotland 216; Wales 74; and Ireland 660'... (this) works out at one for every 3500 inhabitants in England and one for every 10,000 in Ireland. Altogether it is a dreadful thought that in one kingdom nearly 4,000 human beings should be incarcerated, against whom no crime is alle(d)ged'.

The Crown debtors were, according to the report '...deserving compassion in full as great a degree as any other description of victims of hopeless poverty'.

Just weeks later, two unnamed city watchmen were despatched to Hereford to bring back a prisoner who'd done a runner from the City Gaol the previous June. John Jones had been chanced on by three out-of-work lads who'd walked the 26 miles to Hereford in the hope of jobs; sadly for him, one of them had been his cell-mate at the time of his escape from Worcester and no doubt with his hopes set on financial rewards from the justices, he'd raised the alarm. At the time of his arrest, Jones had levelled a pistol at one of the Worcester watchmen '...either for intimidation or a worse purpose' noted the *Herald*. The escapade not only indicated just how dangerous life had become for the city's chosen few, but particularly the low esteem in which they were held.

In the same edition, a single paragraph was to herald (no pun intended) major changes in future years. At the time, it went completely unremarked on and read, simply: 'The Marquis of Lansdown (sic) is said to be engaged in a revision of the Police System with a view to its improvement'.

Henry Thomas Petty-Fitzmaurice, 4th Marquess of Lansdowne *(note differences in spelling between his official, and his locally-reported titles)* had succeeded Sir Robert Peel as Home Secretary in this year and continued in the role until the following year when Peel again resumed the office. The two shared similar interests, and no doubt notes, with regard to legal reform in general and policing in particular.

It's not known quite why the City Corporation's plan to offer the Freedom of Worcester to Robert Peel some sixteen months earlier had failed, but August this year saw a return to action. The City was fortunate that the son of the Recorder, the Earl of Coventry, was Lord Viscount Deerhurst, a close confidant of the great man, and he was co-opted to act as go-between in renewed attempts to offer the greatest honour Worcester could bestow. On August 26th, the City, via Lord Deerhurst received his reply...

*'I beg to be permitted to express, through your Lordship, my grateful sense of the distinction which has been thus conferred upon me, and to assure those who have, in the most flattering manner, indicated their confidence in me, that I am justly proud of their approbation and good opinion'.*

All very proper and stiffly formal, it was simply signed 'Peel'.

Whether or not the Commissioners had been hoping to press him on the possibility of creating a professional Worcester City police force *two years ahead of the same in London* will never be known for sure as, contrary to popular belief and other histories of policing in Worcester, Robert Peel apparently failed to back up his gratitude to the 'ancient and loyal City of Worcester' by a personal visit, and all that remains is the plaque on the wall in the Guildhall, the future Prime Minister taking his place alongside Lord Nelson, the Duke of Cambridge, Colonel Ellis, Viscount Sidmouth and the Duke of Gloucester.

At least his praiseworthy predecessors had all had the good grace to accept the honour bestowed on them *in the place it had been awarded*. It seems that the Home Secretary and MP for Tamworth was just too busy with affairs of state and escalating crime levels to pay a visit, and the award of the City's greatest honour appears to have been offered, accepted and conducted solely by proxy and post.

While the Home Office was struggling to keep pace with the exploding levels of crime – not just in the City but throughout the United Kingdom as a whole, one critical amendment this year being that a person convicted of felony for a second time would be liable for transportation for life – conditions in Worcester Gaol remained typically dire. The year's accounts showed that during the year, the guv'nor William Griffiths had managed to wangle himself a £25 increase in salary – now up to £150 putting him on a par with his counterpart at the County Gaol; the clerk and four turnkeys now commanded £339 19s 4d up from £252 and even the Chaplain had recorded a significant increase in salary – £250 up from £120. It's likely the Commissioners had not been over-impressed with the watchmen's performance over what had been a fairly uneventful year: their comparatively pitiful remuneration remained unchanged at £36 8s.

HONORARY FREEMEN
FROM THE YEAR 1800
1802 LORD NELSON
1802 DUKE OF CAMBRIDGE
1814 COLONEL ELLIS
1817 VISCOUNT SIDMOUTH
1819 DUKE OF GLOUCESTER
1827 SIR ROBERT PEEL

The *Journal* began the year with a hard-hitting article simply titled **'Increase in Crime'** and outlining that '...the very obvious and alarming increase of crime, notwithstanding the various efforts made to check its progress, is the subject of very general observation, and has attracted perhaps more attention at this moment from circumstance of late Sessions' Kalendars being in many instances heavier than they were ever before known to be', adding that its prime cause was likely to be the rapid spread of population and 'other causes referable to certain mistaken practices that have of late crept into the treatment of the poor'. It was hard-hitting stuff, but a fair reflection of the times.

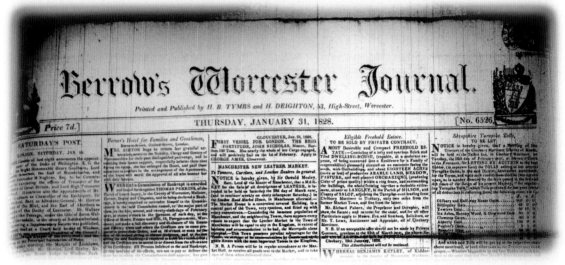

Prize-fighting – denounced by all except the sometimes 20,000-strong crowds that flocked to witness the events – continued to be a popular sport in Worcester despite the *Journal*'s description of one event as 'a disgraceful and demoralizing scene', while the winter claimed a raft of deaths by fire, for the most part children and old folks, the coroner's reports making distressing reading.

Hydrophobia – rabies – was also rife in the city, but magistrates stopped short of ordering the destruction of every dog found on the streets, as their Birmingham counterparts had decreed, while the year was also to witness a rise in deaths from smallpox.    January alone saw 9 prisoners hauled into the County Gaol awaiting trial at the Sessions and 23 for the Assizes, due to be held on March 10th.

**Tommy Watkins** and **Joe Orchard** continued to serve the city well: in February they played a key role in nailing Ann Harwood resulting in a twelve-month prison sentence.  Her crime? Stealing a piece of handkerchief and a piece of flannel.  At the same session, Henry Clark was charged with selling improper books which were brought into the court in a linen bag, sealed with the judge's own seal.  Trouble was, he'd done a runner and the constables were ordered to search for and apprehend him.

The following day, Worcester housemaid Lucy Edwards was cleared of murdering her child.

In March, a neat piece of detective work by **Joe Orchard** – described by the *Journal* as 'one of our police officers' – showed him to be a remarkable individual. He'd picked up two lads, both giving their names as Davis, but by some determined sleuthing he discovered that one's real name was Jones, that they'd escaped from Hereford Gaol and that a chalice dated 1637 that they had in their possession had been stolen by the pair from the treasury of Christ Church in Oxford.

April proved a trying month: early on, the lock at Sidbury claimed yet another young life, this time 5-year old William Guest, while an unnamed watchman was fined 5s '...for having, under pretence of discharging his duty, most insolently and unwarrantably interrupted a respected individual, whilst returning with his wife to his house, at a reasonable hour'.  In other words, overstepped the bounds of his duty.

To balance the equation, the same court fined another (*unnamed*) individual 5s for interrupting (*another unnamed*) Watchman in the execution of his duty'.

By the middle of the year, observers were noting that the solitary confinement of prisoners '...has been found to be more irksome to criminals than the severest labour, so that experience as well as an examination of the constitution of the human mind, concur to convince us that the seclusion and silence of a solitary cell are more terrible to criminals and more likely to deter them from a repetition of crime than any other species of punishment'. Noted the *Journal,* 'the Magistrates appear (to agree) as we observe that the late Sessions they awarded it to several of the prisoners'.

At the end of the year, guarded praise for the watchmen where they operated, when the *Journal* highlighted the difference between the patrolled parishes and those still unpatrolled and calling for a statutory extension of police measures City-wide – typically what was fast emerging as the Blockhouse (*'abused to the most disgraceful purposes'*) and the Tything (*'nightly in total darkness because a few individuals did not contribute towards the lighting of it).* These and other inconveniences should not be permitted to continue any longer unremedied'.

The policing system, such as it was, was beginning to make its mark.

# 1820

What was to become a hum-drum year on the home front – although a policing milestone year at national level – proved a slow-starter. As the *Herald* termed it, January's proved '...an exceedingly light calendar, both as regards the number of prisoners and the nature of their offences' – and that may or may not stand witness to the growing success of the city's burgeoning force of mayor's officers and constables.

Not that it was to remain that way. Over the next few months, they found themselves dealing with the usual round of:

- **petty thefts,** including 13-year old James Walters who stole 3s 6d from servant girl Mary Vickers, sentenced to fourteen days' confinement to solitary labour and once privately whipped; and 11-year old Laurence Harrison and Richard Hailes (14) both sentenced to seven years' transportation for stealing the clothes of James Smith who'd stripped off for a swim in the Severn at Pitchcroft and returned to find his clothes filched

- **suicides** – or, as in the case of ex-bankers' clerk James Knight who'd slashed his throat in a Mealcheapen Street house in 'a truly appalling case of self-murder and within half an hour of the deed he became a corpse' (*Herald*). In November, Mary Savage, wife of the porter of Edgar Tower, dosed herself with a quantity of arsenic. Verdict: insanity

- **a heavy catalogue of deaths by clothes catching fire**, both children and in the tragic case of tailor's wife Mary Cox, an 80-year old who '...on Tuesday last was sitting by the fire side with her husband when a live coal fell from the grate on her gown and she became instantly enveloped in flames... neither the unfortunate victim herself, or her husband (both being little short of 80) were enabled to extinguish the flames and she was burnt in so dreadful a manner, that after enduring the greatest torture for about fourteen hours she was relieved from her suffering by death. Mr [Richard] Cox was much burnt in the hands in his feeble endeavours to assist his ill-fated partner

- **sudden deaths:** in the same edition, the tale of 108-year old Elizabeth Griffiths found dead in her bed in the Blockhouse and adjudged, in the quaint wordage of the time, to have died 'by the visitation of God'

- **fatal accidents** including one involving the Birmingham and Bristol mail coach that overturned at the breakneck speed of thirteen miles an hour – one hour being the time it took to travel to the City from Bromsgrove

- **lunatics** including William Lewis, landlord of the Druids Head in Merrivale who travelled to London and stormed Sir Robert Peel's office, claiming his rights as the King of England. Peel was out at the time and Lewis was locked-up for his own safe keeping

- **fatal prize fights** including one in a field at the top of Rainbow Hill involving two men named Jones – one nicknamed 'Lippy', the other Samuel, alias John Ashley, who died after a slug-it out scrap for a 30l stake that lasted 1 hour and 20 minutes over 60 rounds. It resulted in the death of Samuel Jones, a charge of manslaughter against 'Lippy' Jones *(six months' gaol)*, sentences for both combatants' seconds, and led to Plaisterer's Arms *(Dolday)* licensee James Overbury committed for trial as timekeeper *(one month's gaol)* and losing his licence.

It could also have spelled the end of 'star' Mayor's officer **Joe Orchard** who was called on by the magistrates to answer questions as to why he'd failed to put a stop to the scrap that had attracted more than 2,000 spectators.

Fortunately for him, he was able to prove that he was out of the city at the time, engaged on other business.

## Peel's Nine Principles – still the bedrock of modern policing

By far the furthest-reaching events of the year occurred 120 miles away in the capital when Home Secretary Robert Peel introduced his Nine Principles that still form the basis of modern policing:

1: to prevent crime and disorder, as an alternative to their repression by military force and severity of legal punishment
2: to recognise always that the power of the police to fulfil their functions and duties is dependent on public approval of their existence, actions and behaviour, and on their ability to secure and maintain public respect
3: to recognise always that to secure and maintain the respect and approval of the public means also the securing of the willing co-operation of the public in the task of securing observance of laws
4: to recognise always that the extent to which the co-operation of the public can be secured diminishes proportionately the necessity of the use of physical force and compulsion for achieving police objectives
5: to seek and preserve public favour, not by pandering to public opinion, but by constantly demonstrating absolutely impartial service to law, in complete independence of policy, and without regard to the justice or injustice of the substance of individual laws, by ready offering of individual service and friendship to all members of the public without regard to their wealth or social standing, by ready exercise of courtesy and friendly good humour, and by ready offering of individual sacrifice in protecting and preserving life
6: to use physical force only when the exercise of persuasion, advice and warning is found to be insufficient to obtain public co-operation to an extent necessary to secure observance of law or to restore order, and to use only the minimum degree of physical force which is necessary on any particular occasion for achieving a police objective
7: to maintain at all times a relationship with the public that gives reality to the historic tradition that the police are the public and that the public are the police, the police being only members of the public who are paid to give full-time attention to duties which are incumbent on every citizen in the interests of community welfare and existence
8: to recognise always the need for strict adherence to police-executive functions, and to refrain from even seeming to usurp the powers of the judiciary of avenging individuals or the State, and of authoritatively judging guilt and punishing the guilty
9: to recognise always that the test of police efficiency is the absence of crime and disorder, and not the visible evidence of police action in dealing with them

In essence, the ground-breaking directions amount to the still firmly-held principle of 'policing by consent' and are still considered universally unique in establishing a system of policing based on co-operation rather than fear.

For all its well-meaning ideologies, the police both in the Metropolitan area where the so-named force was formed on September 29th this year, and throughout the regions, not least lawless Worcester, still remained unpopular: there were fears that they would be a military force, crushing freedom, there was widespread objection to paying money for them and even when it became clear that this was going to be the new way and that here was a case of fait accompli, like it or not, there followed a raft of demands to keep such forces under local control.

It's from this period that the nickname 'bobby' in reference to a policeman is drawn from the Principles' chief formulator, Robert Peel: it remains a popular term to this day.

Mid-October this year, 'Watchman (Tommy) Davies' gets some recognition from the *Herald*, his actions resulting in six months' hard for serial offender, Worcester lass Mary Ann Darke *(cutting, right)* '...single woman, indicted for stealing a sovereign and a farthing from the person of William Mogg... a waggoner in the employ of Mr Jolley'.

Another body destined to keep the everlasting wheel in motion...

WORCESTER CITY SESSIONS, OCT. 19, 1829.

MARY ANN DARKE, aged 22, single woman, was indicted for stealing a purse, containing a sovereign and a farthing, from the person of William Mogg. Mogg is a waggoner in the employ of Mr. Jolley; the prisoner a woman of the town. In the night of the 8th of August, the parties were together in the Bull Entry, when the prisoner contrived to abstract the purse from Mogg's pocket. The prosecutor almost immediately discovered his loss, and apprized Davies, the watchman, of it, who very shortly after apprehended the prisoner, and on her person the stolen property was found. Mogg positively identified the farthing. *Guilty— Six months, hard labour.*

JOSEPH SMITH, aged 31, labourer, was found *guilty* upon the most conclusive evidence, of stealing, at the Coventry Arms public-house, an umbrella and other articles, the property of James Bannister. A record of this prisoner's conviction of a felony at the March assizes for the present year was put in, and he was sentenced to *seven years' transportation.*

FRANCIS HOUSEMAN, aged 24, labourer, was charged with stealing two dead rabbits, the property of Benjamin Downes. The prisoner was seen to take the rabbits from the cart of the prosecutor, whilst standing in the fruit market, on Saturday, the 10th inst. Houseman was convicted of a felony at an adjourned

**1830**

The City Gaol's accounts, published on January 23rd., shows a healthy state of affairs, if a wide variance in salaries between the top (the Chaplain at £250 and the Gaoler and the Keeper of the Bridwell at £150 pa each) and the bottom, the lowly watchmen, the year's salaries for two amounting to £36 8s.

Other expenditure during the previous year had included salaries of Clerk and four turnkeys (£343 8s); surgeon (£80); matron (£30); female turnkey (£31 4s) and woman waiting on the prisoners (£13); bibles and prayer books for the use of prisoners (£13) and an unusual one reflecting the sad state of the economic climate: 'conveying and maintaining Irish vagrants' (£665 10s 5d).

And then a deeply disturbing case following the discovery of a baby's body in Barbourne brook...

INQUEST UPON THE BODY OF A NEW-BORN CHILD, FOUND DEAD IN BARBOURNE BROOK.

A jury, most respectably composed, over which Wm. Smith, Esq. presided, assembled at the Talbot Inn, in the Tything, last night, for the purpose of investigating how and by what means a female infant child, apparently new born, the body of which was found on Tuesday last, in Barbourne Brook, adjoining to the Old Water Works, came by its death. The investigation lasted six hours, and, although it proved not to be, as at first dreaded, a case involving the crime of MURDER, still circumstances were developed in the enquiry which exhibited it as one as flagrant in depravity and moral turpitude as ever became the subject of enquiry before such a tribunal. The body was discovered, as stated above, about middle day on Tuesday last, locked in the ice. It was first wrapped in a white pocket handkerchief, and then covered with an old blue cotton gown, the whole being slackly secured round the neck with a piece of

Extensive enquiries pointed to the child's mother being no more than a child herself – 13-year old, Elizabeth Inight who was in the service of 67-year old tailor Thomas Whiteley, and further questioning led to the charge '...that she had secretly delivered herself of it, and then destroyed it, and put it away to hide her shame. The rumours... reached the ears of the parish constable [John Taylor] who caused the apprehension of the girl'.

In court, Elizabeth Inight firmly stated that Whiteley was the father and that he'd been in attendance at the birth and immediately took the child away from her – all of which he'd violently denied. Unfortunately for him, not a soul in the room – least of all the 15-strong jury – believed him, a sentiment forcibly rammed home when the child's body was displayed in open court as critical evidence and '...he was desired to look upon it, which he did with the most perfect indifference and apathy'.

On the other hand, surgeon Thomas Carden presented his evidence and belief that the child had been still-born: accordingly, the case was dropped and both were released. Noted the *Herald*: '...as regards the girl Inight, we have no doubt few who peruse this will murmur at such a result. We can easily anticipate that far different will be the case of the latter and that one feeling of regret will prevail that such an offender should go unpunished. We have reason, however, to believe that the delinquent will not altogether escape the deserts his iniquitous conduct merits. It has been subsequently ascertained that he is subject to a charge of misdemeanour, it has been resolved to prosecute him thereon and, we have no doubt, he is by this time again in custody, preparatory to an accusation of such nature being preferred against him before the proper tribunal'.

He was later charged with perjury.

The same day, Michael Toll was executed at the County Gaol for the murder of Ann Cook. Reports the *Herald*, on the gallows he was '...firm and collected; and suffered himself to be bound and the rope adjusted without betraying any violent emotion. About eighteen minutes past twelve, the signal given, the drop fell and in a few seconds afterwards, he was a lifeless corpse'.

In February, another policing milestone when the costs of implementing the City of Worcester Improvement Act and particularly empowerment to appoint parish watchmen were published and the general feeling was that it was not, after all, going to be as financially crippling as at first thought – 9d in the pound for the first year and 6d in the pound for subsequent years. Reports the *Herald*: '... the bill bears evidence of having been ably and carefully framed. Its provisions are clearly and distinctly set forth and while they embrace all necessary to obtain the objects in view, they are free from aught which, if enforced to the letter, can be deemed frivolous or vexatious. Such an Act has long been needed, and we have no doubt that it will be found beneficial in its operations'.

The following week 13-year old Thomas Spragg was the only prisoner up for trial at the City Sessions. Charged with stealing a quantity of spirits from his employer, chemist Edward Evans of the Foregate he was sentenced a month's hard and also to be privately whipped.

A provident stroke of luck befell an unnamed watchman in May when he overheard a private conversation between two Irish hawkers and their Worcester landlord involving 'several parcels of French brandy, clandestinely introduced here for sale without having first paid the duty'. Several gallons of fine brandy were impounded and the Irishmen committed for trial.

The same week, possibly the first report of the death of a serving officer: this was the ever-dependable **Tommy Watkins** watchman of St Helens for the previous eight years and for whom getting beaten-up was a regular event. The final time it occurred had been at the races the previous August when, typically,

he'd gone in head-first to apprehend a gang of sharpers and predictably came off worst, suffering injuries from which he never recovered. According to the report, he left a widow and five children and the County magistrates immediately ordered 10l to be paid to the family. It's not recorded what the city's contribution was – if anything at all, which is the most likely.

Mayor's officer **Joe Orchard**, on the other hand, was going from strength to strength. In August he successfully investigated a daring robbery at a City tailor's shop resulting in the apprehension and subsequent gaoling of two notorious villains Thomas Baker and Edward Williams, and the next week proved instrumental in nabbing two more noted thieves, Stevens and Bayliss, for a spate of robberies including a violent affair at the Waterloo Tavern in the Blockhouse. Both were later transported.

The next week 17-year old Thomas Turner was executed at the County Gaol for the rape of child Louisa Blissett in front of a huge crowd of onlookers: '...the unhappy malefactor made no confession further than that he hoped the Lord would forgive him. After hanging the usual time, the body was cut down and will be interred tomorrow, in the event of no application from his friends being made for it'. (*Herald*).

Later in the year, the Duchess of Kent and her daughter Princess Victoria visited the city: it was the only time the future Queen was to set foot in her 'Faithful City'.

On October 29th came the inauguration of a new society that, while no-one knew it at the time, was to play a major role in the formation of the city's first real police force within three years: the 24-strong Mendicity and District Society 'with the two-fold object of diminishing the number of travelling beggars and relieving cases of extreme distress amongst our own poor at their own habitations'.

# 1831

Extreme cold heralded the start of a year that, history was to show, did much to speed-up the creation of a professional police force in Worcester – as well as everywhere else – by demonstrating in no uncertain terms that the masses were a force to be reckoned with and that when pushed, anarchy and disorder would result. The conditions had run coal stocks low – so low that prices shot up from 9d a cwt for the best quality to 1/- for coal of inferior quality. The knock-on effect was that the traditional hand-out of coal stocks to the poor at times of dire need was also hard hit. The masses were not pleased and discontent was rife – but there was worse to come.

The City's rival 'sheets', the *Herald* and the *Journal*, ran much the same tales of the news of the day:

● Worcester's support for the new King, William IV due to be crowned later in the year: George IV had died in June 1830
● a gang of con-men 'of the Hebrew persuasion' in the City offering guns of particularly poor quality 'so shamefully got up that they offer immediate danger to all who may venture to discharge them'
● a crop of daring daylight robberies carried out by known Birmingham gangs
● **Joe Orchard** ingeniously tracing the theft of a horse from Cripplegate House to Bromsgrove where the trail apparently fizzled-out
● an increased spate of suicides and accidental deaths, including those of several boys ice-skating on the canal, and more properties destroyed by fire and deaths from burning
● an upsurge in petty crimes as desperate families struggled to survive the cold and the increasingly harsh times. At the same time it was estimated that 80,000 women in London alone had been forced into prostitution solely in order to survive.

Then, after the ice and snow had melted, came the usual misery of floods after the river rose 12 feet in as many hours – a calamity 'scarcely paralleled in the memory of persons living in the vicinity of the river'.

1831 was shaping up as a difficult year for Worcester; law and order was breaking down and the Mendicity Society was finding itself hard-pressed to cope with the sheer numbers banging its door (*at the House of Industry on Tallow Hill*) demanding food and shelter.

The situation had reached such a pass that the almost unheard-of, not to mention grossly unforgiveable crime of plundering churches hit what passed as headlines in the news-sheets' columns: at the end of February, a quantity of valuable books was stolen from St Nicholas Church. Found guilty of the theft, 39-year old cabinet-maker 'of creditable appearance' James Handley was sentenced to the vicious term of twelve months' hard. Outbreaks of influenza in May and cholera later in the year, also hit hard.

As the year wore on, the city recorded another worrisome increase in robberies – including raids on the properties of some of the City Commissioners, hardening their resolve to beef-up policing measures for a city where crime had now reached crisis-point.

Meanwhile, the pressures on the Mendicity Society continued to increase at a time when expectations had been for a marked *decrease* with the coming of the summer months. In one week alone there had been 100 new applications at the Tallow Hill 'workhouse' – *33 more even than Birmingham the same week* – and in its first nine months, the Society had had to deal with 2,421 people demanding assistance, including 82 'foreigners', mostly Scots and Irish. Those that were refused regularly resorted to violence against property and people in order to secure some kind of accommodation – more often than not the City Gaol.

Then, as thoughts of a new-look professional police force began to form, a spate of events occurred that did as much to pave the way for what was to become Worcester City Police as any other single factor: riots in the streets in the wake of the Reform Bill proposed for the following year. The proposal had been to extend voting rights to those who owned properties valued at more than 10l. The House of Lords opposed the idea and delayed its passing for more than a year while those who remained disenfranchised noisily said so – and took to the streets to record their displeasure. Result? Anarchy at its ugliest...

Angry mobs united in disapproval, buildings were attacked, shops looted, and anybody standing in their way viciously assaulted. For the better part of a week starting on November 3rd, the city was in a state of uncontrolled riot and Mayor Henry Clifton was forced to adopt extreme measures to counter the threat.

To his credit, his actions proved effective – to the point that it could be argued that the City Police force came into being in all but name at this time. Almost immediately, he'd issued a handbill:

> '...inviting the citizens of this city to co-operate with the Magistrates in preserving the peace by enrolling themselves as special constables. The invitation was met with most creditable alacrity by our fellow citizens and (the following night, Friday 4th November) 400 of our gentlemen, and others, had been sworn in. **(See extract from the List of Special Constables, right)** These were divided into four sections, over each of which a captain was appointed; short staves were provided for the whole, with a letter to place in their hats denoting their section and also to serve as a badge; and in charging them with their duties on severally taking their oaths the Magistrates took occasion to urge... firmness and decision in acting but at the same time forbearance and good temper. Besides these arrangements, the regular constabulary force of the city was placed in an efficient state, the customary guards at the city and county gaols were strengthened (portions, we believe of the staff of the Militia being posted in each, and at the former the Sherriff's javelin-men were placed) and at the Bishop's Palace, the College Green in the vicinity of the cathedral and other places likely to be singled-out for attack, large bodies of constables were stationed under appointed superintendents'. (Herald)

With the rioters running wild and every attempt to reason with them violently rejected, Henry Clifton ordered the church bells to be tolled – the signal for the constables to wade in – or, as the *Herald* put it, '...sallied forth and encountered the rioters, and the streets immediately became the scene of conflicts in every direction'.

Even the enrolment of the 7th Hussars failed to halt the carnage and mayhem and at 2am Henry Clifton was forced to read the Riot Act from the steps of the Guildhall: it was met with a stone being slung at him, hitting him on the head. The action spurred the specials and the Hussars into determined action and the riot was eventually put down, although with brutal results. Captain Bathurst himself had gathered two of the ringleaders – one with his bridle, the other with his sword-arm – and rode down Broad Street *at full gallop with the men dragged along*. Order was restored by Sunday evening although it again flared up the following day and night by which time the taste for fight was gone and the City's prisons were graced with the presence of dozens more new inmates under sentence of several months' hard apiece.

Despite a riot and plans for mass escape from the County Gaol on Christmas Day – only averted by the governor, J. Nelson Lavender, clapping a dozen ringleaders in irons – 1831 had proved an important, although brutal and bloody, year in the city's policing history.

1832 would prove equally so...

# Special Constables. 1831

| Names | Trade &c | Residence | Remarks |
|---|---|---|---|
| Corbett James | Draper | Broad Street | |
| Powell William | Carpetmanf. | Cross | |
| Matthews John | Ironmonger | Broad Street | |
| Anson John | Waterman | Dolo.. | |
| Wainwright John | (F Workes Esq.) | St Cle.. | |
| Also Thomas | Glover | Butt.. | |
| Harvey Ralph | (F Working) | Lower G.. | |
| Bishop John | Grocer | Broad .. | |
| Butt Thomas | Surgeon | Infir.. | |
| Taylor John | Mason | St.. | |
| Pemberton Isaac | Brushmaker | Broad.. | |
| Parker John | Atty at Law | Infirm.. | |
| Crane Saml Senr | Gent | .. | |
| Whitehouse John | Cordwainer | Crip.. | |
| Clarke Charles | Ironmonger | Bro.. | |
| Parry Thomas | Smith | Ang.. | |
| Twin Thomas | Pensioner | St.. | |
| Holland Francis | Bricklayer | G.. | |
| Palmer James | Porter | St.. | |
| Booth Benjamin | Pensioner | St.. | |
| Onslow George | Combmaker | On.. | |
| Hill Edward | Confectioner | Nea.. | |
| Allen George | Pastrycook | Br.. | |
| Shuck William | Hatter | | |
| Calvin John | Do | | |
| Starratt Lillington R. | Do | | |
| Davis Ed | Linendraper | | |
| Helius John | Pastrycook | | |
| Sawyer Jas | Innkeeper | | |
| Suggins John | Wireworker | | |
| Ostland Rich | at Bradleys | | |
| Hounsell Robt | Do | | |
| Green Edward | Do | Do | |
| Newton Edward | Chandler | Do | |
| Dobbins Richard | Cooper | Do | |
| Leonard Thomas | Grocer | Do | |
| George Thomas | Do | Do | |

**... HERALD.**

... EVENING, NOV. 11.

WORCESTER DISPENSARY.

... MORNING, November 20th, 1831, the ... SERMON will be Preached at the Parish Church ... by the Venerable THOMAS SINGLE-... N, D.D. Archdeacon of Northumberland and Prebendary ... , and a COLLECTION afterwards made for the WORCESTER DISPENSARY.

### DISTURBANCES AT WORCESTER.

We have this week a task of mingled pain and pleasure to discharge—of pain in relating the situation of alarm, disquietude, and terror, in which this city has been placed in the interval since our last, by disgraceful and violent acts of outrage and tumult;—of pleasure, in announcing that, thanks to the promptitude, energy, and decision of our excellent Mayor (Henry Clifton, Esq.) and his brother Magistrates, conjoined with the ready and firm co-operation of their respectable fellow-citizens of all classes, these proceedings were speedily checked in the outset, soon altogether suppressed, the nefarious aggressors completely foiled and defeated in their infamous designs of rapine and plunder, and the city restored to its wonted repose and tranquillity.

The combined circumstances of the County Reform Meeting taking place on Saturday last, its being market day, and also the anniversary of the Gunpowder Plot, leading our authorities to anticipate the congregation of a large number of people, and that from various intimations they had received, the day was intended to be marked by proceedings of a nature calculated to lead to the interruption of the public peace, they promptly applied themselves effectually to the adoption of such measures as should enable them effectually to meet the dreaded evil, should it unhappily arise, subdue it in its bud, and avert from the city those fatal and deplorable consequences which, for the want of the like timely precautions, had been so recently experienced in another part of the kingdom. Accordingly on Thursday, a handbill was issued from the Public Office, inviting the inhabitants of the city to co-operate with the Magistrates in preserving the peace by enrolling themselves as special constables. The invitation was met with most creditable alacrity by our fellow-citizens, and, by Friday evening, 400 of our most respectable tradesmen, as well as many professional and private gentlemen, and others, had been sworn in. These were divided into four sections, over each of which a captain was appointed; short staves were provided for the whole, with a letter to place in their hats, denoting their section, and also to serve as a badge; and in charging them with their duties on severally taking their oaths, the Magistrates took occasion to urge, should it unfortunately occur that their services were required, firmness and decision in acting, but at the same time forbearance and good temper. Besides these arrangements, the regular constabulary force of the city was placed in an efficient state; the customary guards at the county and city gaols were strengthened (portions, we believe, of the Militia being posted in each, and at the former also the Sheriff's javelinmen were placed); and at the former also the College Green, in the vicinity of the Cathedral and other ...

WCiCo/WAAS

# 1832

The fragile peace was maintained as 1832 dawned – just – but given the hard times and the changing world, it wasn't long before more instances of organised violence again united the special and regular constables and the Military, and once more involved the reading of the Riot Act.

Men put out of work by the coming of the railways and the canals had directed their frustration and anger at buildings, property and people associated with the new companies and the problem had prompted the passing of the Special Constables Act – tersely summed-up as '*an Act for the Payment of Constables for Keeping the Peace near Public Works*' [permitting] *the appointment of special constables for keeping the peace, and for the protection of the inhabitants and security of the property in the neighbourhood of such public works*'.

The 400 armed citizens employed as Specials had remained in force, putting down sporadic incursions into the peace, often with unwarranted violence.

But then another issue exploded into all-out conflict threatening more of the same... hundreds of labourers that had been employed along the Severn as bow hauliers – a thankless and gruelling profession that involved *manually* hauling the flat bottomed boats when there was insufficient wind – had rebelled against the Act of Parliament now permitting the use of horses on river and canal towpaths and had begun violently disrupting waterborne traders going about their lawful business.

With river and canal traffic on a major up, the bow hauliers' gravely-deteriorating situation erupted in June when they blockaded the river at One Acre Piece a mile north of the city, close to what's now the Slip. The Specials now found themselves overwhelmed by the sheer numbers of protesting labourers gathered in vicious protest – as the *Journal* put it, 'a considerable and formidable mob' – and the Mayor was again forced to call in the military, this time the Scots Greys, not known for their easy–going ways, commanded by Maj-General Campbell.

'*Several of the men most active in the affair singled out by the Constables were taken into custody but they were speedily rescued; one of the constables was thrown down and his shoulder much injured. Mr Williams [John Williams, one of five Magistrates ordered to take charge of the protest] now read the Riot Act and again warned the people to disperse; the horses were once more brought out to be yoked to the vessels, but still to no purpose... [the Scots Greys, some dismounted others on horseback] were again ordered to clear the towing path which they soon accomplished whilst, under the protection of the dismounted [soldiers], the horses were affixed to the vessels, and the special constables and others rushed into the mob and captured the ringleaders. Nine were taken and placed in the care of the military*'.

All the time, recorded the *Journal*, and all the way to the County Gaol where the men were conveyed pending trial, the specials and the soldiers were pelted with stones, for the most part by women but also reinforced with yet more labourers and hauliers who'd been besieging the entire length of the Severn between Bewdley and Gloucester.

**(Left)** *One of the staves issued to the Special Constables at a time of mounting civil disorder, now preserved in the Guildhall (Worcester CiCo)*

Clearly, somewhere along the line the cost of maintaining order on the streets and towpaths was going to lead to a head-on situation, and once the shockwaves created by publication of the cost of the year's 'special' policing measures – some 400l more than the previous year – had subsided, it's likely that the City's resolve to better channel available cash into a new, improved and permanent standing police force, of sorts, had hardened.

While the times had been gravely clouded by the disruptive actions of determined workers gathered en masse to create mayhem as an alternative to unemployment and starvation, the situation on the streets had similarly spiralled out of control.

A *Journal* report at the end of the year (right) stated:

*'... scarcely a night passes but robberies of the most daring character are openly committed in our streets and thoroughfares. In the New Road, leading to St Johns on Thursday evening, two persons were attacked, one of whom was plundered of 15 sovereigns; at the Cross on the same evening, a gentleman was knocked down by a gang of villains, doubtless with the intention of robbing him... in Broad Street, shortly after nine, a man was observed by a boy to enter the shop of Mr Brookes, shoemaker, and carry off 12 pairs of clogs. The boy kept his eye on the fellow, until he saw him go into the Woolpack public house, in Doldy, and he then gave information to the police of what he had witnessed. The officers immediately went to the house in question, but the thief had fled. Their visit, however, had one good effect – that of discovering a number of dissolute characters playing at cards. The landlord, Hales jun. was in consequence summoned before the Magistrates, on Saturday, and find (sic) 50s and 7s 6d expences (sic) for keeping bad hours, and harbouring notoriously bad characters...'*

Later events would show that this was Martin Smith and that one of the notoriously bad characters' found in the Woolpack – a pub with a questionably iffy character right up to its closure as recently as 1968 – would almost certainly have been Thomas Evans, aka Butcher Tom. The same report lists several more gross felonies all on the same day including Benjamin Berry, 'a well-known character who has been more than once charged with robberies'. He had been seen to enter the premises of perfumer Mrs Bradford on the Cross and carry off her till. From this date, the fates of all three – Martin Smith, Thomas Evans and Benjamin Berry – were to be linked for the next seven years at least **(see pps 6-13, 53 and 378-381)**

1832 had seen 121,318 people in England and Wales committed for trial at the Assizes and Sessions – 101,638 men and 19,680 women. 9,302 were sentenced to death; 460 executed; 9,316 transported for life, 3,103 for 14 years, and 14,436 for 7 years; and 2,214 ordered to be whipped. More than 60,000 had been committed to gaols.

If ever there was time that a permanent professional police force was needed, this was it.

The city rose to the challenge with not perhaps as much determination as evident desperation...

# 4:
# The Sharpe years

## 18th January 1833 – 14th April 1835

If the crime tally for 1832 was considered shocking, that of 1833 would prove even worse...

This year alone was to see 20,829 men and women transported for various terms, imprisoned or whipped for various offences, and 1,419 sentenced to death.

The harsh state-of-affairs was clearly stated: get caught after having stepped out of line, and life was simply not worth living – or so the authorities would have you believe. The fact was that in just too many cases, chances of getting caught and being faced with paying your dues was, for the most part, a risk worth running. Everybody was in much the same boat and crime was a burgeoning business.

The nation had been plunged into economic chaos, crime was now everyday and for many had become a condition of survival, with the result that chancers were on every corner, the streets were dangerous, and the overall situation was fast becoming desperate.

In the capital, Home Secretary Sir Robert Peel's early Metropolitan police force had been making some inroads into quelling a population hard-hit by economic and political circumstances and 120 miles north-west, the need for something similar was plainly evident: what had sufficed for a policing system during times of comparative stability was clearly out of its depth during these new troublesome times of disruption and discontent, and the old order had been found lacking in virtually every respect.

Besides, having to call in the army to quell civilian rioters and troublemakers was considered a step too far and served only to harden the antagonism of the population-at-large to the old order and its old ways.

The fact is that the Government had been making too many wrong decisions, economic woe was rife and the hardest-hit was the poor. Reporting the second annual meeting of the Worcester Mendicity Society set up two years before to provide temporary relief and shelter to the increasing number of families turning to the authorities for help just to survive, the *Worcester Journal* noted that in the previous year, 3937 people had applied for relief, of which 2593 had been supplied with provisions and lodging at the House of Industry, aka Workhouse, on Shrub Hill; 1067 were supplied with provisions only; 101 had failed to take

...in these cases, some parishes have adopted... in these ends, some parishes have adopted...
...of publishing the names of the defaulters, and as it appears to have been attended with good effect, surely the example cannot be too generally followed.

The nightly patrole formed in All Saints' parish, with the view, so far as regards that parish, to operate until the new police establishment is organized in checking that system of outrage and plunder by which our city has lately been disgraced, commenced its duties on Wednesday evening. The list of members includes 120 names of the most respectable inhabitants and substantial tradesmen of the parish, and the arrangement is for four to go on duty from five to ten in the evening, and then to be replaced by six others, who continue from ten till one. Already the benefits to be expected from the plan have been manifest. Wednesday evening, about half-past nine, as the first-mentioned party were going their rounds, they found a decently dressed female engaged in a scuffle with a man whom she asserted had robbed her of between four and five pounds. The woman firmly held him, notwithstanding his struggles, and two other fellows were endeavouring to release him; however, upon the patrol appearing, all three made off. Two got clear away, but the third was captured, and yesterday morning he was taken before the City Magistrates. He stated that his ... that he came from Plymouth, ... produce no licence, ... so un-

NEW POLICE.—The new day-police for the city is now in operation. It consists of an Inspector and four men, some of whom are on duty in the streets from the morning until the time the watchmen come on. Whether any new arrangement will be made with a view to render the night-watch more efficient, is not yet determined. The Inspector will shortly report to the Commissioners his opinion upon that point. The good effects of having an active and intelligent person at the head of the police, have already become manifest. In consequence of information given by the Inspector, William Steele, the landlord of the Druid's Head in Merry Vale, has been fined ... the same plan, and we doubt not, ... throughout the different parishes in the city, ... foregoing was in type, we have learnt that the ... patrol, aided by the police, last night succeeded in making...

up the lodging tickets issued to them; 143 had been dismissed as undeserving, and 33 had been detected as imposters and committed to prison for varying terms.

Out of the total, 823 were Irish, 74 Scotch (*sic*), 86 were 'Foreigners' and only 1133 could read. In one instance, they'd found a family of seven – father, mother and five children – sharing a single room and one bed in Dolday. Small wonder the Society was already overstretched and in a financial quandary.

The first week of January had not been a particularly good start for Worcester in general: on the first Friday night of the year, the clerk to St Clement's Church, a young man named Barrow, had been attacked on the bridge by seven or eight toughs who'd tried to rob him and, noted the *Journal,* the villains had left him '...so ill-treated that he was unable to attend the Church on Sunday'.

The following night, three yobs attacked another man crossing the bridge and while the victim had managed to lay one of them flat, the other two hammered into him and kicked him senseless.

Earlier the same morning, a countryman emerging from a warehouse in the city was asked by a couple of strangers where he came from and when he replied 'Pershore' the two strangers stated "Just the thing! We want to send something there and if you'll come down to the Druid's Head and have a glass with us, we'll give it to you". The intended dupe was about to fall into the snare when a person came up who knew the fellows, and calling the countryman aside, induced him not to accompany them. But for this caution he would no doubt have been robbed' *(Berrows Journal January 17th).*

And there were others too. Far too many for the Magistrates' liking.

But changes were in hand, and there were encouraging signs that the authorities had plans at least to tackle, and hopefully reverse, the worsening situation. Or so people hoped...

Almost in desperation, the City's Commissioners had already taken on four 'special' new constables, initially to assist in the crack-down on begging and in handing out tickets for a night's accommodation and relief to the growing legions of those who simply had nowhere else to go, but also with an eye to more onerous duties in the future. They were **George Williams, James Douglas, John Leary** and **Michael Fannon** who, alongside the Watchmen were also housed at the Gaol in Friar Street, and their work was gratefully acknowledged by the committee of the Mendicity Society at their annual meeting at the beginning of the year and duly reported in the press.

The same week's *Journal* that carried the report as well as the news of that week's troublesome incidents, also offered a faint ray of hope for Worcester's much put-upon citizens – the encouraging revelation that '... the serjeant of the intended New Police force for this city is arrived from London, and as soon as the arrangements can be completed, the men will commence their duties. There will be a day and night police. This arrangement will give great satisfaction'.

It was accompanied by an almost audible sigh of relief, as: '...the number of robberies and outrages in the streets during the last few weeks has been unprecedented'. The 8-line article was simply headed **'New Police'**.

## A new police force for Worcester

It was the first that Worcester's reading public had heard of the initiative, and while the *Journal* could justifiably be accused of jumping to conclusions, the assumption that the arrangement would give great satisfaction, must on the whole be considered a fair and accurate one.

So as not to be outdone, the *Herald*, published on the Saturday, two days after the *Journal*, carried an expanded version of the story and proved itself at odds with the older, but less well-subscribed broadsheet in at least one element:  was it to be a day **and** night service (*Journal*) or day only (*Herald*)?

The likeliest response is that the *Herald*, with two days to verify the facts and by the sound of it had also got themselves the first interview with the elusive new 'serjeant', is the more accurate – although that's not to say that that was always to be the case.  The edition of January 19ᵗʰ read (*in full*)

> *The New Police established for this city have commenced their duties, but the present arrangement goes no farther than providing a day watch.  The force consists of an Inspector and four men, who, by turns, patrol the streets from the morning until the hour the watchmen come upon their beats, and the Commissioners are waiting for a report from the Inspector on the expediency of extending the system to the formation of a night as well as a day police, or of adopting it partially, so as to render the present night watch more efficient'.*

The *Herald* also presented for the first time the name of the man drafted-in to tame an increasingly lawless Worcester – the available evidence making it perfectly clear that the Commissioners believed that the only solution was to import a no-nonsense hard-case taskmaster from outside, believing that no-one locally, and least of all from the existing ranks of parish constables and watchmen, would be tough enough to handle so exacting a job.

The final decision had probably been borne out of the low opinion in which the existing force was held by the masses and the justices alike, but for all their work over the previous decade, the old spent watchmen and constables must have been desperately disappointed in the Commissioners' response to look not only outside their ranks, but more woundingly, out of the City, for a man mentally and physically big enough for the role.

The new man was 32-year old **Henry Sharpe**, born Newark-on-Trent, a former solder and until now a serjeant in the Metropolitan Police established just four years earlier, and the *Herald* carried a brief, but interesting pen-portrait of him – sadly, the only one we have... *'He appears an intelligent active man, possessing a thorough knowledge of the duties of his appointment, and he has already shewn that the city may depend upon his discharging them fearlessly and honestly'.*

Editor William Holl may or may not have regretted those words in the months, and events, that followed, but in the meantime hopes were rising that the city's increasing crime tally could at least be curtailed.

The next week, the *Journal* amended its ambiguity on the force's expected hours of operation, and covered itself by adding: '...whether any new arrangement will be made with a view to rendering the night-watch more efficient is not yet determined'.

At least, there remained one key point on which the two news-sheets wholly concurred – that the Commissioners were prepared to await the new man's observations on the topic of hours.  In the meantime, it was 'as you were' for the existing Watchmen who must have been wondering a) quite how they fitted into all this, and b) how they were going to feed their families if their worst fears came true.

With typical new-broom application and ex-military organisation, **Henry Sharpe** appears to have set-to his new duties with a vengeance, arranging and co-ordinating the activities of the interim four-man team that he'd inherited and weighing-up the pros and cons of a 24-hour professional police force.

The following week, the *Herald* carried more details about the new police – including the all-important detail that the plan was for the men to be dressed uniformly, and that clothing was already being prepared for them.  While there was some leeway in local uniform detailing, the Home Office had laid down some guidelines in respect of the new forces' dress – purposely aiming to avoid similarities and mistaken identity with the army and other military forces by stipulating blue as the predominant colour and regulating that officers carried no visible means of armoury such as a cutlass or sword, a short staff or nightstick considered sufficient both for their **de**fence and, in the unlikely event that it might ever arise, **off**ence.

Sir Robert Peel's overall vision had been the establishment of an ethical police force characterised by intelligence, persuasion and respect rather than brute strength, and the chief element in attaining such a grand master-plan had been the creation of the new body's image not as 'them and us' but rather as 'from among us' – a citizen in uniform going about his duty with the common consent of the community he served and thus, provided he stuck to the rules, entitled to the respect of the people whose safety could be left in his hands. A noble thought.

*To this day, it's still the bedrock of modern policing, summed up as 'policing by consent'.*

However, within just days of the new force's inception, there was already a thinly-veiled whiff of panic in the tone of a lengthy passage in a press article revealing the warnings the Commissioners had just issued to the new body of men, regarding the perils of drinking while on duty. This was not necessarily a public service announcement: just days after **Henry Sharpe**'s appearance, **Michael Fannon** had been stripped of his duties for drunkenness and sent on his way...

One of the duties of the new force was escorting – the *Herald* termed it 'accompanying' – prisoners to and from the gaols for their trials at the Guildhall. A matter of weeks later, *Herald* editor William Holl printed a report from the Governor claiming that 'in many instances of late, prisoners and constables who brought them to gaol were in a state of intoxication when they arrived'. The report called for a halt on the payment of constables' expenses in such instances and also for certificates, signed by the Governor, attesting to the constables' and prisoners' sobriety at the time of hand-over.

There's every likelihood that **Michael Fannon** had been caught in this way, but it's unlikely ever to be known for sure – although the unfortunate up-shot was already evident: that after the only partially-successful constables/watchmen years, hopes of a miraculous overnight turn-round in policing in the City had received its first body-blow and the new saviours of the city's good name were revealed as mere mortals, fallible and with the same human weaknesses as the rest of the world-at-large.

The magistrates and Commissioners were no doubt livid over the incident that could additionally have been tainted with attempts at bribery – another comparatively lengthy *Herald* article the following week forming an interesting exercise in spin and public relations years before the phrases were coined...

> 'The Commissioners have very properly given some very strong injunctions to the police men against intoxication, and one of their number already found in liquor, has been discharged; they (the police) are likewise forbidden, on pain also of dismissal, from receiving gratuities of any kind from individuals, under any pretence whatsoever'.

The justices not only blamed the erring policeman from whom so much more had been expected, but also issued a scarcely-veiled threat to the publicans who they clearly regarded as being at the heart of most, if not all, of the city's growing catalogue of evils...

'It will become keepers of public houses and beer shops within the city to be circumspect in the management of their houses, as it is one of the more especial duties of the New Police to have a vigilant eye on all places of this description, and to report those in which they may discover gambling going on, not closed at proper hours, harbouring bad characters, or any other irregularities: and in all which cases the Magistrates have resolved to inflict the full penalties'.

Whether **Henry Sharpe** came to the same conclusion of his own accord or whether it was orders from the magistrates is frankly immaterial as virtually from day one, it was already clear where the main thrust of his attention was going to be directed.

Within a matter of days he'd got his first result – William Steele, the landlord of the notorious Druid's Head in Merry Vale, charged with allowing gaming in his house and harbouring notoriously bad characters, one of which was Edward Lloyd, alias 'The Herefordshire Pet' who'd not long before seriously assaulted John Pidduck, one of the All Saints' Patrol.

The catch had netted two outlaws for the price of one and resulted in the come-uppance of a high-profile villain with which to set an example to others.

But for all its promise and encouraging start, the new force was still not generally welcomed, nor was it ever likely to be popular; it lacked public support and needed all the help it could get from whichever quarter it could get it from – first port of call then, as now, being the press that now discovered a rich seam of increasingly lurid stories with which to inform and entertain amid the columns of hop prices, turnpike tolls, society weddings, church sermons and fatstock yields...

The same *Herald* edition that carried the news of William Steele's come-uppance also relayed the information that a thug named David Morris had been '...convicted in the penalty of 5l for having yesterday assaulted William Lloyd, at his house in Lowesmore, and also with assaulting **James Starr,** Constable of St Martin's in the execution of his duty'.

In default of payment Morris was committed to the city prison for one calendar month to hard labour – to which the *Herald* confidently noted that magistrates are '...determined to protect those whom they may appoint to preserve the public peace, and bring offenders to justice'.

It appears increasingly likely that after some consideration, **Henry Sharpe** had quickly made up his mind about working hours and that having seen the nocturnal goings-on in his new adopted city that an after-dark presence was both preferable and advisable – a move that the city's money-men really didn't want to consider as it would also demand an inevitable increase in numbers, (*which they welcomed*) and wages (*which they didn't*). Accordingly, as was to be the case with every chief officer that succeeded him, negotiations with the city's paymasters became protracted and sometimes heated, leading to delays and corner-cutting compromises.

Within a few months he was to get his way, but in the meantime, he must have been desperately miffed when both the *Journal* and the *Herald* gave some prominence to the capture of two notorious city characters, heaping praise on the unpaid All Saints' night patrol and the two unnamed Watchmen that had pulled-off something of a coup from under the noses of the supposed 'professionals', the new police.

## First blood: Butcher Tom and Martin Smith

Martin Smith and Thomas Evans had been found '...carousing in public-houses, with a number of their loose associates, about half-past eleven o'clock, and this morning both were fully committed to take their trials' reported the *Journal*. Martin Evans was charged with the theft of a dozen pairs of clogs from the shop of Brookes' the shoemaker in Broad-street and Thomas Evans, notorious throughout the city as Butcher Tom, had been charged with receiving. This time, though, the *Journal* had got the better grip on the story, editor Harvey Tymbs devoting more than twice the space to the arrests than the *Herald*'s William Holl.

The Assize trial took place in the Guildhall on Saturday, March 2nd: Smith and Evans were each sentenced to 7 years' transportation to the colonies, and the true account forms a convenient – and brutally illustrative – opening and closing of this book (*see pps 6-13 and 378-381*).

The space given to the high-profile arrests now made it even more pressing for the four-man New Police to be given more funding and resources if they were to have any effect whatsoever 'against the forces of outrage and plunder [with] which our city has lately been disgraced' (*Herald*): in the meantime, the uneasy relationship between the professional force and the home-grown patrols of volunteer 'Special Constables' had to suffice.

For obvious reasons – not least, the tightly-huddled communities around the still-existing church – the All Saints patrol remained one of the biggest and most successful of the parish patrols, counting on some 120 volunteers that included some of 'the most respectable inhabitants and substantial tradesmen of the parish'.

The parish's mean and far from sedate streets were patrolled by four Specials between 5pm and

EXECUTION.—This morning, the two y...
James and Joseph Carter, underwent the extr...
of the law in front of our County Gaol, pursuant...
tence passed upon them at the last Assizes, for...
highway robbery, committed on two individuals...
night in the neighbourhood of Bewdley, their o...
rendered doubly heinous by the infliction of most...
ment on the persons of the prosecutors, from th...
which it is doubtful whether one of them will ev...
We mentioned last week the becoming conduct...
the wretched culprits since their condemnation...
happy to say that, up to the last moment of their...
their demeanor was such as became them in th...
situation. Listening with thankfulness to the pi...
and instructions of the Rev. Mr. Adlington, the...
Chaplain of the prison (who, assisted by the F...
Davies, has been unremitting in his attentions u...
they employed every moment of the short sp...
to them in supplicating for mercy at the th...
Maker, conscious their crimes shut out...
their escaping the doom pronounced upon...
earthly tribunal. On Sunday morning last, a...
condemned sermon was preached in the cha...
gaol. The Rev. Chaplain selected his text...
3rd Malachi 2nd v.—" But who may abide the...
coming? and who shall stand when he appeareth...
like a refiner's fire, and like fuller's sope;" and...
he founded a most impressive and suitable discou...
the attention of the whole of his hearers, and...
tears to trickle down the cheeks of even those who...
themselves the most hardened of offenders; the...
who were more particularly the objects of the Re...
man's exhortations, were deeply affected. Wedne...
the day appointed for the final interview, bet...
malefactors and such of their friends as might...
of taking their leave of them previously to the...
James Carter has a father only, and he, it se...
lying at the point of death; the father of Josep...
availed himself of the privilege, and passed some...
cell with his wretched son, taking with him also...
brother, whom the hapless culprit addressed...
anxious and earnest manner, exhorting him...
melancholy fate be ever present to him, and if...
avoid the same ignominious end, never to negle...
done, the observance of the Lord's-day; to...
houses and skittle grounds, and to burn car...
"they have brought me to this." Both sle...
throughout the night, and this morning, at an...
they were visited in their cell by the Chaplain,...
immediately joined in prayer. Shortly after...
conducted to the chapel, where all the other pri...
and female, were assembled; the morning servi...
gone through, and the Rev. John Davies re...
passages of scripture adapted to the solem...
of the day. This concluded, the sacrament w...
tered to the two culprits, which they parto...
great fervour and devotion; and the time be...
arrived for the execution, the mournful proc...
formed to the scaffold. The Rev. Chaplain l...
reading the burial service, and was follow...
two men, who continued incessantly praying, and...
the "Lord have mercy upon us," "Christ l...
upon us." The whole of the other prisoner...
ranged along the avenues leading to the dro...
countenances and demeanour of all of whom g...
that they deeply participated in the awfulness of...
scene, and many of them cried bitterly. It w...
minutes past twelve when the miserable culpri...
signed to the Under Sheriffs, and they were...

10pm, who were then relieved by six others, doing the rounds from ten to one, after which it was assumed, rightly or wrongly, that even the criminals would already have been long before abed. While the system and the thinking behind it was far from perfect, there were clear benefits from the on-going process, and the parishes of St Clement's and St Helens were not far behind in adding their weight to supporting the embryo New Police and promoting law abidance in the city – at least while the official force was struggling to get its act together.

As before, the justices yet again made it quite clear where their attentions should be focused – and again relied on the press to make their intentions abundantly clear: '...we are glad to understand that the patrol will direct their particular attention to the state of (*unintelligible, but clearly relating to public houses*) and lay information against such as are found to keep late hours or harbour loose company. This alone would render the patrol very valuable, for every one acquainted with police matters well knows that almost every outrage and robbery arises from bad characters being harboured at unseasonable hours in public-houses'.

### Pubs and beer-houses 'centres of all crime'

There was no doubt that despite some visible attempt at counter-measures, crime in the city was still on a rocketing upwards trend – and the perception was that the classes that infested the pubs and beer houses were universally viewed as being at the centre of it all.

At a Quarter Sessions meeting around this time, Droitwich's John Pakington who was to be architect of later Beer Acts, addressed the Court proposing that its members petition Parliament to make amendments to current regulations in order to prevent the baneful effects of the pubs and beerhouses which had, he said '...*demoralized the lower classes, and prepared them for the commission of every crime*'.

As an example, he cited what he termed 'the dying declaration of almost every criminal that had suffered the extreme penalty of the law' – a direct reference to the double hanging that had taken place on the ramparts of Worcester's new County Gaol just four days earlier (*see left*)...

James and Joseph Carter, unrelated except by crime, had been hung for highway robbery in Bewdley and as ever, the *Herald* had spared few details in reporting the scene.

*'...the time being nearly arrived for the execution, the mournful procession was formed to the scaffold. The Rev Chaplain* [his name not reported, but actually the Rev. John Adlington who'd been appointed just days before] *led the way, reading the burial service, and was followed by the two men, who continued incessantly praying, and ejaculating the "Lord have mercy upon us" and "Christ have mercy upon us". The whole of the*

*other prisoners were arranged along the avenues leading to the drop, the countenances and demeanour of all giving evidence that they deeply participated in the awfulness of the passing scene, and many of them cried bitterly. It was about ten minutes past twelve when the miserable culprits were ushered on to the platform. Both ascended the ladder with great firmness, and the executioner having adjusted the ropes, they were then placed under the beam, upon which Joseph briefly addressed the assembled spectators, solemnly exhorting them to avoid Sabbath breaking, to abstain from habits of drunkenness, gambling and the association of loose women, all of which sins he said he had been guilty, and by these had at length brought down upon himself his present dreadful fate. His fellow culprit said nothing. The caps were then pulled over their faces, and the Chaplain resumed reading the service for the dead. As previously arranged, at the sentence "In the midst of life we are in death" the signal was given for the executioner to withdraw the bolt and the drop fell. James, who was the heaviest man, appeared to die instantly but a few convulsions were perceptible in the body of Joseph; they were however, of very short duration, and sensation, no doubt, entirely ceased in both at the instant of their suspension. The number of persons who had congregated in front of the gaol to behold the sad spectacle was unusually large, but the greater proportion, as is usually the case, appeared to be women and children. The utmost decorum and stillness was, however, observed throughout the solemn scene. After hanging an hour, the two bodies were cut down and delivered to the respective friends, by whom they were immediately carried away in coffins they had previously procured'.*

Before their execution, the Carters had confessed to John Adlington that they'd probably learned more about crime while *inside* the Gaol than before their committal: '...(they) stated to me that when they were in the day room, there were several individuals who made it their practice to instruct the rest of the inmates in the best and readiest way of committing a burglary, and also instructing them in the slang which thieves and pickpockets &c use among themselves. On the whole, the day-room appears to have very injurious effect on the prisoners in general' (*Worcester Herald*)

Earlier on in the same revealing article, the *Herald* had reported on Joseph Carter's pleas to the chaplain 'in supplicating for mercy at the throne of their Maker (and including) advice to all who followed him to shun beer-houses and skittle-grounds and to burn cards, adding "they have brought me to this"'.

Just a week before the double execution, visiting magistrates had paid a visit to the County Gaol and found that the prison was already seriously overcrowded, with cells built for one convict now housing three.

But at least, the city's authorities had by now largely agreed-with, and had given tacit, if begrudged, approval to **Henry Sharpe**'s demands for a larger and more embracing force paid and equipped to patrol the expanding city *round-the-clock*: fifteen new men, for the most part drawn from the ranks of the existing Watchmen were thus brought in to swell the ranks.

They were **William Sanders, William Hale, William Aston, Richard Bills, Robert Checkett (*or Checketts*), George Nott, William Christian, William Jones, Jeremiah Martin, Joseph Mayfield, John Woodward, John Thompson** and **Richard Winwood,** with two fresh new recruits, **Joseph Hall and William Phillips.**

Not all were to find the tasks allotted to them to their liking – **William Christian** quitting with a month of joining, and little more being heard of either **Richard Winwood** or **John Woodward**, both presumed to have quickly fallen by the wayside. But some of the remainder were to go on to long and distinguished careers with what eventually became Worcester City Police, **George Nott,** later No17, remaining with the force up to March 1860. At last, the times were now marked with real progress and signs were emerging that Worcester might now, fingers-crossed, be getting the professional police contingent its mean streets had for too long been crying out for.

The news-sheets also reflected a note of hopefulness, indicating that some improvement was in the air and that the criminal classes might – *just might, mind* – now be facing an adversary willing to take them on after having had it all their own way for far too long: '...we have reason to believe that some thieves have already left Worcester, under the impression that the active measures now taking place will render their calling an unprofitable one' commented the *Journal*.

Then, as was to happen again and again in Worcester, just as real headway was being made, a set-back occurred, threatening to knock it all back to Square One..

## 140 days on:  Henry Sharpe gravely injured in murderous assault at the Cock Inn

An incident at the Cock Inn in Tybridge Street in the early hours of Friday June 7th this year  was to send shock-waves through the city.  The *Herald* reported the sometimes shocking details, but few readers of the time could decide who was the most culpable or whose side they were on, while even fewer could have foreseen its effect...

Just 140 days into his new job, **Henry Sharpe**, the Nottinghamshire-born hardened ex-Met Police Sergeant brought in to tame the wild and wicked savages of far-off Worcester, and **PC2 George Williams**, one of the original five New Police officers *(and also one of the four in court on the day of Butcher Tom's trial less than three months earlier)* had crossed the bridge and wandered into 'the precincts of our city' – notably, St. Clements which stretched from the river up to the top of Tybridge Street and Cripple's Gate where stood the toll-house for crossing the bridge.  This patch was officially 'Worcester' and was policed: the remainder was wild and wicked St Johns and it was not to be incorporated into the city for another three years.

Their purpose was to keep an eye on the activities of their latest raw and largely untried new recruit, young **PC Joseph Hall** who'd been sworn-in just a few weeks earlier, on March 15th.  As the new Night Constable to the parish, having taken over from its previous Watchman **John Ball** who'd been unceremonially dismissed with the coming of the new force, he was still finding his way around his unaccustomed 'beat'.

Noticing lights still burning at the Cock more than two hours after the proscribed closing time (*the Assize Court held on July 22nd heard that the actual time was 1.15am and that Joseph Hall had already warned the landlord William Smith at 11.15pm about his conduct*) the three uniformed 'New Policemen' walked in and found a reported sixteen men still drinking in there – and worse, creating something of a ruckus.  The *Herald,* as ever, spares few details:

> *'...the consequence was, he [**Henry Sharpe**] spoke to Mr Smith, of the impropriety of permitting such irregularities and said he should feel it his duty to report what he had witnessed to the proper authorities.  He was then leaving, when a number of the men who were in the house, rushed out and falling upon the Inspector, and **Williams** and **Hall**, two of the police who were with him, beat the whole in a most violent manner.  Indeed, we lament to say that Mr. Sharpe was so severely injured as to give rise to fears for his recovery; and both Williams and Hall are suffering considerably from the blows and wounds they received; the latter has a cut on the side of his head which appears to have been inflicted by some sharp instrument'.*

The report concluded that two of those in the thick of the action, brothers William and John Bryan, had instantly done a runner in the direction of Ledbury, and that officers had been ordered to bring them back to Worcester, armed with warrants for their arrest.

As a postscript to the news that only warranted four column inches in the rival *Journal*, editor William Holl added: '...Since the foregoing was in type, we have learnt, that Mr Smith, the landlord, and his ostler, have been committed to the city gaol for further examination on a charge of having taken part in the attack on the officers.  Mr Sharpe, we are glad to say, is somewhat better'.

The following week, the *Herald* updated the situation revealing the news that the ostler's name was Robert Bullock and that the Bryan brothers, William and John, both of whom were described as razor-grinders, had voluntarily given themselves up, all four being held in confinement in the City Gaol until Tuesday the following week when their trial to decide whether or not there was a case to answer was set to be heard in the Magistrates Court at the Guildhall under Aldermen Messrs. Ballard and Shaw.

**Henry Sharpe** was still too badly injured to attend – as the *Herald* revealed, he was '...continuing in so precarious a state that it was until that day that the medical gentlemen by whom he was attended, could pronounce him out of danger'.   He'd been seen by local surgeons Drs. Sheppard and Eli Munn who was so later to visit William Bryan in Worcester gaol.

At the hearing, **PCs Hall and Williams** swore that the landlord William Smith (*who'd come to the Cock from the Albion where in 1827 he'd had the distinction of being the pub's very first landlord*) had been the first to lash-out at the Inspector; that William, the elder of the Bryan brothers and

Bullock, the ostler, also waded in; and that in the fight that ensued, Bullock had hit the police chief over the head with a candlestick.

Young **Joseph Hall** also added that while attempting to protect his chief, he was also stabbed in the head with a knife or chisel, and that an all-in scrap just escalated. **Henry Sharpe** had managed to get a couple of blows in with his heavy night-stick but was then knocked down and while down, the two Bryans kept kicking and beating him with it. The two PCs mounted a commendable fight-back while trying to protect their chief, eventually managing to beat back the attacking mob – and it was only with some difficulty that they managed to break away and drag (*their word*) their badly bashed-about leader home.

In the course of the scrap, **George Williams** had managed to land a blow on John Bryan that had between then and the time of the trial 'rendered him insane at times'.

The magistrates considered the four prime attackers guilty and committed them for trial at the up-coming Assizes. Smith and Bullock were given bail – the former in the phenomenal amount of £100 of his own money and two sureties of £50 each, and Bullock £40 with two sureties of £20 each. Unable to raise any kind of bond, the two Bryans were instantly carted back to the city bridewell.

We regret to have to notice an affray of a very serious character, which took place about one o'clock this morning at the Cock public-house, in Cripplegate, within the precincts of our city. It appears that Mr. Sharpe, the Inspector, was taking his usual rounds over the beats of the police, when he found the above house open, persons drinking there, and much disturbance going on. The consequence was, he spoke to Mr. Smith, the landlord, of the impropriety of permitting such irregularities, and said he should feel it his duty to report what he had witnessed to the proper authorities. He was then leaving, when a number of the men who were in the house rushed out, and falling upon the Inspector, and Williams and Hall, two of the police who were with him, beat the whole in the most violent manner. Indeed, we lament to say that Mr. Sharpe was so seriously injured as to give rise to fears for his recovery; and both Williams and Hall are suffering considerably from the blows and wounds they received; the latter has a cut on the side of his head, which appears to have been inflicted by some sharp instrument. Two of the principal actors in the outrage were young men of the name of Bryan, who went off soon after, as it has been ascertained, in the direction of Ledbury, and whither officers have been sent in pursuit of them, with warrants for their apprehension. We understand, also, that the Commissioners this morning gave instructions to their solicitor to take proceedings against all the other parties implicated in the outrage, with a view to their prosecution at the next Assizes.—Since the foregoing was in type, we have learnt, that Mr. Smith, the landlord, and his ostler, have been committed to the city gaol for further examination, on the charge of having taken part in the attack on the officers. Mr. Sharpe, we are glad to say, is somewhat better.

The *Herald* revealed that Henry Sharpe was '...we are glad to say, gradually getting better, but he still suffers much from the wounds he received to his head, two of which are of a very severe description and we fear it will be some time before he fully recovers from the injuries he received'.

Monday July 22nd – six weeks after the affray – was the date set for the trial, presided over by Mr Chief Justice Tindal. Apparently, **Henry Sharpe** had improved sufficiently to allow him to attend, and his colourful account of the incident, recorded verbatim and in full by the court reporters representing the *Herald* and the *Journal*, took up most of the morning's proceedings.

After hearing the three officers' shocking blow-by-blow account of the tussle that had left five men bleeding and damaged and two more with blood on their hands, both literally and proverbially, surgeon Eli Munn outlined the extent of the specific injuries inflicted on the city's chief of police:

*...I found him much cut on the head. There were two extensive wounds which had penetrated into the skull, and a violent contusion over the right temple. The two first-named wounds appeared to have been done with some cutting instrument; they were nearly two inches in length. There was also a contused wound over the right ear. Mr. Sharpe was confined to his bed for seven days; there was considerable fever; and for the first four or five days I considered him to be in great danger'.*

In course of the trial it became evident that despite the extent of their injuries, **PC Joe Hall** and **No2 George Williams** had acquitted themselves very well in the scrap: PC Joseph Hall testified that in desperation he'd wopped William Bryan over the head with his handcuffs and the defence lawyer with the entirely appropriate name of Mr Justice also made much of **George Williams**' evidence to the point of suggesting to the court that he had used his truncheon 'very unceremoniously'.

He went on: 'Some commiseration might be claimed for William Bryan whose head was dreadfully lacerated, and for John Bryan who had been almost deprived of his reason in consequence of the blow given to him. Both the brothers have marks which will long remain' he said.

But the defence lawyers played heavily on the unpopularity of the New Police, constantly referring-to the assumed 'majority' who clearly didn't much care for the interference of the new regime of law enforcers in general, or their powers to interfere with publicans and the way they ran their houses in particular, and they wasted no time in ramming it home, delivering a damning verdict on the conduct of the new Worcester Police force after just three months' unpopular existence.

The presence of a hungry press no doubt added double weight to the eloquence and Mr Justice QC argued that the incident had only come about because the police and their gung-ho chief had stretched their authority too far. Going for the line of least resistance and what might be viewed as the force's weakest link, he was particularly scathing about young **PC Joe Hall**, urging the magistrates that if they were expecting success to come from the current methods of policing, they'd need to be considerably more selective in their choice of civil officers. "Where such great powers are confided, great care should be taken that those employed are not boys like Hall, but men of age and prudence who will ensure a prudent use of their delegated powers – persons careful, cautious, and humane, who will not violate our homes, or risk a breach of the public peace' he said.

It was, to say the least, well below the belt – not least as young **Joe Hall** in his first weeks as a constable, had stood the test well. Despite the fact that the side of law and order, and one of its number in particular, had come off worst in the scrap, the press sat up and took note. Again, in both senses of the phrase.

It took the jury two hours to reach their verdict: guilty against all four, but with strong recommendations to mercy – *another clear indication of the growing disapproval of the official meddlers in their midst.*

Reading the transcript of the trial, the inference is clear: that given a locally based judge, those accused might have got off with a fine and reprimand as the police had, it could easily be inferred, overstepped the bounds of their duty and had responded with undue force – the tenet 'an Englishman's home is his castle' constantly re-occurring throughout the reports. It's worrying to note that if out-and-out leniency on the grounds of police provocation had been the judicial outcome, there's a possibility the still fledgling force

*Fanciful image of the Guildhall's Court Room from the 1830s (right) and the same room today: scene of City Council and Committee meetings (above)*

might even have foundered there and then...

As it transpired, Mr Chief Justice Tindal was an out-of-towner, a remnant of the old school, a stickler for the law, and no lover of the vice-dens that the pubs and drinking-houses had become. Crucially, he was also a supporter of the local police whose side he unstintingly took.

The defendants' conduct, he summed-up, had been '...most violent and brutal and it was only by the merciful interposition of the arm of Providence that they were not standing at the bar to answer a much more serious charge' he adjudged.

Not everybody in the court agreed and there was some disturbance at the back of the room that was quickly, reported the *Herald* '...repressed by the (mayor's) officers', after which he proceeded to deliver the verdicts.

William Smith was fined £30 which he paid later the same day and was thus released; the two Bryans were sentenced to six months' hard labour apiece, and Bullock to three months of the same: he was to emerge a little over a year later as the ostler at the King's Head (*from 1912 the site of St Johns cinema*).

A separate charge against William Bryan for wounding **Joseph Hall** with intent to murder was dropped by the prosecution.

It was another victory – albeit a close one, and slim at that – for the police.

The general state of affairs and aspirations of the population at large from the time can also be gauged from two reports from the same edition of the *Herald*: one that '...a young man of the name of Thomas Garland, confined in the City Gaol for desertion from the 84th Regiment of Foot, deprived himself of the upper part of his right forefinger (*ie: his trigger finger*) to disable himself from being a soldier. He effected his object by placing the finger on the lock of a door, and then drawing the door so violently (that) part of the finger was wrenched off'.

The other concerned the death of well known Lowesmoor (or Lowesmore as the *Herald* put it, another contemporary spelling being Losemore) coal dealer Philip Boucher from the effects of drinking. One of the witnesses at his inquest stated that he had known Boucher drink eleven quarts [22 pints] of ale within an hour, and a bottle of wine at a draught. Reported the *Herald*: '...while frequently intoxicated, the wretched being said he wished the drink might kill him. His wish was awfully accomplished. Can any stronger argument be adduced in favour of the Temperance Societies, than such melancholy cases as these?'

Another report stemming from the County sessions held in Palace Yard the following week indicates the heartlessness of some local magistrates who'd openly regretted not being able to impose a sound thrashing on four 13-year old St Johns lads named Davis, Stinton, Blundell and Lee, found scrumping apples in an orchard. They '...remarked that the practice of plundering orchards by boys of their age and stamp had got to such a height that it was absolutely necessary some example should be made, and they only regretted that they had no authority to order them at once to undergo a sound flagellation [flogging, or whipping] as a species of punishment most likely to be efficacious in checking their pilfering propensities'.

The mothers of two of the boys were present and said they should be extremely thankful if the Bench would adopt such a course. The four defendants were then adjudged to pay between them fines and fees amounting to 9s, or each to undergo a fortnight's imprisonment'.

### Public sympathy wanes in wake of Cock affair

The Cock affair won the police precious little sympathy from the city's population at large, while the fall-out from the violent incident served only to worsen the new force's already unpopular standing in Worcester. Nor was the sentiment confined to the immediate location: across the entire country where police forces had begun springing up, adverse public opinion had followed, sparking off increasing calls to have the new forces scrapped altogether as being expensive, unnecessary, meddlesome and unpopular. But at least, beyond the Commissioners, Worcester police had won one powerful outside ally, albeit with reservations...

Clearly aware of, and no doubt influenced by, the situation unfolding in his own back yard, 48-year old Whig MP George Richard Robinson – elected as one of the City's two representatives in 1826 and set to serve a further four years to 1837 – jumped to their defence during a heated House of Commons debate on the already questionable future of the newly-formed police forces. While his reported views were in reference to the national situation, they clearly drew heavily on the scandal that had recently rocked the city he represented in Parliament, and on which his comments were evidently based:

"I can easily conceive one class who would have particular and personal reasons for disliking the police (*a comment that, noted Hansard, raised a laugh*) and also another class – viz. the householders, who feel the expense to be oppressive. There might have been some inconveniences and some complaints of a few of the police, but let the House consider how few there has been" he said.

With more than a hint of support for the force in the City he represented, he added that he hoped it would not be forgotten what a vast amount of good they had done, the amount of crime they had probably caused to be avoided, and the mischief they had prevented.

"If any idea is entertained of reverting to the old system I would think it a great absurdity and I would not for one moment entertain such a proposition" he told the House – adding that although he recognised the probability of 'some revision of the present system', it remained his own conviction that the police force was "...a most valuable one under proper regulations, and greater evils than those now complained of would result if His Majesty's Government consents to its abolition" he said.

In the weeks that followed, it became evident that Worcester's New Police had narrowly survived its first real test and could (*as it was to prove correct*) emerge from what might so easily have been a fatal beginning to go on to greater things.

Not so its hard-man inaugural chief, Inspector **Henry Sharpe** who'd been sent in to sort out the lawless locals and yokels and ended-up getting his salutory come-uppance. Instead of moving on and learning from the experience, he appears to have gone in the opposite direction and withdrew from any kind of high-profile exposure, seemingly tinkering with organisational matters and ordering occasional crackdowns on the easy-target pubs and beer houses for petty weights-and-measures offences and for opening beyond proscribed hours.

Despite a major robbery at Allcrofts gloves factory and the escape of a notorious high-profile prisoner Thomas McKenzie, alias Davis, alias Brennan, from the City Gaol in October after serving less than two months of a six-month sentence for robbery (*see 'inadequacies', below*) hardly anything else is heard of Worcester Police or any of its officers or the trials that faced them during the remainder of 1833.

Whether the press had just lost interest (unlikely), or Henry Sharp had retired hurt and sulking, leaving his force rudderless and inactive (possibly), or whether he'd been directed to concentrate on organisational issues and to devote more time to crime prevention rather than solution (inadvisable, but more probable) can't be known for certain, but all the indications are that the City's already hard-pressed Commissioners had realised that they'd misjudged the scale of the job-in-hand, had come to regret the decision to chose a man from outside to lead the local force, and that the year was unlikely to end on a high note.

Very little good news filtered out and the press reports for the remainder of 1833 were nearly all bad and for the most part confined to:

- **the new courts and lodgings,** the plot on Foregate Street having already been bought from Sir Anthony Lechmere for £5230. In July, the shock facts had emerged that in order to save a projected £25,000 at a time of severe economic hardship, the City's magistrates had offered to make any provision required to enlarge and extend the Guildhall to accommodate the County's plans – with the exception of altering the façade – but that the offer had been turned down by their County counterparts who were, noted an observer, 'acting like spoiled children'. Out of 41 architects' plans submitted, the design by local architect Charles Day was eventually chosen, two London architects, Mead and Habershon, coming second and third. One of the first casualties of the agreed scheme was the plan for a huge ornate ballroom, considered extravagant and expected to slash 3,000l off the cost.

- **inadequacies at both the City's gaols**. A high profile prisoner Thomas McKenzie, alias Davis, alias Brennan, had escaped from under the very noses of the new police force housed in the City Gaol, and despite being purpose-built and open little over a decade, the new County Gaol was already full to overflowing. In the autumn, it was revealed that it housed 240 prisoners in 93 cells. Its Governor was Mr Lavender, annual salary £300. His clerk, newly appointed at a reduced rate of £70, down from £80 paid to his predecessor, was Benjamin Stable, later to step up to the role of Governor. For all that, organisation here was considered so lax that there had even been the effrontery of a robbery *committed within the very walls of the gaol!* Worcester hard-case John Matthews had been sentenced to six months' imprisonment for his role in a vicious assault. A model prisoner while inside – with the exception of a charge of stealing some tobacco from a fellow prisoner – he got himself a trusty job, lighting the fire in the office of new clerk Ben Stable (*occasionally, Stables*). It wasn't until the very last day of his sentence that Ben Stable noted that some cash and a handcuffs key had gone missing. Matthews had been brought in penniless but when they released him later that day, Ben Stable had him followed and, to no-one's surprise, his immediate port-of-call was the Three Tuns (*now the site of the MRH Castle Street service station*) less than a hundred yards away, where he was discovered to have offered a half sovereign for his no doubt desperately-awaited first beer. Instantly returned to the gaol, Matthews claimed to have had the coin all the time, sewn up in his 'small clothes' and that he'd retained the key after beating off the four constables that had been sent to apprehend him and that he'd run away with the handcuffs still attached to one wrist. He was returned to his cell and ordered to remain there a further year, no longer a trusty.

## 'Dark-Siders' discover new pastime: baiting the bobbies

Never deserving the description of 'tranquil', the turbulent and still independent parish of St Johns was still accounting for more than its share of lawlessness and with the coming of the police into neighbouring St Clements, the St Johns yobs and trouble-makers – dubbed 'roisterers' – had discovered a new national pastime: baiting the bobbies. At the centre of the worst excesses, the annual Mop – frankly better described as 'Mob' – was ever the cause of a steep rise in the prison's population in succeeding days. This year's Mop proved a particularly raucous affair that could easily have resulted in the first Worcester City policeman to lose his life while on duty...

On previous showings, the presence of the sole parish constable, Mr **Spilsbury** was never going to be anywhere near adequate enough to control the raucous crowds, and this year a well-meaning (but unnamed) magistrate directed that '...as the constabulary force of St Johns was not sufficiently strong, a number of the City Police should be stationed there (in order to prevent) a repetition of such outrageous tumults' (*Herald*).

Far from achieving their desired purpose, the presence of New Police Force rookie recruit PC **Emanuel Onslow** – who, the locals considered, not without some justification, had neither place nor powers here – served only to inflame the mob even more.

Singling-out a particularly ebullient roisterer named William Webley and attempting to escort him to the station-house for arrest for riotous behaviour, **Onslow** and **Spilsbury** started off down the Bull Ring when they were chased by a mob of up to 300 troublemakers, all shouting, throwing bricks and stones at them and jostling them in a violent bid to release their prisoner.

Though the officers were both quite badly injured and streaming blood, they still managed to secure Webley who was later fined 20s for affray. His would-be captors however, came off worst with charges of assault and attempting a rescue: James Witts and Thomas Clarke of St Clements were fined 40s., as were James Beaman, George Withers and Thomas Turvey all of St Johns, and Thomas Beddoes fined 50s. Clarke, Beaman and Beddoes failed to pay and were additionally committed to a month's imprisonment.

The *Herald* begrudgingly spared the officers a small amount of space for having not only risked their lives in the face of almost indescribable danger to themselves, but also for returning later on in the night to

*The setting for most of the courtroom action in this book: once the Police and Magistrates' Court, now the Mayor's Parlour in the Guildhall. The ceiling and side windows are later additions*

capture two more offenders named Robert Lloyd and Richard Roberts who were also convicted of 'a gross and unprovoked' assault on another St Johns man named Lawrence. The two had had a night's lodging in St Johns "cage" (*ie below the Bell Inn where the cells still exist*) it being after twelve o'clock when the affair occurred.

*Watchmen were issued with a nightstick for protection, lantern and candles and a rattle for alerting other Watchmen and members of the public who were obliged to lend all assistance when requested – however potentially dangerous the situation*

### New Police come under increasing criticism

Later that same month, October, the sobriety and honesty of the constables in the new force was again in doubt. Regurgitating the fall-out from the Fannon issue more than a year earlier, the papers reported on allegations that instead of personally escorting prisoners to and from the gaols – for which they received a shilling – some officers instead hired men to do it for a few pennies and then pocketed the difference.

The *Herald* alone makes just one further reference to the increasingly invisible police that year – and that was a paltry case concerning the theft of a bottle of neats' foot oil from a basket left unattended in the Greyhound (*now Old Greyhound and still existing*) in New Street. Reported as having been investigated by officer Horton – who's so elusive his name is nowhere to be found in any other source and so is more likely to have been one of the Mayor's officers, possibly **Joe Orchard** – the thief, 16-year old Cornelius Jones, was sentenced to two months' imprisonment to hard labour, the last fortnight in solitary confinement and once privately whipped. The date was the last day but one of 1833.

It had not been a particularly auspicious start for Worcester City Police. With little to show for a year's work, and with crime statistics still indicating alarming increases both in the city and across the nation, the reputation of the force heralded as the new salvation of Worcester from its lawless ways was already sinking fast. These were only early days, but the force still hadn't made a real mark, crime remained on an unrelenting up, and their chief had rarely been seen for the better part of a year. Worse, they were still regarded as being no better than the Watchmen they'd been intended to replace, regarded as little more than snoops, busy-bodies and interferers, were unnecessary, unwelcome and a drain on the rates, and were closely associated with the lock-ups that everybody knew were absurdly insecure.

Hopefully, 1834 would show some improvement...

**Gained:** *(additions to existing force of Watchmen: William Sanders, William Hale, Richard Bills, Robert Checkett, George Nott, William Christian, William Jones, Jeremiah Martin, Joseph Mayfield, John Woodward, John Thompson, Richard Winwood, Joseph Hall, William Phillips, Edward Harding); Henry Sharpe, George Williams, John Leary, Michael Fannon, James Douglas, William Aston.*

**Lost:** *William Christian, John Thompson, Edward Harding, Michael Fannon*

January started off much as the previous year's had with a hard-hitting report from the Mendicity Society whose work had taken up a huge amount of the new police force's time. At least, the remaining active officers had proved themselves adept at flushing out impostors: several vagrants seeking relief were reported as having been sentenced to seven days' solitary in the City nick for trying it on while another, Thomas Jones, was sentenced to fourteen days' hard for being drunk and using abusive language to the (*unnamed*) officer on the desk.

The first real mention of police uniforms also surfaced in January when the Police Committee – also receiving some media exposure for the first time – met at the Infants School in the Butts and clothing for the year was issued to the men.

Noted the *Herald*: '...the uniform slightly differs from the last, a yellow button, with the city arms, being substituted for the plain white button hitherto worn'.

The police's close continuing tie-up with the Mendicity Society was also underlined when it was revealed that its chairman (*and Governor of the County Gaol*) John Pearkes Lavender Esq., undertook the same governorship on the police committee – but at least he'd applauded their work in its first year: the *Herald* noted that he took advantage of the occasion to '...address the men, and expressed his approbation of their general good conduct and efficiency on all occasions, since their appointment'. The likelihood is that his thanks were due on account of their assistance in helping on the mendicity front which was, after all, the role to which they'd first been appointed.

What rumours circulated about the activities of Worcester's New Police force were humiliating and less than flattering, the talk in the pubs and beer-houses – where clearly they were never going to be seen as knights-in-shining armour, although they probably didn't deserve the almost universal derision they were daily enduring – was that they were meddlesome spoilers of their daily fun and games, unpopular, useless, ineffective and fair game for a bit o' sport.

For all that, just one day in mid-March saw cases successfully brought against John Brown, licensee of the Sun in Lowesmoor; Harriet Smith of the Nelson in (St) Nicholas Street; and George Smith, location unlisted, but based in Friar Street.

The press also remained largely reticent about naming officers or of heaping too much praise on their actions, assuming that heroics and risking their lives were all part of their bounden duty.

However, out of this adversity, it's possible that **Henry Sharpe**, not long before returned to his duties, had found organisational and persuasive strengths: police numbers were growing, the force had assumed general policing duties, now extended to night cover, and the 'New Police' as the force was still termed, was gradually becoming recognised as something of an elite senior service. At the same time, the press were just about beginning to be won over, providing the first independent indications that despite its shaky start, the force might yet still become a body to be reckoned with.

For a while, it even seemed as though the set-backs of the previous year might have been just teething problems and the result of underfunding and undermanning – *but it was a close-run thing and there were still doubts on all sides.*

One of the first examples of the 'new' police officers being identified by name and number, and even indirectly being dubbed a hero, occurred in early March when the *Herald* lavished praise on officer **No 14** who'd staved-off a potentially disastrous fire in a bedroom at the Pack Horse in (*then*) Nicholas-street.

The report relates how the officer got the ostler out of the room and helped put out the fire which had been caused by a lit candle left when he'd gone to bed at 8pm. The *Herald* named him as **Arton** and would continue to do so for some time in the future. The name appears again and again even though no Arton is listed in the available police documentation of the time, so it's possible he's **William Aston**, one of the original watchmen from early 1830s, the mistake possibly arising from the pronunciation of his name as Ar-ston or mis-transcription of shorthand notes: even so, *Herald* editor William Holl or his reporter called for '...the greatest praise for the policeman for his promptitude, and we hope the Commissioners will not overlook his good conduct on the occasion'.

At last! Positive recognition and a much-needed hero identified within the ranks of the still generally unpopular police force.

The same *Herald* edition also carried the tale of a madman named Robert Osbaldeston who in the tap-room of the Crown in Broad Street, had levelled and then fired two pistols at ten feet range at gunsmith William Wood whose shop was nearby. Luckily for him, the shot from the first pistol missed its mark and hit the wall, and the other pistol failed to fire. 29-year old Osbaldeston, the son of another noted Worcester odd-ball dubbed 'The Lunatic Doctor', was tried for attempted murder but acquitted as insane and sentenced to be detained in the city gaol awaiting His Majesty's Pleasure.

*Such were the people the police were now daily dealing with...*

There was more praise for the police a month later when a disastrous fire broke out inside silversmith and watchmaker J. M. Skarratt's shop at no 3, Broad Street when they reported that (*again, unnamed*) police officers had managed to raise the alarm, hammered the door and when they got no reply, broke it down and searched the premises. The officers even assisted the firefighters from the Phoenix Insurance Company who, reported the *Herald* (in an article that they acknowledged had come from the *Journal*) '...were got ready with such extraordinary celerity that within a quarter of an hour one of the Phoenix engines was on the spot and was immediately followed by a Birmingham engine, and another belonging to the Phoenix'. The premises were empty, although detective work by the police revealed that a caretaker named Proctor had returned to the shop after a drinking session and dropped a lit candle that had melted the solder on a gas pipe which had then created an explosion. Damage was put at £1500, but Skarratt's insurance stretched to just £900.

Despite that, Skarratt's was back in business within weeks – extremely fortunately for the city as the firm was to evolve into the mighty Kays, whose relationship with Worcester is worthy of (*and already has been*) cataloguing in its own right – pun very definitely intended!

Unfortunately, whatever successes the new force was now managing to pull off, they were far outweighed by the still unprecedented increase in crime being committed and left undetected – the result being 'no change' in the eyes of the public at large and exposing the police to renewed claims of indolence and uselessness, not all of which were entirely warranted...

On one hand they were making headway as the courts were by now continually full, but on the other, the public were reminded almost hourly that the streets were dangerous and all too often 'no-go'.

As such, in the eyes of Worcester-at-large they were failing, despite what the news-sheets said.

By way of illustration of the scale of everyday street crime, Mr Justice Park assisted by Mr Jervis KC presided over the trials of 43 prisoners in a single 6-hour (3pm-9pm) session in the Guildhall. It saw them hand-down one death sentence, ten transportations for life – eight for fourteen years and two for seven years – alongside seventeen prison sentences of differing lengths. On the up-side, they also delivered seven acquittal verdicts and five dismissals on account of insufficient evidence.

### Robert Lilley executed at the County Gaol

Just a week later, the man they'd condemned to death for murder had his own life snuffed-out at the County Gaol. He was 50-year old ex-soldier Robert Lilley, found guilty of the murder of Jonathan Wall at Bromsgrove the previous November and sentenced to pay the ultimate price. The *Herald* noted: '... the unhappy man having signified that he should say nothing to the surrounding multitude, but wished that his earthly sufferings might be terminated as speedily as possible, the cap was drawn over his face and the platform fell.  His death appears to have been momentary'.  He had left three children.

Worcester Races, held twice yearly for at least a hundred years up to now, was always a thorn in the side for the law enforcers when, much as remains the case, thousands of strangers descended on the city providing rich pickings for hordes of slick pickpockets and thieves, both professional and opportunist.

Tuesday and Wednesday August 4th and 5th this year were no exception. Despite the loudly-voiced disappointment of the crowd at a walkover for a horse named Diana for the 2-Year Old Stakes – the third time in a decade that a lone horse had been entered into the race, securing an automatic 110-sovereign prize for her proprietor and jockey Arthur Pavis – the number of racecourse robberies and other incidents took a sharp fall as for the first time ever, a force of keen-eyed Worcester policemen was visibly on duty.

Reports the *Herald*:

> *'...one of the thimble-rig fraternity ventured to make his appearance and spread his lure on Tuesday, but he was quickly espied by some of the City Police, who kept constantly parading on the ground, and compelled to decamp.  Their vigilance too was the means of keeping the pilfering gentry aloof, and doubtless prevented many robberies.  As the first race was running on Tuesday, a fellow named William Vale snatched a reticule from a carriage, but being observed in the act by two policemen, they immediately secured him.  The property was found on his person and he was taken off to the City gaol where, in the evening, he was fully committed for trial for the offence.  On Wednesday also, during a skirmish in front of the Grand Stand, no doubt purposely got up, Hailes the police-man, detected a youth drawing a handkerchief from the pockets of a gentleman and had him quickly in his keeping, together with a confederate.  On the two were found several other handkerchiefs, three knives and a handsome paper snuff box; both, therefore, are retained in custody'.*

Of course the growing, but still limited, police couldn't be in two places at once, so while they were on duty at Pitchcroft, the thieves, chancers and muggers had a field day elsewhere. But at least, the police were making their presence more than felt.

However, despite their and the city's well-intentioned hopes for a turn-round in fortunes – and typically, as was to be demonstrated again and again, just as it looked as though the corner had been well and truly turned – things were once more about to take a turn for the worse...

Just weeks later, figures indicating a massive increase in crimes committed during the period when the new police force was still that (new) and hungry to make a mark, showed that despite the headlines, they were continuing to fail on an epic scale.  There's a remote chance that they were becoming victims of their own success, but the major issue was that the amount of crime going undetected and unpunished was increasing at an even greater rate than ever before.

As the *Herald* put it: *'...the crowded state* (of the County Gaol), *says little, we lament to say, for the decrease of crime, there being now, including those tried at the Sessions this week, few short of 170 convicts within its walls.'*

At this time too, a gang of counterfeiters was at work in the city and despite their best efforts and demands from rooked traders, the police were signally failing to track them down and bring them to book; street crime, muggings and assaults both at night and now glaringly so, in the day, additionally remained of growing concern; crimes involving the use of firearms were causing heightened alarm in all quarters of the city;  inmates of the City Gaol had initiated a long period of internal disobedience, and house-burglaries and robberies were spiralling crazily upwards – all damning statistics revealing glaring failings in the new force and its officers, just at the time that any snippet of good news would have been most welcome...

On top of that, there followed what might have been a few unfortunate lapses of concentration that all conspired to reflect badly on the force and did little to enhance its reputation.

In June, Thomas McKenzie, alias Davis, alias Brennan the prisoner who'd escaped from the City Gaol the previous October and had been at large ever since, was at last re-captured.  Cause for some much-needed praise for the police?  Not a bit of it:  he'd been found living right under their noses and virtually within their midst, much to the embarrassment of the gaolers who'd failed to recognise him and particularly the police who'd failed to secure him.

As for the City Gaol, a prisoner named James Shaffer, convicted in March for two years for having passed counterfeit coins, slashed his throat with a knife he'd stolen from the refectory and sharpened in the work-room, right under the noses of his gaolers and, again, the hapless police.

## 'Faces' emerge, despite struggles to gain support

Now about to enter its third year of existence, the New Police Force was still struggling to gain some form of public support – but at least the year had seen a couple of its number emerge as astute, worthy and resourceful.

**PC William Aston** had again shone during the year, but in what must have felt like another body-blow for the expectant force was that the man hailed as the most effective law enforcement hero of the day was not one of their number, but actually one of the Mayor's officers...

This was again **Joseph Orchard** who'd already come to prominence as one of the parish constables some ten years before – although the press still encountered problems in distinguishing the difference between mayor's officers, parish constables and now the New Police Constables, all of whom were entirely different entities. **Joe Orchard** remains an oddity: in some reports he's described as a member of the city police force, and in others as Mayor's Officer, and the distinction is never clear-cut.

Having first risen to prominence in his role in breaking up a number of notorious 'mills' (*organised prize fights*) this year had seen him come into his own in a gang-busting case following a stint of robberies with violence committed by three thugs named Bevan, Oliver and O'Neil within the western reaches of the city. Initially sent to apprehend two women thought to have been implicated in another robbery, Joe Orchard's dogged questioning of the pair – one of which proved to be Mrs Oliver – led him to the three gang members who were only arrested after a fearsome fight that took several officers to quell, also involving another Mayor's Officer often wrongly ascribed as a New Police-man, **Thomas Tilt**, who was also gaining some recognition by the press.

**Tilt** and **Orchard** must have been useful scrappers – ever a commendable quality for a Worcester law-man – as, noted the *Herald* '...it was not till (the gang members) were completely overpowered that they submitted to be taken'. When they were charged, the proceeds of several robberies in and around the city were found in their possession.

Just two weeks later, **Joe Orchard** again emerged as a gang-buster par excellence following some diligent sleuthing into a syndicate of horse thieves operating out of Cricklade (*now Gloucestershire, but then in Wiltshire*) but whose activities had regularly stretched as far as the city. Then, some weeks later, after a drunken farmer named Holmes was mugged – or to use the term of the time, 'hustled' – in the notorious neighbourhood around Friars Alley leading into Dolday, it was again Joe Orchard who was quickly on to the case after his suspicions had been roused by the activities of some known rascals.

Sadly for him, it was not to result in a successful outcome as the drunken farmer failed to appear in court to protest the matter of his missing watch and some money, and by the rules of the day, the accused were all allowed to walk away.

**Joe Orchard** again came to prominence after his suspicions had once more been roused by the activities of an ex-window glazer named Keeling who'd been doing the rounds of the city's hardware shops offering a quantity of white lead for sale. Though Keeling claimed to have bought the lead in Manchester, **Orchard** was able to prove that he had, in fact, stolen it from the city's House of Industry on Tallow Hill where he'd sought relief during the days the lead had gone missing.

When a hoard of counterfeit coins was found hidden in excavation works in Bath Road at the end of the year, 36 half crowns, 142 shillings and 36 sixpences were described as 'in Orchard's hands', presumably at the Guildhall and significantly *not* at the police office, still mis-trusted and still housed within the City Gaol.

The police appear to be nowhere in the running – except in one disconcerting element, an escalation of what was later to become a worrying and all too prevalent trend: assaults...

As the year drew to a close, the Tything parish constable [*first name unknown*] **Brookes** had found himself jostled and generally roughed-up in a beer-shop called the Fox that he'd entered and found men still drinking at 10.30pm, half an hour after the proscribed closing time: public houses were allowed to remain open until 11pm. While Brookes made no charge against its owner William Smith (*unlikely to have been the same William Smith who'd been convicted for his assault on **Henry Sharpe** at the Cock the previous year*) or any of its customers for the alleged assault, the landlord was fined 40s and expenses as it had been his second conviction, and he was warned that another conviction during the next calendar year would result in a £10 penalty, while a third would result in a penalty of £50.

Such anti-social shenanigans had been expected on the west-side – after all, this was where the new chief had got his come-uppance, where the Mop was always a night of pitched battles, and where the publicans and beer-house owners thought they could get away with pretty much anything. But this was different: this was a respectable and peaceable suburb of Worcester. The troublesome westside, however, remained a serious thorn in the side of the police – as it would continue to do for several generations more and sometimes still does.

This much is evident from the columns of the *Herald* and the *Journal* – via which, another 'face' began emerging out of the ranks of the otherwise invisible New Police force: **James Douglas**, a name that was to appear with considerably more frequency over the coming years.

One of the original four New Police men appointed at the end of 1832 and inherited by **Henry Sharpe**, towards the end of this year he and the tenacious parish constable of St Johns, the ever-present **Spilsbury,** had brought a successful action against a St Clements' beer-house keeper, Thomas Trimnell, for exceeding permitted drinking hours.

### PC4 James Douglas rises to prominence

It emerged out of a nasty incident at the Bransford Road turnpike when two St Johns men, Fred Lawrence and Thomas Hook, were accused of 'gross and unprovoked assault' on four passengers in a coach. One of those claiming to have been assaulted, Captain William Bund, said he felt obliged to publicly acknowledge the prompt assistance and attention he had received on this occasion from **Mr Sharpe**, the Inspector of Police and the Officer, No 4 – almost certainly **James Douglas**...

'The Rev. Mr Foley remarked that he could also bear testimony to the efficiency and utility of the New Police. Repeated instances had lately occurred in which, by their vigilance and activity, they had been instrumental in detecting offenders and promoting the ends of justice; and it was not the city alone that had been benefitted by their activity, but also the adjacent county. It was, the Rev. Gentleman concluded, a most admirable description of the force' (*Worcester Herald*).

In fairness, the incident would probably have gone unreported but for the prominence of one of the prosecutors, Captain William Bund who was, as luck would have it, the younger brother of Major Thomas Bund, the County's chief magistrate of the time who was later to be the first chairman of the newly-formed Worcestershire County Council. But it was a start, and some much-needed good press – plus evidence that **Henry Sharpe** was still alive and going at least some way towards living up to the role to which he'd been appointed.

Towards the end of the year, **James Douglas No4** was again commended after he and a fellow officer named as **Stoney** (*an all-too common error: the officer was* **George Stoneley**, *a late recruit to the New Police, joining its ranks on 10th October this year and was later to be promoted to sergeant, clocking-up an active 10-year career with the city force*) were patrolling the Shambles when they'd noticed a slaughter-house door at Lea's butchers was open, went in, and butcher Lea himself told them he'd been robbed. The beat-men told him they'd seen a man pass down the street not more than half an hour before '...and upon their describing him, Mr Lea felt convinced this was a man named James Soley, who sometime since lived with him, and that he was the thief. The policemen with one of the servants went immediately to his lodgings, a house of ill-fame in Spa Row, and found him in bed'.

The *Herald* notes '...the vigilance of the policemen on the above occasion entitles them to much praise; but for the information given by them, the robbery probably would never have been discovered'. The *Journal* also covered the story, passing on no praise to the officers and printing the butcher's name as Lee. But they added a chilling footnote to the story that had gone unreported by the *Herald*: 'Sentence of death was recorded'.

Had 1834 proved any more successful for the New Police than the disastrous year of its formation? Barely.

**Gained:** *George Stoneley*

How much of it was **Henry Sharpe**'s influence and how large a role the Commissioners played in determining numbers and procedure is unknown, but the New Police had undergone some formational change in the two years to the beginning of 1835. They were now 18-strong, they were officially termed 'officers' for the first time, and appear to have included the four mayor's officers on 10s a week and two constables assigned to each of the city's seven wards. In addition, the Mayor maintained four Serjeants at Mace elected by the common council and holding offices during the mayor's pleasure. They too had the power to make arrests '... and generally to execute civil process' and were paid a monthly salary of 25s.

With just a handful of exceptions, the old watchmen were no more. Noted the *Journal* at the beginning of the year, 'the establishment of the police appears to have had a very beneficial operation and the peace of the town is very well kept. A magistrate attends at the Guildhall to hear complaints, and a full petty sessions is holden every Monday'. He was clearly a very busy individual.

In the City in the early weeks of 1835, it was a case of life continuing much along the familiar lines – with St Clements and the persistently lawless westside consistently accounting for a disproportionate share of outrage and disorder.

It looks very much, too, as though **James Douglas** was now running the force as chief in all but name. That much is evident in his handwritten *(and punctuation-free)* note dated 2.22am on Thursday 5th March this year in which he complains of two of his officers, **Robert Checkett** *(or Checketts)* and **George Stoneley** who:

> '...refused to take John Turvey to the Station who was drunk and creating a disturbance in Water Course Alley I took hold of him to bring him to the Station and he resisted me I was determined to take him and the officers said I should not and both abused me shamefully I called Williams No3 and we took him to the Station I ordered Checketts and Stoneley to go on there beats and the both said the would not the then came to the Station and forced themselves in I then requested them to go on there beats and the refused and called me everything that was bad and threatened to strike me with there staffs. Onslow No15 and Jones No17 and Williams witness of there conduct towards me. George Nott complains of Stoneley conduct towards him'.

**Robert Checkett** appears to have remained a policeman only until November this year, while **George Stoneley** and **George Nott** hung on to their jobs and were included when Worcester City Police came into being on January 5th next year. **Stoneley** was later promoted Sergeant and served until 12th May 1843, while **George Nott** remained a constable for a further 14 years, retiring 9th March 1860.

*Then, in April, two more setbacks...*

In the first, a new man, *No8* **John Griffiths** and supernumerary constable **Luke Packwood** were severely reprimanded and two separate charges of being assaulted by two brothers, also named Griffiths, thrown out. The charges had arisen out of an incident in which the two officers had been sent in to clear the Queen Adelaide beer shop at the top of Cripplegate found still to be open well beyond the proscribed hour. Far from carrying out their orders to the very letter, the Bench heard that they had sat down and joined the revellers in a chat and accepted their offer of a cordial pint of ale: '...during their conversations, the subject of the police was brought under the notice of the House and their merits and demerits freely discussed. Forgetting the old sentimental adage that "difference of opinion ought not to poison a friendship", the policeman "kicked" at it and a quarrel ensued; during which policeman No8 called him a d––ned rogue, and used other provoking language. Defendant told him that if he repeated so offensive a term he would knock him down; the policeman again used the same epithet to him, and Griffiths then struck him. The defendant further stated that the policeman sat with them more than half an hour. No8 told the Bench that there was another policeman with him at the time, and he wished that he might be examined. **Luke Packwood**, who is a supernumerary policeman, was called in and in answer to a question from the Bench, stated himself

*James Douglas' signed letter dated 5th March this year, preserved in the Hive (for content, see opposite). Within six weeks he was appointed chief of the New Police*

and No8 drank some ale which was offered to them by some persons in the house'.

The comment proved damning and the Magistrates halted the case, stating that the policemen '...had acted very improperly both by drinking in the house and also by remaining in familiar conversation for longer than was necessary to accomplish their purpose of clearing the house at the request of its owner, Mrs Clarke' (*Worcester Herald*).

Then a week later, on April 15th., a 20-word, three-line snippet sandwiched between an article on irregularities at the recent Parliamentary election and the joyous news that Mr Clutton Brock would very likely be joining the Worcestershire Hunt for the up-coming season, delivered the shock and completely unexpected news that (*re-printed here, in full*):

*WCiCo/WAAS*

new Register is formed.
At a meeting of the Commissioners, this morning, policeman Douglas was appointed Inspector, in the room of Mr. Sharpe, deceased.
We h... e that t... is some probability

# 5:
# The Douglas years

## 24th April 1835 - 1st March 1840

It was as blunt as that...

*At a meeting of the Commissioners, this morning, policeman Douglas was appointed Inspector, in the room of Mr Sharpe, deceased.*

The *Journal* didn't bother to report it at all, and by way of contrast, it's interesting to note that the same week, the Mayor and Magistrates also had a further important appointment to make – that of City Bellman in place of James Thomas, also deceased.

James Webley was evidently considered far more newsworthy: the account of his appointment merited a full six lines (*52 words*).

**James Douglas** had proved himself an able and competent officer – although quite what his special qualities were for the role as Inspector and why the Commissioners chose him above **No3 George Williams** for instance, can only be guessed. To his (*and George Williams'*) credit, he'd been one of the four initial New Police constables, knew the ropes, had the respect of his men to whom he was one of their own, and unlike 'outsider' **Henry Sharpe**, was fast becoming a face-around-town. Better still, so far as the Commissioners were concerned, the press recognised and respected him.

A further incentive might be that just the day before his promotion he'd saved a man from drowning – an act of heroism that was not to go unnoticed by the *Herald* that, in the same edition, gave ten times more space to reporting the incident than to his promotion. In dire need of a more positive image, the Commissioners may have opted for the most prominent name to hand.

WCiCo/WAAS

*20 Minutes Past 2 oclock*
*George Nott No 13 complains of Stonelys conduct*
*towards him* James Douglass  J Douglas

silver and copper was found. ...
discovered close to the house in ...
apron. This *Soley* had given to the ...
lived, and on the policemen entering the house, ...
it out of the window. The robbery appears to have been committed at about 11 o'clock. It is probable that *Soley* ...
a better prize at the ... Lead, but ... letter had taken ...
mo... 
te... 
fo... 
A... 
in... 
sto... 
ab... 
fo... 
have been discovered.

On Monday, our active Mayor's officer, Orchard,
saw a man offering at various shops a quantity of white lead for
sale; having some suspicion that it was stolen, he took the
man, whose name is Keeling, into custody; to questions put to
him, the prisoner said he had brought the article from Manchester; but upon searching him in the presence of a Magistrate, Orchard found a paper which led him to suspect that the
lead was stolen from the House of Industry, and such ultimately
proved to be the fact. Keeling had received relief at the House,
and thus got an opportunity of carrying off the lead. He was
apprentice some time ago to a glazier in this city. He will be
re-examined on Friday.

On Friday last, two of our Policemen, Douglas and
Onslow, apprehended a man named John Clarke, on a charge
of stealing a hogshead from the Navigation Inn, Losemore, and
selling it for 8s. and half a gallon of ale. As they were conveying him along the side of the canal to the City Gaol, he
suddenly leaped into the water, apparently with the intention of
drowning himself. Seeing that he would not or could not come
out, Douglas followed him into the water, and with great difficulty got him out, almost in a state of insensibility. He was
taken to the Navigation Inn, where by means of rubbing, &c.
he was restored so far as to be able to walk to the Gaol. He
was brought up to the Town Clerk's office for re-examination
to-day; but he was discharged, the person who lost the property
not having appeared against him.

*Francis Jones* was yesterday examined at the County
Public Office, on a charge of stealing a joint of ...
house of a person named Adams, in the Moors. He ...
for a week, bound in his own recognizance of ...
sureties of 10l. each, then to appear and answer an...
might be brought against him.

COMMITTED TO THE COUNTY GAOL.—B...
G. Talbot, and F. Brown, Esqrs. *John Smi...*
stealing four boltings of straw, the property ...
Kidderminster.—By T. W. Hodgetts, and ...
*John Jones,* charged with breaking into ...

At least, they avoided repeating the costly error they'd made just twenty-seven months earlier with the appointment of Henry Sharpe and his pledges to tame a city of which he'd known precious little and whose inhabitants he'd grossly misjudged. Reading between the lines, the implication is that Henry Sharpe had not endeared himself either to the Commissioners or his men, had shied away from any kind of fight, physical or verbal, in the aftermath of the Cock affray, and busied himself by tinkering with organisation and procedure instead of getting stuck-in to the job-in-hand. It's likely too that as an ex-military man and former member of the London force, he was perhaps just too overbearing for his men's liking.

**But most likely simply because he was a foreigner and non-Worcester-ite.**

At least now they had a new chief, home-grown and promoted from within the ranks.

Something of James Douglas' nature can be drawn from the circumstances of the incident that had immediately preceded his promotion. The *Herald* wrote:

> 'On Friday last, two of our Policemen, [James] Douglas and [Emanuel] Onslow, apprehended a man named John Clarke, on a charge of stealing a hogshead from the Navigation Inn, Losemore, and selling it for 8s and half a gallon of ale. As they were conveying him along the side of the canal to the City Gaol, he suddenly leapt into the water, apparently with the intention of drowning himself. Seeing that he would not or could not come out, Douglas followed him into the water, and with great difficulty got him out, almost in a state of insensibility. He was taken to the Navigation Inn, where by means of rubbing &c., he was restored so far as to be able to walk to the Gaol'.

It all proved to be for nothing as the landlord of the Navigation failed to appear in the Magistrates Court the next day, leaving the Mayor's officers with no choice but to let their man go, but it sounds as though the Commissioners took James Douglas aside and put their offer to him.

### The new chief sets-to

The force **James Douglas** now headed was still 18-strong, serving a population of 19,000 souls, a ratio of 1:1,055. His ever-reliable New Police force colleague **George Williams No3** was still there, and now as second-in-command, became known as 'Corporal'; it's not known what happened to **John Leary,** while **Michael Fannon** had barely lasted out a few weeks after Henry Sharpe's appearance.

From the available scant evidence, the others are likely to have been: ex-Watchmen **William Aston (No2), John Phillips (No4); William Hale (or Hales, No5); William Sanders (No6), Richard Bills (No7), John Griffiths (No8), Robert Checkett (or Checketts No11), George Nott (No17), William Jones, Jeremiah Martin, Joseph Mayfield, John Woodward, John Thompson and Richard Winwood,** followed by replacements **William Phillips, Edward Harding, Emanuel Onslow (No15), George Stoneley (No16), Richard Berry, Richard Dallow, Luke Packwood, Robert Howard and John Drinkwater** for those that had left.

Like his predecessor, the new chief set-to with a vengeance and appears to have made rapid headway...

Within days, the *Journal* reported that 'Mr Douglas, the Inspector of the New Police, apprehended a man named James Powell who had in his possession a fine cock turkey, a gallina (egg-laying hen), two white and one red-coloured fowls. Powell is detained on suspicion of having stolen them and any persons who have lost poultry of this description may see them on application at the Police office'.

A few weeks later, a Severn Stoke farmer named Tibbetts claimed the birds as his, and 37-year old 'old offender' Powell was sentenced to fourteen years' transportation for theft.

At last the editors were substituting their implied hostility towards the New Police and following some of their action with interest. They'd also discovered that by softening the writing style from the usual stilted phraseology that tended to characterise local reporting, it could make some racy copy – at least by the standards of the time.

Typically this, which shows the force in a heroic and diligent new light, reprinted in full from the *Journal* report:

> *A Police Chace (sic) On Thursday evening a ham was stolen from a shop in Mealcheapen–street, by two youths. Information being given to the Police, two of them Checketts, No11 and Stoneley, No16, discovered a young man named James Taylor, suspected of being one of the thieves, in a place called "The Barracks" in Silver-street and a companion was taken at the same time. Taylor made some excuse for going into a room up one of the stairs, to*

*which one of the Policemen accompanied him, while the other remained below with the other prisoner. Taylor watching his opportunity, dashed head foremost through a casement-window and alighted on the roof of a building, whence he rolled on the ground and ran off to his father's house in the Blockhouse. The Policemen followed him thither, and found him up stairs, but, strange to say, he leaped through a window a second time, and again escaped. The Policemen again pursued him but lost sight of him. They, however, lingered about his father's house, towards which, in about half an hour, they saw him coming. They again pursued him, and he took shelter in a brewhouse, where he was finally captured, and taken before a Magistrate, who remanded him till Monday. On that day, as the charge could not be brought home to him, he was committed to the tread-mill for two months as a rogue and vagabond. He is a well-known character. His companion was discharged, in consequence of the character he received'.*

Things were definitely on the up-and-up, journalistically and in terms of police diligence, but there was still a long way to go and crime also remained on an upwards climb – barely surprising given the dire economic plight of the nation as a whole and Worcester's uncommonly low number of officers per head of population. Nor can it be wondered at that some areas of the city still remained dangerously no-go. The state of the streets can be gauged from this, a report of a typical hustle, or 'hocus' – today, mugging – taken from the *Journal* in March and an everyday occurrence:

*'Last Wednesday evening, a man named Brooks, was going down Doldy [sic] when he was met by W[illia]m Knight, alias W[illia]m Parson, in company with another, near the new passage. They asked him to give them something to drink, which he refused. They then pushed him against the wall, and Knight knocked his hat over his eyes, and then they both picked his pockets of a half-crown and two shillings in silver, some copper money and a knife; they then ran off'*

**Emanuel Onslow No15**, was on duty not far away, and he investigated, apprehending William Knight the following night and organising his committal. The other man was never traced.

**Manny Onslow** again made the headlines in early May for his role in the apprehension of Thomas Nixon and Joseph Moreland for the theft of several pairs of shoes. The same week, **James Douglas** was revealed as a conscientious and determined hands-on chief – as the *Journal* termed him, 'our active Inspector of Police' – who took personal interest in the theft of some wet linen off a line near the Albion, made some enquiries, and tracked a suspect down to a lodging house in Doldy' (*Dolday*). 30-year old George Taylor of Carlisle was committed for trial at the Assizes after being chased by Douglas himself and found '...making his way out of the city with the proceeds of his plunder in his pocket'.

The report also reveals something of police methods and gives an indication that they'd forged that most valuable of police assets, a network of informers from the criminal underworld.

Later the same month, tragedy befell one of the old stalwarts, **William Hale** (*or Hales or Hailes, depending on the reporter and the publication)* **No5**, and it occurred in the most distressing manner...

**Bill Hale** had been a Watchman from early 1830 and had distinguished himself as solid and reliable. On his beat near Tallow Hill bridge with another officer (unnamed, but probably **John Griffiths**) at 1 am one Saturday, he was called by a milkman named William Ballenger who'd heard a splash in the canal and the sounds of someone gasping for breath. With no signs of activity, Hale ordered the canal to be dragged and it was an hour before they succeeded in locating a body and bringing it to the surface.

*No doubt to his horror, it was found to be his own wife, Anne, 30 and mother of his three children. He appeared,* reported the Journal with some evident understatement, *to be 'deeply affected'.*

At the inquest later the same day at the Butchers Arms in the Shambles, the Jury returned the verdict that she'd drowned herself while labouring under temporary derangement.

That same afternoon, overworked City Coroner John Brooke Hyde conducted another inquest, this time at the Infirmary, into the death of a market porter named Taylor after his cart had overturned in Friar Street and the shafts had sliced through his thigh leaving him to bleed to death in the street with the police powerless to save him. **Verdict: *accidental death.***

Thug Noah Dayus – a name that was to crop up again and again in ensuing years, occupying several pages of police charge books generally for the same offence, a pathological hatred of the police – appears around now: he'd hammered constable **Richard Dallow** senseless and had also laid into a man named

■ *Inspector Douglas, and officers Hartin (probably William Harding) and Manny Onslow track down a gang of burglars who'd robbed High Street bakers Rouses*

■ *the police have their hands full cornering rabid dogs following an outbreak of hydrophobia in Worcester – they'd shot at least 35 unmuzzled dogs*

■ *Mayor's officer Thomas Tilt investigates the theft of seven wedding rings from St Swithin Street jeweller W. Edwin Palmer, resulting in Sarah Simmonds (24) and an accomplice being transported for seven years*

■ *in August, Manny Onslow is seriously assaulted by a gang of eight and their ringleader, William Chesterton*

William Lane, unfortunately (for him) summoned by Dallow to aid and assist in the arrest and liable to prosecution if he refused. A thorough bad 'un, 27-year old Dayus (*of which more on page 366*) was sent to the City Gaol for six months after which he was ordered to find almost impossible sureties amounting to £80 – £40 for himself and two of £20 – to keep the peace for twelve months.

At a typical Assize day in the city at this time, as many as 20 cases were being heard – no doubt providing a similar number of new inmates for one or other of the city's already overcrowded gaols. The Police and Magistrates court, now meeting six-days-a-week was rarely very far behind in providing a steady stream of contrite inmates.

With **James Douglas** now in firm control of a once-rudderless ship, the police were beginning to make real progress and respect was at last being forged for the way they did their jobs and the apparent impact they were making – *not that it was entirely a one-way street...*

### More murders and two Pitchcroft deaths in the same month

They came in for some criticism when a man died following yet another organised 'mill' on Pitchcroft at the end of August. The third of seven semi-official amateur sets-to that night, 24-year old pugilist Thomas Thorley had tapped an unsuspecting 19-year old spectator named James Williams on the head with his stick and asked him 'will you fight?' – an offer which Williams declined, and tried to walk away. In front of the crowd, Thorley called him a coward – which was just too much provocation for a Worcester man. Turning round, he saw Thorley stripping in readiness for the fight, so he did the same.

Continued the *Journal*: '...Thorley had the best of it by far until the last round, when both fell. The second raised Thorley on his knee for another round, but his head fell on one side. Williams himself urged his seconds to take him to the Infirmary, but they refused'.

Thorley lingered on for about three hours before dying and when house surgeon Cole sawed open his skull at the subsequent autopsy, he found eight ounces of blood on his brain, squeezing it down to half its normal size. Despite showing sympathy for Williams for having been provoked beyond any normal man's tolerance and turning away from the fight, he was nonetheless found guilty of manslaughter, although he later escaped with a minimal sentence.

Horrified at the ruthless loss of life in a public space, the *Herald* in particular slammed the police for inattention and made an impassioned plea for them to keep a closer watch on the Ham 'during the nights of the races, for this is the time when scenes of riot and profligacy are most frequent'.

Another death that same August race-week – this time suspected murder – kept the police, and the news reporters, busy. 17-year old James Sefton who lived at 'Warndon, near Worcester' had been severely battered about the face and neck, his pockets turned out and his lifeless body tossed into the Severn.

He was discovered by a former Watchman, **Leonard Darke** five days later, but despite heavy questioning by the police, **Hales No5** in particular, the two chief suspects were allowed to go despite an accumulation of circumstantial evidence (cuts to the hand, threats to kill etc) but not enough to bring to trial.

*There was, however, to be a further development sparking-off renewed police interest, six months later...*

In the meantime, yet another suspected murder two weeks on, proved an entirely more salacious affair that kept readers enthralled by the proceedings.

Jonathan Stiff had knifed his wife Ann in a fit of rage in their Birdport home after she'd lavished attention on a young lodger, seemingly neglecting her husband and young son. He'd given the lodger notice to quit, but the besotted wife had said that if he went, she'd follow him.

Committed to trial for manslaughter, the magistrates considered Jn Stiff had been pushed beyond the limits of normal endurance and released him without sentence.

There was more praise for the police the following month, September, when a watchman – this time the privately-employed servant of a commercial firm, just to add to an already desperately confusing situation – raised a fire alarm at F. Williams Distillery at 5am one Sunday after discovering some coke well alight and burning a kiln flue.

'Some of the policemen assembled immediately, two fire engines arriving without delay... Had not the fire been discovered in good time, the damage might have been very serious indeed' *(Journal)*.

So far as the police were concerned, some of their number were emerging as heroes and that was good for the body corporate. The reading public was getting to see more of the good works they were doing under their highly active and visible new chief, while a new day and night presence alongside juicy tales of heroism proving the talk of the pubs and beer-houses, the up-shot was that things might well have to change in the wake of this effective new crack-down on the miscreants' fun and games, and that law and order might just be here to stay. The City Council and Commissioners were no doubt delighted.

Then on September 30th, the penultimate piece of the jigsaw – the **Municipal Corporations Reform Bill,** proposing to set straight some of the omissions and clarify some of the ambiguities of its ground-breaking forerunner.

While Worcester was already well ahead of almost all the rest of England and Wales in terms of policing, the Act required 178 Royal Boroughs to have paid police forces in place, each monitored and controlled by a Watch Committee whose members had the duty of appointing constables 'for the preserving of the peace' with powers extended to within seven miles of the borough.

From here on in, the city's already established force, now officially Worcester City Police and considered sufficient to meet the demands placed on it, would be appointed and paid for by the council as opposed to the Commissioners, its cost no longer defrayed by the county rate but instead met from a borough fund.

The amended act also provided for the city to be divided into six wards, with 12 Aldermen and 36 councillors – from which the new-style Watch Committee would manage the 18 constables and unpaid Supernumeraries *(essentially first reserves with first refusal in the event of a vacancy arising, much like today's Specials)* ready to be drafted-in in case of civil need.

The Committee was also obliged to submit a quarterly report to the Secretary of State along with a copy of their rules and other relevant information and now also assumed responsibility for street lighting.

At last, police in general were being given national backing and the full support of the local administration in their area, and Worcester had never needed it more...

The year began as it was to continue when **Manny Onslow** arrested George Pilcher in the Cornmarket on New Year's Day after five brass weights had gone missing from William Bradford's cake and tart shop in New Street. Pilcher was sentenced to three months, the last fourteen days to hard labour.

Two days later, the lads at the gaol-house were shocked when they heard that the bodies of two London bobbies had been found literally frozen to death after being ordered to remain at their posts during an all-night observation of some suspects on Hampstead Heath.

A childish late-night jape that was rapidly turning into an adult craze bubbled-over during the early weeks when **James Douglas** was ordered to instruct his men to keep a close watch, and to crack down heavily, on those who thought it'd be a wheeze to ring the door bells and hammer the knockers of the big houses in High Street and Foregate Street and then run away. That these were adults and the craze a long-running battle between police and the fun-seekers just seemed to add an extra element of excitement to the merry game – not that the already hard-pressed police found it quite so amusing: both the weekly newspapers carried articles on the nightly disturbances, with dire warnings that examples would be made of revellers caught indulging in such nocturnal nonsense.

Whether **Manny Onslow** was allowed a few minutes alone with William Chesterton, thought to have been the leader of a gang that had subjected him to a brutal round of punishment the previous August is not known for sure, but it might be a satisfying thought that he was.

Five of the gang had been caught and fined for the assault, but its ringleader had done a runner. Now, six months on, and assuming the incident had been forgotten, he ventured back into town – and was instantly recognised and hauled into the gaol-house for some serious, er..... *questioning.*

## Murder case re-opened

Another case from the previous August also made a dramatic re-appearance at the same time when a suspected murder file was re-opened after the allegedly murdered man's silver watch appeared in a city centre pawnshop, and was brought to **Joe Orchard** for investigation. Flash young braggart, 17-year old James Sefton (sometimes also Sifton and Selfton) had been savagely beaten, robbed and his body flung into the Severn on the last day of the races, but though there had been masses of circumstantial evidence pointing to the guilt of the two chief suspects, both had been allowed to go.

Now, suspicion fell on 24-year old William Humphreys who, during a week's observation in the city gaol pending further reports after attempting to pawn the watch, came up with several highly implausible excuses as to how he'd acquired it – including having bought it from a wandering jew in the High Street for 2 shillings, having been offered it in the Angel in Silver Street by a stranger, and another that it had been sent him by his mother in Liverpool. Despite piling up even more damning evidence – resulting in an attempt to commit him for Sefton's murder, magistrates believed the capital case would again fail and so committed him on the far lesser charge of suspicion of having stolen the murdered man's watch.

At his trial on March 7th under judge Baron Alderson he was found not guilty, although the crowd in the court thought the verdict a shameful one and made their feelings noisily known.

*The increasing efficiency of the police is illustrated in a report from the City Gaol that same week showing that it held eight prisoners awaiting trial:*

- Jonathan Stiff, 37, charged with killing and slaying Ann Stiff, in the parish of All Saints *(trial Friday, March 4th: discharged)*
- James Williams 19, charged with killing and slaying Thomas Thorley, in the parish of St Nicholas *(trial Friday, March 4th: detained until the Easter Sessions)*
- Samuel Whitaker, 20, and John *(later amended to George)* Smith, 19, charged with breaking into the dwelling-house of John Rouse, of the parish of St Helen, and stealing silver and gold coin of the value of 7l 10s *(trial Saturday, March 5th: guilty}*
- Elizabeth Pritchard, 36, charged with stealing from the person of Jas Mason, a purse containing a half sovereign in gold, and five shillings in silver
- Margaret Scribbens, 27, charged with stealing a hairbrush and one napkin, the property of Mr Pemberton of the parish of All Saints
- Mary Fidoe, 40, charged with stealing five sheets, and other articles, the property of Isaac Jones, of the Hop-Pole Inn, parish of St Nicholas *(trial Saturday, March 5th: guilty, six months imprisonment and warned that a further offence would result in transportation)*
- Ann Dury *(later Drury)*, alias Wall, 27, charged with stealing 8lbs of beef from the shop of Wm Payne in Bridge Street, parish of All Saints.

## Now officially 'Worcester City Police'

For the burgeoning new police force, now for the first time and from here on ever to be known as 'Worcester City Police', the first quarter of 1836 was to be crucially dominated by reform and reorganisation. Now given official backing by the full Council of 36 elected members and 12 Aldermen, the key issue of manning took precedence and **James Douglas** wasted no time in setting his agenda on the table.

Out went ex-Watchmen **Richard Bills, Robert Checkett, William Jones, Jeremiah Martin, John Woodward, John Thompson and Richard Winwood. Edward Harding** had already quit after just a month in the role (*20th October – 22nd November 1835*).

Now the roll was re-shaped to show a clean-sheet with a universal start date of 15th January, chiming with the first scheduled meeting of the new-look Watch Committee.  There was just one annoying draw-back...

For the second time in the force's history, the councillors making up the Committee, under its chairman Alderman Richard Evans who was destined to be mayor two years later, just wasn't ready – or more likely, didn't consider the subject sufficiently pressing to warrant immediate attention, much as in 1824.   At least, unlike on the first occasion, scheduled for March 15th but not convened until the following month, this time there was a meeting of sorts, the press were gathered in excited expectation on the due date, and everyone hoped that this was going to be the first salvo in the biggest broadside yet on the growing evils of crime and disorder – at last!

The *Journal* report was brief and to-the-point:

> **Watching and Police**. *Mr Alderman Richard Evans as Chairman, stated that the Committee were as yet, unprepared with any report.  The subject did not immediately press, as he believed the means were provided for continuing the existing arrangements until Lady-day, and in the interval the Committee would apply themselves to determine what would be the best arrangement thereafter.*

The crucial first meeting actually took place *three months* after originally intended, on April 15th, but at least, it was worth waiting for...

Most notably its first tangible outcome was that the force was deemed sufficient to be competent and capable of adequately policing all the old city boundary.  The 16 constables were to be paid 32s (£1.60p) fortnightly with an extra shilling to the Sergeant, and 30s to the Inspector.  The only additions proposed at the time were three special constables for the Tything and three for St Johns at 3s 6d a week '...until a rate be granted to include the new boundaries, when an augmentation in the police force will be proposed, in proportion to the extra ground requiring protection'.

The official rules governing the police's conduct and procedure were also read out, prompting a few last-minute amendments and suggestions by two members of the committee.

Also taking up an inordinate time at the first meeting was their critical relationship with the press and the possibility of 'perversion' following what the city's elders had no doubt viewed as biased and unfair reporting during both the Sharpe years and more recently under **James Douglas.**

As the reporters were admitted to the committee room (*now the Randall Room*) Mayor John Wheeley Lea set out the terms of their presence: '...the freedom of the press has ever been considered as one of the chief safeguards of public liberty, and also as one of the greatest advantages that an enlightened people can enjoy.  But when that freedom degenerates into calumny or licentiousness, it becomes as great an evil as it was before a benefit.  In reporting, therefore, our proceedings, I claim in the name of the community, as well as in that of this corporation, that the reporters give them in the spirit of truth and justice – that they nothing extenuate nor set down aught in malice'.

While it was no doubt meant as a catch-all and guide for the local media in general – the *Herald,* the *Journal* and the recently-launched *Worcester Guardian* – the latter's reporter and possibly its editor and printer Isaac Arrowsmith saw it as a personal affront, jumped to his feet, and said so, claiming that he felt the mayor's comments were directed at him personally and at the *Guardian* in general.

> *'The Mayor, however, added, that in the observations he had thought it expedient to make, he meant not to allude either to any particular individual or any particular print; neither did he mean in them to advert to what had passed, but he wished them to be considered as intended for general application only, and for the future guidance of the reporters'.*

So there.  The chief of the newly-styled Worcester City Police also unveiled his now permanent force: **James Douglas (Inspector No1); William Aston No2; George Williams No3; John Phillips No4; William Hale No5; William Sanders No6; Richard Berry No7; John Griffiths No8; Joseph Mayfield (***occasionally referred-to as Mason***) No9; Joseph Hall No10; John Drinkwater No11; Robert Howard No12; George Nott No13; Emanuel Onslow No14; George Stoneley No15; (***possibly***) William Phillips No16; Luke Packwood No17.**

The numbers were never regarded as permanent, being re-allocated yearly; nor, even in the case of No1, were they necessarily an indication of seniority or rank.  Subsequent recruits often took over an early number when it had been vacated by a retiring officer and within a couple of years, **James Workman** – who admittedly was to go on to a 21-year career with the force (*19th January 1836 to 7th November*

*1856*) found himself styled No2 despite being a complete rookie and up to a few weeks before, a mere Supernumerary.

The police:population ratio remained much as before the Reform Act at 1:1117. By comparison, Bristol City Police, also officially formed on January 1st this year had a complement of 307 patrolling its municipal borough, population 59,034, ratio 1:192 *(Source: Population and Policing in Bristol c1835 )*

The terms of the new act still allowed the Mayor to retain his officer and four Serjeants-at-Mace – and still does to this day – although it's difficult to determine quite how they sat with the police as they were still not only considered part of, although essentially separate to, the constabulary, but also had similar status including full powers of arrest.

Certainly during this point, Mayor's Officers **Joseph Orchard** and **Thomas Tilt** were still highly active members of Worcester's policing arrangements – to the degree that the newspapers still struggled to distinguish them from the regular ranks of policemen: even the uniforms, while different in many respects, could at first glance be mistaken as being one and the same.

Within a matter of weeks, **Manny Onslow** had been promoted to Sergeant – the second in the history of the force, behind **George Williams**.

But at least the city had a new name to look up to in its mixed-success saga of good over evil: the official title *'Worcester City Police'.*

So would the new-look force – still seemingly undermanned, but at least with a clear road ahead for expansion as per circumstances dictated – be able to live up to all the hopes and aspirations now expected of it? **James Douglas** for one was determined that it would, and with the backing of his hand-picked men – the first time such an advantage had presented itself to a commanding officer – there was every hope that yes, it would.

*Proving it began on day one...*

## RACK ALLEY.

Rack Alley – the rump end of which still exists – was a notorious passageway cutting though the old city wall and linking the ever-dangerous Dolday with the Butts: it also provided a near daily reminder to the police and the public that dangers still abounded for the unwary on the city's streets. So much was forcibly hammered home to an unsuspecting youth named Edwards who, en route to Bristol to join a ship destined for Demerara, stopped off in Worcester one night, picked up a girl (*unnamed*) and accepted her invitation to accompany her to the alleyway for an unspecified purpose.

The *Journal* picks up the tale...

*'...on their return down the alley they were met with a man named John Onions who was acquainted with the girl, who struck Edwards a blow which knocked him down; a scuffle ensued, in the course of which Edwards lost his purse, containing twenty-nine sovereigns. He called out "Murder", and Onions and the girl attempted to run away'.*

Luckily for him, not so the girl or Onions, the ever-reliable **Joe Hall No10** was close by. Edwards had managed to hold the girl and the rest of the force had tracked down Onions within half an hour. Just one of his 29 lost sovereigns – to all intents £1 which the newspapers were now printing as '£' – was recovered: it had fallen from the girl's dress when she was searched at the City nick. Edwards was sent on his way sadder, poorer and no doubt considerably the wiser, but probably full of praise for a police force whose workload was *six times greater per man than that of the city he was headed for.*

The force's newest recruit **Luke Packwood No17** came in for some well deserved praise in April after standing all-night vigil –10pm to 6am – outside the house of a man named Thomas Hill who he suspected of stealing potatoes. Nabbing him in the early hours of April 18th in possession of two sacks of potatoes, he took him into custody then marched him to a field off Northwick Road where his shoes perfectly matched prints found round a plundered burrow. Noted the *Herald*: 'great praise is due to the policeman for his vigilance as we understand that many depredations of this kind have lately been perpetrated'.

At the time, **Luke Packwood** was aged 30 and he'd have needed every single one of his 16s a week as he was married to Priscilla, also 30 and they had four children: Lucinda and Herbert both 5, Luke jnr 4, and Emily 2. Another former Supernumerary, he'd already been an official member of the force for almost all of the previous year. Five years on, Worcester's first official (1841) census shows the family living in Spa Row off Carden Street in the Blockhouse, with three more children: Joshua then 4, Samson 2 and Henrietta 1. He remained a constable and quit the force on March 1st 1844. *More on p351.*

The increasing number of policemen bringing cases to the Magistrates court caused a row in the Guildhall in April when magistrates lodged a sulky objection to the mayor that the room to which they'd traditionally retired to consider their decisions – *today the Green Room* – had been commandeered by the police. On several occasions they'd had to pull rank and shoo them off '...whilst the Bench were deliberating upon their decision; and there was no place to station them except the landing at the foot of the stairs and on the staircase where they choke up the approach to the office, and make ingress and egress difficult' (*Journal*).

The Town Clerk decided to defer the matter 'for a future day'.

## Chief remains very much 'hands-on'

**James Douglas** was showing himself an altogether different proposition to his predecessor. Chief or otherwise, he remained very much a hands-on copper as in the summer of this year he played a prominent role in the arrest of 36-year old carpenter William Curnock, committed for trial for stealing timber from his employers. The court heard that he'd personally taken control of the case, individually apprehended him, brought him before the magistrate for charging, searched his premises where he'd found dozens of articles buried and otherwise cleverly concealed, and acted as chief witness. Curnock was later sentenced to six months in prison, the first and last in solitary.

As already made provision for, the force's ranks were swelled by another six officers in September, ahead of extensions of the city boundary to include St Johns and Claines – then referring to the entire north-eastern reaches of the city from the old city wall at Lowesmoor and including what's still termed Claines but then also including Rainbow Hill, Blackpole, Warndon, Ronkswood, Nunnery Wood and St Peters.

They were: **George Brewer** *(also Brewers)* **No18; John Silvester No19; William Dyer No20; Thomas Chipp No21; William Cowley No22; and William Henry Incell No23** – one of which was to gain notoriety and only one other of whom was to go on to anything approaching a remarkable career.

The former, **William Dyer No20** sounds a complete chancer and a liability, but the latter, **Tommy Chipp No21,** proved to be a remarkable copper and eventually, chief.

It might just be proof that the police had become viewed as all-purpose, all-seeing upholders of good over bad at this time, or it might just have been plain stupidity created by out-and-out financial stinginess – a common trait of the City Corporation over the years – but when the state of the city's streets came in for some harsh criticism from official quarters and calls were made for the appointment of a Streets Surveyor to take control in the autumn, some bright-spark suggested the role could be taken over by the police.

The notion had its supporters and detractors despite the obvious observation that the addition of such a duty could have no possible effect other than to interfere with their more immediate work-load. Even so, the issue was referred to the Watch Committee whose reaction can be guessed.

*The matter appears to have been buried and never brought up again.*

Events of a more personal and pressing importance were now taking up the officers' time that September – one nasty case in particular. With strong echoes of the fateful events of a little over three years earlier, their chief had got himself into a fight, and had come off worst, hammered with his own heavy night staff by the men he'd gone to arrest.

*And with a clear sense of déjà-vu, there were fears for his continued future...*

At 11.30pm on the 24th., a boatman named Jeremiah Jones staggered into the station-house claiming to have been roughed-up by some rowdies in the Castle and Falcon (*later The Falcon*) in Broad Street, and robbed of cash and his watch. **Sgt Manny Onslow** accompanied Jones back to the Falcon where they were joined by **Inspector Douglas**: '...and from the information they obtained, they went to the Sun, in Bull Court, at about a quarter past one on Sunday morning. When they had obtained admittance, they proceeded into the attic where they found the prisoners, (Maria) Bardin and (William) Phillips, partly undressed and another man named Francis Bradley; when the officers determined upon searching the prisoner Bardin, Phillips was seen by both Onslow and Douglas attempting to pass something to Bradley, which proved to be Jones' watch' (*Journal*).

The upshot was that **James Douglas** made a grab for the watch, the two men set about him, his staff fell out his pocket, he was walloped over the head with it by Bradley – noted the *Journal*, 'from the effects of which he will be some time before he recovers' – and the two men escaped.

**Sgt Onslow** called for medical help for his chief, secured Maria Bardin in the city gaol, and rounded-up six officers, marching them into St Johns where Phillips' brother was known to live.

When they got there, the Phillips brothers pelted them with stones, leaving **Joe Mayfield ('Mason') No9, and Bill Hale(s) No5** cut and bleeding. Despite that, they stormed the house and dragged them, as like as not literally, back into the city and the station-house. On Monday morning, the Phillipses, Elizabeth Kepax who'd initiated Jeremiah Jones' first encounter in the Falcon, and Maria Bardin, later amended to Martha Barden, were all hauled before the magistrates and committed for trial at the Sessions. Richard Baylis, landlord of the Bull and Sun was also summoned to appear before the Bench and severely reprimanded both for allowing persons of bad character to frequent his house and for not rendering the prompt assistance which the case required. An oaf called Davis who'd also tried to interfere with **Sgt Onslow's** attempt to haul Phillips to gaol was also charged with obstruction but discharged after a reprimand. Elizabeth Kepax was discharged (*but was to re-emerge in notoriety on several occasions during later years*); Barden and Phillips were sentenced to seven years' transportation apiece.

*Such were Saturday nights in Worcester, but there was no time for sitting still and taking stock...*

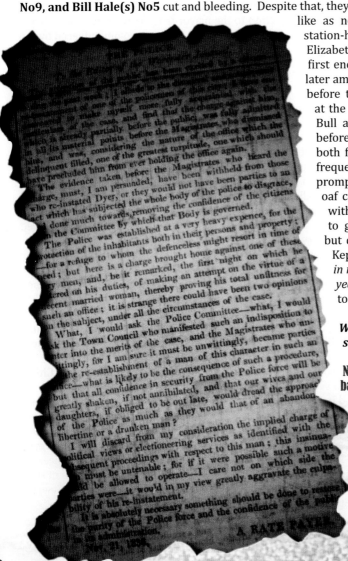

### New copper, No20 proves to be an altogether bad penny...

Towards the end of this year of crises, the potentially most crippling of all occurred – dividing the city, plunging the whole force into disgrace and progressing a long way towards the complete erosion of trust and confidence in the city force. As if a charge of sexual assault by one of its officers wasn't bad enough, the incident imploded with allegations of callous anti-police manipulation by self-interested political factions, vacillation by the magistrates under pressure, dirty tricks and tactical voting by the Town Council, and a cover-up by the police chiefs. *No-one was going to win this one...*

On his first night out, **William Dyer, No20**, was accused of forcing his attentions on 'a decent married woman' by name of Andrews. It would appear that he'd mistaken her for a common prostitute and that she'd remonstrated, told him she was not the sort of woman he'd mistaken her for and showed him her wedding ring – which only spurred him on, '...offering her money as an inducement to comply with his criminal purposes' (*Journal*). He didn't get his way and Mrs Andrews went about her business, laughing about the issue to one of her work colleagues the next morning. Next thing, there were angry scenes at the Guildhall where Mrs Andrews had been brought, seemingly against her better judgement, to lay a charge of assault against Dyer. The magistrates ordered the Watch Committee to implement his instant dismissal, **James Douglas** was in no state to initiate the sacking, but still refused to comply without a proper hearing, and without clear guidance from his superiors, **William Dyer** was permitted to continue with his duties until further notice.

The move prompted outrage from sections of the anti-police community, many of whom probably had a vested interest on revenge, and resulting in a torrent of outraged and vitriolic letters to the press.

Commented 'A Rate Payer' in a letter dated Nov 21st., the affair '...has subjected the whole body of the police to disgrace and done much towards removing the confidence of the citizens. All confidence in security from the Police force will be greatly shaken if not annihilated... and our wives and daughters, if obliged to be out late, (will) dread the approach of the Police as much as they would an abandoned libertine or a drunken man'.

Three weeks later, 'One Of The Insulted Citizens' asked '...whether we must servilely submit to the extraordinary determination of a Town Council to have Policeman No20 forced upon us with the aggravation too of having our money forced from us for support of such a character?'.

## Also this year: 1836

■ *No17 Manny Onslow proves himself a scourge on beer-shop owners keeping their premises open for longer than proscribed*

■ *One week in July alone sees charges brought against the George in Silver Street, the Prince William in Clap-gate (later the King William IV Vaults, aka 'King Billy' still in living memory in St Paul's Street), and the City Tea Gardens in Withy Walk*

■ *the same month sees Joe Hall No10 savagely attacked by William Chesterton – very likely the same gang-leader that had beaten-up Manny Onslow the previous year. He was sentenced to seven days' gaol*

■ *William Derrett, miller at the County Gaol for the previous fifteen years, hangs himself within the confines of the prison after being charged with dishonesty*

■ *the races provide a steady stream of miscreants and new prison inmates, Joe Hall again emerging a particularly active officer*

■ *Sgt Onslow yet again plays a major role in the apprehension of two boatmen, William Lessemore and Thomas Dyson accused of murder of one of their own, Samuel Edge, dragged out of the Severn in September. Both committed for trial.*

■ *George Stoneley No15 comes in for praise both from his superiors and the Bench when he is attacked by three men in the Dog & Duck in St Nicholas Street yet still manages to get the better of all three and secure them in the Station-house; the three were fined £2 each and expenses*

■ *Michaelmas Sessions in October are particularly busy and the police '...whose vigilance and activity was generally acknowledged', earn some well-deserved praise*

■ *in November, No7 Richard Berry is commended for a rescuing a drunken Thomas Kedward who'd fallen off the North Pier (Parade) into the river*

The matter raged on for weeks with accusations and hot-tempered denials from all quarters involved. No-one emerged with their reputations intact – least of all the police. Dyer remained with the force, but only for another eighteen months: by June 1838 he was no longer a city policeman. Nor was this the last that Worcester was to hear of **William Dyer**: in mid-1842 and by now punchy, stout and a drunkard, he was beaten-up in the Shades in Diglis Street by 20-year old George Perry who'd had enough of his constant bullying.

The *Herald* reported that Dyer had had: '...the worst of the fight and the best of the swearing'.

*Gained: (second, third and fourth intakes, supplementing the original sixteen with a start date of 15th January) Thomas Baylis, Charles Bowyear, James Workman, John Evans, George Williams, John Mason, Willliam Phillips, George Brewer, W. H. Incell, William Dyer, Thomas Chipp, John Sylvester, William Cowley, Charles Smith, Joseph Norman, George Jones*
**Lost:** *William Aston, Joseph Mayfield, John Evans*

1837

The **Dyer** case and the integrity of everyone associated with it was still rocking the city as 1837 dawned: even plans for a new all-embracing County force, bringing together the various outlying town and rural forces springing up, was tainted by the affair – a letter to the *Journal* openly warning that such a force would be a 'prerogative standing army, permanently-established... hating and hated by the people and trained to suspicion, falsehood and craft of every kind; it would constitute the most terrible of all weapons in the hands of an ambitious aspirant to tyranny'.

It was strong stuff, but typical of the scale of distrust and contempt in which the police were still being viewed nationally, regionally and, largely as a result of one rogue policeman, locally.

The City Police still had much to do to regain the ground lost in the previous hot-tempered months, and it's unclear whether or not **James Douglas** was around to play his hand in repairing the damage done to his demoralised force: the implication is that he was still indisposed from the hammering he'd received at the Bull and Sun three months earlier.

Everybody was tainted by the fall-out from the affair – and walking round on tippi-toes for fear of making the situation worse. Even a fire at John Young's warehouse in the Trinity in which the police had played a heroic and active role in bringing under control – thereby saving neighbouring premises including Farley's Bank, Freame's warerooms and factory, warehouses belonging to Archer and Co. and West, and the private home and stables of John Lippitt Esq., – only drew faint praise from the press with no individual singled-out for praise except for 'Mr S. Pumphrey jun., son of the agent to the Birmingham Fire Office'.

The attitude was echoed on the streets, and even reaction to what otherwise would have been hailed as exceptional sleuthing was muted – typically, a case in January when the ever-diligent **Manny Onslow** managed to find a stash of £15 stolen from a guest at the Three Tuns and very cleverly concealed in the stables there. Despite 'decently-attired' Irishman Thomas Mulvaney's strongest protestations to his innocence, Onslow had managed to trace a catalogue of similar crimes by tracking scores of transactions at various city pawn-shops and Mulvaney was committed to the city gaol to take his trial for theft.

Nor were the magistrates, hoping to keep a low profile after their shameful part in the Dyer affair, prepared to step out of line, proving themselves reticent to be seen to side with the police for fear of accusations of partialism in cases where there was even the slenderest sliver of doubt.

One such was when **PC John Silvester No19** was jostled, challenged to fight and struck over the head with a pair of boots by a Leech (Lich) Street shoemaker named Wadeley who he suspected of having broken into a property in the same street late one night. Despite corroborating evidence of a supernumerary (later full PC) named **George Jones** and two other witnesses '...the magistrates thought it best to dismiss the case' (*Journal*).

Even the mayor's four Sergeants at Mace now appeared to want to distance themselves from the force, presenting a claim for loss of fees occasioned through some of their former paid duties now being handled by the police – but at least, here the corporation voted unanimously to reject the claim and censured the four serjeants for having made the claim in the first place.

That same week, the County Gaol held 34 prisoners awaiting trial, the City Gaol 8. Two prisoners had attempted suicide by hanging, but both had failed.

The inadequacy of the Guildhall as the site of multiple courts also surfaced in March when the proceedings of the County Assizes were noisily interrupted by a string of chained prisoners being led by the gaoler from the cells below to take trial in the Police and Magistrates' court (*now the Mayor's Parlour*). The incident sparked-off an angry exchange of letters between the new Mayor, surgeon Christopher Henry Hebb and John Pakington, Chairman of the County magistrates and later architect of several Beer Acts, and the two were never to enjoy a cordial association again. Luckily, the new County Court and Judge's Lodgings buildings in Foregate Street were nearing completion.

## Deaths, murder, suicide and assault in March

During the same week in late March, the new police were kept busy with a spate of intense activity involving four comparatively high-profile cases:

- *a number of beer-shops operating illegally and reported by a couple of professional snoopers who had to be taken into custody for their own protection when their identity was made public*
- *the suspected murder of a 4-year old boy, shot on a barge moored on the canal at Lowesmoor*
- *the suicide of 23-year old Emma Skarratt under Tallow Hill bridge just days after she'd buried her baby*
- *and a vicious attack that had left one of the city's most prominent licensees, John Jeremy of the Angel (later renamed the Plough) in Silver Street, almost blinded.*

The police were also called in to restrain the crowds at the emotional and hot-tempered public execution of murderer, 29-year carpenter William Lightband at the County Gaol: '...he fell apparently dead, but in about half a minute a violent convulsive movement of his whole frame excited a cry of horror from the crowd, which covered every visible spot of ground. A few struggles, as if gasping for breath, followed, and in a few minutes he ceased to live' (*Journal – to which editor Harvey Tymbs had sniffily appended the note 'May it be a lasting and useful lesson to those who are following a similar course of life in rioting and drunkenness'*).

At least, chief **James Douglas** was by now back to fighting fitness and again in the thick of things, personally taking control of a case involving four hardened criminals from Birmingham on a spree of picking pockets and passing counterfeit coin.

At the centre of it was a 10-year old lad, Michael Condlie, described by the police chief to the Bench as a dexterous pick-pocket and thief who Douglas partly undressed in court to show them the special pockets sewn into his trousers to conceal his swag:  '...Douglas said that the lad had been the most artful young rogue that had ever been before the Bench (*the wording is almost too coincidental that this was precisely the same month that the first chapters of Charles Dickens' latest masterwork Oliver Twist were published as a serial, not reaching its conclusion until 1839*).

The boy had been remanded in the city gaol for several days before any other gang member, in this case the boy's mother, came to visit him. At the subsequent court hearing, she, the boy and a known local fence named William Crump were all discharged on lack of evidence – a further illustration of the mistrust still being felt between the force and the Bench.  **James Douglas** must've been livid.

Another tale involving a child and **James Douglas** also merited a snippet around the same time...

Emily Evans had attracted the chief's personal attention on several occasions as he'd done tours of the city late at night and sensing that she was little more than a common prostitute had had her committed to the City Gaol for seven days '...with a view that some means might be taken to save her from further infamy and ultimate ruin'.  She was aged just 12.  Faced with little alternative but to commit her for the statutory seven days, the Magistrates took special care to commend the chief for his conduct '...and in the hope that something might be adopted to extricate the child from such wretched practices, determined to send her to prison that her parents might be written to' (*Herald*).

***Then, just two weeks later on June 22nd., a key historical event...***

## Maintaining order following news of old Sailor King's passing

The popular old 'Sailor King', William IV had died and the nation was to have a new monarch, this time, a queen, Victoria. Worcester went wild and the police were sent in to maintain some semblance of law and order at the formal announcements of the old king's passing and the accession of a new monarch.

The same day, George Taylor keeper of the Paul Pry beer house in the Butts and Charles Rea, keeper of the Rose and Crown beer house in Sidbury were each fined 40s and costs, for allowing the sale of beer during hours not authorised by the Bench, while at the Falcon in Broad Street another (*unnamed*) member of Worcester City Police was coming in for what was by now an all-too common experience: a severe beating by a member of the public he'd been appointed to protect.

As ever, the *Herald* spares few details, the colourful journalistic style of the time adding an almost music-hall veneer on what sounds like a painful episode for the copper, as ever in the firing line for all the city's worst excesses. It's more than possible that the fanciful scribe was John Noake, a *Herald* reporter and sub-editor at the time, later Magistrate, councillor, Mayor and Aderman and acknowledged cataloguer of all things Worcester, rightly regarded as classics of their kind. It's worth re-printing in full...

### DEATH OF THE KING.

We deeply regret to state, that His Most Gracious Majesty, WILLIAM THE FOURTH, expired at Windsor Castle, on Tuesday morning, soon after two o'clock. Below we give, in a connected form, the official announcement of this melancholy event, with an account of the proceedings connected with the Accession of our young Queen.

The *London Gazette Extraordinary*, published on Tuesday forenoon, contained the following :—

WHITEHALL, JUNE 20.

A Bulletin, of which the following is a copy, has been received by Lord John Russell, one of his late Majesty's Principal Secretaries of State :—

" Windsor Castle, Tuesday, June 20, 1837.
" It has pleased Almighty God to release from his sufferings our most excellent and gracious Sovereign, King William the Fourth. His Majesty expired at twelve minutes past two o'clock,

*'James Bryant, a stalworth (sic), strapping (so the policeman felt) six-feet-high fellow, was charged with being riotous and disorderly, and trying the strength of a massive iron fist while practising a series of gymnastic feats on the eyes and temples of a policeman. The policeman, whose memories of James' powers seemed to be refreshed by his presence, stood at a very respectful distance from him while he stated that at half-past nine o'clock he was called into the house of a publican named Irish, the sign of the Falcon, Broad Street, to look after a skrimmage, and there sure enough, was James Bryant, a little the worse for liquor, and every thing within reach of his fist the worse for that. Glasses couldn't stand in his sight – an empty one was his abomination. It trembled for its very existence, a cold fit came on it and it shivered in pieces, and pewter pots went to pot. Irish himself **[Robert Stracey Irish, landlord of the Falcon 1836-42]** pat-riot as he was, felt that he couldn't stand before him and James, like a bull in a china shop, had it all his own way. On the policeman attempting to take the prisoner into custody, he demurred, planted his two feet against the counter by way of a lever, and in that position, like another Archimedes, if he couldn't lift, he thought he could beat the world before him. The policeman succeeded however, in loosing his hold of the counter and in attempting to bring him along the prisoner collared him – that might be in joke – but then his blows were so thick and heavy, that he considered him in earnest. On getting the prisoner into the street, he flung himself on his knees, and cursed him a great deal more to the prisoner's satisfaction than his (the policeman's) and finally, after much struggling, he succeeded in lodging him in the station-house. The prisoner, in his defence, admitted that he was a little fresh on the night in question – he was sorry, so very very sorry indeed – but his wife was near her confinement.*

*'Mayor (**Christopher Henry Hebb Esq**) – What has that to do with your getting drunk and assaulting the policeman?*

*'Prisoner – Nothing at all, your Worship, only Betsey – that's my wife your Worship – was in that way, a little "family way" of our own – and –*

*'Mayor–Oh! I understand you; you anticipated the christening and got drunk – isn't that it?*

*'The prisoner looked very dewy, stroked down his hair, peeped into his hat, – then rubbed and "owned the soft impeachment". He could assure their Worships it was all a mistake and if he was let off this time, as he was a teetotaller and a man of his word, he wouldn't do it again for six months to come – a teetotaller's word might be taken for that time. Upon the prisoner's expressing his regret, and giving the promise that he would reserve such riotous demonstration of his satisfaction till Betsey's accouchement, his uncommon reason for a common assault was admitted for this time...'*

In other words, he got off.

July, the month after the new queen's accession, proved a bad one for the force when two prominent stalwarts moved on: **John Drinkwater and George Williams**. They were replaced by **Thomas Evans** (*28th July*) and **Henry Griffiths Dunk** and **George Richardson** both on August 11th

It set the pattern of police activity for the remainder of the first year of Victoria's reign.

1837 had been a roller-coaster year for Worcester City Police, but they'd survived. Just.

It had seen 250 prisoners locked-up in the City gaol for crimes committed within the City boundary: 114 for felony, 24 as vagrants, 2 as reputed thieves, 28 for assaults, 11 as prostitutes, 1 for bastardy, 43 for various petty offences – typically, drunkenness and illegal pawning – and 27 as debtors. Of these 86 could neither read nor write and 39 could read only.

At the same time, the County gaol (*in Salt Lane, later Castle Street*) saw 749 committals involving 370 awaiting trial, 4 military deserters, 22 under the game laws, 7 under revenue laws, 5 for bastardy, 72 vagrants, 21 under the Malicious Trespass Act, 16 under the Larceny Act, 2 under the local police act, 53 for assaults, 27 for want of sureties, 2 for re-examination or charges under summary jurisdiction but afterwards discharged, 97 for various petty offences, and 51 debtors.

The year had also seen the City Police play a key role in the re-capture of an escaped convict, 20-year old ex-bricklayer Thomas Phillips, at large in Worcester after breaking loose from the Curriers Arms in Angel Street where he and Rice, the Governor of Brecon Gaol, had put up for the night en route for the hulks at Woolwich.

A failing this year was to make a charge stick against Arthur Clarke, keeper of a beer-house in St Johns for staying open after allotted hours. Clarke and his solicitor F. T. Elgie, maintained that police powers didn't extend into that particular area of St Clement, the information was held to be fatal and the case was dismissed. Everyone, and none more so than the police, hoped for better things in 1838...

*Gained: Thomas Evans, Henry Griffiths Dunk, George Richards, all three former Supernumeraries.*
*Lost: John Drinkwater and George Williams*

## Also this year: 1837

- *investigations begin when 3-year old Thomas Poole of the Blockhouse is burned to death*

- *Louisa Court throws herself into the canal and drowns at Gregory's Mill after a failed love affair*

- *objection to the licence of the Virgin Tavern being renewed because of constant rowdy behaviour*

- *James Douglas himself violently opposes the re-granting of the licence for the Druids Head in Merrivale '...on the grounds of opening hours being very improper, that characters of the worst description are harboured there and that it adjoins two brothels, and is in the immediate neighbourhood of many others'*

- *a Little Witley farmer named Joseph Boughton is relieved of the massive amount of £90 after consorting with three good-time girls Ann Glover, Elizabeth Kepax, and Mary Kepax*

- *early form of rta (road traffic accident) on the bridge when a horse and gig knocks over and kills Ann Ross*

- *arrest of James Cullis, a serial flasher targeting young girls*

- *Mary Wheeley of Claines is murdered by her husband Thomas by poison administered in a glass of ale drawn at the New Inn*

- *scores of robberies and sundry other assaults, accidents, gory suicides and attacks on the police*

The year began much as the previous one had ended – beer shop convictions and assaults on the police...

Early on, Edward Pardoe, keeper of the Nag's Head beer-shop, Sidbury, was fined 40s and expenses, for allowing his house to be open after 10 o'clock and then two days later, John Harris was charged with assaulting **No4, John Phillips**. It was the usual tale: man goes for a drink or two on a Saturday night (*in this case, the Green Dragon in Newport Street*), he gets a bit tipsy, one things leads to another, and suddenly he's no longer in control. Seems he got a bit rowdy, broke several glasses, refused to pay when asked to do so and was then confronted with a dutiful copper whose orders were that he should be locked up for the night – generally an easier-said-than-done mission. Continues the *Herald*: '...he was then given over into the custody of the officer **Phillips**, whom he struck very violently over the head. From these injuries Phillips stated that he had not recovered, and was unable to perform his duty'. Fined 2l and 2s.6d costs

At least **Manny Onslow** was continuing as he'd begun, with some fine detective work. Noticing some pewter pint and half-pint measures and a pudding dish in Matthews Ironmongers in Broad Street, his suspicions that they'd been stolen led him to the arrest of four juveniles, all of whom were later convicted of thefts from the Foundry Arms and Johnsons Bakery in Sidbury.

This was another case that **James Douglas** had taken a personal interest in, seizing the opportunity to comment to the magistrates about the appalling decline in moral standards displayed by Worcester's youth: with another clear reference to Oliver Twist, he said that the boys had been 'harboured and encouraged' by a notorious character named Argus who kept a cider shop in King-street, frequented by youngsters of both sexes and implying that the establishment amounted to little more than a brothel and vice den: shades of the new fictional villain of the hour, Fagin the Jew.

The entire force was out on duty and its work clearly cut out on 28th June this year for the coronation of Queen Victoria, 53 weeks after acceding to the throne. The day was packed with dozens of incidents demanding their intervention – including the bizarre death of Michael Cummings, who, on returning from the Coronation Festivities, fell over a low wall into the open cesspit shared by several families in the shadow of St Andrews church. The unpleasant duty of extricating his body was left to an (*unnamed*) police officer. Verdict: Accidental death.

Their conduct on that no doubt otherwise joyous and incident-filled day was such that the Watch Committee voted a 5-shilling bonus for each man, totalling £8 10s 0d '...in recompense of the additional duties imposed upon them on the day of the Coronation, and the very effective and creditable manner in which they discharged them'. It also demonstrated that bridges were being built in the improving relationship of all those involved in the wake of the unfortunate Dyer affair.

### Fatal punch-up at Hope & Anchor leads to licensee's manslaughter charge

More solid policing work followed in the weeks following the Queen's coronation when Charles Goodman, licensee of the Hope & Anchor (*now Severn View or Vue Bar*) was convicted of manslaughter after a stand-up fight between him and confectioner Edward Hill outside the pub's front door.

Though they'd been old friends and drinking partners for some years, a row broke out one Saturday evening over a half-crown loan that Goodman refused Hill; Hill challenged Goodman to a fight and the two went out to settle the matter in the time-honoured way. Despite trying to persuade his friend to calm down, Hill persisted in his wish to fight Goodman, whose patience cracked and quickly knocked him down, promptly retracing his steps back inside.

A few minutes later, and after threatening another man to a fight, Hill raced back inside and again challenged Goodman to finish the fight. In the street again, Goodman – who was, by all accounts a much larger man – hit him twice more, both times with his left hand to the right side of his face, but this time Hill fell on the pavement and cracked his skull. He died in the parlour of the Hope and Anchor – scene of the crime, the post-mortem and the inquest – in the early hours of the next morning.

The court proved lenient – but it was not to be the only violent death here during Victoria's reign.

The police were only too well aware of the Newport Street pubs in general, and the Hope and Anchor in particular. Merry Vale (*or Merrivale, the area around St Andrews church*) was another notorious area considered no-go so far as the new police were concerned: but when the officer assigned to its policing was also **William Dyer** – who wasn't to know it, but was in the final few weeks of his career as a PC, probably a deliberate ploy by **James Douglas** as a way of getting rid of an officer that had frankly become a liability – anything could happen. Which it did in August...

Sent in to quell a near riot in the Hen and Chickens (*not that that was in itself anything unusual: there was a riot every night in the Hen and Chickens. For details of its location, and much more of its violent nature, see Bob Backenforth's Worcester Pubs then and Now Vol 2 p411-13*), to his credit **Dyer** had not shied away but had waded in, grabbed hold of one of the battling protagonists – a drunken chimney sweep named Richard Sharples, hence the subsequent *Herald* headline '**A Black Job**' – but was then set upon and repeatedly knocked down by a mob including two brothers, bricklayer George and hop-porter Tommy Smith, both of whom were later fined 20s including costs or 14 days' imprisonment.

The same night, **George Brewer No18** also got a hammering in the Star beer-shop in Sidbury. His attacker, a braggart named Henry Barton with vain ideas of being a star pugilist, had smashed-up the beer shop after threatening to take on all-comers and oddly enough, after finding no takers, set about the PC charged with the unwelcome task of calming him down and escorting to the station house. On the receiving end of a flurry of kicks and punches, it was all in a night's work.

### Drunken cop up before the Mayor

Then, the following week, yet more of the kind of black publicity the Commissioners dreaded – particularly at so sensitive a time so far as the police's slowly-improving reputation went – and **James Douglas** could frankly have done without: a policeman found reeling about the streets, completely incapable through drink. Worse, all the indications were that he'd been plied by some individual who knew what he was doing and wanted to make an example of the still-tarnished force, or – *nightmare of nightmares for him and for James Douglas* – that he'd frequented some drinking establishment criminally outside permitted hours, an area highlighted as priority crack-down for the police. The *Herald* identifies him as William Jones, but the roll of the time shows only ex-Supernumerary George Jones who'd joined the force in the fifth intake, as late as 21st October 1836.

Luckily for him, he'd gone off duty at 5am having done his night's stint otherwise it would have meant instant dismissal. The ever-observant *Herald* told the tale, clearly with another heavy veneer of what was later to be called spin-doctoring:

'It appeared, from the evidence of Inspector Douglas and others of the force, that the man went off duty that morning quite sober, at five o'clock, and was brought to the Station-house in a state of intoxication at the time stated, by an officer who found him in the street in that condition. The man explained that he had been for many months a member of the Temperance Society, and unfortunately he had fallen into temptation from the circumstance of an old comrade meeting him on the road home. He admitted his fault, but appealed to his general good character as extenuating his conduct. His statement was completely corroborated and it appeared he was invariably in the habit of refusing to partake of anything in the shape of liquor, even to a glass of ale; besides, the man was of excellent character, in consideration of which, and the extenuating circumstances of the case, he was acquitted, with a very severe reprimand from the Mayor'.

The mayor this year was surgeon Christopher Henry Hebb.

## Also this year: 1838

■ *No17 Manny Onslow returns empty handed after a running chase with a suspected thief as far as Lower Wick where he eventually caught him, searched his house but found nothing*

■ *a serious fracas at the Dolphin in Copenhagen Street (later the site of the new police station-house) involving nearly 20 people, all members of three Irish families sharing a yard*

■ *the usual round of objections to licence renewals on sundry grounds*

■ *St Clements parishioners revolt over charges for upkeep of New Road*

■ *250 prisoners admitted to City Gaol and 749 to County Gaol over the year*

It was yet another image disaster that did nothing for the police's reputation at a time when they needed it most; the wonder was that despite the catalogue of bad news centred around the gaol and the station-house, the police kept bouncing back for more. It was probably a case of having no choice...

The ever-dependable **Joe Hall No10** was next to get another beating, a known thug named Benjamin Cook, dishing out the kind of treatment that was becoming so depressingly frequent, it'd be tempting to think that the reporters had wagers on who could come up with the most fanciful description for the next week's edition, this from the *Herald*:

> ***City Police Monday Drunkenness - its Doings, and Their Consequences.*** *Benjamin Cook was charged with behaving in a very unbecoming manner, for a married man and a father, on Saturday night, while under the influence of the "Jolly God"... there was a further charge of changing the position of policeman Hall from the perpendicular to the horizontal, thereby bringing him prone on mother earth to the injury of his person, and the bedaubing of his habiliments. Prisoner expressed contrition for his misconduct, and was liberated on promising to become a tee-totaller, and paying for cleaning said policeman's garments'.*

It would have been comical were it not so serious. It was also becoming too commonplace. The following week, the *Herald* began its description of a typical Monday morning in the Police court:

'A stranger in the Justice-room this morning, would have been apt, from the number of disorderlies introduced to the Bench, to set down our really quiet and well-conducted population for something very much the reverse, and considering that two nights' and a whole day's imprisonment in the station-house are known to await delinquents, it is really wonderful that the most thoughtless should put themselves into the force's mercy on Saturday of all nights in the week'

It then listed a catalogue of the better part of a dozen cases heard that day – and could have done the same for the following five days, ditto the next week and ditto every week of the year.

October this year saw a momentous occasion – the desperately needed move to the force's own Station-house. Relations between the police and the increasingly quirky and unpredictable Guv'nor Griffiths of the City nick had strained relations to breaking point – and anyway, the force's growth had made a move all-but critical.

The premises selected was the former Militia HQ in (St) Nicholas Street bounded by Queen Street on the west and Watercourse Alley on the east, and it was to serve as the base and central police station for the next 25 years.

The forbidding grey stone building itself went on to out-survive Worcester City Police by some half a dozen years, falling to the bulldozer in 1971 as part of the planned City Walls Road, and will be fondly remembered as the later premises of Gardner's Bakery.

Its site is now the north-western corner of the Cornmarket car park.

### Actual charge book 1838-41 still survives

Coinciding with the move to new premises, a new **Charge Book** was begun on 27th of October, cataloguing the stream of suspected felons being brought into the station-house. The original has survived and it's preserved in the Hive, providing a fascinating insight into the force, its

| Number of Charge. | Hour when brought to Watch-House. | Persons Charged, Name and Address of. | Charge, Nature of. | Persons Charging, Name and Address of. |
|---|---|---|---|---|
| 27th Oct. 3162 | 4 07 | Jerimiah Carrol | charged with Strikeing the officer in the execution of his duty | Williams No 3 |
| 27th Oct. 3163 | — | Jerimiah & Ann Murry | charged with attempting to rescue Carrol | Williams No 3 |
| 27th — 3164 | 4 20 | Ann Hurst | drunk & disorderly in Broad St | Chipp No 21 |
| 27th — 3165 | 4 48 | Joseph Jones | drunk & beating his wife | Packwood No 17 |
| 27th — | 4 30 10 | Thos Hill | drunk & fighting in Sidbury | Sylvester No 22 |
| 27th — | 4 30 11 | William Wall | drunk & disorderly in Sidbury | No 22 |
| 30 | | John Pope | Stealing a Slat | Sylvester |

WCiCo/WAAS

day-to-day existence and the expectations of those employed in the furtherance of law and order in the new queen's Faithful City.

With the dubious honour of being the first entry in the book, is Jerimiah (sic) Carroll, charged with 'striking the officer in the execution of his duty'. The officer in question – **George Williams No3** – seemingly did his bit, went back on his beat and within minutes had returned with two more offenders, Jeremiah and Ann Murray, both charged wth attempting to rescue his previous prisoner. **Tommy Chipp No21, Luke Packwood No17**, and **John Silvester No22** all made additional arrests on the same night *(above)*.

The next few days also saw hauled-up:

- *Ann Hurst, charged with being drunk and disorderly in Broad Street*
- *Joseph Jones, drunk and beating his wife*
- *Thomas Hill, drunk and fighting in Sidbury*
- *William Wall, drunk and disorderly in Sidbury*
- *Peter Lamison and Thomas Harrison, charged with vagrancy*
- *Richard Webb and William Dowling, charged with obtaining a shilling under false pretences*
- *George Taylor, vagrant*
- *Richard Walker, charged on suspicion of felony*
- *William Bishop and Joseph Field, charged with being drunk in Foregate Street*

By the end of an otherwise unremarkable year, the state of crime and disorder had reached such a pitch and its officers stretched to such a degree that even the generally resourceful **James Douglas** felt obliged to ask the Magistrates to take a harder line with erring landlords thinking they could flout the laws regarding late night drinking. Although the public houses were obliged to close at 11pm and the beer-houses an hour earlier, too many were remaining open beyond those hours with the result that, said Douglas '...it would be impossible to keep the city in that state of peace and quietness so desirable at night, if (any later) hours were countenanced by the landlords'.

The only way ahead, he'd decided, was to make an example of one of their number: sadly for John Griffiths of the Black Boy in Leech (Lich) Street, he was the man duly selected. He was handed a severe fine, ordered to publicly agree to be more prudent than hitherto, and to pass the word on to his colleagues.

*Gained:* -
*Lost:* *William Dyer, William Cowley*

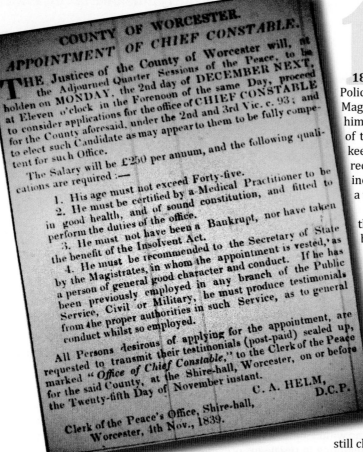

COUNTY OF WORCESTER.
APPOINTMENT OF CHIEF CONSTABLE.

THE Justices of the County of Worcester will, at the Adjourned Quarter Sessions of the Peace, to be holden on MONDAY, the 2nd day of DECEMBER NEXT, at Eleven o'clock in the Forenoon of the same Day, proceed to consider applications for the office of CHIEF CONSTABLE for the County aforesaid, under the 2nd and 3rd Vic. c. 93; and to elect such Candidate as may appear to them to be fully competent for such Office.

The Salary will be £250 per annum, and the following qualifications are required :—

1. His age must not exceed Forty-five.
2. He must be certified by a Medical Practitioner to be in good health, and of sound constitution, and fitted to perform the duties of the office.
3. He must not have been a Bankrupt, nor have taken the benefit of the Insolvent Act.
4. He must be recommended to the Secretary of State by the Magistrates, in whom the appointment is vested,' as a person of general good character and conduct. If he has been previously employed in any branch of the Public Service, Civil or Military, he must produce testimonials from the proper authorities in such Service, as to general conduct whilst so employed.

All Persons desirous of applying for the appointment, are requested to transmit their testimonials (post-paid) sealed up, marked "Office of Chief Constable," to the Clerk of the Peace for the said County, at the Shire-hall, Worcester, on or before the Twenty-fifth Day of November instant.

C. A. HELM,
D.C.P.

Clerk of the Peace's Office, Shire-hall,
Worcester, 1th Nov., 1839.

**1839** started well when, at the first Police Court of the year, Prosecuting Magistrate Charles Sidebottom himself openly acknowledged the role of the new Worcester City Police in keeping gaol numbers down, despite recent boundary changes that had increased the city's population by a third.

Since 1832, committals to the City Gaol had see-sawed between 198 (1834-5) and 309 the following year. In 1838 the number had been 236: '...and when it was considered that the city jurisdiction now extended over at least a third more inhabitants than prior to 1835, the fact was very gratifying, as well as very creditable to the improved system of policing' the *Herald* reported.

The same month, **James Douglas** was given special orders by the Mayor and still chairman of the Watch Committee, Richard Evans, to instruct his men to keep a special eye on 'the wicked and mischievous practice of throwing oil on ladies' silk dresses by some paltry miscreants'. The Mayor himself had offered 20 guineas reward in the hope that the worst of the japesters could be apprehended and brought to account.

The year also saw the passing of the **Rural Constabulary Act** allowing county areas to establish police forces *if they chose*; unlike the trend-setting City, Worcestershire wasn't up there among the first echelon in the queue to sign-up would-be constables – that honour went to Wiltshire although the County wasn't seriously far behind, being one of the first eight to take up the option. Accordingly, this year saw the creation of Worcestershire Constabulary, whose 'patch' meant that Worcester was isolated and effectively an island within when it came to police matters, just as it was in administrative concerns. The arrangement suited the city, but was to lead to all manner of troublesome issues over coming years.

In remarkably short order, the rules of the County police were quickly published – although the model set by the City force had already been established and the rules mirrored, almost word for word, those of the City constabulary, now entering its fourth year, but with its roots considerably further back. The major difference was in manning levels: the County force was to have one Chief Constable, 10 Superintendents or Sergeants, and 30 Constables.

The Chief Constable was to be no more than 45 years of age, while Superintendents, Sergeants and private Constables had to be under 40 years. The other requirements were much as had always been demanded by the city force. In order to be considered, applicants had to stand five feet seven without shoes; be able to read and write and keep accounts; to be free from any bodily complaint and to be of strong constitution and generally intelligent. Game-keepers and even ex-gamekeepers as well as wood-rangers, bailiffs, sheriff's bailiffs or parish clerks, or anyone who had worked for, or was related to publicans were excluded from selection.

The Chief Constable was to be paid not to be less than £250 nor more than £500 a year; Superintendents not less than £75 nor more than £150 a year, and Constables not less than 15s nor more than £1 1s a week, all exclusive of any permitted allowances. Additionally, the first (and third) year's 'clothing and accoutrements' included one great coat with cape and badge, coat and badge, two pair of trowsers (sic), one pair of boots, one pair of shoes and hat stock. The second (and fourth) year would see the addition of another coat and badge to ditto, another pair of trowsers, one pair of boots, one pair of shoes and a hat.

Constables were also issued with a staff '...and where the Justices deem it necessary, a cutlass'.

Top priority was to appoint a Chief Constable, and as if having learned a sharp lesson (no pun intended) from the City's gross oversight of 1835, the *Herald* and Worcester's other papers duly ran the advertisement to find the right individual. It read:

Salary £250 a year his age must not exceed 45; (he) must be certified by a Medical Practitioner to be in good health, and of sound constitution, and fitted to perform the duties of the office; he must not have been a Bankrupt, nor to have taken the benefit of the Insolvency Act; he must be recommended to the Secretary of State by the Magistrates, in whom the appointment is vested, as a person of general good character and conduct Producing testimonials etc. All persons desirous of applying for the appointment are requested to transmit their testimonials (post paid) sealed-up, marked "Office of Chief Constable" to the Clerk of Peace for the said County, at the Shirehall Worcester on or before the Twenty-fifth day of November instant'.

It was signed C A Helm D.C.P., Clerk of the Peace's Office, Shirehall, and Richard Reader Harris, an ex-Metropolitan Police officer with a keen eye for crime detection was the man they chose (*pictured right*).

All of which, for the time being at least, was of only passing interest to the on-going lives of the City Police, whose day-to-day existence had been continuing at the same highly-charged pace as before.

*Richard Reader Harris*

### 'Alarming and ruffianly' attacks on the police

If anything, life on the streets was becoming even tougher and attacks on the police seemingly a rite of passage for Worcester's increasingly troublesome population – as a report from the *Herald* at this time graphically illustrates:

> *Police affray   Alarming and ruffianly attack on City Police*
> *'...an outrageous and determined attack upon the police in Broad-street, on Monday last, and for which seven of the individuals concerned therein were committed to take their trials at the ensuing sessions. On Wednesday, two of the prisoners, Robert Featherstone and Robert Smith and yesterday two others, John and William Rathbone, were liberated upon giving satisfactory bail for their appearance at the sessions. William Onions, a most notorious character, who is known to have taken part in the affray and the man who escaped apprehension by the police by swimming across the Severn, remains presently at large'.*

Others subsequently summoned for their part in a savage attack on **George Williams No3** and a new man, former supernumerary **Thomas Evans, No23** who'd been recruited on July 28th two years earlier, were

## Also this year: 1839

- cock-fighting ring busted at the Rising Sun, Cripplegate

- James Douglas visibly wilts in court and eventually drops all charges of drunkenness and child cruelty against a St Johns couple Mr and Mrs Thomas Smith '... because she kept up such a yelling that the Inspector, trembling for the good name of [the Station-house] fairly turned her out to get rid of her clamour' (Herald)

- armed robbery at the Sebright Arms

- a spate of fires in the Moors sparks off search for serial arsonist

- uproar as the cost of transporting convicts to the hulks for transportation to the Colonies is revealed as £156 18s

- major storm puts an end to the summer's exceptional heat-wave and creates havoc in the City. Man struck by lightning and instantly killed during a storm over the city (another bolt also killed a cow near the Virgin[s] Tavern)

DARING AND ALARMING ATTACK UPON THE CITY
POLICE.—Robert Featherstone, Robert Smith, John Rathborn, William Rathborn, John Bradley, Thomas Bradley, and William ———, were placed at the bar this morning, charged with a savage attack upon Evans, 23, Williams, 5, and others of the City Police force.

Evans deposed that he was on duty at the Cross last night, at half-past twelve o'clock; he heard a noise, and traced it to Friar's Alley, where he saw the seven prisoners, together with others to the number of at least twenty persons, engaged in a disturbance. The prisoners John Rathborn and Thomas Bradley were fighting. Witness attempted to stop the fight and disperse the mob. One of the rioters said "Oh! you are that b———y rogue Griffiths, are you?" and then Featherstone came up and forcibly wrested witness' staff from him, using so great a degree of violence as to break the thong by which it was secured to his wrist. Featherstone struck witness with the staff on the head and body; and on his springing his rattle for assistance, Williams, No. 3, came up. The prisoners then fell upon Williams, and Featherstone struck him some violent blows, knocked him down repeatedly, and kicked him most brutally. Featherstone broke Williams' lamp to pieces, tore it away from his girdle, and threw it at his head with great violence. Finding they were unable to cope with the ruffians, who by this time were throwing brickbats and stones at them, the police officers retreated for more assistance, and having been joined by Workman, No. 2, and supernumerary Kinnaird, they returned, and then the prisoners ran away down Newport-street. The constables pursued them, and met them returning, armed with poles, rails, and palings, to the number of from twelve to twenty, and being still unable to overcome such a mob, the police again retreated, and having procured further assistance again returned to Newport-street, when the prisoners ran off, and one of their companions, dressed in a light smock-frock, and not yet caught, jumped off the North Quay into the Severn. The river was heavily swollen, and the police were apprehensive that the fellow must have been drowned, but it appears that he was observed to get to shore.

Williams and Workman corroborated the preceding testimony. The first presented very visible tokens of excessive bad usage. He had a large bruised wound in his head, and many bruised contusions on his face and other parts of his body. The identification of the prisoners was complete, and each was distinctly sworn to by the witnesses as having been actively engaged in striking, kicking, or throwing brick-bats at the police.

Mr. R. P. Holmes, baker, residing next door to the Falcon, in Broad-street, spoke to the violent character of the disturbance. He was awoke that night, about a quarter-past 12 o'clock, by a noise in the street, got up, and saw a number of people engaged in a disturbance, and striking the police; heard Williams exclaiming, "don't murder a fellow—don't murder a poor fellow." The brick-bats were flying in great numbers at the constables, and the mob seemed principally incensed against one of them, a little man, whom he noticed running up Broad-street. The disturbance of the peace was most alarming, and the usage of the police by the mob most shameful. The affray having been immediately reported at the station-house, serjeant Phillipps, in the absence of the Inspector, proceeded at once to search for the offenders, and by half-past two o'clock he had secured seven of them—the prisoners now at the bar. Four of them he took on board barges, two in their parents' houses, and the principal offender of the whole, Featherstone, he apprehended in a low lodging in Turkey; and it is material to notice that in the same house, but in another room from that in which Featherstone was abed, the police discovered the truncheon which the prisoner had forcibly taken from policeman Evans—thus making out a strong prima facie case of felony against him in addition to that of ———

WCiCo/WAAS

brothers Jake and Thomas Bradley and William Mann. ***See Charge Book extract, p.358.***

The *Herald* spared few details when it came to graphic descriptions of the scale and ferocity of the violence directed towards the hapless constables (*cutting, left*), **Williams No3** reportedly pleading for his life with the heartrending words *'dont murder a fellow, don't murder a poor fellow'.*

Small wonder the City gaol was bursting at the seams. In October this year, visiting magistrates, Charles Sidebottom and George Allies prepared their report of conditions at the gaol and found that standards were pretty much up to the required levels – even though those levels were not particularly high.

*Today it would be called 'ticking the boxes'.*

They also reported that during the previous seven years – Michaelmas 1832 to the current year, 1,781 prisoners had been committed to the gaol, a yearly average of 254. It was signed by both (*see above*).

In November, Guv'nor Griffiths gave his formal undertaking that all Rules and Regulations '...have been **Generally** (*upper-case as written, italics mine - BB*) complied with as far as practicable except that part which relates to Learning Prisoners to Write. The Prisoners are very orderly'.

Dated November 9th this year, it was also signed by the Guv'nor 'isself...

WCiCo/WAAS

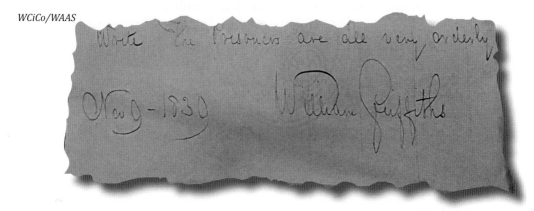

Given the shocking incidents of street crime, it will come as a no surprise that manpower turnover reached a critical new high this year – seven new constables prepared to put themselves in the daily firing line, although it has to be stated that not all went on to enjoy illustrious careers with their new employer. The County force was also on the lookout for new men.

**Gained:** *John Woodward, Edward Kennard, Thomas Bateman, James William Mitchell, Benjamin Best, Thomas Jones, John Price*
**Lost:** *Joseph Hall, William Phillips*

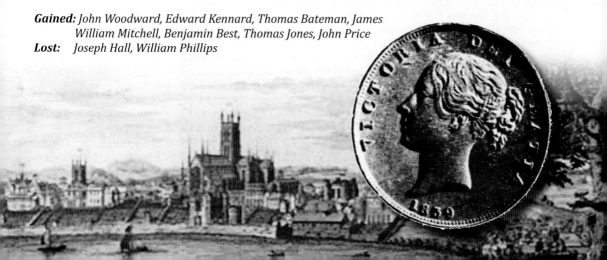

The *Journal* began the year by breaking the shocking news that '...50,000 drunkards die yearly in this country, and the one-half of the insanity, two-thirds of the pauperism, and three-fourths of the crimes of the land are the consequences of drunkenness'.

In the city, in the first hearing of the year Robert Featherstone, Robert Smith, John Radborn, William Radborn, William Mann, Thomas Bradley and John Bradley were arraigned on a charge of assaulting **No3 George Williams**, while in the execution of his duty (*see previous page*). The first prisoner was sentenced to six months' imprisonment, and the remainder for a space of three months.

A fascinating document survives in the Hive dated January 14th this year. It's the frontispiece to the 1839-47 Charge Book, serving as the official sworn statement of the men and officers of the police force of the City and Borough of Worcester, demanding that they shall:

> '...well and truly serve our Sovereign Lady the Queen in the office of Constable for the Borough of Worcester so long as you shall be employed as a Constable for that purpose according to the best of your skill and knowledge. So Help you God'.

It looks very much to have been prepared by **John Phillips** in his own hand and was also signed by him and **James Douglas** several times as well as by PCs **John Jackman, William Bradford, John Woodward, Edward Kennard, Thomas Bateman, James William Mitchell, Benjn Best, Thomas Jones, John Price, John Golland, Joseph Harrison, and Edward Walton.**

Meanwhile, with the new Chief Constable Richard Reader Harris firmly in the driving seat, the County force was also in expansive mood. The City police had always been reticent about advertising for constables – besides, Worcester was compact enough for word to get around without resorting to paid-for advertising. Almost of necessity, their County counterparts became adept at the art of harnessing the Victorian equivalent of 'Sits Vac'...

## A bombshell: James Douglas quits without warning

Nothing exceptional was expected to emerge from the first Watch Committee proceedings on January 15th – just the day after Charles Sidebottom had witnessed the signing of the oath of allegiance by fourteen constables and the chief – and the meeting looked set to consist of the usual tenders for uniforms and a report on the inevitable Christmas outrages and how the police had coped manfully in the face of impossible levels of seasonal and commonplace disorder.

**But the members were in for a shock. Out of the blue, James Douglas suddenly quit...**

He'd never really recovered from the vicious bashing he'd received in the Bull and Sun and in its wake, never appeared to play the gung-ho hero he'd always aimed to live up to.

Now there was real concern for his future.

The Committee appears to have taken his resignation with a mixture of surprise and disappointment, and the *Chronicle* duly reported:

WORCESTERSHIRE CONSTABULARY.
WANTED, TWENTY-FOUR YOUNG MEN to fill the OFFICE of CONSTABLES. Persons desirous of the above situations must send their Certificates, properly authenticated, to the Constabulary Office, 15, Britannia-square, Worcester, on or before TUESDAY, the 10th of NOVEMBER next. The Candidate must be 5 ft. 7 in. high, under 40 years of age, able to read, write, and keep accounts, and be generally intelligent, and must procure a certificate of good conduct for at least the last five years. No Person need apply who has been dismissed any Police Force and cannot produce a certificate of good conduct during his service therein.
Forms of recommendation may be had by applying at the above Office. All Letters to be post-paid.

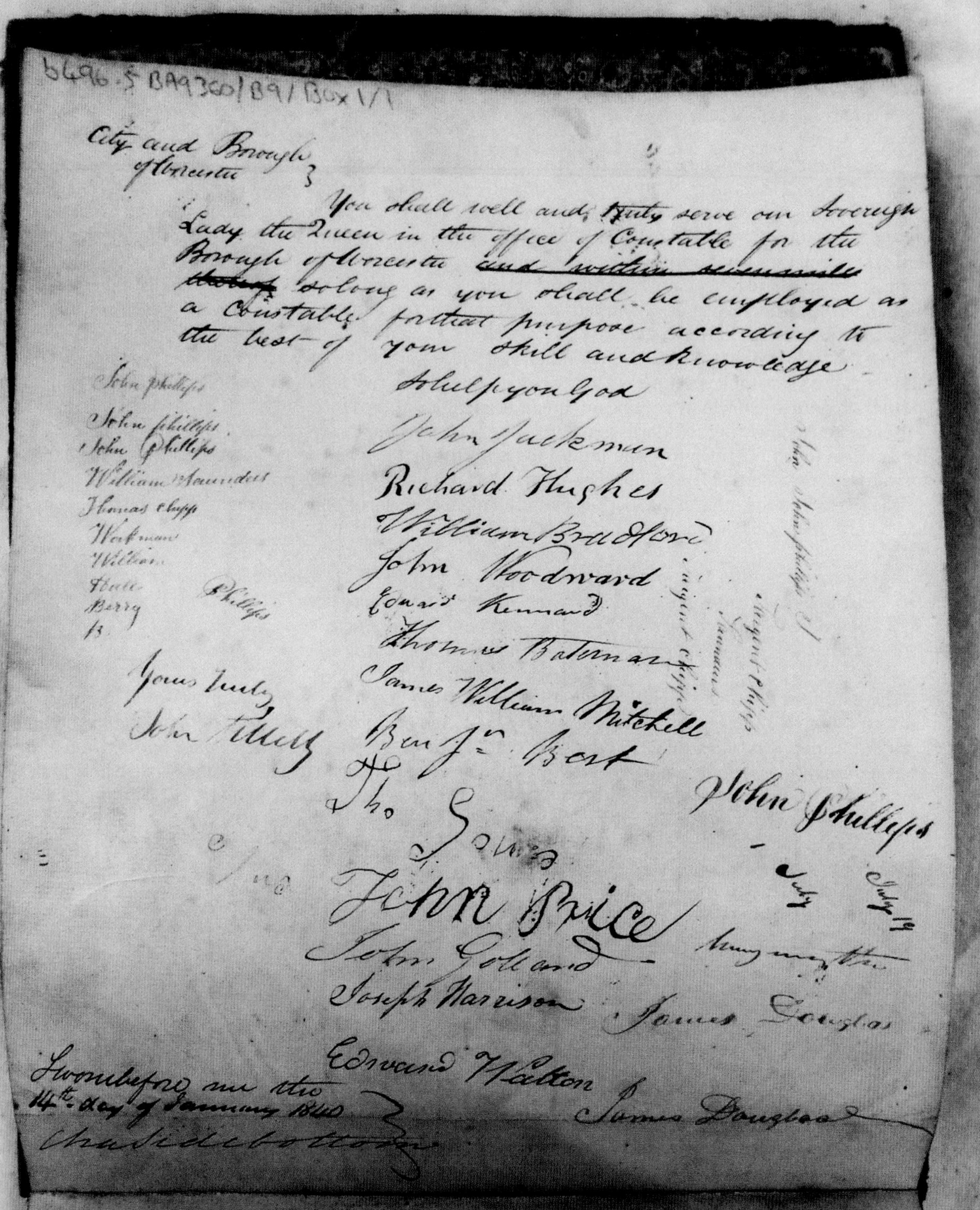

b496.5 BA9360/B9/Box1/1

City and Borough
of Worcester

You shall well and truly serve our Sovereign Lady the Queen in the office of Constable for the Borough of Worcester ~~and within seven miles thereof~~ so long as you shall be employed as a Constable for that purpose according to the best of your skill and knowledge

So help you God

John Phillips
John Phillips
John G Phillips
William Saunders
Thomas Chipp
Workman
William
Hull
Berry
B

Phillips

John Jackman
Richard Hughes
William Bradford
John Woodward
Edward Kennard
Thomas Bateman
James William Mitchell
Benjn Best

Yours truly
John Tilley

Tho Jones

John Brice
John Golland
Joseph Harrison
Edward Walton

John Phillips

James Douglas

Sworn before me this 14th day of January 1840
Cha Sidebottom

James Douglas

Fascinating document dated 14th January 1840 and a rare link with the early heroes of Worcester City Police with the signatures of two chiefs (John Phillips and James Douglas), reference to a third (Thomas Chipp) witnessed and approved by high-profile Police Magistrate Charles Sidebottom. The day after it was signed, James Douglas (bottom right) had signalled his intention to quit and had left the force by March 1st.

(Worcester City Council/WAAS)

*'A communication was read from Mr Douglas, signifying his intention to resign from his situation as Superintendent of the City Police force, on the ensuing 1st March, and a special meeting of the Committee was appointed to be held on Monday last, to take the appointment of his successor in the office into consideration'.*

It was clearly a traumatic week for the force: in addition, former Supernumerary **PC George Jones** *(21st October 1836 – 24th January this year)* was instantly sacked for 'great want of energy in the transaction' after allowing a highway robber named Edwards, suspected of a murderous assault involving firearms, to escape after Home Secretary Lord Normanby had offered a £50 reward for the assailant's apprehension, and supernumerary **Benjamin Best** was chosen to replace him.

It was also decided that day-watch officers would wear a band on their right wrist to distinguish them from those of the night-watch. Contracts were also taken for clothing: Henry Davis for each suit £2 14s 6d each; R Baker, hats, 11s 6d each; Mrs Nicholls shoes 11s a pair.

Now the Corporation was charged with finding a successor – but they weren't alone in the task: for the first time, the press took real interest in the key decision – the two foremost weeklies, the *Herald* and the *Journal* altogether expectedly coming out on different sides of the fence.

Concerned at lowering standards and dwindling successes on the streets, the *Journal* began advocating for another tough outsider to come in and tame a City that seemed to be going backwards instead of forwards in the sphere of law and order – just as the County had, just the previous year.

The *Herald*, on the other hand, perhaps mindful of Henry Sharpe's ill-fated regime and the impact he'd had on his officers, began campaigning for a recruitment from within...

> *'We trust that the principle adopted in the City of London Police, of promoting members of the force from within, will be carried out here. It appears to us to be the only way of proceeding and the one most calculated to improve the efficiency of the Police, and strengthen their desire faithfully to discharge the duties of the office'*

There was one final controversy surrounding **James Douglas** before he walked away. On 11th February, Edward Davis No12 of the County Constabulary stationed at Upton Snodsbury, was drinking in the Red Cow in Birdport *(coincidentally, 100 years on destined to be the site of the new Police Station House, by then in the new thoroughfare called Deansway)* when he was challenged by outspoken Socialist, anti-police agitator and troublemaker John Roberts who abused him. The *Herald* report implies that it was on account of his uniform but it's not made clear, although later events would suggest that he was uniformed. Seemingly the day before, Davies had been involved in a scuffle with some railway navvies and it could well be that the confrontation was a continuation of that.

Whatever the reason, Roberts called him a thief 'and a great variety of equally abusive names'.

There's also conflicting reports, for the most part denied by the crowd of witnesses in the Red Cow, never the most law-abiding of pubs, but verified by Elizabeth Harris who'd called in to fetch her husband home, that Roberts had even slapped the clearly very patient constable.

Being Worcester folk, they favoured neither the forces of authority nor the loud-mouths and show-offs who thought they knew better than

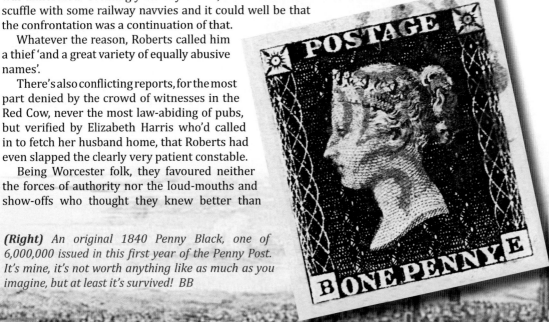

*(Right) An original 1840 Penny Black, one of 6,000,000 issued in this first year of the Penny Post. It's mine, it's not worth anything like as much as you imagine, but at least it's survived! BB*

anyone else: such hot-heads went right against the grain and overstepped what most of the citizens, then as now, considered acceptable.

Understandably, Worcestershire Constabulary No12 Davies' temper eventually snapped. He upped, hit John Roberts, handcuffed him, dragged him outside, again hit him over the head and shoulders with his truncheon and hauled him to the St Nicholas Street station house.

There they were met by the notice-serving Inspector, **James Douglas** who, having heard both sides of the story and Roberts' threats of a counterclaim for assault, shooed them both away and refused to take either case – the implication being that he suspected the County force would come off badly and he had no wish to upset his County counterparts (*with good reason... see below*)

When they heard, the City magistrates were furious that he had taken his unilateral stance – effectively pre-empting a magisterial decision – and had he not already tendered his resignation, there's the distinct possibility that they may well have ordered him to do so.

As it transpired, PC Davies was hauled into court and later fined 10s with 11s costs and allowed a week to pay it in. As a PS to the story, Davis wasn't to last much longer as a policeman either: he was dismissed on the 26th May (*Bob Pooler - From Fruit Trees to Furnaces, p12*).

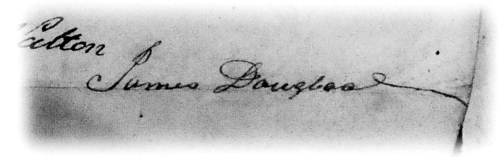

WCiCo/WAAS

For **James Douglas** it was the final act in an up-and-down career with the City police, dogged with a few setbacks that demonstrated a much more recent observation, but still just as relevant then – *that everyone gets promoted to his (or her) level of incompetence.*

He had been a good, true and dedicated policeman, but his tenure as chief of police was, to say the least, mixed – and frankly, all was not well while he was in charge. Perhaps he'd been just too gung-ho and hands-on for the corporation's liking.

In the spirit of general goodwill and not without an eye on good public relations, the next week the Police Committee '...expressed their high sense of the diligence, zeal and general propriety of conduct manifested by Mr Douglas, the late Inspector, by awarding him a gratuity of £10 and desiring that he should be furnished with a copy of the resolution signed by the Mayor as Chairman. At the Police Office on Friday, Mr Sidebottom on behalf of himself and the other Magistrates bore testimony to the activity and perseverance of Mr Douglas, and passed a high encomium on his character generally'.

He'd been chief for four years and 11 months – *but the ex-chief still held one more surprise...*

In July 1844, he came out of semi-retirement in Dudley, and was appointed inspector of Evesham Borough Police, remaining in post up to February 1850 when Worcestershire began policing Evesham by agreement.

In many ways it's a pity that, unlike Richard Reader Harris his counterpart at the County whose formal photograph shows a stiffly formal Victorian gent with a gaze that'd pierce steel, James Douglas hadn't seen fit to have his portrait captured by the new-fangled wonder of the day, light pictures (*later photography*).

What remains is a few copies of his spidery signature, the one above apparently scrawled just the day before his resignation from Worcester City Police.

It's all we have.

# 6:
# The Phillips years

## 1st March 1840 – 4th July 1849

**John Phillips** was the third chief in a little over seven years, and in common with both his predecessors **Henry Sharpe** and **James Douglas**, little is known about the circumstances of his promotion to Inspector and his elevation to the role of head of the police. He doesn't appear to have been a watchman or supernumerary although he was included in **James Douglas'** initial batch of hand-picked officers with a common start date of January 15th 1836.

Even so, his name is rarely prominent among the press reports of front-line cases and gung-ho action – with the exception of a nasty assault he'd been subjected-to in early 1838 (*see p86*), the implication being that his strengths were in organisation and administration rather than muscle and brute force. Whatever the appeal, he must have displayed qualities that struck a chord with the members of the Watch Committee that was still reeling from the fall-out from the **Dyer** affair as well as renewed general criticism – most of it stemming from **James Douglas'** absence and recuperation from the beating at the Bull and Sun, and the revived memories of the ill-fated **Sharpe** experience.

Despite the expected PR-influenced praise for **Inspector Douglas**, the force's reputation was still see-sawing – one minute the saviours of a grateful city, then following yet another unfortunate incident, considered inefficient, not up to the role and unable to hang on to its officers, for the most part all legitimate observations.

WORCESTER POLICE FORCE.—At a meeting of the
[Wat]ch Committee of the Town Council on Friday [mo]rning
[la]st, it was unanimously agreed to appoint Sergeant [Phillips]
[Ins]pector of the Police Force of this city, vacan[t by the]
[resi]gnation of Mr. James Douglas, and at the same [meeting]
[Wil]liam Sanders, No. 6, was elected Sergeant vice Phil[lips pro-]
[mot]ed. There can[not] be a doubt that Inspector Ph[illips has]
[ful]filled every duty [...] a[...] ted to him with [...]
[...]ness and faithfulness, a[...]a [...] of the
[ard]uous duties of a Police Officer, and we are always pleased
[to re]cord the acknowledgment of desert. Sanders is also an
[offi]cer of great trust and competence, and deserves to be re-
[war]ded by promotion. By the kindness of Mr. Burges, the
[Chi]ef Commissioner of Police at Birmingham, Inspector Phil-
[lip]s has been for the last month incorporated and acting with
[the] new force there, in order to obtain an insight into its mode
[of ]regulation and management, with a view to the introduction
[of ]any portion of the system th[...] [advant]ageous
[to a]n improve[...] [...] held a
[for]tnight a[...] [...]r high
[...]ase of the [...] [co]nduct
[ma]nifested [...] [rega]rding
[...] a grati[...] [...]hed
[...h] a copy [...] [Chair]man.
[On] the Poli[...] [...]
[...] Wednesday, Mr. Sidebottom on behalf of
[him]self and the other Magistrates bore testimony to the activity
[and] perseverance of Mr. Douglas, and passed a high encomium
[on ]his character generally.
[...] a report of the County business transacted at the

WCiCo/WAAS

With the times far from conducive to having a token chief who, when he wasn't mixing it with all and sundry, was either absent nursing an injury or being insubordinate to the wishes of his superiors, they needed someone to pull it all together and hoped **Sergeant John Phillips** – less unpredictable and volatile have-a-go hero than solid back-room organiser – was going to be that man.

Almost all that's known about him is that he was aged 35 when he took up his post on 6th March 1840, married to Mary Ann 29, with children Samuel 11, Mary 9, Eliza 5, and Fanny 4.

His official start-date was March 1st and since **James Douglas'** resignation, he'd been attached to the new Birmingham City Police force '...in order to obtain an insight into its mode of regulation and management, with a view to the introduction of any portion of the system that may appear advantageous or an improvement into the body here'.

**PC William Sanders No6** was appointed sergeant in his place – and both were highly praised by the *Chronicle* in the week of their respective promotions:

> '...there cannot be any doubt that Inspector Phillips has well deserved his present
> advancement by course of vigilant, laborious, and unremitting attention to the discharge
> of the arduous duties of a Police Officer, and we are always pleased to record the
> acknowledgement of desert. Sanders is also an officer of great trust and competence, and
> deserves to be rewarded by promotion'.

The Police Committee couldn't afford to get it wrong: these were still troublesome times on the home-front, locally and nationally. At both levels, crime remained massively on the up – in England alone, offences committed against peace officers in the furtherance of their duties were up nearly a fifth over the previous two years, 4,154 convicts had been transported, and another unexpected trend – one in four of all reported crimes was now being committed by women.

Worryingly, and closer to home for the new Superintendent and the City Corporation, new figures showed that locally, the number of women to men in the City was well above the national average of 13:12: the Worcester of the day showed the ratio at $14^1/_3$:12. In fact, the population of the city had escalated to 26,425 – the previous ten years alone had shown a 37% increase, a figure that was reflected in the number of admissions to the City Gaol that had this year reached an all-time high of 117, *more than twice the number for 1837.*

But while some observers despaired for the future of civilisation as Worcester had known it, the tally nonetheless represented a fair result for the police. Reporting the latest gaol statistics, the *Herald* commented '...we defy a more interesting text for comment to be presented to the rate-payers than the startling fact here proved, that beyond all doubt or cavil, detected crime has more than doubled during the short space of three years'.

### New chief begins with a vengeance – and shows himself kind-hearted

As per his predecessors, **John Phillips** appears to have wasted no time in knuckling-down to the job in hand. He also comes over as an altogether more kind-hearted soul than either of his forerunners...

On the Saturday night of his first week he took himself on a walk about town, observing the goings-on and the variety of folk milling about the centre. While out and about, he'd come across 'two dirty-looking vagabonds apparently in distress', William Burrows and William Johnson, brought them to the Station-house, gave them shelter and the next day took them to the House of Industry for relief. They stayed there just a night, so the new chief must've been less than pleased when the two were brought back to the station the following night, Monday: this time it was on a charge of attempting to commit robbery at several shops. Both were committed as rogues and vagabonds; Burrows for two months, and Johnson for six weeks' hard labour.

Then, still in his first week, the new chief had taken pity on a poor-looking husband and wife who'd been remanded on suspicion of stealing some ribbons. Noticing them in a cell, he enquired when they'd last eaten and when they said it had been some days previous, he sent out for some food which he paid for out of his own pocket. When the issue was raised at their hearing in the Magistrates court the next day, the Town Clerk replied that the Watch Committee had made provision to supply prisoners on remand with food: *'...Phillips, who was not previously aware of the order, and who had given (them) food at his own expense, promised to act on the order in future'.*

For the police, big-hearted new chief or no new chief, it was life as normal, and any good news was to be welcomed. ***It did not get off on the best of starts...***

Early on, stalwart **George Stoneley No16** found himself accused of an uncharacteristic loss of concentration after a prisoner he'd nabbed, 39-year old Frederick Lawrence, suspected of stealing a purse containing two sovereigns, a half sovereign, four half crowns and three shillings from George Lardner at a notoriously low dive in Powick Lane called the Painters Arms, escaped his clutches and did a runner while in custody and en route to the station-house.  Luckily, the no doubt embarrassed officer had managed to keep hold of his hat which he returned to the Painters Arms with orders to the landlord to report back if Lawrence made a return for it.  The following week's *Herald* reported the news that '...next morning (*Stoneley*) having gone there to see if prisoner had called for his hat, in a few minutes prisoner walked in when he again apprehended him'.

A fortuitous stroke of luck – but it was all for nothing.  After an eloquent defence, Lawrence was found not guilty of the theft and released, his hat no doubt having been duly returned to him.

At least, the relationship between the City force and its new County counterparts was riding high: the first Worcestershire Police Committee report levelled praise in the direction of its longer established neighbour, Chief Constable, Richard Reader Harris noting '...I have much pleasure in adducing that the City police have, on all occasions, manifested a zeal and promptness in communicating with and rendering every assistance to, the *(County)* Force, which must tend to facilitate the detection of crime and apprehension of offenders'.

An advertisement for County constables, placed in several of the weekly Worcestershire news-sheets, resulted in 24 being taken on in a single batch, swelling the new rural force to 64 including eight sergeants, and the good relations and spirit of co-operation that had started well under **James Douglas** was to continue, at least in the short term, under **John Phillips,** although it was not always to remain so.

During Worcestershire Constabulary's first operative year, one PC had been dismissed, another allowed to resign, six fined and one reprimanded.  212 prisoners had been apprehended for the previous quarter of whom 103 had been summarily convicted, 60 committed for trial and 49 discharged.  Harris – whose new and untried force was three times the size of its city counterpart – no doubt believed he was speaking for both forces when he commented to the Magistrates that he believed (they) had '...the approval of a great body of the rate-payers who already felt the good effects of an efficient police' and to a large degree, he was probably right.

Even so, he had clearly watched the shaky evolution of the City force with close interest and probably feared some sort of comparison with **John Phillips'** now well-drilled officers as he felt obliged to hedge his bets by warning that the men of the County police had still '...not attained the degree of proficiency to which only experience can lead them in the execution of the arduous duties which they have to perform'.

However, he added that he was confident that they would not only do so – and soon – but that the benefits the public had a right to expect from them would also quickly become apparent.

But for all his confidence in, and implied respect for, the City's 'ceruleans' – a gorgeous term penned by the *Herald* in reference to the colour of their uniform, cerulean blue – already the ebullient Chief Constable of the neighbouring Worcestershire County force was making ominous noises that he and his successors would reprise over and over, voicing a note of warning that was to become a regular thorn in the side of the City Police for another 127 years...

 These were early days and Harris was not yet in a position to make any demands – least of all as his force was still raw, untried and was yet to make a mark.  But it was plain to see where he was headed and at the end of the year he made his first request for an amalgamation of the City and County contingencies – with himself as Chief, of course.

Instantly rebuffed (*see next page*) he fired-off a sulky and petulant note to the City Council that frankly did little to endear him and probably did his cause, however well-intentioned, more long-lasting harm than good...

- rash of cases brought against coin counterfeiting gangs in the city, typical sentence for passing dud coin, three months' hard

- police investigate death of jobbing butcher Thomas Houton, felled in the Shambles by a single punch by a man named Clayton for no apparent reason

- murder suspected when the body of Louisa Leicester, 35, of Lark Hill is found in a coffin with the lid screwed down and the funeral already organised just hours after she'd died

- Humphries, driver of the Birmingham Mail coach, acquitted after running over 8-year old Richard Jones outside the Crown (now Barbourne Health Centre) in Droitwich Road

- PC21 Tommy Chipp emerges as a no-nonsense enforcer when he tangles with eight navvies in The George in Silver Street. In May, he is appointed Supernumerary Sergeant

- capital convictions in England and Wales is the lowest in decades, 54, with 3,699 prisoners transported to the colonies. Four out of five crimes (41%) is committed by under 21s

- labourers William Hall and Thomas Barnes granted mercy and accordingly minimally sentenced to a month's hard labour apiece for stealing a teaspoon

- police seize over 1,000 copies of local scandal-sheet 'Paul Pry' after claims that it contained 'the most abominable attacks upon the character' (ie libels) of two Worcester women and a man

- Insp John Phillips reveals the number of licensed public houses and beer houses in the city to be roughly equal – 150 of each, total 300

- PC18 Richard Hughes' disbelief of a tramp passing himself off as a retired sailor is questioned in court after the Bench decides the vagrant's story is true '... because everything about him had a sea smell'

- PCs 18 Richard Hughes and stalwart No7 Richard Berry (15th January 1836 – 24th February 1860) clash with Mayor's Sergeant-at-Mace Harper after he'd been found drinking beer in the Blue Bell in Moor Street out of hours.

- prostitute Sarah Loveland glasses (with a china jug) William Walker in the Red Cow after accusing him of drinking her beer

- police investigate attempted murder of a guest (unnamed) who'd been given a pie baked by his estranged wife in the Unicorn in Broad Street, subsequently found to have been generously laced with strychnine

- PC18 Richard Hughes and No1 William Hale seriously roughed-up by brothers George and Henry Edwards in October

- Tommy Chipp and by-stander Jeremiah Fudger who he'd called on to assist in tackling drunk and disorderly Cornelius Bevan, both knocked unconscious in the Falcon in Broad Street. Bevan, sentenced to a week's hard for the assault was a professional prize-fighter who was to die within two years in a bout on Pitchcroft, p 110

- attack on PC16 George Stoneley by John Phelps who was described in the Herald as '...using all manner of unmentionable and ferocious doings with the head and other important portions of the body of said No16, which neither flesh and blood, or the dignity of a constable, could stand'.

## County force issues first amalgamation hint – and firmly told 'No!'

"I regret exceedingly that the authorities of the Borough towns decline an amalgamation with the County Constabulary. I was led to believe that the boroughs would take into consideration the great and decided advantages which must necessarily result from an entire uniform system of Police and be induced to give the measure a trial, for I am satisfied that until a consolidation takes place, a completely efficient force can never be established in the county, for the more disjointed the system, the weaker it is and less good the result. I believe it an indisputable fact that the present system adds, and this in no trifling degree, to the benefit of the thief for where there is a link wanting in the chain of communication, there the thief will derive his particular advantage and support"

– Richard Reader Harris (right)

This was only to prove another so-so year for the Worcester City Police, the first report following the usual post-Christmas dock filled with contrite revellers, concerned not with the arrest of some high-profile criminals, but the mundane subject of clothing. The *Herald* reported that '...contracts for the clothing of the City police for the ensuing year, were entered into by the Watch Committee this morning; viz., clothes including great-coat £4 2s each suit, Mr Henry Davies Newport-street; hats 10s 6d each Mr Baker Broad-street; shoes 12s a pair Mrs Nicholls, Corn Market'.

In fact, even the newspapers' customary glee at reporting police matters seems to have faded into a glum reticence. Either that, or **John Phillips** had failed to be an inspirational leader or to have left the generally impressionable press less than impressed. No-one can be quite sure.

Then the force's reputation sank to a new low in February when a complete blank was returned following an exhaustive investigation into the 'diabolical' attempted murder of the entire family, nine in all, of the Reverend Joseph Webster of Merriman's Hill. Worse, the reverend's solicitors Cameron and Foley of Palace Yard made the failure even more public by posting an ad with £100 reward – matched by the Government, plus a free pardon for the offender's accomplice – for information leading to the conviction of whoever it was had laced their soup with a liberal dose of arsenic. Despite the reward, no culprit was ever traced.

> ## ATTEMPT TO POISON!
> *FURTHER REWARD of £100 offered by her Majesty's Government, making, with the former, £200.*
>
> WHEREAS, on Tuesday, the 9th of February, 1841, a diabolical attempt was made to POISON the FAMILY (nine in number), of the REV. JOSEPH WEBSTER, of Merriman's Hill, near Worcester, by introducing a quantity of Arsenic into Soup, of which the Family partook, which nearly caused the Death of the whole.
>
> Any Person or Persons who will give such information as may lead to the conviction of the offender or offenders, will receive the above Reward.
>
> Any Accomplice (not being the actual offender) making such disclosures as shall lead to the conviction of the principal, will be entitled to the above Reward, and HER MAJESTY'S FREE PARDON.
>
> Apply to Messrs. Cameron and Foley, Palace Yard, Worcester.

Another reward around the same time was for a much lowlier 10s, offered for the capture of whoever had daubed 'obscene and disgusting sentences' on walls in the passage from High Street to the Shambles (*later, Golden Lion Entry*).

At the census this year – the first in British history, recorded on the night of June 6th – **John Phillips** was shown as Superintendent of Police living at the (St) Nicholas-street station house with his growing family. Also living nearby in the Trinity was **Edward Kennard**, Policeman aged 41 with his wife, laundress Frances and sons William and James, 15 and 8. *More of him later....*

The census had revealed that the population of England to be 14,995,508 – an increase of 14.5% over previous decade; the population of Worcester is put at 26,425 (12,010 males and 14,415 females) and the number of houses in Worcester at 6,164.

### Tommy Chipp makes his mark after Angel Street scrap ends in ostler's death

On 25th July, **Tommy Chipp** rose to prominence in the handling of a murder case - later reduced to manslaughter –in which he'd played an active, some even said contributory, role.

Former tailor Emanuel Maiden, 35, had been licensee of the Shakespeare for some six months. He was known to have been a man with short fuse; in just his few short months at the Shakespeare, January to July, he'd made it clear from the start that he would stand no messing and had already notched-up a record for having a ready fist for anyone thinking they might disturb the peace of his new venture – or worse, those that meddled with his family. Unfortunately on both counts, such a man was 25-year old John Fisher, an ostler at the Star Hotel and who, Maiden believed, not without some justification, had been more than close to his wife of ten years, London-born Kezia.

Maiden had already banned Fisher from the Shakespeare as a result of having been found in here in a compromising position with his wife, but Fisher, who sounds like a bit of a chancer, still crept back in to visit his illicit alleged lover on several occasions when he knew the landlord was out.

*Such was the state of affairs when the two met up in Angel Street at midnight on July 25th this year...*

Maiden was already pretty far gone, having been in the nearby Waggon and Horses and then the Currier's Arms outside which he was talking to a group including George Wall, a man named Boyce, and Fisher's brother-in-law John Darke, when he spotted his presumed cuckolder. There was some heated banter between them that initially resulted in Maiden at first believing that Fisher was a constable, but on closer inspection commented *'...no, it's not a policeman, it's a bastard'.* Fisher then approached the group and asked Maiden what he meant by calling him a policeman and a bastard – with the result that a full-scale row erupted, first Maiden warning him 'If you come near me I will split your bloody head', before calling Fisher 'a common hostler fellow' and telling him to go home to his horses – with Fisher responding that Maiden wasn't worth a horse, before making some further remark, probably alluding to his wife.

The row attracted the attention of **Tommy Chipp** – Supernumerary Sergeant, although still on PC's wages – and there the tragedy might have been averted as the ever-reliable 'Chipper' approached the party, grabbed Maiden by the arm and told Fisher "Do you go home; don't wait here".

As he turned to go, Maiden shook off Chipp's grip, chased Fisher across Angel Street to the door of the Horn and Trumpet and the two fell heavily to the ground, with Maiden on top.

The event had also been partially witnessed by Richard James Lloyd, superintendent of the Worcester Rural Police, who was in a bedroom at the Curriers' Arms who deposed that '...on hearing a noise he threw up the window and heard one man call another a d — d rascal; the other said he was not, but that the other was a swindler; one party then accused the other of owing him a debt, which the other denied; one of the parties said "Damn your eyes, I'll do for you." I then drew my head in, and afterwards heard a race and a scuffle, in which something sounded like a blow, and then a heavy fall' (*Berrows Worcester Journal*).

The unfortunate Fisher who was a regular at the Star Tap, much frequented by ostlers and flymen whose masters and employers enjoyed the far greater comforts of the adjoining Star Hotel, was dead and **Chipp**'s statement proved central to the subsequent manslaughter hearing:

> *'I saw Maiden pursue the deceased, get up to him, and close with him, when they both fell. I was then about 30 yards from them. As I approached them Maiden was on his hands and knees, getting up. Fisher was lying on his face, with his arms extended and doubled about his head. He was lying across the flags, with his head near the curb stone (sic). I rose him up in a sitting posture; there was blood flowing from the back of his head, and he was quite insensible. Maiden then came up, and putting his hands in a fighting attitude, said, "Mind, let me go at him;" there were then seven or eight persons standing by him. I said "No, I won't have that;" I then turned towards Maiden, and would not allow him to come near the deceased. I did not see Maiden held by anybody at this time. I then carried deceased home, assisted by Mr. Wall and others, to the yard of the Star Hotel.*

The post-mortem held at the Star Hotel the day after the fracas by surgeon John Henry Walsh had revealed that a '...portion of (Fisher's) brain, about the size of a goose's egg being mashed, apparently by some act of violence'.

Further probing also showed that Fisher's skull was the thinnest Walsh had ever seen, 'except in museums'. When this information came out at the subsequent trial, Maiden's defence team asked for the proceedings to be terminated and their client released, but the judge refused. After only half an hour's deliberation, the 15-strong jury found him guilty of manslaughter but with a strong recommendation for mercy. He was sentenced to the mitigated punishment of one month's gaol, significantly without hard labour.

At least, the Brewster sessions on September 2nd, provided some interesting copy for the bored reporters when '...some very important conversation took place on the Bench regarding a very interesting point to "mine hosts" and hostesses. [Police Magistrate, Charles] Sidebottom said that complaints had been made to him of the publicans in St Johns, for keeping late hours and for unruly conduct. [Mayor, Edward] Evans thought they should make a few examples to check others; but upon the whole it was the opinion of the

Bench that altogether the public houses in the city were tolerably well conducted. Mr Sidebottom alluded to the terms of the licence.

'Among other things which the publican was not allowed to permit in his house was "tippling". Now who could define that? To drink is to tipple, but all drinking is not tippling; and to say that a public-house keeper might not lawfully permit tippling was to say that his house should be shut up. A most unreasonable law is that which must compel publicans to restrain their customers from drinking luxuriously' he'd jokingly commented.

*Gained: William Hyslop, Richard Hughes.* **Lost:** *George Richardson, Benjamin Best*

## Also this year: 1841

- Herald warns 'young rascals had better mind their goings-on for the future' after a spate of stone-throwing incidents against carriages in the New Road

- police investigate death of another 8-year old, Thomas Walters, run over by a horse and cart outside the Talbot in the Tything

- several boats on the Quay are set ablaze in a spate of arson attacks

- Sgt. William Sanders has a gun pulled on him by Samuel Barber in an altercation in the Plume of Feathers in Copenhagen Street, he is also punched by Barber and his mate Edward Grey before PC16 George Stoneley intervenes to even-up the score

- ostler Richard Link suspected of murdering his girlfriend 19-year old housemaid Mary Sneed found dead in the Shades in Mealcheapen Street, poisoned with arsenic

- spate of youngsters' deaths in the canal after low temperatures result in weeks of ice

- toughie 13-year old John Hiam has 10 years' transportation sentence

commuted to 7 years in the Reformatory at Parkhurst after several felony convictions

- 15 years' transportation passed on man nicknamed 'Nitts' for theft of a gun at the Crown & Anchor, investigated by Supt Phillips and Sgt Chipp, both of whom are mercilessly grilled by his defending barrister but fail to crack in court

- PC Luke Packwood severely beaten up by boatman Thomas Mott in the Black Horse, Lowesmoor

- 10s reward offered for information leading to arrest of obscene graffiti daubers who struck twice in Shambles Entry in the same week in April

- spearheaded by John Phillips and Tommy Chipp, springtime offence against erring pub and beer house landlords results in spate of summonses for illicit gaming and exceeding proscribed hours

- PC Luke Packwood again gets painful come-uppance and comes off much the worst when he tackles four drunken women in Grope Lane – Rebecca Roden, Elizabeth Wheeler

(both sentenced to a month's imprisonment), Susan Denson (fourteen days) and Mary Wright (dismissed)

- police presence demanded when crowds descend on Pitchcroft for one of the first known organised cricket matches, Kidderminster (74 runs) v Ledbury (21 runs)

- gang of youths calling themselves 'The Night Larks' embark on nocturnal crime spree

- assiduous investigation by Tommy Chipp clears John Wright of charges of rape and robbery laid against him by thorough bad 'un Mary Evans, real name Susan Addy (details in Worcester Pubs Then and Now Vol II p52-3)

*Early Merit badge*

Even the naturally gloomy and hard-pressed magistrates had cause to view the prospects for the coming year with increasing caution.

With Britain's economic fortunes already bleak and diminishing, the courts between Christmas and the first week of January had been 'unusually scanty and devoid of interest, and there has been less than the average amount of drunken disorderlies brought before their Worships', noted the *Herald* – with the rueful observation that the unusual state of affairs and thin list of prisoners was less attributable to a new sense of sobriety by Worcester's working (or idle) masses than the fact that cash was tight.

Or, as they colourfully termed, it '...more a drought in the Exchequer of the abusers of alcohol than a prudent adoption of temperance'.

The same *Herald* edition also carried the news that the previous two years, 1840 and 1841 had seen the number of murders in England rise to 156 – with chances of being murdered 1:200,000, re-equated to 1:19,000 for anyone aged 20-plus. Hardly surprising more people were staying sober.

With the exception of **Tommy Chipp's** promotion to Sergeant (*from Supernumerary, ie Probationer and thus still paid PCs rates*) news from the City Police was proving hard to come by, the local press seemingly more interested in the doings of the County force that had already, just two years after its inauguration, outgrown its base in Britannia Square and was to move to another close by the County Gaol in Salt Lane that gave greater accommodation, albeit with an increased rent. But though the quarter to the previous December 25th had seen an upturn in activities and corresponding success by Harris' men – the return indicating a small improvement on the previous term – the County force was now also beset by precisely the same problems that had dogged the City Police in its early days.

With echoes of the Fannon affair, a serving officer had been found drunk and had allegedly committed an assault, both accusations strongly denied: that he was a Superintendent rather than a lowly constable ought really to have made the reaction even more final, but instead the officer, Craig, was simply moved from his post at Stourbridge to a similar role at Upton-upon-Severn. The decision was not popular, smacked of a cover-up and sparked outrage from all quarters, the anti-police contingent having a field-day at this windfall opportunity for renewed criticism – much as it had in the city after the Dyer affair.

Inevitably, the fall-out rubbed-off on the entirely separate City force – and there was worse to come for the new rural police...

Chief Harris himself was now being accused of neglect of duty and of being poor value for his £380 a year salary. This time the accuser was no sly anti-police campaigner, but actually Thomas Bund – high profile and ebullient member of the Police Committee who would also go on to be the first Chairman of Worcestershire County Council: that the police chief went on to publicly call him a liar and to query his motives in open session, gave the anti-police faction even more ammunition to hurl against them.

The press reported every move and yet again the County chief had done himself more harm than good.

### A damaging blow: PC22 guilty of serious charges

In February, the kind of headlines **John Phillips** really didn't want to see; *'Serious Affray. Bad Conduct By A Policeman'.* The incident revolved around a drinking session first in the Mitre in Lich Street and then in the Crown in Friar Street that had turned nasty. That it involved on-duty constable **No22 Edward Kennard** (sometimes also *Kinnard* and *Kinniard*, a former Supernumerary who'd joined the force on Oct 7th 1839) made it hard to sweep under the carpet, while the charge against him – initially one of serious assault that could easily have been interpreted as attempted murder, as well as clear perjury – gave the case instant notoriety, once more threatening to put the entire City police force on the rack...

A tailor named Thomas King, who also lived in Friar Street, claimed he was beaten up by the policeman in the kitchen in the Crown. Though Kennard denied the whole affair – particularly claims of having been treated to ale late at night by King – several witnesses came forward to testify that they'd seen them drinking together in several inns that night, Kennard being on duty the whole of the time. Despite that, the PC stuck to his lies, even adding a smokescreen to the effect that he: '...was told by two men that there was a row in the Crown that he ought to quell; accordingly, he went there, knocked and was admitted when he saw four or five people (*they were later named as Boaden, Knight, Sandels and Chapman all regulars of the Crown*) in the kitchen, drinking but perfectly quiet when a man in a corduroy jacket threw some ale in a man's (*King's*) face who then struck out at him'.

The fact was that it was **Kennard** that had attacked King for refusing to treat him to more ale – indeed, had subjected him to such a beating that his injuries were considered life-threatening. At the subsequent court hearing which King was still too bashed-about to attend, the magistrates took the unusual step of visiting his house after the surgeon treating him had considered his patient 'in a considerable degree of danger' with several broken ribs and serous facial injuries.

The *Herald* report concluded: '...the policeman had forestalled punishment by resigning' on February 18th, but this was not the last heard of the disgraced PC (*see Also this year, 1844*).

Perhaps it was lack of action or success, the disgust felt over the Kennard case or a combination of any number of issues, but once joyously-reported heroics of the City police were now giving way to some harsh criticism – the *Herald*'s editor William Holl adding an acidic post-script to a report on a 'hocussed' (*mugged*) Kempsey butcher named Richard Amphlett, accusing the City force of being unable to distinguish between intoxication and poisoning, and of callously – even, implied the outraged editor, *criminally* – withholding medical aid to a sick man.

Unusually, **Tommy Chipp** was also to come in for some personal vitriol over the affair. Holl's sense of outrage and disgust was immediately evident, not only in the title of the piece ('*Immediate Reform Needed*') and the opening paragraph '...(Amphlett) was brought between two police officers into the justice room in a condition in which we hope never to see another human being in that or any other room', or even the length of the article, half a column stretching to almost 1,000 words, but also that he felt the post-script sufficiently important to warrant his own personal signature.

The article described Amphlett in court as being:

> '...unable to stand, restlessly turning his head from side to side, momentarily raising up his face to the light then dropping his head on his bosom, his face pallid and livid by turns, his eyes closed, his mouth shut, with lips quivering convulsedly, the man seemed to us to be suffering the extremes of agony, the seat of disorder apparently being in the head, and to be verging rapidly to the limit of endurance, that point where we can suffer no more, for nature there steps in and with tardy kindness, relieves us by steeping the aching brain into insensibility. The police were called upon to explain this horrible appearance when we heard with amazement the following extraordinary statement. Between one and two o'clock on Sunday morning, Amphlett was found by the officer on duty in Birdport, resting, in an upright position, against the wall at the mouth of an entry in which is situated a low brothel. He was insensible and at first taken to be intoxicated; a stretcher was procured and he was conveyed to the Station-house where he was put into a cell with another man. Sergeant Chipp stated that they thought he would have died during the night and we are informed that the other prisoner, believing the man to have died, actually gave the alarm and for some time it was actually believed that he was dead'.

To which William Holl's signed post-script levelled a new degree of criticism at the police, not least **Tommy Chipp**'s testimony that, far from dragging him into court, that they'd expected to find a corpse the following morning: '...a very grave question arises out of this case. Is it that Worcester police cannot distinguish between a man suffering in a poisoned stupor and being simply intoxicated? There may be instances of great similarity in the symptoms of both, we believe there are; but even admitting the policemen on duty at the Station House ascribed these symptoms to the effects of drunkenness, were they justified in allowing the wretched patient to remain without medical aid? We entreat the attention of the authorities to this matter, in the name of humanity, and also to the absurdity, we ought to call it by a much stronger term, of dragging a man evidently in the greatest suffering, from his sick bed to the justice room in such circumstances as those which we have detailed. Signed ED. WH'.

In the autumn, a shocking testimony to the state of Worcester at the time. **PC Joseph Hall** – the same young Joe Hall who'd been recruited under Henry Sharpe nine years earlier, but was not to see out the decade – heard a commotion while on duty on the Cross at 2am and tracked it to notorious boozer, the Severn Trow in Quay Street. Rushing there, he found '...an assemblage of thieves, bargemen and others, standing at the door, with a large jug of ale which was being handed round and drunk amidst a most uproarious admixture of oaths, obscenity, quarrelling &c. Defendant (*licensee Sarah Grove who'd only taken over a few weeks earlier but was to have her licence blocked by **Inspector Phillips** at the next Brewster Sessions*) was at the door and received the jug from one of the party. The disturbance was of considerable duration and the officer was most grossly insulted'.

Shocked at the treatment and roughing-up received by his meticulous PC, **John Phillips** personally took charge of the case. Sarah Grove was charged with allowing disorderly conduct in her house – including the harbouring of two men wanted for rape. It was, reported the *Herald*, 'yet another of many other occasions most disorderly conduct has been carried forward in the house', and she was fined £1 with 12s costs.

## Final setback reserved for the last day of the year

The year had been far from an auspicious one for the force, and it held one more set-back, reserved for the very last edition of the year. It was yet more news of the kind John Phillips could have gladly done without...

The headline itself – ***Outrageous Assault upon a Policeman*** – was everyday, but it wasn't until the final paragraph that the full weight of the story became evident. It read (in full):

> 'Early on Tuesday morning, Thomas Phelps of the Blockhouse and Henry Jones of Dolday, together with two women, were in Pump-street making a noise and upon the policeman on duty there No1 William Hale, requesting him to go home quietly, Phelps gave him a tremendous blow in the face, which immediately streamed with blood. Hale was about to draw his staff in self defence, when Jones seized his arm and Phelps beat him about the head in a fearful manner. Hale however, gave his assailant one blow upon the head and finally secured him. They were both brought before [magistrates] F Hooper and C Sidebottom Esqrs., in the course of the morning when Phelps was fined £5 and costs or a month's hard labour, and Jones £3 and costs or three weeks. Not being prepared with the money, they were both sent to gaol. What is rather odd, Jones is a supernumerary policeman; his chance of promotion now, we should say, is very small'.

Attacks on the police were nothing new, but when one was carried out by one of their own number, and in the course of resisting an arrest, the reflection on its members was devastating.

It could have been the relentless barrage of assaults, continued derision on the streets, the lack of respect for the uniform, failure of the authorities to be seen to support their activities, criticism from the press and sections of the public, lack of leadership or any number of associated internal and outside influences, but the personnel of the force was rapidly changing, and officers were coming and going with disappointing regularity.

What's more, the average term of office was shrinking: several constables had come and gone having served less than a year. Of the 32 officers that had been elected during the course of 1835-6, only 9 remained – from the initial intake, stalwarts **John Phillips** still Inspector, **No1 William Hales, William Sanders, No7 Richard Berry, No17 George Nott, No16 George Stoneley** and **Luke Packwood**; of the second intake only **No3 James Workman** remained (*John Evans a supernumerary from the second intake, quitting just three weeks after taking on his beat*); none remained from the third intake and only one from the fourth.

At least, this was the ever-reliable **No21 Tommy Chipp** who was popular and his promotion to sergeant the previous year had been generally welcomed as well deserved. That year, he was living above butchers Tandy's shop in the Shambles with his wife Ann, both aged 30, daughter Lucy (5) and son Edward (2) who was also to make his mark with the police, but more of that later...

**Gained:** *George Fudger, George Sanders, (unknown) Bradford - none of whom survived the year as numbered constables, although Bradford was allowed to continue serving on reduced pay. He remained in post up to 3rd October 1852*
**Lost:** *Edward Kennard*

# Also this year: 1842

- Metropolitan Police establishes its first criminal investigation department (CID)

- city police called in when an unnamed woman is attacked by a furious cow with a calf by her side in Foregate Street

- police condemn 'stupid countrymen' who venture into some of the city's low dives in a state of intoxication and are left to the mercies of streetwise girls who make off with their cash

- the entire force is put under orders keep a watchful eye on 'the common practice for filthy fellows to commit disgusting nuisances in passages &c leading from our public streets and attention of the police has been called to the same, and future offenders will be fined not exceeding £5 for such disgraceful conduct'

- city police, particularly Sgts Tommy Chipp, William Sanders and PC1 William Hale, come in for credit after gang-busting initiative in the wake of robbery at Webbs Warehouses in the Trinity cracks John Attwood ('Three-Finger Jack's) notorious gang of thieves based at the Horse and Jockey in Pump Street

- so many suicides by drowning in the river that the news-sheets coin a new phrase 'making a hole in the Severn'

- 'some excitement created in the vicinity of Tallow Hill' is how the Herald describes the finding of a new-born baby girl's body in the canal near the bridge. She'd had her skull smashed and had been tied up in sacking

- another suspected murder the following week with the discovery of 2-year old Elizabeth Bishop, found head-down in a water butt. Three years earlier her brother had been found drowned in the canal

- serial offender Elizabeth Fowles is committed for a month after being found drunk and insensible by PC No1 William Hale in the street 'with her person exposed'

- city in uproar when it is reported that a pair of hacked-off hands 'with parts of the arms still attached' has been found on Pitchcroft two weeks after the severed sleeves of a bloodstained coloured cotton gown had been found near the Cattle Market and handed to PC16 George Stoneley. Two lads, James Harris (8) and John Palmer (12) confess to making it all up, the older lad laying all the blame on the younger one

- barely a year after joining, former Supernumerary William Hyslop No 11 is gravely injured in a fracas with two boatmen, James Perry and Abner Smith outside the Union in the Blockhouse

- the summer proves oppressively hot and humid, keeping the force on its toes – and occasionally on its backs – in quelling the daily outbreaks of violence in the most populated areas of Dolday and Birdport. It was to have a demoralising effect on manpower

- in one of the last cases of its kind, William Tolley, Clerk to the Racecourse, is summoned for allowing a person under 21 to ascend his chimney for the purpose of sweeping it

- No18 Richard Hughes again gets a beating – this time at the hands of Birdport hard-case Henry Hardwick after attempting to separate him from his wife who he'd been severely pummelling. A month's hard.

- two nights later, veteran PC No17 George Nott (15th January 1836 – 9th March 1860) is severely beaten in Birdport by japester John Wedgbury who'd blacked his eyes and then run away laughing. 21 days' hard

- at Christmas, No11 William Hyslop again comes off worst in a tussle with glover Edwin Whittall in Lich Street

The new year was only hours old when the police were called in to tackle a fire that, had they not responded so quickly, would have completely destroyed the Rein Deer Inn (*later Reindeer and now shops in Reindeer Passage*).

Throughout the opening weeks of the year, police were also kept busy with a spate of violent incidents: a baby's body with its head smashed and face flattened had been found in a drain leading from the Albert beer-house in New Street, and there was another case of suspected murder on Pitchcroft.

In consecutive weeks in April, a notorious rough-house known as the Jolly Waterman in Birdport became the focus of intense police interest: **PC Luke Packwood** who was to last barely another year with the force, had had the misfortune of encountering a troublesome boatman dubbed 'Chilley', William Chillingworth – and, as most did when pitched against the hardened bruiser, he came off rather the worst '...Packwood stated that on the night in question, about ten o'clock he heard a very great disturbance at the Jolly Waterman, Birdport-street and going into the house saw the defendant (*Chillingworth*) in the act of fighting with another man; he was requested by the landlord to turn them all out, and that after doing so he was standing by the door when the defendant threw a stone at him which hit him on the left side, and ran away'. As Chilley had been in trouble for similar offences in the past, he was fined £5 and in default sent to the City Gaol for a month's hard labour.

Then, a fight that began in the same pub and was continued on Pitchcroft the following day, resulted in the death of one of the protagonists, local shoemaker Cornelius, known as 'Neely', Bevan, and manslaughter charges against the other, gipsy knife-grinder John Cuff from Liverpool and his 'seconds'.

## Another manslaughter charge after fatal Pitchcroft 'mill'

It began with Cuff singing songs in the Jolly Waterman (*also known as the Leather Dressers' Arms*) and Bevan scoffing at their delivery. Bevan broke off a piece of his pipe and threw it at Cuff before hitting him two or three times and the two going 'six or seven rounds' in the parlour. With that scrap undecided, Bevan challenged Cuff to fight for 2s, but Cuff said he never fought for money. They agreed to meet on Pitchcroft the following day when the tussle lasted about half an hour with Bevan – though considered well 'up' for most of the scrap, ended with the local bruiser mortally injured. Mr. Cole, house surgeon at the Infirmary where Bevan was carried on a hurdle, told the court that Bevan was labouring under all the signs of apoplexy and that there were several severe contused wounds on his head. His left eye and nose were much swollen and there were wounds to his neck. The post-mortem revealed 'a large quantity of extravasated blood on the right side of the brain which was no doubt the immediate cause of death'.

The jury immediately returned a verdict of manslaughter against John Cuff in the first degree, and against his seconds, local men Reuben Hathaway, William Cooke and Richard Morgan in the second degree.

Two weeks later, two 14-year old lads, Abraham and Jones, avoided swelling the numbers at the City Gaol when they promised never to offend again after being hauled into court on the serious charge of stealing manure in the streets, the scamps!

Then some more harsh and unwelcome criticism for the police, resulting in a severe reprimand and near-sackings for two constables after an assault on the ever-reliable **Sgt George Williams No3**, by a drunken farmer known only as George. Earlier on the Saturday night in question, **PCs William Hamshere**, just three years in the force, and **Henry Griffiths Dunk**, his senior by three years had been seen drinking gin and ale with the farmer outside the Kings Head in St Johns, considered at the time to be the parish's premier drinking house (*and now the derelict site of the former St Johns cinema and later night-clubs*). Partially to their credit, they'd refused to be treated *inside* the inn, but had nonetheless taken full advantage of the farmer's jovial hospitality in an al fresco foursome in the street with the keeper of the Malvern gate, Mr Field.

When Farmer George was later found dead drunk and fighting mad at the Malvern turnpike, the two PCs called for assistance and were joined by **Sgt Williams** – who, the evidence suggests, was teetotal, a rarity for a city policeman, and harboured a special dislike of drunks, St Johns drunks especially.

Doubly galling for him, the farmer viewed the other PCs as his new friends and in their defence, set about the sergeant with a flurry of kicks and blows. In court the next day '...the Bench thought that Dunk and Hamsher (sic) were much to blame for the poor farmer's insobriety and reprimanded them accordingly, while [George] was fined 5s for being intoxicated'. To which William Holl again appended a sniffy post-script: 'the conduct of the two policemen underwent investigation before the Watch Committee this (Friday) morning when they were both severely reprimanded'.

It was not to be long before **William Hamshere** (*also represented as Hamshire and Hamsher*) again made the headlines...

### PC William Hamshere horrifically disfigured after being shot in the face

On December 19th this year he'd taken a load of buck-shot full in the face after he'd attempted to arrest a man in Watery Lane in the ever-troublesome parish of St Johns. He'd survived, but was not in a good way and was barely expected to live-out the week: he surprised them all and continued as a serving officer, although horribly disfigured, until 1850.

The case shocked the city and the Mayor William Lewis led a campaign, of sorts, to offer a reward to find the man who'd stoop so low as to shoot a policeman in the face with the evident aim of eliminating him. Addressing the full Council, he almost apologetically asked that if the Government would match their offer, would the Council be minded to grant £50 by way of a token reward? The response was that yes, they would – but only on the condition that the Government would do the same. If Whitehall was not forthcoming in that respect, then neither would the city and the whole deal would be off.

The phrase 'half-hearted' comes to mind, as does several

£100 REWARD.

WHEREAS, WILLIAM HAMSHER, Police Constable of the City of Worcester, was FIRED AT and WOUNDED by some Person, with a Gun, loaded with Powder and Shot, while on Duty near the Watery Lane, in the Bransford Road, in the Parish of Saint John in Bedwardine, in the City of Worcester, between the hours of Two and Three o'Clock in the Morning of TUESDAY, the 19th of DECEMBER last. NOTICE IS HEREBY GIVEN, that whoever shall give such information and evidence as shall lead to the discovery and conviction of the Person who fired the Gun, shall receive a Reward of FIFTY POUNDS from the Corporation of Worcester, and a like Reward of FIFTY POUNDS from the Government.

The Secretary of State will also advise the grant of Her Majesty's gracious Pardon to an Accomplice, not being the Person who actually fired the Shot, who shall give such information and evidence as shall lead to the same result.

WM. LEWIS, Mayor.

Guildhall Worcester,
5th January, 1844.

## Also this year: 1843

- *PC Joe Hall comes in for praise for halting a charity scam known as 'the begging petition trick' involving the London School for the Blind*

- *14-year old gin drinker, petty criminal and seasoned house-thief John Hunt is transported to Australia after police crack-down on illicit gaming – this case, against the licensee of the Cross Keys in Sidbury, Robert Gell, investigated and prosecuted by the chief, John Phillips himself*

- *good and bad news for PC Luke Packwood: the day after winning praise for apprehending Zachariah Whitehouse for theft at the Old Greyhound, he meets his match in Aaron Dayus 'of fighting notoriety' in what the Herald terms 'a bit of a shindy' in Lowesmoor*

- *rookie cop PC James William Mitchell (29th November 1839- 2nd August 1844) is beaten up when he attempts to separate John Bristow and his wife in a heated 'domestic' in the Blockhouse. At the same time, a Herald article titled 'Married life in King William St' indicated that a wife's lot '... consist(s) of grubbing round for money and getting regularly wopped – which is the custom of the place'*

- *police mount search for a man named Blissett after the body of a new-born boy 'with his head smashed and his face flattened' is found in a drain leading from the Albert beer house in New Street, which he'd kept up to then*

- *spate of acts of 'atrocious cruelty' committed by boatmen on horses, donkeys, and mules on the canal towing path reported to police*

- *shameful conditions at County Gaol are revealed including gross mismanagement, corruption, theft, falsifying of accounts and men being put on the treadmill 'to amuse (visiting) ladies'*

- Elizabeth Loveland, described by the Herald as 'with nothing very lovely about her' and 'familiar to frequenters of our police office' again summoned for d&d and is 'adequately rewarded with a month's board and lodging with Guv'nor Griffiths'

- dud sixpences widely circulated in the city, investigated by PC18 Richard Hughes

- massive thunderstorms on 9th August result in major damage to scores of properties on the Blockhouse: '...crash succeeded crash without intermission' reported the Herald

- police out in force for the visit to the city of Queen Adelaide, widow of William IV, later the same month

- seven cases heard on the same day after riots erupt between warring families in the Blockhouse – later notorious as 'the Charles Street Wars'

- attempts to tutor prisoners in the City Bridewell in reading and religion scrapped after they're met with 'lukewarmness and indifference'

- at the end of the year, a new recruit who'd joined in August, began making a name for himself as a solid, no-nonsense feet-first copper: this was No 22, Edward 'Grubber' Grubb, who remained with the force for ten turbo-charged years (4th August 1843 – 4th March 1853)

- **Gained:** James Wheeler, Edward Grubb, James Davis

- **Lost:** George Stoneley, Thomas Jones, William Hyslop

others... Luckily, the response from London was positive and the city drew-up the required advertisement.

Also that month, (*December*) **Sgt Tommy Chipp** on desk duty at the station-house is requested to a) arrest and detain for the night, and b) call a doctor to attend to Jeffrey Paul Handley who'd been dragged there by St Johns chemist Augustus Wrisberg.

The two men had been drinking in the Bell Inn and when Wrisberg put down his sovereign to pay for his corner, Handley had picked it up and swallowed it. Not quite seeing the joke, he now wanted his ex-friend arrested for the theft of his sovereign.

The *Herald* merely notes: '...the sovereign has been recovered with the aid of a physic'.

In Christmas week, **PC No8 Thomas Bateman** (*later Sergeant*) was called in to investigate a major disturbance in the Lord Nelson in Powick Lane created by something rarely seen in the city, a black face '...in the shape of a stalwart African, sable in hue but not of Nubian jet'.

His name was not revealed but he was said to have been creating a disturbance which was probably not much more than a natural retaliation to the boisterous curiosity and excited attention that he'd created: either way, it had got out of hand and had turned nasty. **Tommy Bateman** – described as 'one of the elite of the police force' – was called in to clear the house and, reported the *Herald*, '...turned the son of Afric's (sic) burning clime out into the street where not even the change from the sea-coal and tobacco-impregnated atmosphere of the Lord Nelson kitchen to the dank outdoor atmosphere of Birdport had the effect of bringing the brains of the burning zoned son of earth to reason; he showed fight in the street and was forthwith taken off to the Station-house... (*in court*) he displayed considerable horror at the idea suggested by one of their worships of being accommodated with a few weeks' lodgings at Mr. Griffiths' hotel (*the City gaol*) naïvely adding that "...him neber see inside of Englis gaol till yes'rday and no like it much very at all".

***Verdict: discharged on promising to leave the City within two hours.***

But now, the police were finding themselves swamped and under intense pressure as the result of a sudden and violent upwards turn in street disorder and every other crime and misdemeanour leading to, and associated with it, and it was all down to one cause.

Navvies.

## 1844

Hassle caused by armies of drifting labourers – navvies, short for navigators – was nothing new in the city.

For more than thirty years they'd been quartered in the City, initially in large numbers for the construction of the canal and, on its completion in 1814, a depleted, although still dangerously active congregation demanded for the waterway's continual

# 'work like a donkey, drink like a mule, act like an ass...'

*...the navvies returned with a vengeance, and with them came a marked and almost overnight re-escalation in street crime and violence and everything else associated with gangs of rootless men on the loose. Not that these were normally peace-loving citizens out on a weekend spree: they were, for the most part, desperate labourers of whom not too many questions were asked. Included were hard-drinking Irish and Scots, ex-militiamen and deserters, convicts returned from the colonies, and absentee fathers lured by the promise of good money, regular work in the open air, and anonymity...'*

**WORCESTER CITY POLICE.**

MONDAY.

THE NAVIES.—It was rather a matter of surprise in the Justice-room of the Guildhall this morning, that Inspector Phillips was not provided with at least a leash of navies for presentation. The worthy officer, however, explained that this rather singular privation arose from no *laches* of him or his body of gentlemen in blue, but was the result of a novel arrangement come to ... ... ... bunching ...

... had rece ... ed 25s. in t ... ... landlac ... was owing to her, and drunk the balance. "Why," said the Mayor, "how much was left of your wages?"—Navie: "Some your shillin or summat thereabout; I know it warnt much more."—"Did you drink the whole?"—"Did I drink the whole! Lor bless thee your shillin dunna take much drinking."—"Well, if we let you off this time without a fine, will you promise not to get drunk again?"—"What! I ... romise the ... its no use, how can I tell ... ... ...

display, we presume], and paid the ... ...

NAVIE, No. 1.—Henry Copley, a navie, was charged with having been drunk and very disorderly, about half-past eleven o'clock, on Sunday afternoon. Hall, of the city force, described a scene of great riot and disturbance in Birdport, owing to the prisoner's conduct; and Inspector Phillips represented to the Magistrates that the navies required so much of his men's time and attention that the property of ... rate-p ... ... often ... ... ... un ... of doors.

"NAVIES" IN TROUBLE.—Two "navies," named Jones and Williams, were charged with having been drunk and disorderly on Saturday night. There was nothing beyond the customary folly usually shewn by such patients in the one fellow's case or demeanour at the bar, and he was dismissed with a brief reprimand. The other was rather a marked man of his "order." He related, by way of accounting for his state and condition, the following tale. Saturday ... arr ... ... pay day at the ... ... it is, the ...

**WORCESTER CITY POLICE.**

MONDAY.

BRUTAL ASSAULT.—Charles Turner, an excavator, but not a regular "navie," was charged with striking Mrs. Eliza Leonard, of the Gloucester Arms, Copenhagen-street, a violent blow in the face on the 10th inst. It appeared that the prisoner had broken a half-pint glass and refused to pay for it. Mrs. Leonard insisted on his paying, and he then struck her a violent blow ... the nose, blacken ... th eyes and knockin ... ... ... Mrs.

... navigators," many of whom we have had lately among us, may be depended upon for fact:—A "navey," some six feet three inches in height, and of Herculean build, went into the shop of one of our shopkeepers, and asked if they had got any "whirlers"—which is a corruption of wheeler—that is, stockings without feet. "No," quoth the shopkeeper, "but we have got some famous big and strong stockings as will just suit such a man as you." "Let's ... ... ... rejoined the "navey." ... counter

need for maintenance. Now the final phases of the Severn Improvement works including the construction of locks at Diglis and Bevere brought them back in droves to the city that was vibrant and alive with the attractions of drink, women and mayhem.

They returned with a vengeance, and with them came a marked and almost overnight re-escalation in street crime and violence and everything else associated with gangs of rootless men on the loose. Not that these were normally peace-loving citizens out on a weekend spree: they were, for the most part, desperate labourers of whom not too many questions were asked. Included were hard-drinking Irish and Scots, ex-militiamen and deserters, convicts returned from the colonies, and absentee fathers lured by the promise of good money, regular work in the open air, and anonymity.

As a result, at the end of each day – and most especially every second Saturday as that's when the men received their fortnight's pay that could amount to as much as 25s after the 2s a day allowance had been taken from it – it's thought that as many as 500 hardened, thirsty and largely aimless and otherwise unattached labourers descended on the City for as much pleasure as they could wreak out of it.

Suicidal was the man that even attempted to get between them and their goals, and aside from drunkenness, a disregard for decency, morals and the law in conjunction with the perceived need to fritter away every last penny on self-seeking pleasure, the only other trait they shared was a dislike of authority – police uniforms especially.

As if the situation wasn't already bad enough, at the same time also came the boatmen, often toughened ex-matelots, plying their trade along the Severn and the man-made waterway, added to which the City additionally became a garrison town with as many Militiamen billeted on unwilling homes and pubs.

*Thus the scene was set for daily bouts of lawlessness and disorder on an unimaginable scale – all of which the newspapers of the day were only too ready to relate to their reading publics.*

Few days now saw the dock at the Magistrates' and police court devoid of one, two or often more hardened and rarely penitent rough-necks being brought to book, and scarcely one edition of any of the weekly sheets – the *Herald, the Chronicle*, the *Advertiser* and the *Journal* – went by without at least a dozen references to the scourge of the coarse and ever-ready strangers that had descended on an unsuspecting Worcester, turning the City into a location as flammable and volatile as anything the Wild West could throw up. Virtually every page carried a story containing one or more tales of some navvie-related misdemeanour, the routine of navvie following navvie into the dock to receive much the same penalty (*5 shillings*) for having committed much the same offence (*drunk and disorderly, or riotous and creating a disturbance*), had become so predictable and tedious that the reporters simply referred to the cases as 'Navvie No1' or 'Navvie No2', and busied themselves more with fanciful descriptions of hardened features and Herculean frames than the salient issues of each alleged misdemeanour.

This is typical of the time, under the headline '***The Most Brutal Of Navies***' (sic):

> '*Samuel Davis, navigator, a native of Somersetshire, upwards of six feet high, most powerfully built and altogether the most savage looking of the excavators we have seen...*'

He'd been charged with, yet again, assaulting a Police Constable, this time **No18** in discharge of his duty after he'd been found near Hardy and Padmore's Foundry drunk and asleep. Miffed at being so rudely awaken, Davis felled the PC with a vicious flurry of kicks and punches. It wasn't his first time in court: he'd not long before been released following two weeks on the Crank after a nasty incident in the Angel in Silver Street (*later the Plough, demolished as recently as 1971*). Having turned up there already drunk at nine am on a Sunday, he'd been refused a drink and as a consequence he took hold of servant girl Mary Green round the neck and threw her across the street. He then fell down on the girl who was severely bruised by the encounter and lucky to escape with no bones broken.

Said the *Herald* '...she is a young girl; her face bore marks of severe injury and altogether we do not recall a case of more disgusting brutality'. Editor William Holl in another of his customary footnotes added that the sentence was 'not a tithe (*tenth*) of the punishment the brute deserved'.

Just the following night, another navvy, William Brown of Painswick was convicted of being riotous and disorderly in the Angel. He was unable to tell the Bench 'to within a couple o' quarts' how much ale he'd drunk and was fined 5s and 8s costs.

The Angel – indeed, the Cornmarket in general – was fast becoming the focal point for nightly hassle, demanding a hefty police presence and not just at weekends either. Whether the navvies came first, or the good-time girls, is open to conjecture but the Angel was evidently the favourite haunt of the prostitutes living and working at the notorious 'Barracks' brothel in nearby Watercourse (inevitably, dubbed

*Inter*course) Alley – one notorious serial offender Phoebe Gardner well known in the police's black books and on one occasion, sent straight back to gaol for having been disorderly and breaking a glass on the same day she'd come out after serving fourteen days.

The reporters were even coming to recognise the regular attendees in the dock and to refer to them by the nicknames adopted by their mates. Among these was Henry Copley better known to all and sundry as 'Nottingham' and a regular at the station house after wreaking havoc and mayhem in one or other of the public houses. He was also known for another habit – his prodigious appetite (the *Herald* more accurately referred to it as gluttony) that had prompted one reporter to comment that '...Nottingham is decidedly one of those persons whom one would much rather keep for a week than a fortnight. The fellow expressed a desire to have his "breckast (sic) afor a-goin' afore the beeks" and it took all the coin in his possession to provide the materials...' He'd actually devoured 4½ lbs of beef steaks in a very cannibal fashion, the meat scarcely warmed through, adding half a quartern loaf to his monstrous meal.

'Wedgie' (*real name Samuel Wedgbury*) was another navvie scrapper and hard-case but after several years of taking on all-comers he'd become punchy and no longer able to take on four or five opponents at the same time and still be the last man standing. On one occasion this year, **PC Joe Hall** had found him drunk and disorderly in Merrivale one Saturday night: '...he had his clothes off in pugilistic fashion and was just about to "get it kindly" from a lot of navies (sic) who "owe him one" when Hall took him off to the station-house for his own safety. The next day his case was dismissed with an admonishment for his future conduct.

But though the magistrates had done their business, the navvies still considered theirs unfinished. *He was found drowned in the Severn just days later. No-one was ever charged in association with his death.*

### Police – and courts – swamped with never-ending catalogue of navvies' misdemeanours

Now, with rape, bastardy, criminal damage, assaults on the police and a never-ending catalogue of d&d and riotous behaviour threatening to swamp the courts and bring the city's legal system to its knees, it's no wonder that **John Phillips** was forced into making almost daily appeals to the Magistrates to show a heavier hand in dealing with the occupying armies that required so much of his men's time and attention that the property of ratepayers was, he said, often left comparatively unprotected.

'The Bench saw the force of the Inspector's complaint, but could do nothing further than adjudicate on the case before them' meekly reported the *Herald*.

Not that all the issues were created by the rough-necks: occasionally, the navvies themselves were the victims. In one instance, a sub-contractor named Burgess had absconded with £16 4s intended as the wages for 28 men. Desperate for cash, the workers clamoured around the Guildhall for some kind of judicial enforcement, but the best the Bench could come up with was no doubt well-meant advice to send after Burgess and to recover the money 'by the ordinary proceedings to recover wages'. Some hope.

The lawlessness on the streets also gave rise to the temporary re-appearance of The Lambs, once the scourge of the Watchmen (*see p28*) but now made up of home-grown thugs like Reuben Hathaway and James Jones intent on extracting some kind of revenge and getting their own back on the occupying troublemakers, particularly when found stumbling back to their mean lodgings alone after a night's hefty wenching and quenching. A string of late-night muggings served only to inflame the situation, leaving the Birdport pubs – home turf for the navvies, particularly the already-notorious Glovers Arms – the scene of nightly ruckus and mayhem, some of it appallingly vicious.

Extremely rarely, although not completely unknown, in company with the navvies were the navvies' wives who created trails of havoc of their own: just one this year was Mary Stone, arrested and charged by **Sgt. Tommy Chipp** '...with breaking seven and twenty panes of glass in her landlady's windows, small ones to be sure, but twenty-seven of them, last night. Chipp was called in to put an end to her breaking propensities, and finding her tipsy and outrageous, conveyed her to the station-house. The woman intimated that although the drink had raised her spirits somewhat above the regular blood heat, it was jealousy that had elevated them to breaking point (when) she asserted that she had found her husband's arms too lovingly around her landlady's neck. The case was adjourned to see if the husband could be induced to pay for the misdeeds of his wife' (*Herald*). Whether he did or not, is unrecorded.

The next article on the same page told the tale of a young girl named Bullington, in court '...to charge a lusty young navvy named Charles Rawlings with being the father of a child she held in her arms. Charles at once admitted the parentage and was ordered to pay 1s 6d a week towards the bantling's support'.

The same day, three further charges of pick-pocketing both by and from the navvies came before the ever-patient Bench, and the day after that, a rape case involving three labourers Coley, Boden and

Doughty whose crime, if not already serious enough, was apparently overshadowed by the unforgivably ungentlemanly act of one of the men giving the (*unnamed*) girl a kick in the mouth.

By now, the situation was at breaking point and **John Phillips** at the end of his intellectual powers as to what to do next. But then, in the middle of this year, his organisational flair kicked in and he came up with a brainwave...

It was not infallible, there were clear flaws in the plan and it demanded a large dose of mutual co-operation and even self-sacrifice on the part of the unpredictable strangers. But it was worth a try.

The wheeze he came up with was that if they stayed out of town on Sundays and confined their orgiastic revels out of the jurisdiction of the City magistrates, the police and magistrates could – *just could mind, no guarantees* – be persuaded to take a softer line the other six days of the week.

Quite where they were to go and what they were to do when they were there was not mentioned, but what did he care so long as the problem wasn't his?

The arrangement worked fine for two weeks, the reporters welcoming the unusually quiet Monday mornings in the dock. But then it was soon back to the old order.

Virtually the next week, **Sergeant Tommy Chipp** and a posse of other officers found themselves roughed-up by a gang of labouring men at the Albion – the haunt of hard-cases and ruffians over much of its life. He and PC Staite of the neighbouring County force had chased a man called Potts, suspected of a robbery, into here but quickly found themselves 'surrounded by a host of his butty workmen... by whose contrivance (*the suspected man's clothes*) had been substituted for a fustian jacket for the purpose of disguise. But their attempt proved abortive as the accused was at once recognised by a scar on his face'.

Hoping to protect his friend from the police, one of the gang, Ralph Poynton 'had the audacity to follow the officers with threats and menaces to the door of the station-house' where, notes the *Herald* with a touch of smugness, he too was locked up for the night and next morning. **Tommy Chipp** was clearly not the man to be messed with. Potts' case was heard before the full Bench of magistrates the next day.

Another officer not totally overawed by navvies throwing their weight about was **Sergeant William Sanders**. Called in to sort out a violent labourer aptly-named John Tussell who'd demanded a bed at the already-notorious Glovers Arms in Birdport and when asked for pre-payment by gaffer John Dunn not only smashed him in the face, but also swept a number of glasses off the bar and started wreaking havoc on everything else in reach, the no-nonsense old stager and ex-Watchman tried to calm him down and when that failed, laid him flat and carted him off to the station house.

Tussell was fined £1 with expenses or 14 days' gaol.

### 'Frightful calamity' as 12 navvies drown in the Severn

Then, on August 10th., 'a frightful calamity' – as the *Herald* described it – occurred that brought a temporary truce between the city and its hordes of rampaging and generally unwelcome visitors.

It happened on the Severn when a flat-bottomed fishing boat used to convey the workmen from Worcester bridge to the Severn Improvement Works at Diglis tipped over at around 6.45 on a 'gloomy and rainy' Monday evening. Fifteen men who'd just completed an additional hour to their normal day's work of constructing a stank on the St John's side of the weir, were in the boat: only three made it back to the riverbank. According to the *Herald*, the boat had '...proceeded in safety nearly across the river when (it) came in contact with a rope attached to a barge moored off the left (ie St Johns side) bank, and stretching across the river. At this point one of the sufferers (*it later transpired to be Richard White, one of the twelve who drowned*) had hold of the rope either to lift it over the heads of the people in the boat, or else to assist by holding on in dragging the boat across, and then occurred the fearful calamity, and no less than twelve fellow creatures met an untimely death'.

The boat had tipped over, precipitating all fifteen exhausted navvies into the Severn. After an all-night search, the last of the bodies was brought out at midday the following day.

The entire city and its occupational army was united in shock and grief, but the police were all placed on standby just in case: wherever the navvies gathered, anything could happen.

Two days later, the police were mustered in force when the Whitehall at Rushwick was the scene of the inquest into eight of the drowned navvies. They were: Thomas Packwood (28) from Ombersley; George Poulson jun (19) from Cheltenham; John Pegg (24); Charles Child (19); George Smith (25 – later discovered to be an alias for John Jones); Charles Moscow (23); Henry Mancks of Solihull (21) and James Marshall (45 – described as 'married, his wife keeping a public house at Liverpool and having five small children').

The *Herald* described the inquest scene: '...to the right of the stable on entering, the following five were laid on benches – Packwood, Child, Marshall, Smith and Moscow. On the left were Mancks, Poulson and

Pegg, who had been identified by friends and prepared for interment. The scene altogether presented a most appalling spectacle, several of the bodies having their faces bruised and otherwise disfigured from the drags or other implements used in searching. A pitiable scene took place in this sad receptacle of the dead shortly after the Jury left. The wife of Pegg, a young woman very recently married, rushed into the stable and called frantically for her husband, adjuring in terms sufficient to melt a stone, the cold and lifeless corpse to speak to her. Her cries and lamentations were heart-rending and so violent that she was, of necessity, although with difficulty removed from the spot' (*Herald*). The jury that included several prominent Worcester publicans found the likeliest reason for the boat's overturning being the shift of weight when all fifteen navvies stooped down to duck the rope that stretched across the river 3 feet off the surface. Verdict on all: Accidental death.

Following the inquest, a cortège left the Whitehall carrying seven of the eight for burial in four graves in the churchyard at St Johns, while that of Mancks was conveyed by the railway for interment in Birmingham.

The inquest on the other four – Richard White (21); Charles Baker (21) from near Brighton; Mark Lewis (27) from near Walsall; and William Rose (24) residence unknown – was held later the same afternoon at the Anchor, Diglis where the navvies kept up a silent vigil – much to the relief of the massed ranks of police.

It could all have been so different.

The costs of the funerals of all twelve navvies were met by the Severn Improvement Scheme contractors Grissell and Peto; George Chamberlain of the Star Hotel also gave two hearses 'gratis for the melancholy occasion'. One of the navvies was usually called Smith and was buried in that name but was later named as John Jones; two were married – Pegg, as we've heard, and James Marshall whose wife kept a public house in Liverpool.

*Just a few weeks later, the opening of Diglis Lock signalled an end to the temporary truce.*

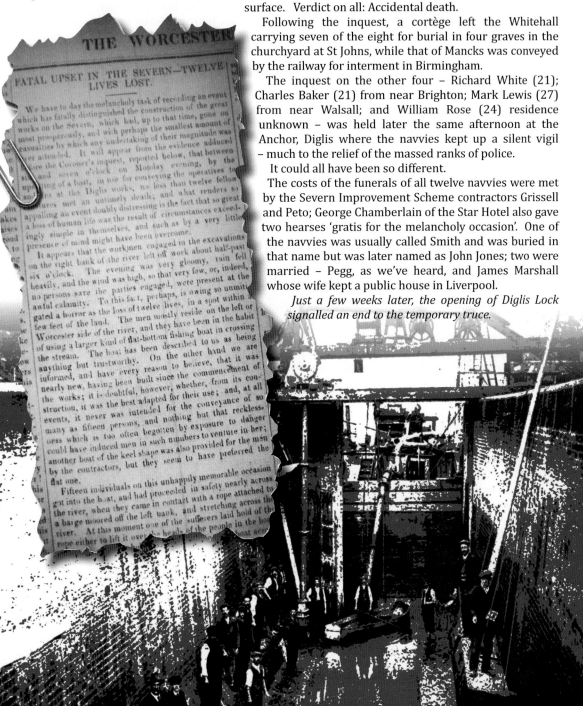

**THE WORCESTER**

**FATAL UPSET IN THE SEVERN—TWELVE LIVES LOST.**

We have to day the melancholy task of recording an event which has fatally distinguished the construction of the great works on the Severn, which had, up to that time, gone on most prosperously, and with perhaps the smallest amount of casualties by which any undertaking of their magnitude was ever attended. It will appear from the evidence adduced before the Coroner's inquest, reported below, that between six and seven o'clock on Monday evening, by the upsetting of a boat, in use for conveying the operatives to and from the Diglis works, no less than twelve fellow creatures met an untimely death; and what renders so appalling an event doubly distressing is the fact that so great a loss of human life was the result of circumstances exceedingly simple in themselves, and such as by a very little presence of mind might have been overcome.

It appears that the workmen engaged in the excavations on the right bank of the river left off work about half-past six o'clock. The evening was very gloomy, rain fell heavily, and the wind was high, so that very few, or, indeed, no persons save the parties engaged, were present at the awful calamity. To this fact, perhaps, is owing so unmitigated a horror as the loss of twelve lives, in a spot within a few feet of the land. The men mostly reside on the left or Worcester side of the river, and they have been in the habit of using a larger kind of flat-bottom fishing boat in crossing the stream. The boat has been described to us as being anything but trustworthy. On the other hand we are informed, and have every reason to believe, that it was nearly new, having been built since the commencement of the works; it is doubtful, however, whether, from its construction, it was the best adapted for their use; and, at all events, it never was intended for the conveyance of so many as fifteen persons, and nothing but that recklessness which is too often begotten by exposure to danger could have induced men in such numbers to venture in her; another boat of the keel shape was also provided for the men by the contractors, but they seem to have preferred the flat one.

Fifteen individuals on this unhappily memorable occasion got into the boat, and had proceeded in safety nearly across the river, when they came in contact with a rope attached to a barge moored off the left bank, and stretching across the river. At this moment one of the sufferers laid hold of the rope either to lift it over the heads of the people in the boat

The first vessel through was the 'Sarah' belonging to Mr Luke Maybury who, reported the *Herald*, '...kindly accommodated a number of his fellow citizens with a sail down the river to join in this interesting ceremony cheering of spectators and salute of cannon'.

The locks, allowing vessels to pass in the astounding time of less than five minutes were an amazing feat of engineering ingenuity, 150 feet long by 30 feet wide and 34 feet deep with 32-ton lower gates that could be worked by one man by the ingenious means of balance beams – the first ever applied to a canal anywhere in the world and for which the locally-based resident engineer Leader Williams won the Telford Silver Medal this year. The same week the lock at Bevere was opened 'so that now all the locks are open and the navigation of the river on the new principle will soon be in operation'.

The river also continued to prove a constant source of attendance for the already hard-pressed police force as the City at this time had been hit by a spate of drownings, both accidental and intentional.

Under the title '***The Drowning Mania***', The *Herald* gave space to a number of deliberate and attempted suicides – suicide being criminal offence and as such notifiable to them.

Just a week after the navvie tragedy, a failed suicide David Jones had been pulled out of the river at the top end of Pitchcroft where he'd attempted to drown himself. The *Herald* reported: '...he had latterly been living very temperately till the day in question when shame and mortification at being detected by his mother drinking in a public house, threw him into a fit of phrenzy, under which he committed the rash act.' Noted the editor: 'He has been sufficiently punished by a severe visitation of fever'.

### 'Horrible murder' and suicide in Pheasant Street

As the summer wore on, the reading public of Worcester had a more juicy titbit to follow than the trials of being a lawman on Worcester's still lawless streets; in fact, the City was, according to the *Herald*, 'thrown into a state of painful excitement in consequence of it becoming known that a murder had been committed' in the otherwise comparatively quiet quarter of Pheasant Street', and for several days, The Cock and Magpie pub became the focus of attention when it was the scene of the inquest into two deaths.

HORRIBLE MURDER IN THIS CITY, AND ATTEMPTED SUICIDE OF THE MURDERER.

Early on Wednesday morning last, this city was thrown into a state of painful excitement in consequence of its becoming known that a murder had been committed in the course of the previous night, in Pheasant-street, Lower-..., and that the murderer had made a desperate attempt at suicide. The unfortunate victim, Joseph Hooper, was a child of about six years of age living with his...

The facts were these: six-year old Joseph Hooper had had his throat slashed by his deranged and hard-drinking 45-year old uncle Jabez (also Hooper) who then turned the razor on himself, dying a day later.

With typical drooling attention to detail, the *Herald* described the inquest scene:

> '...the corpse (of 6-year old Joseph) was lying on the trestle (presenting) a ghastly spectacle. From the left ear extended a deep and broad gash, past the front of the throat in the direction of the right ear. The wound was to all appearance as deep as long – in fact the hapless little fellow's head was nearly severed from his body. His flesh and garments were covered with blood'.

In the summing-up, the boy's mother (*also the murderer's sister-in-law*) deposed that some of her husband's family had been '...afflicted in their intellect, and some members had been confined in a lunatic asylum on that account', as Jabez had. She added that when he'd been drinking his acts were like those of a deranged person.

'The Coroner then briefly addressed the jury and after a short consultation, they returned a verdict to the effect that the deceased destroyed himself by cutting his throat during a fit of temporary derangement'.

Around this time '***Grubber***', as the ne'ers-do-well had already christened **No22 Edward Grubb**, was forging a name for himself as a tireless copper, not afraid to wade-in and mix it with even the toughest customers, navvies included. Throughout his time with the force, his gung-ho attitude was to land him in hot water with the magistrates, and several times he was warned about his 'free and easy dealing with the liberty of the subject' after applying what many considered to be excessive force in bringing his man to book. After one particularly heavy tussle this year in which he'd set about Thomas Glover while allegedly drunk – a charge refuted by his chief **John Phillips** who said he was merely 'excited from running after drunken navvies who keep the whole force in a ferment' – the *Herald* remarked on his efficiency as a policeman but added: '...he has evidently very magnificent notions of the powers and privileges of a policeman. They get him into scrapes'. Even so, he was a good man to have on the side of law and order – as scores of incidents in which he always, or nearly always got his man, readily bore out.

Towards the end of the year, **PC13 James William Mitchell** who been promoted from the ranks of Supernumeraries at the end of 1839 had his private life exposed in the press, the *Herald* report (below) telling the tale:

> *'Bastardy Clauses No II – An order of 1s 6d a week was made upon Police Constable Mitchell, No 13, for the support of the illegitimate child of Sophia Walker, of which he was proved to be the putative father. It was stated that Mitchell is a man of singular acquaintance with the laws that govern paternity. His wife had been seduced from him some years ago, and had born (sic) three or four children to her seducer; and Mitchell is actually now supporting those children. – [He is not legally bound to do so.]'*

**Gained:** Herbert May Evans, Edwin Short, John Fudger, George Powell
**Lost:** Richard Hughes, James William Mitchell, Luke Packwood, William Hale

## Also this year: 1844

- City gaol accounts include prisoners' clothing £133 12s 6d; surgeon's bill for leeches and trusses £11 1s 4d; books £25 3s; keep of the miller's horse and yard dog £15 12 2d

- Edward Kennard who'd resigned two years earlier rather than face a possible attempted murder charge, is beaten up by a gang of graceless thugs that included bully-boy William Downes in the doorway of the White Hart (now Hand in Glove). 'A more brutal nor wanton assault never was committed' (Herald)

- PC No2 (initially, No3) James Workman investigates when 30-year old thug, labourer George Hipwell, steals the 7¹/₂d (3p) from enterprising 7-year old Joseph Gough's night's takings for selling 'baked taters, all hot' in the Lord Nelson

- Sgt Bill Hale takes over the duties of town crier and bellman Webley who'd fallen down some steps and broken his leg

- the force tries try to distance itself from landlords' refusal to take in billeted militiamen, but the number of soldiers either creating trouble to get a cell-bed for the night makes it impossible

- drunk Edward Sellis brags that he had 'put it into several of 'em' referring to a spate of attacks on PCs in St Johns, but meets his match in the ever-reliable No3 George Williams

- in February, off-duty Sgt William Sanders, is called into the Raven in Droitwich Road to find the landlord, 38-year old John Hutchinson had put a shotgun against his chest and pulled the trigger with his toe. He'd died reciting the Lord's Prayer

- punch-ups between 'cads' of the Unicorn, Bell and Crown Hotels – generally drawing huge crowds – show alarming escalation: the fights prove so vicious that often teenaged combatants are regularly sentenced to a week's hard

- PC1 William Hale (sometimes Hales) is described as 'an officer who always conducts himself moderately and temperately' has his '...teeth loosened and features deformed' by 4s 6d a day stonemason John Worthington in the Glovers Arms. Fined 20 and 7s costs: 'far too lenient' howls the Herald

- in separate incidents, No22 Edward Grubb and No2 James Workman are both warned about excessive use of their truncheons in settling often unpleasant altercations. In one in Angel Street, Grubb is jostled by more than 30 onlookers after a 10-minute public scrap with labourer Thomas Slater

- house burglaries in the autumn running at an unprecedented rate, although the police emerge with some credit in tracing their perpetrators

*Herald* readers were treated to a delightful tale of come-uppance in the first edition of the year involving a stroke of luck for **Tommy Chipp** and seven years' transportation for navvie James Hayward, 19 (*below*).

As if the police hadn't already got enough on their collective plate, the City had been hit by a spate of shoplifting, often the work of professional gangs. The *Herald* reported that the trend was '...so common and haberdashers and linen-drapers have suffered so severely by this species of depredation, that they have for some time past adopted a means of quickening the vigilance of a shopman who may be serving a suspicious customer in a manner which excites no attention in the mind of the party suspected. The shop-walker calls out "two-ten" which to the uninitiated, sounds like intimating the price of an article; but the real import is that the shopman is to keep his *two* eyes fixed upon her *ten* fingers'.

HAYWARD, James, aged 19, labourer, was indicted for stealing a purse and ten shillings and sixpence, from the person of Maria Brace, on the 2nd of November last, in the parish of All Saints. Mr. Huddleston, for the prosecution, called Mrs. Brace, who proved that as she went down Broad-street, on the Saturday night named, with a purse containing 10s. 6d. in her pocket, she felt somebody fumbling about her clothes, and on putting her hand behind her a hand was withdrawn from her pocket. She seized the hand; it was the prisoner's. He got away from her, however, and ran down Friar's Alley. She gave information to the police; and Sergeant Chipp and other officers went down to the "Swan," in Quay-street, and apprehended a lot of fellows they found therein, in the hope of having the rogue among them. The sequel proved the correctness of this opinion; for Mrs. Brace, as soon as she saw him, picked out the prisoner as the man who robbed her. Before she came, however, Chipp had not told prisoner what was the charge against him; and upon the prosecutrix exclaiming "That's the man," he said "You're a d—d liar." Chipp asked "What for?" The prisoner replied—"For saying I robbed her on Saturday night." "Aye, where was that then?" quoth Chipp. "Why, in Broad-street, to be sure." Prisoner, in defence, attempted to show that there was not sufficient light in the street so enable prosecutrix to recognize him; but this was disproved. Found guilty; and likewise proved to have been previously convicted. Seven years' transportation.

In March, **John Phillips** took control of a case of attempted murder when one of three (*unnamed*) youths 'of the humbler class' that had hired a horse and cart for the day for a trip to Kempsey was found badly burned. The other two were questioned under suspicion of having deliberately set fire to him, but were released on lack of evidence when they said it had been an accident that had occurred when they were 'experimenting' with cigars and a fusée box.

The same month, the County police came in for general, if muted, praise for having been '...the means of the detection of crime in the rural districts and among Magistrates and respectable famers it was admitted that, so far as the force went, it was effective, but that all agreed that it was numerically insufficient'.

A proposal to swell the force by 20 more men including the promotion of one to superintendent and two more to sergeant was accordingly approved, with the bulk of the new men destined for Dudley that, it seemed, neither Worcestershire nor Staffordshire really wanted within its policing boundaries. The town, ever a troublesome hot-spot, remained within Worcestershire – although by a quirk, the castle remained in Staffordshire.

## Murder, sorcery and witchcraft suspicions surround babies' deaths

In June, the police were called on to control angry crowds gathered for an inquest into the controversial deaths of Eliza Batchelor and her new-born baby boy '...who'd died within hours of each other under circumstances which gave colour to many vague rumours afloat upon the subject' (*Herald*).

At the $8\frac{1}{2}$ hour inquest, during which time a noisy crowd clamoured and jostled outside the Guildhall, the jury heard that Eliza had probably died during childbirth and that when the child was born it fell to the ground '...with not the slightest attention paid to it' even though it was still alive half an hour later when

Mrs Mary Freeman, alias Dovey, whose son William was thought to have been the father, took the child downstairs to wash it. It was dead within minutes.

The Jury were divided whether to charge the Doveys with wilful murder through neglect, or manslaughter through gross negligence – the route they eventually took, Coroner John Hyde admitting he was unclear '...whether upon this verdict he should issue a warrant for their apprehension or not'. For all that, the city's outraged population had already made its mind up and wanted the Doveys unceremonially strung-up. It took the presence of half the police for much of the day to disperse the blood-hungry crowds.

Just weeks later, more controversy surrounding a child's death had the city's population once more up in arms and clamouring for judicial revenge: that the circumstances also involved implications of witchcraft and a secret 'witch's brew' added an extra dimension to the already sad tale. 2-year old George Hooper had been scalded when he'd tipped a bowl of boiling water over himself. Deeply concerned, his parents summoned their Silver Street neighbour Ann Jones, who passed herself off as having magical healing powers, to apply her own special potion and when the boy eventually died, she was arrested on suspicion of having hastened his death.

In court to answer charges of manslaughter she vehemently refused to reveal the contents of her magic cure claiming that she'd be cursed if she did, but later analysis showed that the secret ointment was little more than a quack remedy 'of a simple and harmless nature'.

The very last *Herald* of the year saw **PC Joe Hall** – still patrolling the bear pit that was St Johns – again come in for heroic praise after he'd risked his life by following skinner James Pritchett into the river following a dash for freedom.

That this was a cold December night makes his actions all the more selfless and determined to nail his man. Undoubtedly one of the City's great coppers, he was later promoted to Sergeant but was to die while still in service in May 1849 after contracting fever following another heroic river rescue.

- murder suspected when the body of new-born girl is found in a box placed by the side of the house belonging to clerk to St John's parish, Edward Munn. 'The police are still vigilant in their enquiries to discover the unnatural parent, but hitherto unfortunately without success' reports the Herald

- The Herald states that 'teetotalism is far from universal' in Worcester after a typical Saturday night's revels mean packed courts on Mondays

- city publicans are warned about renewing their annual licenses (10s) for billiard and bagatelle tables

- PCs posted at either end of what's now Cheshire Cheese Entry to stop courting couples taking their activities to obscene levels

- Sgt Bill Sanders and No22 Edward Grubb sent by night mail train to Cheltenham to liaise with the town's police in the apprehension of highway robber 24-year old George Schwamenscrüge, later found with £219 stolen from a dupe in Worcester. He was later transported for ten years

- murder again suspected when Harriett Greenway is found dead on the boat she shared with her husband on the Upper Quay. She was later found to have drunk herself to death, not having been sober for several days previous

- police out in force in June when fire breaks out at the back of the Old Greyhound and completely destroys Nicholson's organ building factory causing £1,000 loss. He was uninsured

- the final quarter for the year shows 148 births, 149 deaths and 82 marriages

DESPERATE ACT.—Last night, between nine and ten o'clock, Policeman Hall, when on his beat near the Bell, St. John's, had to interpose his authority to prevent a young man named James Pritchett, a skinner, from maltreating his wife. Pritchett accompanied the officer down the New-road to near the Bridge, abusing and threatening him for his interference, when he suddenly rushed to the Quay and plunged into the Severn. Hall instantly followed him into the water, and, with the help of a man named James Jones, succeeded in bringing him safe to shore; but he had got into the deep current, and though Hall is an expert swimmer, he was so encumbered with his heavy night duty dress, that his humane intentions were not accomplished without some peril to himself.

*PC Joe Hall, a Watchman from the early days, proved himself to be one of the City's great coppers, with a string of selfless actions. He was later promoted to Sergeant but was to die while still in service in May 1849 after rescuing a would-be suicide from the river*

Christmas had seen an alarming increase in the on-going cad issue and the first *Herald* of the new year carried another bracketed post-script from William Holl that also included a veiled criticism of the force:

*'...the conduct of the omnibus cads and stable boys has reached such a pitch that it can no longer be tolerated. The police have the power to prevent the nuisance by insisting that they shall not congregate on the footway in front of the inns. They are clearly, when standing thus in groups, an obstruction to the passage of the streets and liable to be removed as other nuisances are'.*

As usual, following the long line of d&d-ers in the wake of the busiest Christmas festive period than many could remember, the annual issue of supplying the City police with uniforms also came up for some attention.

The first week's newspapers of the year outlined the fact that '...the Watch Committtee, on Friday last, received contracts for supplying the police with clothing for the ensuing year, when the following tradesmen were appointed to supply the under-mentioned articles and the prices annexed:– Mr H Davis of Newport-street a coat and two pair of trowsers £3; Mr Baker, hats [**note:** *still not helmets*] 10s 6d; and Mr Wadely, Lich-street, shoes 10s 6d a pair. The whole of the above articles were of excellent quality. Several tenders for the coats &c were sent in by linen and woollen drapers, but the committee appeared unanimous that they had travelled a little out of their province and were infringing on another business and consequently were not disposed to entertain their contract' (*Herald*).

Once more, the city was abuzz with tales of a yet another shocking murder when the body of high-profile solicitor and married father-of-three William Finch of Foregate Street was dragged from the canal at Tallow Hill in February.

Despite all manner of lurid tales about his past and of miffed clients/adversaries exacting the ultimate toll for a court case that had gone wrong, the jury at his two-day inquest at the New Inn in George Street found that in all likelihood he'd deliberately drowned himself through pressure of work and fears of an up-coming case going against his client, John Brown of the Sun Tavern (*later the site of the Bridge in Lowesmoor. More about this case on p320,* ***Bob Backenforth's Worcester Pubs Then and Now*** *Vol II)*

However, one real, and very bloody, murder case this year had required no imagination whatsoever – that of kitchen-maid Susan Tolloday in the Guildhall Coffee-house *(now the Tourist Information Centre where some readers may have purchased copies of this book).*

HORRID MURDER.—An appalling murder was committed at the Guildhall coffee-house, on Saturday morning. The cook, whose name is John Smith, and the kitchen-maid, Susan Tolloday, who was only between 20 and 25 years old, were engaged in the kitchen, the former in preparing some ducks for dinner, and the latter in cutting some French beans, when a quarrel having arisen, Smith cut her throat with a knife, dividing the carotid artery and the jugular vein. The...

(Courtesy: Worcester City Council)

## 'Horrid Murder' in the Guildhall

A messy blood-and-guts incident, the press reported every gory detail, despite the murderer – cook John Smith, 30 with a wife and five children – instantly admitting his guilt and regretting his action in the Station-house literally next door, where he'd been locked-up pending his appearance before the Magistrates.

Headlined by the *Herald* as 'Horrid Murder', the ensuing article reports that he and his victim were engaged in the kitchen, he in preparing some ducks for dinner, she in cutting some French beans, when he lashed out and slashed her throat, dividing the carotid artery and the jugular vein.

'The poor victim rushed upstairs, where she fell dead, bathed in blood. Smith immediately gave himself up, acknowledging his crime: and it transpired that the deceased had upbraided him with stealing a pound of tea, and with acting harshly towards a person by name of Riley and his wife, the latter of whom had been kitchen-maid at the Guildhall coffee-house and against whom he had threatened legal proceedings, they having borrowed money of him without re-paying it'.

No doubt the city police, already under intense pressure with the hurly-burly of daily life and now yet another murder to contend with, gave thanks that while hardly a sedate backwater when it came to drunken and generally violent weekends, Worcester was in an entirely different league to Liverpool where on the Monday of the same week, Liverpool Police court had dealt with 60 drunk and disorderly cases!

During the course of the year, the same three names now repeatedly began to emerge as a three-handed hard-man hit-squad, wading-in wherever a tough line was required: **Tommy Chipp, Edward Grubb** and **James Workman** – sometimes singly, but often in trio.

It's notable that assaults on the police during this and the previous year had shown some reduction and while the tally-sheet was never going to return a blank, the three front-liners' reputations for no-nonsense like-for-like retaliation accounts for the number of incidents at least being kept in check.

Typical, and far from unusual, is evident when, at the end of the year the navvies' favourite, the Angel in the Cornmarket, again made the headlines – again for the wrong reasons. Since the navvies' first appearance more than two years before, it had won its

## Also this year: 1846

- Police pressurised with calls to close-down of one of the City's most notorious brothels 'Victoria Barracks' in Quay Street. £10 reward is offered for information

- Sgt Bill Sanders has his leg broken in a violent altercation with tailor Thomas Smith – who'd attempted to gate-crash a Masonic Ball – on the steps of the Guildhall

- the Herald calls for the return of the ducking stool as punishment for would-be suicides who throw themselves in the river and then have a change of heart and need to be rescued

- cholera outbreak and several deaths attributed to '... pig-sties, wash-houses and cess-pits in Warmstry Slip'

- boxing matches on the Quay become 'a pretty general custom among the disorderly portion of the populace' particularly on Sundays. Police regularly called in to break them up and disperse crowds. In one, Grubb and Hamsher are severely criticised for being too heavy-handed in their treatment of spectators and suspects

- at least ten suicides and accidental drownings in the river during the early summer months prompts the Herald to resurrect its phrase 'making a hole in the Severn', first popularised in 1843

- 'Grubber', sent in to investigate coal missing from boats moored at Lowesmoor Wharf, comes face to face with notorious hardman Thomas 'Chilly' Chillingworth who after trading punches, draws a knife on him: the Herald merely reports '... the officer eventually succeeded in capturing him and gave him over to a fellow officer'. He then coolly goes on to arrest two of Chilly's accomplices

- Ten Bells in Dolday, Half Moon in Diglis (later Severn) Street and Mug House Hylton-street (later Road) identified as topping police 'Black Books'

- John Phillips orders his men to clear Worcester Bridge – now the favoured location for 'women of the tramp kind who at all hours of the day and night accost almost every male that crossed the bridge, with improper solicitations'

- high-quality fake half-crowns prevalent in the city, PC Henry Griffiths Dunk investigates

- new iron steamer 'Sabrina' plies between Worcester Quay to Kempsey, Upton and Tewkesbury on market and race days, with pleasure trips every evening except Sunday. A legal loophole permitting on-board drinks to be sold outside normally permitted hours is to be the cause of all manner of violent affrays over the coming years (and sometimes still does)

well-justified reputation as a rough-house best avoided by decent folks – a reputation that lasted up to its final demise even as late as 1971 by which time it had been re-christened The Plough.

Three navvies, Barnaby Megrary, William Gerby and John Evans had spent much of the day getting drunk and being boisterous in there, and when they later had the virtually inevitable disagreement in the kitchen, they at least took the gentlemanly course of sorting it out in private. The chief objection – at least in landlord Charles Such's eyes – was that they'd locked themselves in a room with the purpose of slugging it out amongst themselves '...leaving the landlord with no chance of putting them out. The police being called in, **Sgt Chipp**, with **Grubb** and **Workman** broke open the door and collared the combustibles who were forthwith removed to the station-house where they remained the whole night'.

Nothing out of the ordinary there – except for the fact that at the end of their shift, all three policemen appear to have remained vertical and while possibly blooded, at least not notably injured and largely intact for the next night's shenanigans when, like as not, it'd happen all over again....

*Gained: George Pursell, Richard Haycox, George Vaughan, Charles Lloyd*

# 1847

Another year, another day, another violent anti-police incident – this time in the Boat in Lowesmoor when a mob of navvies including William Smith, George Stephens, John Wilson and Edward Woodward crowded round **PCs Edward Grubb** and **George Powell** *(2nd August 1844 – 21st September 1849)* and physically barred their way into the pub where'd they'd been sent with a warrant to arrest another of their number, George Thomas.

The four ringleaders surrounded them and refused to let them go until the warrant was read out to them '...Grubb replied that he would read the warrant to any two of them in a private room, but he was not going to show it to them in the midst of a crowd. They then pushed him away from the prisoner and Powell added that they opened a window in the kitchen, formed themselves into a circle of three deep round Thomas, and pushed him out into the yard so that he escaped'.

The ringleaders were convicted and fined between 45s (*Stephens*) and 10s (*Woodward and Wilson*) while Stephens' defence had been that he'd tried to advise Thomas to go quietly to the Station-house. 'Powell replied that he *[Stephens]* had certainly used those words but added "Your conduct did not agree with your words; you stood in the doorway, putting your arms and feet so as to prevent me from getting out to look after my prisoner". Smith's defence was "I never mislested ne'er a one on 'um"' (*Herald*). It concluded 'Mr Chipp, *the acting superintendent of police* was ordered to report the landlord's conduct next licensing day when the Magistrates will have some serious chat with him on the subject'.

It was yet another navvie-related incident in a daily catalogue of navvie-related incidents, but the report additionally underlined two further issues now seemingly pressing: that anti-police feelings was continuing to run high with assaults on the police still an everyday occurrence, but perhaps more significantly, that **John Phillips** was flagging in – and by the sound of it, increasingly absent from – the role for which the City Corporation had expected so much from him.

## Fears for chief's health – and future

Luckily, the ever-present **Sergeant Tommy Chipp** had broad enough shoulders to step into the temporarily-vacant post. Not many months later, it was to become a permanent arrangement but, for the present, life went on as normal on the City's still-volatile streets.

Early in the year, a particularly vicious attack had left ex-Supernumerary **PC John Fudger** *(7th July 1844 – 28th January 1850)* who'd been called in to quell a disturbance at the Barracks brothel and had been hit, kicked, bitten and generally roughed-up by hard-case William Cotterill, unable to continue his duties for several weeks. The affair was only ended with the timely appearance of **PCs No17 George Nott** and **George Jones** wading in to effect a rescue. Cotterill was sentenced to 21 days for the attack while Francis Stephens and Barracks' inmate Phoebe Gardner who'd both tried to intervene, were additionally charged with obstruction.

The following week, **PC John Doughty** who was to go on to a chequered, but mostly celebrated 30-year career with the force (*14th February 1845 – 26th March 1875*) was set on by Charles Goodman in Newport Street. The next week **PC George Powell** came off much the worst in a tussle with Thomas Charles in the Glo'ster Arms in Copenhagen Street

Just three days later, yet another Powell – this time navvie Charles – was fined 5s for being drunk and creating a disturbance in the streets during divine service '...and on Grubb requesting (him) to desist, Powell was very abusive'.

Then the following week, echoes of an all-too familiar event – the police chief, albeit on this occasion acting in a *holding*, rather than an *actual*, role got himself roughed-up by a raucous and unruly pub crowd. This was the rough-house that was the Falcon in Broad Street where the ruckus he'd been sent in to quell was already over, but with nothing better to do, the crowd now turned its boisterous attentions on the no-nonsense Sergeant now acting police chief, a man named Joseph Sager proving the pushiest and most abusive. Even without calling in his usual side-kick reinforcements – a feat that sets **Tommy Chipp** in a rarified league of his own plus just a handful of others in the annals of Worcester City coppering – he'd managed not only to subdue the mob, but also to get its gobby ringleader outside, quite understandably dishing back some of the treatment he'd received inside.

Back at the Station-house, the miffed fruiterer lodged a complaint of assault. Heard before the Bench the next day, the *Herald* simply noted: 'the charge was instantly dismissed'.

Noted trollop-about-town was Catherine Egan who also regularly demonstrated a pathological hatred of the police. She and **'Grubber'** had a long-standing mutual dislike – as a beautifully-crafted *Herald* article this year reveals:

*'Catherine Egan of most disorderly fame, was charged with having been drunk and disorderly at eleven o'clock yesterday morning in Birdport (just as the churches were going in). Constable Grubb proved that he was sent to the Mason's Arms to clear the house before shutting-up during Divine Service; there he found Egan intoxicated and very disorderly; she refused to go home and was so outrageous that he was compelled to carry her to the station-house. Egan had an entirely different version of the matter. She said "No, no, no yer Hanner. I goes to fetch me a quart o' ale and they 'buses me as usual, whilst I does nothing at all, at all. I'm shore uv id yer Hanner. It's the infant as is there along iv me as knows it's thrue; but Musther Grubber, the Peeler, whiniver 'ee claps 'is eye on me, sis 'ee, "Is it Egan? We'll station her" an' 'o that, 'ee sazes me an' puts me in the hole". Egan kept all the while pawing a child, which she would carry into the dock with her, in a curious bear-like fashion. The youngster seemed a well-fed little fellow with a mouth as splendidly shaped for swallowing a "Murphy" as if he had been born in his mother's "dear counthry". He sung out occasionally, either because his dam caressed him too roughly, or perhaps from catching an awful vision of the majesty of the Mayor's state sword **(the actual, pictured left)**. The magistrates, having been troubled with the defendant far beyond all reasonable bounds, sent her down to gaol for a month's hard labour, with an intimation that the strictest application of the law would be used in future when she was convicted of offences, so that she has the agreeable prospect before her of being very soon in a position to have twelve months' imprisonment'.*

Weeks later while being escorted, yet again, to the Station-house charged with being a common prostitute, she bit '...policeman [No 7, Richard] Berry's finger with considerable savageness. Her tongue did not appear to have lost any of its glibness, but rather to have acquired fresh power by constant usage' ran the ensuing press report. Another seven days' hard.

**Richard Berry** is another of the notable names of the current force, having been in at its inception as a Watchman, recruited to **Henry Sharpe**'s initial squad in March 1835, retained as one of the elite of James Douglas' burgeoning force (*as No7*) and would continue, still a PC until 24th February 1860. By contrast, **Richard Haycox**, appointed PC on 9th October the previous year quit just a day short of a calendar year (*8th October this year*). Several weeks before, he'd been the subject of 'a fierce and brutal attack' by two men who were later fined £5 and £3 for the offence and he never returned to work following injuries inflicted him and damage inflicted on his watch. He was paid 30s for the injuries he'd sustained and allowed to resign.

■ *young lad George Edwards ordered to be 'well-whipped' and to pay 3s expenses for bathing in the Severn contrary to the bye-laws of the city. The same week, travelling stationer David Brown is drowned while bathing 'at Diglis'*

Despite the well-deserved **Chipp-Grubb-Workman** reputation still riding high, the catalogue of almost daily assaults on the police was fast regaining momentum, and it's to their eternal credit that the bruised front-liners continued to turn up for their duty day-in, day-out – no doubt half-expecting to be involved in some extreme nastiness, almost certainly involving bloodshed and probably their own, before their next shift was out.

Throughout it all, it's plainly evident that Worcester was fortunate in having such a dedicated band of policemen whose perseverance is supremely commendable. In the middle of all this, it'd be interesting to know quite what the reaction was in the St Nicholas Street Station-house on the morning the following letter appeared in the *Herald*:

*SIR – having lately admired the improved appearance of your handsome town, I crave permission to notice a difference betwixt its policemen and those of the metropolis which, I think, upon enquiry, should not be allowed to exist. It is the practice by the Worcester policemen of carrying walking-sticks or switches. When the Metropolitan force was established, it was considered of the greatest importance that nothing should be seen in their hands from the effect which the bearing of any, even the smallest, stick is known in exciting ill-will'.*

It was signed A Traveller and dated 1st September 1847.

Worcester's propensity for continually assuming the worst in cases of unexplained death again re-surfaced in August with the discovery of coal merchant's wife Jane Salmons at their home in Lowesmoor: '...the evidence given, though not warranting an inference that such was actually the case, must nevertheless give rise to strong suspicion that the marriage vow, as it related to

■ *scavengers emptying a mixen at Pitman's Entry (Tything) discover the decomposed body of an infant boy with his skull smashed and a rag pinned around it. Inquest held at the George and Dragon*

■ *PC William Bowen, now constable of the Esplanade, orders – and later summonses for disobedience – Robert Jones to immediately douse a fire he was using for singeing a pig just yards from boats moored on the Severn, one of which contained 70 uncovered casks of gunpowder*

■ *in the same September week, commendable police work results in three felons sentenced to lengthy transportation terms: David Roberts (10 years) for robbery at the Commandery; John Johnson (10 years) for stealing a jacket at the Horse and Jockey in Pump Street, and George Marsh (7 years) for robbery in Broad Street*

■ *sweep John Rook is sentenced to 14 days for assaulting PC (later Station Sergeant) John Doughty in the Hole in the Wall, Merrivale*

■ *arson suspected (later amended to accidental death) when body of Joseph Cobley is found in burned-out shell of outhouse at 13 The Moors. A hardened drunk, he was later found to have died after knocking over a lit candle while in a stupor. Two empty gin bottles were found nearby*

■ *the same week, police are called in when the body of another celebrated drunk 'Blind Robert' Wormington was found dead in bed. The previous night he'd gone to a privy and was unable to find his way out and had been found where he fell in temperatures of –3°*

■ *police called in to trap a large monkey that had escaped its owner Sam Badgery of St Johns and had been on the loose for several days, terrorising the neighbourhood and even seeing off two bull terriers sent in to trap it. The creature was eventually shot and cudgelled*

the deceased and her husband "to love and to cherish" had not by any means been complied with. An inquest was of course summoned on the body and was held on Monday evening last, at the Crown and Anchor Inn, Silver-street, before J. Tymbs Esq., (Deputy Coroner), and an intelligent Jury'.

Despite a mass of livid bruising covering almost the whole of her body – quite explicitly detailed in the *Herald* – the 'intelligent' jury returned the verdict that she'd died from epileptic fits, accelerated by ill-treatment and drunkenness. Her husband William was duly released from the police cells where he'd been held in on suspicion of murder. None – least of all the police and no doubt William Salmons himself – could quite fathom-out how they'd arrived at the verdict.

It was almost a case of déjà-vu in the autumn when a fire that destroyed tailor James Ings' Friar Street house and business and almost took with it the Cross Keys Inn next door (*now Tudor House Museum*) also resulted in his wife Jane's death. While the Norwich Union Brigade, heroically assisted by the police were battling to contain the flames from spreading to the other timber-framed properties in the historic old street, she'd fallen while attempting to escape by climbing into an open window on the first floor of the Cross Keys. Her skull horribly smashed, she was killed instantly, but the unfortunate husband was long the subject of a whispering campaign that implied that he could have done more to save his wife – or worse, that he had actually pushed her.

Despite some real progress on the law and order front, it had not been a particularly satisfying year, with manpower levels continuing fluid.

*Gained: James Griffiths, John Cook, John Bowen (none of whom were not to out-last the year), George Poole, Joseph Bullock, John Johnson, George Martin (Constable for College Precincts), John Jackman, Robert Burden, George Phillips, Henry Davis*
*Lost: Charles Lloyd, George Vaughan, Richard Haycox, George Jones, Sgt William Sanders*

# 1848

The year began with predictable monotony with yet another scathing *Herald* editorial about the scourge of the navvies and an outline of just a few of the dreadful incidents they'd been involved in over the abnormally turbulent Christmas period that had again seen the police stretched to the limit of their capabilities, not to mention perseverance. When it came to the increasingly unwelcome navvies, the press certainly didn't mince their words and it'd be interesting to see what reaction would accompany a similar editorial today.

William Holl wrote: *'...there can be no question that their order does present as low a state of morals, or indeed considerably lower than could be found among the operative class generally. They are but too likely to be tempted into evil courses – poaching, housebreaking and highway robbery, we fear too many...'*

His gutsy editorial then lists five cases of gangs of navvies that had waited for unsuspecting passers-by on the roads leading into the city over the Christmas period, and their inevitable criminal results.

The Sunday of the second week of the year took an even sharper turn for the worse. After just 28 days as a PC – 17th December to January 14th this year – former Supernumerary **George Phillips** attacked and severely knocked about another (*unnamed*) officer **No19**.

The officer v brother officer was bad enough, but it took on a dark new dimension when in his ill-considered defence, **George Phillips** admitted to having been drunk at the time – barely a move geared to securing his position in a force already committed by oath to clamping down on the evils associated with drink. Result? Not only sacked for the wanton and motiveless assault, but also handed the indignity of a 5s fine with 8s expenses with the option of fourteen days' gaol. With the force's reputation teetering on the brink of 'brave lads but foolish losers', he'd needed to be taught a lesson.

Then, not quite the worst scenario of all, but nudging very close: was one of its highest-profile stars and crime-busters not far off being promoted to sergeant, nothing but a common thief himself?

## High-profile PC nothing but a common thief?

The question, involving **Edward 'Grubber' Grubb**, was raised and spread like wildfire after it was revealed that his next door neighbour in the Trinity, shoemaker John Knowles had left town for a few days and had left the key to his house with the gung-ho copper and his family: when he returned, he'd found his house ransacked and cash, jewellery and other valuable trinkets missing.

Things had never looked quite so bleak for Worcester City Police than they did at that precise moment. Casting his mind back, **'Grubber'** recalled a visitor of his wife's the previous Saturday, Charlotte Gill living at the rear of the George and Dragon (*now Dragon*) and that for a moment she'd been left alone and may have had access to the key. Summoning **PC John Fudger** for moral support, the two tracked down Charlotte Gill, broke down her door and found the missing items.

It was a close-run thing and the City Police – and, no doubt **PC22 Edward Grubb** most of all – breathed a hefty sigh of relief. Charlotte Gill was committed for trial.

The policemen's work was never done. The very next week Mayor Edward Webb ordered an (*unnamed*) policeman to enter a house on the Lower Quay where a notorious prostitute Mary Lilley, nicknamed 'Great Western' had died several weeks earlier – a *very gross subject* as the reporter called her: '...she was without friends and being in debt for rent, the landlord put in a distress for the house and the few goods that it contained, but these were barely sufficient to pay the expenses. Her corpse has ever since remained in the house untouched and no-one interferes to have her buried'. The guardians had refused to have anything to do with the matter because she'd been possessed of goods at the time of her death, and the authorities only acted when they feared that disease would be the result of leaving her putrefied body any longer.

In April, another '*was she murdered or was it just a tragic accident?*' poser kept the force occupied – even though the rest of the city had already made its mind up.

**No20, George Poole** who'd only joined the force five months earlier had been alerted to a body floating in Swan Pool, now the site of Sainsbury's in St Johns: '...he went through a gap in the hedge, and by means of a long pole which he procured, succeeded in bringing to the shore the body of a female. She was quite dead, and might have been so some hours. The dress of the deceased did not appear to have been disturbed, and her hair was in place. The body was seven or eight yards from the side of the pool, which is about eight feet deep in water', reported the *Herald*.

Asking questions among his colleagues, **No 8 John Doughty** said he'd seen a woman answering the same description the previous evening arm-in-arm with a man. She was later discovered to be 19-year old Caroline Williams with a reputation as something of a flighty maid, and known to consort with several of the lusty young lads with whom she was known to frequent The Bell (where she'd been the night before her death) and several gin-shops in town.

Two of her swains in particular – William Jenkins who'd 'kept company with her' for six months, and William Lampitt, both admitting to intimacy – were heavily quizzed by the police as they suspected murder, but after having heard that the deceased had threatened to take her own life on several occasions, the jury under John Hyde returned the verdict that she was 'found drowned in the Pool; but how or by what means (she) got in the Pool no satisfactory evidence has been given'.

### WORCESTER CITY POLICE.

#### MONDAY.

VIOLENT ASSAULT ON THE POLICE.—William Vaughan was charged by Police Constable Powell with assaulting him on Sunday night, in Merry-vale. Powell deposed that he was on his beat in Broad-street, about nine o'clock on the above night, when he heard a cry of murder, and on going in the direction he heard the cry come from, found the prisoner and another man fighting opposite the Hen and Chickens. He ordered them to desist and go away, when the other man ran into the Hen and Chickens, but the prisoner would not go away, and threatened to knock the policeman's eye out. On Powell attempting to take him to the station-house a struggle took place, and prisoner threw him down, and kicked him violently in the face and about his body. Complainant got up several times, but was again knocked down and kicked by the crowd. Powell's hat was also cut, apparently with some sharp instrument. Policeman Burden also deposed that he was called to the row, and found Powell bleeding on the ground by the side of the prisoner. Burden, with the assistance of another constable, succeeded in taking the prisoner into custody, and on the way to the station-house he threatened to knock Powell's brains out. Witness also stated that, on arriving at the station-house, he missed his pocket handkerchief, which was subsequently found in the prisoner's possession. The charge being fully proved, the Bench fined him £3, and, in default, he was committed to gaol for a month's hard labour, the Mayor intimating to him that he may then be brought up on the charge of stealing the handkerchief from Burden.

*PC George Powell (2nd August 1844 - 21st September 1849) appears to have been set on with a rare regularity – this instance (left) one of several, in the notorious Hen and Chickens in Merryvale in September this year.*

But for all their good deeds, intelligent sleuthing and willingness to tackle every unpleasant task hurled their way, the police still remained target #1 in all-comers' firing line, while the courts remained swamped and overburdened with hearing the never-ending stream of cases being brought before them.

It was all becoming very mundane and routine, the repetition of case after case all with the all too common thread leading the Bench to become complacent, dishing out fines in place of gaol sentences, no doubt on account of the costs of incarceration and increasing prison overcrowding.

Certainly the justices come over as being far more forgiving than the local newspapers thought seemly – *Herald* editor William Holl particularly denouncing the local Magistrates as 'soft'.

After another day of hearing yet more navvy-related incidents, the usual fine of 5s being the general outcome, he stormed '...there was not a redeeming feature in (any of) the cases and such extraordinary clemency as was extended was only calculated to give such pests of society an idea that the law is administered very favourably for their order in the city and so will, as far as it goes, promote the growth of such bad weeds in these quarters'.

Worse than that, violence directed towards the police who were battling on all fronts and not always succeeding, showed precious few signs of ever letting up. On the same mid-April night, and at the same location – the New Inn in the Shambles – two officers had been given a seeing-to in two different incidents: **PC No18 John Johnson** who was to last less than two years with the force (kicked and hammered by Richard Lockley), and **Supernumerary Frederick John Wood** (or *Hood, and yet to join the full force*) ditto by old offender James Chapman who was sent to gaol for a week.

Just a week later, another disgraceful assault, covered with almost obscene attention to detail by the 'tell-it-like-it-is' *Herald* (left).

At least no-one could turn a blind eye to the horrors awaiting almost every copper on the streets – which, thanks to the frugality of the Corporation, manpower remained at the very minimum recommended number of police per head of population; small wonder the front-line officers' frustration was plainly evident and often exploded into returns-in-kind when situations became just too heated for comfort.

## Assaults continue unabated – case after case...

In the middle of the year, **Sergeant Tommy Chipp** again found himself having to answer a charge of adrenalin-fuelled over-reaction after he'd arrested a Blockhouse leather stainer named Thomas Phelps who then accused him of insulting him in the street and tearing his waistcoat: '...the Bench having referred the matter to the Watch Committee expressed that in their opinion there was not the slightest ground for complaint against the officer, and dismissed it accordingly'

**'Grubber' – PC22 Edward Grubb** who a few years later was to go on to greater things (see p. 342) – was still allowing his heart (*or more accurately, his fists*) to rule his head when under the extreme provocation presented by near-daily events. On one occasion around the same time, the *Herald* combined editorial comment with straight reportage after his now-legendary temper had got the better of him – to the point that at first it's difficult to know whose side the *Herald* had favoured:

> **Might and right.** *A policeman ought to be a man of no passions, a perfect disciple of Loyola, in whose breast all the possible agitations of humanity have been stifled. For example, Policeman Grubb went to put an end to a row in High-street on Saturday evening but made a mistake in the party who had been fighting, upon which a man named John Clarke set up a shout of derision, in which the rest of the crowd joined in chorus. Grubb was not perfect: his bile rose and he ordered Clarke off. Clarke, however, would not go;– he was an Englishman, and why mightn't he stand where he liked as long as he liked? Grubb then proceeded to clear the street, and pushed Clarke once or twice who said if he did it again he would knock the front part of his skull in. Grubb could stand this no longer, and walked him off to the station-house. The Bench read Clarke a long lecture and fined him 1s with costs for sticking up so pugnaciously for his right to stand in the street'* (Herald)

More provocation and another paltry fine for a thug who considered the forces of law and order fair game. To make matters infinitely worse, things were far from perfect inside the Station-house too...

Instant dismissal was not always the outcome for policemen found drunk while on duty, and the Inspector and the Watch Committee could resort to other recourses at their discretion including fines – usually docking a day's pay – reprimands, and admonishments.

The available charge books contain scores of instances of officers being found drunk while on duty, and

*Extract from the Approbation Marks book entry for John Doughty, showing his first offence – the loss of his rattle, lamp and staff: it was not to be his last. See p 338. (Worcester City Council/WAAS)*

June 7th this year shows **PC John Doughty** (*appointed 14th February 1845 but destined for a stellar police career, and promotion to Station Sergeant*) was just one among many. To compound the issue he had also lost his rattle, lamp and staff – yet he was 'severely reprimanded' only, on account of being his first offence. It was not to be his last.

The fact remains that being a policeman, exposed to some of the worst elements day and night, and not knowing what dangers lurked around the next corner, was a trying business that'd test the patience of a superman, let alone a man generally of only passable intellectual powers, just about able to read and write and who'd likely been chosen for his size and ability to handle himself rather than his intelligence or well-defined powers of diplomacy and forbearance. There were exceptions, but they were precious few and far between.

One of these was demonstrably not **Richard Jackman** (*or **Jakeman** as he's reported*) who just a matter of weeks after having been promoted to PC from the ranks of the Supernumeraries found himself face-to-face with Thomas Knight of Church Walk, St Clements at closing-time one night. He was already in the process of 'escorting' another prisoner named Hardman to the Station-house on a charge of drunkenness when Knight intervened '...and charged Jakeman with ill-using Hardman, upon which he was taken into custody and a struggle ensued in the course of which, Jakeman with his staff struck the prisoner a violent blow on the side of his head and inflicted a dreadful wound, in fact nearly knocked his eye out. The prisoner was taken to the Station-house and on being brought up this morning was fined 10s and 10s expenses, and allowed seven days to pay it in' (*Herald*).

 *Noted the editor: 'After the case was over, we believe a private intimation was given to Inspector Phillips that the policemen ought not to use their staves in so violent a manner'.*

Given the amount of provocation they faced day-in, day-out, seven days a week – there was no such thing as a weekend shift or days off, for the police it was a never-ending grind – it's difficult not to side with the hard-pressed officers. The Corporation was little help and the press constantly proved ever ready to throw-in a barbed jibe about heavy-handedness and lack of self-control. But at least the Magistrates stood alone in offering a degree of support and understanding.

That was largely to be expected as they were an active party to the police's activities in what was becoming an increasingly difficult – it could almost be termed intolerable – situation on the streets.

The report of a typical Monday morning Police court at the end of this year beautifully demonstrates the variety of cases being tackled by the police over the course of just a normal weekend...

> '*This morning, that dolorous portion of the Courts of Justice called in England "The Dock" and "Bench of the Accused" in France, was crowded with a very miscellaneous assemblage of both sexes and a variety of ages from the young courtesan to the dissipated aged crone; and the youthful culprit in his teens to the used-up man of vulgar life, whose days had extended, in spite of difficulties, beyond the allotted span'.*

First up that day was a Patlander – Irishman – named James Smith '...charged with vagabondising after midnight on Saturday. He was found asleep in Cooken [Copenhagen]-street between twelve and one o'clock and on being awoke, it turned out that he was drunk. The [unnamed] policeman started him for home but a short while afterwards found him... in Bull Entry. His defence was, "If you plase, sor, oi was lost moi way an' oi kem from Dorsetshoire".

*To which the reporter had added a comment of his own: 'A Dorsetshire man speaking pure Connemara was a phenomenon worth setting free, so Mr Smith was discharged'.*

As if the hordes of fighting navvies, drunken boatmen and sadistic Militiamen hadn't already changed the character of Worcester almost beyond recognition, the previous few years had seen yet another unwelcome addition – the dreaded Irish, looking for a new start in the 'haythen counthry' after the potato famine had driven them to seek new lives elsewhere. It's hard to say how true the rumour had been that many had ended up in England because they'd heard that America lay just across the sea and had started from the wrong coast, but the fact is they were here, they were unpopular and where the Irish went, fighting was never far behind.

Those that had gravitated to Worcester had settled in the poorest area around Dolday and Merrivale in the shadow of St Andrews church where the cost of lodgings was cheap and the landlords weren't too fussed either about the origins of their tenants or where they'd found the price of a room – honest toil (*rarely*), hocussing (*mugging, often*) and begging (*mostly*).

The utter frustration of the police and their exasperation after yet another weekend of street fights and violent affrays is plainly evident in an article at the end of this year when they issued a stark warning to

## Also this year: 1848

- court held on Boxing Day '...occupied in clearing off the balance of the Christmas festivities and administering penance to those who had gone beyond the sober proprieties of joy' (Herald)

- in May, officers investigate case of 55-year old lodger at the Bear, poisoned with arsenic

- the same week, police were called to John Liley, driver of the Sovereign coach to London who'd collapsed and died in the back parlour of the Horn and Trumpet

- City Commissioners slammed for 'reprehensible nature of false economy in leaving the streets in darkness during the summer months' following a spate of burglaries

- police investigate death of baby boy found in the Severn opposite the Rectifying House, 'wrapped in a black handkerchief, having a brick weighing about 4lbs placed in it for the purpose of sinking it' (Herald). The same week, the decomposed body of a navvy aged about 30 is also dragged out of the Severn

- on a single day in June, 124 cases and several cases of summonses were heard at the city's Small Debts Court

- police investigate when 40-year old Joseph Roebuck, town councillor, manager of Pickford and Co and father of five, slashes his own throat with a razor

- 'Grubber' in more trouble for over-use of force. Fighting 'cad', ostler James Jones claims he was '...strangled till (he was) black in the face, till people shouted shame on you. You never tells us to away, but you russles us at once, like a bull at a gate, just as you likes'. Seven days hard labour for fighting

- John Phillips summons the owners of several beer houses who'd misread the terms of the new Beer Act believing they were allowed to remain open until 11pm (rather than 10pm) when the provision was for London only

- Tommy Chipp has charge brought against him for violent conduct, insulting in the street and ripping the waistcoat of Blockhouse leather stainer Thomas Phelps. Complaint dismissed after a full hearing

- spate of summertime drownings in the Severn. After one, the hat of an unidentified man is put on display at the Dog and Duck in the hope that someone might recognise it. No-one did

- ruckus at the races results in Supt Phillips being roughed up with a forceful blow to his head and one of his eyes gouged by a petty thief named Byrne, later arrested by Tommy Chipp

- midwife Elizabeth Jones charged with manslaughter after death of Ann Hill during a botched delivery

'Employers and Others' that nearly 200 Irish labourers were to be found in the city's 'dark parts'.

The day before, **Tommy Chipp**, had had to intervene after '...crowds of these men collected in idle knots on the pavement, obstructing the passage and rendering it unpleasant for people, especially females, to pass. He had to threaten a forcible clearing of the streets before he could get the men to "move on", and he believes that unless the greatest energy is displayed by the [police] force they will be unable to cope with the influx of disorderly elements'.

To which William Holl added yet another pithy post-script 'we suggest that it would be well in employers of labour to require some kind of character [reference] in persons applying for work when strangers in the city, and this irrespective of their being Irish, English or Scotch'.

Then again, the press often viewed the 'Scotch' and Irish as one and the same, considering them both as bad as each other. In one instance towards the end of the year, William Holl no doubt chose his words with a craftsman's touch in an article headlined '**The Celt Plundering the Sassenach**'. In it, he almost poetically described one Scottish marauder by name of Dick Dixon as '...a hideous, blear-eyed, red-haired hatchet-faced man'. The very last Police court of the year revealed another fascinating tale, reprinted here in full:

> '*Paddy moving. James Collins, a begging Celt caught in the act, was allowed to take himself off from the dock, on a promise to be off "afther favrin some other place, shure, wid his blessed prisince"'.*

In December, the battered body of 15-year old Mary Ann Staight had been found in a ditch near Spetchley crossroads and the tale was to enthrall the city for the next three months...

**Gained:** *Frederick John Hood, William Jordan (Extra Constable assigned to Lowesmoor Wharf), Joseph Banner, Eli Merrick, Joseph Thomas, John Willoughby, John Bennett, Ezekiel Gummery*

**Lost:** *Henry Davis, George Phillips, Robert Burden*

# 1840

Early on in the year, **PC George Powell** who was to resign in September this year had come in for a severe admonishment and warned about his future after a battling Tallow Hill housewife Mary Price charged him with assault. Called to what today would be termed a 'domestic', he found that Mary Price had already given her brother-in-law a bloody nose and was making a grab for her husband when the PC stood between them, marched her outside and, she claimed, 'shook me dreadful'.

The action then moved next door where Mary Price had removed some of her furniture to prevent it from being taken by her seemingly no-good spouse: '...I followed them upstairs in my neighbour's house and my husband being determined to remove them I broke some of the ware. Upon this the policeman threw me on the bed, knelt upon me and held me by the wrists so as to force my own nails into my neck. He threw me down the first pair of stairs, telling the neighbour in whose house we were to catch me. He did so and then pushed me out of the house. I was so excited that I could not remember anything more'.

Though she claimed **PC Powell** was 'tipsy' at the time, none of the witnesses corroborated her statement and while supporting her in the salient facts, Sarah Perkins, Betsy Perkins and Harriet Knight all played down the amount of violence used – another neighbour named Hardman additionally stating that the policeman did no more than was necessary to restrain her extreme violence.

'After a very patient hearing, the Magistrates concluded to dismiss the case, telling the policeman to go on no such errand for the future without an order from his superior'. Even so, it was publicity of a kind the force could do without.

'**Grubber**', the ever-dependable PC, soon to be Sergeant, **Edward Grubb** was still wading-in boots-first where the situation demanded it, and sometimes even where it didn't. Ever the first to be called in to sort out a tight situation, he'd been instrumental in bringing a whole catalogue of prisoners to book, few of whom had been prepared to go along quietly without some 'persuasion' from the ever up-for-it constable. It's thus inevitable that he was viewed as a legitimate target for a growing army of miffed miscreants queuing-up for their chance at revenge.

Such an opportunity arose later this year when he was escorting four prisoners accused of highway robbery from the Station-house to the Guildhall when '...a loose-looking fellow named Charles Pennell railed upon the officers and threatened to give Grubb "something for himself" ere long. Grubb had suffered the fellow's insolence for a long time patiently, but the threat of future violence was more than he chose to take without a reprisal, so he captured the fellow and brought him before their Worships'. Pennell was discharged with a warning – no doubt pending the next time.

### Another public spectacle: Robert Pulley hanged for murder

Maybe what the city needed was another visual public warning of the perils of not toeing the line – and it came on March 26th with the execution of 49-year old labourer Robert Pulley, convicted of the murder of 15-year old Mary Ann Staight the previous December. It was the first public hanging at the County Gaol in twelve years, the fortieth in its history and also the last, although hangings behind the gaol's walls continued here until well into the twentieth century.

Mary Ann's mother had died when she was eight and she'd been brought up by her aunt Mrs Roberts in Broughton (Hackett). On the afternoon of Tuesday 5th December 1848 she'd been sent to fetch some tea and sugar from the little shop at Egdon a mile away and had the misfortune of meeting up with Robert Pulley who battered her over the head with a satchel filled with stones. The following morning she was found dead in a ditch [along what's now the A44 Evesham Road about three-quarters of a mile from Spetchley crossroads] by a young lad out bird-scaring, with her provisions scattered all around her. Robert Pulley had known her and had been stalking her for some time and he was arrested the next day in Pershore after bragging that he would soon be dead and that he'd forever be remembered for what he'd done.

At his trial in the first week of March this year, he'd declined any kind of legal representation but was assigned the services of a Mr Cooke, the cost of his defence defrayed by the County Sherriff. The guilty verdict was never in doubt and came within a matter of hours, during which time Pulley had remained so impassionate and unmoved that there were fears for his sanity. Despite urgent pleas for mercy made by the City's Mayor Richard Padmore and the whole corporation, neither of the city's two MPs managed to secure any kind of commutation of the sentence and Home Secretary Sir George Grey ordered it to go ahead. As usual, Salt Lane (*now Castle Street*) was impassable for hours as whole families clamoured get a close-up view of the condemned man's dying moments: an observer put the crowd at more than 4,000 – for the most part women and children. Few were disappointed and one enterprising resident had even offered ringside seats from his home at 3d a time with the promise of 'a very good view'. Reported the *Herald*:

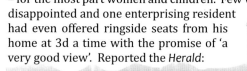

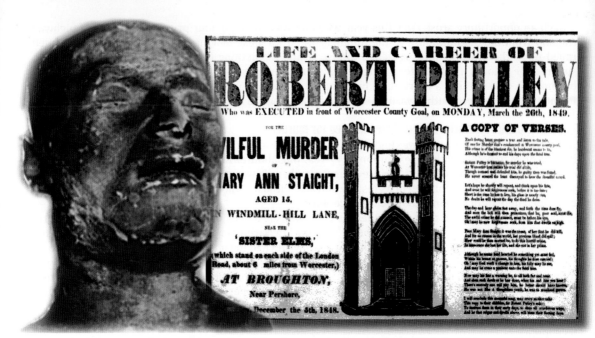

*Cast of an executed Worcester murderer's head now in the George Marshall Medical Museum. Possibly that of Robert Pulley, the marks of the rope are clearly visible*

*In about five minutes life had departed... the body having been suspended for an hour was cut down at a quarter past one, and placed in a coffin on the scaffold, in the clothes as they stood, with the exception of the shoes, which were removed. It was afterwards removed to the cell which had been last occupied by the convict, where a cast of the head was taken by Mr J Stephens, sculptor, of this City. The craniological development was as follows:– Good perceptive powers, with great firmness; destructiveness, moderate; amativeness, very large; with a considerable development of concentrativeness; benevolence moderate; and the organ of veneration appeared depressed in consequence of the extent to which firmness and self-esteem developed. It is rather singular, but philoprogenitiveness was well developed also. Time and tune there was very little of, with a moderate development of the organ of language. After it had been made thus slightly the object of science, the body was again coffined and taken to a grave dug in the north-west corner of the gaol, into which it was contained without further ceremony or funeral rite".*

Presumably, it's still there.

In life, Pulley was described as 'remarkably short (*he was four feet eight and his coffin measured four feet eleven*) and intelligent beyond his fellow workmen'. The cast of his head remains in the museum at the Infirmary. He was one of 356 committed for the same offence that year; how many murders had gone unsolved is not recorded. Additionally, there had been 573 committals for rape, 2,357 for burglary, 615 for arson and 759 for forgery. Crime remained on a steep upwards climb.

In the city, the early months had also seen a major epidemic of housebreakings, causing the police to issue a warning to householders and shopkeepers about the 'large number of thieves and rogues in the city, for the purpose of pursuing their avocations'.

It's likely that word had spread that policing in Worcester was no longer what it had been, and that the odds of being caught and subsequently punished had favourably lengthened.

In May, ever-dependable **Sergeant Joe Hall** died of fever after he'd plunged into the Severn in another selflessly heroic bid to rescue a would-be suicide. Within weeks his widow was forced to contact the City Council for distress assistance and was referred to one of the charitable organisations as a deserving case. *Then, what many had been anticipating for some time...*

**Insp John Phillips**, born 1805, died after several intermittent bouts of illness on Wednesday July 4th. He'd been police chief for 9 years and four months and his funeral at the burial ground at Tallow Hill (*now the municipal car park of the same name*) was pegged for the following Sunday when not only the whole of the police force turned out in solemn procession, but so did a large crowd of spectators.

Neither the *Journal* nor the *Herald* appear particularly moved by his passing: the *Journal* scarcely made any reference at all while the *Herald*'s response (*below*) was similarly muted, dismissing the announcement of his death in just five lines, while the same edition carried a 15-line article on the passing of local circuit judge Mr Justice Coltman who'd died of cholera on the same day at the age of 69.

Whether or not the cause of John Phillips' death had also been cholera is no known for sure but the disease had swept through the city, carrying off dozens of folks particularly in the vicinities of Copenhagen Street and Diglis: it had also appeared at the Workhouse, with three new cases and several deaths reported in the same week as **John Phillips**' passing.

The fact is that he was he was unlikely to be missed: he'd been an absentee chief for much of the previous two years, his role carried out in all but name (*but not rank or pay*) by **Sergeant Tommy Chipp** who, it was thought, would step up to the now-vacant post of chief almost as a matter of course.

It was not to be quite so cut-and-dried, and the next four months were to see Worcester City Police brought to the very brink of extinction...

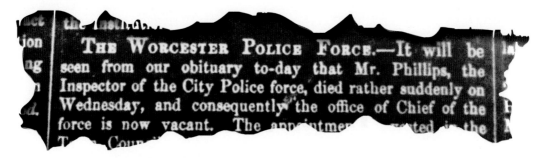

THE WORCESTER POLICE FORCE.—It will be seen from our obituary to-day that Mr. Phillips, the Inspector of the City Police force, died rather suddenly on Wednesday, and consequently the office of Chief of the force is now vacant. The appointme...

## Also this year: 1849

- police investigate suicide of painter George Insull who'd poisoned himself after earlier attempts at drowning and slashing his throat had failed

- Tommy Bateman rumbles gambling den at the Mitre in Lich Street

- Worcester calculated as having 38,000 yards of streets, courts and alleys

- boat hauler William Dowling gaoled for a month for assaulting veteran PC George Williams before John Doughty comes to his rescue. Tied to a truck for transport to the station house, he slips his waistcoat and jumps into the river

- 'smashing' rife in the city, credible counterfeit half sovereigns (10s/50p) in wide circulation

- three men including George Evans, boots at the Unicorn, charged with interfering with the police after PC George Poole who was to quit not long afterwards, is roughed-up by a crowd attempting to rescue a prisoner he had in his custody

- summertime sees an escalation in burglaries and deaths by drowning in the city

- Sgt Tommy Bateman leads an anti-vice team to storm the Lord Nelson in Birdport and finds eight prostitutes and a dozen men

- unnamed PC investigates wanton mutilation of horses at Sir Offley Wakeman's house The Blanquettes

- the same week sees the start of investigations into two more child murders in the city

- Clever detective work traps the Jones Gang, headed by three brothers Sidney, Lindley and Leonard who'd waged a long campaign of terror, robbery and extortion

- parents advised to soak children's night-clothes in a strong solution of alum, following a spate of accidents and deaths in fires

- Edwin Jones appears in court '...with his face curiously veined with scratches which came to a focus at the corner of his mouth, the extreme point of the chin was also bitten off' – punishment meted out by two women for assaulting his wife

- crime wave hits the city, 'thieves and rogues' gaining entry to properties by prising open cellar gratings

# 7:
# The Chipp years

## 21st November 1849 – March 16th 1861

The vacancy created by **John Phillips'** passing started an instant media war of words with the following Thursday's *Journal* urging the Town Council to look to London and the Metropolitan Police for his replacement – a strong indication that outspoken Harvey Tymbs considered the force to be failing in its allotted role under **John Phillips** and erstwhile **Tommy Chipp,** and now needed a firmer hand in the superior's seat.

The *Herald* two days later, took an entirely different stance, describing the *Journal's* call as 'a very extraordinary course' and criticising its rival for its gall in offering even a word of advice or suggestion to the Town Council.

In William Holl's eyes, Worcester-born-and-bred **Sgt. Tommy Chipp** was the man for the job, and he stated his case in no uncertain terms:

> '...we should not have deemed it necessary to interpose a word of advice or suggestion as
> to their [the Council's] choice in filling up the office, but for the fact that in a contemporary
> a very extraordinary course has been recommended. The Worcester Journal advises
> the authorities to engage one of the Metropolitan police "regardless of expense"; and to
> encourage Mr Sgt Chipp by raising his pay to the salary of the late Inspector. Now even if
> these were times of as great prosperity and plentifulness of money among the rate-payers as

this Committee. It recommended that th
les at present receiving 16s. a week sho
ded into three classes; the first to receive
ond 16s. 6d., and the third 15s. The f
iled that the Committee had unanim
Superintendent Mr. Chipp to head the
weekly salary of 32s., taking effect fro
January, 1850. Some discussion was ri

*they are notoriously the reverse, we would object to such a course, because a Metropolitan police officer could bring nothing with him to Worcester appertaining to the efficient discharge of the office of Inspector which may not be learned in this city; while he would labour under the very serious disadvantage of being entirely deficient in local knowledge. Besides, from many years' observation of the manner in which Sgt Chipp has discharged his duties as second officer of the force, we are satisfied in bearing our testimony, such as it is, to his perfect fitness to perform efficiently the office of Inspector. His local knowledge cannot be excelled; his general acquaintance with the duties of Chief of Police of a city or a district, we believe to be quite equal to that of most persons that could be selected from the Metro force itself, and his character for steadiness, sobriety and general good conduct are entirely satisfactory. In these circumstances we shall indeed be surprised if the authorities follow the advice so strangely volunteered by our contemporary'.*

As it transpired, his words turned out to be prophetic – but in the meantime, the vacancy had also sparked-off a yet another renewed request from an unwelcome area, Worcestershire Police – and this time it appears that the City was edging towards caving-in and throwing-in its lot with the larger force...

### Worcestershire Constabulary's renewed amalgamation calls come close to succeeding

Its Chief Constable, Richard Reader Harris had been fuming at the rebuff he'd been given the last time of asking for an amalgamation of the two distinct police bodies, and he wasted no time in penning his official letter to Mayor Richard Padmore, repeating his view that the vacancy now presented another not-to-be-missed opportunity for amalgamation and setting-out the perceived advantages of such a move.

He was, he said, satisfied that it would lead to the suppression and detection of a great deal of crime, and would promote the efficiency of the officers. In a bid calculated to appeal to the council's perpetually-fretting financial decision-makers, he added that the move would additionally result in a saving to the city of £200-£300 a year.

Given so powerful a set of arguments *for* the proposed 'marriage', it's clear that at least a proportion of the City members were now becoming inclined to go along with the suggestion, and the *Herald* was urged to comment two weeks after John Phillips' death that: '...we are requested to mention that the appointment of Serjeant Chipp to the Inspectorship of the [City] Police force is merely temporary, the Watch Committee *contemplating a new arrangement with the view of putting the force on a different footing'.*

The debate appears to have raged on for months, during which time Worcester City Police came within an ace of losing its hard-won identity. But again, reported the *Herald*, the final Council debate held to thrash-out the issue once and for all, proved to be 'desultory' with the leading speakers coming out strongly *against* surrendering the privilege and power of self-government, and the merger was again rejected. It had been four months since John Phillips had died, and now the *Herald* summed it up in five perfectly-chosen words representing journalism at its tersest and best: 'Unanimous, and the subject dropped'.

But once again, it had been a close-call, and Richard Reader Harris' response can only be imagined.

The *Herald*'s earlier foresight now proved accurate and **Sergeant Thomas Chipp** who'd joined the New Police in the fourth intake on September 23rd 1836 and had been acting Inspector during **John Phillips'** intermittent absences, was nominally appointed Inspector on 21st November although his official start date was set five weeks ahead at January 1st 1850. The Watch Committee's decision had eventually proved unanimous although there had been dissent from some members: as the *Herald* put it 'some discussion ensued upon the merits of the arrangement' and it's likely this was in consequence of his proposed new salary, 32s a week, almost double his previous sergeant's rate.

Despite the usual tight-fistedness entrenched within the Council and the clear economic pressures facing the city and the nation as a whole, the Committee also took the advantage of the change at the top to review the salaries of other ranks. The course they chose was a first at the time, and not without merit, literally and metaphorically...

In place of all constables receiving the same 16s a week regardless of personal qualities or length of service, they now devised a new three-tier arrangement of First, Second and Third Class constables at 18s, 16s 6d and 15s a week.

The number-crunchers also looked rather sniffily at a letter written by **John Phillips**' widow 39-year old Mary Ann claiming that her husband's death had left her in an almost destitute condition and that as she was incapacitated by illness from finding any employment, would the Council be so kind as to assist in placing her in some small way of business, or provide for her in any manner it might think fit?

No it wouldn't, came the reply – probably a reflection of their opinion that the force had been under-achieving in recent years under her late husband's absenteeism, although mayor John Wheeley Lea volunteered to head a subscription on her behalf. At least it covered the cost of his burial.

Now former Sergeant, **Tommy Chipp** was officially the new chief: he was one of the lads, he'd proved himself in many a set-to on the streets, he had their respect, and he was the fourth to be appointed to the role. But before the appointment became absolute, there were still 40 days to the end of the year.

Christmas Eve was, according to the *Herald:*

> *'...never more noisy than the one just passed. Bacchanalians of all degrees seemed to occupy the streets from midnight to morn and parties of singers, dancers, shouters and mere noise-makers contributed to a jumble of very frightful dreams in those good citizens' heads who managed to sleep at all, but we think this must have been a very diminutive minority. In (a riot in Dolday) which Sergeant Tommy Bateman was trying to quell, one man named Edward Maund came up to him and with an evident view to make confusion worse confounded, accused the sergeant of robbing him of a pocket handkerchief. Bateman pushed him away, and happening to be drunk, he necessarily followed the laws of inert matter, by tumbling lengthways into the gutter. When he recovered his perpendicular, he heaped on the officer a torrent of abuse, which the latter at last ended by walking him to the station-house. Just as they arrived there, a woman rushed up and declared they shouldn't lock her darling up or she would be locked up with him. As she too was drunk and of foul speech, the police accommodated her also, and there they both spent a very dummy Christmas Day'.*

The following morning, Boxing Day, each received seven day's imprisonment.

On the last day of the year, a thief broke into the Railway office in Broad Street and stole a cash box and some loose change, having removed a pane of glass from a window shared with the Unicorn Hotel.

January 1st saw **Tommy Chipp** formally take up his office as Superintendent of Worcester City Police. The same week saw 9 new paupers admitted to the Workhouse, 4 discharged, 2 inmates giving birth and 1 death. The so-called House of Industry housed 287 unfortunate souls – 58 fewer than the corresponding period the previous year. During the year, 2,577 Worcester beggars had asked for assistance via the Mendicity Society, 1,294 beggars had been relieved with provisions, and 202 with provisions and lodgings. All this on an income of £63.

Almost immediately the new chief was in trouble with the magistrates when he was personally sued by a horse dealer named Dee for the return of £8 8s he'd confiscated after a fracas following a failed deal in the Cross Keys in Sidbury. It wasn't until the end of a lengthy court case which the police chief's main witness had failed to attend that it was revealed that he had, in fact, returned the money to the injured party. *But it was not the best of starts.*

Nor did it take long for the usual crop of anti-social situations to pick up and gather momentum on the streets.

On his first night on the Worcester beat after serving with Birmingham City Police, the newest recruit **PC Richard Edmund**s (*or Edmonds*) got himself badly beaten-up in Powick Lane where several gangs

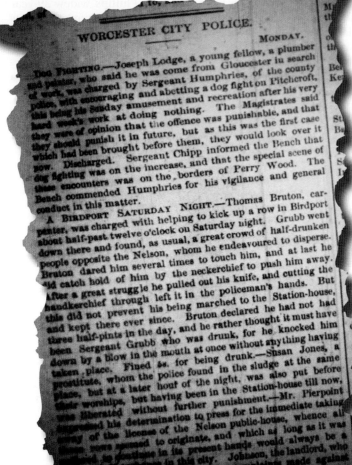

*Just another Saturday night in downtown Worcester, 1850*

had gathered for a mass pitched-battle of their own. He'd stumbled on several fights going on but instead of turning and running when they saw the new beat bobby approaching, the large crowd – none of whom had ever seen him before and, because he was so new, wasn't wearing the requisite uniform trousers, although he was wearing his numbered top-coat and carrying the standard police lanthorn – the pugilists and their spectators alike forgot their differences and turned their attentions to the new constable *en masse.*

His presence had angered those that thought he was a policeman and those that thought he was an imposter. While very severely bashed about, he remained with the force, but left after 2 years. It's interesting to note that his previous spell with Birmingham City Police had lasted 7½ years – the assumption being that he'd come to Worcester for a more sedate life. *If only he'd known...*

Just a few weeks later, **Sergeant Thomas Bateman** was stabbed by a tailor after being called on to turn him out of a house in Clap-gate. For a while it was touch-and-go whether or not he would survive the life-threatening injuries he sustained, but though he remained off-work for some months, they eventually put an end to his police career.

### 'Grubber' gets his come-uppance

It was all-but inevitable, but about the same time, **'Grubber'** finally got his come-uppance – albeit at the hands of **three** people, not normally a bar to his securing his quarry but this time one was armed with a lethal weapon. Reports the *Herald* (*reprinted here in full*):

> **Brutal Conduct**. *Between twelve and one o'clock on Sunday morning, as two men and a woman were quarrelling in High-street, Sergeant Grubb interfered and requested them all to go home. This appears to have provoked the men, both of whom, after much abuse, attacked the officer, and one of them struck him a severe blow on the cheek with a large stone which he held in his hand, and which was afterwards found to weigh nearly two pounds. The brute ran off and was followed, but Grubb was too much injured to keep up the pursuit and thus both fellows have for the present escaped but we trust they will soon be in the hands of justice. We are sorry to say that Grubb was severely injured'*

As is still the way of official bodies, figures and statistics are life-blood: performance needed to be scrutinised, reviewed and revised on a regular basis – then, much as now, so as to keep people in a job. At the end of **Tommy Chipp's** first year in office, the tally was calculated and taking all factors into account, his

# Also this year: 1850

- **murder by opium poisoning suspected when 70-year old Matthew Doughty is found dead and rumours circulate that his son had administered the fatal dose. Verdict: 'Died by visitation of God'**

- **organised dogfighting on the increase in Worcester with 'encounters' at Pitchcroft and on the outskirts of Perry Wood**

- **the ancient Worcestershire games of bowls and quoits under threat following renewed police vigilance against skittles and nine-pin bowling in City public houses**

- **skins and hides left on the pavements in the Shambles '...present a filthy spectacle, cause confusion and danger, and are intolerably offensive to the olfactory nerves of every one within a moderate distance of the disgusting heap' according to the Herald. Police also given authority to clamp down on '...a species of street music calculated to drive people crazy – such as hurdy-gurdies, bagpipes and ground-down barrel-organs and the sooner they are put down, the better'**

- **calls to suppress the number of brothels in Worcester gains momentum and the police charged with keeping a closer watch on their activities. A Street Walker's List is prepared, noting all the fallen women 'registered' to the profession**

- **'young boy' named Ford sentenced to fortnight's gaol and a whipping for stealing lead from the roof of a blacksmith's shop in the Blockhouse**

- **spate of drownings in the canal at Sidbury, the latest being the 4-year old daughter of the landlord of the Cross Keys in Friar Street, prompts magistrates to issue call for improved safety measures**

- **salary of the City Bridewell Gaoler and keeper is revealed as £300 – the same as the Chaplain. The Surgeon receives £125**

- **Worcester's newly-appointed Inspector of Nuisances removes 50 improperly-sited pig-sties in clamping down on 178 reported nuisances in his first few weeks in office**

performance rolled-out as good – so good, in fact, that the Watch Committee took the entirely unexpected step of awarding him a surprise salary increase. Nor was it just a token amount: the main recommendation to the Town Council was that it should be upped from 32s a week to 40s – a 25% pay rise in just his first year that had also seen a near-doubling in income from his 18s a week Sergeant's pay.

It was a tangible expression of the high esteem they'd very quickly come to hold him in and, so far as the Council was concerned, vindication of their decision to promote from within, much against the *Journal's* plea for a tough import from the capital. Chief among their stated reasons was that he had brought the police force into 'an excellent state of discipline' – a rare feat, given the liking for booze and diffidence that had come to characterise a higher proportion of its front-liners than **Tommy Chipp** might have liked: that very same week **PC John Doughty** had again been found drunk on duty and severely reprimanded for not coming to morning muster.

There was, of course, another determining factor – the small matter of the £200 savings he'd delivered to the body corporate via some unspecified 'judicious arrangements' – one of which was the establishment of the superannuation fund in March that already amounted to £38 12s 6d. *One small catch: he wouldn't get it straight away, but they would be mindful at some stage in the future.*

At least, there was some immediate compensation...

Having checked-out the salaries of the heads of police in comparable-sized towns of Gloucester, Shrewsbury, Leicester and Wolverhampton, finance bosses in the city were no doubt horrified to discover that with the exception of Shrewsbury, all were on significantly higher rewards. Having arguably done the dirty on him in respect of his pecuniary rewards, the Committee instantly felt obliged to make an almost derisory token award of 10 Gns 'in respect of the lowness of his salary hitherto'.

It's interesting to note that recruitment this year – 11 new constables 3rd Class: **Charles Partington, Richard Edmonds, William Holtham, William Brooks, Thomas Hawker, Philip Derry, Frederick Hardy, Eli Emanuel Hughes, James Clarke, George Wadley and William Presdee,** almost all of whom had originally served as Supernumeraries – was the highest in the force's history thus far.

It's also notable that they were all brought in to replace officers who'd left.

What delights might 1851 have in store...?

As usual, the issue of the force's clothing supplies occupied a few column inches in the year's first editions.

'The Watch Committee of this city on Friday last fixed upon the following tradesmen to supply each member of the city Police force with the following clothing viz:– a body coat and two pairs of trousers for £3, Mr William Humphries Angel-street; a hat for 8s 6d., Mr William Wilks, High-street; and a pair of shoes for 10s, Mr John Booker, St Clements-square'.

At the same time it was revealed that there had been 591 deaths in Worcester the previous year.

A report early in the year showed that there were around 13,000 policemen in England and Wales, but despite some notable successes locally and nationally, there was still no legal compulsion on local authorities to establish police forces, and some had proved remarkably slow on the uptake.

Locally, while the navvies' work was largely at an end with the completion of the Severn Improvement Works – mercifully leading to a large-scale exodus from the city as they wandered off in search of work elsewhere – a small army of labourers still remained for the maintenance and upkeep of new railway lines and this had soured much of the relief felt by their departure.  Accordingly, conditions facing the front-line police officers remained tense and unpredictable.

In the first week of the year, the police were called on to halt a bull 'of very red colour' that had gone on the rampage along Sidbury and up the High Street where it was cornered and shot.

Yet again, **'Grubber'** – now promoted to Sergeant and well-deserved too – stole the headlines early in the year when he was set upon by a mob while tackling a desperate and violent drunk named William Hughes who was so intent on resisting arrest that even the hard-man Sergeant had trouble quietening him down.

Coming off much the worst against Hughes and his rabble-rousing mates, he charged a bystander named Henry Davis to aid and assist him in the name of the law – a legal requirement when called on:

> '...Davis refused to do so and instead, rather incited the people to resist the officers.  It appeared that Davis had been a Supernumerary Police-officer at one time.  The magistrates ordered him to be summoned to show cause why he ought not to be punished for his refusal to aid the police and stated that all persons should know that it is illegal to refuse their assistance when charged in aid of keeping the Queen's peace'.

Henry Davis had clearly not been cut out as a fearless have-a-go police hero: his term as a Supernumerary had lasted a shade over two months from starting to quitting (*31st December 1847 – 10th March 1848*).

The census on Sunday 30th to Monday March 31st March, shows 42-year old **Tommy Chipp**, profession Superintendent of Police, living at the Police Station-House at 1 Queen Street with his wife Ann who appears to have gained four years more than her husband aged 46 (*the previous census 10 years earlier had showed them both aged 30)*; children Lucy (15), Edward, scholar (11), and younger children William, Alfred and Ann.  Also living here was house-servant Mary Harper, 21 and 'passing through' (ie: in gaol, possibly just for the night but maybe for a longer term) prisoners Elizabeth Child (24), Benjamin Preece (43), William Greenway (48), Mary Berry (14) and Ellen Butler (21).

Next door at number 3 resided **Edward Grubb**, Sergt of Police (42) his wife Mary (46) and their niece, farmer's daughter Elizabeth Jones.

The census showed that the City's population was 27,528: 12,401 males and 15,127 females.

There was more evidence of **Tommy Chipp's** concern for abandoned youngsters when he took into custody, for his own safety as much as anything else  '...a poor little wretch, a boy of 8 years old, found wandering about on Saturday with no other clothing than a ragged shirt, (who) said he got his living from singing, sometimes earning 6d and the most he ever earned was 2s 6d'.

A fine example of reporting a total non-story also appeared in the *Herald* about this time: *'The business before the Bench today was of no interest'.*  Ho-hum.

At the races this year, supernumerary **PC Michael Cusack** who'd joined in March was set on by 'a gang of profligate vagabonds who used him very violently finishing by perpetrating a most filthy act in his hat'.

It was never proved if a man named Philip Boucher was the man who'd done the dirty in the police headgear, but the very sight of him in Queen Street a few weeks later prompted the rookie bobby to lash out at the man who he'd suspected as having humiliated him in the eyes and the public and worse, his mates at the station house.

His action sparked off a full-scale ruckus that immediately escalated into **Cusack** also laying flat Peacock landlord Charles Hughes who'd come out to see what the commotion was all about. With upwards of a dozen men now laying into the constable, it was only with the intervention of **PC15 Joe Banner** that the mob was broken up. Boucher was sentenced to 14 days' hard, Cusack immediately quit the force. He'd been a bobby for nine months.

With the navvies largely gone and life settling down to some semblance of normality – such as it was in a still-volatile city that was growing outwards in every direction and beginning to take on the look of a smoke-belching industrial metro-land – an issue that had always been there without troubling the courts overmuch until now, began to make its unruly presence felt. Kids.

*Gained:* Jesse Frankling (quit after14 days), Michael Cusack (also quit in December), George Sanders

## Also this year: 1851

◼ in the first Police court of the year, Tommy Chipp himself testifies against a man named Fuller who'd hit his wife so hard in a heated 'domestic' that he'd knocked her eye out

◼ PC Richard Edmonds is knocked down and kicked when he caught Thomas Jones, a groom at the Angel 'with his mouth grimly applied to the cask (of cider)'. One month's hard

◼ magistrates throw out a case of two prostitutes, Pratt (first name not listed) and Mary Bromwich found fighting '...but there was immediately disclosed so much immorality on the part of the complainant that the Magistrates would not entertain the matter further (Journal)

◼ criticism for police after bringing would-be self-poisoner David Howell to the station-house and left overnight to 'sleep it off'

◼ police arrest John Collins, son of former Angel St Johns landlord Joseph Collins for murder after his friend is shot

◼ police ordered to keep special watch on boys congregating on the bridge and dropping large stones on pleasure steamers passing underneath

◼ Sgt Tommy Bateman, called in to the Barracks brothel in Watercourse Alley finds Mary Ann Bush with her throat cut and her attacker, labourer John Waters in the process of slashing his own throat

◼ PC James Workman arrests 17-year old William Pearse for arson after the Fish Inn in Friar Street is almost destroyed by fire; Sgt Tommy Bateman investigates rape of 7-year old Mary Devereaux in St Johns

◼ PC John Doughty testifies to finding body of Charles Reeve who'd slashed his throat and bled to death over fears of missing money

◼ drunk Charles Crockett accuses Sgt Bateman of stealing a valuable recipe for ginger-beer while in the station-house

◼ on the same day in October PC22 Philip Derry and PC12 George Sanders are beaten up by men they'd arrested

◼ two days later Derry is fiercely attacked by prostitute Hannah Hitchens who'd lain down in Phillips's butchers in Little Angel Street after he'd been called in to remove her

◼ PC14 Richard Edmunds summoned by young lad Henry Burrows to take charge of a baby's body dragged from the canal near Gas-hill (Rainbow Hill) bridge. The next day Supt Chipp stated that Hannah Sharp had been arrested on a charge of murdering her new-born son. Discharged on lack of evidence

◼ PC17 (later Sergeant) Herbert May Evans and John Doughty both severely hammered after being sent in to the Hen and Chickens to disrupt an organised mill (prizefight) being held there and the crowds then turned on them

Under the headline **'Street Pests'** an early *Herald* edition this year commented that: '...Young Worcester was probably never so bad as at the present time: the precocity in mischief of every kind of young rascal is absolutely stupefying and would require the entire devotion of a special police... and it is bewildering to a degree to imagine what level of badness future generations may attain'.

Prophetic, given that this was a century before the phrases 'teenagers' and 'juvenile delinquents' had been coined.

The report went on to list several nasty incidents involving minors including one of a boy named Carwardine 'a habitual pest of the Butts and Shaw-street' who'd set a dog on another boy, while adult families in and around Little Park Street had organised themselves into vigilante groups to tackle 'a daily species of martyrdom from the tricks of the idle juvenility of the place'.

*Contemporary Punch cartoon, entitled 'The Advantage of taking a Shortcut Through a Court'.*

*(Reproduced with permission)*

A growing menace common on nearly every street and the scourge of every bobby on the beat in every quarter of the city was the incidence of boys playing a popular game called Tip-cat – but try as they might to make examples of the hordes of youngsters, some as young as 8, daily threatening people and property with their antics, it was like pouring water into a bottomless bucket.

When a 10-year old, Patrick Glover, was hauled up in court, the Magistrates hoped to make a stark example of him, thereby allowing the *Herald* to run a complementary description of the sport's finer points:

*'...it is played by striking a cylindrical bit of wood about three inches long, and pointed at both ends, on one end, so that it flies up from the ground and then the player hits it while in the air with a bat, sending it sharply, point foremost, in any direction. When played in a thoroughfare, it is very dangerous to passers-by and indeed many persons have been injured by it. Glover [the 8-year old brought before the court to be made an example of] was frightened out of his senses almost, and let off without further punishment, but all "tip-cat" players had better take notice that the police have orders to apprehend anyone found offending in this way; and that none hereafter shall escape fine or imprisonment on conviction'.*

It had little effect: later in the year, naval officer Admiral Powell had been thrown from his horse in the city after it had been struck by a tipped 'cat'. While calls were renewed for the police to drag-in all offenders, Police Magistrate Charles Sidebottom advised the Mayor to circulate handbills warning that the same fate awaited all boys so offending.

The old childish misdemeanour of ringing bells and running away also continued to be a repetitive nuisance – oddly enough in Worcester a favourite pastime of raucous adults after a night's boozing. On October 24th **PC Herbert May Evans** was commended for his role in apprehending three men '...from disorderly conduct in the streets and ringing bells and destroying bell pulls'. He was awarded 10/- for his 'fidelity and extraordinary diligence' on the occasion.

December 10th this year also saw the appointment of a remarkable officer.

The city would long have cause to remember **PC** (*later Detective and then Superintendent in his own right*) **William Richardson...**

At the end of the year, *Herald* Editor William Holl yet again came out fighting against over-lenient sentences being handed down by the Bench. After another soft sentence (*in this instance 16-year old 'Juvenile Savage' Josiah Griffiths, fined 10s or gaoled for 14 days for beating up a younger boy*) he wrote:

> '...a private flogging would have been less dangerous and more punishing. Daily floggings in private, bread and water diet with hard labour, might affect a man by fear; mere imprisonment without labour, good lodging and a fair diet which the law as it stands orders, seem rather like an encouragement for his criminality rather than punishment'.

**Gained:** *Henry Smith, Thomas Goodyear, William Walker, John Cecil, James Burrow, Thomas Moule, John Etheridge, Richard Jones (none of whom were to last the year), Andrew Hooper, George Archer, Richard Bennett, John Pitt, Samuel Twigg, William Richardson*

**Lost:** *William Presdee, Philip Derry (no22)*

## Also this year: 1852

- *in the same week (May), the New Music Hall (later Public Hall) opens in the Cornmarket, and floods devastate the city – the river level coming to within a couple of feet of the 1795 plaque (then the highest reach of flood water)*

- *four bobbies, unnamed with the exception of Sgt Doughty, attempt to take prize-fighter James Smith into custody for attacking his wife, who then attacked them all with a poker*

- *Sgt Grubb arrests servant Sarah Poulteney for concealment of birth after a baby's body is found in a mixen (dung-heap) at the Bird-in-Hand on the Cross*

- *PC2 James Workman testifies in the case of 18-year old Henry Farley found guilty of stealing a handkerchief and transported for seven years*

- *St Johns tailor James Jones prefers to pay £4 fine and expenses rather than a month's imprisonment for hammering Sergeant Bateman who was attempting to search him after being found 'melancholy drunk' in Broad Street. It was his second attack in similar circumstances in a matter of weeks*

- *on the same day in July police recover two bodies dragged out of the Severn in separate incidents. One was 14-year old Edward Price, the other was an unidentified child sewn up in a cloth bag brought back by a terrier dog that had been thrown a stick to fetch*

- *known Birmingham thieves offer a pair of stolen gun barrels to a man they met in the bar of the Golden Lion in High Street – sadly for them, it was Tommy Chipp himself!*

- *Chipp also plays highly visible role in policing Worcester races. Not a single misdemeanour reached the courts*

- *on the last day of the year PC John Bennett apprehended (as the Herald reported 'seized by the throat') suspected thief George Belcher who'd tried to swallow the evidence – a half-crown, four shillings and two sixpences.*

While life continued in much the same vein and at much the same breakneck (*no pun intended*) pace as in previous years, Worcester City police appear to have been chipping away (*another pun, this time wholly intended*) at consolidating its role and getting to grips with the job of keeping a still largely lawless city on the straight-and-narrow, and at last signs were emerging that they were beginning to make some headway – at least so far as was humanly possible given their limited resources and inadequate financial backing.

Much of this must be put down to the quality of the new recruits coming up through the ranks: rarely now would the force be content to take on any volunteer who'd wandered in off the streets and asked for a job, and this is probably one of the greatest legacies of **Tommy Chipp.**

Having been there, done that and knew the score, he was proving selective in his choice of men and the force was now reaping the benefits. 1852 had seen the highest number of new recruits ever – 14 between February and December, just two less than the entire complement the New Police had stood at just 16 years before.

**William Richardson,** appointed on December 10th the previous year was a remarkable find and his progress proved equally outstanding: he was raised to PC 2nd Class just three months after being appointed, and 1st Class just a few weeks after that (April 15th).

February 18th this year saw another remarkable and equally outstanding new recruit **Benjamin Holmes,** standing at 6' 7". He was also raised to PC 2nd Class in April this year (the 29th – two weeks after **William Richardson**, but after only two months as PC 3rd Class).

This year was also to see the selection of two more exceptional constables – from an intake of just five – who would go on to earn a high reputation with their colleagues and with the world at large: **John Hunting** and **Charles Vaughan**, about both, more later.

### 'Chipper' proves shrewd organiser and judge of character

It was already evident that despite the *Journal's* unwarranted fears, **Tommy Chipp** was turning into a shrewd organiser and judge of character at a time that the force needed it the most.

March 18th saw PCs **John Doughty** and **Herbert May Evans** appointed Sergeants, moves also proving popular with the men. As **Tommy Chipp** had by now come to realise, with the right people behind you, anything's possible. Even, some day, taming Worcester.

Overall, this was shaping up to be a year of good, steady progress for Worcester City Police – a fact that wasn't going unnoticed by their County counterparts in Salt Lane or by the City's go-ahead mayor, ironfounder and factory boss Richard Padmore now in his second year as mayor (*he'd first served 1852-3*) and was to go on to greater things including Governorship of Worcester City and County Bank, and Liberal MP for Worcester.

That said, for the police the road ahead was a rocky path strewn with some disheartening set-backs along the way...

On May 27th **PC William Richardson** had been severely censured and fined 5/- for interfering with boat–owner, publican and well-connected man-about-town Thomas Maybury on his way home '... and assaulting and ill-treating him at half past two o'clock this morning while on duty'. Some people thought themselves above the law and immune to the attentions of its officers.

*WCiCo/WAAS*

Then a few weeks later, more of the kind of publicity only the anti-police faction wanted to see... two coppers, **PC20 Andrew Hooper** and **PS3 George Williams**, slugging it out in front of a crowd of onlookers. To make matters worse, Hooper was much younger than his superior who'd already logged more than 20 years service, while he had only been lifted from the ranks of the Supernumeraries three months earlier. It sounds very much though, that the experienced and super-dependable **George Williams** who was to go on another six years with the force, got the better of the hot-headed young upstart and gave him something of a sharp public humiliation because Hooper, seemingly the instigator whose conduct, commented the *Herald,* was 'of the most reprehensible kind' was fined 10s and ordered to be restored to duty only after being severely admonished by the Mayor as to his future conduct.

*Then a bit of a blow...* 'Grubber' was leaving the force, and the city, after almost ten years in the thick of things: he'd been appointed Superintendent of the Hereford Division of Police and was Worcester's loss. He was going to be a hard act to follow. Immediately, his mates at the Station-house opened a subscription for 'a suitable testimonial of respect on the occasion of his leaving this city'.

By the end of the year, explosive growth in the city had led to the police:population ratio sinking to well short of the recommended level. London could count on 1 officer per 225 souls; Dublin 1:273; Glasgow 1:537; Bristol 1:564; Manchester 1:675; Birmingham 1:712; Liverpool 1:761; and Newcastle-upon-Tyne 1:1,100.

By comparison, Worcester stood at 1:1,500 and barely surprisingly, things were starting to get out of hand again.

After a spate of brutal street robberies – what would today be called 'mugging' but was then popularly known as hocusing – the *Herald* penned an altogether new term for the growing trend that was beginning to cast a dark shadow over the city and reflect badly on its image: 'thugging'.

In a hard-hitting editorial commenting on the state of affairs on the streets, the *Herald* came out highly critical of the police's failure to get to grips with the worsening situation, Irish labourers living 'in dark parts of Worcester' said to be between Blackfriars-alley and Newport-street and Broad-street to the Butts, blamed for most of the action.

*Gained: Benjamin Holmes, John Hunting, Jesse Sanday, William Hall, Charles Vaughan (see p 155)*
*Lost: Samuel Twigg, John Pitt, Edward Grubb*

## Also this year: 1853

■ *Sarah Sirrell accuses Sergeant Bateman of being drunk when she handed in a watch left behind by a client from the previous evening. When she admitted to being a prostitute, she was disbelieved and shown the way out*

■ *veteran Sgt George Williams praised for talking his next door neighbour in Pheasant Street, George Ricketts, out of hanging himself*

■ *Supt Chipp and PC (later Sergeant) Herbert May Evans weren't so timely. Called in to break down a door at the New Greyhound they were too late to save 37-year old George Woolf from poisoning himself with a fatal dose of acid*

■ *PC10 John Bennett proves himself a scourge of erring publicans with a spate of reports on licensees keeping irregular hours, earning himself a reputation as an over-zealous snoop*

■ *Supernumerary PC John Hunting savagely assaulted by 'A Rough One' Thomas Crane who'd already beaten up a soldier and the landlord of the Gloucester Arms in Copenhagen Street, but put up such a commendable fight he's admitted as a full PC within weeks (June)*

■ *unnamed PCs halt attempted murder of a woman by her husband James Jones just returned to the city after 7 years' transportation to Australia. During his absence she'd had two more children*

■ *Supt Chipp warns that the force is unable to cope with the influx of 'disorderly elements' – a reference to Irish and Scots immigrants*

■ *mayor Richard Padmore offers £30 reward for information on assault of Rev George St John in Britannia Square, adding to £10 already offered by the police*

■ *Herald report 'A Queer Lot' reveals that on the same day 'a bronze black-tressed Hindu, a red-haired Irishwoman and a blue-eyed English girl occupied the dock in a batch this morning' (August)*

■ *Herald editor William Holl again criticises police for 'appearing to take no notice of harpies of their class, [ie prostitutes] who prowl every night on Worcester bridge'*

■ *Tommy Chipp ordered by the mayor, acting on a request from Captain Lavie, to caution every pawnbroker in the city about receiving militia uniforms, pledged by deserting soldiers*

There's every chance that the *Herald* journalist behind a lusciously-written description of a Monday morning in the police court early this year was none other than John Noake, (1816-94). Born in Dorset, he'd come to Worcester in 1838 to work on *Berrow's Worcester Journal*, and lived in the city for the rest of his life, later working on the *Worcestershire Chronicle*, and finally as sub-editor of the *Worcester Herald*. He was in later years sheriff, mayor, alderman, and magistrate and his books, *'Jottings'* and *'The Rambler'* – two of ten he wrote covering all aspects of his adopted County after, it was said, he'd found documents in a chest in the tower of St. Swithin's Church that shed new light on the history of the city – are, by general consensus, the starting point for any work on the city's rich history.

Whoever it was, the picture it paints provides a revealing insight into the start of most weeks around this time...

> We would not recommend anyone very desirous of entertaining an exalted idea of human nature to look for models of mankind among the crowd of Monday folks who usually begin the working week by a lounge before his Worship the Mayor. Indeed, if he would foster and preserve any remains of esteem for his kind, he had better give even the exterior of the Guildhall a wide berth. Behind the dock he will find an abundance of food for contemplation, most of it presenting an unpleasant look deeply impressed in the callous, sharp-set, but wicked, vacant and minor dark shades of the human face divine, a sea of which he will usually have before him. Today there were more than the usual full complement and this difficulty, if it were one, was easily solved by the number of the accused enclosed in the dock whose short and simple doings of police retaliation were about to be revealed by the ministering men in blue.

Here, the 'men in blue' are seen as heroes, but they were not always so warmly regarded – certainly not by those that had attracted their attention, and least of all by those that had paid a price for so doing.

It was all too easy for the ne'ers-do-well to lay trumped-up charges – drunkenness, heavy-handedness bordering on assault, theft and even sexual advances – against them in the quest to mitigate or even divert the blame for their own dire offences.

Mostly the charges were laid before the Superintendent who could, and generally would, wave through some of the more fanciful claims; at other times he had little choice but to bring the matter before the Watch Committee who had powers to deal with the matter with powers right up to dismissal, and in extreme cases where some gross outrage was alleged, all the way to the Bench where the hard put-upon PC had to take his place in the dock alongside the real criminals.

**PC 10 John Bennett** was one such early this year after having taken two men and a boy into custody for no reason other than that he '...fancied he saw a sufficient portion of the "Brummagem prig" character about them to warrant a close watch'.

Already viewed with suspicion and regarded as an over-zealous snoop (*see previous year)* he'd also reckoned that the bundle of clothes they were carrying was certain-sure proof that they'd been involved in a robbery. Though they were found to be entirely innocent and the bundle no more than legitimate samples of cloth they were carrying as bona fide tailors, they laid a charge against **PC Bennett** of robbing them of their liberty and excess of duty, both physically and verbally, during their journey to the station-house. The Bench was clearly in benevolent mood that day and Bennett was lucky to get away with it following an admonishment.

But then serendipity played a hand and Bennett was to get his own back in a curious manner...

The three suspected 'prigs' had been lodging in the Coventry Arms (*now Cardinal's Hat*) in Friar Street and its landlord James Nottingham had asked them to make up a suit from some material he had: the next night the three absconded with the material and having overheard that they were headed for Tewkesbury, he happened to come across **John Bennett** in the street and asked him if he'd care to accompany him in a bid to recover his stolen property. His guess was right and they found the three Brummies there. Threatening to have them apprehended, they returned the cloth and gave James Nottingham a watch to pay his expenses and to drop the matter.  For **No10 John Bennett**, the look on their faces was, apparently, reward enough.

Storm clouds were gathering during the middle of this year with Government-backed calls for enforced centralisation of city and borough police forces with their larger, and in some cases – as in Worcester's – newer and less well-established County Constabularies.

Town Clerk John Wood was tipped-off about the looming coup by John Howard, his counterpart at Portsmouth whose force was also on course to be swallowed up into the wider Hampshire Constabulary, and wondered if, by chance, the city might like to be part of a united deputation to oppose the move – ominously backed by firebrand Lord Palmerston – on the grounds that the contemplated measure was an unjustifiable attack upon the rights and liberties of municipal corporations and an unconstitutional interference with their privileges and independence.

Too right they would, came the official response, and the entire Town Council wasted no time in making its stance clear – that '...the amalgamation of police in municipal boroughs and counties would be an unconstitutional interference with the rights and privileges of corporations, as depriving the burgesses of control of the police and that it was calculated to lead to consequences unfavourable to liberty, and to detract from the just and beneficial influence of municipalities'.  Strong stuff...

They also agreed to petition against the measure, and to leave the city's two elected MPs in no doubts about the necessity of rendering their assistance in the protection of their rights.  Their biggest fear was that the move would as good as place control of every force in the hands of the Home Secretary, a breach of the principles that went all the way back to the milestone Statute of Winchester (*1285*).

For the time being, the issue faded into the distance. But it was never going to disappear forever and would swallow them whole in the end.

During all this, life went on much as before at the Station-house.  Constables came and went, some voluntarily, some with a little extra help; the Watch Committee was kept busy with allegations from within and from outside regarding officers' conduct, and Superintendent **Thomas 'Chipper' Chipp**, no doubt missing his old friend **Edward 'Grubber' Grubb** – who, not long after taking over at Hereford had had a nasty accident when he was thrown from his horse en route from Leominster and was lucky to survive – still revealing himself as a sympathetic leader of his men and still very much hands-on and able to mix it along with the best (or worst) of 'em, as the *Herald* reveals:

*'A scavenger named John Vale was charged by Inspector Chipp with drunken and disorderly behaviour.  On Saturday night, the Inspector found him in a liquor-shop in Angel-street, in a decidedly riotous condition, and when the officer attempted to eject him, he squared away at Chipp, but the latter then struck him in self-defence.  The prisoner had nothing to say, and quite as little in his pocket to pay.  His wife however appeared and pleaded his case powerfully, and it appearing that he had several children, and that it was seventeen years since he was last drunk, the Magistrates thought it a legitimate case for the exercise of leniency and he was discharged'.*

## 1854 worst year yet for assaults on police – but worse still to come...

Not all of **Tommy Chipp**'s men managed to end their shifts in an upright position, and 1854 proved to be the worst year yet for assaults against the police.
*Just a few among them were:*

● **Charles Vaughan No19,** who'd only been appointed in December the previous year and was still PC3rd Class.  Called into the Royal Oak in Carden Street to arrest a Militia deserter, he was unfortunate to find notorious hard-case 'Tinker' White standing between him and his quarry: '...whereupon White said he should not be taken away and struck **No 19** several blows in the face.  White had no defence besides being very drunk at the time and he was fined £2 or fourteen days' imprisonment to hard labour'.  A few days later **Vaughan** was called into another dragon's den, the well-avoided Ten Bells in Dolday to arrest another notorious character named Lloyd who'd absconded six months earlier and was still wanted for an assault on Mrs Ackrill of the Brewers Arms in All Hallows.  During a massive free-for-all also involving two of Lloyd's mates, they'd managed to wrest his staff from his hand and, as the *Herald* put it 'two frightful blows inflicted upon his head, from which the blood streamed copiously.  He managed nevertheless to recover his staff and then struck Lloyd with it so violently that he fell to the ground insensible. The policeman is not able as yet to resume his duty'. On May 12th **Vaughan** was awarded a gratuity of £2 for outstanding diligence and exertion during the incident, alongside a commendation from the Magistrates (*cutting, below*). They were not to be his only commendations for bravery and application to duty. On October 13th he was raised to PC 2nd Class.

- **William Richardson** who came off worst, as most did, against a man the *Herald* termed 'An Old Customer' Noah Dayus who was fined 10s and 7s 6d costs or fourteen days' hard
- **William Dance**, a Supernumerary who ended up floored in the Hare and Hounds in College Street after a flurry of punches from Queen's Own Worcestershire Yeomanry Cavalryman Herbert Hughes after he'd heard men drinking after hours. Luckily, **PC Benjamin Holmes** was also within earshot and waded in to his rescue. Result: Hughes was fined £1 and 7s 6d expenses. But for **Dance** it was all too much and he quit the force. He'd been an officer for just nine weeks.
- **PC20 Andrew Hooper** who'd been allowed to return to his duties after having a go at **PS3 George Williams** less than a year earlier, had been severely kicked in the face by a drunken boatman and old offender named Francis Morris in New Street: '...a tussle ensued and [Morris] had the best of it; he threw [Hooper] down, knelt upon his stomach and was beating him when **Supt Chipp** and **Sergeant [Herbert May] Evans** came and put a stop to his violence. Fourteen days' hard. Hooper was back in action the very next week. He and **PC17 John Hunting**, had been called into the Ten Bells (again) following reports of noted hard-case John Smith – or, as the *Herald* reported it 'at other times John Newman or John anything-else but his right name when it may suit his convenience' – was beating-up his live-in lover Ann Williams. The *Herald* recounts a horrific tale of attack and resistance that ended up with John Hunting getting a serious kicking. Fourteen days' hard.

es,                    o
and was          arged.

MONDAY.
agistrates present, the Mayor, (C. Bedford, Esq.), T. Chalk and E. Evans, Esqrs.

FEROCIOUS ASSAULT UPON A POLICEMAN.—In last *Herald* was stated that a very grave assault had been committed on City Policeman Vaughan by a man named Lloyd, in the Ten Bells public-house, Doldays, and we have now to state that that offence formed the subject of an enquiry to-day before this Bench in the investigation of a charge against Robert Groves, andlord of the Ten Bells, for having resisted Vaughan in the execution of his duty. Defendant was assisted by Mr. Bentley, citor; Mr. Chipp, the Inspector, stated the charge on ehalf of the prosecutor.

Vaughan deposed.—About half-past two in the afternoon last Tuesday I went to the Ten Bells, Doldays, to apprehend man named James Lloyd, under a warrant. Mrs. Ackrill, the complainant against Lloyd, went with me to point him out. I found Lloyd in the kitchen; two men were drinking with him, and other parties were in the house. Mr. Groves was in he kitchen. I asked him to aid and assist me. He said " it is of no use, there are three, you must get more force." I told Lloyd I had a warrant to apprehend him. He said—" Then you'll not have me," to which he added—"Neither you no any three; it will take three to take me." The other two men who were drinking with him said—" There are three of us ere, and it will take all your force to take one out." I said should try my hand, and with that I went and caught hold Lloyd. The other two men, with Lloyd, began to beat me, nd one got on the form of the settle, and kicked me in the ins. The other people, except a short bandy-legged man, ft the house when I first caught hold of Lloyd. I said was no use resisting me, I had a duty to perform, and I should do it. Groves said " Leave the man there and fetch more        force       I refuse        I should

On Sept 29th **Joseph Banner** was appointed Supernumerary Sergeant.

Earlier, there'd been sadness in the Station-house when an old favourite, **Sergeant Tommy Bateman** died aged 48 following injuries he'd received after being stabbed in a fight while in the execution of his duty. **Superintendent Chipp** led the tributes when he said that for many years he had been an active and intelligent officer. His death had left a widow and several children in very poor circumstances and the police chief began a campaign to raise a collection on their behalf.

Shocking though it was, 1854 was not to go down in posterity as the worst year for crime or for assaults on the police: they weren't to know it, but that particular accolade was not very long in coming. **If they had, it's likely December 31st would have seen several more resignations...**

*Gained*: George Sedgeley, Edward White, William Dance (who was to last just 10 weeks), Alfred Weston (7 weeks)

*Lost*: Tommy Bateman, Richard Bennett, George Sanders

## Also this year: 1854

- a first for normally dour Police Magistrate Charles Sidebottom who raised a laugh in court when one of dozens of pick-pockets rampant in the streets was caught red-handed. Instead of improving street lighting as was suggested, he volunteered that ladies should have their pockets in a more secure position than was now the fashion

- the new Health of Towns Act comes into force requiring all common lodging-houses to register – 16 complied, one declined, and two were disapproved as being totally unfit for lodging purposes

- scarlatina is rife in the city – the three children of George Arden at 25 The Tything all die in the same week

- four 15 year-old lads are charged with raping 16 year-old Ann Hawthorne at Lark Hill

- police on the lookout for a gang of 'sharpers' who secure jobs as barmen and waitresses and then when their confederates visited, tendering just a small coin for drinks or food, were given change for half a crown and often more

The year started off on a violent note and it was to continue the same way.

There were many dark interludes to come, but it's fair to say that this year was to prove among the most infamous in the history of Worcester City Police with seemingly all-out war being waged on its officers during the execution of their duty by all-comers who thought they stood a chance. In some cases it was a matter of revenge, in others it was some thuggish, and generally drunk, opportunist who'd taken a dislike to the uniform or its wearer's unwelcome intrusion and held a different viewpoint to the officer's that a night in the cells and an appointment with the Magistrates in the morning would be the best course.

It's possible too that some officers, tired of constant abuse, were toughening-up – to the point, at times, of overstepping the bounds of retaliation in respect of their duty.

Even so, the upshot remained the same: no officer was safe and the city was in danger of becoming a pitched battlefield involving the police v the rest. Whether one incident sparked-off the hot-tempered catalogue of assaults is not known, and whether it was the civvie faction or the uniformed police that began the viciousness with the other merely retaliators, is frankly neither here nor there, but never before had there been so many assaults on the police in so short a time; nor is it likely that any town of comparable size has ever, before or since, seen so violent a reaction to the body of men appointed to maintain law and order on the streets... and so dismally failing.

What made it worse was that in all the reports in the following cases, hardly any one of the hundreds of witnesses and spectators of sometimes brutal fights came to the assistance of the police whether voluntarily or when requested, despite refusal carrying a penalty on a par with that doled-out to the thugs who appear to have declared open war on the constabulary and its officers.

*As a consequence, these were Worcester's darkest hours in many a long year, and a shameful reflection on the upright citizens of the once Faithful City.*

### Worst year yet for assaults begins with a murderous attempt on 6' 7" PC Ben Holmes (January 13th)

The mayhem started at lunchtime on Saturday January 13th when one of the force's fastest-rising stars, **PC Benjamin Holmes** had been called to the Pheasant in Pheasant Street to eject a troublesome ex-railwayman named Richard Margetson, one of six dismissed from the railway company that morning that had descended on the town with the object of getting blind drunk and had ended up fighting him in the

**WORCESTER CITY POLICE.**

MONDAY.

Before the Mayor (J. Goodwin, Esq.), C. Sidebottom, W. Lewis, and T. Chalk, Esqrs.

THE ASSAULT UPON P.C. HOLMES.—Henry Jones and Oswald Hill, both in the service of the Oxford, Worcester, and Wolverhampton Railway as goods guardsmen, were to-day brought up in custody on the charge of being concerned in the ferocious assault committed upon Holmes, one of our city police, on the night of Saturday, the 18th instant, as detailed in our last. Mr. Clutterbuck attended on behalf of the defendants. The following evidence was adduced :—Sarah Mason, servant to Mr. Davis, at the Railway Hotel, deposed that Holmes and Price called at that house on the night in question. Price was drunk, but Holmes was quite sober. Holmes had on a dark over-coat. [This coat had been lent to Holmes by Price, the County Court bailiff, whom he was accompanying to assist in arresting a party against whom he had a warrant, and is an important feature in the case as respects that part of the evidence given by Hoyle, a night yardman at the Shrub's-hill station, at the examination this day week of Kerns and Meek, the two other railway men charged with being concerned in the affray, and are at large on their recognizances, in which he (Hoyle) said " that when the party came out of the Prince of Wales Tavern, he saw Holmes pull his coat off and challenge the best man of the lot."] They were there but a few minutes, and then went to the Prince of Wales beer-house. About ten minutes afterwards, witness heard a noise went out, and saw a crowd, some of whom were saying, "Kill the b——." Holmes was then against the wall, and the people were round him. Saw the prisoner Jones hit Holmes with his fist on his face, which knocked him down ; and another man, in a goods guard's dress, gave him a running kick on the cheek while he was on the ground. Other persons threw stones at Holmes, who got up .... his staff, and struck the prisoner Hill on the fore.... asked witness to feel the lump, and then said,— I'll ... him b—— ... for himself ; ... on which he went up to ... and struck him, but did not knock him down. Jones ... ent up and took Holmes's staff from him, and put it ... is coat sleeve. Witness said to Jones, " For God's ... n't hit the man any more ; " to which he replied by ... king expressions, and hit Holmes on the head with ... , and then said he would turn the staff out of sight ... , and then said it was Jones's blow that knocked ... not say whether it was Jones's blow that knocked ... down, but when he was down ....

street – *not a notably intelligent thing to do as Holmes, just 22, stood a massive 6' 7"*

The outcome was largely foregone, and with Margetson safely esconced in the Station-house to sober-up over the weekend pending his Monday morning appearance before the Bench, Holmes went back on duty.

At 11 pm the same night he'd been requested to accompany Henry Price, Bailiff to the County Court, who had a warrant for the arrest of a man known to drink in the Railway Arms on Shrub Hill. At first the gathering was cordial – after all, the copper was in plain clothes and barely cut an insignificant figure: witnesses later said that there were about 40 men drinking and singing in there, and despite some banter from Holmes about the singing of a railwayman named Jones, the warrant was duly delivered and he and Henry Price the bailiff went to leave, their duty done.

Sadly for them, the Railway Arms and the neighbouring Prince of Wales were both railwaymen's pubs and one of the drinkers had been in the Pheasant earlier in the day. Now fuelled up with booze and with revenge in mind for the treatment levelled at their incarcerated ex-colleague Richard Margetson, a free-for-all erupted, spilled out into the road and drew with it the baying customers from there and the Prince of Wales, all kicking and punching the lone police constable. Henry Price had scuttled back into the Railway Arms and locked himself in a room. The Court was later to hear that **Holmes** – described by his chief as '...a steady man exceedingly good-tempered and by no means pugnacious' – was sober, having consumed a pint of ale and 3d worth of rum during the whole evening, but that Price was drunk. The son of Henry Knott, landlord of the Prince of Wales, also described the fight in which **Holmes** was surrounded by the men with his back to a wall. First he was hit by railwayman Henry Jones who landed a mighty blow to his face that knocked him down and that a 'short, stiff man (who) had on a dirty slop' took a running kick at his head.

Despite that, **Holmes** got up, drew his staff and lashed out at the crowd, striking Oswald Hill, later fined £3 for his part in the assault, on the forehead. While still fighting-off the rest of the stirred-up mob, Hill said "I'll give the b———— one for himself and rained punches on **Holmes** who again went down. He then said they all waded in 'kicking him like a football'. Henry Jones then hit him on the head twice with his heavy-duty railwayman's night lantern – for which he was sentenced to a month's imprisonment for attempted murder.

Other witnesses testified to seeing '...marks of blood covering several feet of wall opposite the Prince of Wales Tavern' where Holmes was carried into and **Tommy Chipp** – himself no slouch when it came to mixing it with troublesome customers as he'd shown on many a heated occasion – later said that Holmes' injuries were so bad that he saw little point in administering any kind of first-aid, instantly calling for professional medical help. Miraculously, Holmes survived but as it transpired, he was off work for two months as a result of the murderous attack.

Nobody was held that night, but the Watch Committee immediately offered a reward of £10 'for the discovery of the wretches that so maltreated Holmes', and three railwaymen of the Oxford, Worcester and Wolverhampton Company stationed at Shrub Hill, were soon arrested: Hill, Jones and another man named Meek. In addition to their sentence of a week's gaol apiece (*and Jones' month on the greater charge*), all were immediately sacked.

**And there were others.** *Lots of them*. They included:

● **Supernumerary William Berridge** attacked on the same day as Holmes, by Richard Griffiths alias Morgan – described with typical Herald observation as *'...an itinerant vagabond whose extraordinarily ugly face seems to be an index of his heart'* – after he'd been called in to halt Morgan's ferocious attack on his wife in Broad Street. Sent to gaol for 21 days' hard labour.

● **PC Charles Vaughan** *who, literally the very next day, was on the receiving end of a kicking in the Boat in Lowesmoor (now the site of Co-operative Funeral Services). Sent in to arrest George Smith who'd been beating his wife in there and had also set about landlord James Hobro, another boozer named Cooper intervened and placed himself between Vaughan and Smith, knocking down the lawman before both ended up kicking him while he was on the floor.* **PC William Richardson**, *patrolling nearby was called in and managed to get Vaughan outside. Sentence: seven days' hard.*

● **PC John Hunting** *who only managed to beat a retreat with judicious use of his staff after being sent in to the Boar's Head in Newport Street at closing time to deal with two drunken squaddies quartered there, Archibald M'Quillan a private in the 80th Foot, and James Shuard. He'd been violently kicked, bitten and beaten after the soldiers had kicked-off when refused more ale*

● **Tommy Chipp and two other officers** *who were escorting some prisoners through town and were set on by a mob of militiamen in an attempt to release them.*

● **PC John Hunting** *again, savagely kicked by three drunks named Bedford, Spalding and Edwards, one of which was a soldier, after he'd cautioned them for singing in Broad Street '...and making night hideous with their noise'. Each was fined the statutory 5s and costs or seven days' for drunkenness – a paltry verdict that again sparked-off William Holl's now legendary ire, calling the punishment '...absurd. A police officer, while*

*preserving the peace by apprehending a drunken brute, is knocked down by another and then beaten by three brutes, for which they are fined 5s! We ask any reasonable being to say if the Magistrates, by such a judgment, protected the police?'*

● **PC John Newell,** *only recently appointed PC 3rd Class after being a Supernumerary, who came off badly against two boatmen. Both received a month's hard and the PC quit a few weeks later having clocked-up just ten months, spanning February to December*

● **PC John Knott** *who the same night '...was attacked in a very unprovoked manner in the yard at the Glover's Arms and bruised his face and eye badly. James Sayer, a rough-looking fellow in a smock-frock who "does anything" for a living was charged with the assault. His defence was that when drunk, as he was then, he was mad, his head having been cracked in an accident'. Fined £2 or three weeks' hard. Repeated again at the end of the year by plasterer Edward Ludlow*

● **PC George Sedgeley**, *battered, kicked and bitten by Robert Tyler who'd already laid a militiaman flat in a free-for-all in Merryvale*

● **PC James Workman**, *a veteran from the second intake of 1836 after tackling mad lodging-house keeper Tommy Link who'd threatened to destroy his wife and children by cutting off their heads. On being taken into custody, he kicked the officer violently, and it required the assistance of another policeman to apprehend him. Sent to gaol for three months (more on Link, p.367)*

● **PC (unnamed) 13** *sent to the Swan in Lowesmoor to eject drunken Mary Brown '... but he found he had a tough customer, for she got his finger into her mouth and made him extremely anxious to withdraw it; she also lay down and intimated that her only mode of transit to the station must be by being conveyed thither'. Fourteen days' hard.*

● **PC Andrew Hooper** *challenged to fight by drunken thug Joseph Griffiths in the Angel* in St Johns. Hooper was knocked down in a flurry of punches and while prostrate and defenceless, kicked severely in the ribs.

● **PC William Berridge** again, this time in the Hole in the Wall, Merryvale, the Herald recounting a blow-by-account out of which Berridge emerges with his honour intact although possibly not his teeth. He was hit several times about the shoulders and face by Henry Barber, thrown down by his brother John Barber and knocked down three more times – although he never let go of either of his two prisoners even when a third man named Knight also waded in. Enter **Benjamin Holmes**, now restored to full duty after the attempt on his life earlier in the year. Reports the Herald 'the three prisoners were soon lodged in the station-house'

● **PC John Doughty**, called in to '...quell the disorder created by a drunken mob when Meg Merrilees (alias Elizabeth Batter, a fighting virago with a pathological dislike of police officers) came out of the Lord Nelson and used the most obscene and abusive language towards him. He at length took her into custody but soon found that he had a more than ordinary customer to deal with while the blue-jacket could have no other thought than that his end was near at hand. When they arrived as far as the Bell Hotel, the PC got two Militiamen to help him, but the united efforts of this trio were barely sufficient to convey Meg Merrilees to the station. The poor officer declared to the Magistrates today that when he got to the station, he "might have wrung his shirt" so perspiring and so exhausted was he from the battery he had suffered' (Herald).

The races this year also proved a particularly troublesome time for the police: there had been a tip-off that the city was about to be invaded by 'pickpockets and sharpers who were expected to come from Birmingham and other places in order to make a harvest upon the unsuspecting visitors to the racecourse this week'.

As a preventive measure, **Tommy Chipp** had called in a posse of 'clever detectives from various large towns' to assist. The result? On the first night alone, the station-house was crowded to overflowing with predatory ne'ers-do-well from Worcester and further afield. The following morning more than twenty were hauled up before the Bench. Birmingham detective Enoch Palmer had recognised three villains from his own doorstep '...of the class called card sharpers who infest the railways and railway stations and swindled by means of tricks with cards'.

The justices' workload was such that those arrested were allowed to leave if they promised to return to Birmingham on the first train – which they did, with a police escort to make sure they kept their word. Charles Sidebottom had again raised a titter in the court when he remarked that the prisoners were such smart-looking men that he was surprised he had jurisdiction over them.

The others, plus a similar haul the following day, included smashers (*counterfeit coin passers*), tricksters, illicit gambling table operators, pick-pockets and Isaac William Townsend, described as '...a young man possessing a careless nonchalant manner, a light drab moustache, and a swellish Brummagem suit of clothes' who was also charged with acting as a bonnet (*lookout*) to two illicit roulette tables.

### Drunken Militiamen – aka squaddies – fill the hassle void left by the navvies

But far and away the greatest problems in this particularly troublesome year stemmed from the antics of drunken off-duty Militiamen – *aka squaddies* – who, like the navvies a decade before, continued to wreak mayhem on the streets most nights; it was a rare morning following that the frustrated Magistrates weren't forced to call in the commanding officers, generally Captain Elrington, a regular observer in court, or Adjutant Lavie to take away their occasionally penitent soldier for the administration of tougher martial, rather than civil, law. Not that the soldiers, some of whom were stationed in the Barracks in Silver Street (*today's site of the former Territorial Headquarters*) always had it their own way: the city remained home to some home-grown hard-cases of its own – many only too ready to have a go at the noisy and unruly strangers on its streets.

This year, the militia had demanded fresh billets 'within a mile of the depôt in St George's Square' for an additional 4 sergeants and 700 men with every public- and beer-house obliged to take in its share: nine instantly returned the order papers – the Wheatsheaf in London Road, Goodyer's beer house in Sidbury, Mug House, Hylton-street, Crown & Anchor, Lower Hylton-road, Doughty's beer-house in St Johns, Cooper's beer-house, the Apple Tree and the Cock, both in St Clement's-street (now Tybridge Street) and

*Appointed 9 December 1853*

## MARKS OF APPROBATION.

| DATE. | PARTICULARS. |
|---|---|
| 1854 May 12 | Awarded a gratuity of £2 for extraordinary diligence and exertion used by him in apprehending a man named Lloyd (a notorious character) in which occasion he was severely beaten by Lloyd and two other men — he also received a commendable recommendation from the Magistrate on the occasion |
| 1854 Oct. 13 | Raised to 2nd Class |
| 1856 Sept 12 | Raised to 1st Class |
| 1862 Feb 21 | Commended for his skill & tact and promptitude in discovering several robberies lately |
| July 11 | Commended by the County Magistrates for his perseverance in apprehending a man for stealing geese and awarded 10/- by the Committee |
| 1864 Sept 2 | Appointed a Sergeant |
| 1870 Nov 7 | Commended for steady and attentive conduct at a fire |

*Approbation Book entries for PC19 (later Sgt)* **Charles Vaughan**, *9th December 1853 - 7th November 1870*

the Herefordshire House in Bransford Road whose landlords demanded a crisis meeting with Police Magistrate Charles Sidebottom the very next morning. The following day, the Bench officially ruled that while the practice of billeting was a great hardship on the publicans, they could not in the present instance afford them any relief.

The *Herald* noted: '...the applicants then retired, expressing their intention of memorialising (ie petitioning) for the removal of the Militia into camp or barracks'

The landlords of the Shakespeare, Lamb and Flag in the Tything and Three Tuns in Salt-lane all complained that they'd been lumbered with more than their fair share of coarse and unruly soldiers; John Hill, landlord of the Fountain in Angel Street had been fined and severely cautioned for flatly refusing to take any more, and one night in the middle of the year, John Pearse, landlord of the Angel in Silver Street, *(later the Plough)* had threatened to kick down the stairs all the militiamen billeted there because of their bad language and uncouth habits that had included polishing their boots in the kitchen over the joints of beef roasting for the inn's paying guests.

At least the sustained uproar and barrage of complaints had prompted the Militia to look for a plot of land as the site of new barracks, and there were reports that such a site had been found at Norton.

In the meantime and for the next two years, the soldiers and their uncontrolled – not to mention incontrollable – ways continued to create constant hassle and mayhem for a police force already over-pressed in trying to tame its existing resident population that this year was put at 27,677.

During the year there was 251 marriages, 540 births, and 733 deaths – of which 42 were from cholera and 13 from diarrhœa.

To make matters worse, the Mormons had targeted Worcester, sweet-talking the ladies of the house into giving up all their (*and their husbands'*) worldly goods in return for a new life in far-off America, while the city was also being swamped with counterfeit coins – particularly some well-crafted fake half-crowns (2/6d) that had been cleverly electro-plated on an iron base.

The police warned the population at large '...to provide themselves with a pocket magnet and where suspicion presents itself, to apply it to the coin. If it is of iron material, it will adhere tenaciously to the magnet'.

**Gained:** *William Berridge, John Newall, Joseph Herbert Mann, George Haynes, Alexander Clarke, James Drew, Thomas Perry, George Young*

**Lost:** *Alexander Clarke (served just four months), John Newall (ditto ten months)*

The first bad news of 1856 appeared in the first editions of the year. Two publicans, Edward Kirk of the Pheasant, and Edward Robinson of the Dolphin in Copenhagen Street had laid charges of excess of duty and the use of improper language on the part of **PC William Richardson** while on his rounds on the penultimate day of 1855: both pubs had been found open well beyond the approved hours, the Dolphin at midnight and the Pheasant at 1.15am.

The enquiry took some time and in the end, the Committee came to the unanimous opinion that '...the officer had not gone beyond his duty or otherwise misconducted himself in either case', and dismissed both complaints.

The police had long been wary of Edward Kirk who'd earlier been licensee of the Berkeley Arms in Bank Street and theirs was a mutual dislike: sadly for him, the Pheasant was more dependent on the police than vice-versa and it was the same **PC Richardson** who was called in just a few weeks later to deal with a charge of pick-pocketing against Jane Shaller who was eventually sentenced to six weeks' hard labour for the offence. A similar sentence was also imposed on tailor William Davis, alias Stevens, for stealing scarves and other items out of a carpet-bag belonging to a lodger there, Patrick Cregan.

Over the years during his tenure of the Pheasant (1855-62), Edward Kirk had had numerous occasions to demand police intervention, and it's a tribute to their sense of duty that they never failed him – although it must have given **Tommy Chipp** a rare moment of pleasure when they were called into the Post Office in Shaw Street to eject the noisy and drunken landlord during Christmas week. Though they got him outside, he constantly threatened to return, so Chipp held him in custody until 9pm by which time the Post Office had closed.

March this year saw **Tommy Chipp** engaged in an incident that can be looked on as either an heroic adventure or a strange and ultimately tragic case that demonstrates either his genuine care for people and the lengths he was prepared to go to in order to secure justice, or alternatively that his was an overblown sense of duty.

Wealthy coal dealer Joseph Hodgetts of Tallow Hill had returned from a three-day business trip and found his house stripped of every stick of furniture and his wife, four children and a grandchild that was the offspring of a deceased daughter, all missing. Also gone was his entire savings, £314 cash. A note informed him that his wife had joined the Mormons who had been actively door-knocking to gain converts in Worcester over the previous few years, had given them all their worldly wealth and that the family was now on its way to a new life in Mormon Utah.

A distraught Joseph Hodgetts knocked on the door of the station house for advice and, touched by the tale, **Tommy Chipp** immediately agreed to go with him to Liverpool in the hope of heading-off the next America-bound Mormon vessel. With the Mayor's approval, they caught the next express, arriving in Liverpool at 3am. There, the local police told him that the family was booked with the Enoch Train, due to sail at 4am – but when they arrived at the quays, she'd already set sail.

At 9am **Tommy Chipp** saw a steam tug called the Great Conquest pull alongside the quay and asked the captain if he'd seen the Enoch Train: he had, but he said, chances of catching her up were slim. Even so, with the lure of £25 of Hodgetts' cash – half if he failed – he'd try. The good news is that they caught the vessel; the bad news was that the 'Mormon slime', as the *Herald* later reported their leaders, refused to give up any of its hundreds of new converts and that neither the police nor anyone else could force them as the ship was now in blue water, on the high seas and out of the jurisdiction of Her Britannic Majesty's constables.

The chief Mormon even taunted Chipp by saying that if he could find Mrs Hodgetts and her Worcester brood on board, he could have them. Never the man to resist a challenge – and entirely to his credit having come so far – Chipp tried, but failed. The *Herald* omits to outline quite how it came about, merely commenting '...chance, however, befriended him in a way that we shall not tell for obvious reasons, but at length the foolish mother and her misled children stood on the deck, devoured by the yearning eyes of the unhappy father'.

The two eldest daughters, 18 and 15, elected to remain on board, en route to '...a land morally poisoned, a country of sin and death' (*Herald*) – but the rest of the family returned to Worcester *sans* a farthing in ready cash.

In the city, things hadn't altered much. A mob had attacked **PC 3rd Class William Beddoe** just days after he'd been promoted from the ranks of Supernumeraries, kicking him while he was on the ground after he'd attempted to arrest a man called Munn whose father had waded-in and hammered him to the ground in the Shambles.

The incident once more fuelled William Holl's anger as he appended the comment '…unfortunately in Worcester, mobs are ever ready to ill-treat a fallen officer and to frustrate the ends of justice'. The son escaped but Munn Snr was ordered to pay 5s costs but released from further charge, prompting another terse observation and media criticism of the Bench: 'Mistaken leniency, we fear'.

That same April week the police were involved in the suicide of John Sefton in the Ewe and Lamb in Angel Street. Up to the day before, he'd been drillmaster of the County police but was sacked over allegations of some missing cash, got blazingly drunk and had spent the previous night in the cells at the Station-house. The next day he was dead, having written a tragic letter to his estranged wife before swallowing poison.

And still the assaults went on: **PC William Berridge** being repaid for his concern over the welfare of a wife and daughter, Esther and Margaret Murtock being assaulted by the father Dennis by having the entire family as well as a neighbour, Mary Barrington, 'most unmercifully' kicking, punching and hitting him – first with a pair of tongs and then with a poker at 2am: they even managed to kick him, literally, down three steps out of their Merrivale hovel. By chance, **PC James Drew**, due to be promoted to sergeant later this year, '…came up, and by his aid further violence was prevented, though Berridge is bruised all over his head and body. Vomiting blood, he was subsequently off work for several weeks. In court, Berridge was described as 'one of the steadiest in the corps'. Dennis Murtock was sentenced to 14 days for the assault, although he complained all along that Berridge had 'committed the most wanton and altogether unprovoked attack it was possible to conceive' and suggested that the officer had probably been hallucinating.

On August 1st **Benjamin Holmes** (*appointed 18th February 1853*) was elevated to detective and the Approbation Book, ***below,*** shows his progress – a remarkable feat given that he was fortunate to have survived a savage beating at the hands of a mob of inflamed railwaymen little over a year earlier. He was undoubtedly another of the City force's great officers and later civic sword-bearer.

WCiCo/WAAS

*Appointed* 18. February 1853

6

MARKS OF APPROBATION.

| DATE. | PARTICULARS. |
|---|---|
| 1853 April 29 | Raised to 2nd Class |
| 1854 Octr 2 | Raised to 1st Class |
| 1856 Augt 1 | Appointed Detective |
| 1861 July 12 | Appointed Station Sergeant |
| 1862 March 21 | Rewarded £1 on the recommendation of Mr Inspr Crompton for courageous conduct as an attack being made upon him for which two men were tried and convicted |

WCiCo/WAAS

There was cause for a personal celebration the same month when **Sgt John Doughty** – already in his 11th year with the police and another decade ahead of him *(14th February 1845 – 26th March 1875,* a remarkable achievement) was able to claim that he had a grandmother *and* grandchildren living at the same time. Former Fish Street fruit-seller Jane Doughty had just died at 104, having had four children all of whom she outlived, twenty-five grandchildren, fifty great-grandchildren and four great-great-grandchildren.

The *Herald* reported that 'up to the last she could see and hear well enough and was only a little bent with age, and her neighbours do not recollect her taking ale till the day before her death when she expressed a wish to have some and she drank a good draught'. *A lesson to be learned, perhaps?*

Clearly, it was only going to be a matter of time before the constant assaults and mounting absences through injury took their toll on the efficiency of the force – and that occurred very publicly in June when a formal complaint was lodged with the Watch Committee after a Sunday night fight between a carriage lad ('cad') and a Militiaman outside the Star Hotel, drawing a huge and raucous crowd and continuing for 25 minutes before being broken up by the police – led by **Sgt Doughty** who'd just lost his grandmother.

Hauled before the committee to answer charges of neglect of duty and inefficiency over the delay, **Tommy Chipp** '...explained to the committee that on the night in question, a number of his men were unable to come on duty through illness or injuries they had received while executing their duty, and although every regular officer and supernumerary that could be employed went on their beats, there still was no-one who could be put upon the beat where the disturbance occurred'.

He also added his regret that nobody had even bothered to send to the station, probably little more than 100 yards away, to fetch an officer to quell the row.

Though the committee recorded their regret that so violent a disturbance should have occurred in the first place, they exonerated the police from blame in the matter.

On June 5th, the force had gained a new supernumerary, soon to be promoted to the full ranks: this was **Edward Chipp**, one of eight to be admitted during the course of the year, and son of the chief. The following month, Edward Kirk again called the police into the Pheasant to solve the mystery of a missing – he alleged, stolen – watch, and the same week it was **Tommy Chipp's** turn to get a hammering.

### A common tale: chief wades in to a scrap – and comes off worst

ASSAULTING MR. CHIPP.—A labouring man from Hallow, named Augustus Williams, was charged by Inspector Chipp with having assaulted him late last night at a liquor-shop in Silver-street. The fellow was making a row and using shocking language, when Chipp went to apprehend him, but he showed fight in so ferocious a manner, striking Chipp about the head and other parts, that it was with some difficulty, even with the assistance of two other officers, he was taken to the station. Fined 5s. and 5s. costs, or 14 days' imprisonment.

*5 shillings (25p) fine for duffing-up the chief of police. Justice 1856-style*

A labourer named Augustus Williams had been kicking up a stink in a beer shop in Silver Street just as the still hands-on Inspector was passing by. Attempting to put him out, Williams '...showed fight in so ferocious a manner, striking Chipp about the head and other parts, that it was with some difficulty, even with the assistance of two other officers, he was taken to the station. Fined 5s and 5s costs or 14 days' imprisonment'.

Ever in the front-line and not always for the right reasons, **PC William Richardson** was appointed Detective on August 1st 1856. It proved to be a good move: not long afterwards he was awarded £1 for his adroitness and diligence in apprehending a gang of thieves later convicted at the Assizes, although at the same time he was cautioned to be more circumspect in the future for allowing a prisoner charged with rape to escape through neglect of his duties.

The year had seen 113,746 men and women committed for trial in England alone: mostly for offences against the person. There were 757 cases of forgery and currency offences', 310 murders, and sundry shooting and stabbing cases, manslaughters, concealments of birth, 'unnatural crimes and attempts to commit unnatural crimes', rape and carnally knowing girls under 10 years of age, hundreds of cases of abusing girls between the ages of 10 and 12, assaults with intent to ravish, abduction, bigamy, grievous assaults and common assaults, suicides and attempted suicides of which a high proportion was described as being prevented by the police and others.

There was also 474 major fires, and 19 executions. In addition 6,376 soldiers had been sent to military prisons where the average confinement was 53 days.

A new phenomenon that was to account for many hours of police time and not a little additional grief for its officers also now emerged: inter-cad rivalry. The origin of the word cad is unknown – Google offers several possibilities, but as stated in ***Bob Backenforth's Worcester Pubs Then and Now Vol II***, the likeliest derivation is from 'carriage lad', feisty and pushy young men, usually hired by the coach operators or hotel proprietors to tout for business by whatever means from the rapidly increasing number of visitors just arrived either by stage or the new-fangled railways in the city and in search of a room for the night.

As if the aggressive treatment of their would-be customers wasn't already the cause of a great deal of irritation and friction, sparking-off a rash of complaints to the police, the rivalry amongst themselves daily erupted into stand-up slug-it-out scraps attracting huge crowds. Inevitably it was the police's lot to break up the fights and the unruly mobs that had gathered round to watch – who then turned on the police for breaking up their innocent 'fun'. The result was that Broad Street – site of the city's three main central hotels the Crown (*still there*), the Unicorn (*now the passageway into Crowngate*) and the Bell (*cleared to make way for Angel Place*) all standing within a few yards of each other – became the scene of almost hourly pitched battles that more often than not had ended up with one or more of the original combatants prostrate and bloody on the floor and just as likely a bobby in blue, bruised and battered for getting between them and doing his duty.

*If more steady than spectacular for the City force, 1856 had at least been a milestone year for the police generally...*

The year had seen the introduction of the **County and Borough Police Act** making policing a statutory requirement, stipulating that local forces would be funded by central government distributed to local authorities. Another key element of the Act that was to have an impact on the City and its County counterpart was the formation of a central inspectorate of constabulary appointed to keep an ever-watchful eye on the efficiency and effectiveness of each force with a direct line to the Home Secretary himself.

Worcester City Police and Worcestershire Constabulary were included in the Midlands District – far and away the biggest of the three sectors, covering 25 counties and now administered by Maj-Gen William Cartwright considered to have been the toughest and most influential of the Inspectorate's first three inspectors (*source: 'The History of Her Majesty's Inspectorate of Constabulary – The First 150 years'*).

The other two sectors were North – which covered just 9 counties, and the South.

Statistics showed that at the time Worcester police:population ratio to be hovering around 1:1,000. Birmingham was running at 1:646, Liverpool 1:393 and Manchester 1:540 although crime levels in St Ives in Cornwall and Pwllheli in Wales demanded a police presence of 1:6,500 and 1:3,034 respectively.

Locally at least, and taking all elements into account, 1856 had proved to be a more satisfying, and satisfactory, year for Worcester City and its police force.

If only they could maintain the same rate of progress. Sadly it was not to be...

***Gained:*** *James Foote, Thomas Berrow, Richard Halford, William Phipps (not one of which was to last out the year) also Joseph Phillips, John Inight, William Hill, John Wall, William Beddoe, John Sanders*

***Lost:*** *James Workman, Andrew Hooper*

## Also this year: 1856

■ *a curious statistic emerges early on when it is revealed that inmates at the Union (ie Work)-house – cost of maintenance 3s per pauper per week – are smashing windows and being generally insubordinate in order to be transferred to the city gaol – ditto 4s per head per week – because they are better fed and given less work to do*

■ *in the same week, Eliza Cox attacks PC James Drew with a shard of glass after she'd smashed a window while resisting arrest, and PC George Sedgeley narrowly averts serious injury when James Gough, recently returned from 14 years' transportation to Australia had a pan of boiling water knocked out of his hands as he was about to throw it over the prostrate bobby*

■ *PC John Hunting commended for apprehending Worcestershire Militia deserter, drummer Thomas Maund*

■ *Tommy Chipp is awarded £40 raised by donations for his tenacity in pursuing the Mormons*

■ *police under pressure controlling crowds at the funeral of five workmen overcome by fumes at Worcester Distillery*

■ *police investigate suspected murder of 19-year old Lucy Tredwell found in the canal near Blockhouse bridge with her skull caved in. Despite several of the subsequent jury claiming 'there was not the smallest doubt the case was one of wilful murder', chief suspect ex-boyfriend William Thomas is acquitted on lack of evidence*

■ *police investigate death of two workmen, Charles Ogbourne and William Jones, after scaffolding collapses in the cathedral during extensive renovations*

## WORCESTER CITY POLICE.

MONDAY.

Magistrates present—The Mayor (J. Weaver, Esq.), W. Lewis, T. Chalk, R. Padmore, C. Sidebottom, and J. W. Lea, Esqrs.

REVIEW OF THE POLICE CHARGE-SHEET.—There were nine occupants of the dock this morning—to the credit of the fair sex, all of the masculine gender. The names of Wm. White (pugilistic notoriety) and John Hunter (little known hereabouts) were first called. They were jointly charged with drunkenness and violently assaulting Policeman Berridge. It appeared, however, from the statement of Inspector Chipp, that Berridge was too unwell to attend, and the case was remanded till Friday. It was stated that about eleven o'clock on Saturday night the inspector and P. C. Knott were called into the Falcon Inn, Broad-street. Found the kitchen full of people; White and Berridge were on the kitchen floor, struggling together. Hunter stood by, and Berridge recognised him as having also illused him. Berridge appeared to be very much distressed; he complained of his back, and has since been off duty.—No. 3 was Robert Corbett, employed at the steam saw-mills at Diglis, against whom a charge was preferred by Policeman Banner of being so drunk in Angel-street, at half-past one o'clock on the previous day, as to jeopardise his life. It appeared that two companions in almost as intoxicated a state as himself were endeavouring to assist Corbett along, but the latter fell into a sewerage cutting. Fortunately at this juncture Banner stepped up and rescued him. Fined 5s.—Next came a respectable-looking man of about 50, named John Cotterell, a labourer, of White Lady Aston. His offence was also drunkenness. The police met with him in an advanced state of incapability at half-past eight o'clock on Sunday morning, in the Corn-market, with £2. 11s. in his possession. His plea was that he required change, and that in order to get it he and a companion had partaken of two half pints of gin. Fined 5s.—An ostler at one of the inns, named John Parry, was No. 5. At half-past twelve o'clock last night an officer found him in Birdport lying in the gutter and unable to render any account of himself, so he was stationed, and £2. 11s. 6d. was found upon him. Fined 5s.—Nos. 6, 7, 8, and 9, were respectively Wm. Finnin, John and Thomas Moore, and Edward Connor. They are employed at the waterworks. Finnin was first charged with being drunk and disorderly at the top of Broad-street, at 12.45 this morning, and, in consequence, was taken into custody by Policemen Ledgley and Banner. But before this charge had been fully entertained, a married woman, named Elizabeth Knight, stepped forward to prefer a charge of robbery against Finnin. She stated that on the road to fetch her husband from the Coach and Horses, in the neighbourhood of Hylton-street, Finnin, whilst in the company of others, snatched at a piece of linen placed in the body of her dress, and took thereout a half-sovereign, after which he ran off and she was unable to overtake him. Immediately upon this accusation, a young man presented himself before the Bench and declared that he had seen Nos. 7, 8, and 9, drinking together in company with Finnin near Worcester bridge, on Saturday night, and that something was taken from Finnin's pockets, which he (witness) believed to be money. Hereupon Finnin declared to the Bench that he had not lost any money; and as the two Moores and Connor were equally confident that they had not robbed Finnin, but merely so far interfered with him as to prevent his falling into Severn, the Bench felt that there was no alternative but to discharge Nos. 7, 8, and 9, and they were released accordingly. Finnin was remanded till Friday.

# 1857

Chief's son **Edward Chipp** was now one of the force – and it didn't take long for him to get noticed. Within days of joining, he'd brought to the station-house a 'teaser' (*stoker*) from a glass works charged with wilfully breaking windows in Bridge Place. John Webb, described as 'a strong, young, devil-may-care vagabond from Dudley' admitted he'd broken the windows in order to get a bed for the night as he'd hoped the militiamen would have found him and he'd have volunteered to join-up there and then: sadly for him, it was the police, and the chief's son, anxious to make his mark. Still, he managed to get his bed for the night, in the station-house, plus thirteen more during his term on the Crank, all courtesy of the Bench.

He'd be joining the ranks of the 136 prisoners, 85 men and 51 women, sentenced to terms in the City Gaol this year: of these, 3 boys and 2 girls were under the age of 15, and for 64 it was not a new experience: only 72 were there for the first time while the violent nature of the times is evident in that 98 of the total were for there for assault and/or Union (*Workhouse*) disorder.

The following week, **PC John Hunting** who was to see-off the year on a high note, came in for praise after following two men he'd suspected of being involved in a robbery, prising them out of their hiding place in a yard in Quay Street and bringing them to book. He'd only found them when he heard one of the men, concealed behind some barrels, say 'he'll never find us here'.

But his night's work wasn't without some personal cost. He'd taken them both on but had been kicked and punched in the face several times. Two more for the Crank.

Quay Street again lived up to its notoriety just three weeks later when the *Herald* reported, (*in full, for the simple reason that the journalism is glorious*):

*A sewerage labourer calling himself William Tandy who presented a bloody head and frock, and a maniac look, was charged with being drunk and assaulting PC12 John Sanders very early on Sunday morning. The officer was passing through Quay-street when he saw the besotted fellow sitting against a wall, as though in deep meditation on the course of human events, but, on requesting him to progress homewards, he responded by striking the officer a violent blow with his fist and when apprehended he hit, kicked and knocked him about like a galvanised body. Fined 5s.*

The very next case in the court (*and the next report in the Herald*) was that of John Dondon: '...half tramp, half mason, in possession of a superabundant black beard and features indicative of laziness and Bacchanalianism, also fined 5s for assaulting a PC in Broad-street yesterday morning, shortly before one o'clock'.

As the autumn approached, a single day came close to rivalling the fateful January in 1855 that had proved so bad for the police.

Noted prostitute and court-house regular Ann Gomer had had been found drunk and violent in the Mug House in St Johns (*for its location, see Bob Backenforth's Worcester Pubs Then and Now p48*) and set about two policemen – **PC Sanders** (*unclear whether John or Benjamin, both of whom were in service at this time*) and **PC Ward** (more likely, **Wall** who just a few weeks later was severely reprimanded and made to apologise after unjustifiably taking Sarah Palmer to the Police Station and detaining her there for some time). They'd been summoned to turf her out after she'd already flattened the landlord, William Stalworth.

Later the same day the ever-dependable **William Berridge** had come unstuck in a scrap with a thug named Richard Griffiths who was drunk and disorderly in the Leopard in Broad Street and was only hauled-off with the timely intervention of **Sergeant John Doughty**. Still on duty at 1am **Berridge** had had to intervene in a squealing cat-fight between two battling whores, Sarah Ann Baker and Bridget Ann Bridges and came away with sundry facial scratches to accompany the bruises he'd received earlier on.

It was all in a day's work.

The actual report of the following Monday's activities in the Magistrates court tells the tale better than any current recounting, and demonstrates the scale of the problems confronting the police on any given night *(see cutting, far left)*.

The situation of police v the rest of the world had reached such a state that mayor James Weaver took the opportunity of the Brewster Session to lash out at victuallers for their complacency and lack of backbone in assisting the police being called out to quell disorder, drunkenness and other violent incidents in their premises: '...there is not the disposition on the part of licensed victuallers which there ought to be. The Bench is therefore often embarrassed and the police frustrated in carrying justice into effect. When summoned the police readily attend and get maltreated, knocked about and suffer considerable violence'.

### 'Men in blue we never see here...'

Just a few weeks earlier, *Herald* editor William Holl had turned his usual broadside on the police into a rant about lack of police supervision in Hylton Road (*then, Street*) following gangs of urchins committing regular nuisances: '...we have in vain begged as a personal favour a little police supervision of this disturbed district, but men in blue we never see here... bands of graceless boys block up the pavement, pester the shopkeepers and other tradesmen, annoy passengers and advance themselves as unruly characters at an alarming rate. It is frightful to think what kind of men such scamps are to grow up into'.

The ever-thorny subject of police costs and numbers came up for discussion around now. The annual cost of running the force was revealed as £1,249 2s which would be stretched to £1,519 16s if the committee accepted the suggestion of HM Government's newly-appointed Inspector of Police for the Midlands District, Major-General William Cartwright, that the force needed some new blood.

With the Government allowing a grant to cover a quarter of expenses for clothing and salaries, they decided that the year would see a surplus of £109 6s and voted to boost the roll by recruiting two more officers, bringing the city in line with the Inspectorate's recommendations.

As the year drew to a close, **James Barker,** a PC for a matter of weeks, apprehended a 60-year old Distillery worker James Munn at 2am on the Quay in Hylton Road (*then Hylton-street*) and when he asked him what was in a bladder-like bundle he was carrying, Munn set about him with it: it was later revealed to be grain, valueless but nonetheless a heavy weight – and worse, removed without permission.

A serious barney then ensued with both men up and then down again until the constable got the better of the older man by hitting him across the head with his handcuffs. An allegation was made in court that Munn, a useful scrapper and ex-prize fighter, had been deliberately placed as a dupe by some anti-police faction – to which William Holl added his usual terse footnote along the lines that any repeat '...would see the jokesters laughing all the way the treadmill, by which time their smiles would have started to fade'.

Another officer emerging as a useful scrapper was **PC John Hunting** who during Christmas week this year laid flat two drunken revellers, Edward Crisp a known offender and police-hater, and George Wickham – both of whom fancied themselves as pugilists but on this occasion had taken on the wrong man.

It happened at the top of Dolday after the duo had emerged from a raucous night's boozing and, reported the *Herald* in the final edition of the year, '...the gentleman in blue tooled Crisp in self defence, effecting some very well defined but not very ornamental alterations on the surface of Crisp's corpus'.

In a gorgeous phrase for laying them flat, the *Herald* reporter commented that the PC '...measured their lengths on the stones'.  Beautiful!

*Gained*: Edward Chipp, Charles Cotton, John Alfred Ross (quit after seven weeks), Benjamin Sanders, James Fielders, Thomas B Meredith

## Also this year: 1857

- *Herald reports that the Watch Committee of Bath Council had given permission for its constables and others to sport moustaches*

- *Bench orders Tommy Chipp to clamp down on boys engaged in the latest craze of lighting rags and throwing them about and he orders several officers to patrol in plain clothes to make an example of a few offenders*

- *Supernumerary constable John Inight – reported as 'Knight' in a Herald report when he is bashed about by drunken gardener Benjamin Linton who he'd attempted to arrest in the High Street and had ended up with a broken knee – quits after a few weeks*

- *Herald describes Worcester's streets as 'the worst in the kingdom' for street nuisances and 'thugs using diabolical and obscene language', gathering on street corners*

- *the term 'juvenile delinquent' is used to describe boy thief Thomas Blower, caught by PC Ledgley (sic – actually, Sedgeley). Precisely 100 years on, Frankie Lymon and the Teenagers release their song professing not to be one.  In November the newspaper also refers to 'Tom and Jerryism' referring to young Worcester troublemakers*

- *PCs (later sergeant) James Drew and Bill Berridge investigate suspected child murder after a baby's body is found at a hovel in Merryvale; the very next day the body of a baby girl, wrapped in a piece of apron and stuffed into a bag is also fetched out of the canal near Blockhouse bridge*

- *police cells full to overcrowding with drunks following an unusually rowdy Easter in which several constables are assaulted and generally roughed-up*

- *chief's son PC Edward Chipp emerges with great praise for tackling and disarming a labourer named Gipsy Jack (Joseph Moule – see p366) who'd followed him into the street with a candlestick, threatening murder*

- *new 'in' place for young people, Crystal Palace Liquor Vaults on the corner of Angel Street and the Butts rapidly emerges as violence hot-spot with several police call-outs every night*

- *PC17 John Hunting investigates case of child cruelty after a starving, vermin-ridden child is found in a Dolday hovel; the previous week a married couple had done a runner from a neighbouring property owing several weeks' rent and officers brought in to break down the door had found a baby's body in a coffin amid all the other rubble*

- *spate of swans being injured by boys throwing stones, sparks extra police vigilance on the riverside*

- *PC Edward Chipp again rises to prominence when he investigates baby's body wrapped in flannel and sewn into a calico bag found in a privy in St Andrews Square*

- *police station-house and cells referred to as 'Chipp Castle' in a report on Christmas rowdyism.*

The first Watch Committee meeting of the year contained good news...

Worcester City Police had been officially graded as 'efficient' by Maj-General Cartwright and the Inspectorate, and the recent increase in numbers had resulted in the granting of the certificate to that effect, whereby the Government would continue to pay for a quarter of the running costs amounting to some £300.

Manpower consisted of **Superintendent Chipp** on £1 15s a week and house rent-free (*he lived on the first floor of the Station-house*); two sergeants at £1 3s; two detectives at £1 3s, one supernumerary sergeant at £1 2s, seven 1st Class constables at £1, seven 2nd Class constables at 18s 6d, and six 3rd Class constables at 17s. Clothing for the men was an extra.

They'd seen fit to reject one of the Maj-General's recommendations though – the appointment of **Tommy Chipp** as a relieving officer for vagrants.

The year had begun with a major epidemic of pick-pocketing – few instances of which had the police any chance of solving. January 28th also saw **PCs No16 George Young** and **No26 James Barker** involved in the investigation of an unpleasant suicide in the Brewers Arms (*now the Imperial*), immediately opposite the Station-house. In fact, the room where James Wylde had taken the fatal dose of laudanum immediately overlooked the police HQ.

It was quickly followed by the death of an old favourite, **George Williams**, the old No3 and ex-Watchman included in Henry Sharpe's four-man first squad from 1833 and probably from two years before that.

He was aged 60 and, reported the *Herald* '...his death is very much regretted by the police, who, we understand purpose (sic) to defray the expenses of his funeral by a subscription among themselves and friends'.

Another departure was the chief's son Edward in February. He'd joined Gloucestershire Constabulary and within weeks 'the zealous discharge of his duties' had led the force's Captain Lefoy to promote him to assistant detective officer.

The early part of the year was also characterised by a marked blitz on Worcester publicans thinking they could flout the law in respect of closing times: the early weeks saw well-publicised cases brought against John Henry Johnson of the Odd Fellows (*later Farriers*) Arms in Fish Street, and Joseph Lydiard at the Dog and Duck on Henwick Hill (*later Hylton Road*); the 80-year old pub closed for good two years later.

Again the police's on-duty drinking issue re-surfaced; on April 9th Supernumerary **Sergeant Joseph Banner** was cautioned as to his future conduct for drinking in the house of a citizen in company with **PC Richard Berry** while still on duty.

The markets, particularly The Shambles, had always been hassle hot-spots and **PC Joseph Phillips** volunteered for, and got, the role of Market Constable. In April he was obliged to bring a private case against his Blockhouse neighbour Edwin Griffin after he'd warned him about his '...abominable language, whereupon Griffin collared the officer, spit in his face and threatened to pull him over the fence'. Fined 5s and 10s costs or 14 days' imprisonment.

In what was becoming all too tediously regular, a single weekend in May saw several officers quite seriously bruised and battered in a catalogue of cases brought before the Bench the following Monday morning. They included:

- **Bill Berridge** again, severely set upon by George Herbert, a farm labourer from Martley who'd got drunk in town, joined the militia but then had a change of heart and did a runner with Berridge assigned to drag him back to Worcester to face charges of desertion

- **Unidentified PCs 23 and PC40** both kicked and grossly assaulted in a free-for-all in the Pack Horse, and yet again,

- **PC John Hunting** who, after asking drunken sewerman William Hands to move on from a doorstep in Angel Street,

*'...he refused to do so and catching hold of Hunting's arms, ripped one of the sleeves of his top coat. A struggle ensued, the constable and his prisoner fell to the ground, and after much difficulty with the assistance of PC Drew, prisoner was taken to the police-station. When there, he refused to be searched, ripped the other sleeve of Hunting's top coat and behaved very violently'. Fourteen days hard.*

Calls to a notorious brothel dubbed The Barracks in Watercourse Alley also accounted for virtually nightly visits from the police – often several times in the clamp-down on outrage and mayhem among the girls, their minders and their customers, almost always involving fights and general disorder.

The police rarely needed to be called: they left a window open at the rear of the station-house which backed onto the incident-packed alley and it proved more effective than an alarm. Just one regular among scores was Eliza Paine, particularly noted for her disgusting language.

The thorny issue of boys playing tip-cat in the streets and throwing stones stepped up when 20 panes of glass were broken in St Martins Church causing an indignant outburst by the Rev. Wheeler, demanding tougher police action. **Tommy Chipp** told the Bench that '...whenever the officers caught the lads they gave them a good caning, and the Town Clerk said that was decidedly the best course to pursue as the magistrates had no power to prevent boys playing in the streets or to punish them unless some specific set of damage were proved. The Mayor (*Josiah Stallard*) said that the conduct of boys in the city generally had become intolerable'.

### Summer and autumn of discontent

The summertime – as virtually every summertime up to then and for at least the next century – saw the city descended on by tinkers and travellers, drawn by the season's casual hop and fruit-picking opportunities. Paydays were inevitably action-packed and lively – particularly in the pubs and beer houses, one notorious gipsy family, the Lovells, virtually guaranteed to be taking up several cells in the station-house during August and September, year after year.

September saw **PC4 John Doughty** attacked by Julia Briscoe '...who alternates between gaols, union-houses, police stations and common lodging houses, she being a tramp of the most inveterate kind. She will attack any man and come off with e-claw [*poss transcription of equal? BB*] so that the officer had a dreadful piece of work to accomplish on Saturday evening when he was called into Bryant's lodging house, Copenhagen–street to suppress a row in which she was the principal agent. The tigress scratched his face, kicked him violently and behaved so badly that even the by-standing women assisted the officer against her. Sent to gaol for a week'. **Doughty** later described her as 'the strongest woman he has ever met with'.

The same session saw **Tommy Chipp** brand William Holland as 'the biggest coward in Worcester' for attacking his wife yet again, this time in broad daylight in Broad Street: the *Herald* also labelled him as 'a great bull-headed fellow with apparently as much of the "milk of human kindness" in him as might be extracted from a millstone'.

The autumn saw **Bill Berridge** yet again stretchered-off after a kicking in the Brewers Arms in Merrivale, the culprit Mark Henry who'd also brutally assaulted the landlady Mrs Price sentenced to a month on the Crank.

**Bill Richardson, PC No14 James Drew** and **No16 Ezra Franklin** all emerged bruised and battered from incidents at the same time – in Franklin's case by fighting woman Caroline Newman who'd been brought to the Station-house in a drunken state but once there had attacked other prisoners and kept up a constant hammering by kicking on her cell door. Sent in to remove her heavy-duty boots '...she became still more obstreperous – then it was that Franklin got sadly knocked about' reported the *Herald*. Ten days hard.

On November 22nd **John Hunting** met his match in blacksmith Samuel Mables, his brother James, their mother as well as a man named Bennett and several others – ten in all. They'd all taken it in turns to kick and punch him while he was still on the ground in a Tybridge Street alleyway, and left him for dead. To his credit, not to mention his constitution and recuperative powers, a week later he was back at work.

The next week it was **No14 James Drew**'s turn – again beaten-up in the Bridge in Bridge Street by a navvy named James Sutley who was sentenced to seven days' hard for the assault. The *Herald* reported 'we have since been told that Drew's hurts are more serious than at first imagined, and that fear is entertained that he will be laid up in consequence'.

Not all the action against the constables was physical: following the autumn races, two young Malvern men, cousins George and Thomas Mitchell accused **PC25 Charles Martin** who'd only joined in February this year (*and was to quit in February next year*) of stealing cash, a handkerchief and a woollen muffler from them. Confused as to the officer's actual identity, **Tommy Chipp** laid on an identity parade of his officers at the station house where George picked out PC **Martin**, but Thomas disagreed, claiming that '…the one who robbed us had sore eyes and bushy whiskers'.

In a lengthy action that also saw the involvement of **PCs James Fielders** and **Charles Vaughan,**

> *'the magistrates said that they believed the statement of the two boys to be most false and unfounded, that the charge against Martin was altogether groundless and that he (Martin) left the court without a stain on his character. Mitchell protested that what he stated was perfectly true and was advised to keep better hours and company in future'.*

The last week of the year proved as action-packed as every Christmas week traditionally had – with two more PCs nursing bruises and at least one counting himself extremely lucky to be seeing-in 1859.

This was **No24 Richard Fowkes** who'd only been appointed in April this year. Just weeks after joining and still a PC 3rd Class, he'd distinguished himself and his selfless conduct praised after rescuing a girl named Griffiths from drowning in the Severn at the imminent risk of his own life. He'd been raised to 2nd Class in July this year. Called in to clear the Apple Tree in Tybridge Street at 12.30pm, well after appointed hours, he and **Ezra Franklin** (*also appointed this year on 12th March*) got all the customers outside with the exception of one, boatman William Dowling.

The *Herald* tells the tale:

> *'…he ordered the officers away, followed them into the street, and was very abusive. After a great deal of persuasion, he still refusing to go home, Fowkes collared him whereupon Dowling drew a large clasp-knife from his pocket and threatened to cut off the officer's hand if he did not loose him. Suiting the action to the word, he aimed a blow at the policeman's hand and the officer received a cut in his little finger which would have been more serious had he not snatched his hand away. Then Dowling aimed another blow at him with his knife, which would have descended on his face or breast had not the other officer, Franklin, parried it. Franklin was then soon thrown on the ground and the prisoner then ran away up a passage, followed by Fowkes who collared him in the garden; a struggle ensued, but the prisoner being very strong speedily threw the officer and bolted again. Fowkes who is but a spare thin man and a poor match for the heavy weight and savage determination of his antagonist, with a courage which is highly creditable to him, got on his legs again, and once more pursued and collared his man. Both fell to the ground and Franklin then came up; subsequently the assistance of other officers was obtained and with great difficulty, Dowling was escorted to the station where he held up his fist and threatened to knock Fowkes' head off. The prisoner who is a violent character and has been frequently before the Bench on charges of assaulting his wife and others, said in defence that the officer pushed him in the gutter first and that he took out the knife to scrape the mud off his clothes'.*

One of his witnesses damaged his case by describing the two officers as 'the most sanguinary brace of "blues" ever known'. Fined £2 with 8s 6d costs or a month's hard. It appears he paid rather than submit himself to a month on the treadwheel. It was neither the first nor the last time he would be involved in a tussle with the police.

## Also this year: 1858

- more serious assaults this year: PC William Hill who resigned not long after, PC Richard Berry in March, Richard Fowkes (April), James Fielders (April), and PC Charles Martin (September)

- forged £5 Bank of England notes cause financial chaos

- Mary Bromage clocks up 50th d&d, calling the police her enemies

- police avert lynching of Odd Fellows (later Farriers) Arms landlord John Johnson following rumours that he'd murdered his wife Sarah. The subsequent autopsy suggested natural causes, but the crowds thought otherwise

- Tommy Chipp personally conducts investigation into the murder of bullying militiaman George Turner, stabbed by young ostler Joseph Barnard in the Hope and Anchor (now View Bar) later sentenced to a month's imprisonment without hard labour

- the same week another baby's body is dragged out of the canal at Sidbury. In court Sgt John Doughty produces the few miserable rags the baby was found in

- '5-year old' William Perkins sentenced to a month's hard labour for theft, followed by five years at a reformatory (See next page)

street, and at other places, this morning, was sent to gaol for seven days' hard labour.

WEDNESDAY.

Before C. Sidebottom, Esq.

JUVENILE POCKET-PICKING.—Wm. Perkins, 5 years old, who had been remanded from last week on the charge of taking a purse containing 3s. 10d. out of the pocket of Mrs. Teague, whilst she was dealing at the shop of Mrs. Oakey, Shambles, on the 30th August, was sentenced to a month's hard labour, and at the expiration of that time to be sent for five years to the Hinkley Reformat...

**It must be true - it said so in the Herald...** *5-year old William Perkins sentenced this year to a month's hard labour plus five years in a Reformatory for picking pockets. Stretches the credibility, though...*

**Gained:** *Ezra Franklin, James Barker, William Hill, Charles Martin, Richard Fowkes, John Phillips, Thomas Roberts, Peter Bullock, George Humphreys, William Arkwell*

**Lost:** *George Williams (after 22 years), Joseph Phillips, Edward Chipp, Charles Cotton, Thomas Roberts (after three months), George Humphreys (after three weeks)*

Again, another bad start to the year when in February **PC Charles Martin** was sacked a month short of completing his first year. He'd offered his resignation after having been reported by a brother officer following visits to three pubs and having a drink in each while on duty.

'Martin, in defence, alleged that he was ill and sought some liquors to comfort him, but a surgeon refused to certify as to his illness; and consequently the committee declined to accept his resignation, but at once discharged him, with the forfeit of the whole of his pay'. Although reserving their strongest condemnation for the landlords who'd served him, the *Herald*, indignant as ever with officers displaying an over-fondness for drink while on duty, used the opportunity to lob more warning shots across their bows:

> '...we trust this will prove a salutary warning to others, as the police force should only consist of those in whom the utmost confidence can be placed for sobriety as well as honesty and good character. It may be useful to publicans to warn them that they subject themselves to a heavy penalty for knowingly harbouring police officers in their houses while on duty, besides jeopardizing their licences'.

The fact is that Worcester folk in general and a high proportion of policemen from day one right up to the very end $134^1/_2$ years on, were notoriously fond of their beer and sometimes more. Pressures of the job plus the weight of temptation given the number of pubs per head of population inevitably played a hand, but it still remains surprising just how many officers were prepared to take the risk of being found out.

On May 12th this year, **PC First Class William Berridge** was fined 10/- admonished and warned that future delinquency would result in more severe punishment after being found in a public house while on duty and afterwards making use of bad language and abusing his Sergeant.

It was pretty much everyday, and even up to the end (*1967*), a high percentage of Worcester City's policemen maintained an eminently-deserved reputation for enjoying a pint or two, on- *and* off-duty.

The same week, 180 vagrants were housed in the Workhouse and 1,011 had received out-door relief.

Another month, another nasty assault by a gang of drunken thugs, the victim this time **PC William Hawker** after just a few months with the force: the assault prompted him to jack it in as soon as he'd recovered. It occurred in the King's Head in Sidbury and the worst offender, out of a mob of possibly a dozen or more, was 'a great, lungeous brutalized railway labourer' (*Herald*) named William Cooke.

Shocking as Hawker's injuries proved to be – as the paper put it 'he is quite a young man, and by no means a match in bulk or weight for his powerful antagonist', the worst aspect of the case emerged as the crowd's antagonism to the young copper who'd been called in by the landlord's son to sort out a drunken out-of-hand mob, reached danger level. While he was down and being unmercifully hammered by Cooke, pack instinct kicked-in and they all just turned on him, spurred on by yells of (quote) 'Go into the b-------

policeman and give it to him'.

The sheer ferocity of the attack led shocked magistrates to issue an order to **Tommy Chipp** '...to apprehend everyone who could be identified as having taken part in this outrage'. Cooke, whose only plea was 'tipsiness and know-nothingism' according to the news-sheet, was fined £2 and costs or in default, three months' hard. It was no-win for the police. A few weeks later, a low lodging-house keeper named George Ballinger lodged a complaint with the Bench that **Sergeant Banner** and reliable beat bobby **PC George Sedgeley** who was also later to be promoted to Sergeant, had:

> '...refused to quell a disturbance in his house and he brought witnesses to prove that the officers were at the time in the Falcon public-house in Broad-street, to which house he went to engage their assistance in a drunken row at his own house but could not get them to do their duty. The officers, in defence, said that they went to the Falcon by request to clear that house and were just on the point of coming out when Ballinger arrived there; that he wished them to turn some men out of his house who had gone to bed drunk, but one of the officers told him that the best thing he could do, if the men were gone to bed, was to let them stay there; and lastly, that Ballinger harboured fellows of such rough character at his house that it was not expected that the police should always be dancing attendance upon him to free him from the consequences'.

On June 17th **Joseph Banner** was appointed full Sergeant – a popular move – but on the same day, **John Doughty** was censured for supineness and indifference in not taking effective steps to apprehend a gang of burglars suspected of a robbery at Alderman Price's warehouse and not immediately informing the Superintendent and detectives.

A few weeks later (*July 15th*) **PC 1st Class George Young**, now in his third year with the force, was fined 5/8d and severely reprimanded for soliciting a solicitor (*a lovely phrase, that!*) for a cash hand-out in a prosecution which he'd conducted.

Yet another complaint of a policeman failing to do his duty swiftly followed – this time **PC26 James Barker** who'd refused a request to take a man into custody as he had no grounds so to do – and was also unceremoniously slung-out by the Watch Committee, but not before the complainant, dentist McGregor of Laugherne House, had dashed off furious letters to all the papers alleging woeful police inefficiency.

The affair took up almost a whole column in the *Herald*, who accused the *Journal* of being misled by the complainant, who in turn hurled insult at the *Chronicle* for having run the story in the first place.

## Popular Bill Hale No5 and later Bellman, dies

The same week, a former Watchman from 1830 who'd served under **Henry Sharpe** and **James Douglas'** No5, **William Hale,** died from erysipelas (*of which we shall be hearing more before long*) and bronchitis. He'd been the City's bellman and one of the Mayor's officers after he'd quit the force at the end of 1844, and when he was buried at Tallow Hill Cemetery, the police attended en masse as a mark of respect.

A lovely Hale-tale appears on p 336 of ***Bob Backenforth's Worcester Pubs Then and Now Vol II*** (*2015*) when he was reported to have been taking a quiet stroll down Lich Street and invited in by the new landlord of the Black Boy, John Page (*there, 1853-58*) '...to give a judgement on the quality of some ale, which there were none fitter than a Bellman to decide' (*Herald*).

While in there, an ex-offender called Sanders (*Herald description: 'an ancient Visigoth'*) with a hatred of officialdom '...poured his abuse upon the unmeddling Bellman. Hale admonished him to silence, but he thereon got up from his seat with a centrifugal motion and applied his fist to the cryer's crying organ. It did not require much violence on Hale's part to lay the offender low'. After he'd left, Sanders followed him into the street, severely slashed his ear with a knife '...and made the blood gush forth in horrifying torrents' leaving Hale no choice but to put him down again – this time until someone came along to revive him to his senses. Sanders was sent to prison for a fortnight.

It was also proving to be **William Richardson's** year: on September 29th, the Watch Committee expressed their commendation for his meritorious conduct in risking his life in the execution of his duty during a stand-off in the City Gaol, and two weeks later (*October 16th*) again commended him for the 'prompt and efficient discharge of his duty in the apprehension of a burglar convicted at the last Assizes for a burglary at Ald. Price's'.

On the downside, a prisoner named James Westwood had died in the cells at Worcester station-house on November 2nd and a large proportion of Worcester was only too willing to believe it had been at the hands of an over-zealous policeman. A major enquiry was set up to investigate the circumstances and it

## SUPPLEMENT

### TO

# THE WORCESTER HERALD.

### SATURDAY, NOV. 5, 1859.

**SECOND EDITION.**

**THE FATAL AFFRAY AT THE ANGEL INN, SILVER-STREET.**

**VERDICT OF MANSLAUGHTER.**

*(Continued from Principal Sheet.)*

The adjourned inquest on the body of John Westwood, whose death at the police-station on Wednesday morning last, and the subsequent enquiry before the jury on Thursday evening, is reported in the principal sheet of this day's *Herald*, was held last evening (Friday), at the Pack Horse Inn, before Mr. R. T. Rea, coroner. Mr. George Bentley again attended for the prosecution, and Mr. George Finch for Mr. Pearse, who was not himself present. There was considerable excitement manifested, and the inquest-room was crowded.

The first witness examined was—

Emma Evans, of Tarrington, Herefordshire, now a prisoner under remand in the city gaol, who deposed—On Tuesday evening last, about nine o'clock or from that to half-past nine, I went into the Angel Inn to get a supper, and partook of it in the bar. I had finished my supper, but the landlord's brother and a female who I believe assists in keeping the house, who were supping at the same time, had not finished. I heard a noise in the kitchen, cursing and swearing, and I heard the landlord speaking at the same time. This continued for some time, and I heard a person, but I do not know who that w:s, say, "If I had a gun I would shoot you," and some one said, "Shoot me, would you?" Almost immediately upon that the landlord came into the bar, and Collins followed him, rushing in upon him directly. Immediately before this I saw that the landlord's brother was kicked in the face. He was sitting close to the door, and looking towards the kitchen, with his head turned round the corner. Collins struck at the landlord with his fist in the bar. Before this

passed me by the door, and went into the bar. He went towards the landlord, who had the poker uplifted as before described, standing near to Collins. He told Pearse, "You shan't hit my baiby down." The landlord told him to stand back, but he stepped over Collins and went nearer to the landlord. His hands were down and open, and he put himself in no menacing position whatever. The landlord immediately knocked deceased down with the poker by a blow on the head. Deceased had a cap on, which fell off after he was struck. Both men were on the ground at the same time, and for about ten minutes. During this time the landlord retained possession of the poker and stood near to the fire-plate with the poker uplifted as before. I saw a man named Haines come in and go towards deceased to pick him up. The landlord said, "Let the b—— lie, or I'll serve you the same." (Sensation.) The row then ended. I staid at the bar door for about two minutes, and then went back into the kitchen.

By Mr. Finch.—I have been in Mr. Pearse's employment, and was discharged.

Mr. Finch.—What were you discharged for—do you know?
Witness.—Because he beat me.
Mr. Finch.—What did he beat you for?
Witness.—Because I was gone too long to the Bowling-green.
Mr. Finch.—What state were you then in?
Witness.—As sober as I am now.
Mr. Bentley.—What did he beat you with?
Witness.—With a great big stick.

Alfred Haines, gardener, of Evesham, deposed—I went into the Angel Inn about nine o'clock on Tuesday night. Westwood and Collins were both there at that time. There was a noise in the kitchen, and the landlord said he would put Collins out. I saw Collins follow the landlord into the bar, and then heard a disturbance in the bar, and went to the door, where I saw Collins down on the ground on his hands and knees. I saw Westwood leave the kitchen and go into the bar. He said to the landlord, "You shan't hit my mate like that." I afterwards saw him lying on the bar floor. I went towards him and said, "Oh, dear, oh; that man is dead I should think." Pearse said, "Oh,——, let the b—— lie," and he told me to step back or he would serve me the same. I stepped back. At that time Pearse had the poker uplifted

there, and there was no doubt that he was struck by Pearse. That was the state of the facts. The very moment that the deceased was on the ground the offence was completed—there was an end of it. Having already said that in his judgment the instrument with which Pearse armed himself was unnecessary, and that he did not retreat, but stood in the bar, as he was proved to have done—there could be no ground in his opinion for the jury coming to any other reasonable verdict than that Mr. Pearse did feloniously kill and slay the deceased—that was, that he was guilty of the crime of manslaughter. But if, regarding the circumstances and the evidence they had heard in the case, they would reasonably come to a different conclusion, they would do so. Mr. Rea then alluded to one or two unimportant discrepancies in the evidence of the witnesses, as being amongst that class of discrepancies that very frequently arose in such cases, and further remarked that whilst on the one hand he considered Pearse must be committed on the charge of manslaughter, still it was not a very bad case of that kind—not one of those grievous cases which should have called for that public demonstration and that noisy kind of expression which he had heard in coming to the inquest the previous evening, of persons calling out to hang Pearse without "book, bell, or candle." The jury had, he again observed, calmly to consider the circumstances of the case, and if they agreed with the opinion he had expressed, they would return a verdict of manslaughter, or, if not, if they thought the case could be reduced, and that it was not a felonious but an excusable slaying of the deceased, they would return their verdict accordingly. He suggested that the room should be cleared of the public whilst they were deliberating.

The Foreman said that he thought that course was unnecessary, and almost immediately afterwards, having consulted his fellow jurors, said their unanimous verdict was that of "MANSLAUGHTER." The Coroner's order of commitment against Pearse was then made out for him to appear for trial at the next assizes.

Mr. Finch applied that the prisoner might be admitted to bail.

The Coroner said that he would grant bail under a recent Act of Parliament, and he had great pleasure in stating that this power was now given to Coroners to accept bail, for in his own experience he had even met from £15 to £16 in

---

emerged that he'd been brought there blooded and insensible after a typical Saturday night pub brawl in the navvies' favourite, the Angel *(later the Plough and still within living memory)* in Silver Street.

Westwood and another man named Collins had tried to pick a fight with several soldiers in the tap-room, and were first ordered to be quiet by landlord John Pearse and then ordered out. Collins retaliated by following Pearse into the kitchen and starting a major argument in which John Pearse's brother George was also on the receiving-end of a kick in the face. As the fight spilled into the parlour, Pearse picked up a poker and a witness, ostler William Martin, saw the two tussling, with Collins 'fencing' the poker with his fists: '...Collins then rushed up to the landlord who then struck him down (with the poker)'.

Telling everyone else – including the soldiers and a young prostitute Emma Evans released on remand from gaol earlier that day – to stand back, the single blow felled Collins, at which John Westwood went to help his pal. While he was in a kneeling position, Pearse also hit him over the head with the poker. Pearse's fate was sealed when an observer with a deep-seated grudge against the otherwise model landlord testified that while both men were lying injured on the floor with Pearse standing over them with the poker raised, he told gardener Alfred Haynes who'd observed '...oh, dear, oh. That man is dead I should think" and Pearse said "Oh,–––, let the b–-s lie" and he told (Haynes) to step back or he would serve him the same' – a comment that produced gasps in the court.

Westwood and Collins were taken to the city gaol, both walking, although awkwardly – Collins because he was drunk, and Westwood because he was still bloodied and dazed from the blow. When another prisoner, Francis C. Stephens was flung into the cell they shared – now making it six prisoners in there – he asked Westwood to move over. When he received no response, he was found to be dead.

No charges were brought against any constables and the force was absolved of any blame in Westwood's death, although persistent rumours circulated for a long time afterwards.

In March the following year, John Pearse was gaoled for a year *without hard labour* for manslaughter.

On November 18th **PC 1st Class James Drew** was reprimanded for receiving property from a prisoner in the charge of the Governor to the Gaol which he was assisting, and refusing to give it up. Despite this setback, he was appointed Serjeant on July 12th 1861.

*Gained: William Hawker, George Smith, Alfred Greenall, Stephen Edwards, Frederick Moule (all three quit after less than a month), George Robins, Charles Clements, James Williams*
*Lost: Peter Bullock, Charles Martin, William Hill*

## Also this year: 1859

- in January PC (later Sergeant) John Wall breaks down door at the Church Tavern (later Fleece Inn, now Durrants) in Mealcheapen Street to discover body of suicide Catherine Yarnold

- Herald renews attacks on police for leniency in dealing with boy nuisances and repeats calls for tougher action and increased use of the birch

- grave concerns expressed by police at renewal of the licence for the Crystal Palace, gin shop, scene of almost nightly disorder and violence

- Det Bill Richardson investigates city-wide spate of clothes-line thefts. This was to prove a good year for him

- Sgt Herbert May Evans arrests Esther Greenwood for being drunk in the Cornmarket and singing obscene ballads, printed copies of which she sold

- Tommy Chipp intervenes in the case of flyman Henry Griffiths for setting his dog on 'Old Worcester' one of the first swans introduced on the Severn swannery some years earlier

- police investigate discovery of another new-born baby's body, found in a privy in Sidbury

- Det Richardson praised for apprehension of gang of professional pickpockets

- crowds turn violent inside and outside the Guildhall at the trial of Thomas Harris and his sister Sarah following the suicide of his wife Emily and their two children all drowned in the Severn. Tommy Chipp forced to give protection and provide transport for their return to gaol

At the beginning of the year, it was reported that there was now more than 200 separate police forces in England and Wales.

In the wake of the previous November's Westwood incident, accommodation at the Worcester station-house came under the spotlight. Following the unfortunate man's death and associated rumours, they'd increased ventilation in the cells and put in some form of lighting. Plans were also put in hand to build a third cell for women by taking up two of the rooms used by **Inspector Chipp** as bedrooms which would be replaced by giving him the two rooms used by **Benjamin Holmes**. No mention was made of what was to happen to the Station Sergeant or his family – but of more concern to the Watch Committee was the element of cost that had now entered the equation and set alarm bells ringing at the Guildhall.

The council's more frugal members instantly put a halt to the plans on the excuse that the lease on the former Militia HQ could be up the following year and that at the present time, further expense on the building would be inadvisable.

**William Richardson** was still riding high: in February he was involved in the detection of a driver named Joseph Kettle in the employment of St Nicholas Street fly proprietor Thomas Honess who, after having been paid 10s for fares, then jumped on a train to Birmingham and blew the lot on drink, having to be dragged back to the city three days later in irons.

*He'd left the fly and its horse at Shrub Hill station all that time.*

On the same day as their return, poor **PC16 Ezra Franklin** was again coming off worst in an altercation with two slug-it-out women he'd been sent in to separate. Typically, the two, Ann Jenkins and Ann Band, turned their flying fists on him and '...Jenkins who had been the worst of the two, was fined 10s and 3s 6d costs or seven days' imprisonment.

Just a few weeks later (*March 27th*) more publicity of the kind **Tommy Chipp** had been hoping to avoid – and more evidence of in-fighting amongst his officers. That these were two of his most prominent and visible men hardly helped the situation and no doubt he'd have far preferred to have had the affair hushed-up and dealt with from within. Sadly it was too high-profile for that and went all the way to the Watch Committee – drawing attention to the fact that at the police HQ all was not running as smoothly as originally believed. It had centred on an allegation by the ever-confrontational **PC William Berridge** against the equally belligerent **Detective Bill Richardson**, accusing him of drunkenness and otherwise improper conduct.

Reports the *Herald*:

> *'...the committee were fully occupied for three hours when they passed resolutions stating their opinion that there was no foundation for the charge, and that Berridge had been guilty of traducing the character of Richardson in making the charge against him in a manner to destroy his efficiency as an officer, instead of bringing it to be investigated by his superior officer or the committee. They also resolved to reprimand Berridge and he was to be informed that upon a repetition of such conduct he would be discharged from the force'.*

But the year had not yet finished with **William Richardson**, or **William Berridge...**

Just a week later, **Berridge** was commended for taking on two drunken boatmen who'd been fighting in Quay Street, who then both turned on him, knocking him down with a string of blows – despite which, he still managed to better the two. In court the next day, he even pleaded for leniency for William Walkley, the worse of his two attackers, and he walked away with just the usual fine of 5s for drunkenness.

The same night **PC John Sanders** had been hammered by punches and kicks in the White Horse in Silver Street by stonemason Richard Langley who blamed 'summat pernicious in the ale' for the assault. Fined 10s and 3s 6d costs.

Ever a contentious and controversial policeman, on April 20th, **John Sanders** was ordered to resign within a fortnight or be discharged for insulting Charles Williams landlord of the Holly Bush while in uniform and calling him a liar at the top of his voice. On May 4th he attended before the Committee and expressed his regret for his conduct and apologised to Mr Williams who expressed his desire that he might be reinstated in consideration of his previous good conduct. For once, the Committee listened.

In one week alone in April, five separate attacks on policemen were reported to the court, prompting Police Magistrate Charles Sidebottom to remark that '...assaults on the police this week (are) more than usually numerous, and of a more aggravated character, than (he) ever before remembered in Worcester'.

One of the worst was in the apparently mis-named Dove in Lowesmoor where **PC24 Richard Fowkes** was called in to quell a near-riot with fighting-mad Noah Dayus jun taking on all-comers. Though **Fowkes** managed to quieten the temper of the Dove, as he reached the corner of Pheasant Street '...Dayus came up and after making some remark struck him a violent blow in the face. Afterwards he knocked Fowkes down and kicked him on the eye while his wife hammered the constable's head against the stones. Prisoner managed to escape to his own house, which was near, and there issued threats'.

With a warrant out for his arrest, he gave himself up the next day. Fined £1 with 6s costs.

Others throughout the year – and almost a random selection on account of the sheer number of reported incidents, many of them of an exceedingly violent nature – involved:

● **No3 Charles Clements**, still less than a year after joining, kicked and seriously roughed-up in the now-notorious Crystal Palace liquor shop where fighting was an almost nightly occurrence (*see* **Bob Backenforth's Worcester Pubs Then and Now** *Vol II pps 262-3 for a long list of complaints and assaults here*). A few weeks later, he was also set on by three drunks outside the haunt of noted pugilists including hardened professionals, the Duke of York in Angel Street. Not surprisingly, he was seriously banged about before being rescued by **William Richardson**. At the hearing in which the main aggressor, 'sportsman' (ie: probably a professional fighter) Charles Pollard was fined £1 and expenses, **Tommy Chipp** described Clements as an excellent officer, young but useful, and not drunk as stated nor the worse for liquor (*pity in a way, as the application of some prior anaesthetic might have been welcome!*)

● **No 22 James Hill**, only four months on the beat, first attacked by Edmund Bishop with a length of wood that he'd been using to beat his wife, then attacked by the wife while Bishop went upstairs to get a foot-long iron spike '...which he said he would run into my heart if I interfered', then an almighty tussle in which he was knocked down, kicked several times in the ribs, followed by more threats that he would wash his hands in Hill's blood before he was done.

- **PC James Fielders** too ill to attend court the following day and also a week later after a major set-to with boatman Thomas Penney in Quay Street
- **Sgt Benjamin Holmes** whose attacker Henry Burton opted to pay the fine of 10s and 3s 6d rather than 14 days' hard, but then pleaded for return of some part of it to purchase food for himself and his wife and was eventually let off on payment of 2s and a promise to leave Worcester immediately
- **PCs Arkell, Meredith, James Hill, Banner, Berridge and Vaughan** all severely hammered in separate incidents throughout the year

Not that many of the other constables were entirely squeaky-clean in their dealings with the public this year. In March **PC No 7 William Wild (*or Wilde*)** was found drunk while on duty in St Johns and later of committing 'a savage and wanton assault on blacksmith Mr. Perkins'. Instantly suspended, he did a runner from the city, failed to report in and was sacked by the Watch Committee. *He'd been a policeman for less than two weeks.* The same month, a returned convict George Newman claimed that he was assaulted by **PC James Hill,** who'd only joined the force two months earlier, who was, he alleged, drunk. His claim was unanimously dismissed when he was hauled up in court for two separate assaults on the police: **Hill** and, in a separate case, **Tommy Meredith**.

On June 10th., **Sgt Joseph Banner** was reprimanded and fined 5/- for drinking ale in a public house after 12 o'clock on Sunday morning and allowing one of his men to do likewise.

On the positive side, March had also seen **PC24 Richard Fowkes** awarded a guinea gratuity for courageous conduct in saving the life of Elizabeth Griffiths who'd attempted to drown herself in the Severn, and on October 5th **William Berridge** was allowed to keep the 10 shillings sent anonymously to the station house with a request that it be forwarded to him for his actions in bringing a drunken man to the station-house. On the down-side, on November 23rd he was censured for exceeding his duty taking a prisoner, Ellis, into custody on a false charge.

Just the previous week, more of **Detective Bill Richardson's** unpopularity emerged when **Sgt. John Doughty** had been severely reprimanded for '...assaulting **Detective Richardson** while on duty, refusing to receive the charge of this officer and using abusive language. Fined £1 and ordered to be more careful in the control of his temper and future action in the discharge of his duties. At the same time, **William Richardson** was reprimanded for using abusive language to **Sergeant Doughty** while on duty'.

*Below: Det. Bill Richardson's Marks of Approbation [extract] (WCiCo/WAAS)*

**Gained:** James Hill, James Hawker (quit after eight weeks), William Wilde (dismissed after just a week), William Bayliss (quit after a month), Charles White, John Winwood Tandy, John Brown (all three ditto - two months), John Knott, John Cullis, George Moule (dismissed then re-instated), Frederick Dolvere, Charles Incell

**Lost:** James Williams, George Robins, George Knott, Richard Berry

- *in the first weeks, PC (later Sergeant) John Sanders No12 was brought in to stop two jockeys galloping their horses up and down Lowesmoor in mock races. They said they were trialling the horses as part of a sale*

- *cocky 11-year old Jack Sheppard of Copenhagen Street sentenced to five days solitary and 'low diet' in gaol after retaliating to the Bench that he 'didn't care if they cut him into little pieces and salted him' following a severe reprimand for wayward ways*

- *before mayor William Haigh '...John Johnson, a tall pale young man in a state of so-soism insisted on PC (12, John) Sanders finding him a lodging, which he duly did – at the station'*

- *time is running out for the Crystal Palace after PC Charles Clements is gravely assaulted by Samuel Trehearne inside. 'The magistrates said that assaults on the police were getting too frequent and must be prevented'*

- *the same day PC22 James Hill is assaulted by Edmund Bishop after he'd responded to calls of 'murder' from a house in Hand's Entry off Newport Street*

- *neat work by PC3 Charles Clements involving apprehension of a man who'd taken the King's Shilling from Pte. Thomas Goddard of the 24th Regiment of Foot and did a runner, showed him to have joined up eighteen years earlier, deserted, court-martialled, re-enlisted, deserted again and sentenced to seven years' transportation from which he'd just returned. He called himself Henry Boddis but his real name was Guise*

- *the last day of the year saw notorious drunk Jemmy Gomersky in court the day after his release following 7 days' imprisonment on the same charge (on that occasion, he'd gone with PC 25 Charles Insell without resistance). This time he accuses PCs 10 and 22 of throwing him down and dislocating his shoulder. See p371*

On January 15th the Watch Committee expressed their gratification of the prompt action used by **Det William Richardson** following a city centre blaze discovered by **PC Ezra Franklin** who was also praised for his 'assiduity and distinguished conduct in attending a fire in Foregate Street'. It was to prove a good year for both officers, both coming in for commendations for their actions.

Just a few weeks later, **Det. Richardson** came in for even more praise for his detection work in a robbery of a quantity of clothing from a public house in Sidbury, and February saw the Mayor Joseph Wood present him with a written citation on behalf of the entire city, in recognition of '...his conduct, his honesty, his sobriety, and also of his activity and skill in the detection of crime (in Worcester)'

On the other hand, **PC Ezra Franklin** (*appointed 12th March 1858*) was fined 1/- for neglect of duty. He'd earlier been praised for excellent behaviour during an assault being committed on him and the resulting conviction of two men that had seen him promoted to PC 1st Class.

*Then another shock of the kind that was following an all-too regular pattern...*

### Tommy Chipp dies suddenly

**Tommy Chipp** died on Sunday March 10th, quite suddenly even though the previous two years had seen him absent on numerous occasions due to increasing bouts of illness. He was 52 and had been overtaken by an attack of erysipelas – a bacterial disease also known as 'St Anthony's Fire'.

For the passing of the chief of the city force, the press was again remarkably muted in its comment on the deceased superintendent: the testimonial to **William Richardson** the same week garnering more column inches, a more prominent place in the newspapers and massively more praise for its subject.

In a subdued 16-line report, the *Herald* noted '...(**Superintendent Chipp**) was a very civil and well-behaved man and a useful public servant and though he might not possess many of the requisites of success for a competitive examination, he was practically as well posted in his business as many more showily gifted functionaries. We are sorry to learn that his widow and family are left in very poor circumstances'.

DEATH OF INSPECTOR CHIPP.—Mr. Thomas
Chipp, Inspector of the police force of this city, died on
Sunday morning last, from an attack of erysipelas, in his
52nd year. The deceased had been ailing for a considerable period, but his decease was somewhat sudden at last.
He was a very civil, well-behaved man, and a useful public
servant, and though he might not possess many of the
requisites of success for a competitive examination, he was
practically as well posted in his business as many more
showily gifted functionaries. We are sorry to learn that
his widow and family are left in very poor circumstances.
He was buried in the new Cemetery yesterday (Thursday)
afternoon, by the Rev. C. Bullock, rector of St. Nicholas.
The Mayor's officers, the whole of the city police force, and
several inhabitants of the city, attended as a mark of
respect.

On the day of his funeral (*Thursday , March 14th*), the Watch Committee met to discuss his successor
– three candidates having already emerged as possibles: **Sergeant Herbert May Evans** who'd just
notched-up 17 years with the force and had been appointed interim superintendent pending a permanent
replacement; **Detective William Richardson** who never appears to have been out of the front line over
the past two years, and Superintendent Phillips, head of the Worcester Division of the County force.  In
the intervening period, they followed established procedure and resolved to appoint **Sgt. Evans** to take
temporary direction pending selection of a permanent superintendent.  They also voted to consult Maj-
General Cartwright for his advice '...and any further information he can give as to the salary and class of
man usually appointed as superintendent in cities or boroughs of equal magnitude'.

The chief of the Inspectorate quickly responded by saying that the new chief's salary should be £120 a
year (£2 6s 8d [£2.34p] a week) exclusive of house rent, and that whatever course they took in respect of
the latter, it should be either within, or very close to, the station-house.

**Tommy Chipp**'s funeral was marked by a full turn-out of the police force and Mayor's officers plus,
noted the *Herald* with telling lack of enthusiasm, 'several inhabitants of the city'.

He'd left a widow, Ludlow-born Ann, now 55 who was now claiming straitened circumstances – not least
as she was about to lose her salaried role as female searcher and was also about to become homeless. The
Watch Committee voted to allow her £60 – 5s a week for five years – but the ever-frugal Council knocked
that back to £50 while moves to make up the shortfall from the Police Superannuation Fund were also
rejected because not all the officers agreed:  *it was now emerging that at least in later years, Tommy Chipp
had not been so popular nor so efficient as generally believed.*

For the time being, and at least until a new chief had been selected, Ann Chipp and her remaining
brood Alfred (15), Ann (12) and Fanny (8) were allowed to remain at the station-house and the following
month's census on 7th April showed they were still living there, 1 Queen Street with servant Jane Bunn
(18).  Next door at number 3 lived Detective Police officer Cumberland-born **Benjamin Holmes** (28)
with his Worcester-born wife Lucy, a milliner aged 24, son Thomas (4) and daughter Elizabeth (2). Their
immediate neighbours included a trunk maker, shoe binder, carter, seamstress, laundress, whitesmith,
carpenter, labourer/excavator, bricklayer and several glovers/gloveresses.

If the prospect of shelling-out £120 a year gave the frugal council members sleepless nights, another
report the same week must have given them nightmares:  *the crying need for a new police station.*

The St Nicholas Street former Militia Drill Hall, had served as the force's main station-house since they'd
moved out of the over-cramped and oppressive City Gaol in 1838 but now it was considered dirty and
dilapidated and no longer fit for the residence of a superintendent or for the transaction of day-to-day
police work.  Additionally, there had long been complaints of prisoners who'd been locked up overnight
in the cells being carted through the streets to the Guildhall the next morning and besides, while already
cramped, plans for the widening of the street meant that the building was about to lose some of its length
and frontage.

The choices were to knock it down and start again – which the city could probably afford, just – or to
look for somewhere new for a police HQ, a move which would probably involve borrowing money, a route
the notoriously frugal Council would be unlikely to feel inclined to follow.

**But first, they needed to find a new chief....**

# 7:
# The Power years

## 10th May 1861– 6th February 1884

The vacant post was advertised nationally and 26 hopefuls submitted applications, whittled down to four, all already high-ranking police officers – Jesse Lister, Inspector of Leeds police; Matthew Power, ex-lieutenant in the Irish Revenue Police; George Rogers, Chief Superintendent of police at Swansea; and Robert Gifford, Chief Constable of Berwick.

The three local candidates that had first emerged as possibles – **Sergeant Evans, Detective William Richardson**, and Superintendent Phillips of the County force – were all, apparently, rejected. No doubt desperately disappointed, **Herbert May Evans** who'd run the force in the meantime, immediately resigned and was gone within the month; Superintendent Phillips continued to head the Worcester district division of the County force and was later to play a major role in the apprehension of a madman accused of the attempted murder of one of the City force – but that was three years down the line.

But the great *'what might have been?'* question-mark hung over the clear rejection of Detective **William Richardson's** application. For all the praise and glowing hopes for the future at his testimonial just three months before, **Det. William Richardson** was also gone a little over a year later, although admittedly to a Superintendent's role at Stratford-on-Avon.

The chosen four candidates were invited to Worcester for the formal selection process on May 10th and paid travelling expenses. On the day itself, the thermometer had dropped to minus 10 degrees: was this a sign of the cooling relationship between the city, its police force and people it had been appointed to protect?

Irishman **Matthew Power,** seemingly between jobs at the time, was the man they selected and was immediately appointed. It's likely that the members of the Watch Committee were sensing some regret and possibly disappointment in the three previous chiefs all drawn from the ranks of existing City officers, and that perhaps the *Journal* might – just might – have been right after all.

Certainly, **James Douglas** had quit before he was pushed, **James Phillips** had died a broken and unfulfilled man, and now opinions were divided about the success, *or otherwise,* of the force during **Tommy Chipp**'s easy-going rule, particularly during the previous two years.

# PART II.

## DUTIES.

### CHIEF SUPERINTENDENT'S DUTY.

The Chief Superintendent, under ⟨…⟩ the Watch Committee, will be the ⟨…⟩ of the Po⟨…⟩ Force, and will take the entire c⟨…⟩and of the men. It will be incumbent on him tha⟨…⟩ shall be able and ready to give instructions to the ⟨…⟩cers and men on all points relating to their respec⟨…⟩e duties. He will endeavour, by personal intercou⟨…⟩ to make himself acquainted with the ability and gen⟨…⟩ character and behaviour of all the men. He shou⟨…⟩ firm and just, but at the same time kin⟨…⟩ must take care that the stand⟨…⟩ ⟨…⟩gulations, and all others given out fr⟨…⟩ to time, are promptly and strictly obeyed. M⟨…⟩ be done by himself and under his own im⟨…⟩ nspection, and, as he will be held responsible ⟨…⟩eneral performance of the duties of the Police, he ⟨…⟩ give clear and precise instructions ⟨…⟩er ⟨…⟩

He wi⟨…⟩ide at the ⟨…⟩ion. **Residen**

He ⟨…⟩ muster the men for n⟨…⟩uty at a quarter **Muster** before ⟨…⟩ o'clock at the Station ⟨…⟩, and see that **night** they ar⟨…⟩ean, sober, and in every resp⟨…⟩fit for duty, wit⟨…⟩taff, hand-cuffs, lantern, call,⟨…⟩d all other p⟨…⟩nts, and, having informed ⟨…⟩h man of the n⟨…⟩&c., forming his b⟨…⟩ will dismiss them u⟨…⟩nd of th⟨…⟩jeants to their respective bea⟨…⟩ to the Station-house at such hours ⟨…⟩ time to time fixed, for inspection and dism⟨…⟩ by the Superintendent or Station Serjeant.

*1861 cast-iron handcuffs [courtesy Bob Pooler]*

Then again, they may just have seen something in 35-year old **Matthew Power**'s physical and psychological make-up that appealed – despite, on the face of it, being the least-qualified of the four candidates. The other three were all heads of existing provincial forces – one English, one Welsh, and one Scottish – and all were well experienced in equivalent positions and ready to make the next move; meanwhile **Matthew Power**'s most recent position had been in Belfast and before that in America. He was also a subordinate rather than a principal, and was some distance removed from the day-to-day running of an English borough constabulary.

No doubt the committee members had their reasons, one possible explanation being that the force was crumbling as it stood, and someone needed to gain the upper hand – and quickly, the implication being that immediate availability may well have proved the deciding factor, rarely the most advisable course.

*As events were to show, this time they appear to have got it largely, if not perhaps spectacularly, right...*

### New chief declares no-nonsense stance from Day One

**Matthew Power,** married to Mary Elizabeth two years his senior and daughter of an American consul, and with two daughters, Georgina and Elizabeth, wasted no time in setting-to, making it clear from the outset that here was a man who was going to take no messing...

Within three weeks, he'd produced a critical report on the overall state of the force for the Watch Committee. To call it damning would be overkill, but it remained notably hard-hitting for a man who'd only been in the role for a matter of days and had yet to win the trust of his men.

It came up for discussion at the next Watch Committee meeting on Friday, June 22nd.

First, he claimed that for a city of 31,123 heads and 28 miles of streets with 151 public houses, the ratio of one policeman to 1,192 souls was woefully inadequate and immediately put in for an increase in numbers, describing Worcester as 'insufficiently guarded'.

Possibly shocked by the intensity of the report, but more likely swayed by the new chief's warning that Major-General Cartwright who was due to visit the County within a matter of weeks, would probably withhold its certificate if the force's efficiency was undermined by lack of manpower, they immediately agreed to an augmentation. However, with typical Worcester Corporation frugality – *for which, read 'tight-fistedness'* – it was inevitably a compromise, unilaterally deciding that **two** additional posts would be sufficient rather than the *four* that **Matthew Power** had requested.

Alongside a sideways promotion that made **Detective Benjamin Holmes** a station-sergeant leaving **William Richardson** free rein as detective, the revised arrangement would give the city one superintendent, two station sergeants, three sergeants, 21 constables, one detective and an improved police:people ratio of 1: 1,071.

The new chief was also immediately shaken by some of the working arrangements that at their worst included the station officer coming on duty at 1pm, remaining there for 24 hours and then taking his turn on night duty, and suggested a number of switches in rota patterns – most of which were agreed to with the exception of any that required an increase in expenditure.

Naturally the new chief had also put in for an increase in financial rewards for his men – the *Herald* reporter, as usual, telling it like it is: '...[the proposals] were agreed to with the exception of the paragraph as to pay'.

One proposal that *did* win approval that day however – and would go on to have long-lasting effect – was that officers should wear white gloves while on duty, a nice touch that was to stand the test of time.

Three weeks later, Maj-Gen Cartwright duly reported favourably from his scheduled visit, inspecting the County force in the morning and the City men, mustered in the yard at the Guildhall, in the afternoon.

Reports the *Herald*: '...the gallant officer expressed himself highly pleased at the conduct of the men and their efficient discipline, stating that he considered an evident improvement was already perceptible in the condition of the force and the recent alterations in the organisation, according to the recommendations of

*An elegant touch that stood the test of time: white gloves became a visible hall-mark of the City police this year – and gave the force a sartorial edge for the next 106 years*

Mr. Power, were likely to be attended with good effect'.

It was a different tale at the city gaol where a visit by the Government Prison Inspector Voules the same week had resulted in a highly critical verdict – so bad, in fact, that the prison governors and the Town Council instantly distanced themselves from it and slammed its writer as unjust after having, they claimed, spent just a few minutes visiting and '...producing a report made up of statistics which he finds in documents'. Even so, admitted the city authorities:

> '...the Worcester city prison, although not a model gaol of the most comfortable and coddling class, is economically and religiously conducted, and preserves withal something of the true character of such a place – a terror to evil-doers.'

Quite what **Matthew Power** made of the organisation he'd inherited isn't recorded: one thing that's clear right from the start however, is that he was going to take a much harder line on discipline than **Tommy Chipp** whose sympathies had always lain with his men who'd regarded him as one of their own and as such, something of a soft touch. Not so the new man whose every act left them in not the shadow of a doubt that things were going to change and that anything – or more to the point, *anyone* – standing in the way of the uprated efficiency and standards he demanded would be unceremonially eliminated.

It was clearly a case of starting off the way he meant to go on, and first in the firing line was **Bill Richardson**, cautioned on June 14th for disobedience of his orders. The two were clearly embroiled in a personality clash of the first order – to the point that it could only be one or the other. The force would never be big enough for both: within weeks **Richardson** had been asked to consider his future with Worcester City Police following more instances of insubordination, and the die was cast.

On the same day, **PCs Charles Vaughan and George Moule** had been found trespassing in the Arboretum Pleasure Gardens at 5am and both fined 10/- for shooting rooks instead of patrolling on duty, while **PC Richard Fowkes** found himself carpeted before the new chief, severely reprimanded and fined 5/- for being in the Rising Sun at 2am on a Sunday when he too should have been out on his beat.

***It was clearly not going to be an easy ride for the new chief or for his systemically undisciplined constables.***

Five weeks after taking office, he'd sacked **PC Charles Clements** who, within a week of completing his second year had been cautioned and fined a day's pay for being absent from night duty. He'd asked for an hour and remained absent all night. Bad move: the following day he deserted with part of his clothing, Matthew Power intervened, and **Clements** was instantly discharged.

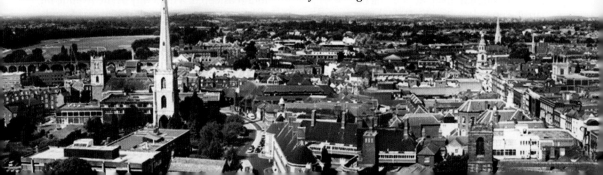

That same day, June 28th., **Matthew Power** also severely reprimanded **PC 3rd Class John Cullis** and warned him for his future conduct after he'd been found 'drinking ale and amusing himself' in the Garibaldi while still on duty. On September 6th, he was fined 10/- and joined the ranks of jobless ex-policemen after being found playing cards in the Royal Oak.

June 28th was also the first day on duty for **John Stringer No21**. Before the end of the year he'd been raised to 2nd Class but was not long after downgraded to 3rd Class for being drunk while on duty and disobeying orders.

From the spate of admonishments, demotions, censures and sackings, it was already clear that the lax state of the force he'd inherited had come as something of a shock, not to mention an out-and-out disappointment to a rigid taskmaster like **Matthew Power,** and that the toughest possible discipline was going to be the only remedy.

Perhaps he didn't like what he was seeing, but also on June 28th have-a-go hero **John Hunting**, veteran of eight heavy-duty slug-it-out years in the front line, had sent in a certificate of incapacity for service in the wake of several nasty injuries sustained during a catalogue of assaults while on duty. In consideration of his good conduct, length of service and overall state of his health, he was relieved on full pay – not that he was to enjoy his semi-retirement for long: he died on October 20th and a gratuity of £10 allowed to his widow from the Superannuation Fund.

- July 26 **Charles Incell** resigned after less than a year

- on August 9th well-respected **PC William Berridge** was severely reprimanded but escaped dismissal after being found asleep in a fly in Angel Street at 2am while still on duty. The action left him angry and disillusioned and he started to look for another job. A useful, intelligent and able officer, he was to find it quite quickly

- August 23rd **William Arkwell** who'd been raised to 2nd Class on July 12th was reprimanded for coming 15 minutes late for muster when going off duty and being under the influence of liquor

- the same day constable **Richards** – his first name appears not to have been logged, even in the Approbation Marks book – was dismissed for being drunk on duty and losing his hat. Ordered to pay 17/-

- **PC John Boyd** was also dismissed that same day after being found guilty of immoral conduct

- September 15th saw **PC 3rd Class George Moule** – who a few months earlier (*March 14th*) had been severely reprimanded and fined 5/- for shooting rooks with **PC Charles Vaughan** instead of being on patrol – up before the chief when he was again cautioned and ordered to be more careful in future after using unnecessary violence towards prisoner James Beard while accompanying him to the Station-house. Within a year he was found guilty of a gross falsehood in the furtherance of his duty and instantly sacked

- September 20th **George Tomkins**, appointed just fourteen days earlier, was fined 10/- and dismissed for keeping a watchful eye on a gentleman's home and receiving a reward for doing so without reporting his additional nefarious duty

- on the same day **PC 1st Class James Fielders** was fined 5/- after being found drinking in the Old Peacock in the Trinity while on duty – not a clever state of affairs as the Peacock was the off-duty PCs' local, sited less than 50 yards away from the station-house. Chances of getting away scot-free must've been less than slim and it was indicative of the complaisance the force had slipped into under **Tommy Chipp.** Fewer than three weeks later, (*October 9th*) Fielders was suspended and afterwards resigned after having been found drunk and asleep while on duty

- also that day, **PC William Carloss** was fined 5/- and admonished for going into the Gilbert Arms public house Diglis, and sitting down to drink. He too later resigned

- two weeks after that, **PC 3rd Class John Spencer,** appointed only three months earlier, was fined 5/-and reprimanded for leaving his beat at an early hour and being found asleep in a doorway at the Avenue on the Cross. Two months later, he was found to be drunk while on duty, fined 2/3d and severely censured

- on October 19th., **PC 3rd Class Herbert Burch** (*appointed August 9th*) was fined 5/- for sleeping on his beat while on duty and allowed to pay over five fortnightly instalments, but on Nov 29th he found himself charged with insubordination and writing an insulting letter, and discharged

- November 29th **PC Isaac Clarke** had three days' pay stopped and was discharged for carelessness

- on December 13th., **Richard Fowkes**, now raised to PC 1st Class was fined 2/6 for want of zeal in the performance of his duty

- twelve days earlier had seen PC 3rd Class **Charles Hill** (appointed October 18th) admonished for deserting from the force. On December 27th he was dismissed for coming off duty intoxicated and absenting himself from duty without leave

- the same day, **PC 1st Class John Wall** was fined 2/6d for being absent from duty without leave

On July 12th one of **Matthew Power's** new organisational measures came into effect: **John Doughty** was appointed Station Sergeant alongside **Benjamin Holmes,** and the new chief hoped to see some immediate improvement in the conduct of his men. Sadly for all concerned, it was not to be ...

## Matthew Power's Blue Book, published in November and still regarded as the model of its kind

Yet despite all this frantic heavy-duty manning and personnel activity, Matthew Power still managed to put his mind to the creation of the **Worcester City Police Blue Book,** published in November this year and still regarded as the model of its kind.

Officially *'the General Regulations, Instructions and Orders for the Government and Guidance of The Worcester City Police Force as framed by the Watch Committee and Approved by the Town Council',* it was, in short, the force's all ranks cast-in-stone bible and rule-book, extending to 40 printed pages – and it demonstrated in the clearest of all possible terms that the new chief had a clear vision of how his men were to conduct themselves from here on in, and Lord have mercy on anyone thinking otherwise.

In its introduction, he stated:

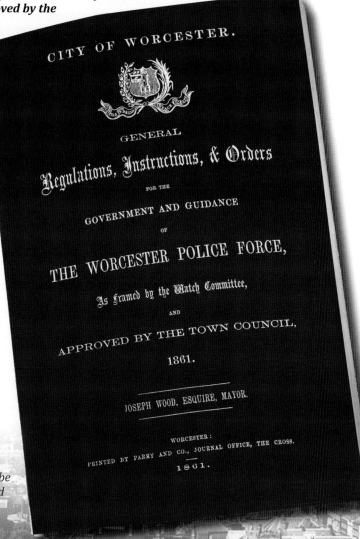

*'...the following general instructions for the different ranks of the Worcester Police Force* [sic, at the time consisting of the chief himself, one detective, 5 sergeants, 8 First-Class Constables, 9 Second Class and 4 Third Class, 28 in all] *are not to be understood as containing rules of conduct applicable to every circumstance that may occur in the performance of their duty; something must necessarily be left to the intelligence and discretion of individuals, and according to the degree in which they show themselves possessed of these qualities, and to their zeal, activity and judgment on all occasions, will be their claims to future promotion and reward.*

*'Main objects to be attained are*

CITY OF WORCESTER.

GENERAL

Regulations, Instructions, & Orders

FOR THE

GOVERNMENT AND GUIDANCE

OF

THE WORCESTER POLICE FORCE,

As framed by the Watch Committee,

AND

APPROVED BY THE TOWN COUNCIL,

1861.

JOSEPH WOOD, ESQUIRE, MAYOR.

WORCESTER:
PRINTED BY PARRY AND CO., JOURNAL OFFICE, THE CROSS.
1861.

*these: –– First, the prevention of crime; second, its detection; third, the apprehension of and punishment of offenders; and all persons engaged in this service are especially to bear in mind that the prevention of crime is the main object of their appointment; to this great end every effort of the Police is to be directed. The security of persons and property, the preservation of the public tranquillity, and all the other objects of a Police establishment, will thus be better effected than by the detection and punishment of the offender after he has succeeded in committing the crime. This should be constantly kept in mind by every member of the Police Force, as the guide for his own conduct.*

*'It is expected that every member of the Force will behave himself with civility to every one with whom his duty may bring him in contact; he must be careful on the one hand not to interfere with that which does not concern him, and on the other, not to permit anything to be neglected which it is his duty to notice. His veracity should be unimpeachable, as this must affect his credibility as a witness; untruthfulness is one of the most serious offences that can be brought against a Constable.*

*'He must be firm in the discharge of his duty, and be careful never to use more force than is necessary for his own safety and the performance of his immediate duty. He must ever retain that perfect command over his temper which is an indispensable qualification in a Police Officer, and which ought ever to be preserved under whatever provocation.*

*'As no Constable can be promoted who cannot write a good official report or letter, no matter how exemplary his conduct, it is in his interest to devote every hour which he can spare from his duty to reading, writing and general mental improvement'.*

The remaining pages then go on to list 22 conditions of every officer's appointment; chief superintendent's, station sergeants' and sergeants' duties – *perhaps surprisingly including provision to allow any of his men to obtain 'moderate and necessary refreshment at public houses provided they pay for or what they have at the time'* – and outline of 38 Constables' duties, and also lists offences by which '...commission of any of them by a Constable will lead to severity of punishment or dismissal', instructions in case of fire, and 15 pages of General Instructions.

What a year it had been.... by any stretch it had proved a roller-coaster for Worcester City Police – and none more than its new Irish superintendent who must have been left wondering what kind of heathen and

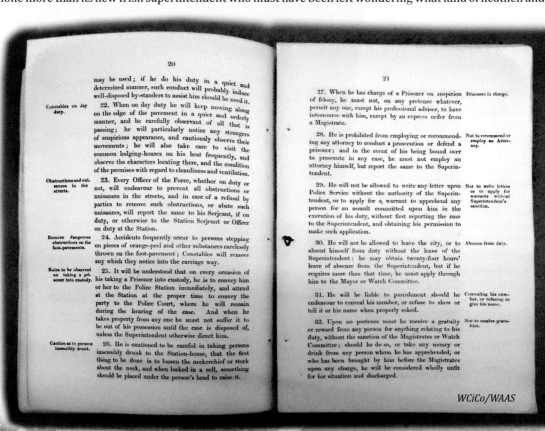

WCiCo/WAAS

lawless town he'd stumbled on, and quite how he was going to face another year with the insubordinate and headstrong characters he'd been expected to work with.

Matthew Power's hard-line first nine months had seen some significant change and a rapid bout of sackings, resignations and replacements – 15 between April and December. No doubt he hoped that among the replacement probationers would be promising new future constables – although he'd probably have settled for men with a basic sense of reliability and attention to duty rather than undisciplined stars.

And then there had been the Blue Book – tough but unequivocal. Was there ever a more eventful year for any other police force anywhere in the Queen's dominions? Unlikely.

**Gained:** *William Carloss, Thomas Croft, John Stringer, Herbert Burch, John Spencer, ? Richards, John Boyd, George Tomkins, George Moule, Charles Smith, Charles Hill, Alfred Vine, James Quinn, William Reeves, Isaac Clarke*

**Lost:** *Thomas Chipp, Herbert May Evans, John Hunting, Thomas Meredith, Charles Clements, John Cullis, Frederick Dolvere, Charles Incell, Herbert Burch, ? Richards, John Boyd, George Tomkins, Charles Hill, William Reeves*

## Also this year: 1861

- **PC10 Ezra Franklin praised for prompt action at a fire in Foregate Street (January) and commended for excellent behaviour during an assault being committed on him and the resulting conviction of two St Johns men, Thomas Burrow and Richard Williams**

- **PC Charles Vaughan tussles with currier John Flemming in the Cross Keys Friar Street, found with two goat skins he'd stolen from his employer William Price of Carden Street**

- **unnamed PCs charge Red Lion (Sidbury) barmaid Emma Clarke with stealing from her employer (six months' hard)**

- **William Richardson comes in for praise for detecting a long line of petty felonies**

- **PC14 John Stringer tangles with notorious hard-case 'Gipsy Moule' after more unpleasantness in the Bell in St Johns**

- **Charles Vaughan again comes off worst in a violent to-do at the New Inn in the Shambles**

- **unnamed PC26 who on St Patrick's Day (March 17th) apprehends Irish navvie Richard Morse who, in addition to several other drunken japes had 'exposed his person in the street', later claiming to have given up the drink for a year but 'moi toime was up yisterdiy'**

- **another unnamed PC apprehends a Gloucester boatman named Hewlett for shooting a swan on the river and was taking it home for dinner**

- **PCs George Moule and Richard Fowkes intervene in separate incidents in the city on the same night and both emerge bashed-about and unable to continue duties for some days**

- **PC George Young strips and dives into the canal to save a would-be suicide, 74-year old labourer William Ross**

- **unnamed PC called to examine and later remove the corpse of carpenter William Jackson who'd been taken ill in Sidbury, given a chair to sit on and forgotten about for five hours – during which time he was found to have died of apoplexy**

- **constables ordered to keep a watch on men and boys bathing naked in the Severn, officially limited this year to the north end of Pitchcroft between the hours of 8pm and 8am**

- **PC John Cullis praised for arresting Irishmen Patrick MacNamara and Thomas Brown at a bodged burglary at Skarratts' silversmith shop in Broad Street**

- **PC William Hill and Sgt James Drew both severely bitten by 'inhuman wretch' William Prince later charged with vampirism after also biting Sam Badgery, landlord of the New Market Tavern in the Shambles, in the face**

- **PC William Berridge and Sgt James Drew subdue Rising Sun (St Johns) landlord John Barrel who was intent on murdering his wife**

- **PC2 Arkell (actually Arkwell and not entirely squeaky-clean) investigates a robbery at the Lamb and Flag in the Tything**

- **PCs Tommy Croft and Richard Fowkes praised for raising the alarm to a fire at the White Horse in Silver Street, later extinguished by a contingent from the whole force led by Matthew Power himself**

- **Charles Vaughan sent to Warwick to apprehend Charles Smith wanted for highway robbery and attempted murder involving two prostitutes, Mary Williams ('Cockney Poll') and Phoebe Hughes**

- **At the end of the year, police called in to control the crowds besieging the Guildhall for news of the passing of Prince Albert, the Queen's Consort**

After the easy-going, but in many ways damaging Chipp years, **Matthew Power'**s first nine months had been a major culture shock for the men of Worcester City Police – some of whom must have been wondering quite who'd be next for the chop.

A typical legacy of the Chipp years surfaced in the first Magistrates' court of the year when **PC John Stringer,** just six months after joining the force so had not served under the previous chief, charged beer-house keeper Richard Baylis of the Shades in Diglis with selling drink on a Sunday afternoon – a privilege extended to fully licensed houses only. Baylis brought in **PCs Charles Vaughan** and **John Sanders** who lived nearby, to corroborate his defence that **Tommy Chipp** had always instructed his officers to turn a blind eye to such goings-on provided the establishments were otherwise peaceful.

Surprisingly, the case was thrown out at **Matthew Power'**s suggestion as he claimed the resulting publicity would suffice, but he made it clear that the law was the law and that, however potentially discomforting, he was now chief and things were going to change...

Yet for all the tough measures he took with his force of headstrong officers, all the new chief wanted was the best men doing the best job – for whom only the best would be good enough. For them he would give his best. To that end, early this year also saw him arguing strongly with the city paymasters for cash rewards for three officers – **William Richardson, William Berridge and Ball** (*sic – actually **Sgt John Wall**) – that had been opposed by tight-fisted members typically demanding to know if there was anything '...extraordinary in the conduct or proceedings of the officers to render them entitled to more than their regular pay?'

To his credit, he presented a determined case on their behalf and, backed by Mayor Joseph Firkins, won over the opposers.

He was also fastidious about his men's appearance, making further suggestions about improvements to the uniform and suggesting 'a neat and comfortable tunic and forage cap in place of the unsightly tail coats and hats' that was little changed since the Watchmen days.

Six tenders for tunics were duly submitted – John Tasker of Lowesmoor proving the successful bidder. Mr Thomas' tender for lace-up boots at 13s 6d a pair was also accepted as was Mr Chaplin's tender to supply caps at 1/9d each for night duty – '...but the question of substituting a cap for the hat at present worn by the policemen was deferred for further consideration' *(Herald)*.

However, his attention to detail, the cost of the men's uniforms and even his own, were to cause him to clash, sometimes quite heatedly, with the more frugal members of the 23-man Watch Committee right up to the end of his Worcester years.

In February, **Joseph Banner** was made permanent station sergeant – but almost immediately after taking up his role he was hauled over the coals for allowing a prisoner to escape. To make matters worse, the chief made a deliberate show of heaping praise on **PC (later Sergeant) John Sanders**, fulsomely commended for his role in re-apprehending the absconder.

In March, two resignations – **PC Henry Davis** after fourteen days and **PC William Berridge** after seven years. The first one, while not perhaps preferable given the problems of attracting suitable replacements, he could cope with, but the loss of **Berridge** was going to be keenly felt; after feeling the sharp edge of the Power-play for something that he considered merely trivial and would probably have been overlooked in the Chipp years – *being found asleep while on duty* – he'd landed himself a new job as Streets Superintendent, being selected from 18 candidates at a salary of £70.

While **Matthew Power** was still struggling – and not always succeeding – in reining-in some of his mens' worst excesses, he displayed not the least concerns about making enemies either within the force or outside, or the position of those whose toes he was prepared to tread on in order to bring his men up to the rarefied standards he'd set for himself and expected from them.

As ever claiming to be driven exclusively by his demand for more efficiency and the best interests of the force, he even dared to cross swords with the megalomaniac future Sheriff John Lloyd Bozward after

William Berridge

OFFENCES.

| DATE. | OFFENCE. | PUNISHMENT. | REMARKS. |
|---|---|---|---|
| 1859 *May 1?* | *Being in a Public House while on duty and afterward making use of bad language to and abusing his Sergeant* | *Fined 10/- admonished and told that another delinquency would be visited with severe punishment* | |
| 1860 *March 27* | *Publicly showing a letter in a Public House reflecting on Detective Richardson's character* | *Reprimanded and informed that upon a repetition of such conduct he would be discharged from the force* | |
| 1860 *April 20* | *Insulting Mr Williams of the "Holly Bush" in the public street (High Street) at midday while in uniform and calling him a liar at the top of his voice* | *Requested to resign his place or in a fortnight without his usual fee discharge* | 1860 *March 4. Resignation being this minute received he expressed his regret at his misdeed, conduct and apologised to Mr Williams. This together with his active and zealous conduct on a previous occasion this minute and his promise to carry on the minutes of this minute...* |
| 1860 *Nov. 23* | *Exceeding his duty in taking J.F. Wise into custody on a false charge* | *Censured* | *See minutes* |
| 1861 *Aug? 9* | *Sleeping in Nash's Fly in August Street while on duty at 2 a.m. of the 19th inst.* | *Severely reprimanded police indiscretion* | |

WCiCo/WAAS

**Detective William Richardson** again allegedly overstepped the bounds of his duty during a swoop on a brothel said to be populated by girls as young as 11.

The *Chronicle*, never the most diplomatic of the city's newspapers and ever inclined to blow a modest story out of all proportion, had come out sensationally against the determined detective with all guns blazing, quoting councillor Bozward as accuser-in-chief and alleging that he had the full support of Matthew Power. It was a bad, and as it turned out, presumptuous, reflection on the new chief which he sought to put right in no uncertain terms the next day, dashing-off letters to all the editors angrily denouncing the councillor's actions and protesting '...against being associated with anyone in proffering a complaint having reference to the discipline of the force the command of which I am charged. I can only say that as long as I occupy the position I do, my actions shall be exclusively prompted by what I conceive to be beneficial to the public interest, unbiased by friendship or antipathy'.

The letter was dated March 13th 1862 and the *Herald* instantly supported him and, significantly **Bill Richardson** '...whose alleged excess of professional zeal is... an almost infinitesimal amount, if not nil' they wrote.

With the city's top-selling newspaper on his side – the *Herald* was now selling some 7,000 copies weekly compared to the *Journal's* 3,700 (and the *Advertiser* and *Chronicle* considerably less) – **Matthew Power** won the day and the charges against **Detective Richardson** were dropped. But there was more to come from the go-getting and occasionally controversial detective before the year was out.

March 21st this year saw two officers each receive £1 for courageous conduct and both for the same reasons: being attacked by two people, all four of which were bettered by the officer concerned and subsequently arrested and convicted. They were **PC 3rd Class John Spencer** and, in yet another vicious encounter that still seemed to characterise his daily grind, ever up-for-it **Sgt. Benjamin Holmes**.

*Above:*
*PC 1st Class* **William Berridge,** *appointed 2nd February 1855, resigned in March this year, having had enough of the Power-play. He'd been censured for something that he considered merely trivial and would probably have been overlooked in the Chipp years – being found asleep while on duty*

Stirring-up a revival of painful memories of 1855, attacks on the police were again on the up, and in April a particularly nasty assault on **PC Charles Smith** brought home to the reading public the dangers now daily being encountered by the men of the force in the execution of their duty...

Called into the volatile bear-pit that was Dolday in order to apprehend a desperate character, also by name of Smith, following a violent assault on a woman that had additionally involved some significant damage to property:

> '...the officer was attacked not only by the prisoner but by a lot of others who knocked him down, kicked and severely ill-used him while the prisoner bit and kicked him, tore his coat into shreds and tried to bite him in a ferocious and beastly manner between the legs. The officer fortunately avoided this attack, but fully expected that, what with the prisoner and the mob, his latter end was come. The prisoner was fined £2, and in default 21 days' hard labour; and he retired from the dock in custody, observing that he had fought for his Queen and country which he apparently thought was sufficient excuse for attacking any of Her Majesty's subjects ad lib' (Herald).

### Most pressing demand of all:  the need for more space

Around this time too, another matter was occupying the new chief's attentions, less than a year after taking over – and no doubt wondering quite what he'd let himself in for. But at least this one offered a measure of increased comfort:  *the proposed new Police Station that had started to become pressing in Tommy Chipp's later years but was now reaching the critical stage.*

A survey of the St Nicholas Street station-house by the City's Surveyor Henry Rowe '...had found that in consequence of the dilapidated condition and imperfect arrangements of the station, it would be much better to erect a new building than attempt to modify the present one'.

The estimated cost was put at £1400 – but then with typical Worcester caution, Alderman John Lloyd Bozward, later Sheriff and chairman of the Streets Committee, seconded by Alderman Josiah Stallard, proposed that room might be found in a Cooken (*later Copenhagen*) Street yard and other properties owned by three spinster sisters, Susannah, Candia and Rebecca Pumphrey, adjoining the Guildhall and that such a location would be better for all concerned as it would spare the police the problems associated with transporting prisoners to trial between the gaol, station-house and Guildhall.

Then, two further factors emerged that, so far as the Council was concerned, clinched the matter once

*Work begins on the City Police's first custom-built Station House in Copenhagen Street this year. It is sited between the Guildhall (right) and the ever-troublesome Dolphin Inn separated by Court No3*

*Dated 1861*

*The Misses Pumphrey — and — The Mayor Alderman and citizens of Worcester.*

*Agreement for purchase of property in Cooken Street in the City of Worcester.*

*Left: cover of the agreement between the City Council and the Misses Pumphrey (WCiCo/WAAS) 1861. See also page 214*

and for all: i) that such a move would also permit just one police officer to remain in attendance instead of four or five, and ii) that the cost of acquiring the yard and its eighteen dwellings would be 'not more than the present station would fetch if sold'.

The latter consideration made it No Contest so far as the money-minded council was concerned: accordingly, deal done. Moves had been put in hand to finance the project on January 9th this year, and now site acquisition and preliminary work was about to begin.

The same month, Maj-Gen Cartwright presented his report on the Midlands police forces to the Home Office. Although it applied to the year to September 1861 and thus only included **Matthew Power**'s first six months, it painted a reasonably commendable image, highlighting some improvement as well as co-operation with the county much more satisfactorily carried out than formerly. The report pointed out that the number of indictable offences in Worcester (*as opposed to the daily stream of misdemeanours that was running in the high-hundreds*) '...is returned at 129, apprehensions at 103 and the committals at 38; but the inspector [Cartwright] thinks these statistics unreliable owing to the head constable having been appointed within the year. If correct, the committals, in proportion to the offences, are far below the common average of detections'.

Not all good, then. Even so, by comparison, Worcestershire Police came off worse, barely earning a mention save the damning-with-faint-praise comment that 'a great many changes have taken place (that) must have been detrimental to its efficiency. The force is reported to be efficient, but the formation of a small reserve is recommended'.

**Matthew Power**'s claim to be driven exclusively by sense of duty, unbiased by friendship or antipathy, now stepped up a gear – all the way up to Guv'nor Griffiths 'isself.

The practice of men from the city force being seconded to the Gaoler to escort prisoners from the bridewell to the court-house had been established for more than thirty years, three men regularly being taken off their normal duties for just such a purpose. But when **Matthew Power** asked to replace the three originally assigned for the Summer Assizes this year because two were required as witnesses in a hearing at the Magistrates Court that same day, William Griffiths threw a fit, refused to accept their replacements describing them as untrustworthy, and detained the original constables all day despite repeated urgent requests from the police chief whose patience had by now cracked and had stormed on the Shirehall demanding their release.

The next day the Guv'nor whizzed-off several messages about the police chief's unacceptable conduct – letters that **Matthew Power** considered unprofessional and impertinent – while both lodged heated complaints about the other's behaviour to the chairman of the Visiting Magistrates.

It was left to the Watch Committee to pick up the pieces of what they termed '*a squabble between Mr. Supt. Power and Mr. Griffiths, City Gaoler*'.

When the results of the previous year's census were released, showing the national population to have swelled to 10,309,873 (*less than one-sixth of today's*) and the city's to 31,123 (*just under one-third of today's*) a 10% rise in ten years – General Cartwright lost no time in writing to the Watch Committee warning that the city had increased so much in population that additions to the police force must be now considered necessary.

He said that taking all the circumstances into consideration, he felt it to be his duty to suggest a further increase of *two* constables – echoing **Matthew Power**'s earlier warning that without such an increase, Worcester City would not be granted its crucial certificate of efficiency.

The letter caused uproar in the Guildhall, references being made to the recent Police Act requiring one constable to every thousand of the population and councillors claiming that Worcester should not be treated the same as Birmingham, Manchester and other large manufacturing towns and could easily survive with a far lower complement.

### First Brewster Sessions report paints grim image of the City

This year also highlighted **Matthew Power**'s increasing grip on the contributing factors relating to law and order in Worcester with what's believed to be the first Superintendent's report to the Licensing Committee, later known as the Brewster Sessions, traditionally held at the end of August or early September. With the increasing number of pubs and beer-houses – every one of which was considered to be the very source of crime and mis-doing in Worcester, a belief short of the mark, but frankly not by a lot – he'd acquainted himself with every one and was thus able to comment on whether or not each of the 161 licensees applying for a renewal of his/her licence was deserving of it. In the face of the report, the *Herald* commented that '...nearly all were granted, but complaints were made against the Duke of York (*Little*

WORCESTER CITY POLICE.

MONDAY.

Before T. Chalk, Esq. (in the chair). E. Webb, J. Wood, and J. Coucher, Esqrs.

HOME MISSIONS WANTED.—Despite the efforts of teetotallers and moderate people, the sin of drunkenness among the lower orders seems still to be the besetting one, and there is no diminution in the length of the police sheets in reference to the obscenities and intoxication with which the Sabbath is usually ushered in. For instance, here is a copy of the sheet for Saturday night and Sunday last :—

1. Henry Forester, labourer, of Wadborough, drunk and incapable, in the Tything. 12.30 a.m. (Sunday morning.)

2. Charles Ross, shoemaker, Silver-street, "D.D." in the Tything, 1.30 a.m.

3. William Vincent, brushmaker, Union-street, "disorderly, fighting, and assaulting a man unknown, in Friar-street," 10 p.m."

4. Thomas Connor, bricklayer, formerly of Kidderminster, drunk, and breaking a window at the Hen and Chickens, Allhallows, 2.15 p.m.

5. John Jones, from Ireland, drunk, and assaulting Mr. Jos. Reynolds, landlord of the above-named inn, same time.

6. Samuel Severn, wheelwright, drunk, and threatening the life of his wife and children, near Dolday, 12.40 a.m.

7. Eppey Teale, disorderly prostitute, in Sidbury, 1.45 a.m.

8. Elizabeth Minton, ditto, ditto.

9. Martha Landon, of Watercourse-alley, refusing to leave the streets, 2 a.m.

10. Catherine Ricketts, "no home," disorderly in Silver street, 2.20 a.m.

No. 1 was brought into the station between nine and ten o'clock on Saturday night, with his head fearfully cut, but he couldn't or wouldn't say how it was done. A surgeon was sent for, and a fee of half-a-guinea incurred for the city to pay, and when the youth's head was "strapped up" he was let go again comparatively sobered down by blood-letting. [...]

*A typical Monday morning court list after a typical Saturday night's revels*

Angel-street); Horn and Trumpet (*Angel-street)*; Fountain (*Angel-street*, licence suspended for a week); Pheasant, New-street (*suspended for a week, as the landlord was not in attendance*); Plough (*Silver-street*); Ewe & Lamb (*Angel-street*); Falcon (*Broad-street*): Rising Sun (*St Clement-street)* suspended for a week; spirit vaults at the corner of Bridge-street; Ram Tavern (*Tallow-hill*); and Crystal Palace (*Butts*).

All were what might today be termed 'the usual suspects' as the same names, plus a few others, cropped-up virtually year-in, year-out in police black books on licensing day.

In most cases this year, the objections centred on the loose company they attracted and that in some, music had been added to the other attractions, contrary to the order of the magistrates.

Then, as now, there's no pleasing all the people all the time, and despite official praise from the top for his thoroughness and application in producing what's clearly a highly authoritative and insightful observation of the city's drinking establishments of this year (*of which far more in the existing volumes of 'Bob Backenforth's Worcester Pubs Then and Now'*) several landlords instantly condemned **Matthew Power**'s initiative as intrusive snooping and unnecessary police over-zealousness that had now gone several steps too far on the part of its new – and an outsider at that – no-nonsense superintendent.

The Mayor, Jos. Firkins Esq., felt obliged to intervene and '...defended the Superintendent against this imputation, observing that the thanks of the citizens were due to him for the fearless and impartial discharge of his duty'.

But the report was just the beginning of a tough new crackdown on the pubs and beer-houses that had been allowed to get away with far more under **Tommy Chipp** than frankly they should have. The previous months had seen the constables at the sharp end once more warned in the strongest terms of the consequences of getting drunk or even being seen drinking in any of the licensed premises, and a renewed warning went out to every publican regarding the penalties that could be expected of harbouring a police officer knowing him to be on duty. So far as **Matthew Power**, if not perhaps so fervently his boys in blue were concerned, priority #1 was that they and their rowdy establishments were going to have to toe-the-line or pay the consequences.

A typical Saturday night/Sunday morning charge sheet would include ten and often more d&d and similar related cases (*see Herald cutting above from May this year*).

**Matthew Power** had made it clear all along that friendship and the risk of making enemies were of no consequence to him: he'd come to Worcester as a stranger knowing hardly anything about the town or anyone in it. Home-grown **Tommy Chipp's** regime had been too easy-going by far, but this new way was a shock to the system akin to an earthquake. Inevitably, his Irish aggression and rigid ex-military by-the-book discipline had set him on a collision course with several sections of the community and it was only a matter of time before matters came to a head: *as it transpired, several came together at once...*

Clearly, first to feel their feathers ruffled were his men – first among many being one he really needed on his side: **Detective William Richardson**. Already twice during the course of this, his second year, on March 10th and on April 4th the chief had had cause to give his top 'tec severe admonishments for his conduct – in the first instance alleging indiscipline and subversive conduct, and in the second of insubordination and using insulting language, for which the chief wanted his pound of flesh, making **Richardson** publicly apologise and to await formal acceptance of his apology by the Committee.

It was, frankly too much to stomach and **Bill Richardson** duly delivered the news that he was off: he'd been appointed Superintendent at Stratford-on-Avon and was leaving Worcester after 10 sterling years. For all the personal setbacks and growing distance between him and his erratic, if essentially dependable detective, the chief allowed **Richardson** £10 out of the Superannuation Fund as a reward for his 'extraordinary diligence and exertion in the execution of his duty'.

### Manpower problems escalate

On the same day, **PCs George Moule** and **Samuel Shipley** were both dismissed, the former for blatantly lying about a prisoner, thus jeopardising a forthcoming case, and the latter for absenting himself from the City without first asking permission – although **George Moule** was later (*ie four years later, 1866*) reinstated.

February had seen **Charles Vaughan** commended for his skill, tact and promptness in discovering several offences and again on July 11th for his perseverance in apprehending a man for stealing geese for which he was awarded 10/- gratuity by the Committee. Later this year though (*September*), Vaughan found himself yet again up before the chief, cautioned to be more careful in the future and charged with neglect of duty after not being quick enough in apprehending a man he'd been watching, later caught in the act of assault with intent on a young girl 'of tender years'.

**John Stringer No21** (*also No14*) was also censured on September 18th for allowing a prisoner to drink ale while in his custody on their way from the police station to the gaol. Over the next few years, **John Stringer** was to become no stranger to the chief's office or his metaphorical carpet, although in July this year he brought a case of attempted bribery against publican Henry Mason of the Cross Keys in Sidbury.

Yet despite all the set-backs and appearance of the

## Also this year: 1862

■ *PC10 Ezra Franklin again severely beaten up in the Bell in St Johns by a gang of thugs led by cordwainer William Hardman, 30*

■ *major fracas with Irish navvies in the Duke of Wellington leaves four PCs injured and nursing grievous wounds – John Spencer (stabbed), Benjamin Holmes (bitten), William Arkwell, and John Knott (bruised)*

■ *Ezra Franklin called in to investigate sudden death of Sarah Coxell wife of Railway Bell landlord found horrifically burned. Murder suspected but not proved*

■ *No16 George Young recovers body of man missing for a week, Edward Walter, from Diglis Locks*

■ *PC (later Sergeant) James Barker wins reputation as the scourge of the beer houses after a string of cases against erring landlords*

■ *PC Alfred Vine quits after six months following savage assault by boatmen in Lowesmoor*

■ *murder of Emily Jones of the Blockhouse whose body was found in a pond in Perry Wood*

■ *unnamed PC investigates highly suspicious death of Arthur Walters, 8, found dead in a well with fractured skull and broken arm although no charges are brought*

■ *PC Frederick Francis Trickey quits after eight months after being roughed-up by a baying crowd in Birdport*

■ *police called in to investigate three sudden deaths on the same day, two later found to be natural causes, the third resulting from a kick by a horse*

■ *police investigate body of new born baby girl found dead in the Garibaldi, St Johns*

■ *PC George Moule laid-off after 'a severe blow at the back of the head by some cowardly ruffians amongst a mob'*

■ *Henry Hopton, a plasterer working on the new police station falls from his bench and dies instantly*

■ *PC Thomas Croft in just his second year (of 30) is rescued from a mob by PC John Goodwin who served just one day under a calendar year (10th January this year to 9th January 1863)*

- **intelligence between City, County and Birmingham police prevent a 'fancy' – organised prizefight – due to start at 5am on Pitchcroft**

- **Sgt John Doughty breaks door down at music seller Mr Baldwyn's High Street home and discovers body of American housekeeper 57-year old Charlotte Savage: later verdict, suicide**

- **PC James Hill beaten up by navvies in the White Horse**

- **PC Charles Vaughan has face gouged and severely bitten by labourer Charles Hewlett in a fight. The next day he's on duty investigating the theft of £45 from a city businessman**

- **in November 150 navvies and railwaymen besiege Shrub Hill Station. Edward Jarrett is later charged with the attempted murder of keeper of the refreshment rooms Thomas Watton, witnessed by PC Francis Rudniski (a full account in Bob Backenforth's Worcester Pubs Then and Now Vol II pps 185-7)**

force falling apart at the seams, progress was being made, a lot of useful ground had been covered and this hadn't gone unnoticed at the Guildhall. For all the frantic internal to-ings and fro-ings of men, one day in civvies, the next in uniform and vice-versa, the courts were satisfyingly full to overflowing, the Magistrates had more than enough on their plates, and the gaols were finding it tough to cope with a never-ending influx of inmates – all of which, while seemingly disadvantageous to all concerned, conversely reflected favourably on the efficiency of the new smartened-up constabulary.

Accordingly, and at the insistence of the Bench of Magistrates, on November 29th the all-too critical Watch Committee took the remarkable step of recording their '...approbation of the marked improvement which has taken place in the appearance, discipline and efficiency of the men employed in the force since **Mr Power**'s appointment which were considered highly creditable to the exertions and talent of their officer'.

**Gained:** Henry Davis, Thomas Broadfield, John Gardner, Frederick Francis Trickey, Samuel Shipley, William Buckingham, George Danford (none of whom survived the year), John Goodwin, Charles Augustus, Thomas Hall, Thomas Brown, Francis Rudniski, Charles Matthews, James Morris, Thomas Tolley, Thomas Barrett, William Charles Preece

**Lost:** James Clarke, William Richardson, William Berridge, James Fielders, William Carloss, Isaac Clarke, George Moule, Samuel Shipley

## 1863

In January, the new police station next to the Guildhall and separated from the troublesome Dolphin Inn by Court No3 was ready, and the Big Move began.

First in was **Matthew Power** whose family's private quarters – 'a commodious dwelling house' as the *Herald* termed it – were at the front, overlooking Copenhagen Street, and **Sergeant Ben Holmes** and his family's were '...ditto at the rear'. Also included was the chief's office, large charge room, six cells (*compared to the St Nicholas Street station, still unsold at the time of the move, that had two, both measuring less than 10ft x 10ft*). There was also a new feature: heating. The final bill came in at just £39 over budget – the Council's frugal money-men expressing themselves delighted that that was all.

While the glowing report from the Watch Committee had been welcomed, the previous few months had been trying for the men on the beat to say the least, and the two weeks up to the 23rd January this year had seen 71 man-days lost through sickness and injury with six constables absent at its black worst.

The roll at the time consisted of thirty: the chief, five sergeants, eight 1st Class constables, eleven 2nd and five 3rd – but of major concern was that there were four unfilled vacancies and no-one with the required mental and physical attributes was coming forward to fill them. When asked why, **Matthew Power** was unwavering and adamant: the job was just too much for his existing force and his men were simply overworked.

That half of them also came in for a hammering from ruffians at least once a week no doubt played a part too. The upshot is that even the ever-cautious Council realised that they were going to have to loosen the purse strings some way further if the new chief was going to be allowed to do his job and law and order was to be maintained on the streets.

Whether reluctantly or prompted by the Magistrates now so fulsomely impressed by the change in attitude being displayed by the men on the beat, they agreed to a 1s a week across-the-board rise, upping the new rates to 24s for sergeants, 21s, 19/6d, and 18s for the class-ranked men and 17s for probationers on the understanding that they would be raised to 3rd Class at the end of their first month.

**Matthew Power** was also told that, instead of relying on persuasion or recommendation, for the first time he'd be allowed to advertise the vacancies and the new rates in the local newspapers.

For all that, the difficult manpower situation had scarcely been helped by **Matthew Power**'s insistence on weeding-out those he didn't feel were up to his – and his no-nonsense Blue Book's – exacting standards, and there was still to be no let-up in his drive to stamp-out laxity, inefficiency and behaviour considered below-par and unacceptable...

*Tommy Croft aged 46 and his inattentive dog in 1884*

On February 6th **James Hill** resigned after almost exactly 3 years with the force following a severe censure for absenting himself from duty all night having asked for an hour only. He'd been raised to PC2nd Class in July 1861, but downgraded to 3rd Class for a month the year before for being in a public house for an hour and a half without leave.

On April 2nd everybody's favourite sergeant, **George Sedgeley**, resigned on account of ill-health and a gratuity of £12 allowed from the Superannuation Fund, plus his clothes. He'd joined nine years earlier and appointed Sergeant on July 12th 1861, but even he had been susceptible to the usual human temptations: the previous year, he'd been fined 5/- for being in the White Hart for half an hour while still on duty.

### Chief comes in for criticism in manpower decisions

**Matthew Power** was to come in for criticism and accusations of error of judgement when he appointed **James Barker** and **John Sanders** as replacements for the out-going sergeants **Banner** and **Sedgeley** in May.

Several members of the Watch Committee said that **Charles Vaughan** should have been awarded one of the two vacant posts, but it later emerged that he'd been canvassing members for their vote and this had disqualified him from consideration.

The chief's recommendation of **James Barker** to take **George Sedgeley**'s place was probably no less controversial, however. **Barker** appears to have been a loose cannon whose waywardness was surprisingly tolerated by his superiors.

On his plus-side, he's shown to have been appointed on 11th September 1857, raised to 2nd Class in April the following year and First Class July 1861, his progress to Sergeant taking just three lines of the Approbation Marks book.

On the debit side, a string of offences is recorded against his name. Between October 1858 and October 1866, he's either reprimanded, admonished or censured *seven times* for neglecting to comply with orders (*fined 10/- and allowed to be paid by two instalments*); improperly accepting money and being in a public house after hours (*reduced from Sergeant to PC 1st Class for a week*); being in the Gloucester Arms on a Sunday morning at prohibited hours and drinking therein a glass of bitters (*admonished and cautioned to be more diligent in the future*); concealing information from his superintendent regarding a man suspected of stealing from his employer and going to the suspect's house to wait for him, absenting himself from duty; insubordination and insolence. For the final offence, admittedly still three years away (*October 26th 1866*) he was allowed to resign and granted 14 days 'for the purpose'.

In June this year, **PCs Tommy Croft** (*pictured above, photograph taken some 21 years later in 1884 when he is 46 and clearly a man not to be tussled with*) **John Stringer** and **Alfred Vine** were elevated to PC1st Class; PCs **William Charles Preece** and **John Whitehouse** from 3rd to 2nd Class.

Every one was to go on to a distinguished career with the force. On the downside the same week, **PC Charles Smith** was reprimanded and fined 2s 6d for being in liquor while on duty.

The next month (*July 3rd*) **Matthew Power's** own performance during his two years at the head of the force came under scrutiny. The verdict? Outstanding.

He had, formally recorded the Watch Committee, efficiently discharged the duties of his office. Better still, they reckoned, the force had never been in better or more efficient shape and there was a marked improvement in both the prevention and the detection of crime:

> *'...the Committee therefore felt it to be their duty to recommend the Council to advance the salary of Mr Power by the addition of £30 per annum, fully believing that he had rendered very valuable services to the city by the earnest devotion of his time and talents to the performance of the duties of his office'.*

Praise indeed – and vindication of the tough line he'd taken with his men. Nor had it gone unnoticed by the Committee that the force had grown since his appointment or that he had additionally promoted himself to Detective, thus effecting a saving of £15 to the ratepayers!

Even so, the decision to up his salary to £150 plus his accommodation, coal and light, was not unanimous: almost half of the 23-man committee disagreed and in a heated debate that revealed more about the city's tight-fisted administrators than the efficiency of its law officers, voted against the move.

*Hard helmets replaced soft hats this year: the first featured a protective ball at the crown and 'black' accessories and plate (Malcolm Price)*

One (*Alderman Minchal*) even went so far as to say that he thought the increase was premature, that he considered £120 a year ample, and that he thought the police chief would have had the courtesy to wait longer than two years before putting in for a rise. He also thought the cost of his uniform, £14, nothing less than a public scandal: '...Mr Cordle was of the opinion that **Mr Power** should not wear any livery at all' reported the *Herald*. And there were more grumbles bordering on open hostility too...

As the all-in cost of the police force now amounted to £2,229 a year – one-eighth of the city's official receipts – Councillor J H Sanders claimed that the City would be better off by actually **reducing** the number of officers on the streets, a comment that sparked outrage in the committee room, not least as a new report showed that even with the increase in manpower, the force still remained insufficient in number both for the discharge of their duties and in meeting the recommended police:population ratio demanded by the Whitehall paymasters who picked up 25% of the tab. The objections were defeated, but the 13-10 'yes' vote showed that, so far as the people and leaders of Worcester were concerned and in the face of seemingly glowing references to their evident success, Worcester City Police and their Irish-born chief were still far from home and dry.

The Watch Committee meeting two weeks later was a rather less heated debate but still contained two elements indicating festering concerns about the way the force was being run. Reports the *Herald*: '...Mr Sanders gave notice of the following motion for the next meeting:– "That in future Mr

Power be requested to lay before the committee a statement of the distribution amongst the force of all moneys passing through his hands".

The other business had reference to complaints against members of the police force'.

It was in the middle of the year that **Matthew Power**, ever conscious of his men's appearance and a stickler for a smart turn-out at all times, began trials for a feature that some years down the line was to distinguish the constables of Worcester City from every other force but two: *its distinctive helmet.*

A variety of different hat styles had been the order of the day for the city's boys in blue, but with increasing violence being directed towards the police, the new thinking was that something more protective was needed, and new-style headgear based on the Prussian military helmet was ordered for men of all ranks and even the chief himself, with a ball at the crown and 'black' accessories (*pictured left and below*).

In the same week that a sailor named Joseph Pulley killed a man named George Griffiths in a fight over a game of bowls in the Blockhouse, **Sergeant James Drew** was awarded 15/- for his conduct and devotion to duty in saving the lives of five females at a fire in Broad Street – although the next year was to see him finished as a policeman following an attempt on his life that came within an ace of succeeding.

## Also this year: 1863

- PC John Spencer, beaten up by George Norman in the Shambles on Boxing Day, quits after just eighteen months and three serious assaults

- PC Charles Augustus is assigned to plain-clothes duty to clamp down on young lads staging impromptu boxing matches in the streets

- police control crowds celebrating the wedding of the Prince of Wales (later Edward VII)

- baby's body fished out of the Severn investigated by Charles Vaughan leads to arrest of Elizabeth Dovey, later charged with murder

- PC Francis Rudniski and Sgt Charles Vaughan both gravely assaulted by 'determined fellow' Maurice Flemm, also accused of whipping up the crowd to assault the officers in a running battle in Lowesmoor

- police investigate body of new-born child found 'wrapped up in a rag bag' at Haywood's florist in Broad Street

- City force collaborates with County to investigate 'outrageous' spate of thefts of bells from churches

- PC Edward Bettington gets the first of several beatings by Blockhouse gangs that results in him quitting the force next year after just 13 months

- PC (later Sergeant) Thomas Tolley let off charge of assaulting passenger Joseph Coley at Shrub Hill station

- sailor Joseph Pulley charged with manslaughter after a fatal fight with George Griffiths in the Blockhouse

- police investigate death of 2-year old Kezia Hill found drowned in 'a pan of soap suds' in the Blockhouse

- unnamed constable drags body of John Langford out of Severn. Verdict: suicide

- Matthew Power stumped in court when Magistrates ask how many times 'old offender' Mary Bromwich had been convicted of being drunk and disorderly. Response was that it would task the entire constabulary powers to answer it. Agreed on 'more than twenty'

- just days after joining, PC Herbert Osborne is exposed to the realities of being a bobby on Worcester's streets, when he's beaten up by 'ragged youth' Edward Blissett. 21 day's hard

- police ordered to clamp-down on cab drivers charged with driving dangerously in order to get their fares to the stations for trains after several high-speed accidents

- City and County police again collaborate over serious assault on a woman on the riverbank near the Ketch culminating in fears that her attacker later drowned himself in the Severn

*(Below) collar 'dog' in black. All ranks were issued with special cleaning solution as part of Matthew Power's drive for his men's sartorial elegance on the streets*

As already implied, the year had been a bad one for fires in Worcester and as fire prevention was a related issue that also came under the policing remit, **Matthew Power** had devoted some of his time to perfecting a fire escape system that he now patented – seemingly under his own name rather than that of his employers, although quite how that squared with the council is not recorded.

During the last committee meeting of the year, one of the patented systems was commissioned exclusively for the city's own use.

That same meeting also saw **PC Abraham Gibbons** (or *Gibbins*) dismissed after just four months for neglect of duty on Christmas Eve; new recruit **PC Herbert Osborne** fined 5s for being drunk while on duty – although he was to go on to a 20-year career with the force; and dependable **PC Ezra Franklin** commended for his promptitude in apprehending at Ledbury two prisoners charged with theft.

In the last quarter of the year, 131 (*out of 309*) people had died in the city from an epidemic of scarlatina. Overall, it had been a bruising year for Worcester Police and the man charged with bringing it up to the topmost reaches of efficiency – anything less being considered a failure in his eyes. For all that, it was satisfyingly evident that in some areas – if not all – he was gaining the upper hand and succeeding...

*Gained: Charles Cook, Richard Payter, Jabez Griffiths, Richard Thompson, John Handley, John Watkins, Abraham Gibbins, (none of whom saw-out a year), John Whitehouse, Edward Bettington, David Morgan, William Creese, William Underwood, Herbert Osborne, Thomas Williams, Charles Smith, Thomas Cole*

*Lost: Joseph Banner, George Sedgeley, George Young, James Hill, John Spencer, John Goodwin, Francis Rudniski, Charles Matthews, James Morris, Thomas Barrett*

**Matthew Power**'s patented fire escape made its debut at the Guildhall early in January when it was twice put through its paces for the benefit of the Watch Committee – once to show its operation from outside (*ie from the rescuers' point-of-view*) and again from the inside, (*ie: the rescuees' point of view*). Noted the *Herald*: '...the committee expressed themselves much pleased, and ordered the machine to be paid for'.

The same month Guv'nor Griffiths' City Gaol yet again came off very badly in every respect in comparison with the County Gaol, being described as vastly inferior and massively below the standards demanded by new Government regulations...

> 'The cells are too small to allow constant confinement day and night, so that during the day the prisoners are to a great extent associated whereby the penal character of the gaol is much reduced, and great contamination of young offenders necessarily occurs by intercourse with adepts in crime. The walls are constructed so that conversation can be held by one prisoner with another in the adjoining cell, and as the male and female cells are much mingled, it is evident that much mischief must arise from this defect... there is no separation between the prisoners on the tread-wheel, it is impossible to maintain discipline and consequently punishments for bad conduct are very frequent. Instead of deterring from crime, it is greatly to be feared that it promotes it'.

Guv'nor Griffiths had been formally summoned before the House of Lords Committee on Prison Discipline the previous year, and when asked to explain why the prison was failing in every respect, he laid the blame firmly at the feet of the City Council – although a trawl through all records up to then actually revealed that he'd asked for no improvements there for at least the past ten years.

The City absolved itself of all blame in the damning affair.

The appalling inadequacy of the gaol now prompted demands from several quarters to close the ageing city bridewell and amalgamate it with the County Gaol – a call instantly rejected by Ben Stables, now installed as Governor at the latter on the grounds that though they had 272 available cells, even that number was still inadequate for the County's own need which was nearing 300.

In March, just a week after being presented with a new mayoral chain that he pledged would subsequently be left to the city in perpetuity (*pictured, right*) mayor Alexander Clunes Sherriff started off what would become an annual feature: the mayors' dinner for the police.

It was held at the Bell Hotel in Broad Street (*since demolished to create the opening of what would become Angel Place*). Small drawback this first year – the mayor couldn't make it: it was instead hosted by **Matthew Power**. 'The dinner was all that could be desired and the wine excellent', reported the *Herald*.

While assaults and incidents directed against the police continued at no less a pace than the previous years, an incident at the end of April took the crisis to a new low: four men in their twenties – James Williams, Isaac Small, Charles Teague and Frederick Smith – had laid into **PC Herbert Osborne** after he'd been called to the Wheat Sheaf in London Road to turn them out for rowdiness.

Williams had tried to throw him on the fire and then hit him three times in the face; **Osborne** fought back and threw him out; then the other three set about him while Williams returned wielding a whip-stock; **Osborne** retaliated by drawing his staff and hitting him twice over the head; Small ran off and **Osborne** chased him. As they returned, Williams had climbed onto a wagon parked outside the Wheat Sheaf and from there whipped **Osborne** who was still trying to fight off the other three: '...a general scuffle then ensued in which the officer was thrown to the ground and kicked in a brutal manner. Osborne's clothes were greatly torn and there was a lot of blood on them... he has received several injuries'. He was also off duty for several weeks as a result. At the trial, Teague's solicitor claimed that **Osborne** had exceeded his duty: the Bench were having none of it. After three hours, all four defendants were sentenced to terms of hard labour.

And then the assaults took an even more severe turn for the worse: **Sergeant James Drew** had been shot in the face, virtually outside his own house...

### Sergeant James Drew shot in the face

Off-duty, he'd been working in his garden in Moor Street (*then called Moorfields-street in the parish of Whitstones, Claines*) at 11 am on Tuesday, April 12th when he heard cries of 'Murder' coming from the direction of Pitchcroft where there'd been a mustering of the Militia. Also running up Moor Street at a furious pace was a man who'd just jumped the railings leading to the Moors and behind him followed a posse of people giving chase. Ever mindful of his duty, he joined the chase and when the man ran up an alley leading to the house of a neighbour named Griffiths, Drew took the crowd's request to assume control of the situation, calmly walked up to the man who he already knew by sight:

> '...and collared him. The prisoner made but little, if any resistance, but allowed Drew to take him peaceable (sic) into the street. Drew turned his head to see if any other pursuers were following to assist him. The prisoner observed this, drew a firearm from his pocket [it was later revealed to be a loaded six-ball Lefacheaux revolver valued at 15s that he'd stolen earlier that morning from Perrins gunsmiths in Mealcheapen Street] and shot the officer point-blank in the face. Drew let go his hold on the prisoner, staggered and fell against the rails and blood commenced running from his nostrils. Prisoner then ran up the narrow walk leading to Britannia-square and witness saw no more of him'.

The would-be murderer, 21-year old Walter S. Jones, a GWR engineer based at Shrub Hill, was followed by a young lad who he also threatened to shoot but ran away before he was able to carry out his threat. The gunman was later found hiding in a garden in Britannia Square where Superintendent Phillips – the same man who'd put in for the chief's job at Worcester three years earlier – overpowered and disarmed him, literally dragging him to the County station in Loves Grove.

Though **James Drew** later said he'd felt nothing more than a pin-prick, he was in a bad way; he was unconscious for two days, his jaw was smashed, he'd lost four teeth and there were real fears that he might not survive. It also transpired that a 13 year-old girl, Emma Ball had also had a lucky escape: as she ran away after rejecting Jones' advances on Pitchcroft moments earlier, he'd levelled a shot at her from six yards range. The ball hit her in the left hand and bounced off a piece of iron she'd picked up and was

THE EXTRAORDINARY CASE OF SHOOTING IN THIS CITY.

On Tuesday morning, the young man, Walter H. Jones, charged with shooting Police-sergeant Drew and the girl Emma Ball, with intent to do them grievous bodily injury, as stated in last week's Herald, was taken before the City Magistrates on remand from Tuesday, the 13th inst., when the case was further gone into. There were present on the Bench A. C. Sherriff, Esq., Mayor, and T. Chalk, R. Webb, ... J. Comber, Esqrs. The prisoner was placed between two policemen in the dock, and securely handcuffed. He seemed to look on calmly during the proceedings, but his countenance was not set at indifference, nor was there on the other hand the slightest cast of wildness in his face; and he gave one the idea of repressed intelligence that would have obeyed the great law of action but for the compulsory quietude of surrounding conditions. His features are not regular, nor strongly marked, and they have something of the air of the engineer's workshop. To look at him one would not be ready to think him capable of committing deeds involving so much cruelty and ferocious indifference to human life and suffering as the fearful acts of the morning of the 12th inst., so that taking those naked facts themselves, the mild visage of the prisoner, and his antecedents, it would perhaps be impossible to imagine more unsatisfactory ... ements in the means ...

carrying home. Jones – who'd shouted "There, that's you finished!" – was lucky not to be tried for two counts of murder.

In court it was revealed that the revolver was capable of firing a bullet 100 yards before it dropped and would seriously injure a person from 50 yards' range. The hearing was delayed several times pending Drew's slow and painful recovery – at least to a condition sufficient for him to take the stand – although the preliminary hearings on the twin charges of stealing the revolver and of wounding Emma Ball went ahead on 6th May when Jones, revealed as a surgeon's son, was committed to the up-coming Assizes.

But even by then Sgt. Drew was not considered fit enough to take the stand so the justices agreed to allow more time and to permit him to make his statements at the City Gaol – from where the Herald eventually described the scene: '...the injured man [Sgt. Drew] was led into the room and apparently was very weak and debilitated. His head was bandaged and being unable to stand during the investigation, a chair was provided for him by the side of Mr [Richard] Woof, the Magistrates' clerk. The prisoner was in charge of one of the turnkeys and appeared as unconcerned as ever'.

Jones was committed on the charge of shooting with intent.

That self-same week, **Matthew Power** had also reported to the Watch Committee that:

- **PC Richard Fowkes** was now very much better and would probably be able to resume his duties in a fortnight after some vicious handling by a family of gipsies in St Johns (*it was later revealed that his injuries were far worse than originally thought and that he was instead likely to be off for six months as a direct result. He was put on two-thirds of his pay [14s a week] until his return)*
- **PC Herbert Osborne** was also commended for 'excellent conduct when attacked recently by several men at the Wheat Sheaf: the magistrates considered that Osborn (sic) acted with much forbearance and when urged by the bystanders to use his staff, did so with the greatest forbearance and command of temper. They thought it a proper case in which to commend the constable to the committee's consideration'. He was later allowed a gratuity of £1 for his actions
- **PCs [William] Underwood** and **[Charles] Smith** were recommended by the chief for promotion to 2nd Class; and the permanent appointment of **PC [George] Guise** who had been a month on probation'.
- on the down-side at the same committee meeting, the 'loose cannon' **Sgt James Barker** was reprimanded for neglect of duty.

In July there was talk of murder followed by suicide after **PC (*later Sergeant*) John Whitehouse** had been called to the scene when the bodies of a man and woman, William Crompton and Harriet Hill were discovered lying close together in the river under one of the bridge arches. They'd earlier been involved in a fight over a penny with a man named Inight in the Queen Caroline pub, but with no sign of injuries on the woman's body and no cries for help, all combined with their known penchant for regular bouts of drunkenness, it was concluded that they'd either fallen off the boat called 'The Fanny' that they shared as home, or had perhaps been involved in some bizarre suicide pact.

Clearly, despite the troubled times and problems in finding suitable recruits, **Matthew Power**'s crackdown on erring constables had been continuing unabated, with little mercy being shown to those found lacking: the following week also saw two more PCs discharged as unfit for duty, **Richard Jones** and **Thomas Perry**. Then, more tragedy on August 18th when **Sergeant John Sanders** drowned in the Severn in an incident not entirely without the whiff of scandal...

### Sergeant John Sanders drowned in the Severn

He'd gone off night duty at 6am, changed his uniform for his day-clothes with the intention of taking a row on the river

*'...as had been his custom on several mornings in each week recently. At the Severn bridge he hired a small boat "The Faithful City" and rowed towards the locks at Diglis. On his return he overtook a young woman in the service of Mr Fanning, postmaster of this city, whom, though a stranger to him, he invited to ride in the boat as far as the landing-place at the bridge. The young woman at first hesitated, being afraid of the water, but ultimately entered the boat, which the deceased had drawn near to the shore, close by the residence of Mr. E. L. Williams [now the Diglis House Hotel]. Instead of taking a seat in the stern, she sat at the bow of the boat and the weight of her body sank the head of the boat unduly, while it raised the stern almost out of the water ...and he and the young woman were precipitated into the water. The poor fellow was unfortunately drowned before assistance could be rendered him'.*

'The girl was rescued and brought to shore as the weight of her crinoline dress had kept her afloat and she'd managed to cling to the side of the boat.

'The deceased was a married man, but fortunately has left no family besides an afflicted widow to mourn his loss" the *Herald* concluded.

**John Sanders**, who'd been appointed 10th October 1856, raised to 2nd Class December 4th 1857, and 1st Class December 2nd 1859 and appointed Sergeant April 2nd 1863 had been commended by the Committee the previous year for great promptitude in the re-capture of an escaped prisoner. He hadn't been squeaky-clean throughout, mind. While still a PC 2nd Class, he'd been fined 6/- and told that more delinquency would result in more severe punishment for being in a public house while on duty, and a few months later (*July 1859*) he was

■ cholera takes a huge toll on the city with more than 250 deaths in under a year

■ no clues found on a man's body dragged out of the Severn at Diglis in the opening weeks, excepting a label, 'Woodhall 49'

■ PC (later Sergeant) George Archer first on the scene after labourer John Ford (53) murders 'poor miserable creature of a woman' Elizabeth Hull in the yard of the Rising Sun. She'd been hit on the head with a shovel

■ the next week a young (unnamed) lad calmly walked into the station-house carrying the body of a newborn baby he'd pulled out of the canal in the Arboretum and carried through the streets to report it

■ robbery at Pickford's of Sansome Street investigated by Sgt John Doughty now in his 19th year (of 30)

■ investigation begins into an 'impudent daylight robbery' at a packed Elephant and Castle when thieves enter via a back window and walk off with cash and goods worth nearly £40

■ more police time taken up with picking up mangled body parts in the wake of an increasing number of accidents and suicides involving trains

■ PC John Stringer in his third year resists bribe to bring Edwin Hyett of the Landsowne Inn to trial for selling out of proscribed hours

■ another newborn baby dragged out of the Severn in March, found in a bundle weighted down with a brick

■ PC George Guise who lasted just six months with the force (April to October this year) investigates a case of stabbing involving noted Dolday hard-man Walter Vipond. The tables were turned as on this rare occasion, as he'd been stabbed by his wife Mary Ann

■ on the same June night Sergeant James Barker and PC William Keith are both assaulted, the first on Pitchcroft after trying to break up an illegal roulette game and Keith, later to gain notoriety, in the Chestnut Tree

■ it was a bad summer for assaults, over the next few weeks, PCs Thomas Brown, John Whitehouse, David Morgan, George Guise and Sgt Ben Holmes all reporting injuries

*Bizarre tale involving* **PC Charles Vaughan.**
*Worcester citizens always liked their news spiced-up for maximum effect!*

**DISCOVERY OF HUMAN REMAINS.** — A human hand was last week picked up by a dog and brought into the yard of the Plough Inn, in Silver-street. Of course the most exaggerated rumours were soon afloat in the town, and strange stories told of the sudden and mysterious disappearance of a man from that neighbourhood some years before. P.C. Vaughan, to whom the relic was handed over, took it to Mr. Everett, surgeon, who said that the limb had evidently been preserved for anatomical purposes, wax having been injected into the veins. The lovers of the marvellous were no doubt disappointed at this solution of the mystery.

reprimanded for soliciting a solicitor – *lovely phrase, that* – for a gratuity in a prosecution he'd conducted. Earlier this year, he'd investigated the theft of tripe and entrails of a cow, the property of Mrs Elgar of the Shades Inn Mealcheapen Street; the log for August 18th this year reports 'Accidentally drowned and a gratuity of £10 from the Superannuation Fund awarded to his widow'.

Just a week later, **Charles Vaughan** in his 11th year with the force was at last promoted to Sergeant in his place, and after just over a year's service, **PC William Archer** was raised to first class: by the end of the year he'd put in for promotion to sergeant but the final decision was postponed for a fortnight.

Off-duty **PC William Morris** went up in the chief's books after he called into a Birdport barber's for a shave one Sunday morning and found several people sitting around drinking beer: they'd been nipping into the Plume of Feathers next door via a shared internal door and were being illegally served with beer. The barber and the landlord were one and the same man, Joseph Birbeck. Morris had only joined in July this year but despite this early success, he'd had enough by the following March and quit.

In October, miffed Shambles shoemaker William Harrison brought a charge of trespass against **Charles Vaughan** after the newly-promoted sergeant had run into his shop while chasing suspected thief and wife-beater Thomas Nash who was hoping to make an escape through his premises. Harrison's wife had also taken a stick to the tireless copper claiming that all policemen were 'the biggest thieves out'. **Vaughan** had also made a counterclaim in his own name of assault while in the execution of his duty. Verdict: Harrison to pay 2s and 8s costs or a day's imprisonment.

The final Watch Committee meeting of the year proved to be another heated affair:
- they ordered a surgeon's report into the condition of **PC John Whitehouse**, who'd cried-off absent 35 nights during the year citing rheumatic fever, and agreed to allow him to continue another fortnight pending the surgeon's report
- acting-sergeants **Ezra Franklin** and **John Wall** both posted charges of neglect of duty against **PC Charles Smith**, for not being at the appointed places to meet them (*downgraded to 3rd Class*)
- **PC James Barker** was yet again cautioned as to his future conduct after a charge of using 'obscene language and for other foolish talk'. He'd been asked to resign by **Matthew Power** in order to save his character, but refused
- **PC Thomas Brown** was charged by **Sgt Holmes** with neglect of duty for not having made his 'points' (*ie scheduled meetings*) for several nights and admitting to having 'succumbed to sleep' although the charges were dropped after the chief himself had intervened and said that his recent conduct had been exemplary. Instead he was fined 5s and reprimanded.
- the same meeting also saw **PC Thomas Williams** granted a gratuity of 5s for detecting and apprehending two thieves the previous week.

Maj-General Cartwright had once more judged the City force 'efficient' at the start of the year, but that was the sum total of the good news for much of the year.

Friday, 3rd March proved a black day for the force: three PCs were dismissed for drunkenness.

They were **Henry Clements** who'd served a fraction over a year; **William Morris** who'd served just eight months; and **Amos Morgan** just four months. The meeting of the Watch Committee two weeks later was only slightly more encouraging: £1 gratuities were awarded to **PCs Thomas Cole** and **William Underwood** for their part in detecting a robbery at Webbs pawnbrokers in Broad Street: in recognition, **Underwood** was later promoted to Sergeant.

**PCs John Whitehouse** and **Thomas Williams** were elevated from 3rd Class to 2nd.

After being shot in the face the previous April, Kidderminster-born **Sergeant James Drew** never returned to work and on September 29th he was superannuated at £1 5s a week from the city funds on account of the injuries he'd received at the hands of the madman Walter S. Jones. He was 36, and married to Ann six years his senior: they're thought to have been childless.

Meanwhile, **PC Richard Fowkes'** injuries inflicted in February the previous year had been found to be far more serious and longer-lasting than at first thought, and following a corroborative report from a surgeon that his absence was entirely due to the injuries he'd sustained as a result of execution of his duty, he was allowed an extension to the period of reduced pay – although he never returned to active duty and was superannuated out of the force at the end of September this year.

He'd been an active constable during his $7^1/_2$ years as a Worcester City policeman (*9th April 1858 – October 3rd 1865*) although his track record was not entirely without blemish. Just weeks after joining and still a PC 3rd Class, he'd distinguished himself and his selfless conduct praised after rescuing a girl named Griffiths from drowning in the Severn at the imminent risk of his own life. Raised to 2nd Class in July that year and then 1st Class by November 1861 he was demoted to 2nd Class in November 1863 for drunkenness and using abusive language to **Sergeants Holmes** and **Sanders**. Prior to then, accusations levelled against him included being in a public house for half an hour while on duty (February 10th 1860); being in the Rising Sun at 2am on a Sunday while on duty; want of zeal in the performance of his duty and disobeying orders (*February 6th 1863*); and being found asleep on his beat and insubordination to his sergeant.

In February the previous year (*1864*) he'd been fined 5/- and severely reprimanded for again being found asleep while on his beat. He and **James Drew** were both pensioned-off on the same day – Friday, September 29th – as the result of injuries received,

- Sgt Ben Holmes investigates baby's body found in a black bag tied with string left on the footway between the reservoir and railway cutting at Rainbow Hill

- Sgt Charles Vaughan sent to Pontypool to arrest James Phillips to answer manslaughter charges

- PC Charles Clements breaks up a fight in Mealcheapen Street but when he's walking one of the combatants back to the station house for charging, his ankles are dragged from behind, he falls on his face and is kicked several times by his prisoner and James Parsons

- the following week PC Amos Morgan is set on by brewer 'Chalker' Brown and the wife he'd been beating up as well as her mother and the lodger named James Burbidge

- PC Thomas Brown gains an admirer when he cautions Ann Smith for being drunk in Broad Street one Saturday in April, despite orders to leave him alone, she persists in following him everywhere on his beat so he takes her into the station-house where she is later released uncharged

- the same month, shocked boatman Charles Stephens appears at the station-house with a box containing the body of a new born baby he'd found floating in the river. Verdict returned: 'Wilful Murder against person or persons unknown'

## 1866

The first week in January was a troubled time that saw a flare-up in sectarian violence directed both by and towards the growing numbers of Irish that had settled in the city, with the Blockhouse the chief battleground. In one unpleasant anti-Irish incident, the police were called in to Providence Street where a full-scale lynching was about to take place.

John Hoskisson, William Snow, Henry Hopkins, John Day, James Wilson and the notorious Collins brothers Thomas, Jesse and Aaron had besieged the house of Irishman Thomas McCurnock, smashing windows, lobbing a hail of stones and threatening to drag him out and throw him on to a large bonfire that had been built in the street – complete with an effigy of the marked GWR fitter.

They were quickly joined by a massive hooting crowd, none of whom were on the Irishman's side, almost every one baying for the Patlander's blood: a Mrs Hopkins is reported to have yelled 'let's light it in his guts' and the Irishman's wife had been hit by a large stone thrown by William Snow through a smashed window. Reports the *Herald*: '...the noise was terrific and street was crowded'.

Enter the police. With judicious use of staves, they managed to beat the crowd back and arrest the ringleaders – **PC William Charles Preece** emerging with some glory. Charged under the old City Act with riotous proceedings, the instigators were each fined 9s while Snow, seemingly the ringleader, was fined 14s.

The following week, the *Herald* erroneously promoted **PC Alfred Harrison**, who'd only been with the force since the previous

> ...pleaded guilty, and was sentenced to 14 days' hard labour.
> STREET OBSTRUCTION.—Mr. Elgar, music-seller, of High-street, charged by Inspector Harrison with causing an obstruction by leaving an empty case in the street opposite his house, was fined in the expenses, 7s. 6d.—R. Daniel, fruiterer, for a similar offence, was fined 19s., including costs, it being his second offence.
> VAGRANCY.—W..........................charged with vagrancy in

May, to Inspector when reporting on the cases of two High Street traders charged with obstruction. The first, fruiterer Richard Daniel was fined 19s and costs, it being his second offence. The other, who'd left an empty case in the street opposite his house at no 7, was fined expenses only, 7s 6d. His name was William Henry Elgar, described as a music seller whose wife handled the catering side of things at the Shades in Mealcheapen Street where they'd met. Their 9-year old son Edward was presumably at school at the time.

In the same edition, a report implying some police brutality, denied by the police (*inevitably*) and, as the complainant was an out-of-it drunk, dismissed by the Bench (*expectedly*). John Carey's was the first case heard on a Monday morning following a riotous weekend and, according to the newspaper '...(he) was apparently suffering badly from his Saturday night's break-out in the drinking line and had a black eye... charged with having been drunk and riotous and resisting **PC15 [*unnamed*].** Said he:

> "*Please your Honour, I've been 40 years in Worcester and was never here before. I've been a teetotaller for seven years but two quarts of cider on Saturday quite overcame me. I don't know if I resisted the officer, but I was very badly used in the cell". There was no proof of this bad usage, and as he was so excessively "gone" in his liquor as that he might have fallen about and received any damage unconsciously, the Bench took no notice of his complaint and fined him 5s; allowed a fortnight to pay*'.

The string of similar cases heard on the same day alongside assaults, soliciting, family desertion and theft, accounted for most of the rest of the column – a massive slab of words and cases in a broadsheet paper measuring $29^1/_2$ inches depth (x $23^1/_2$ inches width).

The city at the time was not a particularly healthy place to be. There had been a spate of yet more fires demanding police supervision – in one, on March 2nd **Charles Vaughan** and **John Stringer No14** had been commended for sturdy and attentive conduct.

New figures had shown that at 28.4 per 1,000 people, Worcester's death rate was higher than it had ever been: even the cholera years hadn't seen it rise above 23.2. Much of the blame was put down to the mode of drainage and open cesspits festering in increasing numbers. Chairman of the Streets Committee John Lloyd Bozward commented: '...open cesspools are hot-beds of contagion and they (the city engineers) have made an open cesspool under the city and called it a drain and are crying out that everybody should connect their drainage with the large one'. In typical Council style, the matter was passed on to the General Health Committee. And so on.

● On March 29th. **PC No13 Charles Smith** had been permitted to resign after leaving his beat and going home while on duty; earlier in the year he'd been fined 2/6d for neglect of duty for not making his [rendezvous] point on Dec 30th (1865)

● April 13th saw **PC No7 Thomas Brown** discharged for assaulting a man while under the influence of drink and fined £10 7s 6d costs by the magistrates for the offence: earlier this year he'd been fined 1/- for being late for muster (Jan 5th), and reduced to PC2nd Class on Jan 19 for taking a man into custody without just cause, being at the time the worse for drink

● April 27 **Thomas Tolley** fined 3/- for leaving his beat while on duty

● On May 25th **PC No21 William Preece** was fined 2/6 for being drunk on duty. Just a few weeks earlier (Feb 2nd) he'd been suspended for two days without pay for insubordination in disobeying the lawful orders of the Superintendent

● A bright spot, however on May 11th when a formal record was made of the energy and perseverance displayed by **PC No23 John Whitehouse** in apprehending Benjamin Dalton Wilkins at New York for forgery. It was a long way to go to make an arrest, but his passage and time had been paid for by the injured party, the Worcester Old Bank. On the day of his return, he was appointed Sergeant, but his joy was short-lived: he died of chloera while still serving, in November this year

The same month **PC Thomas Cole** was on duty in Friar Street when he was foiled in what he thought was sure to be a promotion-winning arrest. The *Herald* report, reproduced here in full, tells the tale.

> "*About half past two o'clock last Saturday morning PC Cole was on duty in Friar-street when he heard a noise in a fowl-pen in a yard adjoining the Cross Keys Inn. He concealed himself and just as he was in the expectation of securing a thief, he saw emerging from the entry not a burglar, but a large dog with a fowl in its mouth. The officer, who was greatly surprised and not a little disappointed, immediately started after the canine thief, and succeeded in pressing the animal so closely that it was glad to drop its ill-gotten booty which was minus nearly all its feathers. The officer picked up the fowl and returned it to its pen*'.

**Matthew Power** had kept something of a low profile for the previous twelve months at least, and even the rate of police censures and admonishments appears to have slowed down. It's possible he'd now found his 'dream team', but that's unlikely: new recruits this year, drafted-in to replace out-going officers, still numbered 13, more than one in three of the total complement.

*Any similar-sized organisation showing a 40% turnround in staff in the same year would appear to have major, some might say terminal, problems.*

Thus, the more plausible solution is that the chief was busying himself with improving organisation and systems for the benefit of his men.

The continual problem of the growing number of public- and beer-houses in the city was never going to go away though, and in his report to the Brewster Sessions in September he said that some of the 185 public- and 84 beer-houses (*269 in all, a slight reduction in the previous year's 276*) had been conducted 'in the most objectionable manner'.

During the year, 24 ale- and 7 beer-house keepers had been proceeded against for offences against the tenor of their licences and 19 of the former and 5 of the latter fined. Of these, he singled-out landlord John Foss' Masons Arms in Diglis as the worst of all – a damning accusation considering the near daily violence, disorder and assaults on the police at the likes of the low-dives and crime nests that were Lord Nelson and the Glovers Arms. In February this year, John Foss had been convicted of '...so reprehensible a practice in the conduct of his house that the convicting Justices considered that the circumstances should this day be specially mentioned'.

Sadly, the *Herald* omits to shine any more light on the specific nature of this reprehensible crime but it proved sufficiently damning for the magistrates to take the dramatic step of formally suspending his licence – at the same time adjourning the consideration of eight others until the following Friday.

At that session – at which John Hill of the Fountain also stood next to John Foss to have his licence determined – mayor Thomas Southall told them both that '...the magistrates had taken into their careful consideration the applications for licences, and they felt they would not be doing the duty confided to them by Act of Parliament except in receiving a promise from each that they would dispose of their business within six months to some suitable person'.

Neither was given any say in the matter or leave to appeal.

Two recently-recruited constables now emerged as particularly vigilant in executing their duty in respect of erring landlords, although neither went on to enjoy particularly glorious careers with the force: these were **PC George Lamb** and **PC William Keith**.

In one September week alone, **George Lamb** charged three publicans with illegal activities after walking in and finding people drinking outside proscribed hours: these were Susan Packwood of the Mug House in Hylton Road, Charles Goodyear of the Chequers King Street and John Barnes of the Oak in Bransford Road. All three cases were proved – unlike two more brought that same week by PC Keith. That's not to say that the landlords he charged, William Woodward of the Shades in Diglis (*now Severn*) Street and Edward Hill of the Albion in Bath Road, didn't have cases to answer, but **Matthew Power** had found it necessary to intervene pending a more serious charge and had both of Keith's charges dropped rather than face criticism over the conduct of the officer who was already in serious trouble and was about to be given his marching orders (*or more accurately, allowed to resign although they amount to much the same thing*).

It was the kind of issue **Matthew Power** had been dreading, and it turned out to be every inch as bad as he feared...

To you
and me,
a whistle;
to the
bobbies on
the beat, a
'call'.

*Courtesy
Bob Pooler*

## Power's 'worst scenario' comes true

It involved the Holly Bush on the Cross – already the notorious haunt of prostitutes and scene of nightly disorders generally, but by no means exclusively, involving the mis-named 'fair sex'. The removal of the station house to the Guildhall had taken the brake off the general lawlessness and disorder that typified most of Worcester's pubs in this area, and a free-for-all had developed in the street outside when a set-to in here between three battling women spilled-over to involve upwards of a dozen slugging it out in a fracas that also included the landlord Henry Baker in the affray. Then within two weeks of each other, prostitute Ellen Bevan threw a glass at William Browning during a stand-up fight in the bar and was fined £1 including costs, and Sarah Hartwright was fined 5s and ordered to repay the cost of two panes of glass she'd broken in there while drunk and disorderly.

But the most damaging incident occurred this year, resulting in uproar in the court when the chief witness (*and prosecutor*) of Henry Baker, again charged with permitting after-hours drinking, was found to have been one of the drinkers. *Worse, he was a policeman on active duty!*

The court heard that **PC Keith** had called in, having seen a light on well after the proscribed closing time, and boots Alfred Wall had called barmaid Elizabeth Snow to bring some matches and a glass of ale for the bobby, who said he didn't drink beer and asked instead for a glass of whisky, which he drank. This was the charge laid against the landlord. **Matthew Power** who was in court, immediately saw the implications of the sham trial and the wrong messages it would send out to the public at large, and instantly intervened with a request to withdraw the case against Henry Baker – to which the Bench agreed – offering to dismiss Keith on the spot. The Magistrates preferred to leave the case in the hands of the Watch Committee who later allowed **PC Keith**, who they viewed as being guilty of wilful and corrupt perjury, to resign.

Nor was 1866 a good year for **Thomas Croft, No23.** Between April and December he was admonished and fined on three occasions: for neglect of duty in not removing an obstruction in the street (*April 27*); loitering while on duty and fined 1/- (*September 28th*); and being drunk on duty and fined 2/6d (*December 21st*). Any other time, and possibly any other officer, would have been dismissed by **Matthew Power** for the string of offences, yet **Tommy Croft** clung on, progressing to greater things.

As for **Matthew Power**, was he beginning to lose his grip?

Far from untypical conditions of the time – not to mention a typical night's work for a beat bobby – also emerged in a case chaired by MP and ex-mayor Richard Padmore in October, reprinted here from the *Herald*, in full:

*Charles Walters was charged with assaulting his wife last evening in Friar-street. PC Harmer [Joseph Harmer had only been appointed at the end of June so was still a considered a rookie: he was raised to 2nd Class on October 26 this year but was to quit, with an apparently clean sheet in January 1869] said that at 11 o'clock the previous night he heard a child crying and on going to see what was the matter he saw defendant dragging his wife about by the hair of her head. It*

## Also this year: 1866

■ murder suspected when the body of a little girl, Mary Ann Roberts, was found in outhouse in Commandery Street, Blockhouse

■ two unnamed PCs despatched to Droitwich to apprehend Engine Works fitters Morris and Webb, that had done a runner after their landlord had gone to their works to demand back rent and they set about him, leaving on the canal bank severely injured

■ in July, PC Thomas Tolley interrupts carpenter Thomas Bryant in the act of raping Elizabeth Cosnett in St Oswalds Walk after responding to several cries of 'Murder'

■ 5th August Sgt Ben Holmes disarms Joseph Austen Yeates who'd threatened Swan with Two Nicks (then Necks) landlady Rhoda Sanders with a loaded gun, later charged with attempted murder

■ just days after his first 'beat', PC Charles Pountney brings in a fighting drunk who's later found to be 'The Worcester Model Working Man' teetotal lecturer and staunch anti-drink campaigner Henry Powell. Fined 5s

■ unnamed PCs alerted to smells from Diglis lock-house find an accumulation of dead dogs and cats fished out of the lock and kept on the premises of the Canal Company, lock-keeper remanded

■ Detective George Lamb and PC Thomas Williams commended for apprehending a gang of nine Bristol pickpockets in town for the Music (Three Choirs) Festival

■ Matthew Power directed to produce posters warning publicans of swift action if found guilty of holding Christmas raffles

■ on the last day of the year and in his first month as a PC, Henry Harding is made to walk a straight line in the charge-room to prove he is not drunk after fighting with (and, seemingly, beating) James Burton and Thomas Cope in the Bell in St Johns

*also appeared that it was customary for him to get beer, and then go home and beat her severely. The wife however could not be induced to appear against him. Defendant pleaded drink as the cause and was sentenced to two months' hard labour'*

On October 26th the 'loose cannon' **Sergeant James Barker** was at last allowed to resign and granted 14 days 'for the purpose' after absenting himself from duty, as well as insubordination and insolence.

By the end of the year, **George Lamb** had been appointed detective and he had the misfortune of being called in to the Wellington beer-shop *[later Duke of Wellington public-house]* in Birdport to investigate reports of a man violently beating a woman, Caroline Skinner, in there.

What the report hadn't made clear however, was that the man was Frederick – alias Nobby – Hardwick, probably the city's hardest hard-case of the time and ex-prize fighter, and that he was roaring drunk. Worse, he hated the police with a passion: '...Detective Lamb stated that he went to the beer-shop when the prisoner became very violent and kicked witness severely on the legs and was altogether so violent that it took three officers to take him to the station. He said that he would wait for him (Det. Lamb) if it was for 20 years'.

Hardwick was fined £1 4s 6d and in default a month's hard, and at the end of that time to find sureties to keep the peace against the officer.

The same night, **PC Francis Harvey**, another rookie from the 1864 intake, was also severely beaten up – as the *Herald* gloriously reported it 'knocked him staggering along the street' – by dyer George May who'd claimed that whatever a policeman said, being an Englishman gave him the unequivocal right to stand anywhere, and in any condition, he wanted.

The last court of the year proved to be much the same as the first and virtually every other, **PC Herbert Osborne** faring much as many of his brother officers had fared throughout the year having been vigorously slapped about by a drunk and disorderly prostitute miffed at having her nightly activities watched and presumably cut short. The only variables were the names and locations: in this case, Sarah Hartwright and Broad Street. Plus ça change.

*Gained: John Richard, George Millichap (neither of which saw out the year), Thomas Green, William Futrill, John Colley, Edward Hodges, Charles Thomas, Thomas Trueman, Joseph Harmer, George Lamb, Charles Pountney, Robert Boulton, Henry Harding*

*Lost: James Barker, Charles Smith, Thomas Brown, John Whitehouse, Samuel Westwood, John Richard, William Keith*

# 1867

After the usual round of Christmas rowdies and d&ds (drunk and disorderlies) the first court of the year was overshadowed by a worrying case for the police: **PC12** who'd only joined the force at the end of August (31st) was charged with assault.

This was **Charles Pountney** who, in just his first few months had earned a reputation as a hard-line copper who took no messing from anyone: small wonder he'd found himself assigned to the gruelling St Johns beat where a hard line and big boots were not only required, but also a pre-requisite of survival.

On December 11th he'd been reprimanded for not making his point (*the pre-arranged regular 'meet' with his sergeant*) and then while patrolling past the notorious Rising Sun in St Clements (*now Tybridge*) Street on Boxing night, he'd challenged three men who emerged from here at 9.30pm.

The men – John Pitt and Daniel Taylor, both labourers, and William Taylor, later said to have taken no part in the ensuing action – said they were singing, but **Pountney** maintained they were shouting and disorderly and ordered them to make a little less noise. It was too much for the revellers who, by the sound of it, had had their fill of the pushy policeman and saw a chance to get one back on him:

*'Pitt immediately took him by the collar, seized his neck and tore the coat he wore at the time, ripping the collar off and some of the buttons. The prisoner kicked him on the legs, bit both his hands severely and also bit a piece out of his coat. Taylor then assisted the prisoner*

*and kicked him. They all three had a struggle and (Pountney) drew his staff and struck Taylor on the head. He threw Pitt down and drew his handcuffs, but they were immediately taken from him and have not been seen since'.*

The *Herald* then reported how Taylor ran up the street towards St Johns and returned with an unruly mob from the Cock and the Bush who pelted the PC with stones. In a surprise later twist, several witnesses came forward to say that it was **Pountney** that had been the aggressor, first knocking Pitt's head against railings and hitting him twice with his staff after straddling him on the ground. Both sides' solicitors withdrew to consider the next move and agreed to abandon all claims.

This was not to be **Pountney**'s year: on February 1st he was fined 2/- after being found asleep on his beat; two weeks later he was off with illness caused by excessive drinking and fined three days' pay; on March 15th he was fined one day's pay for again failing to make his rendezvous point. Then finally on April 26th he was sacked for once more not having made his point at Blockhouse bridge five days earlier. He'd denied the charge and tendered his resignation, but his case was considered so bad that it was not accepted – thereby precluding him from applying for a post with any other police force.

**Matthew Power** was still not the man to be messed with – nor would he ever be – and no doubt the customers in the St Johns pubs breathed a sigh of relief while they waited to see who was next in line for more of the Rising Sun boot-treatment.

Not, of course, that hassle was anything new at the Rising Sun: **PCs William Berridge, George Moule**, and **Sgt James Drew** (*and* **PC Lewis Barnes** *before long*) had all been victims of assault in here over the previous few years, and just months before, John Ford had murdered his live-in lover Elizabeth Hull in the home they shared backing on to the Rising Sun's yard.

On March 15th **PC Frederick Hall** was appointed to the force – and was to prove a grave disappointment to Matthew Power. Within four weeks (*April 12th*) he'd been found drunk while on duty, fined 2/6d and allowed a month to resign. But before that time was out, (May 11th) he was again found drunk on duty and dismissed.

In May, a notable piece of legislation received the royal nod: this was the **Worcester Prison Act**, signed-off by the queen on the last day of the month and paving the way for the union of the city's two prisons – one of which was falling well below the standards expected of any penal establishment and had become a national disgrace. At the same time, plans were drawn up for the enlargement of the County Gaol 'to admit of the Amalgamation of the Worcester City and County Gaols' – all of whch required full Whitehall debate, subsequent approval and not a little expense.

WCiCo/WAAS

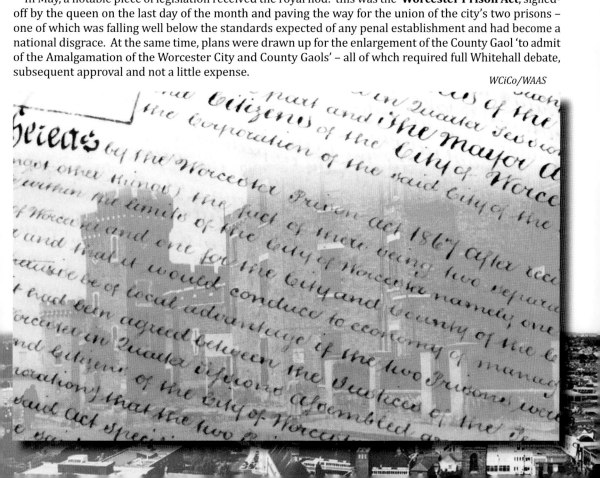

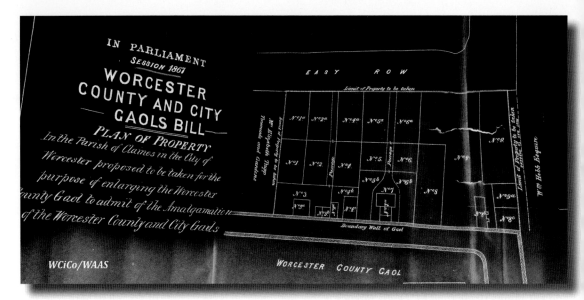

IN PARLIAMENT
SESSION 1867

WORCESTER COUNTY AND CITY GAOLS BILL

PLAN OF PROPERTY

In the Parish of Claines in the City of Worcester proposed to be taken for the purpose of enlarging the Worcester County Gaol to admit of the Amalgamation of the Worcester County and City Gaols

WCiCo/WAAS

EASY ROW

WORCESTER COUNTY GAOL

The Friar Street/Union Street site of the old city gaol was acquired by philanthropist and Squire of Abberton, William Laslett who paid £2,250 for the freehold of the half-acre site that included blocks of cells, mill-houses and the notorious (*and still working*) treadwheel, with machinery, fence and boundary walls, metal fences and gates, hospital building, governor's house, outbuildings and offices, pumps, and iron and lead mains and pipes. It was a good buy: in July 1824 it had cost the city £2,139 for its purchase and conveyance of the land and £10,439 for the buildings, while an inordinately massive amount had also been swallowed-up in improvements and additions. Now its life as a prison was at an end.

Laslett's plans for it were to include the siting of almshouses for a significant portion of the city's deserving poor. When he announced his intentions he received a huge roar of support, but pending extensive re-building, the chosen few were temporarily housed in the same dingy spaces up to then considered unworthy of even the city's lowest of the low.

In Castle Street, the move had demanded the acquisition of land sufficient to allow the construction of fourteen new cells, to be built on the space between the existing prison walls and Easy Row (*see above*).

### Publicans complain of police victimisation

In true Worcester style, many of the pubs were proving just too hard to handle, and publicans were becoming tetchy with what they were increasingly coming to view as police victimisation – several claiming that they were being too closely watched by the officers who were bringing too many cases to the Magistrates court for no better reason than that they were an easy target for a force that they claimed was now failing in every other respect.

The issue came to a head in the middle of the year when Fred Ellis, newly-installed landlord of the Grandstand on Pitchcroft, was fined for selling beer at illegal hours. In the wake of that case, he summoned **Matthew Power** and as good as accused him of dirty practices by having constables hidden in the grass to observe who came and went from his establishment, and more importantly, **when**: after many had been found to be calling in during out-of-proscribed drinking hours, he countered that the drinkers were boaters who hired pleasure boats from here – and as such were bona fide travellers out of the scope of the Beer Act. He won his case, but hardly surprisingly, the action served only to increase police vigilance at the Grand Stand: **PC *(later Sergeant)* Charles Thomas** charging him with a similar offence on Good Friday the following year, this time making the charge stick.

On July 21st **PC Henry Moseley,** appointed only weeks earlier, was reprimanded for using unnecessary violence to a prisoner in custody.

The year's final edition of the *Journal* contained a letter to the editor that give a mixed indication of the efficiency and worth of the police in a year that had not been marked by any significant success: indeed to some, it appeared to be a year of going backwards, and none was more aware of it than **Matthew Power.**

With memories of the narrowly-avoided Providence Street lynching still fresh in people's minds, anti-Irish feelings had escalated in Worcester and the police were on full alert. With an unusually large Irish population in the city, they'd been made aware of the threats posed by the Fenians, forerunners of the IRA and guided by the twin goals of making Ireland a self-governed republic with the justified use of armed force as the only way of achieving it.

Now, after discovering more than a comfortable number of Irishmen carrying guns in the city – *they'd said for their own protection, although there were fears over how long it would be before* **de***fence turned to* **of***fence* – the police feared serious revolt, sensing that an uprising, geared to sending a stark and unmistakeable message to HM's Government that Ireland was hell-bent on home rule at any cost, was being planned in Worcester.

There were letters in the local and national papers – one, a scathing and violent attack on the revolution-driven enemy in Worcester's midst calculated to stir up armed revolt against the militant force actively committed to achieving independence with bloodshed if necessary. It was unsigned, but widely believed to have been written by Belfast-born **Matthew Power** himself and went all the way to a parliamentary commission to discover its source.

The commission never released its findings, but it had had one effect in Worcester at least – a growing call for the city's police to be similarly armed.

The Irish question aside, the move was welcomed, to a man, within the force, given the number of continuing assaults and the reception afforded to the police in the execution of their day-to-day duty.

The trouble was that many – including the press – questioned whether, in the light of some unfortunate recent lapses in discipline, Worcester City Police could be trusted with the general issue of firearms: the majority thought they couldn't and that the move would create more problems than it sought to solve. A letter from 'A Ratepayer' voices the opposing argument:

> '**Sir** – Certainly, Sir, arms ought to be provided for the police.
> In times like these it is not Fenianism alone that we have to
> dread; but there is a spirit of lawlessness which influences other
> desperate characters besides Fenians. There ought to be a number
> of revolvers provided in the case of need, and I am sure the
> ratepayers will be glad to pay for them.
> I have heard it said that some of the police are not fit to be trusted
> with firearms. Trust them, Sir, then, who are experienced and safe
> officers, and those only when there is reason to believe they may
> be required. Vagabonds and murderers ought not to know which
> man is armed and which is not' (Berrows Worcester Journal)

He ended by calling for some of the police to be given arms 'at all events'.

It was not only the police coming in for some stick by the public at the end of a fairly dismal year: the city's Sanitary Committee was also condemned over the general state of Worcester having '...failed in many respects, either through want of guidance, efficient officers, or through economical considerations. If some demon of pestilence had been specially engaged in accumulating material suitable for the reception and propagation of plague seeds, he could not have done more than had been done in some "back slums" of our otherwise clean and handsome city. Wells with sewage matter percolating into them, cesspools unemptied for many years, streets undrained, byeways unswept, crowded dwellings unventilated and a host of abominations in every parish... much remains to be done before Worcester is in a sanitary condition creditable to her wealth and station, or thoroughly healthy as a place of residence'.

**Gained:** *Henry Evans, Frederick Hall, John James, John Abraham, Michael Murt (none of which survived the year) Henry Moseley, John Carter, Frederick Thompson, John Walker, Edward Henry Dowdeswell, Charles Page, Frederick William Thorne*

**Lost:** *Alfred E Byng, Edward Hodges, Thomas Trueman, George Lamb, Charles Pountney, Robert Boulton*

## Also this year: 1867

■ *PC Henry Harding is beaten up inside and outside the Bell, St Johns, despite butcher David Hooper offering to stand James Burton and Thomas Cope half a gallon of beer if they desisted*

■ *61st Rifles deserter John Pugh surrenders to Sergeant George Archer after three years on the run*

■ *Berrows Journal cracks a joke 'why is a hotel ghost like a policeman? Because he is an inn-spectre' (tee-hee!)*

■ *Lowesmoor coal dealer William Dayus charged with attempted murder of his wife*

■ *Worcester LVA's 100 members complain of Matthew Power's 'French spy system' using officers in plain clothes to trap publicans. A number of charges involving late hours and refusing to admit the police are thrown out*

■ *raid on Horn and Trumpet led by Sergeant Charles Vaughan reveals 22 known prostitutes operating out of here*

■ *police investigate robbery at Shrub Hill Station refreshment rooms*

■ *PC John Stringer investigates curious case of the mysterious extinguisher of public lamps in London Rd*

The 'should they/shouldn't they?' arms debate raged on over Christmas and in January the *Journal* reported that a special meeting had been held, chaired by the mayor William Webb to hammer out the issue. The Sheriff, three aldermen and eight councillors duly decided that special constables would be armed with staves at a cost of £27 8s 6d and that six revolvers and 30 cutlasses would be provided for the police – albeit only for use in emergencies of such dire nature that they '...appear to call for the adoption of such a course, and then with such authority as it is provided by the law'.

The full Council agreed and placed an official order to that effect – with the proviso that the weapons could only be drawn from the Superintendent's office on receipt of a letter signed by the mayor.

Public opinion was hugely in favour of the weapons and particularly of the guns – not least through fear of the Fenians' growing militancy both nationally and nearer to home, although the *Journal* took the side of the minority antis, not on the grounds of protection not being needed against what it termed 'the criminal attempts of those skulking cowardly ruffians the Fenians', so much as the paltry number of guns being proposed.

Likening the suggested provision of half a dozen revolvers to the five biblical barley loaves (and two fishes) and suggesting they'd be of as much use against the Fenians' 'blunderbuss slugs and revolver bullets', they raged

*'...anything more utterly contemptible we cannot conceive than a respectable city arming its protectors with six pistols; why, it would have been wisdom compared with this to have had the curious old defensive armour now hanging empty in the [Guild]hall furbished up and fitted, so far as it would go, to the backs and bellies of the pick of the fine-looking military fellows, now comprising the city force'.*

In the council chamber, the old **Matthew Power** v John Lloyd Bozward mutual animosity bubbled over several times as the firebrand councillor openly accused the Irishman police chief of stirring up anti-Fenian sentiment in Worcester, creating disorder rather than suppressing it.

Life went on for the force – and it wasn't getting any easier. In the very midst of the Irish question, two men, Charles King and Henry Archer, summed-up what would appear to be Worcester's general attitude when they deliberately tried to provoke two on-duty constables into some form of action – preferably violent so that the whipped-up Saturday night crowd would instantly turn on them.

Given the short temper-fuse of some of the officers, there's a good chance they'd have succeeded with potentially fatal results; unfortunately for them, the two they picked on were both experienced and rather more even-tempered officers 1st Class – P**Cs William Phillips** and **Thomas Tolley,** the latter of which (*pictured right from a photograph dated 1884, by which time he'd been promoted to Sergeant*) had already been commended for his forbearance and good temper under circumstances of great provocation when he was violently assaulted by a man who was later sentenced to 9 months' imprisonment.

First, King drew a large crowd around him in Broad Street

*Thomas Tolley*

before approaching **PC Phillips** and asking him to go and get him some beer. Barely surprisingly, Phillips refused: '...(*King*) said "what's the use of putting a fool like you in the streets if you can't find any drink?"'

Sensing the trap, Phillips walked away. Not long after, Henry Archer tried it on with **Tommy Tolley** who he'd asked for a light and had been refused. Told to move on, he stood his ground and hurled abuse at the copper, saying that he had more right to be in the street than the police had. While **Tolley**'s track record to date had been far from exemplary – in 1863 he'd been fined 7/6 and severely reprimanded for getting drunk on his beat while on duty and then going home without reporting himself, and in April 1866 he'd been fined 3/- for leaving his beat while on duty – he too saw the ruse, although he did manage to get Archer back to the station-house and into the magistrates court. It's not revealed how, without inflaming the mob, but in any case it proved futile. His charge of provocation was dismissed.

Nonetheless, it was typical of the mood of the city and the more the police did, the tougher it got and the less it was recognised.

*As for approval? Not much chance of that...*

Just the following week a regular drunk-about-town and old offender Emma Wall was again charged with being drunk and disorderly in Broad street, lay down in the road and stated that the only way they (*the police*) would get her to the station-house would be on a stretcher. Asked to explain herself in court the next day she stated – and the reporters duly reported – '...that the police had walked about the streets long enough doing nothing and she intended giving them something to do now'.

Her eighth time before the Bench on the same charge, she was sentenced to gaol for 14 days.

At this time too, the magistrates continued to show their sadistic side: a young boy, Henry Creese was whipped for stealing a fish from Mr Burroughs, Pump Street.

## A not very flattering statistic: four hours as a city bobby, sacked and sent to gaol

With the coming of the summer – July 17th this year showed record temperatures for the city – appeared a new and not very flattering statistic for Worcester City Police: the shortest time from appointment to dismissal, just 4 hours! At 10am on his very first morning, a Monday, **PC Henry Naylor** was, according to the *Herald* '...sent on duty for the first time. After going on his beat he appears to have visited every public house he passed and by 2 o'clock was incapably drunk in Silver-street.

'P.C. [*Tommy*] Croft heard of the defendant's being in such a state in Silver-street, and he took him to the police station. He was charged with being drunk on duty'. Clearly guilty, he was hauled up before **Matthew Power** and instantly dismissed, additionally being sentenced to seven days in gaol.

*Could it get any worse for the city police?*

Given the number of internal charges brought against members of the force succumbing to the temptations of drink before, during and after coming on duty, the publicans were keeping a sharp eye on what **Matthew Power** would have to say about them and their activities at this year's Brewster Sessions. Whether intentionally or not, it was not all bad. At 300, the number of public- (*190*) and beer-houses (*110, which also included refreshment houses*) was the highest it had ever been and would ever be, and from here onwards the tally was to show an annual decline.

There had been 28 proceedings against licensees and 26 convictions, and **Matthew Power** commented that '...although the criminal statistics show that there is much drunken and riotous conduct in our streets, especially on Saturday nights, it is satisfactory to observe that there is less of it than formerly' – a reference to the fact that nine years earlier (1859) 484 people had been charged with drunken or riotous behaviour in the city; the current year's tally was 245 – which he countered by:

on the subject, but he thought the Magistrates had the power to make the order, and they were fortified by the opinion of the editor of the *Justice of the Peace*, who had been consulted on the subject. They therefore made the order as prayed.

## WORCESTER CITY POLICE.

MONDAY.

Before T. Chalk and J. Stallard, Esqrs.

THE D.D. SQUAD.—The list of delinquents this morning consisted chiefly of persons who had indulged too freely in "John Barleycorn" on the Saturday night, in fact in most instances they had extended their orgies far into the Sunday morning. In the dock, after spending the Sabbath in durance vile, they presented a truly woe-begone appearance, with contrition strongly pourtrayed in every feature; but what was to them a source of apparent misery, from the ludicrous position in which they found themselves, was in many instances the means of producing much amusement to the many admiring spectators who usually spend "Saint Monday" in the Police-court or its suburbs in the absence of anything better to occupy their time, and so find amusement at the expense of others' misery. The first defendant who was called upon to answer the charge of being incapably drunk was Richard Teague. The officer in charge stated that at an early hour on Sunday morning he found him in the High-street quite helpless, and as he was unable to give any account of himself, or to give a tangible reason for his preference of the gutter to a couch, he was speedily accommodated with an asylum at the station. Teague is an old offender, but in extenuation he said that he had not been there for drunkenness since March last, and begged hard to be forgiven once more, as he was on tramp, and had the beer "stood" for him by a comrade. He was, however, reminded that since his last conviction for a similar offence he had not been in the city until the day on which he was again found in the same condition. He still pleaded to be let off, and promised to abstain for the future, but the Bench were obdurate, and fined him 5s., and in default he was sent to gaol for seven days.—Samuel Cameron, a respectably attired man, came next, and was charged by P.C. Harding with being drunk and riotous on Saturday night. He admitted the offence, and obtained his discharge on payment of 5s.—William Minton, labourer, was then charged by the same officer with being drunk and fighting in the Shambles at midnight on Saturday. The officer said that his attention was called to a disturbance, and on arriving upon the scene of action he found defendant fighting

- William Garton, described as 'the worst boy in the Blockhouse' fined 2s 6d for playing pitch and toss in the streets

- body of baby boy dragged out of the canal at Lowesmoor

- the next week another is found in the Severn, while 51-year old William Reynolds and 22-year old Allan Birchley are drowned in separate incidents, and John Yeates is rescued after getting into difficulties

- in court, noted drunk about town Jemmy Gomersky (see p371) threatens to have revenge on the unnamed officer who arrested him and is ordered to return to the court after his 7 days' incarceration

- investigating a dog-snatching incident, PC Alfred Harrison concluded the case by charging the victim Sarah Field with using profane language on a Sunday

- County PCs Cowell and Bellamy have lurcher dogs set on them when they apprehend a gang of poachers in St Johns

- PC Herbert Osborne investigates arson attempt at the Coach and Horses in the Tything

*The DD (drunk and disorderly) Squad, as reported by the Herald, September 19th this year*

'...I must however add that this number is considerably **above the average for towns in equal population to that of Worcester**'.

Race week this year proved one of the worst ever for crime and Worcester crowds described as the worst in the country – magistrate and Alderman Stallard commenting: '...why can they *(the race-goers)* not behave as others do? At Doncaster, for instance, they hardly knew that on the Sunday that it was race-time, everything being as quiet as on any other Sunday, whilst in this city [he was] quite sure that there were more cases come before the Magistrates of offences committed on the Sunday than on any two days of the races'. Drunkenness, general rowdiness, theft, fraud, illicit practices, illegal gambling and assaults had been so bad that the Bench was already looking to curtail the event for future years.

To that end, **Matthew Power** had been asked to provide a list of those selling drink on Pitchcroft during the run of the races, but admitted that as he had to rely on the memories of his officers, he could not guarantee its entire accuracy.

Some interesting facts to emerge this year: nationally, there was 1 birth to every 30 living souls; 6 out 100 were out of wedlock; 26 out of 100 children would not live to see their fifth birthday; 104 boys were born to every 100 girls (*the reverse was the case in Worcester*). In every marriage, one in five men and one in three women was unable to write; average age at which people got married was 25.5 for men and 24.3 for women. Average life expectancy at birth was 39.9 for men and 41.9 for women although once they'd passed their critical 5th birthday, it increased to 49.8 and 50.3; for those that had reached 40, expectancy was 60.1 and 67.3. Reach the magical 50, and this further increased to 69.5 and 70.8. Domestic servants could expect to be paid £6 a year.

It was also a bad year for crime: 332 people had been committed to the City gaol in its final year, and 1,497 to the County. Despite this, the proportion of crimes being detected was dismissed as 'average'.

*Gained: William Brayley, John Thompson, James Phipps, Samuel Fitzsimons (none of which were to see-out the year), William Andrews, Henry Willis, Henry Naylor, Charles Hunt, Lewis Barnes, Jabez Waldron, Thomas Chapman, George Milward, Charles Newman, Edwin Adams, ? Burnham*
*Lost: James Quinn, Thomas Williams, Thomas Cole, Frederick Thompson, John Walker, Charles Page*

On the continuing subject of statistics, the *Herald* reported early in the year that the city of Worcester now amounted to 965 acres, its population stood at 32,000 and was policed by a force of 31 representing a ratio of 1:1,032.

A sergeant, **John Walker** about whom very little is known, had been appointed Assistant Relieving Officer for the casual poor of whom 6,613 had been provided with assistance during the previous year, representing an annual increase of 1,242. Times were hard. Desperately so.

During the year, 14 Worcester city constables were to resign, three to better themselves and one to emigrate, and two constables had been dismissed. It represented almost half the force.

In all there remained 14 vacancies – a view commented on by the *Herald* as 'a very unsatisfactory number in proportion to the strength of the force. This is not to be accounted for as there is every encouragement to the men to remain, both by pay and promotion, and the force is well supervised. The station-house is in good, excellent order'.

The year before, Maj-Gen Cartwright had described Worcester City Police merely as 'efficient'.

Nor was the year to show much improvement: 17 new constables were to be taken on just to maintain numbers. In all, the latest report showed that despite **Matthew Power** trying to put a brave face on things, all was far from well.

The mayor's Sergeant-at-Mace Thomas Hanbury had died and a major debate now arose in the Council chamber as to whether the post and that of the three other mayor's officers was still relevant and not an anachronism in this day and age of the city's own police force.

Regardless of the message it conveyed, the councillors cited the James 1st charter and unanimously agreed that yes, it was: the following year the high-profile Sergeant's role was to be handed over to the equally high-profile **Benjamin Holmes** who quit the force after nearly eighteen years' service as PC 3rd, 2nd and 1st class, Detective, and as of 12th July 1861, Station Sergeant. His loss was going to be keenly felt.

At the same meeting, and seemingly taking up less time than the Sergeant-at-Mace post, was the similarly-unanimous decision to buy the Dolphin Inn and sixteen adjoining tenements for £950: the City council already had plans for the site.

The final *Herald* edition of the year looked like the final *Herald* edition of *every* year: awash with the misdemeanours of Worcester citizenry at play and enjoying its favourite sport: getting drunk and/or baiting the police. Just two at random: Irishman Michael Foley, who appeared in court as he'd been arrested (*by PC John Edwards, just nine months into his job*) the night before, stripped to the waist and ready to fight anybody. At 9 the next morning, **Station Sergeant John Doughty** – now in his 24th year with the force and still with six more to go – took him his regulation breakfast, a pint of coffee and the usual quantity of bread:

*'...the prisoner grumbled at the amount allowed him and said it was "a baby's breakfast".*
*The sergeant then went into the cell to take the bread and coffee from him in order to show them to Mr. Power, when the prisoner attempted to throw the coffee over him and to strike him. The sergeant was compelled to strike him in self-defence. The prisoner said that the complement of food brought to him in the cells was just about half what was produced in the court. This Mr. Power and*

Sergeant [Charles] Vaughan who saw the breakfast as it was being conveyed from the cell, denied. The Mayor [Francis Woodward Esq]: you have been here before and I am sure my brother magistrate will agree when I say that your assault upon the sergeant was a most unprovoked one. You were provided with a most excellent breakfast: one, in fact, that I should be glad to partake of myself. For your assault upon the officer you will be fined 20s and costs, or in default sentenced to one month's imprisonment with hard labour. Prisoner: How much? Mayor: Fined 20s or sent to prison for one month. Prisoner: Excuse me, but I would sooner drink the money if I had it than pay the fine'.

Next up: '...an unfortunate character named Emma Bird, who presented a miserable appearance in the dock, being but indifferently clad, with hair dishevelled and a face long a stranger to soap and water, was charged by **PC [Henry] Willis** with being guilty of disorderly conduct in Foregate-street early this morning. The offence having been fully proved, the prisoner was sentenced to seven days' hard labour'.

The same month, Susan Pearce, serving nine months hard, died on the treadwheel at the County Gaol.

*Gained: Frederick Beard, William Franks, George Gibbs, James Farley, John Morris, Samuel New, ? Dancey, Thomas Adams,, ? Young, (none of whom were to see-out the year) John Edwards, George Firth, Thomas Wallace (pic, opposite) Richard Smith, John Richards, John Fitzsimmons, William James, George Stanton*
*Lost: George Archer, Joseph Harmer, Joseph Carter, William Andrews, George Milward, Charles Newman, ? Burnham, Benjamin Holmes*

**Also this year: 1869**

■ *child's body found by two boys in a box near the old cemetery on Tallow Hill*

■ *police investigate attempted suicide of George Morris and attempted murder of his son after he'd jumped into the canal with his son in his arms*

■ *manslaughter case opened after William Weaver dies in a fight at the Express Tavern in Lowesmoor. An inquest was also held here into the death of 4-year old Ada Blanche Davis, scalded by a pan of boiling water*

■ *infant child found drowned in the canal near Tallow Hill bridge*

■ *crime increasing at unparalleled rates and the pubs and beerhouses cited as the chief reason*

# 1870

Early in January a classified ad appeared, just five lines sandwiched between a wheelwright wanted for constant employment and a single man with four years' good references seeking employment as a baker and confectioner, seeking recruits (*left*).

Just the week before it was revealed that the cost of keeping 91 lunatics at the Asylum was £158 9s 8d although in recent weeks, the report noted, two had since died.

Since January the city had experienced four months of drought; up to Whitsun, there had been just three days of rain. Fever was rife: in St Johns churchyard alone there had been

WANTED, by a Single Man, a Situation as BAKER and CONFECTIONER, with four years good reference from his last employer.—Address, F. M. No. 67, Worcester-street, Kidderminster.

WANTED, a few YOUNG MEN for the WORCESTER CITY POLICE; age not to exceed 25; height not less than 5 ft. 9 in. without shoes.—Applications in candidates' handwriting to be addressed to the Head Constable.

WANTED, for constant employment, a good WHEELWRIGHT.—Apply to Joseph Cook, near Kidderminster.

WANTED, by a respectable experienced Man, a Situation as FARM BAILIFF; highest reference.

93 burials the previous year compared to an average of around 50 a year during the previous decade. To the beginning of June this year, there had already been 39 more – of which 21 were children under seven. The crisis prompted one resident to implore, via the *Herald* '...surely the wails of mothers who have lost their little ones, and anxiety for the living, should excite some sympathy in the hearts of the most rigid economists, prompting them to alleviate if possible such distress, even though it would necessitate an appeal to the susceptible pockets of Worcester ratepayers'. Effect? Unknown. Presumed outcome? Unlikely.

As for the police, it was business as usual, on the same day in August, **PC 3ʳᵈ Class John Barnet Bridges** had been dismissed after just five weeks' service for assaulting a woman who'd called him in to expel an intruder at her Tything home, while **PC Lewis Barnes** – *later to go on to some notoriety* – was severely reprimanded for insisting on the same woman accompanying them to the station-house against her will.

At the following week's annual Brewster Session (*August 25ᵗʰ*) **Matthew Power** brought it to the attention of the justices that in the city there was now 196 premises licensed for the sale of spirits and 86 for the sale of beer or wine: '...being in round numbers one to 119 of the population of the city'.

But the news was, for the most part, good: during the previous year '...nothing has occurred in regard to any particular house to call for special action. Informations have been laid against the keepers of 24 ale or beer-houses and 12 have been fined in sums varying between 10s to £2, and seven in costs only. The number proceeded against is less than usual and the proportion of convictions to complaints is much below that of previous years' he reported.

But was it the much-needed sign of having turned the corner and that the police had at last regained the upper hand? Not a bit of it. The police chief was sufficiently savvy to recognise that the prime reason was not so much due to improved management than the difficulties of enforcing a spate of new legislation in the wake of several new Beer Acts. The impact had been that '...conduct which was formerly supposed to warrant proceedings is now necessarily unheeded'.

Towards the end of the year, **Matthew Power** placed notices in all the newspapers warning of the consequences of people being found on licensed premises after hours and of withholding or giving false name and address when requested.

### Plans for more station-house extensions get the go-ahead

Though Matthew Power and his growing band of police officers had been in the custom-built station-house for just nine years, it was already evident that the facilities were just not going to be enough and following the previous year's decision to purchase the ever-troublesome Dolphin Inn next door and 15 adjoining tenements, the deal was struck with its owners and plans drawn-up to make way for a brand new complex, purpose-designed for a force trying manfully to cope with a city growing at an unprecedented rate.

*Gained: Thomas Bettington, Thomas Yarnold, Henry Hill, Daniel E Gibbons, John Barnet Bridges, Abraham Willetts, (none of whom were to see-out the year), Thomas Goodwin, William Cadd, Edwin Oakey, James Harden, Thomas Soles, Henry Joyner, George Davis, George Wall, William Greenhill*
*Lost: Charles Vaughan, John Stringer, Alfred Harrison, John Edwards, George Firth, John Fitzsimmonds*

*(left)* **Tommy Wallace**, *recruited the previous year, went on to serve the force with great distinction up to his retirement in 1896 when he was forced to resign after surviving a murder attempt in a tale worthy of Boys Own Comic stuff*
*(See p310)*

*Main pic*: the Copenhagen Street Station-house, pegged for extensions this year; **left** OS map showing completed works and **below,** cover of conveyancing agreement between the City and the trustees of Michael Wyatt's Charity. **Note:** the two nearest upstairs windows [facing Copenhagen Street] were the private quarters of successive Chiefs, and later my office as Press Officer for the City Council, 2003-5. BB

WCiCo/WAAS

## Also this year: 1870

- PC Henry Moseley quits after just two years following gross assault by four men in St Johns, each fined £5

- the same night PC Hollerton (probably mis-transcribed) is saved a beating at the hands of John Leveridge in the Union Lowesmoor after intervention by town crier Chas Poole, and PC Lewis Barnes is attacked by Sam Teague of the Rising Sun St Clements (now Tybridge) Street

- police investigate malicious letters implying Journal editor Rev Charles Boutell is leaving the city

- PC (later Sergeant) William James rumbles the password for getting served out of hours in the Roebuck – rubbing a brick against the wall and responding 'Glover' when asked who it was. Five men arrested for drinking out of hours

- PC Francis Harvey investigates widespread 'smashing' – coin counterfeiting – in the city, dozens of shops and pubs duped by gang led by Patrick Grogan, scores of innocent passers-on also prosecuted

- nuisances investigated by the police led by Sergeant William Charles Preece at the races include a 6-legged horse, 'The Extraordinary Fat Woman' and gangs of professional pick-pockets from Birmingham

- police called in to investigate a dead baby claimed by its mother, barmaid Louisa Perkins, to have fallen out of her arms at the top of the cellar steps at the Sandpits in St Johns (now the Bedwardine)

- landlord of the George and Dragon, Tything accused of rape of his servant girl Louisa Lucy, aged 13. Discharged as she was found to have been a willing party

# 1871

By the closing weeks of the pevious year even some members of the public and, worse, some councillors had been busy reviving yet another call for the amalgamation of the city and County forces – one elected member in particular pointing out that the officers of Worcestershire Constabulary tended to remain longer with the force than their counterparts in the City.

As an observation it could scarcely be considered revelatory given the daily dose of violence and disapproval suffered by **Matthew Power**'s men, but when tempered with the corresponding news that 'some of the County officers, several of whom are advanced in years, will soon retire; and as such an event would, in my judgment, be a favourable opportunity to carry out such a scheme...' it took on a new urgency with support beginning to grow within the Council, several prominent citizens, and the county authorities.

The letter writer had been in the know about the affairs of the County Constabulary – and that it was in turmoil. Just a week later, the County Police Committee reported the intended resignation of its Chief Constable Richard Reader Harris on medical grounds on January 2nd.

The very next day the ad appeared in the *Herald* and other papers calling for applications for his successor. The right man would be under 40 and provided he lived either in or close to the county town and devoted his whole time to the discharge of his duties, he could look forward to a salary of £400 a year with £10 expenses (*in the same edition, the City was also head-hunting – this time for an Inspector of Nuisances and Sanitary Inspector, salary one-fifth of the police chief's: £80*).

Citing his inability to continue fulfilling the arduous duties of his office '...and praying for the liberal consideration of the magistrates in awarding him a pension' Richard Reader Harris was stepping down after 31 years. Under him the force had grown to 187 men.

It seems he wasn't going to be missed. "There were no long speeches describing his loyalty, or the sadness that was felt at losing his services. Neither were there warm expressions of good wishes in his retirement. Rather an unemotional acceptance of his departure' (*Bob Pooler – From Fruit Trees to Furnaces. A history of the Worcestershire Constabulary, Blacksmith Publishing 2002*).

There were 120 candidates for the post, whittled down to 10 invited to interview on 27th February, where they were further reduced to three. The man they eventually chose was Lt-Colonel George Lyndock Carmichael (*pictured, right*) and unlike almost all of the others, he'd had no police training but was instead a career soldier with the 95th (Derbyshire) Regiment with whom he'd seen action at Alma, Inkerman and Sebastopol in the Crimea. The *Herald* mis-reported his name as Lt. Col Macmichael.

In Worcester, the Inspector of Nuisances and Sanitary Inspector's role had not proved so popular and had attracted just 46 applications. It went to George Hobbs, for the past six years invoice clerk at Shrub Hill Station in the employ of the Great Western Railway Co.

The Worcestershire Constabulary proceedings were no doubt followed with interest by **Matthew Power** and his own band of 'fine-looking military fellows, now comprising the city force' as they'd been described by the *Journal* not long before, but for now there was a more pressing issue: **Matthew Power** had entered into an unwise war of words with the city's best-selling newspaper the *Herald*, and the other newspapers had been sucked-in too...

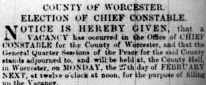

COUNTY OF WORCESTER.
ELECTION OF CHIEF CONSTABLE.
NOTICE IS HEREBY GIVEN, that a VACANCY has occurred in the Office of CHIEF CONSTABLE for the County of Worcester, and that the General Quarter Sessions of the Peace for the said County stands adjourned to, and will be held at, the County Hall, in Worcester, on MONDAY, the 27th day of FEBRUARY NEXT, at twelve o'clock at noon, for the purpose of filling up the Vacancy.
Candidates for the Office are desired to send formal Applications, accompanied by original Testimonials, to the Clerk of the Peace, at his Office, in Worcester, on or before the 4th day of FEBRUARY, 1871.
No Candidate will be eligible over the age of 40.
The Salary attached to the Office will be £400 a year, and £100 a-year for allowances.
The successful Candidate will be required to devote his whole time to the discharge of the duties of his Office, and to reside in or near the county town of Worcester.
WM. NICHOLS MARCY,
Clerk of the Peace.
Worcester, January 3rd, 1871.

Concerned at the rising amount of undetected crime, he'd resorted to what some had already condemned as underhand methods to trap offenders, additionally introducing a 'spy' system that was to re-surface quite spectacularly a few years later: some high-profile cases had seen several publicans charged with the illegal sale of alcohol at the races, a jeweller in St Swithins Street, an auctioneer in High Street and a post boy at the Post Office had all been caught committing crimes that had actually been set up by the police – in one case involving a policeman's wife: the post boy had been caught out by a decoy letter that had virtually invited him to steal it.

The *Chronicle*, the *Journal* and the *Herald* were all frankly appalled at what they termed 'police-manufactured crimes'. The ever-outspoken *Chronicle* called it 'the trap system inveigling people into the commission of an offence against the law'; the *Journal* described it as 'unsatisfactory', and the *Herald* dubbed it 'odious and infamous', later receiving a letter from the furious police chief charging the paper with irresponsibility and guilty of popularising crime. The articles were, he said, '...infinitely more dangerous than the practices which they inveigh; they tend to popularise crime; they contain no expression of condemnation of it, while they make the criminal an object of interest'.

The *Herald* fought back with a haughty self-righteous editorial as did the others. It was a war no-one could win.

## Manning levels at crisis point

Volatile manning levels continued to be a constant thorn in **Matthew Power**'s side. 1870 had seen 15 new faces to replace the same number that had left, and so far this year the turn-round was occurring at much the same pace. Despite the numbers, suitable candidates weren't exactly beating the door down to become police officers in a violent and unpredictable bear-pit like Worcester city.

The situation was barely helped when the tough, although generally genial HM Inspector of Constabularies General William Cartwright had been succeeded by a new by-the-book man, Colonel Charles Augustus Cobbe, a fighting ex-soldier who'd seen active service with the Ceylon Rifles, the 95th Regiment and then the 3rd Regiment West Riding Police before joining West Riding Constabulary where he'd risen to the rank Chief Constable.

Following his first inspection of the City force this year, he not only *requested* but also physically **demanded** the addition of more men, claiming that the current complement was inadequate for the population and that the one officer to 1,000 inhabitants ratio was not an arbitrary figure or a preferable state to attain, but was instead cast in stone and as such inarguable.

Faced with frankly no choice save shouting down a legally-binding Government demand, moves were made to bring the ranks up to scratch with two further recruits, no doubt reluctantly.

As if they weren't already crippling, the duties put upon the police continued to become increasingly onerous – two in particular, not so much crimes, more street nuisances: noisy newspaper boys and, outrage of all outrages, people throwing down orange peel in the street. To read the editorials and the insistence by the press on the police turning on the full force of action, one could be forgiven for thinking that these were capital offences: *on newsboys* '...hawking their sheets through the agency of youths whose lungs are in their early vigour. Just imagine the unspeakable effect – second only to the South American forests when all the beasts and birds therein conspire to render night hideous!' (*Journal*). *On orange-peel:* '...nothing that can be said or done seems to stop the criminal recklessness of those people who, while eating oranges in the streets, cast the peel on the pavement... a wickedly thoughtless habit' (*Herald*).

Small wonder the police force were demoralised and jacking it in in droves. Then again, it could have been the press getting their own back at **Matthew Power** over their criticism of his tough, hard-line methods.

On a more serious note, the *Herald* had also come out strongly against the more evident and physical nuisance of 'gangs of young men and fast youths taking possession of the pavement and linked arm-in-arm in one line, [that] drive all the other passers-by into the mud of the gutter'.

Worcester and its wild youth had come out very badly in comparison with the large manufacturing towns of Yorkshire, Nottinghamshire and Lancashire where, noted the *Herald*, '...in none of these towns is "modern mohawkery" that is, obscene language and disgusting behaviour, so fully developed'.

The editor's dig at the force was scarcely concealed:

> *'... we don't wish to be hard on the police, who are generally expected to perform all kinds of impossibilities, but really there never seems to be any attempt on their part to bring street*

*walking into a civilised mode, or to clear the corners of our thoroughfares of the gangs of roughs who are always assembling there, and insulting or obstructing the peaceable and respectable citizens'.*

The *Herald* even put forward the notion of placing two plain-clothes detectives on the streets on Saturday and Sunday nights, and even when **Matthew Power** pointed out that attempts at detection would be futile and the 'detectives would very soon be the detected' – with who knows what results – the *Herald* still called for a trial, if only on Sunday evenings for a couple of months. It was a notion that they admitted was almost hoping against hope: '...for (we) have moved so often in the matter without results that it may be that the present call upon the authorities, like others, will be disregarded'.

It was – but it was clear that relations between the press and the police had turned sour at a time that the chief needed all the help he could get.

A common nuisance for the police, particularly around harvest time, was the number of itinerant gipsies, ever ready to fleece unsuspecting customers using any number of a series of well-known dodges. The old fortune-telling trick was a constant source of trouble with the impressionable young girls and maids-in-service – until a regular offender, Sarah Lee, picked on the wrong woman, mother-of-two Mary Ann Thorne. When she suspected she was being duped and was refused her request for her money back, she went straight to her husband to enlist his help: sadly for the travellers, who were quickly persuaded to be on their way, the husband was **Sergeant Frederick William Thorne** of the City police.

*The gipsies are said to have put a curse on him for his intervention – and curiously, he was to die quite suddenly and tragically two years to the very day while still serving as sergeant.*

In October, plumber Robert Redding walked up to **PC (*later Sergeant*) William Phillips** who was on duty in Broad Street, and confessed to murdering Nancy Meredith on Pitchcroft six years earlier after a walk along the river resulting in a struggle in which, he said '...I pushed her in and there the poor girl was drowned. It wur through me 'er lost 'er life'. Though drunk at the time *(he later said he'd been drinking from 6am and it was now near midnight)* he was cautioned about the implications of his confession – which he repeated several times over, adding that he hadn't had a moment's peace since the crime – and duly locked-up.

**Also this year: 1871**

■ *On New Year's Day, 11-year old John Huson drowned in the canal near the Arboretum after falling through ice*

■ *Matthew Power receives a personal letter from the Home Secretary complaining of the city's laxity in granting too many aid tickets 'to vagrants, mendicants and other improper persons'*

■ *despite his constant badgering for amalgamation, city police donate towards testimonial for Richard Reader Harris, retired as head of the County force after 31 years*

■ *in the same week PC Edwin Davies is found drinking in the Swan in Pump Street when he should have been on duty, and PCs Edwin Oakey, Henry Willis and Thomas Goodwin are found in similar circumstances in the Old Greyhound*

■ *Sergeant Thomas Tolley, PC Wallace and another unnamed constable wade into 50 spectators of a free-for-all scrap between rival gangs in Quay Street (now site of the fountains)*

■ *PC Francis Harvey tackles and disarms Joseph Hunt who'd stabbed a man with murderous intent in the Fish Inn*

■ *Detective William Underwood investigates arson attempt at the Saracens Head*

By the time he'd sobered-up, he banged on his cell door and begged to be released saying he'd made up the whole thing as a way of getting back at his nagging wife. Referral to the County police force proved that Nancy Meredith was entirely a figment of his drunken imagination. Remanded in custody for a week he was brought back to face the wrath of the Bench for wasting everyone's time, expense and trouble, Charles Sidebottom warning him '...I wish I had the power to give you what you deserve – to be tied up and flogged for telling this gross lie. You are a disgraceful fellow but you are discharged and I am very sorry that I am compelled to discharge you'.

***Gained:*** *George Evans, William Howse, (both of whom had quit or been sacked before the end of the year) Samuel Grosvenor, Joseph Owen, William Woodward, John Lewis, John Eate, George Ewins*
***Lost:*** *George Stanton, William Cadd, James Harden, Thomas Soles, George Davis*

The year began with a raft of sobering tales about the number of assaults on the police in the execution of their duty in the County force: 82 compared with 56 and 59 in the previous two years.  With fewer constables but a higher concentration of population, attacks on the officers of the City force was running at an even higher proportion.  Christmas had been particularly bad: in one incident an angry mob of around 40 had surrounded **PC John Richards** after he'd separated two men fighting in Sidbury and not only had they both turned on him – but one, Herbert Price had also incited the entire mob that had surrounded them to join in to resist his arrest.

In the first week in January an unnamed PC had also been called in to investigate reports of a mother, 'simple-minded' Fanny Marshall, neglecting her child. Though they took the child into care, the infant died the next day.

The first Watch Committee meeting of the year saw **Matthew Power** recommending the promotion of two sergeants to the rank of inspector at 30s a week, but true to form, the members declined to make a decision, probably on the grounds of the increased wage bill, holding over their verdict for months to come.  Beyond that, according to the chief, he had no other recommendations to make regarding the force's composition: as it turned out, 14 more constables were to be recruited this year to replace out-going officers. The situation was still far from good and dissatisfaction within the ranks was plainly evident.

As an indication of how bad it had become, two brothers **George** and **James Baldwin** had both joined the force in March this year – George on the 8th and James on the 22nd.  They both quit in very short order – George on March 22nd having lasted just 14 days and James rather more enduring, remaining in post until April 19th, less than a month.

Worse, the entire complement was now pressing for a wage increase and pestered the chief to apply to the Watch Committee for rises between 1s to 3s a week and improvements in their conditions – including seven days' holiday during the year. The sound of jaws dropping in the Guildhall could probably have been heard in the High Street, but the men in the ranks were adamant and made their case on the grounds that provisions were increasing in cost and that their opposite numbers in Manchester and Sheffield had received an increase similar to the one they now sought.  The application was considered sufficiently important to warrant a special committee meeting just to hear the arguments for and against when, the committee pledged, **Matthew Power**'s proposal regarding inspectors would also be considered.

They failed to reach any kind of decision on either count.

### Aunt (19) and niece (17) guilty of conspiracy to murder

That same month, the force was kept occupied with the tragic case of 17-year old Elizabeth Banks who had conspired with her aunt Leah, just two years older, to murder her new-born baby girl at the Wheelwrights Arms in Hylton Road a month earlier. Both were facing a 10-year jail sentence if found guilty...

After being tipped-off by the Wheelwrights' landlady, widow Martha Mabels who emerged something of a heroine in the eyes of the public, some assiduous sleuthing by **Detective William Underwood** *(pictured, right)* found evidence that the baby girl had been poisoned and that though the fatal dose had been bought in Worcester and administered by Elizabeth, the method and procedure had been devised and sent by the aunt who lived in Hartpury, Gloucester.

A damning piece of evidence was a letter from her that stated:

> *'...mind no-one else don't have a say as it is strong poison and the child will gradually waste, and in a few days it will be dead; and of course no doctor or anything of the kind will not be wanted but it will be took in the night and put in the Cemetery and no-one will have no suspicion. Burn the paper you get it in as soon as you get it home and put it in some plain white (sic) as there will be a label on it.  Tell them at the druggists you want it to take stains out of clothes'.*

(below) Detective (later Sgt) **William Underwood**, conducts investigation into a child's murder at the Wheelwrights' Arms, Hylton Street (later Road)

## THE CHARGE OF CONSPIRING TO MURDER.

The adjourned hearing of the charge against Leah and Elizabeth Banks, aunt and niece, both of Hartpury, Gloucestershire, of conspiring to murder the infant child of the latter, took place this morning. The Court was densely crowded, the extraordinary disclosures which the evidence revealed, exciting much interest. The prisoners were apprehended nearly a month ago, but the weak condition of Elizabeth Banks, caused by her recent confinement, rendered it undesirable that she should undergo the excitement and fatigue of an examination. She is a slender-built girl, not more than 17 years of age, and still appeared very weak. Her aunt, Leah Banks, was stated to be but 19 years of age. Both evinced considerable coolness and unconcern during the examination. Mr. Pitt, solicitor, Worcester, prosecuted, and Mr. Clutterbuck defended.

The evidence was damning and the two were committed to trial for conspiracy to murder after **Matthew Power** himself travelled to Hartpury to interview Leah Banks and bring her to Worcester. The jury took a lenient stance and she was sentenced to three calendar months' imprisonment and Elizabeth to four, both without hard labour.

Then in November a crushing blow that again speaks volumes about the wiliness and power-play (*no pun intended*) of the Council. Even though the men still had not won their pay rise, the chief thought he'd try again, this time on his own account.

In the light of his findings earlier in the year, **Matthew Power** had put in for an increase of £30 a year – taking his salary to £200. The rise had been approved unanimously by the Watch Committee – always a good sign – and was, he believed, largely a done-deal and in-line with the salaries of chief constables in other towns, as he demonstrated: Leamington with a population two-thirds that of Worcester £350 a year; Coventry £225; Dudley £180; Walsall £250 and Birmingham £700. In Liverpool and Manchester, salaries were even higher. The chief of the Metropolitan force was commanding something near £1,000 year.

How would the Council's money-men react? Yes, Mr Power is an excellent officer; yes, crime is down by a significant margin; yes, we appreciate the improvement in the force and its impact on cleaning–up the city; but is he worth £200 a year?

**Matthew Power** thought so and so did at least some of the city's decision-makers. Better than that, his timing was good and the police's reputation was riding high. As ex-mayor Richard Evans Barnett addressed the council:

*'...Mr Power is an excellent as well as an old officer and has served the city faithfully for 12 years. (We) all know what his services are worth and can appreciate the improvement in the police at the present time compared to what it was formerly and Mr Power might fairly be congratulated upon the diminution of crime that has taken place since the force came under his control. He is active, vigilant and painstaking. If we compare the state of crime in the city with what it was when Mr Power took office we will find that burglaries have become quite exceptional and conspicuous by their absence. It was a common thing at one time for jewellers shops to be broken open and valuable property stolen and it is a subject of sincere congratulation that none of these crimes are ever heard of (now)'.*

It's evident that the wage comparison examples **Matthew Power** had chosen had been selective, as is entirely to be expected, but then the city council showed its resolve and proved to be several jumps ahead of him. Councillor (*later Alderman*) James F. Airey – who suggested £10 rather than £30 as he '...objected to paying more than 20s even for the best sovereign ever coined' – had done some research of his own and produced details of comparable pay from four towns slightly larger in population than Worcester and therefore, he pointed out, a little in their favour: Oxford with a force of 38 men £165 a year with an increase of £5 a year until it reached £200; Exeter also 38 men £175 a year; Wakefield with 36 men, £175 a year and Carlisle with 34 men £174 18s.

In addition, he argued, the supplements of rent, coal, gas and other emoluments would take the Worcester superintendent's salary to £255 which, he said, in the present burdened state of the city they would not be justified in giving. Besides, when he came to call it a day he (**Matthew Power**) would eventually be entitled to a superannuated pension '...whereas the refuge of the traders of this city in case of decay would be the big house on the top of Tallow Hill' (*the House of Industry, aka Workhouse*).

It proved fatal. Put to the vote, the proposal was comprehensively lost 7 to 27 with three abstentions – one of which was his old adversary John Lloyd Bozward. An appeasing amendment proposing payment of the increase in a series of instalments as at Oxford was also defeated.

Worryingly, the next item on the agenda was consideration of yet another report into the desirability of amalgamating the county and city forces – and given the potential savings such a move offered, alongside the mood of the city's mean-minded money-men that had just voted overwhelmingly not to entertain the chief's latest demands, the entire future of Worcester City Police could have come to a grinding halt and the whole body swallowed-up, all in the space of one bleak and fateful afternoon. However, it appears unlikely that the debate on that particular issue amounted to much as the *Herald* gave the entire matter just four lines, concluding that the movement '...on being put to the vote, was lost'.

It's interesting to note that earlier in the year the councillors had voted for major improvements at the Guildhall; admittedly they'd turned down the idea of complete re-build projected at between £20,000-£30,000 but were still embarked on a course of renovations set to involve something approaching half that much. The final estimate was £11,543 4s – the lowest quote (*of nine*). The highest had been £14,973. On completion, the final bill came in at £14,217 7s.

There was no time for sulking; there was serious police work to be done...

The 1872 Beer Act had come into effect in the autumn of this year and its effects had been considered quite far-reaching. At the annual Licensing session at the end of August – headlined for the first time 'Brewster Sessions' in the *Herald* report of August 24th – **Matthew Power** reported to the Bench that there were '...183 houses licensed in this city for the sale of spirits, and 73 for the sale of beer or as refreshment houses with wine licences. Of the former, 23 have been proceeded against during the past year for offences

## Also this year: 1872

- a fire at the Guildhall Inn, facing the station-house, put out by unnamed policemen alerted by smoke in March

- Detective William Underwood follows boatman John Baylis to Stourport and arrests him in connection with a robbery at the Bear Inn in Tybridge Street. Fourteen day's hard labour

- police called in to shoot a horse injured in Cemetery (later Astwood) Road after taking fright and bolting at the new-fangled train passing nearby

- despite having been being kicked and punched, PC Smith was reported to the Watch Committee for assaulting gardener William Badgery in the Angel in St Johns

- PCs Henry Harding and Lewis Barnes commended after spotting and extinguishing a fire at the Swan with Two Necks (sic)

- PC (later sergeant) William James talks Louisa Dudley of Severn Street out of committing suicide by poison

- PC Price (more likely William Charles Preece, later sergeant, pic right) discovers a baby's body in a canalside hedge near Lowesmoor

- PC Francis Harvey apprehends two naval deserters in Shaw Street. Their ship HMS Thalia had sailed from Plymouth several days before

- already wanted for desertion and for having committed several robberies in Monmouthshire, a man named Summers is recognised and arrested after asking for a relief ticket at the station-house

- PC William James rescues two children, one with a broken thigh, thrown ten feet out of an upstairs window at the Crown in Friar Street by their drunken mother Ann Parsons

against the tenure of the licence, and 19 fined: of the latter, five houses have been proceeded against and three fined'.

The new Act specifically laid down that on Sundays, Christmas Day, and Good Friday all licensed premises were to remain closed until 12.30pm., between 2.30pm and 6pm., and after 10 o'clock at night. On all other days they had to close at 11pm sharp and remain so until 6am.

The Act also markedly increased penalties for erring landlords for offences including transgressions against under-measures ('...all sales not in cask or bottle or in quantities less than half-a-pint must be in measures marked according to the Imperial standard'); selling to persons under 16 years of age; permitting drunkenness, or violent, quarrelsome or riotous conduct on licensed premises; knowingly permitting prostitutes to resort or meeting in licensed premises and remaining longer than necessary for the purpose of obtaining reasonable refreshment; knowingly harbouring a constable or offering him to remain any part of the time appointed for his being on duty; supplying any liquor or refreshment to a constable on duty whether by gift or sale unless by authority of some superior officer of that constable; suffering gaming or unlawful games, or using the house in contravention of (*a different*) Act for the suppression of betting houses'.

The law referring to police powers in respect of licensed houses was also ramped-up – to the point that constables now had the power to enter every room at all times 'and take account of all intoxicating liquors stored therein'.

Loftily noted the *Herald*: '...the determination to close all licensed houses at eleven o'clock at night may have very good effects. It can hardly be said that such a restriction is any infringement on the rights of a British subject. As far as the licensed victuallers are concerned, we believe that the arrangement will be, if not a profit, certainly a comfort to them'.

*Gained:* George Evans, Jeremiah Pearson, George Baldwin, James Baldwin, Joseph Weaver, Mark H Durant, (none of which lasted-out the year) William Hitch, George Hill, John Spencer Morris, Edwin Davies, John Pugh, Matthew Hunt, Amos Nottingham, Thomas Hickman

*Lost*: Joseph Herbert Mann, Richard Smith, Thomas Goodwin, William Greenhill, William Woodward, John Lewis, John Eate

*William Preece, recruited November 28th 1862, went on to serve up to October 1890 with major distinction*

# 1873

It was not one of the best starts to a year. **William Charles Preece** *(pictured above)* originally No21 when he'd joined 28th November 1862 and a popular and active sergeant for the previous six years, had been demoted to the ranks for another misdemeanour. He'd always been prone to displaying a fiery side, but now he'd gone too far. In his first year he'd been severely reprimanded for being asleep on the College Green while on duty and then a few months later he'd been suspended and severely censured for assaulting **PC George Archer** – a contemporary, originally **No5** and similarly prone to the temptations of drink. The next two years had additionally seen him fined 2/6 for being asleep on his beat, suspended for two days without pay for insubordination and disobeying the lawful orders of the Superintendent, and fined 2/6 for being drunk on duty.

He'd first been sacked but in view of his popularity with the men and his 11-year record, **Matthew**

*Hard-man
John Pugh
No8 -
sent in to
tame the
hard-men
on the
St Johns
beat*

**Power** had had him demoted but allowed him to retain his job. When he promised to mend his ways, the Watch Committee agreed to re-instate him to sergeant but ordered him to forfeit a fortnight's pay.

The *Herald*'s report of the matter was sandwiched between the adoption of some new police rules (*unspecified*) and the putting out to tender for the supply of police overcoats and boots.

The courts were full of the usual d&ds, the women every inch as bad as the men, **PCs No8 John Pugh**, who was to go on to a 16-year career with the force, and **Edwin Adams** assigned to the ever-lawless St Johns beat, both emerging with some credit.

During the early months the City was also badly struck by disease – smallpox, measles, scarlet fever, diphtheria, whooping cough, diarhœa and other fevers had carried away 71 out of the 214 deaths recorded in the previous quarter alone. The city's population had soared to 32,410, that quarter showing 49 more births than deaths – which at 214, the highest in some years, was made up of 20 in public institutions, 11 had been enquired into by the coroner, and 5 were due to violent means. In the Worcester Division of the County, Foot and Mouth disease was also rife.

**Detective William Underwood** again had his work cut out when he had the thankless task of deciding whether or not a gun was discharged intentionally or accidentally after a woman named Harriet Fudger was shot in the hand at her home in Foundry Street. Alerted by staff at the Infirmary where her injuries were found to be serious, he questioned her when she implicated a man named Bache living in Lansdowne Street. When quizzed, Bache replied that he and some friends had found the gun 'in the meadow going up to the canal bridge' and that it had gone off accidentally while larking about. Some astute detective work unearthed the gun in the closet at the Pheasant in New-street, and Bache was later tried for wounding.

The next few months proved typical for minor internal breaches: in the same week, PC **No3 Herbert Osborne** who was no stranger to the chief's black book, and **PC13 William James** who was to go on to a 33-year career with the force, were both restored to good service pay after being fined for [*unspecified*] breaches, and **PC No18 Alfred Ewins** who'd only joined on January 1st this year was fined 5s for being in the Mount Pleasant Inn without any reasonable cause, and was permitted to resign, which he immediately did.

1873 seems only to have been a so-so year for the force, its highlight being the annual inspection by Colonel Cobbe at the Guildhall in September. The entire complement of 32, minus one of five sergeants (on leave) and an unfilled post, was put through '...various military evolutions which were executed in a very creditable manner, and apparently to the satisfaction of the inspector. The books, cells &c., were then minutely examined. Colonel Cobbe then expressed his entire satisfaction and intimated that he should report favourably'.

### Sergeant William Thorne dies tragically following gipsy 'curse'

The following week **Sergeant Frederick William Thorne** died, quite tragically: prior to joining in December 1867, he'd been deputy governor of the City Gaol, and he was going to prove a hard man to replace. *Rumours were rife that precisely two years to the day, he'd had a curse put on him by gipsies who'd tried to rook his wife after a fortune-telling scam at the Saracen's Head (see p 215).*

At least, **Matthew Power** was able to take some comfort in returns that showed that over the year there had been a notable decrease in all crimes – with the exception of d&d which had resulted in 215 charges with 174 fined or committed: the previous year had seen 208 with 151 fined or committed. 18 licensed victuallers and 5 beerhouse keepers had been proceeded against under the Licensing Act 1872 of which 13 of the former and 3 of the latter were fined. He put much of the increase in drunkenness down to an upturn in the national economy and more cash now in circulation.

The improved economic situation prompted the entire force to renew their call for a pay rise and an additional reward of good service pay after 10 years, presenting a petition requesting 2s a week across-the-board 'in consequence of the high price of every article for domestic use'.

Tellingly, it was signed by every member bar one: *the chief himself.* It's not revealed whether this was deliberate and a piqued reaction to his own treatment the previous year, or an oversight on account of only having, he said, received the petition the night before the Watch Committee meeting, but before making a decision, the Committee asked him to report back on the comparative rates of constables' pay for Hereford, Leamington, Bath, Oxford, Northampton, Shrewsbury and Worcester County.

It must have been a galling task – not least as he had problems of his own to contend with...

Scarcely surprisingly, dissatisfaction within the ranks had led to several resignations – many of them after a surprisingly short span of service: **PC Richard Preston** after 3 weeks, **Arthur Smith** and **William Heming** after less than three months – and recruitment remained a major problem. Morale had sunk so low that the force was now down to 26 – 6 short of the required number, although two were on the sick list.

Had Colonel Cobbe conducted his inspection at this time, the City would not have retained its certificate of efficiency and could well have found itself disbanded and swallowed up into the wider County force.

*Gained:* Arthur Smith, William Heming Richard Preston (all of which quit within the year) Alfred Ewins, Samel Pagett, John Stanton, Stephen Presdee

*Lost:* Frederick William Thorne, Joseph Owen, John Spencer Morris, Edwin Davies, Matthew Hunt, Thomas Hickman

## Also this year: 1873

■ PC Jabez Waldron called in to separate two grooms fighting in the High Street having decided to 'have it out' while waiting for their respective employers to emerge from a private function and seemingly half the town turned out to watch an epic scrap

■ police investigate strychnine poisoning and death of baby William Henry Griffiths

■ the next week, 6-year old Thomas Anthony Richardson dies after being hit by a brick thrown by classmate Tommy Ranford

■ Detective Bill Underwood investigates spate of window-smashing by boys using catapults. 20 windows had been smashed at the Beauchamp (later Great Western) Hotel on one night alone

■ police take charge of four children abandoned in a house in Dolday

■ PC (later Sergeant) Edwin Oakey ordered to ensure parents of 14-year old Robert King carry out promise to flog their son, otherwise discharged for stealing an orange from a Pump Street fruit stall

■ record number of robberies at the races third week in February. Matthew Power urges Bench to impose maximum sentences possible as a deterrent

■ PC William Hitch threatened with drowning in an assault by Jas Walker of the Arboretum

■ more counterfeit coins in circulation in the city, investigated by PC Amos Nottingham

■ PC Owens (probably Joseph Owen 14th July 1871 – 3rd October this year) jumps into the canal near the Arboretum to drag out bodies of 39-year old Mary Ann Wright and her 7-month old son William of St George's Lane South. Verdicts: deliberate murder and suicide

■ spate of late night anti-social street behaviour prompts Matthew Power to allow constables to patrol the streets in plain clothes during certain hours

■ police called in to break up riots staged by striking tailors in April

■ PC Thomas Hickman beaten-up by boatman William Blake, quits the next day. He'd lasted just four months

■ PC Jabez Waldron hears splash in the canal in Lowesmoor, later found to be pregnant widow Mary Ann Poole, aged 38 who died by drowning and had also attempted to cut her own throat

■ Det. Bill Underwood investigates murder of child wilfully suffocated by its mother, Sarah Rallings

■ police investigate spate of cruelty to horses, five cases in June alone

■ glover George Penney committed to a month's hard labour for abducting a dog owned by Edward Marston licensee of the Anchor, tying it up and setting a bitch on it so that it had to be destroyed

# 1874

In January, the men got their pay rise: better still, and unusually, it appears to have been given with a reasonably good heart although fear of losing the critical certificate through shortage of numbers and the need to attract more suitable recruits, and soon, added some real urgency to the decision.

To bring Worcester City into line with the forces identified – although, typically, only averaged-out – probationer and 3rd Class constables now earned 21s a week; 2nd Class 23s; 1st Class 24s; sergeants 27s and merit class 1s extra.

At least they had an ally in Alderman (*and later mayor, 1867-8*) William Webb who addressed the entire council with:

*'...a few remarks showing the justice of the grant. He then spoke of the efficiency of the police, and the decrease in crime which latter was to a great extent owing to the vigilance of the police who, if intelligent and discreet men, acted as great deterrents as well as detectors of crime. To get men of intelligence they must be paid, some inducement must be given to them to enter the force and to remain in it. It was with great pleasure he saw that the police pay was about to increase'* (*Herald*).

Twelve constables were to be appointed during the course of the year – still a fantastically high turn-round of more than one in three, indicating that despite some clearly measurable success, not all was sunshine-and-smiles at the station-house.

It was always on the cards, but then two weeks later it happened...

### Power assaulted by boatman, but shows compassionate side

**Matthew Power** came in for some of the same treatment his men got on the streets. During a disturbance largely involving horseplay that began with young boys running wild and hitting people on the back with sticks but then began to escalate and turn nasty until it threatened to become a full-scale riot, he'd tackled a 24-year old boatman named Thomas Strain with the intention of disarming him of the stick he'd been wielding.

*PC 14 George Hill, recruited January 1872 came in for praise this year, but was to die while still in service on September 1st 1889*

Strain had a different viewpoint and '...laid hold of him. He (*Mr. Power*) then endeavoured to take [the stick] from the prisoner when he got one of his legs between his (*Mr Power's*) and tossed him over on the broad of his back. Mr. [Police Magistrate, Charles] Sidebottom: "Did he know who you were?" Mr Power: "Oh yes, I was in uniform. I put it on at night so there might be no mistaking me".

The charge of assaulting the chief of police carried a six-month gaol sentence, but when he heard that his assailant had a wife and child and that, after all, he wasn't as badly injured as first thought, **Matthew Power** dropped the charge. Noted the *Herald*: '...the prisoner was discharged with a caution'.

The crusty old police chief – he was now 48 and had headed the force through thick and thin for the past 13 years – was clearly mellowing and showing a more considerate side, of which more, and of an even more revealing nature, was to emerge over coming years.

Over several cases, high-profile City barrister Louis Campbell had shown himself to be no great respecter of the police and their methods, so no doubt **Sergeant Tommy Croft** allowed himself a degree of satisfaction when he had cause to summons him for furious driving of a horse and phaeton in April. It was short-lived: despite three witnesses supporting the charge and the barrister himself even admitting that he 'passed rather sharply round a corner of Broad-street', favouritism, string-pulling and the old boy network kicked-in and the case was dismissed. To make matters even worse, the Bench even turned the affair against the police, warning them about loitering on the corner and that '...unless they stood out of the way of the traffic, they would have their toes run over'.

The next month (June) **PC George Hill** (*pictured left*) came in for glowing praise – although no cash reward – from the entire Council after having '...distinguished himself by his courage in apprehending a prisoner who made a determined resistance'.

Despite the previous year's shock increase, drunkenness showed yet another hike this year – not by a significant margin, but certainly enough to warrant a call from the Licensing Committee for respective members to personally inspect every single one of the city's 232 public and beer-houses. The force's success in clamping down on drinking during illegal hours had notably curtailed the activities, not to mention the income, of many who thought they could get away with flouting the law, and worst in this respect were new licensees, particularly if they'd come to the city from areas where the police had not proved so vigilant, or so effective, in upholding the regulations in respect of permitted hours (*or alternatively, not willing to accept a small bribe by way of kind*).

Little did they know that in Worcester, every PC was ordered to keep a special watch on new licensees in their first weeks and to clamp down swift and hard, and it had proved a remarkably effective ploy, few that had been caught in this way re-offending. By way of countering the police's unrelenting attention, many publicans had instigated a system of 'scouts' or lookouts to provide an early-warning alarm at first sign of an approaching bobby – a move sharply criticised by **Matthew Power** who went on to underline that anyone actively involved in defeating the ends of justice was just as culpable in the eyes of the law as those committing it.

Drunkenness aside, crime generally was still on a mostly downwards trend – a remarkable tribute to the individual officers given the shortages in the ranks – although with more street crimes and misdemeanours involving young people, there was a growing call to re-introduce whipping as an alternative to prison, not least on the grounds of deterrence.

**Matthew Power**'s annual report relayed the good news that '...in no period of equal duration covered by the records of this office has crime been so low in this city'. Good news then – only 826 people had been summarily dealt with in the Magistrates court: even so, it was still down 20% on the same period ten years earlier, while the population had grown by a similar percentage. In the previous quarter, the police had dealt with eight fires and had found 169 private and commercial premises insecure at night. And then the news the Council pay-masters wanted to hear – that overall costs of running the police force was nearly £400 less than it had been the previous year.

In September **PC George Wall** was involved in nasty case of assault when a cat-fight had resulted in Sarah Morris having her eye taken out with the point of an umbrella by Mary Edgington. The fight in St Nicholas Street opposite the Pack Horse (*now Courtyard*) had been over a man Mary Edgington had formerly lived with, and Sarah Morris claimed that her love-rival first hit her over the head with her umbrella and then jabbed it in her eye. The following morning, both took out warrants for the arrest of the other – but when the warrant was executed, Mary Edgington was found naked in bed as she'd pawned her clothes to cover the cost of taking out the warrant.

The PC found himself severely censured by the chief and the Bench for failing to intervene in the free-for-all: '...having witnessed the fight and saw one of the girls on the ground but saw no blows struck. They were both in drink, but not drunk. The Bench thought that the constable ought to have taken both girls to the station-house'.

Later that same month, the city had been thrown into darkness following a gas explosion that destroyed three houses in Rainbow Hill. Records the *Herald*: '...the explosion shook many of the houses in the neighbourhood as though an earthquake had taken place'.

About this time, and for reasons unknown, the newspapers from here on often tended to substitute individual officers' names with a generic description such as '*the police*' or '*a constable*' in their reports: a possible inference – although only a calculated guess – being because some constables had been subjected to threats of reprisal for bringing successful cases to the courts.

Such an outcome was already evident following a tragic incident that occurred in the same area at the same time as the gas explosion; it involved an unnamed constable who'd heroically risked his own life in an attempt to save an 11-year old lad, George Norman, who'd been catching flies and had slipped into the canal near the bridge and drowned. Later admitting to his fear of the police, his younger brother who'd been with him, had run all the way home to Chestnut Street to alert his mother instead of calling for an officer, and when they both arrived back at the spot, the constable had already recovered the boy's body. Remarked the *Herald*: '...the body having been got out of the water, on her arrival life was extinct'.

No doubt the city would have wanted to know the hero constable's name.

In the dock the next day, two 5-year olds, James Franklin and Ellen Blake, were '...charged with annoying Mr Foulkes by knocking at his door. The children were discharged with a caution to their parents'.

Being a Worcester city copper was clearly a light-and-dark experience. 667 people had died in Worcester this year – including 6 between the ages of 90 and 100: 70 had been still-born children.

### Criticism from the law clerks

Harsh criticism had also come from an unexpected quarter – the law clerks. At their annual dinner, generally a far more lively session than those held by their older, more experienced and evidently stuffier employers, the clerks traditionally discussed the burning legal and social issues of the day free of the influence of their bosses who, as a matter of respect, allowed them to discuss any topic and any personality without fear of repercussion. Inevitably this year, the publicans' relationship with the police come up in the discussion, the upshot being that in their view, the licensed victuallers were considered to be '...under the power of the ordinary police constables whose habits and station and intelligence were not suited to the uncontrolled exercise of many of the functions that devolved upon them by the existing law'.

So had claimed James Dracas from Bentley's practice. It was not a kind reflection on the force that he considered too heavy-handed and mentally ill-equipped for keeping order on the streets – a view that was shared by many of his fellow citizens even though it signally overlooked the force's clear successes in cleaning up a wayward Worcester, and that their success often resulted in generating lucrative business for the lawyers. As per usual, the situation continued to come across as Worcester City Police v the rest of the world. Some years on, James Dracas was appointed trustee when printer and publisher Joseph Littlebury was proclaimed bankrupt with debts of £1,319 11s 3d. The police also declined a windfall opportunity to get their own back – *but more of that later...*

*Gained:* Edwin Adams, Charles Carloss, Joseph Bartlett, Thomas Jones, (none of whom were to see-out the year), Joseph Mason, Francis Eli Brotherton, George Spilsbury, Arthur Edwin Sommers, William Tallis, George Clements, Frederick Birt, James Glass

*Lost:* William Hitch, John Stanton, Stephen Presdee

## Also this year: 1874

■ PC Lewis Barnes proves a busy copper in this his final full year with the force. On consecutive days in May he summons hawker John Morgan for trading without a licence, Fred Walters of the Alma in Diglis for refusing to admit him when requested, and Thomas Ogilbie for obstruction at a fire in the Arboretum

■ Matthew Power agrees to pay 13s compensation to publican Josiah Rice of the Masons Arms in Carden street after furniture and fittings had been shattered in an almighty scrap when Sgt William Preece and PC Henry Willis had been sent in to apprehend 'a most violent ruffian' named Bullbrook

■ PC Samuel Grosvenor in his second year (of thirty, he was to go on to become Inspector) is seriously assaulted by labourer James Dunford in St Johns

■ Matthew Power is one of 142 chief constables to put his name to a motion supporting recent moves to limit pub opening hours to 6am – 11pm (from 11.30pm). There was no drinking-up time

■ counterfeit shillings and half-crowns widely circulating in the city cause serious issues with traders in town

■ George John Hopper 17, drowns in the river

■ police remove dozens of barrels of gunpowder found in the cellar of a house in St George's Square

■ new recruit PC Arthur Edwin Sommers confiscates obscene postcards sold at the races by unlicensed hawker Maurice Freedman who's gaoled for seven days

January 1st saw the start of another petulant war of words between **Matthew Power** and the *Herald*. It had begun with little more than a filler during Christmas week, although the *Herald* had laid it on a bit thick, outlining '...the unvarying feeling of terror in passing along the streets' that, they said, were more dangerous to pass along than those in London...

There had been heavy snow and the *Herald* had come out all guns blazing about the danger of boys making slides in the ice. It was all a case of much ado about nothing really – until William Holl remarked on the blind eye he claimed the police had allegedly turned to the issue. It was like lighting the blue touch-paper, and **Matthew Power**'s Irish paddy once more kicked-in. In a hot-tempered letter dated December 28th but appearing in the first edition of this year – more than 1,000 words long, reprinted in full by the *Herald* and then meticulously picked apart, paragraph by paragraph, by the nit-picking editor – it was a nasty spat that frankly did neither any favours. It was, wrote **Matthew Power:**

> *'one of the most uncalled-for, unfair and disingenuous attacks (on the police) that I have seen... the police of this city have 28 miles of streets and lanes to patrol. During the frost there has been but five men to patrol them in the day-time. To my mind, it seems that these men, instead of being subjected to an attack such as you have made upon them, are deserving of the consideration and sympathy of every humane person. The number at present ill*

*More from the Approbation Marks book entry for Sgt. John Doughty who retired this year after 30 years (see next page) [WCiCo/WAAS]*

*attests to the intensity of the cold they have of late experienced. All I can say at present is that I now challenge you to prove the City Police Officers have allowed boys to slide without expostulation... as you may not know the names or numbers of the men you accuse, I shall parade the whole body for you on any day you name for the purpose of identification'.*

With some insincerity, although in line with the quaint epistle-penning conventions of the time, he signed it 'I am, Sir, Your obedient servant, M. Power'.

The *Herald* declined Matthew Power's offer of a personal identity parade and responded with a limp and unapologetic editorial of equal length – but then the following week a third party chipped-in, The *Chronicle* backing the police against the big bully elder-statesman *Herald*: it was followed by another long letter from a furious police chief which a clearly-rattled William Holl declined to print, dismissing it as nonsense and one italicised word – 'N'importe' (*of no consequence*).

To read the letters and subsequent three-sided press reports is like watching three 5-year olds squabbling in a school playground.

On February 26th, **Lewis Barnes**, a clearly troubled bobby with a mixed 7-year record, decided he'd had enough of the force and quit – but it was not to be his last association with the police.

Manpower – and lack of it in sufficient numbers – had been dogging the city force for too long; nor was the County Constabulary immune from its effects... A few weeks after the sliding-in-the-streets issue had calmed down, they too were on yet another recruitment drive. The ad evidently failed to meet its target and was repeated two months later.

March saw the retirement of a real old stager and a great favourite after more than thirty years – **Sergeant John Doughty** who'd joined Worcester City Police on 14th February 1845 and had served under **John Phillips, Tommy Chipp** and for all of **Matthew Power's** years to date. Not that his service record was entirely exemplary: in 1848 (June 7th) he'd been found the worse for liquor while on duty and severely reprimanded for losing his lamp, rattle and staff. Less than two years later, he was

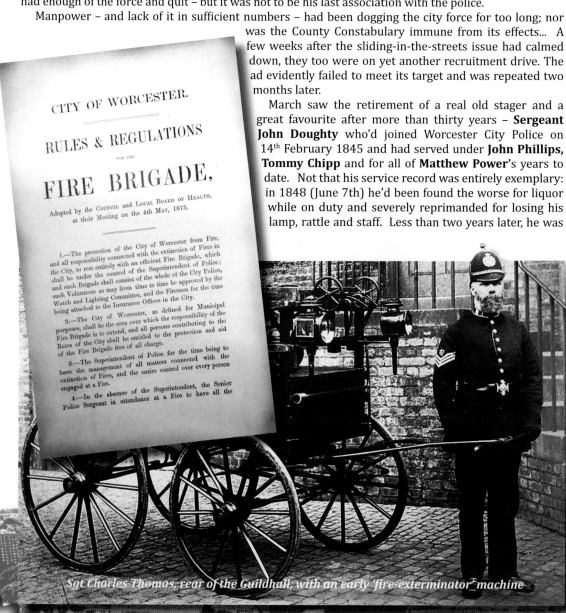

CITY OF WORCESTER.

RULES & REGULATIONS

FOR THE

FIRE BRIGADE,

Adopted by the COUNCIL and LOCAL BOARD OF HEALTH, at their Meeting on the 4th MAY, 1875.

1.—The protection of the City of Worcester from Fire, and all responsibility connected with the extinction of Fires in the City, to rest entirely with an efficient Fire Brigade, which shall be under the control of the Superintendent of Police, and such Brigade shall consist of the whole of the City Police, such Volunteers as may from time to time be approved by the Watch and Lighting Committee, and the Firemen for the time being attached to the Insurance Offices in the City.

2.—The City of Worcester, as defined for Municipal purposes, shall be the area over which the responsibility of the Fire Brigade is to extend, and all persons contributing to the Rates of the City shall be entitled to the protection and aid of the Fire Brigade free of all charge.

3.—The Superintendent of Police for the time being to have the management of all matters connected with the extinction of Fires, and the entire control over every person engaged at a Fire.

4.—In the absence of the Superintendent, the Senior Police Sergeant in attendance at a Fire to have all the

*Sgt Charles Thomas, rear of the Guildhall, with an early 'fire-exterminator' machine*

again found drunk while on duty and severely reprimanded for not coming to morning muster.

He'd been appointed Supernumerary Sergeant in March 1853 and had maintained a clean sheet up to 1859 when within the space of eight months he was censured for 'supineness and indifference in not taking any effective steps in the detection of the burglars who had committed a robbery at Ald Price's warehouse and not immediately informing the Superintendent and Detectives', and later fined £1 and ordered to be more careful in future for assaulting **Detective William Richardson** while on duty and using abusive language.

Despite all that, he clung on to be appointed Station Sergeant on July 12th 1861 and at the time of his retirement on 26th March this year, his pay was £1 8s 9d a week. He was granted a pension of two-thirds, 19s 6d a week, and **Matthew Power** hosted a special dinner in his honour at the Golden Lion in High Street (*now Costa Coffee*) attended by many of his former colleagues.

He was presented with a silver-mounted cane in recognition of his 30 years' service.

### First seeds of Worcester Fire Brigade

1875 was a bad year for fires and the work of a serial arsonist was evident. Exhaustive attempts to trace the elusive 'incendiarist' had drawn a blank and the Norwich Union Insurance Company operating out of its branch office at 50, Foregate Street had offered to pay for a full-time detective from the Metropolitan force to come to Worcester to clear-up the situation that had resulted in 'the extraordinary prevalence of fires during the last few months [*which had*] given rise to much conjecture and anxiety and the inability of the local authorities to trace these occurrences to their origin does but serve to heighten the fears of the inhabitants'.

While the London force refused to allow an officer to come to Worcester with the curious phrase 'she must do it alone', the local Norwich Union manager Alfred P. Watkins had placed his full faith in **Matthew Power** to take whatever steps he might consider necessary to put an end to the continuing spate of fires, and that his company would pick up its share, and more, of the bill.

The following week (*March 9th*) a fire broke out in the Market Hall. Although it was swiftly dealt with, it resulted in considerable damage to the roof – but at least this time there was a positive outcome: acceleration in the formation of the city of Worcester Fire Brigade under the full control of the superintendent of the city police whose duties had all along included those of fire chief but had had to be relegated to a secondary role in preference to day-today policing.

At a city council meeting on March 18th this year '...the subject of a fire brigade and its formation having been fully discussed, it was resolved unanimously that the protection of the City of Worcester from fire, and the extinguishment of fires when they occur will be most advantageously intrusted (sic) to an efficient brigade... such brigade consisting of the whole of the police and the staff of firemen for the time being attached to the insurance offices in the city'.

**Matthew Power** had long held a special passion for fire prevention and rescue and his patented fire escape system had already attracted the notice of several authorities and insurance companies, successive mayors giving their approval for 'live' demonstrations at the Guildhall as required.

Another issue close to the police chief's heart was animal cruelty and when the Worcester Society for the Prevention of Cruelty to Animals (*later, RSPCA*), set up this year and approached him to act as honorary secretary, he willingly took on stewardship of this 'useful and benevolent association' as the *Herald* termed it. Before long, pressure of police work would mean that he would be forced to relinquish that role, but from the start, he proved an active campaigner. One issue he proved passionate about was the bleeding of calves: was it cruel or humane?

**Matthew Power** was in no doubts which, and lashed-out strongly at the city's butchers over what might today be termed 'botch jobs': '...if the bleeding is done properly there could be no cruelty, and no pretence for saying there is [*but, he continued*]... the necks of the calves are sometimes hacked in a revolting manner, and their pain prolonged for several days'. Even so, he added that while his would ever be a tough stance against cruelty to all animals, stopping the practice altogether would amount to an interference with a proper and legitimate trade.

May saw another report of action by a PC who'd been appointed twelve months earlier, but was to go on to achieve fame and not a little notoriety with, and for, Worcester City Police. This was **Arthur Edwin Sommers** (*the Herald reports him as 'Summers', a simple mistake to make*) who'd charged Frederick Hughes, landlord of the Barley Mow in London Road with having his house open during prohibited hours and allowing drunkenness. He reported the landlord as having turned very abusive when approached.

If Fred Hughes had known what was to come, he might have been even more abusive.

## The drink: still the Worcester disease

Drunkenness in Worcester remained a particular thorn in the side of the city in general and the police in particular – and it was still on the up: 150,382 cases had been brought before magistrates in England and Wales alone the previous year and County-wide, out of a population of 270,666, 966 had been proceeded against for drunkenness of which 884 were convicted. In the city, 207 people had been proceeded against and 136 were convicted. There were 982 public houses in Worcestershire, 622 beer and cider houses, and 6 refreshment houses with wine licences; in Worcester city 180 public houses, 69 beer and cider houses and 13 refreshment houses with wine licences.

Pubs and the city force were an enduring nightmare for the chief – a situation that was never to change for as long as Worcester City maintained its own force. Early in July, this year, Charles Page, landlord of the Boat in Lowesmoor (*now the site of Co-operative Funeral Services*), called in **PC James Glass** who'd only been with the force since October the previous year, to help him search the room of lodger here who couldn't pay his bill and was refusing to quit. At 12.30am **Sergeant William Underwood** was out patrolling Lowesmoor and visiting his beat bobbies when he saw Glass come out and the PC related the tale of the lodger and the fight that had ensued in ejecting him – then asking him if it would be alright if he went back into the Boat for a drink the landlord had promised him, a request emphatically denied by the by-the-book sergeant. Despite that, Glass went in anyway when he thought he wasn't being watched – though sadly for him he was: he re-emerged into the street an hour later and was promptly suspended from duty. There were no winners in this unfortunate incident that led to two casualties: **James Glass** was later sacked (*he left on 22nd October 1875 after just 333 days' service*) and Charles Page was fined £2 and costs and was lucky not to have had his licence endorsed for harbouring a police officer who should have been on duty.

A near mirror-image of the same offence also occurred at the same location just eighteen months later (*see p232*).

Early July had also seen the *Herald* report the death of an 8-year old boy named John Bamford Brown who'd been bitten in the face by a bull terrier in the garden of a house at Canalside, Merriman's Hill bridge. The dog was rabid, the coroner returned a verdict of death from

### Also this year: 1875

■ *police investigate a worrying trend of children placing large stones on railway lines near the city*

■ *Matthew Power and PC James Glass (not long afterwards to quit after just a year) each sued for £5 for false imprisonment by Kempsey farmer Stapeley White who'd been arrested on suspicion of being an arsonist. Dismissed.*

■ *police investigate death of 14-year old errand boy, Henry Baker, found hanging from a rope at the rear of Dart's saddlery at 70 Broad Street. Suspicion fell on shop owner Thomas Dart who lived there alone and was known to be a bit strange. Dismissed on lack of evidence*

■ *PCs Edwin Oakey and Amos Nottingham investigate suspected murder after heavily blood-stained womens' clothes found in St Johns, despite intensive search and Sling Pool being dragged, no body is found*

■ *Det William Phillips investigates theft of a pony and trap from outside Shrub Hill Station. Traced to two 14-year old boys later sentenced to prison for a month then to reformatory for five years*

■ *police breathe a sigh of relief as permission is granted for a drinks licence for the new Norton Military Depot where 250 soldiers are to be based*

■ *more fires considered the work of the arsonist in the autumn, demanding use of the police fire truck housed at the station-house*

■ *more railway-related accidental and suicide deaths take up increasing amount of police time*

■ *Arthur Edwin Sommers (left) rises to prominence this year. He was later to be Chief Superintendent and became no stranger to controversy*

hydrophobia, and mad dog disease was again rife in the city, with the police empowered to shoot any dog unmuzzled and on the streets.

This year's Brewster Sessions was not so much dominated by the Superintendent's report so much as an outburst by the new mayor John Longmore's reaction to it. In addition, he very publicly condoned what many others saw as **Matthew Power**'s underhand methods in passing off a rookie cop – and thus unknown to the city's publicans and general army of layabouts and ne'ers-do-well – as a navvy, and sending him on a tour of suspect pubs to keep undercover surveillance on illicit activities.

Despite claiming that in his opinion everything possible should be done to check the drunken habits of the city's population, he wondered if the police chief hadn't gone too far this time. In the police's favour, the Bench had come to realise that people brought before them charged with other crimes were almost exclusively there because they'd been drinking if not already drunk '...and this impressed itself so strongly on his mind, from a lengthened experience, that he considered that no legitimate means ought to be passed which would tend to check the facilities for drunkenness'.

The (*police*) report showed that there were houses in the trade that required very strict looking after – indeed they had seen the conduct of the Chief Constable aninadverted (sic) upon in one of the public prints [newspapers] because he employed a person as a spy. There was no doubt the person was employed as a spy, but the question was whether the Chief Constable was justified under the peculiar circumstances in doing as he did. By this means the Chief Constable detected a publican who could not have been detected otherwise... and a conviction obtained'.

The following month, **Sergeant (*and Detective*) William Underwood** yet again came in for some well deserved praise for tracking down 24-year old good-time girl Elizabeth Wall who'd met wealthy farmer John Owen in the Peacock in the Trinity, wheedled her way to getting him to stand her a few drinks and then to offer her a lift home – she'd said in St Johns, although she lived in Quay Street – and took him under the westernmost arch of the river bridge for purposes unspecified from where she calmly walked off with his purse containing £138 in cheques and coins (about £60,000 today). Sentence? Eighteen months' hard with an order to be kept under police supervision for five years on release.

Noted the *Herald*: '...the Chairman severely admonished Owen who is a white-haired married man, for his disreputable conduct in keeping the company of such a woman as the prisoner'.

**Gained:** *James Willis, Harvey Ford, Alfred Warren, John Ruff, George Richardson, Charles Stallard, Joseph Winwood (none of whom saw-out the year), Sidnam Cole, James Cole, Arthur Blomely, George Lucas, William Taylor, George Hyett, Thomas Booth, Frederick Insell, John Meakins*

**Lost:** *Francis Harvey, Henry Willis, Lewis Barnes, George Wall, George Clments, Frederick Birt, James Glass*

The year began on a high note for the police and, but for one recurring issue that had sharply divided opinion, largely remained there – for the first time in years, if ever.

At the very first full Council meeting the new Mayor, Alderman Francis Woodward

> '...heartily wished them (the assembled councillors) a very happy and prosperous new year and thought it would not be out of place if he took a retrospective view of the proceedings of the council during the past year... another source of gratification was that they had been comparatively free from fires and that they had the advantage of an apparatus for the extinsion (sic) of fires which had been presented by one of the citizens. The efficiency of the police force was a matter of considerable congratulation, and they all knew how well under the superintendence of the Head Constable the force had been conducted'.

Worcester City Police would, he said, bear comparison with any force in the United Kingdom.

In February, an unusual sight – an advertisement for 'a few strong, active, intelligent men for the Worcester City Police. Applications, stating age, height and occupation, to be addressed to the Chief

Officer in the handwriting of Applicants'. Sandwiched between ads for a Stale Dresser, shepherd, coachman and house servants of either gender, it looked, and sounded as though desperation was setting in.

The following week, the Watch Committee approved tenders for shoes (13s 6d a pair, Mr Crump Pump-street); suit of clothes (£3 15s, Mr Butler High-street); helmets, (Mr Butler); and gloves, (Mr Parsons Broad-street).

In May, the whole police spy issue again erupted – but this time the force emerged from it looking cheap, sneaky and underhand.

The police's new undercover agent was 'Mrs Smith' – although who she was, where she was from (*never revealed for fear of reprisal, but Cherry Orchard was reputed to be her location*) and how she was recruited isn't known, but it was her allotted role to collect empty unmarked bottles from the station house and do a tour of the pubs out of proscribed hours on a Sunday, asking for a pint of beer in each and to return the now-filled bottles to the chief. For this she was paid 2s a day, and Elizabeth Cahill of the Boar's Head (*formerly Severn Galley*) in Newport Street was just one of several netted on the same day: also duped that day were Thomas Smith of the Elephant and Castle, Thomas Salmon of the Four Ways Carden Street, Thomas Payne of the Chequers King Street, and Thomas Lucy of the Porcelain Inn.

When the similarity in their cases emerged, with 'Mrs Smith' proving to be the chief witness as one case followed the other, defending LVA brief Mr Pitt halted the proceedings and...

> '...in addressing the Court, strongly denounced what he called the spy system of detecting wrong-doers adopted by Mr Power, and said it was a disgrace to the city, and tended to have a very pernicious and demoralizing (sic) effect. He (Mr Pitt) did not wish to defend the practice carried on by some persons of contravening the law by selling drink during prohibited hours because that in itself was demoralizing, but he contended that the spy system was equally as bad, as that which had been carried on under the instigation of Mr Power induced people to commit crime'

In his defence, **Matthew Power** stood his ground and stated his case – to the effect that this was the only way that he could devise to get hold of the offenders and that after all, he was only countering like with like as a system of posting 'touts' on nearby street corners '...was regularly practised by a certain class of publicans which prevented the police from ever getting near them' (*Herald*).

The court proceedings thus far had taken three hours and when the Bench retired to consider their verdicts, they sided with the police – although they admitted to some distaste for the underhanded methods outlined. However, as they stated, they were '...determined to do their duty and that was to carry out the law'.

All, with the exception of Thomas Payne, were found guilty – Elizabeth Cahill fined the inordinate amount of £10 and costs and ordered to surrender her licence at once.

As for 'Mrs Smith', **Matthew Power** found himself having to ask the Bench for protection for his 'grass' following threats to molest her '...and the Mayor (*Francis Woodward*) said it was a most serious offence for any person to threaten any witness for giving evidence, and if anyone was brought there for assaulting Mrs Smith and the case was proved, he would be punished in the severest manner'.

The issue of using officers masquerading as bona fide travellers in order to catch errant landlords was again to re-surface in 1882, the continuing episodes being viewed as sneaky and underhand and the biggest – to some, the *only* – blemish on Matthew Power's years as Chief.

WANTED, a pick, helve, and hammer STALE DRESSER.—Apply, J. A. Knight, Worcester Wharf, Birmingham.

WANTED, a few strong, active, intelligent MEN for the WORCESTER CITY POLICE. Applications, stating age, height, and occupation, to be addressed to the CHIEF OFFICER, in the handwriting of Applicants.

WANTED, a Man as SHEPHERD, and to make himself generally useful on the Farm. Cottage and Garden provided, and liberal wages given.—Apply to Mrs. J. Cooper, Lowesmoor Wharf, Worcester.

AS COACHMAN, where one or more are kept, to drive a pair. Married, age 28.—Address, G., Post-office, Kington, Herefordshire.

HOME FOR SERVANTS.—MALE and FEMALE SERVANTS may daily hear of SITUATIONS on application to the Lady Principal, College Precincts, Worcester. One Shilling Fee, and a stamped envelope for reply. Ladies' Maids, Kitchen Maids, and Under House-Maids awaiting service.

## Second murder attempt in 10 years at at the Swan with Two Necks (Nicks)

A few weeks later, it was again **Sergeant William Underwood** that grabbed the media spotlight, as did **PC** *(also later promoted to Sergeant)* **Charles Thomas** following a nasty assault in which Thomas Price, landlord of the Swan with Two Nicks *(still then 'Necks')* was stabbed five times with an awl. Though he'd already paid for his bed for the night, shoemaker Samuel Collett had sat up drinking with other guests, his voice getting louder and louder and his language more and more colourful. When asked to moderate his coarseness and several times refused, Thomas Price had tried to give him his money back and put him out of the house, sparking-off the fight in which Collett had threatened to kill the landlord:

> *'...Police Sergeant Underwood and PC Thomas who took the prisoner into custody, said the prisoner was very violent and assaulted them. They ultimately had to carry him to the police station. The prisoner was remanded' (Herald).*

This year, the police were again out in force for the races; previous years had been marked with full court-rooms and overflowing prison cells, and this time they were prepared, ready and waiting. Even the mayor had made provision for a long week of hefty daily sentencing, And...? Sum total of race-related court action that week was '...a lone, single female Bacchante *(drunk)* who had exceeded the bounds of discretion in her convivialities'.

No doubt the word had spread about the new efficiency being displayed by Worcester City Police and the reception would-be miscreants could expect. And rightly so, too...

The following week, the County force was thrown into turmoil with the sudden and entirely unexpected death of John Phillips, 51-year old Deputy Chief Constable of Worcestershire Police for the past five years, Superintendent for the Worcester Division and would-be chief of the City force. He'd allowed some of his men – and had even joined in himself – to tackle a blaze at Shrub Hill Station and had come away with breathing difficulties from which he never recovered. He was succeeded by Supt Checketts of Upton-on-Severn.

On one Saturday night in September, three PCs were violently assaulted: **Thomas Quinney** who was to quit within months, **John Glover** who barely lasted three months quitting in December, and ever-reliable **Herbert Osborne** who was to clock up twenty years with the force (7th August 1863 – 31st August 1883).

The following month, **PC William Smith** was beaten up by soldiers twice within a fortnight.

Meanwhile, the city's population was still growing; in the three months to the beginning of the year there had been 238 births and 187 deaths.

In all it had been a good year for the force. On September 29th., Colonel Cobbe had undertaken his annual inspection and concluded that despite an otherwise shocking 15 resignations, almost half the force – all of which had been replaced: '...the office and cells were in very good order and the force had been efficiently maintained'. 27 people had been apprehended for indictable offences (*one down on the previous year*), 986 were proceeded against in the Police and Magistrates Court (*compared to 1062 the previous year*) with 669 convicted (*705 the previous year*). The convictions included 182 cases of drunkenness and d&d (*177 the year before*) and 29 assaults on the police, an increase of one over the previous year. There were 179 public houses of which 18 had been proceeded against and 13 convicted, and 58 beerhouses (*two proceeded against and one convicted*). Vagrancy had also considerably increased.

**Gained:** *Arthur Taplin, John Dove, Daniel Lake, Charles Miles, Matthew Henry Parsons, John Crockford, John Glover, James Bliss (none of which out-lasted the year) Frederick Tarrant, Thomas Vaughan, Albert Henry Wargent, William Smith, Thomas Harris, Edward Wall, Thomas Quinney, George Wargent, George Roberts, Frederick Goodwin, James Watson (or Walton), George Farley*

**Lost:** *George Ewins, Joseph Mason, William Tallis, James Cole, George Lucas, William Taylor, George Hyett, John Meakins*

## Also this year:

■ *William Stable governor of the County Gaol resigns and his place taken by Captain Tinklar, RN*

■ *Colonel Carmichael's salary upped from £500 a year to £600 – almost three times that of Matthew Power*

■ *the very last Assizes the week before Christmas is remarkable in not having a single prisoner from Worcester up for sentence, although whether this was because the City police had been too effective in crime prevention or not effective enough in detection is unclear*

At the start of the year – which for the first ten months at least, was to prove generally steady with few notable upsets or earth-shattering set-backs, just solid, honest-to-goodness coppering – the force numbered 33: Superintendent, five sergeants and 27 constables that also included a detective.

For the first time in months, there were no unfilled vacancies, the force was at full strength, and its members appear to have been comparatively well disciplined and for the most part, tolerably well behaved.

January saw the new Mayor, Moses Jones, fork-out for the annual Mayor's Dinner for the force, now held at the Golden Lion opposite the Guildhall. 60 guests attended '...and the occasion passed very enjoyably'.

The early months also saw ratification of the formal introduction of the Fire Brigade, and direction to **Matthew Power** to include all the firemen employed by the various fire insurance companies in the formal police drills he staged four times a year and for which they would be allowed 3s 6d instead of 2s up to then. As it turned out, the timing could scarcely have been better for all concerned, as Worcester's notorious arsonist was still unidentified and at large, while the number of fires was increasing at an alarming rate. The year was to see a major city landmark go up in flames.

Then, as it was to continue throughout its entire 134-year life, the old Worcester City Police force malady cropped up again: the booze. Early on in the year, the Boat in Lowesmoor again made the headlines, new licensee Thomas Harris facing a very similar charge to his predecessor eighteen months earlier – this time of attempting to bribe a police constable, **PC William Smith** whose own police career was only to last three years (16$^{th}$ June 1876 – 3$^{rd}$ November 1879). Halting builder Thomas Insull after he'd spotted him coming out of here at midnight the PC had asked his name which Insull refused to give, so the bobby instantly took him back inside and asked the landlord to tell him. Reports the *Worcestershire Advertiser*: '...defendant did not comply but said to the officer "Come and have a glass of something to drink and say no more about it".

'In defence it was stated that Mr Harris did give the man's name and then simply by way of courtesy, asked Smith to have something to drink, but not as a bribe. The case was dismissed'. Thomas Insull was handed the usual fine for being on licensed premises during prohibited hours: 5s with 9s 6d costs – adding that he'd refused to give his name owing to the constable's 'bumptious manner' in asking it.

**Matthew Power** was in a tight spot. He was being driven to clamp down even harder on the nefarious and illicit activities of the pubs and beerhouses that the justices all viewed as being the point from which all things illegal and anti-social stemmed. Conversely and with few of exceptions, his men – in common with most of the entire male population of the Faithful City (**Civitas in Beero et Pubbi Fidelis** *– the city faithful to its beer and its pubs*) enjoyed a drink and were susceptible to the odd kindness extended by the landlords, not to mention payment in kind.

A couple of incidents had cropped up involving (*unnamed*) constables being found in (*unnamed*) pubs when they should have been out exercising their lawful duty – and then the incidents began to mount, this last one proving the final straw. There had been just too many for the chief to ignore and now, if there was a worm eating away at the core, it was going to have to be cut out, regardless of the scars it left.

As a consequence, he took the drastic step of firing-off a warning letter to every one of the city's 237 publicans and beersellers in April '...requesting them, in consequence of several complaints that had been made to him, not to allow any member of the police force to have any drink on credit whatever, or to treat them. Mr Power's object in doing this was to prevent the police from being fettered and rendered less vigilant than they should be' (*Worcestershire Advertiser*).

Sadly for him, the letter had an entirely different effect to the one he'd hoped-for – prompting not a 'message understood' reply and a promise to heed the chief's warning, but instead resulting in a damning litany of even more constables' demands including running-up a pub tab, requests for hush-money and even requests for loans from some of the better-heeled landlords. **Matthew Power** was livid. Instantly, eight of his officers were dragged into his office and given a major dressing-down: one was immediately sacked. It was an episode akin to a bad dream and one he wished had never happened.

Meanwhile, it was not so much police incidents that were taking up increasing amounts of his time, as fire-fighting....

The same week as the sacking, **PC Francis Eli Brotherton** (*pictured right, standing, with ever-up-for-it Sgt Tommy Croft*) now in his third year as a PC to which he would add another 26, rising to the rank of Inspector before calling it a day in 1904, was singled-out for his selfless actions in raising the alarm to a fire in Pump Street.

*Francis Eli Brotherton (right) who served 16th January 1874 to 22nd July 1904, rising to the rank of Inspector*

## Botched fire-fighting results in loss of Theatre Royal

But at the end of November a fire at a noted city landmark kept the entire force and its bolt-on brigades of professional firemen employed by the insurance companies on their toes: the Theatre Royal In Angel Street went up in flames on November 24th.

It was at 6.40 that morning that John Morris, long-standing landlord of the Ewe and Lamb, noticed smoke coming from the premises and was the first to notify the police. Within minutes, Angel Street was impassable with crowds, but, reports the *Advertiser*: '...the police fire-brigade was in active service with admirable dispatch and soon had two hose-nozzles playing from the street into the buildings and on to the adjoining property. The firemen connected with the Phœnix and Norwich and the Liverpool fire offices rendered good service both in front and rear of the theatre'. The *Advertiser* later reported:

*'A sad calamity has befallen Worcester. The elegant model Theatre which three years ago replaced the ugly old building which had so long done duty in that character, has fallen a victim to a fate not uncommon with such structures. On Friday night a classically-founded piece was produced on its boards, and a few hours later the building, with its contents, was a complete wreck, and the city now possesses no local habitation for the representation of tragedy and comedy'.*

During the course of the fire, the Shakespeare next door was also damaged – although more so from water than fire. Luckily, the Theatre had been insured for £3,000 and largely agreed that the fire had been an unfortunate accident, Commercial Union Assurance Company had almost immediately raised the cheque to cover the loss, and work on a new design put in hand.

For all that, the rescue mission hadn't all gone to plan: there were complaints of insufficient water pressure, while the Norwich Union's hose burst, rendering it useless; but for the most part the police had done a grand job in their add-on role as fire-fighters and were duly honoured as such.

Not so at an earlier conflagration at 4pm on November 1st when the Talbot in Sidbury had gone up in flames: unfortunately for the police the incident coincided with the entire force's presence on Pitchcroft for the races. Inevitably, the force came in for a rare bashing for just not being there, although **Sergeant Arthur Edwin Sommers** and **PC Edward Wall** had managed to salvage some of the police's reputation by their prompt actions.

Some of the complaints were so vitriolic that **Matthew Power** instantly threw in his lot as head of the fire organisation, but was later persuaded to back down after a plea from the mayor and four Aldermen, Price, Jones, Woodward and Wood to reconsider: '...it was, they all knew, utterly impossible for any person acting in such a capacity as Mr Power to please everybody, and he (*Mayor, Moses Jones*) felt sure that Mr Power's conduct as an officer had met with the approval and thanks of a great majority of the (Watch) Committee'. (*Herald*)

**Matthew Power** must've been glad to put it all behind him and get down to some solid old-fashioned policing.

***Gained:*** *George Walker, Sydney Harris, William Pritchard, (none of whom out-lasted the year) Henry Harley, Charles Goodyear, George Causier, Henry Barber*

***Lost:*** *Arthur Blomely, Frederick Insell, Thomas Harris, Thomas Quinney, George Wargent, George Roberts*

- murder suspected when body of 'dissolute and immoral' 24-year old Maria Westwood is dragged out of the lock at Diglis by lock-keeper Wilmot. Search mounted for boatman seen in her company earlier, but with no success

- more counterfeit coin in circulation, the new Music Hall in Lowesmoor particularly targeted. The same week the Bell Hotel Glee Club played selections from Handel and Rossini. Father and son William and Edward Elgar are harmonium and second violin, and first violin respectively

- police called in to break up demonstrations of striking joiners in demand of an extra 1d (penny, 0.4p) an hour from 7d to 8d. The employers were offering $\frac{1}{2}$d which, after weeks on unpaid strike, they finally accepted

- Sgt William Underwood recovers body of 7-year old Tommy Fowles, found drowned in the Severn

- PCs Jabez Waldron and Edward Wall violently assaulted in separate incidents on the same night in July

- Matthew Power himself questions legality of pigs' trotter-eating contest at the Concert Hall in Lowesmoor

- fire breaks out in the van used by Mr Winwood for his new removals company based at the inn his sister runs, the Carpenters Arms in the Moors. Neighbours rally round and it is put out with buckets before the police can attend, but is destroyed at a cost of £75

- unnamed PC pumps stomach of attempted suicide Herbert Jennings of Sandys Road who swallowed a bottle of Battles' rat poison. He survived

- PCs Thomas Booth and Frederick Goodwin who was to quit just three weeks later, are both seriously assaulted on the same night in November

- unnamed PC summons 13-year old 'incorrigible' Albert Davis for throwing stones. Sentenced to one day's gaol and six 'cuts' with a rod

- some slick detective work by Det Bill Phillips sees a London teacher in the city for interview as prospective master of the Orphanage in St Johns (later YMCA) sentenced to three months for stealing a 6-guinea coat from a commercial traveller so as to impress the selection panel the next morning. He didn't get the job

1878

Aside from keeping his men in line, his force in shape, and his perhaps unwilling head-ship of the fire brigade, next priority for **Matthew Power** this year was to resign his honorary secretary-ship of the SPCA: the role had been of some personal concern for some time as – as he wrote in his resignation letter: '...I have been of opinion that the desired object would be better attained if the secretary were unconnected with the police because when action by a person in my position becomes necessary, it is apt to be regarded by the general public as the outcome of officialism rather than humanity, its official tendency becoming thereby weakened'.

One of the issues causing concern at the time was a new method of slaughtering animals being tested in the north of the county – but it was popular neither with butchers nor the society's officials: '...the head of an animal slaughtered *by dynamite* being completely shattered by the explosion, the loss accruing to the butcher would be regarded as a serious objection to its use' a report read out at the same meeting as Power's resignation had outlined. His successor was the Reverend D.C.H. Preedy, Minor Canon of the cathedral.

In February the entire japanning department of the Vulcan Iron Works was destroyed by fire and **Matthew Power** condemned the actions of the insurance companies in using their own engines rather than calling on the police to bring into action their vastly superior machines. The incident turned out to be little more than a mis-handled debâcle for which the police came in for more unfair criticism as, with the exception of the few beat bobbies close enough to attend and assist – which they did, willingly and with no small risk to themselves – they were not considered necessary: '...the men are not to blame and they feel that they appear to disadvantage in the eyes of the public' the outraged police and fire chief wrote to the Watch Committee. Despite this, the few local beat officers that were able to assist drew some high praise and were awarded a 'thankyou' cheque for £3 from the Vulcan directors in appreciation of their actions.

Later the same month, there was more embarrassment at the station house when a number (*unspecified*) of police officers had been found sound asleep in St Nicholas Church one freezing night when they should have been about their business on the streets.

The rumour at the time is that they'd gone in there to pray, but it was believed by no-one, and it was to take a long time to live that one down.

## Troubled ex-Pc Lewis Barnes attempts suicide

**Constable Lewis Barnes** who'd quit the force after seven so-so years in February 1875 had taken the licence of a noted rowdy-house originally called the Robin Hood, later the Royal Oak, in an unexpected quarter of the city – York Place. The change of career does not appear to have gone well for the ex-copper who'd taken to drinking heavily while still a PC and now had the means to indulge his weakness to extremes. As the *Herald* told the world in May this year, '...Lewis Barnes, landlord of the Royal Oak, York-buildings, in this city, an ex-policeman, made a desperate attempt to commit suicide last night (a Friday) at 8 o'clock'.

He'd been found lying on one of the benches in the smoke-room, his throat cut, a pillow under his head and a knife beside him. Attempted suicide then being an indictable offence, some of his ex-colleagues were brought in to investigate and Barnes was summoned to court the following week. Witnesses said that he'd been depressed over a fight he'd had with a man named Abel a week earlier, and the scrap had left him injured with what sounds (*in those pre X-ray days*) like a case of broken ribs. He was subsequently bound over in his own recognizance of £20 and a surety of £10 for his future good behaviour.

After what appears to have been a brief drying-out period and spell of getting back on his feet, he was to take over the Crowle House the following year, but doesn't appear to have fared very well there either and he emerged a sad man, dying in the City at the end of 1889, aged just 46.

A shock report into drunkenness around this time revealed that four out of every five crimes committed in the County were the result of drink. Worcester had long been home to a number of vigorous temperance societies passionately opposed to the evils of alcohol, and their voice was beginning to be heard above most others': one of their more outrageous demands on the police at this time cited Luton where the police had closed a third of the public houses and crime and immorality were shown to have diminished by a corresponding amount.

It couldn't happen in Worcester could it... *could it?*

Whether or not the Talbot's licensee Richard Roden held the police responsible for the scale of damage done to his Sidbury pub in the fire the previous year can't be gauged for certain, but it's a fair bet – so when a fight broke out inside and later outside the new-restored Talbot involving noted thug Benjamin Brookes and another licensee, the Fish's George Seville in August, he saw his chance and landed a hefty smack on the side of **PC William Smith**'s head. Bill Smith – about a year into an otherwise unremarkable career with Worcester City Police that would last about another year before he walked away like so many before him, sadder but wiser – had been alerted to the almighty scrap going on outside the surprisingly-volatile former coaching inn, and in trying to separate the two combatants, Richard Roden saw his chance and wallop! blaming a drunken Brookes, who already had a string of convictions for assault, for the blow. Entirely innocent, but too drunk at the time to be able to prove it, Brookes was fined £5 or a month's gaol.

In July, off-duty **PC Jabez Waldron** living at 24 Little Charles Street in the Blockhouse was charged with assault after 64-year old neighbour called John Cleveland accused his son, also Jabez then 11, of being in his garden at 6am and threatened to slap him. The outraged copper went round to tell him he thought he was a foolish old man and pushed him in the direction of his door. Complaint dismissed – but there was a more serious turn of events to come from **Jabez Waldron** and his children (*see December 1879, p241*).

It was Worcester's turn to host the Three Choirs Festival in September this year when only the astutest observers would have taken note of a father and son playing side-by side in the Second Violins – this was music shop proprietor William Henry Elgar and his 21-year old son Edward.

Far more evident was the police presence, this year out in force following a spate of robberies at the previous Festival three years earlier. The ploy must have worked as not a single case of robbery or pick-pocketing was reported throughout the entire Festival: the Council must also have been delighted with the outcome, passing without a single complaint, the force's request for extra payment to cover the additional duties. Even **Matthew Power**'s old adversary Richard Lloyd Bozward felt compelled to stand up in Council and state that he '...could not refrain from saying that the highest credit was reflected on the police by their conduct' during the run of the Festival. They passed the payment of £23 1s 6d of which the chief himself pocketed £5 5s.

The same month saw the fire brigade boosted by another 18 men – members of a volunteer fire brigade recruited by Robert Surman of Broad Street. *Fire, of course, was rarely out of the news...*

In order to avoid a repeat of the disaster that had destroyed the Theatre Royal the previous year, proprietors of the new venture that was already at the planning stage and would be complete by the following April, offered to pay the additional expense of permitting the quarter's patrolling sergeant to let himself in every night after audiences had left in order to inspect the theatre's safety and security. The Watch Committee gave their OK to the plan: in fact, they would probably have given the OK to any plan involving additional cash as estimates for running the police this year had come in at £2,648 5s 6d – £92 8s 2d over the previous year. A proportion of the extra cost had been put down to several pending promotions and the cost of overcoats due to be issued to the men that winter.

At the Licensing Sessions in September, **Matthew Power** revealed that drunkenness in the city was still on the up with 259 cases coming before the courts. For the first time a new element was also to crop-up as playing a significant role in the shocking figures, legitimate licensed victuallers pointing the blame at the growing number of grocers now selling alcohol for drinking *off* the premises as part of their day-to-day trade. It was not to be the last time.

Given the recent shocking drunkenness statistics alongside their relationship with increased crime figures and bolstered by the chief's renewed campaign against erring landlords, this year's session was unusually animated, several constables being brought up to repeat the parts they'd played in a catalogue of reported breaches of regulations: **Detective William Phillips** now in his thirteenth year with Worcester City Police had been particularly vigilant in sniffing-out prostitutes, opposing the renewals of licenses at the Malt Shovel and the Brewers Arms in All Hallows on the grounds of being habitual resorts for the good-time girls; several constables had reported their routine at the Holly Bush where the come-on was that they *stood* at the bar rather than sat down; **Detective Phillips** again, backed up by **PC Herbert Osborne** (whose own record was far from exemplary; over previous years he'd been severely reprimanded for being asleep in the College Precincts while on duty; fined 5/- for being under the influence of drink while on duty with neglect; again fined 5/- and severely reprimanded for being asleep on his beat; fined 1/- for being asleep on a doorstep while on night duty; reduced to 3rd Class, severely censured and warned that repeat would result in discharge for being drunk while on duty; fined 1/- for want of energy in keeping back a crowd at a fire and again severely reprimanded for being asleep on his beat) revealed more tales about prostitutes' activities at the Ewe and Lamb in Angel Street and the Pack Horse (*now Courtyard*) in which they were backed up by **PC21 Henry Harding** (*pictured left, standing behind Sgt William Preece*) – who'd also been fined for being drunk on his beat twice the same year.

**PC Thomas Booth** now in his third year (of thirteen) also described the scene in the Peep O'Day in Cumberland Street where on his late-night patrol he'd found all the lights on, the landlady drunk on the floor and the landlord Henry Cooke asleep in a chair with his head on the table, neighbour Mrs Williams testifying that most nights it was left to her to lock up and post the keys through the letterbox. **Matthew Power** himself said he'd witnessed gambling going on in the Royal Exchange Vaults, while police en masse objected to renewal of the Lamp Tavern's licence to hard-man and police-hater Noah Dayus on account of his not being fit to hold a licence: as a neighbour had put it, he was 'the fearfullest character in all the world'. Curiously enough, every application was granted, although all suspect landlords had been taken aside and warned as to their future conduct.

It had been the busiest Brewster session for years, additionally marked by a number of memorials – petitions – signed by thousands of concerned Worcester citizens, many of whom were taking the pledge and joining the temperance societies.

**A DRUNKEN PAIR OF OLD WOMEN.**—Anne Murray and Mary Rowbotham, two dissipated looking old women, were charged with being incapably drunk on Saturday evening. They were falling down alternately, and the policeman had scarcely raised up one than the other subsided in the puddle. The prisoners, who said they had come hop-picking and would not commit themselves again, were discharged with a caution.

At least there had been time for some levity – as a *Herald* report, re-printed (*above*) in its entirety bears out.

At her trial, gloveress Jane Lewis of Bell-founders yard, arrested by **William Underwood** for murdering her 8-day old baby and concealment of birth, made a courtroom request to allow her to remain in the cells at Worcester in perpetuity because Mr Power and the other officers had been so kind to her and made her so comfortable there. Request declined.

### Death of tireless supporter, Police magistrate Charles Sidebottom

At the very end of the year, a blow: the death of Police Magistrate and ex-Town Clerk, Leeds-born Charles Sidebottom aged 89. He'd presided over pretty much every case brought before the Bench since 1830 – even before Henry Sharpe's days. During that time, he'd achieved huge prestige and respect in his adopted City. Despite a well-justified reputation as a hard-liner who refused to suffer fools gladly – he was a known advocate of corporal punishment for erring youths and children, ordering them to be whipped in the cells when the neighbours complained of the cries of the whipped felons in the yard outside. He'd even considered re-introducing the stocks as the only fitting punishment for the never-ending stream of crime and near-daily violence he was called on to deal with. In later years, he lived at Elm Bank, Lark Hill where he and his wife Mary Abigail had six children and employed six servants. He was still working only days up to his death. A tireless supporter of the police force even in its darkest hours, he was to be greatly

## Also this year: 1878

- concern as a lad named Colman escapes from the Guildhall cells by squeezing through bars

- the same week PCs Henry Joyner and Edwin Oakey cut down a prisoner who'd attempted to hang himself in the cells

- also in February, police investigate when the body of 12-year old James Forrest Dixon of 6 Mayfield Terrace is dredged from the canal at Gregory's Mill, three weeks after he'd gone missing. His throat had been cut

- in March, Mary Ann Higgs of Dolday, arrested for drunkenness and indecency attempts to strangle herself in the police cells

- on 28th., police called in to break up violent gatherings after Conservative John Derby Allcroft wins by-election caused by the death of Liberal MP, Alexander Clunes Sherriff

- George Downes (18) charged with stabbing Henry Perks on Pitchcroft

- murderous attempt on life a County policeman PS Drury only averted when the military is called in to disperse mobs in what became known as the Blockley Riots

- Sergeant Arthur Sommers and PC Sam Grosvenor mount 3 to 11.45 am vigil in the School Board building to trap Queen Caroline licensee William Bateman for out-of-hours drinking – and log 60 illegal customers

- police forced to issue an apology after a man named Lea is falsely imprisoned and later released following a case of aggravated assault in the Crown in Droitwich Road

- PC (later Sgt) William James is lucky to have got off an assault charge after he struck drunken cab-driver Joseph Lloyd on the back of the head in a nasty mêlée at the Farriers Arms in Farrier Street. He said it was self-defence, but even the new mayor Alderman Francis Dingle conceded that he thought in this case the PC had used unnecessary violence, fining Lloyd 6d with 13s expenses rather than six months' imprisonment for assault

- rain, sleet and snow all over Christmas mean that '...general discomfort ruled the day and with closed shops and empty streets, Worcester has rarely looked more comfortless and inhospitable from the exterior'. At least, it results in a quiet start to the year...

missed, and **Matthew Power** was among the long line of official mourners that followed his cortège to the cemetery.

*Gained: Edwin Farr, William Henry Harris, Charles Yeates, James William Underwood, Joseph Pullen (none of whom would survive the year) John Davis, Matthew Tolley, William Wild, William White*

*Lost: Thomas Vaughan, Frederick Goodwin, James Watson, George Goodyear George Causier, Henry Barber*

The first *Herald* of the year contained a report that's worth repeating in full:

> *'Mr Power informed the Bench that some ruffian had written him a post-card, threatening him with personal violence, because of some action taken by the police. The Bench expressed their indignation at the cowardly attack on Mr Power'.*

The poor lamb: being the chief of police was no place for the weak-hearted, clearly.

The County's Chief Constable might have had the greater cause to complain: in the previous quarter to November 30th, the number of reported offences had risen to 1,882 of whom 1,779 people were apprehended or proceeded against, 147 summarily convicted and 402 discharged.

Like the Baldwins seven years earlier, two brothers, **George Henry Reuben Cooke** and **Oscar Cooke** had joined the force on the same day, 10th January this year; both resigned ten days later (*20th January*).

Throughout February, Worcester's reading public had been hearing tales of a heroic stand-off two weeks earlier between a depleted force of Royal Warwickshires that had included several Worcestershire men and a fewer number of South Wales Borderers that had put up a heroic defence against an overwhelming Zulu army put at around 6,000 at an outpost called Rorke's Drift in far-off South Africa.

On that same day (*January 23rd this year*) **PC Samuel Pagett** had had to conduct a defence of his own – although the odds were distinctly narrower – 1:1. He'd had to fight-off a hail of blows aimed at him by waggoner John Bowen who he'd accused of stealing a cart-load of vegetables that he said he'd obtained at the Garibaldi in St Johns, but was later found to have been lying. Six weeks' hard.

The same month, Colonel Cobbe had once more expressed himself perfectly satisfied with the state of Worcester City Police, remarking to mayor Walter Holland that '...the officers, numbering five sergeants and 26 constables reflected great credit on the chief superintendent Mr. Power'.

In April an unnamed constable was brought in to recover the body of a newly-born girl found in the canal near Sidbury by a workman Thomas Henry Attwood. Verdict (*at the inquest, held at the New Inn, George Street*) open, implying murder by person or persons unknown. A far from rare event, it was all in a day's work for the patrolling bobbies – not all of whom were able to handle what they saw and had to cope with during the course of a typical day.

## Violent incident sparks permanent rift between City and County police chiefs

In May, an incident that was to irrevocably damage the relationship between the City and County forces – rarely more than fragile at best, but having notably deteriorated since John Phillips' death two years earlier. More lasting was the personal animosity forever now harboured between their two chiefs, Colonel Carmichael and **Matthew Power** whose fall-out over the issue proved unbridgeable...

Battle lines had been drawn up in squaddies' pub the Albion following a row over a girl that two soldiers had been 'walking out', and the two would-be suitors had set-to as their mates all joined-in in a free-for-all in the road using their belts as weapons. By now having escalated into a full-scale riot in every sense of the word, two City PCs, **Thomas Wallace** and **Samuel Grosvenor** (*pictured, right*) alongside Sgt Major William Perry of the Worcestershire Militia waded in and **Wallace** was reported to have twice hit one of the squaddies with his stick, while **Grosvenor** lashed out at the soldiers who eventually smashed his lamp.

Some officers from the County force then joined in and as like as not, saved the two City bobbies from the entire military rabble turning on them – although they later testified that had their City brethren not intervened with such brute force, the riot would have calmed down of its own accord.

At the subsequent court hearing – reported by the *Herald* under the heading '*Charge of Misconduct against Worcester Policemen*' – Colonel Carmichael had ordered his officers not to attend, but omitted to tell the waiting magistrates and legal teams, and was subsequently rapped over the knuckles for his disgraceful lack of courtesy: the City force also took it as a snub and a clear refusal to support their case. The rift was never going to be repaired.

It's a matter of interest that both City policemen at the centre of the out-of-control and apparently vicious affair, went on to long and successful careers with the city force, both later rising to the rank of Inspector. **Tommy Wallace**, who was Acting Chief Constable for a while, retired from the force on January 17th 1896, with **Sam Grosvenor** quitting on 22nd March 1901, just two days short of thirty years with Worcester City police.

During the summer, **Matthew Power** also volunteered to take on a further duty, hitherto fulfilled elsewhere: control of cab licences. The move followed a spate of complaints that were to be echoed a century and more later under the heading 'taxi wars'. Some things just never change.

In the same week that ex-PC and recovered would-be suicide **Lewis Barnes** took over the Crowle House, **PC Arthur Robert Howard Judge** who'd joined the force on January 20th, came off rather the worst in a set-to with a drunken sweep named George Bedford who he'd accused of breaking windows in a house in New Road. Bedford was sentenced to a fine and costs of 11s or fourteen days' hard in default for the first offence, and exactly the same for the assault on the officer. **PC Judge** just jacked it in and quit, not wishing for any more of the same.

The same day the force was drafted in to solve the mystery of £40 missing from the office at the Star Hotel, and a 42lb salmon caught in the Severn near the city was put on display at Presdee's fishmonger's in the High Street.

At the same time, another charge of police brutality – this time levelled against **PC7 Henry Joyner,** later to be appointed Inspector (*photo, page 242*) – was dismissed by the Bench who heard that the alleged offence had been committed while attempting to drag a fighting drunk named Richard Glover back to the station house for questioning.

At least on that front (*drunkenness*) there was better news: at the Brewster Sessions, an altogether quieter affair than the previous year's, **Matthew Power** revealed that during the year, a mere 202 – ie four people a week instead of the previous year's five-plus – had been charged with the offence: it had been 281 the previous year. But now the Wesleyans were adding their voice to the temperance agitators demanding a reduction in the

*Fearless*
***PC14 Sam***
***Grosvenor***
*takes*
*on the*
*squaddies*
*and sparks*
*a row*
*between*
*two forces*

number of public and beer-houses in operation in the city: 177 with a full licence, 43 for the sale of beer on the premises, 7 for the sale of beer off the premises, 6 for the sale of beer and wine, 2 for the sale of cider, 1 for the sale of wines and sweets off the premises, 10 for the sale of spirits, and 7 strong beer licences.

Technology was coming to Worcester, and the police were interested – if not now, at least in the longer run. At the end of this year, the *Herald* ran a snippet revealing that: '...a company has been formed in Birmingham with the object of establishing telephonic communication between the business centres of Birmingham, Wolverhampton and other towns of the Midlands. A number of leading commercial firms has become subscribers'. At the centre of it all was 'one of Mr Edison's instruments', the new wonder of the age, the telephone.

As for Worcester, the search was on for 40 subscribers that, once amassed would then make the construction of a telephone exchange a viable proposition. There were doubts that figure would be reached, but at least Worcester City Police had its name down on the list, just in case.

The other was the tram and a proposal to set up a series of tramways radiating out of the city had met with some violent opposition that had needed firm police suppression in order to maintain order on the streets: it had been sparked-off by an outcry against the new-fangled mode of transport that would, claimed the protesters and demonstrators, impede the free passage of carriages at the shops and banks.

The plan was for eight identified routes: Tramway 1 from the Cross to the Old Turnpike House near the Cherry Orchard in Bath Road; Tramway 2 from the Cross to Pitmaston Road then northerly to Bransford Road; Tramway 3 Bransford Road 'to and terminating at a point in such road opposite to an inn there called the Portobello Inn'; Tramway 4 The Cross to Shrub Hill 'along the West Midland New Road, along Wyld's Lane into the London-road and Sidbury; Tramway 5: Cross to and terminating at a point on the old Worcester and Droitwich Turnpike Road, opposite an Inn there called The Swan Inn'; Tramway 6 from Lowesmoor, 'opposite to Silver-street, along Silver-street to the Cornmarket, along New-street and Friar-street into Sidbury; Tramway 7 Cross – Angel Street – Old Sheep Market - Shaw Street and Foregate Street; and Tramway 8 Foregate Street to 'where the said Sansome-street meets the said street called Lowesmoor'

Following the demonstrations, attention turned to a campaign of posters being defaced, the consortium behind the scheme based at 13 Cornmarket, offering a £5 reward for the capture

## Also this year: 1879

■ *heavy Christmas snow leads to a flurry of cases of boys and grown men sliding on the ice in the streets, each fined 2s 6d*

■ *police investigate a case of a baby found dead and suspected murder, the child's mother Alice Packwood claiming to have fallen on the ice*

■ *the cold also accounts for a rash of incidents involving children burned by standing too close to fires or scalded by knocking over kettles on a fire*

■ *Det Phillips investigates theft of expensive books belonging to WH Elgar of High Street, unlawfully acquired by William Guise Bennett and identified by Mrs Ann Elgar. He was arrested in the Market Hall Vaults (Shambles) while playing billiards*

■ *annual inspection shows force to consist of one superintendent, 5 sergeants and 26 constables*

■ *police sent in to quell major fracas at the King William Inn after a fight that started over a game of cards escalates into a free-for-all*

■ *murder suspected when another new-born child is dragged out of the canal at Sidbury*

■ *workman William Hardy is drowned in water collected under the gasometer at the Gas Works*

■ *police called in to control crowds waiting to see six Zulu warriors paraded over two consecutive nights at the Music Hall*

■ *commercial and agricultural depression leads to investigations into a spate of often messy suicides*

■ *called in to quell rowdy behaviour at Link's Lodging house in Newport Street, PC Thomas Wallace finds 56 residents – one room contained 11 men, others up to 8 and others sleeping in the kitchen. Alerted, he found a similar state of affairs at Smith's lodging house next door*

■ *202 people convicted of drunkenness this year, a sharp drop from the previous year (281)*

■ *PC (later Sergeant) Fred Tarrant roughed-up by a crowd in the Red Lion Sidbury after he'd arrested a man named Williams on suspicion of stealing rabbits but lost his prisoner after being forced to release him during a tussle with a crowd spurred on by Henry Rammell*

■ *unnamed PC has to fight off 'large retriever' dog that he alleged had flown at him at W B Needham's seed shop Lowesmoor. Needham fined 21s and costs*

GEORGE LEVICK.

**£5 REWARD.**

**WORCESTER TRAMWAY:**

WHEREAS certain evil-disposed Persons are engaged DESTROYING STREET NOTICES, the above Reward will be given for information to the Chief of the Police, Worcester, leading to a Conviction of the Offenders.

of 'certain evil-disposed persons engaged in destroying street notices; the above Reward will be given to the Chief of Police leading to a Conviction of the Offenders'

By the following year, the scheme had been reduced to just two routes – east (*Shrub Hill Station*) to west (*Portobello*) and north (*Vine Inn*) to south (*Berwick Arms*).

At the end of the year, **PC Jabez Waldron** had sent his 13-year old daughter Ann for firewood and when she hadn't returned after fifteen minutes he went in search of her: he found her being indecently assaulted in an alleyway by moulder Henry Stokes of Charles Street who ran away but was caught by the off-duty policeman. The *Herald* merely states 'He was committed to the Sessions'. It's not revealed what condition he was in: but within two weeks, **Jabez Waldron** who'd joined on 22nd May 1868 was no longer a policeman. It's thought he was permitted to resign for reasons that can be easily guessed. Two years later, three of his children, Jabez Davis Waldron, now 12, Alfred aged 10 and Jessie 8 were all in the care of the Union Workhouse, described as having been abandoned'.

It's not known what had happened to him, daughter Ann or his gloveress wife, Mary.

*Gained:* George and Oscar Cooke, Arthur Judge, Frederick Hathaway (none of whom out-lasted the year), Walter Box, Frank Brimble, Alexander Diver, Charles Smith, William Preece, William Stanton, Thomas Sherwood
*Lost:* Jabez Waldron, William Smith, William Wild

**Matthew Power** had always taken a personal interest and not a little pride in the way his officers looked while on patrol – a characteristic that largely continued throughout the entire history of Worcester City Police. But his arch finickiness and insistence on getting the appearance correct, right down to the last button, had had a fatal downside: *cost.*

At the previous year's annual inspection, Colonel Cobbe had noted the difference in the outlay on Worcester City and Worcestershire Constabulary police uniforms and as the Government's appointed inspector whose employers now paid half the cost of police clothing (*up to a few years before it had been a quarter*) he'd lodged a formal complaint about the mounting cost that in the city was half as much again over the Government's allowance. If the County could stay within budget, why couldn't the City?

One of the reasons was that Colonel Carmichael who shared none of **Matthew Power**'s sartorial style and was more concerned with discipline and doing things by the book rather than the appearance of his men, cheerfully re-cycled the uniforms of departed officers by simply handing them down to their replacements. That there might be a massive difference in size between the original owner and its new one mattered not a jot: the result was that County policemen often cut a comical figure in the streets – a situation that'd never do in Worcester where appearance was all.

Hauled before the Watch Committee to explain, **Matthew Power** was ordered to trim the cost of clothing to within budget and to limit price-fixed tenders to Worcester tradesmen only.

The force's strength in January was put at 33 and the County's as 212.

The same week, following an unusually numerous spate of accidental drownings and suicides in the canal, the police's suggestion of a new dedicated – ie police use only – drag-line for pulling bodies out of the water was taken up and the line was unveiled at St Georges Tavern. The timing could scarcely have been better: just days later, it was in use in the search for the body of 41-year old hay-trusser Richard

*PC7 Henry Joyner cleared of police brutaility two years previously, and (right) PC12 Frederick Tarrant, both rising stars of the City Police this year and both set for promotion, long service and stellar police careers*

Fowler who'd fallen into the canal after a mammoth drinking session in the Tavern where, the following day his inquest was also held. It was to be in constant use for all its working life.

March to April had seen a UK General Election (*and a change of Government from Conservative to Liberal*) and early June had seen the Bath and West of England Society's agricultural show held in Worcester for the first time: both events had created a massive drain on already-stretched police resources, but praise for the way the force had conducted itself on both occasions had come from several quarters and in an unusually benevolent gesture, the Council allowed every officer and sergeant a day's pay and two guineas to the chief for each event by way of a gratuity.

On May 11th the police were called en masse to the Railway Bell pub in St Martins Gate to quell a major fracas that had erupted between railwaymen – who saw it as their territory – and an unruly gang of bargemen that had muscled-in and created havoc. It was nasty affair that had ended with one of the railway men, Thomas Cook, being carried off with a broken leg and all bargemen henceforth barred from the pub, but **Matthew Power**'s later opposition to the renewal of landlord Thomas Wood's licence was overruled.

### Serious undermanning fuels visibility complaints

In August, a crisis – and it was not going to go away. The cost of policing had been revealed as at £2,816 in the City (as well as £20,347 in the County with 212 men, Bewdley £94 12s., Droitwich £252 and Kidderminster £1,839). At the same time, a review of the force's structure had starkly exposed the true scale and impact of undermanning: it was damning...

Of necessity, some areas had been left unpatrolled – to the point that there had been a rash of complaints that in some areas the police were '...an unknown rarity (where) sometimes months pass without a glimpse of one being seen'.

In the north of the city, not only were the streets dangerous, but also '...the amount of mischief of a very serious nature being perpetuated without check' daily included property being broken down and destroyed, stone-throwing threatening life and limb, walls chalked with obscene words, garden robberies and householders cutting down fruit trees rather than see them raided of their fruit year after year. Outraged city councillor John Fisher summed it up in an angry letter to the newspapers:

*'...hours pass without a policeman being seen at all; the whole of the north of the city from the Cattle Market to the canal, only one man is in charge; from 6 to 9 o'clock am there has been but one man allotted to supervise the 30 miles of streets; from 10 o'clock until 2 there are supposed to be five men, but one of them has to attend the Police-court; in the afternoon there are seven men if they have no special duty to perform, which they often have, reducing that number. Winter is coming and I deem it essential that residents should consider themselves safe from molestation, either of their person or their property, which at present is impossible'.*

Ordered to report on the scale of the problem, **Matthew Power** had no choice but to come clean: the situation was every inch as bad as claimed.

Besides, Worcester's penchant for lawlessness – well out of proportion to its size in comparison with other towns and cities, and particularly marked among the unruly young – was again getting out of hand and unless things changed, anarchy would be the inevitable result. It was a graphic indication of just how lawless and volatile Worcester had become and that the Government's recommended police;people ratio that sufficed almost everywhere else including the mill towns of the north, was simply inadequate for the now-faithless city.

Nobody was attaching any particular blame to the police: by common consent, **Matthew Power** was doing the best he could with the resources at his disposal – 33 men to a population now nudging 34,000 – but without the addition of five or six more men, the situation would continue to deteriorate to the point of...? Nobody was hazarding a guess.

Even the new Mayor, fearless, outspoken ex-*Journal* and *Herald* sub-editor later to be cataloguer of all things Worcester, John Noake, admitted that no increase of supervision could be accomplished by the present body of men but that on the other hand, an outcry would be raised against the increased expenditure which would necessarily be involved.

How would they get round this? There was some serious hand-wringing in and around the recently-renovated and spruced-up Guildhall for weeks with not a solution in sight. After all, the councillors had the cost of a three-year restoration programme to find.

The tension could scarcely have been helped by yet another once-over from Colonel Cobbe in his annual inspection. Nor was the situation made any easier by coinciding with yet another accusation of police brutality – on this occasion, and not for the first time either, **PC Tommy Wallace** who, witnesses testified, had laid into paper-hanger John Starr of South Street '...struck his prisoner several times, and treated him very badly. The Magistrates dismissed the case and cautioned **Wallace** against violence in his conduct toward prisoners'.

A week later, all available police were out in force in their role as fire-fighters, tackling a blaze at the Paul Pry in the Butts.

The sad state of some of the city's poorer quarters was also brought home when 24-year old **PC (*later sergeant, clocking up 26 years' service*)** Frederick Tarrant, *pictured left,* forced the door of a Dolday hovel and found an abandoned 4-year old child who could neither stand nor speak and weighed just 16 lbs, less than half the average of a healthy child of that age. He was filthy, emaciated, starving and had been left all day with no food: his mother Emma Hopkins was imprisoned for six weeks with hard labour and the boy taken into the care of the Worcester Board of Guardians.

Death and distressing sights were all in a day's work for the city's bobbies – although ex-blacksmith **Fred Tarrant**, already with two sons and another child on the way (*a daughter born a month after the 1881 census*) seems to have copped for more than his fair share. Just a week later, he pulled over a cab and was shocked to find the dead body of another child inside. There was no suspicion attached to the driver Thomas Wood who'd been asked by his boss, proprietor George Hayes to convey the un-coffined body to the cemetery, but the luckless driver was still fined 6s 6d and warned that in such cases heavier punishments would be inflicted.

The year's Brewster Session revealed a marked decline in prosecutions for drunkenness – 177, the lowest tally for some years: there were 176 fully-licensed houses of which 10 landlords had been summoned for various offences, mostly out-of-hours drinking; 54 beer-houses of which two keepers had been fined for the same offence; and 4 cider houses.

*Gained: Charles Bourne, Henry Jones, George Herrington (none of which was to out-last the year) George Bannister, William Heapy, Richard Browning, Thomas Wright, Thomas Bennell*
*Lost: Albert Henry Wargent, William White, Frank Brimble, Charles Smith, Thomas Sherwood*

- twice in the same week police are called to corner cows that had escaped from the market. One, that had knocked down several people was caught by Foregate Street Station, the other ran as far as Claines and nothing more was heard of her

- Matthew Power '...instructed to obtain one of Dick's new Patent Chemical Fire Exterminators and 12 charges for the same for use by the police in the extinction of fires'

- police give full support to the new 'Habitual Drunkards Act'

- 14-year old George Hemming sentenced to a month's gaol and ten strokes of the birch for stealing 12s from Lowesmoor Coffee House

- police granted extra day's pay in recognition of extra work created by the General Election that resulted in two new representatives for the city, Liberals Thomas Rowley Hill and Aeneas McIntyre. Several cases of assault had been reported in St. Johns and there were claims of intimidation, bribery, illegal treating of voters and impersonation as well as a charge of a polling booth having closed before time

- quotes accepted for 34 police capes at 20s each and 34 belts at 2s 4d

- cold spring sparks-off spate of children's deaths and injuries from fires

- PC John Pugh narrowly escapes injury as he's passing a house in Birdport when an iron shovel is aimed at him from an upstairs window. Known police-hater John Graham sentenced to four months' hard

- police called in after horses bolt on sight of elephants being walked in London Road, part of a travelling menagerie that had been halted pending permission to enter the city. Matthew Power personally halts summonses issued against circus proprietor James Edmonds

- PC Walter Box appears in court with a badly scratched face after arresting 'old offender' Emma Eades, later sent to gaol for a month after assaulting the constable. She was also fined 10s 6d

- after another all-in free-for-all (this one resulting in Mary Ann Brace and Sarah Jeynes both being committed to 14 days' gaol), PS William Preece tells the Magistrates' Court that people living in the neighbourhood of the Waterloo Tavern are 'quite as bad as those in Dolday'

- on the same October day police are called to a fire in High Street and the collapse of a parapet wall that fell into Broad Street causing a serious blockage

- the following week they are involved in three sudden deaths on the same day – Peter Stokes (heart attack), Frederick Higham (10) drowned in the canal at Tallow Hill, and the infant son of Lowesmoor cooper Samuel Dunn whose skull was fractured after he and the nurse who was carrying him slipped and fell down cellar stairs (accidental death)

- on Christmas Day PC Alexander Driver is set on by a mob attempting to rescue labourer Walter Beswick arrested for being drunk and riotous in Sidbury. He quit the next year

# 1881

The life-threatening dangers daily faced by the front-liners – not only in their policing roles but in this instance as fire-fighters – were brought home with a vengeance following two fires in the same week early on in the year.

There had been a fire in Barbourne Lane in which **PC Samuel Grosvenor** – another to clock-up a 30-year record with the force, retiring as Inspector in March 1901 – had emerged a hero. Two people, one of whom was the owner of the property that had gone up in flames, Mr. Quarrel (*whose name doesn't appear in the census records of that year, taken on the night of April 3rd-4th*) and Frederick Manning, had both written to **Matthew Power** '...calling attention to the meritorious conduct of **PC Grosvenor**' and enclosing donations amounting to 15s, the better part of a week's wages.

The other, and far more serious, fire that week was at the Music Hall in the Cornmarket that had drawn out every available man and resulted in **Matthew Power** bringing the action of two in particular – **PC Tommy Wallace** (*again*) and **Sergeant Thomas Tolley**, both experienced officers that even up to then had amassed 31 years with the city police – to the attention of the Watch Committee with recommendations for formal recognition and possibly other well-deserved rewards.

Recorded the *Herald*:

> '...Police-constable Wallace was sent up a ladder in front of the hall, and he got on to one of the window-sills to be able to play on the flames with better effect. Sergeant Tolley followed, and as they were standing, a beam fell. They both were struck and Wallace would have fallen into the hall, had not Tolley seized him by the neck. Wallace's hand was much scorched by catching hold of the sash-line weight. He had been with the force eleven years and ought to be promoted to the merit-class. This was agreed to'.

But even with most of the city now hailing the new heroes, there were still voices of dissent – not least, that of the new mayor, Thomas Suffield Townshend who was a noted and outspoken teetotaller, one of 27 contemporary teetotal mayors in England and Wales according to a temperance report, and member of the Total Abstinence Society. Even the Mayor's Banquet this year was alcohol-free. His two-penn'orth was to the effect that as there were no lives lost, the police risking their lives was foolhardy and their actions presumptuous – besides, the proprietor of the Hall had afterwards given them 10s and refreshments!

It's hardy surprising **Matthew Power** yet again allowed his paddy to kick in at complacent officialdom, springing to his men's defence, and dutifully condemning the mayor's comments as 'a pity to check any display of pluck'.

With typical frugality and mean-mindedness, the city agreed to allow 5gns to be shared between the entire force, but to approach the insurance company – already faced with a £2,700 claim for fire damage – for £10, later reduced to cover their award of 5gns as a contribution in recognition of the officers' services. After all, pointed out Alderman Lovesey, they got the city's water for nothing '...and the assistance of the police also'. Motion agreed.

Seemingly of more importance were the complaints lodged by the City Sherriff – the notoriously anti-police and another temperance fanatic Alderman James Airey – of the dangerous habit of throwing orange peel on the street pavements and of a recent 'disgraceful' sports day at the Croquet Ground, Lower Chestnut Street – today's Bowling Club – that had attracted 'the lowest of the low' and demanding to know quite what the police had done about that...

Pte. Thomas Hawkswood of the 29th Regiment wasn't to know it, but when he offered an off-duty constable a drink and the latter refused in the Coventry Arms – prompting a heated exchange of words and an offer to fight and ending with the 37-year old bobby being badly beaten up and bitten on the hand – the man who'd refused him was to go on to become the star of the City force, **Thomas Wallace**, who'd joined Worcester City Police on 7th May 1869 and was to serve until 17th January 1896, attaining the ranks of Detective-Sergeant, Inspector and later Acting Chief Constable. Although his home was in Northfield Street where he lived with his wife Margaret, three daughters and a son and they also took in boarders, he'd called in to the Coventry Arms (*now the Cardinal's Hat*) for a swift 'alf after clocking off.

"Prisoner, who bore a good character in the regiment, was committed for six weeks' hard labour' reported the *Herald*.

## Matthew Power clocks up 20 years' service

The week marking the 20th anniversary of **Matthew Power**'s appointment saw three fires in High Street alone, but at least he and the city council were agreed on one point – that the new and very militant temperance organisation masquerading as a religious association and holding disruptive processions through the city culminating in huge crowds outside the Concert Hall, blocking up Lowesmoor and creating rowdy scenes, was an unholy nuisance that should be hounded out of town.

This was the Salvation Army and its local leader, 'Captain George' had had the effrontery to approach the police chief requesting three officers to control his fervent 'congregation' every night of the week – for which he was prepared to pay. **Matthew Power** flatly refused on the grounds that by doing so, the police would thus cease to be servants of the public. But it was a purely academic move as the situation had deteriorated to the point that he'd already been obliged to post three officers to the citadel (*still called the Salvation Army Hall*) to maintain some semblance of order anyway – and that had already involved cutting short the Army gatherings and even threatening its leaders with obstruction charges.

Captain George was livid – after all, the police actively supported their activities in other towns, so why was Worcester different? Simple: other towns didn't have men of Matthew Power's principles.

Sadly, just two months later, the under-pressure police chief was forced to change his tune in respect of seeking additional payment... The force's superannuation fund had failed and now he was faced with even more financial pressures and needed to claw back extra cash from whatever quarter he could. Three areas where he claimed the police should be recompensed for their time were i) the races; ii) the poor, via the Mendicity Society for their time in handing out tickets to tramps and vagrants and Worcester Guardians; and iii) the Worcester (*part of the Three Choirs*) Festival, all taking up valuable police time which meant that officers were prevented from fulfilling their day-to-day duties elsewhere. Given the resources at his

## Also this year: 1881

- 27-year old brewer's assistant Charles Teague found head-first in a vat of beer being brewed at Malpas, Lewis and Co (later Lewis Clarke's) and ladder found collapsed at the foot of the vat. Verdict accidental death

- James Dracas, now no longer solicitor's clerk but fully-fledged in his own right calls for help to eject drunken clerk Charles Rice from his Foregate Street office. It's unlikely they were aware of his anti-police outburst some years earlier

- ex-Sergeant Benjamin Holmes, now Mayor's Officer, is in hot water after removing the body of Charles Davis found in George Street to the Mortuary where he's later found to be alive

- PC Alexander Diver commended for discovering an illicit gambling den in full session in back room of the Liverpool Vaults, Shambles

- PC Fred Tarrant sent in to investigate offensive smells from the rear of a house in the High Street finds 10 pigs in a sty, three are dead and half-eaten by the others that are starving and in a deplorable condition

- three more 'sudden deaths' (human) investigated on the same day in February

- PC Fred Tarrant (again) overpowers and disarms drunken glover John Yeates who had threatened to slash his child's throat and then commit suicide

- police called in after 10-day old child, a feeding bottle and clothes are found in a cardboard box in the ladies' waiting room at Shrub Hill Station

- suicide at the Stationers' Arms in High Street, found to be George Mason, ex-Porcelain Works gilder

- the same day the body of a child is washed up on fields at Diglis as floods recede

- PC Thomas Tolley accused of using undue force in the apprehension of prisoner, Bench dismisses the case and orders both parties to shake hands

- two fires break out in High Street on the same day, Matthew Power takes control and police extinguish both – one the premises of milliner Wightman's, the other at Bennett's drapers next door to the Golden Lion

- PCs Fred Tarrant, William James and Alexander Diver all severely assaulted on the same Saturday night

- PC Thomas Richard May Bennell is dismissed after just seven months after he and an unnamed recruit walk into the Swan with Two Necks (sic) and orders a pint, the whole proceedings witnessed by Sergeant (later Det-Sgt) William Underwood

- PC (later Sgt) Edwin Oakey cuts down body of Joseph Warren who'd hung himself at the back of a house in South Parade

- Matthew Power personally investigates growing instances of cab-drivers found plying for hire with two carriages of the same number while having a licence for one only

- George Waldron, landlord of the Beehive in Carden Street bares his arm in court to show magistrates bruises sustained when being taken into custody by PC William Heapy

- police bring charge of furious driving in Friar Street against Henry Mapp of Gregory's Mill Street. His trap is estimated to have been travelling at between 10 and 12 miles an hour when it ran over and killed a dog

- in a single incident PCs Henry Harley, Francis Eli Brotherton and Charles Thomas are all attacked and assaulted by drunken battling virago Polly Hoban who also attempts to commit suicide by hanging herself in the police cells

- mother of ten Emma Waldron is shot in the face outside the station house by her husband Sampson after she'd picked up with a soldier Joe Walters, PC Thomas Booth witnessing the whole affair as he was bringing them both in for questioning. Verdict: committed for attempted murder

disposal and the less than unanimous support he received from his employer and paymasters, it was a dodgy situation to be in. But at least he had the support of his men. After all, they were all in the same boat: underpaid, overworked and under-appreciated.

The census this year shows the city's population to have swelled to 45,104 – 9,526 having been added with the extension of the city's boundaries to include parts of St Johns, St Martins, St Peters, Claines and Hallow.

**Gained:** *George Frederick Newman, William Drew, William Littler, George Grubb (none of which was to out-last the year), Edwin Hemming, James Richardson, John Henry Hazleton, Joseph William Troughton*

**Lost:** *Edward Wall, John Davis, Alexander Diver, Richard Browning, Thomas Bennell*

January saw **Sgt. Bill Underwood** sent half way across the world on a case, demanding his absence for 56 days – and still he retuned empty-handed. Armed with a warrant for the arrest of former Great Western Railway employee Arthur Goss for embezzlement, he'd been sent to South Africa but his quarry had got wind of the copper's arrival and did a timely runner. At least, the City police were recompensed for the loss of his services: his pay and expenses were met by the railway company.

**Arthur Edwin Sommers** who had been with the force for seven years and had won a reputation as the scourge of publicans flouting laws in relation to opening times, had been promoted to sergeant. In March, he was further promoted to the newly-created role of Inspector with a relative rise in pay: more would be heard of him in the coming years.

When Colonel Cobbe made his annual inspection the following month – passing his verdict that he was satisfied with its (*and the County's*) conduct generally – he took the opportunity to ask **Matthew Power** if he had anything to say in connection with pay.

Reports the *Herald*: '...(Power) asked whether he should not be entitled to ask for some increase in his salary in June when he will have completed 21 years' service in the force'. The following week, and after some heated discussion, the Committee decided that they might, with propriety and justice to the ratepayers, recommend an increase of £20 which would bring Mr Power's salary up to £250 a year'. The figure excluded his house in Copenhagen Street.

True to form, they weren't going to cave in to his demands for more money without some resistance, and unbeknown to the police chief, the Town Clerk had been asked to contact several neighbouring forces in order to compare figures.

The underhanded ploy backfired and the response came

*(Left) Sgt Charles Thomas recruited February 6th 1866 and set to go on to a 30-year career, retiring in January 1896, comes in for some rough treatment at the hands of battling Polly Hoban in December 1881. He was later to play a key role in one of the City Police's most inglorious episodes*

back that **Matthew Power** was not only on a distinctly average kind of remuneration but that he was also marked out as unique in the number of years' service under his belt.

They duly rubber-stamped his raise dated from May 10th – but then deducted £30 for the rent of his house.

At this time, the City police numbered 34 – precisely the same as the Worcester Division of the County Police: the number of fires in the city was running at four a week.

A rare light-hearted moment was captured by the *Herald* at the end of May when it reported on the comical case of Ellen Reed, described as an old woman of Dolday who'd been summoned for having been drunk at the police station the previous day for which she was fined 5s or seven days' gaol.

'Defendant had a cat in her arms, and upon being asked by the Head Constable what she brought the cat for, she replied that "Purviding the Magistrates sends me to gaol, they will have to keep my cat too, and

## Also this year: 1882

- police called in to break up riot involving 100 boys disrupting Salvation Army gatherings in Lowesmoor

- clever detective work traps 32-year old shoemaker and father-of-four John Jones who'd thrown pepper in the eyes of miller's traveller Joseph Phillips outside the Garibaldi in St Johns and stole his black leather bag containing £72 18s. Twelve months' hard and 30 lashes of a cat-o'-nine tails

- Matthew Power is again accused of planting spies in public houses to trap erring landlords

- police mount search for lad Joseph Wilmot who'd been working in Diglis lock when a massive rush of water swept him into the Severn. His father Thomas was superintendent of the lock and another son also worked for the canals company which was later fined for negligence over his death

- though attacked and injured, PS Bill Underwood disarms a Blockhouse man threatening to murder his wife with a flat iron. Two months' hard

- PC Amos Nottingham orders the river to be dragged after the coat and hat of Samuel Parker who'd earlier been taken to the City nick charged with carrying firearms in a public place and was going to be summoned for the offence, were found lying on the riverbank near the Grandstand. Verdict: suicide and mental derangement. The PC was to quit the force not long afterwards

- PC George Farley asks a young boy found crying in the street what was wrong and he said a man had stolen his puppy. Determined questioning revealed that sweep John Chivers had picked up the dog and had given it as a present to Mrs Richardson at the Market Hall Vaults. 14 days hard. Two weeks later PC Joseph William Troughton is beaten up in there

- police kept busy with four major fire call-outs in a month (May)

- conflict in evidence between PS Sommers and PC Thomas Tolley over amount of time the latter had spent in the Boat in Lowesmoor and whether or not a glass of ale in front of him was his or not, causes embarrassing rift in court

- several distressing drownings of children in the Severn and other accidents including a girl run over by a council dust cart opposite the Anchor in Diglis dominate the mid-year's headlines

- three boys ordered to six strokes of the birch and their parents to pay 5s costs each for stealing books in a summons brought by PS Tommy Wallace

- on the same day PC George Hill is savagely assaulted by Annie Kelley on the Cross

- police out in force for the first day of the Worcestershire Exhibition when 5,200 people pass through the turnstiles. The following night a little known 25-year old local violinist solos 'Polonaise' by Léonard at the Public Hall. His name is Edward Elgar

- PC Frederick Samuel Sheen – so new to the force that he hadn't yet been sworn-in – is ordered by Arthur Sommers to go to the Farmers Arms at 10 am one Sunday and masquerade as a cyclist from Gloucester and the same the next day at the Rising Sun in Bank Street. He is rumbled and ensuing court cases are dismissed against the licensees. Sheen lasts less than three months with the force, quitting on December 12th

- cab driver Henry Wade is found with a stolen cheque for £1,400

- county police forced to recruit new constable for St Peters following increase in violence and anti-social behaviour in the wake of the opening of new militia barracks at Norton

so I brought him with me". She was also charged with assaulting Elizabeth Yeates, a neighbour, which she admitted, and was fined 19s 6d or the alternative of 14 days' hard labour. She chose the latter and was removed with her cat'.

In September, **PC Edward Wall** quit after five years to take over the licence of one of four licensed premises in Grimley.

## Power proves himself an exceptional police chief

Something of the nature of chief **Matthew Power** also surfaced around this time: while his day-to-day grind brought him into contact with folk of every level of society from royalty and the toffs to the lowest of the low-life, the welfare and well-being of his men remained his top priority. He was also a great believer in the prevention, just as much as the detection, of crimes and took it on himself, even without the investigating officer's knowledge, to visit the homes of some of those suspected and accused of breaches of the law if he considered them capable of salvation – which of course, Worcester had additionally thrown up a high proportion of those that weren't.

Where he considered there might be some element of hope, he personally and unaccompanied – not always a sage and prudent thing to do, but he did it anyway – go and bang on their door with a view to a cosy heart-to-heart. To his eternal credit, more often than not it had yielded results, several times resulting in a promise of better behaviour in the future as the alternative to a court appearance and short sentence and the risk of a repeat performance within a matter of months, and so on for the future.

It set Matthew Power aside as an exceptional police chief.

*Gained: Albert Grubb (who was to quit within a few months), Frederick Sheen (ditto 83 days), Thomas Andrews, George Aston, Ernest Albert Heritage*

*Lost: Amos Nottingham, Matthew Tolley, George Bannister, William Heapy, Edwin Hemming*

The year began with the residents of Lowesmoor up in arms over the continuing nuisance that the Salvation Army had become: **Matthew Power** was forced to post a constable on permanent duty in Lowesmoor after regular disruptions of temperance meetings masquerading as religious 'services' – sometimes quite rowdy and even descending into violence with 'Sally Ann' members forced to retreat into the citadel hall amid hails of missiles.

Colonel Cobbe's usual thorough inspection included the entire mustered force, police cells, charge room and office '...and of accoutrements, clothing and books'. All was well. If he'd have visited a week later, his viewpoint might just have been different...

A regular at the station-house, 25-year old Florence Edwards had tottered, in her usual drunken condition, into the nick one Saturday night complaining loudly to **Station Sergeant Charles Thomas** about her treatment at the hands of her live-in lover Higgins in the Dolday hovel they shared.

Kindly Charlie Thomas had been around and he knew the score; he'd been with the force for fifteen years, largely without a stain on his character, and he knew the antics of Florrie Edwards only too well – she already had nine convictions and was, frankly, a drunken nuisance. With patience he tried to cajole her into going off home and making her complaint through the proper channels, the magistrates, on Monday morning: '...but she was in a drunken condition and would not listen to this advice, refusing to quit the station and behaving in very disorderly manner. At last, she was ejected; but immediately afterwards she re-appeared, and was then locked up. Before she had been in the cell many minutes, the sergeant heard her screaming and making a great noise, and on going to see what was the matter, found her violently struggling, and attempting to hang herself with a handkerchief, which she had twisted round her neck. She was, of course, prevented from carrying out her purpose; but twice subsequently she made similar attempts at self-destruction, loudly proclaiming her determination to cut her throat or hang herself. In consequence of this, a constable was obliged to remain in charge of her all night'. One month's hard.

There was, it seems, never a dull minute at the Worcester city nick: it'd be interesting to know quite what American consul's daughter and the police chief's wife, Mrs Mary Elizabeth Power, now 58 and living 'above the shop' with her husband and an unmarried daughter Georgina, 26, made of 'genteel' Worcester.

On December 18th police were on hand to control crowds hoping for a glimpse of Oscar Wilde who was delivering a lecture at the Theatre, following which he was entertained to dinner by the Worcester Pen and Pencil Club at the Star Hotel (now Whitehouse).

It was the end to an up-and down year that was quickly to be overshadowed by other events...

*Gained:* William Tyler, Albert Pritchard, Walter Hawkins Wilcox (none of whom out-lasted the year), James Quinney, Thomas Caudle, Charles Hall, William Henry Lane, George Henry Geary, Henry Rogers, William Buswell

*Lost:* George Farley, Ernest Heritage

## Also this year: 1883

■ *PC (later Sergeant) Joseph William Troughton investigating theft of cutlery from the Shades Tavern in Mealcheapen Street hears that the owner John Crumbie had lost 150 dozen (ie 1800 knives) since taking over, 24 in the previous week alone*

■ *PC Edwin Oakey arrives too late to save 18-year old Elizabeth Hemming from drowning after being alerted by a lad named Henry Neale to a woman deliberately walking into the Severn above the Grand Stand. A County Court summons and a letter addressed to her lover were later found in her possession*

■ *12 months' hard followed by 3 years' police supervision handed down on 22-year old labourer James Simpkins in the wake of robbery at Woods in the Butts investigated by PCs Henry Harley and John Henry Hazleton*

■ *attempt to blow up County Gaol in Castle Street foiled and suspicious black box containing explosive materials defused after the Royal Artillery is called in*

■ *PC Walter Box estimates Christopher Wheeler to be travelling at a furious 12 miles an hour*

■ *on the Cross, one of two similar charges brought the same day. The other was John Fidoe of Laugherne Hill. Both fined 15s including costs*

■ *City, County police and Warwickshire Constabulary collaborate for the first time (West Mercia and Warwickshire are now formally amalgamated) following discovery of baby's body in a canvas bag left at Shrub Hill Station, the girl is later found to have been poisoned with perchloride of iron that had corroded her lips, windpipe and insides. Suspicion of murder falls on her mother Betsy Ann Willis and her mother, both later charged with Wilful Murder*

■ *Sergeant William Preece severely beaten up in the station house while attempting to charge Blockhouse labourer William Vale with assault on a militiaman who he'd earlier knocked through the window of a coffee tavern*

■ *Christmas Day, police called to an incident in which glover John Ross had found his wife in a compromising situation with a neighbour, whitewasher Fred Powell and held a knife at his throat until persuaded to go home*

# 1884

The police had been kept on their toes throughout Christmas which had been particularly bad for rowdiness and violation of licensing laws, at least three subsequent cases brought by **PCs James Richardson, Thomas Caudle** and **Fred Tarrant** culminating in licensees being accused of perjury after lying in court.

The year was just days old when police were also brought in to investigate serious charges being levelled at £250-a-year City Treasurer Henry George. Some £3,430 had gone missing from the treasury accounts although George had tried to cover his tracks and had replaced all but £600 of it: the full extent of his crime was later revised upwards to £4,915. Pending his trial, his son Francis was one of 24 applying for the post left vacant by his father who was languishing in the County Gaol pending trial for the serious charges being levelled against him: to everyone's surprise, he actually landed the job – a move that produced gasps of disbelief in the Guildhall.

The Corporation of Worcester was already in a delicate state: a previous mayor Herbert George Goldingham (1873-4) had died with debts of £50,000 and claims of fraud, and the previous year's mayor Frederick Corbett had been sued at Gloucester Assizes (Faulkner v Corbett) and ordered to pay £140.

In mid-January, solid, reliable **PC (*later Inspector with 30 years' service*) Sam Grosvenor** was passing the Lamb and Flag in the Tything when he was halted by its licensee Julius Sladden who said he was concerned about a guest in an upstairs bedroom that hadn't come down: it was now mid-day. The PC broke down the door and found the man in a fit, but died very soon afterwards. The only clue to his identity was a hat sold by 'Mr Nield of Birmingham' and who he was remains a mystery to this day.

The following week, the City was rocked by another tragic affair of murder and suicide when Eliza Ross, who was already known to the police and lived in a low tenement off Lowesmoor, first gave her baby prussic acid and then swallowed the remainder of the bottle.

Both died what must have been horrible deaths (*Herald headline, right*).

Two weeks later, the funeral of the city's oldest fireman had taken place: he was Richard Williams of Birdport, aged 87 and he'd been with the Norwich Union brigade for more than 30 years. His brass helmet and a union jack was placed on his coffin which was borne on a manual fire engine drawn by four horses, while a heavy contingent of city policemen also joined in the cortège to Astwood Cemetery.

*They weren't to know it at the time, but every man-jack would be repeating the same journey under similar sombre circumstances just the following week...*

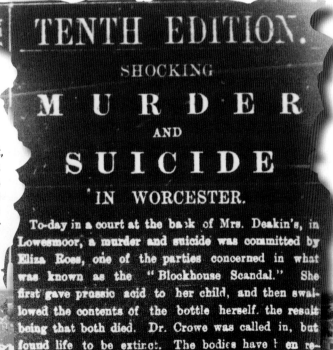

**TENTH EDITION.**

SHOCKING

**M U R D E R**

AND

**S U I C I D E**

IN WORCESTER.

To-day in a court at the back of Mrs. Deakin's, in Lowesmoor, a murder and suicide was committed by Eliza Ross, one of the parties concerned in what was known as the "Blockhouse Scandal." She first gave prussic acid to her child, and then swallowed the contents of the bottle herself. the result being that both died. Dr. Crowe was called in, but found life to be extinct. The bodies have been removed to the Mortuary.

*Brass-helmeted firemen of the 'private' Norwich Union Fire Brigade who toiled alongside the police only when their clients' properties caught fire. Their oldest serving officer had died this year, aged 87*

## An all-too familiar scenario: sudden death of the chief

**Matthew Power** had died suddenly. He was 58, had been chief for 23 years and was still active up to a few hours before he died of an undiagnosed heart condition on Wednesday, February 6th.

The *Worcester Daily Times* that had only been in existence since January 5th 1880 and so had only ever known one police chief, wrote:

> '...during the time Mr Power held the appointment, he succeeded in making the force one of the most efficient in the kingdom; his work was appreciated and suitably recognised by the Corporation. The Watch Committee held absolute reliance on his discretion in all matters affecting the force; and among the public there existed a feeling of confidence in his vigilance, integrity and impartiality. With the men of his force, Mr Power was thoroughly remarkable, exceptional and positive; he never flinched from advocating their claims when he thought it necessary and while on the one hand was intolerant of idle or incapable men, he was at the same time quick to detect and reward them'.

The WDT report concluded that he left a widow and two daughters (*correct*) and that his age was 63 (*incorrect*).

The news of his passing was instantly relayed by **Inspector Arthur Summers** to the Police court due to sit that morning, and was received by the mayor, William Blizard Williamson (*pictured, right*):

> '...he rose with a feeling of emotion to announce the death of Mr M. Power. Just seven hours previously he was alive, commenting on all that was going on around him; now he was lying speechless in the arms of death. It was just two days since he stood in that court and conducted the business of his office in a clear, and thoughtful manner. They (the Bench – that day, mayor, Aldermen Stallard, Townsend, Barnett and John Noake) could not help feeling deeply impressed with the fact that he had been taken so suddenly from among them. Mr. Power was deservedly

## THE LATE MR. M. POWER.
### THE FUNERAL TO-DAY.

The funeral of Mr. M. Power (late chief of police in this city) took place this afternoon; and both upon the route and at the Cemetery an unusually large concourse of people assembled. The *cortège* left the deceased's house in Copenhagen-street about half-past two o'clock. The procession consisted of a detachment of county police, commanded by Deputy Chief Constable Checketts; the firemen of the Norwich Union, in their uniform, under Capt. Sayce; the officers and men of the city police force (wearing armlets of crape) under Inspector Sommers; then came the hearse and a mourning coach, bearing Mrs. Power and her two daughters, who were accompanied by the Mayor (Mr. W. B. Williamson). The procession was joined at the Cemetery gates by representatives of numerous public bodies who were in waiting there. The members of the Corporation present were the Deputy-Mayor (Mr. F. Corbett), the Sheriff (Mr. Bozward), the Chamberlain (Mr. Bach), Aldermen John Stallard, W. Stallard, Townshend, Noake, Airey, Councillors Dutton, H. Day, Wilesmith, Burgess, Price, W. Joseland, Everill, Ball, Smith, Firkins, J. W. Stalworth, and Davies. The city magistrates were represented by Mr. G. Goodwin. Among the public officials were—Col. Carmichael (chief constable of the county), Mr. South-all (town clerk), Mr. R. T. Rea (clerk of the peace), Capt. Lewett (coroner of the prison) Mr. Kitson (in

*respected by all classes of persons throughout the city and, he would say, the county too. He discharged his duty towards the public fearlessly, at the same time courteously and kindly. During the whole of his service, (he) had proved a man of original and uncommon ability'.*

Clearly overcome and as mark of the deepest respect, the mayor immediately adjourned the business of the court to another day.

The Watch Committee was also due to meet that afternoon and **Arthur Sommers** was authorised to discharge the duties of the office pending the appointment of a successor.

The following morning the Worcester Board of Guardians met and the plaudits continued. That the speaker was the Sherriff, John Lloyd Bozward, with whom **Matthew Power** had clashed more times than most folks could remember, added extra weight to the tributes he laid at his feet: he was, he said 'one of the ablest chief constables ever entrusted with the command of a body of police... he had raised the police force of this city to a state of efficiency which gave it rank among the first in the kingdom and he should not be doing his duty if he did not acknowledge the great forbearance and moderation he always exercised in the discharge of his responsible duties'.

To which Alderman Barnett added that he had been '...one of the best public officers he ever knew. While he was very strict and very careful, he was most humane'.

The city had lost a valuable public servant and everyone – the lower elements and the criminal brethren included – knew it. His men were, to use a phrase not in use at the time but altogether appropriate in today's freer and easier-going parlance, completely gutted.

# 9:
# The Sommers years
## 15th February 1884 - 10th June 1892

**Matthew Power**'s funeral on Monday, February 11th saw a massive turnout by hundreds of public officials, a detachment of county police under Deputy Chief Constable Checketts, uniformed firemen of the Norwich Union brigade under Captain Alfred Sayce, and the entire complement of the city force, led by **Arthur Edwin Sommers** and wearing crepe armlets.

Reports the *Daily Times:*

> '...both along the route and at the cemetery an unusually large concourse of people assembled. The cortège left the deceased's house in Copenhagen-street about half-past two o'clock... then came the hearse and a mourning coach, bearing Mrs Power and her two daughters who were accompanied by the Mayor (Mr W. B. Williamson). The procession was joined at the cemetery gates by representatives of numerous public bodies who were waiting there. The members of the Corporation present were the Deputy Mayor (Frederick Corbett), Sheriff (Mr Bozward), the Chamberlain (Mr Bach), Aldermen John Stallard, W. Stallard, Townshend, Noake, Airey, Councillors Dutton, H Day, Wilesmith, Burgess, Price, W. Joseland, Everett, Ball, Smith, Firkins, J W Stalworth, and Davies. The City magistrates were represented

I am Gentlemen
Your Obed Servant
A G Sommers

*by Mr G Goodwin. Among the public officials were Col. Carmichael (chief constable of the county), Mr Southall (town clerk), Mr R T Rea (clerk of the peace), Capt Leggett (governor of the prison), Mr Fitton (inspector of factories), Dr Crowe (medical adviser to the police force), Dr Swete (pubic analyst). Mr H Rowe (city architect), Mr Reece (curator of Hastings' Museum), Mr J Coombs (of the magistrates' clerks' office), Mr G Gibson (chief warder of the prison), Mr A Webb (principal warder), and Mr Harrison (inspector of streets), &c.'*

The report goes on to list a long line of churchmen and licensed victuallers who attended and described the scene in the chapel and the wreaths offered by the Mayor, sergeants and officers of the city police force, magistrates' clerk, clerk of the peace and others. The blinds at the Guildhall remained closed all day.

### Monday, February 11th 1884: entire force musters for first official photograph

It's also likely that the same day saw the staging for the first known official photograph of the entire force mustered in the yard of the Guildhall: it shows 25 constables, 5 sergeants, an unnamed dog – probably Tommy Croft's own – and **Arthur Edwin Sommers**, still in the uniform of inspector, at the extreme right of the front row.

The clue to the actual date is the black rosette armbands worn by the chief and his sergeants who would act as pallbearers later that afternoon. Within a matter of days, the Town Council had appointed **Arthur**

PC24
Walte
Box

PC19
Charles
Hall

PC07
Henry
Joyner

PC5
Henry
Rogers

PC21
Henry
Harding

PC22
Francis
Brotherton

PC18
James
Richardson

PC25
Edwin
Oakey

PC17
Thomas
Wallace

PC26
William
Stanton

PC22
Fred
Tarrant

Sgt.
William
Preece

Sgt.
Thomas
Croft

Sgt.
Thomas
Tolley

**Edwin Sommers** as Superintendent at £200 a year less £30 a year for rent, and a £300 gratuity to Mrs Mary Elizabeth Power out of the Superannuation Fund – although most of the same Finance Committee meeting was taken up with a heated debate on whether or not a special rate might need to be levied to make up the deficiencies of the former city treasurer, still languishing in declining health awaiting trial and on whom no-one wanted to serve the official summons for fear of ensuing manslaughter charges in the event of a fatal heart attack.

Almost instantly, the mayor William Blizard Williamson stated that he considered Mrs Power's £300 gratuity barely sufficient to stand as a fitting testimony to the 'very high esteem in which the late Matthew Power was held by his fellow citizens', and launched an appeal of his own in a bid to push the figure past the £500 mark, with plans for a permanent memorial to his friend the ex-police chief.

A previous mayor Frederick Corbett (1882-3), also added his observation that:

> '...at the time he (Matthew Power) came to Worcester they had been accustomed to chief constables of a very different type, and the more stringent discipline he initiated and enforced gave rise to a great deal of opposition. But he had the tact and ability to smooth away all that opposition and to lay the foundations in a short time of a career of usefulness and success. During the later years of his life, no such thing as criticism or opposition was ever mentioned in connection with the manner in which he discharged his duties'.

PC01 Thomas Caudle | PC16 Henry Harley | PC8 John Pugh

C03 lliam swell | PC26 Sidnam Cole | PC10 Joseph Troughton | PC15 William Lane | PC02 Thomas Andrews | PC006 Thomas Booth | PC23 George Aston

Sgt. villiam derwood | Sgt. Charles Thomas | Supt Arthur Sommers | PC9 James Quinney | PC11 Sam Grosvenor | PC13 William James | PC14 George Hill

In what today might be termed 'a whip-round', the councillors alone immediately contributed a further £130.

It was already clear that Matthew Power was going to be a hard act to follow...

His replacement, Bedworth surgeon's son **Arthur Edwin Sommers** was 37, married to Ipsley-born Harriett also 37 and the couple had two daughters, Sally Maria, 10 and Maud Ellie, 9. At the time of his appointment he'd attained the rank of Inspector having previously been Sergeant, and the family was living at 1 Bowling Green Terrace.

He'd joined the city force from Worcestershire Constabulary in February 1874, having been a constable for two years, and though recently downgraded to 2nd class, he came with a good testimony from Col. Carmichael: his elder daughter Sally had been born in Clent where he'd been stationed. Two years after joining the City, his name appears in a *Police Gazette* article dated Nov 18th 1876 naming him as Station clerk at Worcester during a nationwide search for Charles Gettiffe or George Gittriss, alias Thomas Graham, wanted on a charge of theft.

Just two days after the funeral, **Arthur Sommers** was in court complaining about the number of loose women accosting respectable men on the bridge and along New Road, and outlining plans to crack down on the nuisance after Jane Partridge had been convicted of indecent conduct in Bromwich-walk. Meanwhile, he also made it clear that his predecessor's personal crusade to clean up the pubs and make their landlords unremittingly toe the line would continue with the same tireless diligence under the new regime: if anything, the list of drunks hauled up before the police court actually stepped up a gear, and the next few weeks also saw a spate of publicans charged with allowing gambling to be conducted on their premises.

Within just a few days too, the new chief himself and a large contingent of officers were brought in to keep crowds from obstructing noted 'pedestrian' Edward Payton Weston on his route to the Public Hall where he would have reached the 4,000-mile mark in a planned 5,000 miles in 100 days walking marathon. He'd walked from Birmingham that morning, leaving at 6.30 and arriving in Worcester at midday, completing the course by several laps of the hall, measured out at 26 laps to the mile, in order to reach the 4,000-mile landmark.

The next week the new chief was presenting a charge of bigamy against 26-year old gloveress Clara Collins. He also reported to the Watch Committee that **PC George Knott** superannuated 24 years before had just died and that the eventual charge to the superannuation fund had totalled £578, and that ex-PC **Herbert Osborne** who had put in 20 years' service, retiring at the end of August 1883 and pensioned at 15s a week, was incapacitated for work and unable to obtain a living. Mayor William Williamson pressed for an increase to £1 as the ever-reliable PC had been injured during the course of his duty, but with obvious predictability, while the Council agreed in principle they trimmed the final award to 18s.

Within a matter of weeks of his promotion, **Arthur Sommers** and his family had moved into the Powers' former residence in Copenhagen Street and almost immediately brought up the issue of the now-vacant role of Inspector: Alderman John Noake suggested that the role – *or more likely the additional expense of the role* – unnecessary, but he was overruled and the Watch Committee selected **Sergeant Thomas Croft**

*Worcester Bridge – favoured pitch of the good-time girls from whom few men were safe*

*'...whose conduct ever since he entered the force had been most meritorious. Chief Constable Sommers stated that there had not been a single complaint against Sergeant Croft for eighteen years. The Mayor considered it highly essential that there should be a second in command in the force. He had known Sergeant Croft a great number of years and had always found him most assiduous and courteous in the discharge of his duties' (Worcester Daily Times).*

A few weeks later, the new Inspector, **Thomas Croft,** 46 and originally from Pirton, moved next door to the chief with his wife Phoebe 50, sons Albert and Herbert, and daughter Rose.

An indication of **Arthur Sommers'** all-out determination to curb street nuisances – or then again perhaps an insight into a darker side of his character – is evident in an order for PCs patrolling High Street to carry canes in order to inflict a sharp deterrent to newspaper boys, shouting and aggressively selling their rival titles of which there were now four: the *Journal*, the *Herald*, the *Worcester Daily Times* and the *Chronicle*. On the first day, a lad called Albert Stevens living in Newport Street had felt the cane across his backside before being brought to the magistrates' court where he was cautioned and dismissed. Noted the *Daily Times* '...since Friday this has had a most wholesome effect'.

In the first week of April, a drunken ex-soldier named George Lampitt, alias Fincher was described by the mayor as 'the most ruffianly blackguard he had ever met with' when he'd laid into PCs (*both later Sergeants*) **No17 Tommy Wallace** and **No25 Edwin Oakey** after they'd alerted him to having dropped a sixpence: '...when he used obscene language. Oakey remonstrated with him about it and both begged of him to go to the place where he was lodging when he turned round and deliberately kicked Oakey on the leg, causing him to fall heavily. Witness (*Tommy Wallace*) caught hold of him and taking him into custody told him he had better go quietly to the station. Prisoner, however, became like a madman, kicked witness three times and Oakey a dozen times. Before they got out of Dolday he threw Oakey down and tried several times to bite witness and his fellow constable and his language was most filthy'.

*PC25 Edwin Oakey severely roughed-up this year (and several others) His police career was to end in controversy. Pps 294-8*

He also kicked off in the station house and threw water over another PC. In court the next day, magistrates saw that Oakey's knee 'was swollen to the size of your hat and it seemed that the knee-cap had been knocked out of place by the violence'. Sentence: one month's hard for d&d and using obscene language in Dolday, and six months' hard for the assault on the constable.

In May, Mayor William Williamson was forced to intervene in a full-blown courtroom row after **Arthur Sommers** had objected to the transfer of the Eagle Vaults licence claiming that the new applicant Joseph Malpas, son of the noted wine and spirit merchant whose name he shared, was a drunk, violent and unfit to hold a licence. The LVA's solicitor Arthur J Beauchamp had instantly complained about the excessive number of decisions being taken on the basis of police observations without being backed up by facts or sworn on oath. Due to the mayor's interference, the application failed, but **Arthur Sommers** had made an enemy of the battling solicitor – who, to make matters even worse, was a city councillor not without some considerable civic influence. Before long, it would escalate into all-out war.

In May, an application to build a stable for the chief's horse and trap in Dolphin Yard, behind the station house, was approved by the Council on condition that its cost did not exceed £20.

In August, a graphic demonstration of how blasé the police had become in matters involving babies and others being dragged out of the Severn or the canal is revealed when the *Journal* ran the report of a young lad, Tommy Walker of Little Park Street, who'd found a brown paper parcel floating in the canal at Three Springs and fished it out:

*'...he undid it and discovered inside the naked body of a newly-born male child, and three half bricks evidently placed with the body for the purpose of sinking it. The lad, having become possessed of this unpleasant burden had some difficulty in disposing of it. He at first took it home and was there naturally told to give up the body to a policeman. He found a constable who directed him to the police-station; at the station he was told to take it to the Coroner's office. One Coroner's officer upon whom he called, was in bed; and at length after transporting*

*the body half round the city, he found another coroner's officer to whom he delivered it. No post-mortem examination of the body has yet been made but it is said to present the appearances of having been in the water about a week and a piece of string is tied to its throat'.*

**Det-Sgt William Underwood** was later revealed as the first officer he met, in Carden Street; the desk sergeant was unidentified but Coroner's officers Broomhall who lived in Friar Street and eventually ex-**Sgt Benjamin Holmes**, were identified and criticised for prolonging the lad's ordeal. It was barely a good reflection on any of the adults in the case, least of all the police, for whom there was worse to come...

## Also this year: 1884

- *police investigate death of Charles Rudge who fell head-first down the cellar steps of the Shades in Mealcheapen Street. Verdict: Accidental death*

- *police investigate two suicides in the same week at the end of March. Daniel Baylis who'd sliced his own throat at his house in Silver Street, and James Bishop found in similar circumstances in Fish Street*

- *police investigate murder of baby girl found to have died by having her nose and mouth blocked by the thumb and forefinger of a person unknown*

- *in May, PC27 Sidnam Cole who was to go on to a 31-year career with the force retiring in 1906, is savagely assaulted and kicked while on the ground by plate worker William Corkendale in the Union Inn in Union Street*

- *Arthur Sommers orders the former city Treasurer Henry George to gaol pending trial after several weeks at home following fears for his health*

- *police called in to investigate after decomposed body of a man who'd been lodging at the Talbot in Sidbury and was known to be 'strange in his habits' is pulled from the Severn at Upton*

- *unnamed PC helps trace the mother of a baby girl found wrapped in cloth in a hedge at Crown East to house-servant at the Pheasant in New Street, 23-year old Mary Ann Grubb*

- *spate of suicides on the railway lines in the summer culminates with Sgt Tommy Tolley attempting to identify a man who'd lain his head across the rails in front of the Malvern to Worcester express at Henwick and was later revealed to be his close neighbour and friend of 15 years, saddler and father of seven, Daniel Williams, 45*

- *in June PC19 Charles Hall is savagely beaten by ex-Watchman's son Leonard Darke, aged 24*

- *confusion over regulations regarding the new trams sparks a rash of police appearances in court – cruelty to horses due to overloaded carriages proving the most common. In one case brought by Inspector Croft, three horses had been pulling a car carrying 60 people up the Bull Ring incline*

- *growing resistance to Salvation Army street 'services' results in an attack on PC27 Sidnam Cole by 36-year old Charles Knight who later claimed to have had his shoulder dislocated and his pockets rifled by the PC. Arthur Sommers refutes the charge while condemning the temperance brigade's lack of consideration for others. In July, the SA Captain himself William Booth and his wife visit Worcester*

PC24 Walter Box

- *Emmanuel Cowley sentenced to three months' hard for assaulting PC24 Walter Box and one month's hard for assaulting landlord Martin Boaz who'd gone to his rescue in a savage fracas in the Nelson in All Hallows*

- *two days later Tommy Wallace is kicked in the head and badly cut, and Detective Underwood kicked and assaulted by two brothers Henry and James Guise in the Boar's Head in Newport Street. Four months' hard apiece*

- *in September PC5 Henry Rogers disarms 32-year old Orangeman named William Jones of a Bulldog revolver and a bowie knife claiming he was awaiting orders for an attack on Roman Catholics and Fenians*

- *confusion in store when two PCs both named John Bishop enrol within fourteen days of each other – No15 on 29th September, No2 on 12th October*

- *police out in force to control the crowds on December 16th when the Prince and Princess of Wales pass through the city on their way to visit the Earl and Countess of Dudley at Witley Court*

At the end of August, **PC Thomas Wilks** who'd only joined the force on April 24th was dismissed for perjury, largely at the insistence of Alderman 'Rambler' John Noake 'who pointed out the absolute necessity for truthfulness on the part of policemen' (*Journal*).

And then the worst of all set-backs:  **PC15 David Taylor** who'd also only joined in April this year was sent to gaol for assault and absconding...

The case arose when the rookie cop failed to report for duty and **Tommy Croft** was sent to his house in St Peters and found the PC gone and his wife quite badly beaten up: nor was it the first time.  When Taylor was eventually tracked down and brought to court, his wife toned-down the scale of the assault and would have dropped the case, but he was gaoled for two months with hard labour, largely for the unforgivable crime of absconding from his post as a police officer.  Life on the inside would not have been easy.

At the end of **Arthur Sommers'** first year as chief of Worcester City Police, it was revealed that average daily occupancy at Worcester Gaol was 131 males and 36 females, with the total for the year amounting to 1,641 males and 341 females.  Earlier in the year, 257 prisoners had been housed there in accommodation built for less than half that number.  During the year, three men had been flogged for prison offences; 147 men and 11 women subjected to 'short commons' or dietary punishment; 162 men and 6 women found guilty of idleness; 318 men and 21 women found guilty of other breaches of regulations; and the total combined offences totted-up to 481 by males and 28 by females.  Over the same period, 224 males and 37 females had already been committed once before; 81 males and 22 females twice before; 59 males and 10 females three times before; 36 males and 11 females four times before; 27 males and 8 females fives times; 28 males and 21 females six or seven times, 20 males and 9 females eight, nine or ten times before, and 43 males and 18 females above ten times.  10 males and four women had received sentences of transportation, and occupation of local prisons under sentence of ordinary courts calculated at 160,836 nationally.

*Gained:* David Taylor, Thomas Wilks (neither of whom out-lasted the year), Walter Parry, William Hobbs, John Hughes, John Bishop (No15), John Bishop (No2), George Hooper, George Haynes, William Footman

*Lost:*  William Stanton, Thomas Andrews, James Quinney, Thomas Caudle, William Henry Lane, George Geary, Henry Rogers

*Worcester Gaol in Salt Lane (now Castle Street) and inset, top, the same view today*

The year got off to a good start and every man in the force was awarded an extra day's pay for his conduct during the royal visit on December 16th – the chief himself coming away with a £5 gratuity.

The new mayor Joseph Sharman Wood '...expressed satisfaction at the admirable way in which he (*Mr Sommers*) carried out the police arrangements. It reflected credit upon him, and it must be exceedingly satisfactory to the citizens to know that they had a head of police who could conduct the matter in the way he had done. Mr Sommers thanked the committee for their kindness, and said the conduct of the police individually on the occasion in question was exemplary. He had no complaint with reference to the conduct of any man'.

But in late February emerged yet more evidence of a darker side to **Arthur Sommers'** character than had been revealed up to then. A crowd had gathered at the Sidbury junction with Bath Road around a young man named George Harrison who'd set up a makeshift telescope and was offering a peep at 'a planet crossing the moon' for a penny. As the gathering of intrigued – and criminally duped – would-be stargazers grew to the point of creating an obstruction, **Arthur Sommers** himself intervened, ordered the crowd to disperse and when told by George Harrison that he had been given permission by the police (*he hadn't*), that give him the right to stand wherever he wanted, for as long as he wanted, and that he would do so, regardless of what the copper said and that he wouldn't move even if asked to by the chief constable himself (*which he had*).

Ordered again to move on by **Arthur Sommers**, who by now had identified himself, Harrison firmly stated that he didn't believe him before launching an all-out attack, egged-on by the increasingly hostile crowd: **Arthur Sommers** later claimed that he'd copped the full weight of the crudely-fashioned telescope – described as 'an unwieldy contrivance chiefly made of tin, blackened on the outside' when it was produced in court – after it had been thrown at him by the charlatan astronomer. He also had his hat knocked off, was punched to the ground and kicked several times while down.

The *Journal* report of the ensuing police court appearance is worth quoting, largely in full:

> '..Defendant: No, no, no. I cannot stand and hear such abominable lies. You took hold of me and smashed my telescope before I could speak. The Clerk: You must not speak now. Defendant: but I cannot stand lies. To the magistrates: He was as drunk as an ass... and the people said so. The Mayor: Our decision is that you are committed to prison for two months with hard labour. We are satisfied as to the sort of man you are by your saying the Chief Constable was drunk. Defendant: the people all said he was, or he would not have acted as he did. The Mayor: Oh, nonsense.
>   Ald Barnett (to the police): Take him away'.

Despite the verdict, the lingering questions remained. Was the chief of police lying? Was he drunk? And if he was either, was he guilty of perjury? Doubts were beginning to emerge.

In May, notorious poacher and hard-man Moses Shrimpton was executed in Worcester Gaol for the murder of 35-year old PC James Davis – the only Worcestershire policeman to be murdered while on active duty. He'd been found with his face and neck violently ripped apart in a country lane near Alvechurch. Hangman James Berry – himself an ex-PC – had conducted the execution but it hadn't gone well: he'd misjudged the length of the drop and Shrimpton was all-but decapitated. When Berry journeyed to Shrub Hill Station for his return home to Yorkshire, the police were called in to disperse crowds hoping for a glimpse of the executioner and the rope he'd used – *already reputed to have been used to hang 20 murderers.*

That same week, the City Council agreed to continue the historic role of High Constable after it had been allowed to lapse for a year.

*Hangman James Berry with 131 executions to his name*

## Doubts emerging about the new chief's sobriety

In June, the Chief Constable's methods and even his sobriety were again brought into question in open court when his determined new adversary, solicitor and town councillor Arthur J. Beauchamp violently opposed a charge of drunkenness the chief had brought against two men, William Coucher and Benjamin Brookes, after an incident in the Reindeer in Mealcheapen Street. Again the Bench took the police's side, but private doubts and rumblings about the chief's personal habits were gathering momentum.

The situation was scarcely helped two weeks later when **Arthur Sommers** and Arthur Beauchamp clashed yet again after the chief had opposed the renewal of Thomas Parton's licence for the Crown in Friar Street on account of his not being in court to support his application: *it transpired he was in another court in Shropshire that day answering charges in a murder case.*

The full 34-strong complement of police was mustered at the rear of the Guildhall for the annual inspection the following month when Colonel Cobbe, official inspector of police for the Midlands district, ruled that the force had emerged with flying colours with the exception of one element: '...upon examination of the uniforms, however, he complained of the material of which the constables' day clothing was made as being of inferior quality considering the price paid for it' (*Journal*).

If Arthur Sommers was beginning to foster a drink problem, he was not the only one...

Drunkenness was also on the up city-wide: at the Brewster Session at the end of August, he'd told the Bench that the year had seen 332 males and 69 females dealt with for offences against the Licensing Act – an increase of 59 over the previous year and 100 over the year before that.

In addition, he said, there were 263 licences in force for the sale of intoxicating liquors in the city, and proceedings had been taken against 17 full-licence holders of which twelve were convicted, compared to five the previous year. Unusually, not a single complaint had been lodged against any of the city's beer houses or off-licences.

The September Watch Committee meeting this year proved an important one in the City police's history as it covered the need for structural re-arrangement and additional manpower in the wake of the extension of the city boundary. **Arthur Sommers** calculated that the force's new duties demanded the addition of two sergeants and six new constables to cover the extensions at Barbourne (*one sergeant and one constable*); Rainbow Hill and Newtown (*two constables*); Red Hill, Cherry Orchard, Diglis and Bath Road (*two constables*); Comer Gardens, Comer Road, Oldbury Road and Hallow Road (*one constable*); Happy Land, McIntyre Road and Bromyard Road, (*one constable*). He also recommended that four of the new recruits should be permanently stationed in houses at Barbourne, Rainbow Hill, London Road and Cherry Orchard, the houses rented by the Watch Committee and the rent repaid by the men occupying them. The Committee agreed.

Then in September, yet another set-back for the chief and even more doubts cast on his judgement – this time involving the military and supported by a letter signed by several influential Worcester businessmen and their companies. Echoing the Malpas case eighteen months earlier, Arthur Sommers had opposed an application by the Star Hotel Company for an extension to permitted hours for the week the officers and men of Worcestershire Yeomanry were in town for training. In his forceful objection, he cited incidents that he alleged had occurred in Foregate Street the previous year that included the military causing such an uproar that up to 3am '...no-one could sleep, that the noise they made might have been heard in Salt-lane (*Castle Street*), and that complaints had been made by the residents' – all of which were strongly denied by nine prominent citizens including Chief Medical Officer for Worcester Dr. William Strange, George Joseland and Sons, outfitters Scott and Oram (*next door to the Star at the former Hop-Pole in what's now an estate agents*) and others living in the immediate vicinity.

They concluded: '...we are not aware that any noise or disturbance took place and we cannot find any complaints have been made by residents near the hotel. In testifying to the general good conduct of the Yeomanry on previous occasions, we regret that the justices did not think it consistent with the resolution of the Licensing Committee to grant the application'.

The following week the festering issue took a turn for the worse when the Worcestershire Yeomanry's Colonel-in-Chief Lord Lyttleton personally wrote to Mayor Joseph Sharman Wood laying charges of misconduct by the police chief against officers of the Regiment. Though the press turned up to the Watch Committee meeting at which it was discussed, they were ordered out of the Committee room while the clearly inflammatory contents of the letter were discussed in private. Its allegations have never been made public.

**Arthur Sommers** was beginning to make enemies of some people he really oughtn't to, and some ominous storm clouds were already gathering. For an increasing number of influential notables, wherever

**Arthur Edwin Sommers** was involved from here on, there was always going to be doubts – clear instances of no smoke without fire...

For Worcester City Police, it had been a year of turmoil and mounting opposition:  17 new officers had been recruited – the majority to replace PCs who had left, disappointed and disillusioned, and concerned glances were beginning to be cast in the new chief's direction.

*Gained: William Thomas Onions, Christopher Hardwick, Stephen Hopley, Richard Harper (none of whom were to out-last the year), Albert Smith, Alfred Oldbury, William Charles Fennell, Thomas Baynham, Walter Pardoe, Howard Cooper, Frederick Cook, Richard Robinson, John Slinn, Charles Wood, Francis John Pitt, David Evans, Thomas William Roseblade*

*Lost: William Underwood, Walter Box, Thomas Wright, William Buswell, George Haynes, William Footman*

## Also this year: 1885

- in March, PC21 Henry Harding only recently promoted to Sergeant, and PC23 George Aston are commended for their prompt actions in putting out a fire at the Fish Inn in Friar Street

- in just his second week with the force – he'd joined 28th March – PC Walter Parry meets his match in 32-year old Marion Price who laid him flat in the Farmers Arms, Bridge Place and it takes two reinforcements to take her to the station-house.  The very next night he's involved in an altercation with violent drunk Albert Godd

- County police slated for failing to instruct its officers in 'ambulance work' after 5-year old Elizabeth Allso is drowned in Gregory's Mill pond

- PC John Hughes takes charge of a pram and two children, abandoned on Pitchcroft after their 14-year old nurse Amy Mason of Portland Street drowns herself in the Severn after a reprimand from the children's mother

- calls to Arthur Sommers to clamp down on growing incidents of men and boys bathing naked in the Severn outraging public decency

- City and County police collaborate in investigation of the murder of a new-born boy, found in a brown paper parcel in a hedge on Ronkswood Hill (now Newtown Road)

- PC27 Sidnam Cole no doubt allows himself a smile as William Corkendale who doled-out a severe beating the previous year had his carotid artery severed in a fight with his brother in law investigated by PC Parry

- PC William Hobbs violently scratched and his thumb almost severed by battling drunk Ann Hodgkins when he attempts to arrest her in Broad Street

- Criminal Law Amendment Act allows police more powers to clamp down on brothels.  PCs Tommy Wallace and Samuel Grosvenor deal with dozens of suspect bawdy houses in the Dolday/Newport Street area

- police brought in to control crowds for the visit of Lord Randolph Churchill in October. 600 people are said to have been on the platform at the Skating Rink in the Arboretum and 3,000 in the body of the rink

The year began with **Sergeant Tommy Wallace** being sent to Liverpool to arrest shady character, 29-year old fish dealer named Arthur Jones on a charge of stealing £130 in gold and silver from china and earthenware dealer Richard Pratley of the Shambles after he'd eloped with the businessman's wife, Margaret.  The following week, yet another child's body is dragged out of the canal at Blockhouse Lock.

More evidence of cracks in the force's structure also emerged in the second week of the year: **PC Charles Smith** had been sacked on the 8th January after just three months' service, and when he met **PC Albert Smith** on his rounds at midnight that same night, he first offered him to join him in a drink and when he refused, verbally abused his former colleague before setting about him, and twice knocking him down, banging his head on the pavement. Fined 10s 6d.  The press had a field-day, and it was just the kind of publicity the police could do without.

There was more of the same in February when **Arthur Sommers** – *increasingly being referred-to as Chief Constable even though his official rank remained Superintendent* – lodged a complaint with the Watch Committee about the behaviour of a businessman named Winsmore Hooper who, he said, had called him

*Time for levity: **PC23 George Aston** (rear) tackles a tricky customer. Seen here with **PC14 George Hill***

a scoundrel and ordered him away while he was making enquiries about policing arrangements at a private ball due to be held in the Guildhall. Asked to offer an official apology for his behaviour, Hooper wrote back denying that anything of the kind had ever taken place, that he had no idea he was addressing the Chief Constable – and anyway, that the Chief Constable's own conduct had been far from acceptable and that it was **Arthur Sommers** who should be offering the apology.

It all fizzled out to nothing, but it was one more black mark against the increasingly erratic officer at the head of the city's police force. Even so, there were some light-hearted moments at the station house, typically this from May this year (*Worcester Chronicle*)

*George Jones (48), tailor, Shrewsbury, a man with a wooden leg, was charged with being drunk, begging alms and assaulting a boy named Warr, on the afternoon of yesterday, in Mill-street. Prisoner went to the house of a man named Warr, in Mill-street, asked Mrs. Warr for a penny, and said he should not go until he had got it. He flourished his stick about and struck her little boy. He was very drunk and used most filthy language. PC Aston* (pictured right at the rear) *was obliged to take him to the station in a wheelbarrow, and, as he would persist in sticking his wooden leg through the spokes of the wheel to stop it, the police officer was obliged to hold it in one hand as well as wheel the barrow. At the station he made such a disturbance that the sergeant in charge was obliged to take his wooden leg away. He was sentenced to one month's imprisonment with hard labour'*

Yet despite growing concerns about the chief's judgement in some matters, there were still some plaudits from official quarters. In July the General Election had been hotly contested in the city and there had been outbreaks of disorder and violence at political rallies with threats and attempts at bribery and coercion at polling stations. But for all that: '...Ald (*Richard Evans*) Barnett said he was glad to testify from his own observation, as well as what he'd been told by a number of gentlemen, to the admirable manner to which the police discharged their duties, and to the forbearance they displayed under very trying circumstances. The thanks of the magistrates were due to Mr. Sommers (Chief Constable) and to the whole of the force' (*Worcester Chronicle*).

The Under Sherriff, Mr Warren Tree, had also written to **Arthur Sommers** thanking him on behalf of the Sherriff for the 'excellent police arrangements' made for keeping order at the polling stations: '...the services rendered by the officers were most efficient, and complete order was maintained at every station' he'd noted. Conservative, brewer George Higginson Allsopp was returned as representative for the City.

In June, a common enough occurrence: hard-case Samuel – aka Nobby – Guy (*next page*) kicked off and was hauled up before the magistrates again, having roughed-up several bobbies along the way. He was to continue in similar vein for the next 40 years.

*Hard-man Samuel (Nobby) Guy was at the height of his pugilistic proclivities – the hapless police only too often the victims of his fearful temper, phenomenal strength...*

A SCENE IN COURT.—Samuel Guy, a well-known character, living in Dolday, was charged with being drunk and riotous and resisting and assaulting the police in the execution of their duty, last night, in Dolday. P.C. Cook and P.C. Hughes gave evidence. Prisoner, who appeared very excitable, asked Hughes some questions, and then shouted, "I will pay you out when I come out. I don't care if I get twelve ——— years. I be'ant a thief or a rogue or a vagabond. I'm an old Indian soldier, and it will take the whole police-station to take me If I don't care to let them." The Mayor: You have heard the evidence. What have you to say in defence? Prisoner: I was'nt drunk. I know no more. Chief Constable Sommers said that when he was sober the prisoner was quiet enough, but when drunk he was very violent, and, as he said, very difficult to take to the police station. His clothes always gave way and it was very difficult to hold him. The Mayor recommended prisoner to become abstainer. He was sentenced to three months' labour.

*... and pathological dislike. More bruising tales about one of the city's hardest hard men and scourge of the PCs, p.366*

The same week, a shocking picture of life in the Blockhouse emerged after former PC21, now **Sergeant, Henry Harding** was tipped-off about the plight of six children living with their drunken father in vile conditions in Four-Foot Way, Waterloo Street. Inside the hovel, he and **PC13 William James** found the father, 39-year old riveter Walter Poole:

> '...drunk on a feather bed in the first room. There was a blanket on the prisoner marked 'St Paul's Parish'. (Harding) then went upstairs and found five children lying on heaps of rags. They were in a very dirty state. Tied to a square post, standing in a recess... he saw the boy Walter, aged 8. He was tied around the middle and his feet only just touched the ground, not sufficiently for him to bear the weight of his body on. He had to lean his chest against the sharp edges of the post to rest himself. He said he had been tied there ever since Friday [the bobbies had forced their entry at 11.20pm on Sunday] and he had had nothing to eat except some dry toast yesterday. His ribs were bare; his back was severely bruised down to the buttocks (all) probably caused by thrashing. The knot at the end of the rope produced would cause such bruises. It was evident that the boy had been subjected to great cruelty' (Herald)

It later emerged that Walter Poole Snr regularly tied up his children for a thrashing and that his wife was absent as she was in the Infirmary after he'd given her another good hiding a few days earlier. Six months' gaol. The *Herald* sourly noted: '...when the prisoner was removed from the station-house to the gaol, between four and five o'clock in the afternoon, he was followed by a crowd of people who vigorously hissed and booed him'.

Colonel Cobbe's inspection this year also proved a mirror image of the previous year's...

The entire 42-strong force – now consisting of the Chief Constable, one inspector (*Tommy Croft, 25 years into his service [of 30]*), seven sergeants and 33 constables – police books and cells all again came out with flying colours. The only aspect considered under-par was 'the fit of the clothing'. Possibly it was an indication of the lowering standards all round, but such an observation would never have happened in Matthew Power's day.

At this time too, the mayor Ambrose William Knott who was no great fan of **Arthur Sommers**, ordered – *not requested, but physically ordered* – the police chief to wear his uniform when he was in the presence of the Bench. Even the generally easy-going *Chronicle* professed itself surprised by the edict pointing out that ultra-smart Matthew Power had always attended court *in ordinary dress* and that **Arthur Sommers** was naturally following his example: '...it would be absurd to suggest that the Chief Constable's modest uniform invests the court with additional splendour or reflects new dignity and importance on the administration of justice. Mr Sommers' official dress is of a suitable and serviceable description but by no stretch of the imagination can it be described as brilliant or imposing' ran its outraged editorial.

The mayor's stance was more likely a case of the growing number of antis on the Town Council making it clear to the chief that 'we've got our eyes on you, mate'.

At the annual Licensing Day (Brewster) session, the no doubt uniformed **Arthur Sommers** presented his report – and it proved unique in the entire annals of licensing in the city: n*ot a single complaint to make against any of Worcester's 288 licensees, nor had any one been proceeded against during the course of the year.*

The report was even more remarkable as 10 full licensed houses and 16 beer, cider and perry 'on' licenses had been added to the tally with the new extended boundaries. Even offences against the Licensing Act – drunkenness, refusing to quit etc – were 161 down on the previous year, and Arthur Sommers' friend and patient supporter Ald Richard Barrett pointed out that '...the fact that there had been no complaint against a licence was not owing to inactivity on the part of the Chief Constable. The magistrates knew he discharged his duties very carefully, and was very attentive and painstaking'.

The rosy picture painted on the state of the city's pubs was not echoed, however, in Sommers' report on overall crime in the City for the year to September. During that time 1,080 people – 880 males and 200 females – had been dealt with summarily by the justices, 222 up on the previous year. 612 had been fined, 142 committed to prison without a fine, 10 had been bound in recognizances to keep the peace, 5 boys had been whipped for petty larceny, and 6 deserters had been handed back to the military. The chief also presented his forecast of the cost of running the force for the forthcoming year: £3,373 14s. The current year's budget was £3,130 2s 5d.

**Arthur Sommers**' heavy clamp-down on drunkenness was not only confined to the city's general hoi-polloi – it also extended to his men, as he made clear at a notable and extensively-reported event in September. According to the *Chronicle*, he commented that to his knowledge '...many a young man in the force (has) gone wrong in consequence of there being no convenient place in which they could spend their leisure hours. They sometimes went into public houses and emerged three-parts drunk, and were brought to the station drunk, a disgrace to themselves and the force'.

It was an amazing admission, but it was made at an event geared towards lessening the temptations placed before his officers and, it's a fair assumption, the first of its kind within any police force: the opening of a self-funded institute exclusively for the use of the city's policemen...

The forerunner of what was to become the police club, the Institute – paid for by charging its members $1 \frac{1}{2}$d a week – was also in Copenhagen Street, and it was largely on the initiative of the chief himself that it came about at all. Supported by the Dean and other well-wishers, although significantly *not* by the corporation '...it will be open at all reasonable times for members of the force when not on duty, to hold Bible classes and for the general welfare of the police, both spiritual and temporal. The Dean has furnished the room, and dominoes, chess, draughts and other games have been provided. Friends have given books... and the Institute will supply means for friendly chat and social pipe (*and*) a place where young members of the Force, desiring so to do, may get instruction of every day utility'.

The *Chronicle* made no reference to alcohol being available – suggesting it was not – although it noted that all 41 police officers had joined.

On the same day, **PC William Henry Hughes** who was only to last six months with the force (*March to September this year*) and **PC John Henry Hazleton** whose police career proved rather longer (*15th September 1881 to 30th January 1903*) both came away severely battered after a fracas involving 19-year old gipsy John Smith and fitter George Moran had erupted in the Market Hall Vaults (*now Costa Coffee*) in the Shambles that had already won the reputation of being the most volatile pub in town. The PCs' injuries were such that Smith was sentenced to a month and Moran to six weeks' hard labour.

*(Left) PC21, later Sergeant Henry Harding who investigated a shocking case of child cruelty in the Blockhouse this year*

The year was shaping up as another appalling one for assaults on the police – a particularly vicious attack by two Evesham men, Samuel Haynes and Edwin Rock on **PC John Slinn** in the shadow of Edgar Tower being given the full graphic treatment that included phrases like:

> '...(he) was tripped up and greatly knocked about'; 'Haynes pulled out a razor'; 'Rock took witness' staff from his pocket and struck at witness with it, but instead hit Haynes over the eye. Rock then kicked witness for about five minutes'.

What might have resulted in a murder charge was only averted when another PC, **Hale** (*although more likely to be* No19, **Charles Hall** *17th March 1883 – 28th February 1896*) appeared on the scene: Rock bolted but Haynes was held and was later found to have had a string of convictions for assaults on the police. Slinn and Hall then had the pleasure of travelling to Evesham to arrest Rock – held in the town after an appeal to the County force – and escort him back for charging and trial in Worcester. Both prisoners were sentenced to four months' hard for the attack.

### Another year of disgrace for assaults on the police

Just a week later, **PC William Charles Fennel** (*8th July 1875 – 21st July 1911*) had three fingers almost severed in a fight with Henry Brace of Mayfield Road who also attacked **PC17 Thomas Baynham** inside the station-house. 28 days' hard. The following week, **PC5 William Fennell** was again severely kicked, this time by labourer Edwin Robinson in Friar Street.

The Mayor's celebratory dinner for the police at the end of the year at the Golden Lion in High Street was now a looked-forward-to event, and this year's proved no exception – except that the mayor, Ambrose Knott whose tenure of office was to end the following week to be picked up by Walter Holland, handed over the duties to the Sherriff, Alderman Birley. The implication is that it, like the council's reluctance to be involved in the police Institute, was another deliberate snub to the out-of-favour **Arthur Sommers**.

That said, Sherriff Birley stepped manfully into the breach paying fulsome, if perhaps uncharacteristically muted, tribute to the force and describing them as '...as good and able men as can be found in any corporation in the kingdom'. He also remarked on the continuing good relationship between the city and its county counterparts and stated that he had always found (the men) '...in their places when they were wanted in times of great excitement, and he was pleased to think that they succeeded so well in doing their duty'. Containing telling phrases including *hopes to* increase the popularity and efficiency of the force – clearly implying all was not well – the *Chronicle*'s report notably lacked the all-out enthusiasm that had marked those of previous years.

*Gained: Frank Petty, William Andrews, William Henry Hughes (who were not to out-last the year), George Langstone, Edwin Biddle, Henry Layton*

*Lost: Albert Smith, Alfred Oldbury, Howard Cooper, Charles Wood, Thomas Roseblade*

## Also this year: 1886

■ *in February, PC John Bishop (the Worcester Chronicle is unclear whether No15 or No2 both of whom had joined in the autumn of 1884) is paid 5s and commended for his outstanding courage in separating two dogs in an organised dog-fighting ring*

■ *increasing bouts of violence at closing time in the new patrol of St Johns, forces Arthur Sommers to double police presence in the patch at night*

■ *PC John Glinn (a mis-transcription of Slinn who'd joined the force in September the previous year as part of the intake for the enlarged city and would serve until forced to resign in May next year) is 'kicked, assaulted and bespattered with mud' by hawkers Edward Smith (fined 5s) and James Clavins (seven days' imprisonment)*

■ *in August officers seal the entrance to the Market Hall and accompany John Smith, Inspector of Weights and Measures in a snap raid on vendors selling butter under weight. Nine offenders are proceeded against*

■ *Arthur Sommers leads investigation into a bare-knuckle fighting ring operating above a Bridge Street hairdressers. It was only discovered when they were called in to quell a fight that had broken out among spectators*

■ *more complaints about police failure to crack down on 'loungers' in the High Street impeding free movement*

■ *Chronicle columnist 'Citizen' graphically describes an incident in High Street involving a horse kicking a furniture van and taking 'six policemen and the car-men who were wrestling and struggling with the horse'*

■ *on December 28th Sgt Tommy Wallace orders the filling of Sidbury lock in order to recover the body of drowned lock-keeper George Stanton*

The new mayor Walter Holland appears to have been more impressed by **Arthur Sommers'** performance than his predecessor Ambrose Knott, as in a surprise move at the end of January, he put forward a motion to increase the chief's salary and incredibly, it was approved – although the increase, to £240 year plus free rent of his house, was not necessarily out of the goodness of the councillors' hearts.  It was based on a recommendation from HM's Inspector of Police, Col. Cobbe who'd bluntly informed the corporation that the head of the force was worth more than they were paying him.  Par for the course, ex-Mayor Ambrose Knott had voted against the increase and had tried to get other councillors to do the same.

It's possible that Walter Holland's faith in the force was vindicated the following month when, in line with the ages-old tradition – and for only the third time in more than 40 years – he was presented with a pair of white kid gloves on the occasion of not a single case being brought before the Police court.  That it was a Monday made the event even more remarkable:

> '...Ald Barnett said it was a matter of congratulation for the city that there should be no business before them... for usually on a Monday morning there was a great deal of business.  It spoke well for the behaviour of the citizens of Worcester.  He (mayor Walter Holland) was sure that if there had been any offence committed in the city it would not have escaped the police'.

Col Cobbe's inspection in February revealed that though manpower had grown to 42 – a ratio of 1:960 of the population, or 1:76 acres – four officers had left, eleven had joined, and the city had failed to implement his recommendation for nine sergeants, still standing at seven.  He also noted that the cells and offices were very clean and in good order but that 'uniforms were not as well made as they should be although the prices were reasonable'.  He noted too that the Detective officer (**Det Sgt William Preece**) was paid an additional £6 a year for clothing.

In April, the City lost one of its most enduring and prominent officers, **Sgt Thomas Tolley**.  He'd been with the force since 21st November 1862 and died, still serving, a few months short of clocking up 25 years. The *Worcester Advertiser* wrote: '...the city has been deprived of one of its most valued officers and the members of the force a true friend, whose memory will be long cherished among them, and whose exemplary conduct will doubtless act as an incentive to his comrades, who cannot do better than emulate him in the discharge of those duties they are called on to perform'.

He'd left a widow and six children, four of whom were still dependent, and while the Watch Committee voted to continue paying her husband's salary for a year (£81 9s 4d), mayor Walter Holland proposed raising it to £100 and as a mark of the genuine respect felt for the ever-reliable ex-bobby, the motion was carried unanimously.  *More on Tommy Tolley, p358.*

**PC Francis Eli Brotherton** was promoted sergeant in his place and was to go on to serve more than thirty years, retiring as Inspector in 1904.

It appears that the police in general and **Arthur Sommers** in particular had regained some of the PR ground lost over the previous months as the *Advertiser* grasped the opportunity of **Tolley**'s passing and **Brotherton**'s promotion to print a glowing editorial, demonstrating its stance as firmly in support of both. Its editor stated:

*'...I am glad to learn, on the highest authority, that this very fine body of men bear very favourable comparison with any force in the kingdom, not only in appearance, but also in discipline and efficiency. Time was when it was the rule, and not the exception, for members of the force to be constantly before the Watch Committee for some breach of discipline or neglect of duty. That order of things is now reversed and the Chief Constable now finds himself in the proud position of commanding a body of men that is now so well disciplined that there is absolutely no ground for complaint against any of them. Much of this is no doubt due to the energy and tact of Chief Constable SOMMERS (their caps) who has the faculty of tempering firmness with kindness'.*

For all the media support, the festering Sommers/Beauchamp animosity again flared-up in court in May when the chief supported one of the two **PCs John Bishop** (*it's not made clear which*) who'd been accused of, and summoned for, some rough handling of a cyclist he'd alleged had been riding on the Cross at 10pm without lights. When Charles John Noke of Red Hill found out that **PC Bishop** had reported him and was planning to press the charge, he instantly countered by laying a charge of assault against his accuser claiming he'd been thrown off his bicycle, and instantly employed Arthur Beauchamp to defend him.

Despite the prosecution's combined courtroom testimonies of **PCs Bishop, No17 Thomas Baynham, No18 James Richardson and Arthur Sommers,** the vitriol hurled around the police court resulted in both sides dropping the charges after the poison-tongued solicitor had rubbished both the 'vindictive' police and the unreasonable by-law.

More charges of police brutality arose the following week when Eliza Roberts claimed that a drunken PC had wrenched her arm rendering her incapable of work. Investigations showed that **John Slinn** who'd already shown himself a promising officer had intervened in a Salvation Army meeting that was getting out of hand and when pressed about the incident, admitted that he had used some force against the woman

*Matthew Power's long-standing legacy: officers of Worcester City Police never cut less than an impressive figure when on duty. Unidentified constable on The Cross, c. this year, 1887  CCMH/CFoW*

who was being abusive, and had pushed her in the road: *but then he also owned-up that his actions could well have been caused by some over-indulgence in drink, having met some friends just before going on duty.*

  Permitted to resign rather than be dismissed for drunkenness and rough handling, and thus create a bad impression on the city council, he took that course and instantly joined the Army.

  But despite his gesture, still complaints about the police continued...

  A charge of misconduct against **Inspector Tommy Croft** and (*unnamed PC32*) came up before the Watch Committee on August 20th. Two weeks earlier, commercial traveller Edward Duncan had called into the station-house to lodge a formal complaint against **PC32** for cruelty to a militiaman in his custody. The *Journal* picks up the tale:

> *'...when he informed Inspector Croft of his intention, the inspector, it was alleged, called Mr Duncan a "d----- cad" and threatened that he should be "chucked out". Mr Duncan maintained his statement before the committee; but on the other hand, Inspector Croft and six constables who were present at the time, denied that any such expressions were used. The committee came to the conclusion that Mr Duncan, though actuated by public spirit in preferring the charge, was mistaken and dismissed it'.*

  At the Brewster Sessions, for the second year in a row, there was no complaint laid against any of the city's 287 licensed premises, while only 155 persons out of a population of 42,000 had been charged with offences under the Licensing Act. That said, the picture may not have been quite so rosy as it had been painted:, 108 charges had additionally been brought against 'strangers to the city'.

  Similarly, crime statistics overall for the city showed a small decrease in crime over the previous year, prompting gratification and congratulations from the Mayor. There was also further celebrations at the Guildhall when **Arthur Sommers'** proposed budget for the up-coming year proved to be £104 less than in

*The same view today
(Pic: Amy Bartholomew,
CSM, Nationwide Building Society, Worcester)*

1886: £3,319 4s 8d compared to £3,423 0s 1d.

In all, it had been a far more satisfactory year for the police and for the city as a whole than some previous years.

As commentator Crowquill in the *Journal* summed up the year in its final 1887 edition: '

*...Worcester does not advance by great bounds as some manufacturing towns have done. But it has a wealth of associations, a lustre of tradition... a worthy public spirit and has its part in manufacturing enterprise and especially in artistic work. Its productions go to all parts of the civilised world. It is justly proud of a long history. It need not be in any way ashamed of its recent past. It looks forward hopefully; and I trust that at the end of 1888 I may be able to join in general congratulations on a year of more flourishing trade – manufacturing and retail – than the city has known during the past ten years'.*

**Gained:** John Darley (who was to quit six months later), Frederick John Hawker, William Roberts, John Wilkes

**Lost:** William Hobbs, John Slinn

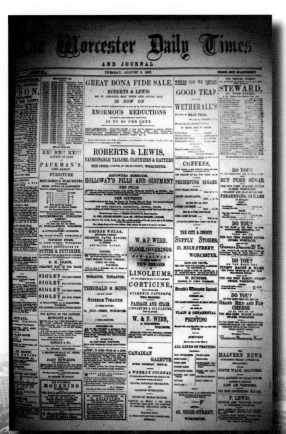

■ on January 7th., PC David Evans investigates shooting in Thorneloe Walk

■ a Liberal soirée at the Public Hall is branded by Arthur Sommers as 'the greatest scandal in the city for some time' when he told the magistrates court that drink was sold indiscriminately, resulting in an unacceptable number of rowdies and d&ds

■ on consecutive days in March, one of the two PCs John Bishop that had been recruited in the autumn of 1884 was kicked and bitten by 'tramp' Mary Baker, and PCs David Evans and John Henry Hazleton were kicked and generally roughed-up by shoemaker James Ball in a very public mêlée in Angel Street surrounded by a hundred onlookers

■ police investigate suicide of Charles Rossiter who'd strangled himself in Worcester Gaol after being convicted of passing base coin

■ police out in force for the three days of celebrations of the Queen's Jubilee on 24th-26th June. The court is jammed with dozens of celebrants charged with d&d and sundry other offences, including assaults on the police

■ in mid-April Arthur Sommers investigates indecent assault of 6-year old Annie Adams by 52-year old George Chapman, Sgt-Maj of the 3rd Battalion Worcestershire Regiment

■ after police investigate a spate of indecent exposure claims levelled at cabmen waiting near the theatre in Angel Street – fines generally 2s 6d plus costs – the corporation is compelled to look for suitable premises 'to provide a proper place of convenience in the vicinity of the theatre'

■ at the end of October, city police liaise with London Police in serving a writ on General William Booth of the Salvation Army for non-payment of £2 18s 8d general rate and 9s 2d water rate in respect of the citadel in Lowesmoor. An order was made for payment in seven days

■ police bring action against Worcester's Medical Officer of Health Dr Strange for false imprisonment of one of his servants who he'd charged with false pretences

■ Christmas proves particularly disorderly with a heavy spate of disorder and assaults

Issues raised about the quality of police uniforms prompted a switch in policy when tenders were sought out of town for the first time. The winning supplier proved to be Dolan and Co of Bond Street in London whose quote for '39 suits of clothing, each suit consisting of a tunic at £1 6s., a pair of day trousers 16s 4d., pair night trousers 14s' surprisingly proved the lowest. Additionally, local firms Butler and Co won the contract to supply 82 pairs of white Berlin gloves at 8d a pair; A J Wilkes for 40 caps at 5s 9d each, and Noakes of St Swithin's Street 82 pairs of boots at 14s 6d a pair.

*PC13 William James, promoted sergeant this year*

**Arthur Sommers** also underlined his good standing with the local press when he was a guest at a lively and apparently musical Press Dinner at the Unicorn and was one of several speech-makers at the event.

The following day, two boys William Bird (9) and Alfred Baddley (8) were submitted to the full court procedure for causing an annoyance in New Street. They were discharged on promising to take care not to annoy people when playing.

In the wake of not always favourable publicity, the police were becoming overly cautious about lapses of standards, and something of the sensitivity to their perceived image – or then again, rabid over-zealousness – is revealed early in the year when newly-promoted **Sergeant (*originally PC11*) Sam Grosvenor** spotted recently-appointed (*February 1886*) **PC Frank Petty** emerge from a side door of the King William IV Vaults in the Blockhouse and instantly marched him back to the station-house for questioning about drinking while on duty. It later emerged that he'd been called in by the landlord James Uncles to investigate a theft of some property and had not been given anything to drink. Even so, rather than lose face, Uncles was charged with harbouring a policeman while he should have been on duty and fined 10s with 13s costs. **Petty** survived until 1893.

The next week a cabman, John Sefton, found himself facing the full force of the law – and **Sgt Tommy Wallace** – for the apparently paltry 'crime' of neglecting to hand over within the specified time a parcel (*as it transpired, of cigars*) left in his cab. Fined 5s.

*Then in March, more embarrassment for the city caused by its wayward police chief...*

A strike by workers F. W. Willis' shoe factory had divided friends that had been workmates for years, and a spate of violence against non-strikers had prompted police action that had additionally sparked-off more angry scenes of violence at picket lines. Enter Henry Broadhurst MP, Secretary of the Trades Union Congress Parliamentary Committee who now penned a vicious letter to the corporation accusing the police chief of strong-arm tactics and of overstepping the bounds of his duty when called in to deal with striking workers. Already an unpleasant situation, Town Clerk Samuel Southall had unwittingly made the situation even worse when he responded by saying that the Chief Constable had acted on his own responsibility in the action he took. It served only to inflame MP Broadhurst even further, prompting his reply to the effect that he took that to imply Council-wide disapproval 'of the extraordinary action taken by the Chief Constable'. Now the entire Council was obliged to take sides in the tussle.

That same week **PC13 William James** (*pictured above*), now in his eighteenth year with the force, was promoted to sergeant and **PCs16 Henry Harley** and **27 Sidnam Cole** raised to merit class after serving eleven years apiece.

Then in April the suspicious death of a prominent Worcester publican enthralled Worcester readers for weeks – not least as it involved salacious tales of his unfaithful wife and her assumed lover...

## White Hart landlord's murder by wife and her alleged lover enthrals the City for weeks

### BERROW'S WORCESTER

#### CURIOUS DEATH OF A WORCESTER INNKEEPER.

##### THE INQUEST : REMARKABLE EVIDENCE.

An inquest was held on Friday afternoon at the Guildhall, Worcester, before Mr. Hulme, Deputy Coroner, touching the death of Henry Powell (52), who was landlord of the Golden Hart, Sansome-street. Deceased died under rather peculiar circumstances. A few months ago he insured his life for £200 in favour of his wife. He then seemed in perfect health, but in a few weeks' time took to his bed for no serious malady that the doctor who was called in could discover. He was seen only two or three times by a medical man, and died this week without having had, since February 14th, any further advice. A certificate of death was under these very peculiar circumstances refused, and an inquest was accordingly ordered.

Mr. Sommers (chief of the police) was present to watch the proceedings.

Mr. Corder, surgeon, Foregate-street, said about nine weeks ago he was called in to attend deceased, who was then suffering from bronchitis. He saw him two or three times subsequently, and on the 14th February he saw him for the last time. He was then convalescent, and seemed in fairly good health. He did not examine him very minutely ; but found nothing more the matter with him than bronchitis and an enlarged liver.

The Coroner : Did you say at that time that he could not possibly recover ?

Witness : No ; I told him to get up and not lie in bed. There was every probability of his recovery. Witness, continuing, said he did not see deceased again. Deceased belonged to a society for which witness was surgeon, and if he had needed witness's advice witness would have been ready to go.

The Coroner : Has any reason been given to you by anyone for your not being called in ?

Witness : The only reason given was that they did not want to trouble the doctor at Easter time.

The Coroner : Who said that ?

Witness : His wife.

The Coroner : Since his death ?

Witness : Yes.

*How Berrow's Journal broke the news (above) and right, the Golden Hart today (2016)*

At 8.50am on Easter Tuesday (*April 3rd*) Henry Powell, 51-year old landlord of the White Hart in Sansome Street died in his bed, not having set foot outside the house since Christmas. He'd been a Staff-Sergeant in the Worcestershire Militia with exemplary service in India, the Cape, Ireland and at home, and had been at the White Hart for a little over three years, having previously run a tobacconists' shop in St Johns and later in New Street with his wife, Devon lass Mary Eleanor, known as 'Nellie'. She was 32 at the time.

His body showed signs of narcotic poisoning, and assiduous sleuthing by **Det-Sergeant William Preece** revealed that his wife had assured his life with the Refuge Insurance Company first for £100 then for £200 – both without his knowledge and with a signature so badly forged that comparisons were later described in court as being 'as different as light and darkness'.

Further investigation revealed that Mary Eleanor had also bribed an insurance official to pass her invalid husband as A1 fit without even seeing him, and that she was the sole beneficiary of his will.

As even more incriminating facts emerged, a man who'd been tending Powell in the three days that he'd suddenly taken for the worse and subsequently died (*while Nellie Powell remained in bed, unwilling to attend to her husband*) was immediately suspected of having also been deeply implicated in what was by now becoming viewed as an open-and-shut case of wilful murder. This was James Henry Keatley 32,

an out-of-work hairdresser and known child molester, living in Bowling Green Terrace until three days before Powell's death when, at Nellie's instigation, he'd moved into the White Hart.  That he was unpaid for his services both as barman and carer heightened talk that he was having an affair with Nellie Powell, but despite the continuing rumours, nothing more of that nature subsequently emerged although several local chemists all testified to selling draughts of laudanum and opium to Keatley who'd claimed they were to relieve an abscess from which he was suffering.  **DS Preece** and his team had amassed a wealth of circumstantial evidence against the pair and 20-year old barmaid in her first job, Helen Humphries, but throughout the police court hearing on April 9th Keatley and Mary Eleanor steadfastly maintained their silence, although at one point the magistrates had had to halt the proceedings as Keatley was giving his two co-accused signals across the court-room.

With evidence now mounting against them, all three were arrested and committed for trial.  According to the *Berrows Journal*, at the Committal hearing, a huge crowd had gathered outside the Guildhall an hour before the trial, with '...hundreds within and without.  The girl Helen Humphries was but little affected.  Mrs. Powell on the other hand was sobbing as she was placed in the dock and continued to do so during the few minutes the proceedings occupied.  When the charge of murder was formally read over to her by the Clerk, she exclaimed "Oh, no sir; oh!" and on leaving the dock after the remand she had to be supported by policemen'.

Keatley was not in court that day:  he was still in gaol where he was just days into a 16-month sentence with hard labour for another indecent assault against a young girl – this time, 11-year old Florence Mason of Portland Street, committed by the steps to the cathedral ferry just two weeks earlier.  He claimed he'd assaulted her so as to be '...sent down so that I may get the Prisoners Aid Society to send me out of the country'.

At the 9-hour committal hearing, charges against Helen Humphries were dropped, but Mary Eleanor Powell and James Keatley were both formally charged with murder.

Before a packed court in the Shirehall in the first week of July before Mr Justice Denman, Nellie Powell kept her widow's veil over her face and Keatley wore spectacles 'to which it was obvious from the way he carried his head, he was unaccustomed' as well as his prison uniform.  The trial lasted 2½ days during which 45 witnesses were called. The judge's summing-up on the fourth day lasted 3½ hours and the jury was out for 35 minutes.

> The Clerk: "Do you find the prisoner Mary Eleanor Powell guilty of murder?"
> The Foreman: "Not Guilty"
> The Clerk: "Do you find the prisoner James Henry Keatley guilty of murder?"
> The Foreman: "Not Guilty"
> The  Clerk : "Do you find Mary Eleanor Powell guilty of anything?"
> The Foreman: "Guilty of manslaughter "
> The Clerk: "Do you find James Henry Keatley guilty of manslaughter?"
> The Foreman: "Guilty"

They were both sentenced to 12 years, and **Arthur Sommers** later received a letter from the Home Office approving of his and his force's actions in the conduct of the case.

In May, **Sergeant (*formerly PC07 and later Inspector*) Henry Joyner** was called in to investigate the decomposed body of a child that had been found at Foregate Street station after 19-year old parcels porter Richard Boulter of Southfield Street had noticed '...a peculiarly revolting odour among the parcels there'.

The 3-day old boy it contained had been strangled and had his skull smashed; the body had been tightly sewn up with linen, then wrapped in a newspaper dated March 25th and enclosed in a cardboard box which had been wrapped in some coarse packing material, tied round with string and addressed to 'Mr Green, Foregate-street Station Worcester, to be called for".  As the *Herald* sourly noted: 'the carriage of the parcel had not been paid', nor had anyone made any enquiries of it. **Sgt. Joyner** had traced the parcel to Reading, but despite **Arthur Sommers** visiting the police there, nothing further was revealed and on

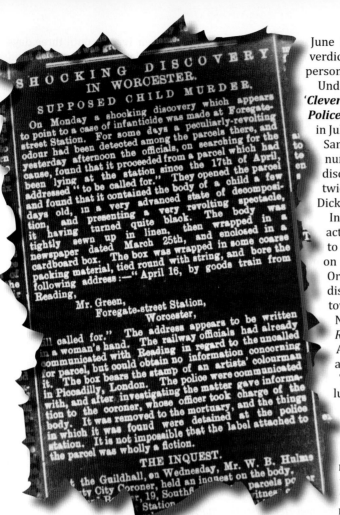

SHOCKING DISCOVERY
IN WORCESTER.
SUPPOSED CHILD MURDER.

On Monday a shocking discovery which appears to point to a case of infanticide was made at Foregate-street Station. For some days a peculiarly-revolting odour had been detected among the parcels there, and yesterday afternoon the officials, on searching for the cause, found that it proceeded from a parcel which had been lying at the station since the 17th of April, addressed "to be called for." They opened the parcel and found that it contained the body of a child a few days old, in a very advanced state of decomposition, and presenting a very revolting spectacle, it having turned quite black. The body was tightly sewn up in linen, then wrapped in a newspaper dated March 25th, and enclosed in a cardboard box. The box was wrapped in some coarse packing material, tied round with string, and bore the following address :—"April 16, by goods train from Reading,

                    Mr. Green,
              Foregate-street Station,
                    Worcester,

ill called for." The address appears to be written in a woman's hand. The railway officials had already communicated with Reading in regard to the uncalled for parcel, but could obtain no information concerning it. The box bears the stamp of an artists' colourman in Piccadilly, London. The police were communicated with, and after investigating the matter gave information to the coroner, whose officer took charge of the body. It was removed to the mortuary, and the things in which it was found were detained at the police station. It is not impossible that the label attached to the parcel was wholly a fiction.

                THE INQUEST.
    the Guildhall, on Wednesday, Mr. W. B. Hulme
    City Coroner, held an inquest on the body.
    ... r, 19, South...           parcels po    r
    ... Station                          itne...

June 13th the jury at the Guildhall returned a verdict of wilful murder against some person or persons unknown.

Under the *Journal*'s complimentary headline *'Clever Arrest of a Burglar by the Worcester Police'*, **PS Tommy Wallace** came in for praise in July for the pursuit and arrest of watch thief Samuel Edwards. Liaising with his opposite number in Cardiff, **Arthur Sommers** later discovered the same man had been convicted twice before under the name of Charles Dickens.

In August, **PC David Evans** took immediate action after baker Harry Hughes brought to the station-house a coat and hat found on railings at the bottom of Severn Street. Ordering the river to be dragged, he discovered the body of noted drunk-about-town and three-times married Joseph Noake of 7, Lower Bath Road (*now Diglis Road*) employed as brewer at the nearby Albion, Crown & Anchor in Silver Street, and the Crown in Droitwich Road.

The same *Herald* edition also carried lurid tales of a series of gruesome murders of prostitutes in London's Whitechapel, ripped apart by what the local press was already describing as 'a serial maniac'. The following week a fourth mutilated body, that of Annie Chapman, was discovered in Hanbury Street. Over the following weeks, details of three more gory Whitechapel murders were graphically outlined in all the local newspapers – not, of course, that Worcester was in any way lacking in lurid news stories of its own....

The year ended much as it had begun – on the subject of uniforms, with the contract being renewed with all the previous firms plus a few additions: tunic, two pairs of trousers and greatcoat for the inspector (*Tommy Croft*) £5 10s, and a suit of clothing for the chief constable consisting of a braided patrol jacket £2 10s, pair of trousers with braided side seams at £1 3s and a greatcoat £2 15s. There were two voices of dissent at the contract going to a London firm – particularly in the light of claims that the uniforms were made in East End 'sweat-shops' – the term in use even then – employing children on starvation wages, but the tenders were approved amid '...great satisfaction given by the clothing supplied by the same firm (Dolan's) and to its marked superiority to that previously made by local tradesmen'.

On the last day of the year, hard-case, wife-beater, general layabout and all-round nuisance Tommy Link made his 50th appearance in the police court charged yet again with being drunk and riotous in Dolday (£2 fine), savagely assaulting **PC Edwin Oakey** (*pictured right*) in the station house 'with a tremendous blow in the face' (£5 fine) and made to pay for smashing the cell window with one of his shoes, as witnessed by **Sgt (*later Inspector*) Henry Joyner**. Total £7 7s or two months' hard. *More p366.*

*Gained: George Bullock (he was to last just two months), Frederick William Peacock, Joseph Williams, John Hall, Alonzo Stone, Walter Foxhall, Richard James Glover. Lost: Henry Harding, Thomas Booth, James Richardson, Walter Pardoe, Henry Layton, John Wilkes*

- police called in to control crowds queuing at the Public Hall to see the Royal American Midgets, 22-inch General Mite and his wife Mrs Mite weighing 7lbs and an inch taller than her husband

- in April PCs Cole and Parry discover the body of gardener Tom Parker (21) in a burned-out building at Smith's Nurseries off Bransford Road

- Mayor Herbert Caldicott shows himself something of a wag when sentencing John Pritchard for theft. When told by the defendant 'I promise never to come before you again', he replied 'I promise you you won't for a month at any rate' before sending him down to a month's hard

- attempted murder suspected when 86-year old Sarah Holder is found in Fish Street having allegedly fallen 20 feet from a bedroom window

- in July PC16 Henry Harley is savagely kicked about the legs and otherwise severely beaten up by ex-soldier John Hobson of Severn Street in his third attack on police officers since his Army discharge two years earlier. One month's hard

- the same day, PCs 22 Francis Brotherton and John Bishop (either 2 or 15) are verbally abused ("you dirty blackguard" was one of the shocking phrases alleged) and set on by drunken sweep

William Francis Whitehouse, now answering his 38th similar charge. Fourteen days' hard without the option of a fine

- in court, Arthur Sommers clashes with the prison surgeon George Hyde who'd overturned his observation that 24-year old Ada Poynter, charged with using obscene language at Barbourne, was insane and thus not responsible for her actions, but that the doctor's diagnosis was that she was 'all right'

- police called in to Gale's booksellers in Foregate Street after complaints about a print on display in the window, revealed as 'Nymphs Bathing' by Munich artist Georg Papperitz. Gale fined 1s and costs for exhibiting an indecent picture

- major police presence in evidence for the second visit of Salvation Army founder and commander General Booth to the SA Citadel in Lowesmoor in September

- more white gloves for the mayor in October, the dock in the police court empty for the fourth time in almost half a century

- hangman (and former police PC) James Berry conducts another execution in Worcester – 71-year old shoemaker Samuel Crowther for the murder of Droitwich gardener John Willis. 400 people gather outside the gaol. It was not to be his last

The world was changing and technology was fast making inroads: in February, the Council gave permission for the Western Counties and South Wales Telephone Company to '...carry wires over the Guildhall, Police-station, Public Library and Market House under certain conditions, one being that the company should permit the use of the telephone at the police-station for all Corporation business'.

Typically, however, Worcester was slow to accept Mr Edison's new-fangled phenomenon and the telephone company's offer.

On February 8th four County PCs – Evans, Pugh, Parry and Robinson – had testified to having been attacked on four separate occasions by a foxhound belonging to Benjamin Wall of the Tything, all having had their uniforms torn. The *Herald* headline ran '*A Dog That Dislikes Policemen*'

Nor had the military lost any of its enthusiasm for tussling with the police. Since the opening of the Barracks at Norton, the everyday and clearly painful issue of dealing with drunken squaddies had eased to a degree, but it was never going to go away entirely and in April the situation bubbled-over in what appears to have been another massive free-for-all in Sidbury that had resulted in **PCs 23 George Aston and Richard James Glover** who'd joined in December and was to quit within eighteen months, both being severely bashed about by several drunken squaddies, of whom William Cooper, William Williams and Thomas Silk, all of the Worcestershire Regiment were eventually nailed and sentenced to civil, rather than military punishment: fourteen days' hard for Silk, a month's hard for the others.

It had begun with a row between Williams and a woman who claimed he'd assaulted her and escalated, drawing a huge crowd – just one man, named Watkins, offering any kind of assistance to the bobbies who were coming in for a rare hammering, dragging Pte Williams off **PC Glover** who he'd knocked down and was sat astride, punching mercilessly. Though a posse of bobbies had managed to drag the three fighting-mad soldiers back to the station-house through lively use of staves, the fracas picked up again in the charge room with civilian prisoners now also joining in, allowing Cooper and Williams to escape.

Williams, still carrying a heavy stick that he'd broken over **Glover**'s head, was caught in Bath Road and Cooper, still wearing snapped handcuffs, had broken *into* the Barracks and was arrested there. At the subsequent police court hearing, ex-mayor William Williamson '...condemned as most reprehensible the behaviour of the crowd towards the police and said that anyone interfering with constables would be severely dealt with'.

By September, *Berrows Journal* was in contact with its sister newspapers the *Daily Times* and *Evesham Journal* by telephone but though the Western Counties and South Wales Telephone Company had offered *free connections* to the city police, the fire station and the infirmary, the offer came with a condition – that 50 other subscribers first needed to be found before they'd go ahead, just as had already happened in Evesham, Malvern, Cheltenham, Gloucester, Bath, Bristol, Cardiff and most other towns in the south-west.

But not only were those fifty not forthcoming, but the company was also now threatening to pull out of Worcester and to withdraw all offers within a month, claiming complete disgust with the city – especially its tight-fisted council and its failure to support and encourage the new ideas '*at least to an extent consistent with their public functions*'.

**Arthur Sommers** was a known supporter of the telephone and he backed a call to the Mayor, Ernest Augustus Day to call a public meeting in order to drum up support. Two months later, the City Council gave in and agreed to accept the telephone company's offer. The police were given the telephone number 9.

A curious case in September resulted in **Arthur Sommers** in particular breathing a sigh of relief as it resulted in the arrest of a serial fraudster John Pritchard who had duped dozens of local traders over previous months by claiming to be gamekeeper to Lord Sandys or other noted gentry, placing large orders with them and asking them to treat him to a drink for favouring them with his employer's custom.

## Also this year: 1889

- in January two newsboys, 11 and 15-year old brothers Walter and Henry Poole each received 'six strokes of the birch-rod' for stealing four dozen copies of Worcester Journal

- former Det. Sgt Ben Holmes, now the mayor's senior sergeant-at-mace is appointed sword-bearer and billet master at the Guildhall

- in March, praise heaped on Det-Sgt Tommy Wallace '...for the able manner in which he had detected crime' in the previous twelve years

- PC John Hughes disarms labourer and serial wife-beater Henry Woodward who had stabbed his estranged wife Eliza in the face in a murderous attempt and believing she was dead, cut his own throat in a suicide bid. He recovered and was sentenced to four months' hard

- on July 3rd hawker James Linton kicks-off in the station house after it had taken four officers to drag him there. PC Frank Petty is hospitalised

- police praise 14-year old Albert Sampson for 'the skill he showed in avoiding a collision with other vehicles' after a horse attached to a spring cart bolted in Bath Road, ran up College Street, High Street, the Cross, Foregate Street and the Tything before dropping dead with exhaustion in front of the Droitwich Road toll house. His younger brother and sister were also in the cart

- PC Fred Tarrant called in to search pockets of man found drowned in the 'side pool' of Diglis lock in a bid to establish his identity. He was found to have come from Kidderminster where he'd left a wife and four children

- Arthur Sommers forced to communicate with every public house licensee in the city about harbouring policemen after two (unnamed, although one was possibly Walter Parry) constables are found drinking while on duty

- PC (later Inspector) Frederick William Peacock sent to Birmingham to arrest two fraudulent horse dealers

- charges of drinking whilst on duty in the Reindeer Hotel, levelled at PC Walter Parry dropped by complainant George Day Snr, who was himself fined 5s and costs for refusing to quit licensed premises when ordered

- PS William James who was to go on to a 34 year career with the police (5th November 1869 – 13th November 1903) and PC (later Sgt) Fred Tarrant put out a fire at a Dolday hovel that had claimed the lives of two boys, 6 and 8

- on Christmas night, PC William Roberts is alerted to a fire on the third storey of 11 Court Dolday. Two children are found dead in a bedroom

Pritchard – described by **Arthur Sommers** as 'one of the most notorious men in Worcester' – had been found by **PC Richard Glover,** alerted by the sound of drunken snoring coming from a field off Malvern Road.  One month's hard.

A few weeks later, ever-reliable **PC14 George Hill** who'd joined the force on January 26th 1872 and was well-respected by all his colleagues died while still in service and his widow awarded a year's salary (£73 14s 4d) as gratuity.

*Gained:*  *Albert Edward Hinett (he lasted 14 days), Thomas Love, George Turner, William Hollis*
*Lost:* *George Hill,  John Pugh, Alonzo Stone, Walter Foxhall*

It had been a distressing start to the year and being unusually cold, the police had been called in to deal with a spate of fires, several involving children that had stood too close to unguarded fires and had been badly burned – in several cases, fatally.  Numerous old and disabled people unable to afford coal for a fire were also found dead from the cold.  In one case, murder was first suspected when 53-year old mother of three, Harriet Cook was found dead in a Dolday hovel. She was later found to have starved to death.

On February 1st, the police at last managed to bring a charge of obstruction against the Salvation Army whose strident temperance and anti-drink sermons in the Cornmarket had become increasingly troublesome, their message deliberately calculated to inflame legions of drinkers leaving the pubs.

The result was often inevitable, but the police were largely powerless to stop them holding their al fresco gatherings, further heralded by drum-banging and an increasingly proficient brass band.  Salvationist John Ellis of Lowesmoor Terrace (*probably the Salvation Army HQ, indicating that he was probably a token offender*) was fined 1s and 11s costs – which, noted the *Herald*, '...someone in court paid on his behalf'.

Another brass band commanding the headlines at this time was Claines Brass Band, sued in the police court for damages of £15 after they'd marched down the Tything as far as Castle Street (*now so-called for the first time, having been Salt Lane up to then*) where they'd startled a horse that subsequently bolted and

*The winters of 1890 and 1891 were remarkably cold, sparking off pleasure for some – skaters seen here on the frozen Severn – but unimaginable grief for others as dozens died from the cold.  Four children died in fires in Dolday  within a  few days at the end of 1889*

knocked down complainant William Davies, causing him to lose eight days' work. Verdict: for the plaintiff plus £4 10s costs.

In March, James Berry was again in town for another hanging at Worcester Gaol – this time a double execution, Samuel and Joseph Boswell for the murder of Frederick Stevens, the Duc d'Aumale's gamekeeper at Evesham. They were the 44th and 45th prisoners to have been hanged in Worcester since 1800, but Berry himself was coming to the end of his own life as an executioner. Trust in his ability to gauge the required drop had been eroding for some time after too many executions had gone gruesomely wrong, and he was effectively sacked as hangman within a year after executing 131 people in his seven years as official hangman. It's notable that he subsequently became an evangelist.

A terse piece of writing and/or editing emerged the following week when the *Herald* covered the far from isolated incident of a far-gone drunk, in this instance 31-year old labourer William Clayton of Barbourne, refusing to quit licensed premises: '...PC Hooper (*George Hooper 20th October 1884 – 18th November 1910*) said that his attention had been called to the Saracen's Head to the prisoner who was standing outside the house. The man was drunk and used very bad language. He refused to go with him to the station and wanted to fight him'. The next details are missing, merely noted by the *Herald*, but every inch as revealing, as **'eventually he had to be conveyed to the police-station on a stretcher'**.

Scores of similar tales could have been, and for the most part were, printed in every edition of the local weeklies and the *Worcester Daily Times*. Worcester remained a desperately tough town that would have gained an even tougher reputation but for a police force tough enough to take it on on its own terms.

Hardly anything is ever heard of any of the police chiefs' wives with the exception of gratuities or a call for financial assistance in the wake of their husbands' deaths, but in March Mrs Harriet Sommers emerged as a personality in her own right having made a 2-guinea donation and as a prominent speaker at rallies calling for a children's crèche serving some of the city's poorer quarters. She was clearly impressive as the crèche duly happened and opened on May 19th at 2 South Parade with provision for 60 children.

It's not known whether the Sommers were overly religious, but in June the chief took a hard, personal and very public stance against Sunday trading in the city, the *Herald* noting:

> '...the prevalence of Sunday trading in some parts of Worcester, chiefly in the lower class streets, has been made the subject of action by the Chief Constable (Mr Sommers). He states that the number of hucksters and small shopkeepers such as greengrocers, sweet-sellers, tobacconists and hair dressers – who keep open on Sunday is assuming such proportions that it is necessary to take notice of it. He therefore gave notice on Saturday to these tradesmen that it was his intention to put in force against them in the future the Lord's Day Observance Act. Mr Sommers says that he was told by the large majority of the shopkeepers that they would be only too glad to close if the others did, and that they only opened because it was the practice of others. A few, however, kept open last Sunday in defiance of the intimation. Mr Sommers says that this decision will not affect the delivery of the Sunday papers so long as they are not cried in the streets'.

Some weeks later he refused to intervene in a private prosecution brought against the Salvation Amy for selling copies of the War Cry on a Sunday.

In June, the old militia v police issue kicked-off again, this time literally when **PC Walter Parry,** who was to quit over the nasty assault, was hammered to the ground, severely kicked and beaten and then humiliatingly rolled in the gutter from Green Hill to the bottom of London Road after he'd cautioned a gang of squaddies including Henry Hammond, William Cox, Albert Jarvis and Albert Lowe all of the 3rd Battalion Worcestershire Regiment, for threatening behaviour and using bad language to Annie Richards 'who lives in the Cherry Orchards'.

Found to have been the instigator, Hammond was arrested at Norton Barracks and despite being bound with three pairs of handcuffs, '...he jumped out of the trap after he had been put into it and it was with the greatest difficulty he was got to Worcester' (*Herald*). Even the chief chipped-in saying that he never knew a prisoner to be more violent than him. 2 months' hard. Cox also received fourteen days and Lowe seven days. Jarvis was released on lack of evidence. The next night, James Hexley and James Murphy of the 4th Battalion were both charged with violent behaviour, **Sergeant William James** who was to go on to a 34-year career with the city police, retiring in 1903, said he had never before had to deal with a more violent man than Murphy. 14 days' hard.

A neat little tale headlined **'The Chief Constable's Compassion'** in July, demonstrated a seldom-seen side to **Arthur Sommers**' nature...

He'd found 35 year old Mary Ann Loosemoore 'wandering abroad without any visible means of subsistence in Copenhagen-street last night. The Chief Constable (*Mr Sommers*) stated that he met the defendant walking in the street and finding that she was mentally affected, he took her to the station, with the view of her being taken proper care of. He feared that if more care were not taken of her she might come to more harm'. The article concludes: '...the Magistrates thought the best plan was that defendant should be sent to the Union (Workhouse) and made an order accordingly'.

In another case a few weeks later, **Arthur Sommers** was forced to intervene when a daughter of blind 75-year old Maria Cox, well known in the city for begging under a sign marked 'Struck Blind by Lightning' removed her mother from the Workhouse where she'd been sent because she said her mother earned a pound a week on the streets. **Sommers** pressed for the magistrates to pay her fare to another daughter's home at Inkberrow out of the Poor Fund, which they did.

On the other hand, his darker side is clearly in evidence the following month when two 14-year old boys, Mark Hodges and James Coyle were sentenced to fourteen days' hard labour, and five more lads ranging from 14 to 18 sentenced to seven days, after he'd ordered **PS Sam Grosvenor, Insp. Tommy Wallace, Sgt Fred Tarrant** and *thirteen* more constables to muster in plain clothes and go down to Pitchcroft following a flurry of complaints about lads gathering there, committing nuisances, swearing and gambling. Though the police had been rumbled and the gang all ran away, seven were eventually hauled-up in court charged with gaming on Pitchcroft – 'a disgrace to the city' as **Arthur Sommers** condemned their action in the courtroom.

In what was now becoming an annual event, the High Sherriff's dinner to the Police force was this year held at the Hop Market Hotel and by the sound of it, some members emerged as capable songsters: '...the evening was very pleasantly varied by some excellent songs by members of the force and thus terminated what all present considered to be a most agreeable and delightful evening' (*Herald*).

Then, on November 12th an incident that would reflect badly on everyone concerned with it.

**Arthur Sommers'** great friend and supporter, Alderman, magistrate and ex-mayor William Blizard Williamson of Sunny View, Battenhall, was found roaring drunk in the Shakespeare in Angel Street and duly charged. In the packed-to-the-rafters Magistrates' court 10 days later, the industrialist failed to show, leaving his defence to, of all people, Arthur Beauchamp who quickly summed up the facts – *yes*, his client admitted being drunk; *yes*, he'd been to a banquet and should have gone home instead of going into the Shakespeare; *yes*, he was in a bad state mentally but that he had a doctor's certificate to the effect that since suffering concussion in a hunting accident, his alcohol tolerance had diminished. Then he concluded that as it was his client's and the one-time First Citizen's first offence, he should be given no more than a warning and the matter closed. It took the Bench barely five minutes to agree that '...the justice of the case would be met by the costs being paid and £5 paid to the poor box'.

The decision prompted 'Rambler' John Noake – another ex-mayor and Alderman, and one of the sitting magistrates that day but clearly overruled – to stand up and wipe the floor with his spineless fellow magistrates, disagreeing violently with the decision, stating that there was neither law nor justice about it, and stating:

> '...we ought not to sit here and accept what some people might call a bribe. He is a man in authority and rather than I should incur the imputation of allowing a brother magistrate to be dealt with in a manner contrary to law and justice, I would myself retire from the Bench. In another part of this hall is the sentence 'Fiat justitia ruat cœlum – let justice be done though the heavens fall. I repeat that and say 'let justice be done though a magistrate suffers'.

The *Herald* noted: 'the speech was received with applause which was suppressed'. Arthur Sommers was in court, but had not been called: he must have been squirming throughout the entire hearing.

*Rear: PC10 (later Sergeant) **Joseph William Troughton** who was to go on to a 25-year career with the City police remaining with the force until 1906, called on to recover a child's body this year.  **(Front):** PC8 **John Pugh,** hard man of the St Johns beat*

The cold continued to wreak havoc well into the new year: on December 29th, **PCs Fred Cook** and **Thomas Love** each carried the body of a boy drowned in the canal at Tallow Hill to the boys' respective homes:  8-year old George Large and 9-year old Ernest Andrews, both of John Street.  They and three other lads had been sliding on the ice when it gave way, Large's father being among a huge crowd of onlookers who'd gathered to witness the two PCs dragging the canal.

The other three boys had been rescued by 'Chilly' – William Chillingworth, bolt-maker and son of notorious boatman, hard-case and police-hater of the same name (*see page 368*) – who'd jumped in to the frozen-over canal, earning the highest praise from all quarters. He was later (*September 1891*) presented with a certificate from the Royal Humane Society for his actions, emerging as something of a city personality for a while.

*Gained: Thomas House, George Lock, Thomas Jaynes, William Teale*

*Lost: Walter Parry, William Roberts, Richard James Glover*

- *in May, police investigate a 'wanton and deliberate' assault on Edward A. Mason, editor of the Worcestershire Chronicle outside Simes' (now Debenhams) in High Street. Bailiff Robert Perks, angered by a Chronicle editorial is fined £3 13s 6d*

- *in June PC10 (later Sergeant) Joseph William Troughton  recovers the body of 10-year old John Meredith from the canal at Chambers Bridge, 200 yards above Bilford Bridge. He'd drowned*

- *Insp. Tommy Wallace is assaulted by shoemaker William Knight, one of two men he caught fighting in New Street and had grabbed both by the collar and was marching them to the station-house. Both combatants laid the blame on the other and were fined 5s and 1s 3d costs*

- *leader of the 'White Horse Gang', striker Thomas Soley (19) ordered to 21 days' hard for assault on PC28 Joseph Williams*

- *autumn sees spate of d&d actions brought against excursionists permitted unrestricted drinking as pleasure boat operators take advantage of a legal loophole that had left their craft outside the scope of the licensing laws*

- *concerns also raised over the condition of Severn pleasure boats following several fatalities in the summer*

- *Arthur Sommers reveals re-introduction of police pub 'black list' after record number of d&d convictions following three years of declining drunkenness. Boar's Head, Albion, Union and Pheasant head the list*

- *gratuities amounting to £27 13s are awarded to the police for their extra work at this year's Worcester (Three Choirs) Festival accounting for virtually round-the-clock duty during the week-long festival*

- *police hold crowds back at the unveiling of the queen's Jubilee statue in November.  No royals are present*

- *in December PC Frederick Cook is menaced by a gang of squaddies in Bath Road. They had taken their belts off and were about to lay into him when PC15 John Bishop arrived and managed to hold off several of them with an ash stick. Thomas Brannon, Harry Watson and Edward Perry of the 4th Battn. Worcestershire Regiment fined 5s or seven days' hard*

- *the year ends as it had begun, police called in to investigate the deaths of several people killed by the cold*

The temperature plummeted to 4°F – 28 degrees of frost – on New Year's Day, eight weeks after the cold snap had set in. The same week, **Insp. Tommy Wallace**'s salary was raised from £1 15s to £2 2s a week, and despite the sweat-shop scandal, Dolan's was again chosen as the supplier of clothing alongside W. Morris of Lowesmoor (*helmets*); Butler and Co, High Street (*gloves*) and Noake's (*boots*).

A matter of days later, one of the force's great unsung heroes, **Henry Joyner** – who'd joined the force on October 7th 1870 as PC07, had been appointed Sergeant and was now Inspector and would continue in the role up to October 21st 1898, a total of more than 28 years – was alerted by a man named Fred Hopkins to a body, still warm, lying across Watery Lane. The man had been shot through the head in what was evidently suicide: his first shot had failed but the second bullet was lodged in his brain. It took the City police, led by **Sergeant Joyner,** two weeks to trace his identity – a long trail involving a registered letter from Ballyford in Ireland, later leading to the revelation that he was Thomas Sullivan, a warder at Prestwich Lunatic Asylum in Manchester until he'd quit a few weeks earlier with failing health. No-one knew why he'd come to Worcester, or why he'd been drinking only minutes earlier in the Garibaldi, and the jury at his inquest in the Guildhall returned a verdict of suicide while temporarily insane.

**Arthur Sommers** had continued to support the Worcestershire Society for the Prevention of Cruelty to Animals as **Matthew Power** had done, and at their 15th annual meeting in February, Hon Sec Philip S. Williams offered '…the thanks of the committee to **Mr A. E. Sommers and the police** under his charge for the very efficient manner in which they continued to check cases of cruelty that came under their notice, as well as for the summonses that they had taken out against grosser cases that they had detected'.

They also praised '…the excellent supervision of **Inspector Croft** and other officers, two of whom were constantly in attendance on market days'. In the preceding year, 15 people had been prosecuted for cruelty to animals in the city alone: just the previous week, labourer Samuel Britton had been sentenced to 14 days' gaol in default of a 23s 6d fine for beating a dog four times over the head with a large stick, witnessed and prosecuted by extra-vigilant **PC (later Sergeant) George Langstone**. The chief himself had also expressed concern about the health and size of the horses used for pulling the trams, and 11 tram company horses valued at 14 guineas apiece had been condemned in one week.

Sunday April 5th was Census day and No 4 Copenhagen Street was shown as the home of **Arthur Edwin**

CITY OF WORCESTER.

POLICE ACT, 18 0.

Scale prepared by order of the Watch Committee, showing the Pensions attai... ...tioned years' service.

**Sommers,** Chief Officer of Police aged 44, his wife Harriett, daughters Sally (17) and Maud (16), and Emily Bevan their domestic servant from Cleobury Mortimer.

Next door lived **Thomas Croft** aged 53, Police Inspector from Pirton, his wife Phoebe (57), sons Albert (24) an engineer's clerk and Herbert (20) a plate worker's apprentice, and daughter Rose (17) a dressmaker – but the big, burly ever-reliable countryman who'd joined on 28th June 1861 just a month after **Matthew Power'**s appointment, had had enough and made clear his intention of retiring after clocking-up thirty meritorious years and being now eligible to a pension. 'The matter was adjourned to the next meeting (of the Watch Committee)' noted the *Herald.*

Two pieces of bad – ie financially damaging – snippets of news in one week was all too much for the anxious money-men to bear: the first had been the suggested closure of both Warwick and Worcester Gaols, meaning that prisoners from Worcester would either have to be sent to Winson Green Prison in Birmingham at the expense of the police, or kept in the city in the Copenhagen Street station-house not only at the expense of Worcester City Council but also with the inevitable demand for new improved premises if it was to stand even the remotest chance of coping with the likely demand. It was all too much and MP George Allsopp was pestered to come to the city's aid, as a matter of the highest priority.

The census had revealed Worcester's population to be 42,937 – 30% up on the tally from 10 years earlier, although the bulk of the increase was put down to boundary changes rather than an unusual increase in fecundity or migration. The Orphan Asylum accounted for 84 people, HM Prison 122, the Infirmary 141 and the Workhouse 266. In the wake of the expanding population, the Council no doubt held its breath for the annual inspection by Col Cobbe, held this year in July. Though deficient by one inspector and two constables, the force was found to be more than satisfactory in every other respect and thus granted its licence to continue operating. 39 men had gathered for the inspection including the chief, one inspector and six sergeants.

City cab driver Henry Wade, 53, was either very unlucky or very stupid or both, as in May he was pulled over by **PC Frank Petty** on suspicion of being drunk in charge of a waggonette. Denying the claim by offering to demonstrate his professed sobriety with the offer to the constable of a ride: '...defendant drove very fast. In Bridge-street, he ran into a truck and then [Petty] took him into custody. He was very drunk. Fined 20s and costs or 14 days' hard labour'.

In September, some welcome praise was laid firmly at the feet of the entire force when the Dean of Worcester Dr. John Gott invited the whole complement to a 'knife and fork tea' at the Deanery – but then left them to be entertained by his wife Harriott Mary (née Maitland). It's possible he'd been called away to matters of higher concern as the following week he announced his elevation to Bishop and a new job: Bishop of Truro. The dinner however, went ahead without him, proved to be a huge success and received ample coverage in the local papers which was probably its prime purpose anyway. He was succeeded by Dr Robert William Forrest of St Jude's Kensington.

In November, the chief, **Tommy Wallace** and more than 20 constables and sergeants said the final goodbye to an old friend – **Det Sgt Bill Underwood** (*left*) who'd retired six years before after 22 years' service (1st May 1863- 10th July 1885). He'd died after four months' illness, and four sergeants bore his pall.

FUNERAL OF A FORMER WORCESTER DETECTIVE — Mr. Underwood, an ex-detective of the Worcester City Police was buried on Tuesday at Elmbridge, where many of his relations have been interred. Mr. Underwood had been ill for four months, and died only last week. Among those who attended to pay a last mark of respect to their old colleague were : Chief Constable Sommers, Detective Wallace, and more than twenty sergeants and constables. Four sergeants bore the pall. Mr. Underwood had risen from the ranks, having commenced his 22 years' service as a constable.

GENEROUS GIFT BY THE EARL OF DUDLEY.—

*Gained: James Matthews, William Price (both remained just four weeks), Charles Lock, Edward Harris, Alexander Millar, Frank Steadman, William Howell*
*Lost: Tommy Croft (after 30 years), Edward Biddle, Thomas House, George Locke*

- *in February, it takes four PCs and two civilians to subdue 'violent as a madman' labourer John Hobson who later claimed to have been bruised and kicked by the police. PC George Langstone is off duty for several days after being kicked and bitten. Three months' prison*

- *in May, Thomas Walton 26, labourer, sentenced to 21 days' hard for assaulting Sgt Fred Tarrant and PC Joseph Williams both left blooded and severely bruised after they'd tried to arrest him for being drunk and riotous in Group (formerly Grope) Lane*

- *a few weeks later, PC Richard Robinson is called to William Turner found in Angel Street outside the chapel (now Tramps) and had died in the Infirmary two days later. He'd been hit in the face for no reason and fell backwards onto the road. Verdict of manslaughter against two men and a woman, Smith, Freeman and Venables*

- *two weeks later PCs George Langstone and George Turner are beaten-up in Shaw Street while attempting to remove drunken 21-year old groom Charles Cockbill to the station-house*

- *in September, Thomas Harris, ex-County PC but now a labourer of Belmont Road, tackles two PCs, Richard Robinson and Joseph William Troughton, and leaves them both badly kicked and injured on the ground. Fined £1 and costs or 14 days' gaol*

- *PC George Langstone is accused of drunkenness by tramp Richard Harper, arrested for begging. Harper: I don't believe you was very sober. I seen you come out of two or three public houses. The officer: I was following you. It was Harper's sixth offence this year. 14 days hard*

- *Arthur Sommers is among the mourners when Edward Arthur Mason, editor of the Journal and ex-editor of the Liverpool Daily Post, Worcestershire Echo, Worcestershire Chronicle and Worcester Herald died. He was 37*

- *on December 29th PC George Locke who had joined on October 13th the previous year quit after a severe going-over and the hands and feet of brothers collier William (27) and labourer Sidney (26) Band in the Prince of Wales in Newport Street. 14 days' hard apiece*

At the beginning of January, sad news: **Benjamin Holmes** simply fell down in his house in Croft Road and died. He'd joined the force on 18th February 1853 and retired as Station Sergeant on 4th November 1870, immediately taking on the roles of the mayor's Sergeant-at-Mace, coroner's officer and sword bearer. 'In his attendance upon the Mayors on various occasions, his remarkable physique was a matter of frequent comment' ran the *Journal*. He'd stood 6' 7".

A few days later, his ex-superior, city Coroner and Clerk of the Peace, Robert Tomkins Rea also died and the police formed a guard of honour at the head of the procession to the cemetery.

*These weren't to be the only shocks this year...*

Eyebrows were raised in court and police statements ridiculed in January when **Sgt Edwin Oakey** stood his ground and several times repeated his assertion that on the first day of the year he'd heard the words of obscene songs being sung by an impromptu gathering of eight merry drinkers outside the Gardeners Arms, more than a half a mile away (*at the point where today's Smiths Avenue meets Bransford Road*).

*'The officer was confident. He volunteered to say that the noise might have been heard at the Cross. The officer produced a four-line verse which he said the men were singing. Asked if his memory was equal to this effort, he said "Oh yes, I could remember 40 lines"'.*

As the evidence descended into farce in the court room with laughter openly ringing around the Guildhall, **Arthur Sommers** intervened and succeeded only in making the matter worse by implying, although not openly stating, that there was more to the case than readily met the eye, before engaging in a full-scale verbal tussle with defending solicitor George Bentley. The eight revellers, who claimed they were merely singing carols, were given the benefit of the doubt and discharged. **Oakey**, in his 22nd year with the force was to have one more tussle with his superiors this year – this time considerably less jocular, to the point of being fatally damaging (*see pages 294-8*).

Also in January, deaths in the city were recorded as 70 per 1,000, with 50 people reported dead in the last week of the month alone. An influenza epidemic was largely accountable, pushing the rate to more than twice the usual average. During the month, 42 children under five had died.

Just weeks after joining, **PC (later Sergeant with 31 years' service) Alexander Millar** had to fight his way through a 200-strong crowd gathered in the Cornmarket to arrest old offender 44-year old Elizabeth Martha Davis for being drunk and disorderly. It was her 26<sup>th</sup> charge for the same offence. One month's hard.

At the Quarter Sessions, it emerged that 90% of the cases before Recorder Richard Amphlett were caused by drink: '...a damnable state of affairs, and drunkenness the ever fertile source of crime' he'd described it.

In March, **PC Thomas Baynham** arrived too late to stop 53-year old Henry Woodward from plunging a knife into his own throat after stabbing his wife Eliza in the neck outside the Malt Shovel in All Hallows after he'd begged her for a reconciliation and she'd refused; she was rushed off to the Infirmary with what might now be termed 'life threatening injuries'. On duty in All Hallows, **Baynham,** who'd been alerted by screams of 'Murder'

> *'...paid immediate attention to the man's throat and hurried him off to the Infirmary too. The house surgeon Mr. Fletcher, promptly treated him and his condition permitted of his being taken back to the City Police Station and charged with the offence (of attempted murder). He remained in custody all night under careful surveillance... he said he thought he had killed her (and) remarked that he wished the knife had gone a lot further and then it would have finished her'.*

It later emerged in court that he'd tussled with **PC17 Baynham** in a futile bid to recover his knife with the comment 'Let me finish it'.

Just weeks later, **PC4 George Turner** on duty in Friar Street was alerted by neighbours to a hovel in nearby Painter's Lane after they'd heard cries for help. When he arrived he found Hannah Westwood heavily bleeding and bruised having been struck about the head and body with a rolling pin, kicked, stabbed in the head and thrown out of the door by her husband, 32-year old slater John.

Breaking down the door and arresting him, he claimed her injuries were all self-inflicted. Theirs was a tale of marital disharmony with violence inflicted by, and on, both sides and despite lurid tales of Hannah Westwood's constant drunkenness and frequent attacks on her husband, John Westwood was sentenced to three months' hard labour for assaulting his wife – *his twelfth conviction for the same offence, according to the court's records.*

Drunkenness, marital disharmony, domestic violence and even worse were also to emerge as the prime features of the next altercation to come to the attention of the police. This time it was much nearer home, instantly grabbed all of the headlines, its fall-out much keener felt, divided the Council, revealed deep rifts as well as inefficiency and cover-up within the police force, and shook the city to its very roots...

WCiCo/WAAS

**The end for Arthur Sommers after drunken assaults on his wife and daughter inside the station-house**

On Wednesday 27th April, Town Clerk Samuel Southall received a note, handwritten in pencil on two sides of foolscap by **Police Sergeant 003 Charles Thomas** from his home 16 Northfield Street. The original is preserved in the Hive *(b496.5 BA9630)* and merits quoting, as written and in full:

> *Dear Sir. Having seen his Worship the Mayor (Walter Holland) this morning in company with Sergts Grosvenor and James, I am requested by him to ask you to kindly lay the following report before the Chairman and Gentlemen of the Watch Committee in reference to the Chief Constable Mr A. E. Sommers.*
>
> *Gentlemen, I beg to report that at 6pm last night, the 26th instant I went on duty in charge of the Police Station and at a few minutes past 11 O clock pm, Mrs Sommers came running into the Charge Room screaming and said I must come to you for protection Sergt he has kicked me and holding her hand on her lip at that time the Chief came rushing into his office in a very excited manner and was swearing at her. and striking at her I protected her and he struck at me saying that he would knock me over her. I caught hold of his arms and held him to prevent him from using further violence to his wife. he was so determined that I had to call Mr. Jaynes who was on Reserve to assist me in holding him. We got him quiet for a minute or two and loosed him and went a little distance from him to go into the Charge Room. when he rushed at his wife and struck her a violent blow on the face and she fell down on the floor and fainted. her eldest daughter fetched her some water. and the youngest daughter ran up the Police Station yard to Mr [Sidnam] Coles house and called him up. at that time he struck his Eldest Daughter a blow on the cheek. and she began crying. He was mad drunk. he then took his watch out of his pocket and put it on the Table saying that he would go out and drown himself or if there was a Razor there he would cut his throat he then went out into High S., during the time he was going on a crowd of People had collected opposite his House in Copenhagen St. I sent PC Jaynes out to see where he went, and he came back and said that he was in High St. I soon after heard him come in the House again.*
>
> *I Remain. Gentlemen your obedient Servant, C Thomas No3'*

In a different hand, it stated: 'Witness **Thomas Jaynes PC No12**'

Whatever other business Samuel Southall had that day had to be relegated to some other time as he dropped everything as the full weight of the allegations sank in. The chief was allegedly mad drunk, he'd attacked his wife first in their house and then in the Charge Room and had also struck one of his daughters and threatened his Station Sergeant. He'd then threatened suicide – all in front of reliable witnesses.

***Save murdering the Mayor, could it get any worse?***

Four days later, including a weekend, he'd called an emergency meeting 'to investigate matters of grave consequence regarding the direction of the City Police'. Eight police officers 'and other persons' were involved and the meeting was held behind closed doors with

WCiCo/WAAS

no press or other parties allowed: his original notes still survive, and some of the following account is verbatim, as written. First in the seat was **Sergeant Charles Thomas** who repeated the claims he'd made in his initial letter, expanding the tale with the additional information that after the assault in the Charge Room and **Arthur Sommers'** excited exit, Harriet Sommers had wanted to follow him and he'd held her back saying that it would only make matters worse. **PC Jaynes** had followed him to the 'Pillar Post Office near the cathedral' (*it's still there*). He also added that the chief had said he'd resign – to which **Sgt Thomas** said he hoped he wouldn't – but that he was very drunk and smelt 'all whiskey'.

*Town Clerk Samuel Southall*

In response to further questions he also added that '...when Chief wanted to go out, Mrs S. rushed at him'. (*In brackets he'd added a note '[**Receipt of money not accounted for**]*)'

**PC Jaynes** corroborated all **Sergeant Thomas'** evidence, adding that there were 15 or 16 people gathered outside the door, having heard the commotion inside.

**PC (27, Sidnam) Cole** stated that he was in bed when Maud Sommers had '...called me up. I got up. Daughter ran into back kitchen. I went into office – chief came out of house said lock up Mrs S. I shall resign tomorrow. Chief very excited and say as to drunk. Very often in house – knows Mrs S. very vile temper – never saw him ill-use Mrs S – I couldn't stand Mrs Ss temper'

**PC No6 Harper** gave evidence of the chief 's drunkenness

**Sergeant (Samuel) Grosvenor** stated that he'd been 'called in by Mrs S and Miss Maud' and asked to withdraw any charge. He also added that Mrs S '...stripped up sleeve of dress and that part of her arm was 'black and blue – took off bodice – showed me bruises on breast – back of neck another bruise – never saw such bruises. Mrs S said she had bruise on back from kick. Mrs S said bruises caused by Chief on 26th April. Heard of frequent disturbances between Chief and wife. Does not know of Mr S's temper'

**Sergeant Harding** gave more evidence of late night drinking and drunkenness.

**PC 17 (Thomas) Baynham** said he saw and heard nothing while on his beat, #13.

Then it was **Superintendent Arthur Sommers'** turn. Quizzing the Superintendent, the Town Clerk's notes read: '10.25 went home. Lay down on couch – Mrs S woke him up – she was in temper – Mrs S stopped me going out – I pushed her away – I threw boot at her – Mrs S ran to charge Room – Thomas & Jaynes came into Hall – they said they had come to protect Mrs S  I said no protectn needed and take her to Powick – Mrs S got in my way – I pushed Thomas aside & Mrs S fell and hit her head.  I never hit Mrs S or daughter'.

Then the Town Clerk noted: 'the Chief elected not to call his wife as a witness'.

The plot had thickened and there was the hint of further allegations to come. Somebody wasn't telling the truth, battle lines were being drawn, and the matter was not going to rest until it had been thoroughly sifted. It might even lead to someone being severely censured. Dismissed, even.

As the press got hold of the story, the city watched events unfold with interest...

Then on Thursday 5th May, events took a startling turn for the worse:  the town clerk received another letter, this time signed not by one, but by more than half of the entire force stating:

*Sir,  We respectfully ask you to lay this Petition before the Watch Committee at their next meeting*
*To the Chairman & Gentlemen  of the Watch Committee,*
*Gentlemen, We, the undersigned members of the Worcester City Police Force, do hereby protest to serve under the present Chief Constable Mr. A. E. Sommers on the ground that we have lost all confidence in him as he is not a truthful and sober man.  We annex our names as follows'.*

It was personally and individually signed by **Sergeants Samuel Grosvenor, Frederick Tarrant and Charles Thomas, and constables Henry Harley No16; Edward Harris No26; William Fennell (***unnumbered but actually No5***); Thomas Love No13; William Hollis No8; Fred Hawker No3; Richard Robinson No30; George Aston No23; Joseph Williams No28; John Bishop No15; F(rancis) J(ohn) Pitt No11;  Frederick Cook No 29; William Teal No20; Frank Petty No31; Thomas Jaynes No12; David Evans No24; Charles Lock No21; Frank Steadman No14; Thomas Baynham No17; Alexander Millar No32; Nathan Harper No6; Charles Hall No19; and John Hazleton No26.**

Recd 5th May 1892

To Samuel Southall Esqr.

Town Clerk. of Worcester

Sir.

We respectfully ask you to lay this Petition before the Watch Committee at their next meeting.

To the Chairman & Gentlemen of the Watch Committee.

Gentlemen.

We the undersigned members of the Worcester City Police Force do hereby protest to serve under the present Chief Constable, Mr A. E. Sommers. on the ground that we have lost all confidence in him as he is not a truthful and sober man

We annex our names as follows.

## Sergeants.
Samuel Grosvenor
Frederick Tarrant
Charles Thomas

## Constables
Henry Harley PC no 16
Edward Harris PC 26
William Fennell
Thomas Love No 13
William Hollis No 8
Fred Hawker No 3
Richard Robinson 30
George Aston. 25
Joseph Williams No. 28
John Bishop No. 15.
F J Pitt no. 11

Fredk Cook No. 29.
William Teal No 20
Frank Petty No 31
Thomas Jaynes No 12
David Evans No 24
Charles Lock No 21
Frank Steadman 14
Thomas Twynham 17
Alexander Millar 32.
Nathan Harker 6
Charles Ball
John Hazleton

Samuel Southall immediately called a crisis meeting of the Watch Committee for the following day (*Friday*) and while much of it was involved with legal procedure as to whether certain statements were admissible or not, and whether **Arthur Sommers'** request to be represented by a solicitor should be approved or declined (*it was declined*), the shocking facts of the case emerged entirely as **Sgt. Charles Thomas** had originally presented them. With typical Council caution, the members decided against a full hearing until the next scheduled Watch Committee – and that was several weeks away.

As the *Journal* noted: '...the Committee spent two hours and a half in investigating the evidence; and they deliberated for another half hour in the absence of witnesses. They were divided as to what course to pursue, and finally the enquiry was adjourned for a month'.

Over the next few days more allegations emerged: that the chief had frequently been seen – and noted in police notebooks – to leave licensed premises, notably the Shakespeare, the Crown and the Bell Hotels, at prohibited hours, in various stages of drunkenness, by officers under orders to arrest parties guilty of such actions; that there appeared to be some irregularities in his dealing with Dolan's, the London firm that supplied police clothing (not pursued); and also that cash intended for the Police Outing fund that had come from at least four sources – the Society for the Prevention of Cruelty to Animals (£7 10s); Ald Hill (£1); Reverend Isaac (£2 2s) and St Johns Cycle Club (£1 15s) totalling £12 7s – had not been accounted for until Arthur Sommers handed it over to **Inspector Tommy Wallace** on April 29th, by which time it was painfully obvious that he was already in deep trouble and would be lucky to survive.

On May 16th., **Arthur Sommers** broke his silence on the situation with a handwritten letter (*also preserved in the Hive*) addressed to The Worshipful The Mayor and the Members of the Watch Committee. It read:

> Gentlemen,
> With reference to the charge made against me, I beg to offer my apologies and sincere regret for what has taken place and I feel that the attack of influenza I had some months ago together with the specially aggravated circumstances in which I was placed in my domestic affairs must plead my excuse.
> I have endeavoured to fulfil the onerous and difficult duties of my office in the past, and I sincerely hope the committee will be able to deal leniently with the charge, and I trust they will afford me an opportunity to discharge those duties for the future, and if you do so, I give you my word that you shall have no cause to regret

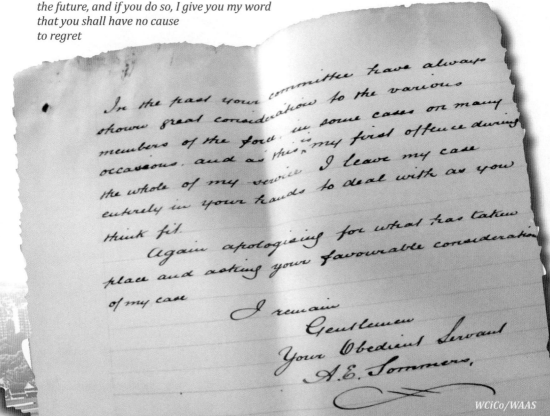

In the past your committee have always shown great consideration to the various members of the force in some cases on many occasions, and as this is my first offence during the whole of my service I leave my case entirely in your hands to deal with as you think fit.

Again apologising for what has taken place and asking your favourable consideration of my case

I remain
Gentlemen
Your Obedient Servant
A.E. Sommers,

WCiCo/WAAS

*the further confidence you will have bestowed upon me.*

*If on the other hand you deem that the state of my health and the provocation I received is not sufficient cause to permit of a renewal of your confidence, I beg most respectfully to point out that this means absolute ruin to myself and family in addition to which I should forfeit the benefit of the Police Superannuation Fund, and the Police Mutual Assurance Association to both of which I have contributed for 20 years and I cannot expect to obtain any situation in a Police Force at my age.*

*In the past, your Committee have always shown great consideration to various members of the force, in some cases on many occasions and as this is my first offence during the whole of my service I leave my case entirely in your hands to deal with as you think fit.*

*Again apologising for what has taken place and asking your favourable consideration of my case.*

*I remain Gentlemen Your Obedient Servant A. E. Sommers*

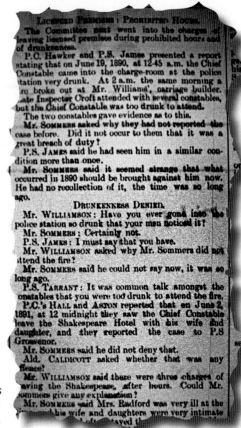

Attached were medical certificates attesting to his state of health and fitness for duty, signed by Drs. Gosling and George Crowe.

The clear assault aside, the worst of the allegations centred on his implied out-of-control drinking: **PC3 Frederick Hawker** and **PS4 William James** presented a report that on June 9th 1890, the chief had been too drunk to attend a fire at Williams' carriage builders and that it had been dealt with by **Inspector Tommy Croft** in his place, and **PS James** said he had seen him 'in that condition' more than once. Several other PCs had also noted similar instances and had been told to take the matter no further for fear of dismissal. There were also allegations of Sommers' hushing-up instances of his friends – including an unnamed Alderman implied, but never actually revealed as the ex-Mayor William Blizard Williamson – and Mr Stretton, Station Master at Shrub Hill, emerging from licensed premises well beyond proscribed hours.

As for the original charge of assaulting his wife, the Committee noted that his letter of apology amounted to an admission of guilt. They decided to take no further action on the Dolan uniforms issue, and put down **Sommers**' failure to hand over several cash gifts as poor organisation and inefficient accounting rather than a deliberate attempt at theft.

Even so, it was staring them in the face: **Arthur Sommers** was clearly unfit for the role of chief, he had lost the trust of more than half his men, the reputation of the entire force was at stake and they were faced with no choice but replace him. He had to go, *but the question was, on what terms?* Certainly, they had grounds to sack him without a penny, or they could allow him to resign and keep either all, or part of his pension. At least, they stopped short of prosecuting him – which would likely have meant prison.

Perhaps with a few wary glances over his shoulder, it was again the ex-mayor, William Blizard Williamson who took control of the situation, remarking that his friend **Arthur Sommers** had '...served the city for 18 years without a black mark against him, and it was notorious (*sic, possibly noteworthy or possibly mis-transcription of meritorious*) that he had brought the police force to a great state of efficiency and they had been complimented on that by Col. Cobbe and had also received the congratulations of Recorders upon the diminution of crime in the city'.

He had been, he said, a most valuable officer, pointing out that the penalty they were being asked to inflict upon him was out of all proportion to the offence. Urging his fellow committee members to vote for the resolution [*to allow him to resign*] he said that not only to discharge a man from the force when nearly fifty years of age and when he was incapable of entering into any other service, but also particularly to

## THE ATTEMPT D SUICIDE OF THE EX-CHIEF-CONSTABLE.

At the City Police Court, on Wednesday, before Ald. Caldicott (presiding), Ald. Airey, and Mr. W. Winwood, Arthur Edwin Sommers (46), Alma Villa, Little Boughton-street, was brought up charged on remand with attempting to commit suicide by taking poison on August 15th. The Court was crowded, and prisoner, who was brought up in custody, appeared to feel his position acutely.

Mr. Halford (Magistrates' Clerk) mentioned to the Bench that the prisoner was remanded on Friday for the purpose of a report being made by Mr. G. E. Hyde, the medical officer at the prison. This report he now read. It stated that Mr. Sommers had shown no symptoms of insanity while in the prison.

The Chief Constable (Mr. Byrne) had no further evidence to offer.

Mr. Matthews, who defended, said he had no observations to make on prisoner's behalf, beyond those contained in his address to the Bench on Friday.

The magistrates retired to consider their decision. On returning into Court,

Ald. Caldicott said the case had received their serious consideration. They had had a very painful duty to perform and they dealt with prisoner as they would have done with anyone else. He had been remanded for a certain time, during which he had had time to consider the offence he had committed. They sincerely hoped that in that retirement he had come to the conclusion that it was a serious offence. They had the certificate from the prison authorities stating that there were no symptoms of insanity, and he was perfectly calm and composed in his mind. He hoped that prisoner had come to better resolutions. He

deprive him of his pension would be a step too far.

The sitting mayor, Walter Holland backed him, stating that he hoped that some way would be found to get out of the position they were in and adding that '...taking into consideration the long and faithful services of the Chief Constable and the efficient state to which he had brought the police so that they were second to none in the kingdom and also the absence of crime in the city, he thought that justice would be done if the motion was carried'.

Not all agreed, but provided more medical evidence could be supplied on his inability to carry out his duties as chief officer, no further questions needed to be asked.

The required letter regarding his fitness to continue was duly supplied and but for a few last minute wrangles on the amount of pension due, that was the eventual recommendation they laid before the full Council to decide on. Under normal circumstances, the chief's pension would have been two-thirds of his salary – £133 a year – but perhaps as a way of appeasing those members who thought the chief deserved to be cast aside with nothing, the ever-frugal Council took a few deductions and recommended his final pension to be fixed at £106 – although even then there were rumblings and a further re-calculation resulted in exclusion of the time he'd spent with the County force: the final figure computed at £95 a year. By a quirky coincidence, in the same week, the Deputy Chief Constable of the County force, Alfred Tyler – also on the same salary as Sommers – retired after 35 years, aged 58. He received his full pension, £133.

All that was required now was to make an inventory of the furniture at the Sommers' tied home; County Surveyor Henry Rowe conducted the survey, reporting from his chambers in Pierpoint Street on May 25th, that the whole of the Sommers' property in the Station-house quarters amounted to £22 13s for which the ex-police chief wrote to City Chamberlain J. T. Rushton that he would accept £18 7s 1d, later amended to £11 7s 1d, further downsized to £7 10s and in final hopelessness, crossed it all out and requested a settlement figure of £7.

His desperation is overwhelming, but with that, disgraced ex-Superintendent Arthur Edwin Sommers, aged 46 and with no immediate prospects, found himself cast aside to make way for a new chief...

To a degree he'd been cushioned from immediate financial ruin as he'd been privately bequeathed the huge amount of £3,800 two years earlier and for a while he dabbled in property, buying three houses in the Arboretum and speculating in other businesses in Worcester – but then realising he'd severely overstretched and miscalculated his situation, the bank began questioning the sudden appearance of an overdraft, with the result that he'd had to sell the houses, resulting in a substantial loss, while none of his investments in local concerns returned a single penny. Almost as a last resort, he then took over The Queen's Arms in Bank Street but within weeks, takings fell from £19 a week to £8. Arthur Sommers blamed the quality of the beer, but with an ex-chief constable in charge of a volatile rough-house like the Queen's Arms, the future could have been predicted: despite living there rent-free, by mid-April he was bankrupt with debts of more than £500 and was forced to live with relatives in Birmingham.

At his hearing on April 15th 1893 – still less than a year after quitting the police and now 47, his assets were enough only to allow payment of 1s 6$^1/_2$ d in the pound, payable by May the following year.

By then he was back in Worcester, living at Alma Villa, 16 Little Boughton Street, desperately seeking a job – any kind of job. With no offers, on August 15th he'd reached rock-bottom and attempted suicide by taking a draft of oxalic acid, bought from St Johns chemist Thomas Silk earlier the same day. Responding to daughter Sally's call for assistance, **PC9 George Hooper** – *significantly, one of those who hadn't signed the protesting petition* – found him lying unconscious on the kitchen floor at 8.15 that evening. Sommers regained consciousness in the Infirmary late the following morning – with his old colleague and 2i/c **Insp. William Joyner** standing over him, with a warrant for his arrest; on his subsequent discharge from the Infirmary, he was remanded in custody at the County Gaol for six days pending a hearing into his attempted suicide and tests for insanity, of which he was cleared.

In an acutely embarrassing switch and dramatic fall from grace at the end of it all, he found himself in the same Guildhall dock to which he'd consigned hundreds of prisoners in his time as a serving police officer, and was bound over in the sum of £25.

As for the future? In 1900 he was still living in Little Boughton Street and described himself as 'agent'. The next year's census throws up no clues as to what the Sommers family did next – but clearly, fate had still not finished with the former surgeon's son from Bedworth...

In April 1911, he was living at 19 Wood Terrace off Sansome Walk, aged 64, described as 'Police Pensioner' and, perhaps surprisingly, still married after 39 years to Harriett, also 64. Living with them was their elder daughter, dressmaker Sally Maria aged 38 and single, and her apparently-illegitimate (*or possibly adopted as her surname is given as 'Sommers'*) daughter Gwendoline aged 4, whose middle name was Maud almost certainly in memory of the Sommers' deceased younger daughter who'd died in November 1903 aged 28. A no doubt broken man beset with tragedy and failure, Arthur Sommers died in Worcester in September 1916, aged 70 friendless and unmourned.

But all that was in the future. For now, Worcester City Police – its image tainted and emerging from the worst kind of turmoil – needed a new chief to repair the damage and recover lost ground and trust. Accordingly, the search for its seventh Superintendent was on. The average tenure of the previous six – Henry Sharpe, James Douglas, John Phillips, Thomas Chipp, Matthew Power and Arthur Edwin Sommers – was just nine years and nine months...

*The spike – Arthur Sommers' legacy or his successor's?*

*(Courtesy Malcolm Price)*

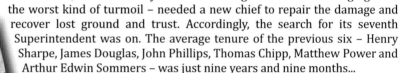

### Sommers' legacy? Introduction of the spike

There's confusion over the precise date of the introduction of the spiked helmet. In his earlier work on the City Police, Insp Colin Glover notes: '...in the absence of any concrete evidence in the records, is it merely coincidence that a uniform similar in all aspects (*to a photograph of Worcestershire Yeomanry dated 1882*) was adopted two years later?'

Whether that's the case – and Bob Pooler is similarly uncertain on the actual date – or whether the actual date was some time later, both former police officers are of the opinion that the force's most distinctive feature was introduced late-on in Arthur Sommers' reign as chief.

An alternative viewpoint is that the style may have been imported when Thomas Byrne took over. As police 2i/c in Blackburn he'd have seen the helmets worn by Manchester Mounted Police – one of just two forces to then that had adopted the spike. Among the few – and earliest – rare snippets available is that in 1898 they cost 7s 9d each, supplied by Worcester firm Butler and Kenwood, High Street.

# 10:
# The Byrne years

## (part 1)
### 10th June 1892 – January 1st 1900

Between the ex-chief quitting and his replacement taking over, the force, under the temporary leadership of **Tommy Wallace**, was to be rocked by yet another scandal at a time when it would prove more damaging than it might otherwise have done – a disastrous charge of theft against two officers, resulting in the downgrading of a PC to 2nd class, and the dismissal of a Sergeant, **Edwin Oakey** after 22 years' service.

Concerned that quantities of cider were nightly going missing out of a barrel in a shed she owned, East Comer market gardener Catherine Hundley laid traps to find the thief – first by placing an empty jug under the barrel marked with chalk, and later by having two of her workmen, Fawdry and Young, stay in the shed overnight in order to nab the culprit(s).

The *Journal* picks up the tale: '...shortly after midnight a key was turned in the lock and the door was pushed open. **PS Oakey** walked in. They [Fawdry and Young] only noticed **PC Hall**'s back in the doorway'. The remainder is a tale of circumstantial evidence: the background and vested interests of the

**Ensemble photograph at the rear of the Guildhall, probably late September 1894**

**Top rank (*left to right*)** *PC5 William Fennell with his hand on the shoulder of PC28 Joseph Williams, PC25 George Phelps, PC16 Albert Smalley, PC7 John Hazleton, PC24 David Evans, PC1 John Hughes*

*Extreme right PC30 Richard Robinson*

**Second rank: (*left to right*)** PC23 George Aston, PC37 John Wyatt, PC33 George Langstone, PC8 William Hollis, PC3 Frederick Hawker, PC32 Francis Gregory, PC19 Charles Hall, PC34 Albert Bradley, PC28 John Hall, PC21 Charles Lock, PC9 George Hooper

**Third rank (*left to right*)** PC2 John Bishop, PC31 Albert Lemon, PC35 William Deakin, PC 12 Thomas Jaynes, PC20 William Teale, PC27 Sidnam Cole, PC13 Thomas Love, PC32 Alexander Millar, PC36 Albert Hargreaves, PC11 Francis Pitt, PC29 Frederick Cook

**Fourth rank (*seated*):** PC26 John Penlington, Sgt 7 Samuel Grosvenor, Sgt 2 Francis Brotherton, Sgt 1 Frederick Tarrant, Inspector Thomas Wallace, Chief Constable Thomas Byrne, Inspector Henry Joyner, Sgt 3 Charles Thomas, Sgt 4 William James, Sgt 5 Henry Harley, Sgt 6 Frederick Peacock

**Fifth (front) rank (*left to right*)** PC17 Thomas Baynham, PC14 Frank Steadman, PC6 Thomas Mound, PC15 John Bishop, PC14 George Turner, PC10 Joseph Troughton

*Insp. Tommy Wallace had been Acting Chief Constable pending Tommy Byrne's appointment. He'd been with the force since May 1869 and was to serve another four years, retiring on 17th January 1896*

two witnesses were never checked; there was no claim that cider was drunk; there was never any concrete evidence that any cider had gone missing at all; and **Oakey** vehemently denied all charges, stating that the door was unlocked and that he was merely checking that no-one had broken in, as per his call of duty as supported by a long list of small donations made to him 'in respect of his vigilance'.

Nor was he ever asked to provide evidence in the form of the key it was implied he'd held. But then another 'witness', **PC Fred Cook**, threw in his two penn'orth and sealed the affair by stating that on at least one previous occasion, **PS Oakey** had invited him into the shed – although he stopped short of revealing the purpose, by implication to drink filched cider.

No doubt keen to avoid another scandal and accusations of cover-up at the worst possible time, acting Chief Constable **Tommy Wallace** hastily brought the case before an outraged Watch Committee. Their reaction was swift and crushing. **PC 18 John Hall** who claimed he was only acting under the direction of Oakey was reduced to PC 2nd Class although he was to continue with the force up to 14th March 1913 by which time he'd been promoted to Sergeant. **Edwin Oakey**, meanwhile, was found guilty and instantly sacked, rendering him pensionless and unemployable. He thought they'd acted harshly and said so.

### Ex-Blackburn 2i/c selected from short-list of six

The same day, June 3rd., the Committee revealed the names of the six candidates selected for interview for the vacant chief's post out of a postbag of sixty-five applications. They were: ex-Deputy Sherriff of Lake, Colorado, and ex-Lieutenant in the Armagh Light Infantry, Supt Lumley, now of the Derbyshire Constabulary, aged *38*; Inspector Spencer of New Scotland Yard, specialising in organising police activity and security at royal functions, *32*; Inspector Walter Thornton of Lancaster and before that of Bradford *31*; Superintendent and one-time detective, Thomas Byrne, *31,* second-in-command at Blackburn; Chief Inspector Sowerby, chief clerk to Leeds Constabulary *30*; and Inspector Bishop of Staffordshire Constabulary based in the Old Hill district who fatally diminished his chances of selection by 'refrain(ing) from circulating his testimonials among the Committee in deference to the forbiddance of canvassing'.

The choice whittled down to two – Byrne of Blackburn and Inspector Spencer of Scotland Yard – the final decision was made on a majority of one. In a 17-word article under the headline *'Election of Chief Constable'* and featured in the 'Latest News by Telegraph' section, the *Journal* revealed the name of the successful applicant. 'At a special meeting of the Watch Committee, today, Supt. Byrne, of Blackburn, was appointed Chief Constable'.

**Thomas William Byrne** was married to Hannah and they had four children, Ellen (*7*), Harry (*6*), Thomas (*5*), and Alice (*2*), and prior to his appointment they'd been living at 96, New Bank Road in Blackburn.

He was, according to the *Journal* the following week:

*'...a self-made man. He has had practical experience extending over a period of thirteen-and-a-half years. His service has been continuous and he has passed through every grade*

*of the police service up to his present rank. He joined the Blackburn force as a fourth-class constable on the 16th February 1881, after having served two and a half years with the Lancashire Constabulary. He held office as a detective from 1883 to 1887, when he was elevated to his present position on the promotion of his chief. His promotions in the Blackburn force were made in quick succession because of the exceptional merit of his service. The Mayor of Blackburn testifies to his being a smart, thoroughly-trained, and competent police officer; while the Chief Constable commends him as a shrewd, intelligent and able officer, of good address and education, and gentlemanly appearance, well versed in criminal law and a good disciplinarian. The Magistrates' clerk acquits him of harshness or unfairness to his subordinates'.*

For all his character references and promises of things-to-come, the new chief was going to need all the personal and professional qualities he could muster if he was going to succeed at Worcester where trust in the police was fading and deep divisions were splitting the ranks.

He took up his post in the last week of June and was '...introduced to the constabulary by the Mayor (Mr. Walter Holland) who remarked, with satisfaction, on the discipline of the force during recent difficulties, and the loyalty of the force to their temporary chief' reported the *Journal* a few days later (*July 2nd*). According to the report, there was no welcoming speech from the mustered men – although it was demonstrated by 'a hearty reception', similarly warmly responded-to by 'Mr Byrne (*who*) said he took it an honour to be at the head of such a fine body of men as he found the force composed of. It would be his aim to maintain the force in that high state of discipline in which it was at present. He said his efforts would be unavailing unless he had the entire co-operation of the men themselves. He told the men they were each units of a whole, and the actions of any one reflected on the force and therefore the credit of the force rested with the individual members'.

At the regular Police Court the same day, he was also introduced to the Bench and magistrates and the usual promises of co-operation and hopes of a long association and the usual platitudes were duly dispensed with.

It didn't take long for the indiscretions of 'the late chief constable' to surface in court: when **PS Fred Tarrant** charged Albert Creese with being found on licensed premises after 11pm – in this case, the Unicorn in Broad Street – the accused countered that the former police chief regularly stayed there later than that: '...the Bench thought the police acted rightly, but the evidence showed there was no breach of the law' curtly remarked the *Journal*. The phrase 'chickened-out' hadn't yet been coined.

Nor was it long before the new chief found himself embroiled in a case geared to test his own leadership qualities to the full: **PC 26 Edward Harris** who'd joined in June the previous year, had been called to yet another nasty fracas at the Boar's Head in Newport Street involving up to a dozen, although some claimed fifteen, drunken squaddies who were threatening other drinkers and refusing to leave. At least one full-blown scrap was already underway in the street, and as the soldiers were unbuckling their weapons of choice, their belts, Pte. John Lee of the 3rd (Militia) Battalion Worcester Regiment stationed at Norton was unfortunate in being the first one caught up with by the gung-ho bobby. He was hit over the head in a vicious swipe and spent 20 days in hospital.

PC18 John Hall

Damning for Harris was that he was alleged to have said *'that's the way to knock 'em out'* as the blow was struck. Despite eminently-justified police claims of constant provocation in that quarter of Worcester, as well as **Sgt Sam Grosvenor's** testimonial that Harris was 'as good an officer as the force contained' as well as a spirited defence by **Arthur Sommers'** old adversary Arthur Beauchamp, Harris was committed to trial on a charge of causing actual bodily harm. Fears of yet another PR disaster in the wake of outraged calls for the PC's dismissal weighed heavily and the new chief and Watch Committee could arguably be criticised for running scared

PC21
Charles
Lock

and acting hastily when they first decided to suspend him from duty, and then, under increasing pressure from the military and fears of reprisals, to summarily dismiss him from the force. With hindsight, the wiser course would have been to have waited because when the hearing came to the Assizes in October, Harris was found not guilty of violent assault and the case dismissed to a round of applause from assembled witnesses. Almost heartlessly, he was never reinstated.

The altercation had happened just two weeks after **Tommy Byrne** had arrived in Worcester and it was not the dream introduction to his newly-adopted home that he'd been hoping for. Nor had he come out of it with any notable credit.

The dream took another sour turn just the following week when 69-year old Thomas Ashcroft accused **PC21 Charles Lock** of a serious assault during an arrest for d&d in Thorneloe Road in which he claimed the PC had kicked and otherwise 'ill-treated' him. This time the Bench took the opposing view and dismissed the drunken labourer's allegations as entirely the figment of his bibulous imagination. But this was a trying time for the new chief and it's possible that for a while he must have rued his decision to quit a comfy role as 2i/c at Blackburn in favour of chief of an unruly and volatile hot-spot like Worcester.

In September, **Tommy Byrne** presented his first report to the Brewster Sessions – and sobering reading it made too. The city had 288 licensed premises and during the year, 225 persons had been proceeded against for drunkenness. Despite the damning statistics, Mayor Walter Holland went out of his way to deliver something of a pep-talk and to *'congratulate the Chief Constable*

## Also this year: 1892

■ police charge Henry Willis, landlord of the Black Lion in Dent Street with indecent assault on a 9-year old, Fanny Hall

■ a week later, cabinet maker Henry Allen is charged with criminal assault and indecent assault on 11-year old Edith Phœbe Davis

■ Tommy Wallace investigates horse-fixing ring based at the George and Dragon in the Tything

■ police out in force to prevent trouble at the General Election held throughout July. George Higginson Allsopp (Con) returned

■ in August an anonymous well-wisher sends Tommy Byrne 10s in the hope that 9-year old Arthur Dutfield, charged with assault, might be let off a sentence of whipping. The offer was declined, the money was advertised for return, went unclaimed, and was donated to a Poor charity. Arthur Dutfield got whipped

■ throughout the autumn, police are called in to maintain order at a succession of Temperance meetings

■ more men and boys are charged with outraging public decency by bathing naked in the Severn. The Journal's Crowquill advises that ladies on boats should avert the spectacle by judicious 'manœuvering of a parasol'

■ another squaddies v civilians free-for-all is broken up by police in Sidbury after a ruckus created in the Old Talbot overflows into the street. Two Worcester men and a private in R Company Worcester Regiment, sentenced to seven days' hard

■ in September, squaddie and convicted arsonist William Hancocks of the 3rd Battn Worcestershire Regiment takes on four policemen, Inspector Henry Joyner and PCs John Hall, George Turner (who was to serve up to 1922) and Frederick Cook, inside the station house after they'd brought him in on a d&d charge and he'd turned wild after his handcuffs were removed. Two months' hard

■ the following week militiamen are banned from coming into Worcester on Saturday nights but just a week after that, PC John Bishop (it's not clear which, No2 or No15) is attacked by six squaddies with doubled-up belts in Bath Road. Four sentenced to a month's hard apiece

■ father of 18 children Enoch Dayus (50) of Pheasant Street charged with two counts of indecency on consecutive days. They were his fourth and fifth charges in as many years. A month's hard labour for each offence

*on the very explicit manner in which he had prepared and presented his report'* – noting his concern at the rise in females being charged with drink-related offences.

The next Watch Committee also received a request from the new chief for an increase in police numbers – although only by one sergeant, and that only because of the recent deaths of three of the Mayor's officers and the additional workload thus created as the service of summonses now fell on the police. Approved. At the same session, **PC Henry Harley** was appointed Sergeant and **PS Charles Thomas**, chief architect of **Arthur Sommers**' ousting, elevated to Court Officer.

With some months now under his belt in Worcester, something of **Tommy Byrne's** essential character as a martinet began to surface. In September he'd issued an order to his constables to ask traders in the Shambles to take up no more than two feet of the pavement when displaying their goods for sale as he considered that free movement was being impeded and that the shopkeepers were guilty of creating serious obstructions on market days. The move instantly sparked-off howls of protest that the chief constable was overstepping his mark, that he was proposing to do away with the time-honoured privilege of displaying goods and that neither he, nor the Council, had the power to sacrifice the ages-old rights of traders in a historic commercial thoroughfare like the Shambles (*picture next page*). Byrne was asked to reconsider – or at least to tone-down – his request and to take a 'commonsense approach' to the issue as in the opinion of many, the Shambles had long been considered as outside the by-laws for street traffic.

A month later, he showed he was not a man to be messed with: John Thompson of Lowesmoor was hauled up before the Bench, charged with obstruction in the Shambles and fined 5s with 14s costs.

In November, **PCs George Turner, William Charles Fennell, Thomas Love** and **Frederick Cook** under the command of **Sgt Sam Grosvenor** all emerged with distinction after tackling a disastrous fire at McNaught and Co's coach works in the Tything (*the site of the former Kays' building*) that despite their gallant efforts was all-but destroyed. **Tommy Byrne**, two inspectors (**Tommy Wallace** and **Henry Joyner**), three more sergeants, **William James, Francis Brotherton** and **Henry Harley** as well as 22 constables, plus the Norwich Union fire brigade and several members of the county police, all joined in the rescue work, displaying '...energetic and well-directed labour under the Chief Constable who fought manfully and unsuccessfully against what appeared at starting to be hopeless odds'.

'The city is rich in latent heroism' also remarked the *Daily Times*.

The damage was put at between £10,000 and £15,000 and sparked-off calls for electric fire alarms to be connected to the police station. Crippling though it was with 32 employees temporarily put out of work, the collateral damage could have been much worse: just two days earlier they'd completed and shipped a new official coach to the capital, commissioned for the use of the Lord Mayor of London.

Still pep-talking, at the last Police court of the year, the now ex-mayor Walter Holland made a special point of remarking on the early successes of the new police chief '...who had prepared the evidence and carried out the cases entrusted to him with business-like tact. He also expressed his thanks to the police for their assistance'.

His successor as Mayor was 31-year old Alfred Percy Allsopp, brother of the city's MP George Higginson Allsopp, and himself MP for Taunton who bore more than a passing facial (*and facially hirsute*) likeness to Tommy Byrne. At the same end-of-year session, 63-year old Alvina Williams was charged by Inspector **Tommy Wallace** with being drunk and incapable. It was her 48th conviction and her fourth in 1892 alone. Fined 20s and costs 3s 6d or 14 days' gaol.

The year had been a roller-coaster for Worcester City Police and a baptism of fire for its new chief. How would 1893 fare...?

**Gained:** *Thomas Byrne, Nathan Harper, George Phelps, John Penlington, Francis Osborne, Albert Smalley*

**Lost:** *Edward Harris, William Howell*

*Sgt Henry Harley, recruited September 1877 was to serve until October 1903*

*(below) PC4 George Turner served up to 1922*

# 1893

It was not the best of starts. The 1½ d *Journal* headed its second edition of the year with a glaring masthead 'literal' (*see inset, below*)

Over the Christmas period, some person, or persons, unknown had been touring Worcester scrawling obscene messages and drawings – not one of which did any of the city's shocked newspapers think fit to describe, let alone illustrate – on walls. It prompted an outraged Council to hastily introduce a new, and 'much-needed' by-law that '...no person shall, within the city of Worcester, draw, inscribe or write any indecent figure, representation, or word upon any house, wall, fence or any other place; and that every person who shall offend against this by-law shall be liable for every such offence to a fine not exceeding 40s'.

For the city to move at such unprecedented speed, the images must have been particularly graphic.

In the wake of the McNaught fire in October, **Tommy Byrne** had been asked to supply his views and recommendations regarding the future of the Fire Brigade and its appliances, and early in January he responded by advising that in his view only a portion of the force should act as a fire brigade but with extra pay for those chosen.

He also recommended that a steam fire engine, 700 yards of hose and a number of other appliances should be bought; that the site of the Dolphin Inn and yard should be used for buildings; that electric alarms and telephonic communication should be introduced; that a few men should live at the station; and that horses should be obtained which might be partly used for other work.

The Watch Committee initially responded by approving *all* of the recommendations until it was calculated that the cost was likely to be £587 a year – to which they instantly recoiled, adding that approval would only be possible '...providing the Fire Insurance companies contributed to the cost in proportion to their interests in the city' (*Journal*), and promptly adjourned for a fortnight.

An outraged Alderman (Walter Caldicott) also pointed out that: *'...there had been more fires in Worcester since Mr Byrne came than in the previous twenty years'.*

*The Shambles,
photographed around this t*

## Ex-chief Sommers still creating waves

The jinxed, out-of-favour and still highly-emotive name **Arthur Edwin Sommers** also appeared in police ledgers for the second time since he'd left the force. The first was when he'd been granted a licence to run the Queen's Arms in Bank Street – scarcely a wise move given the time and energy he'd expended during his tough regime of cracking-down on Worcester's legion of drunks, felons and sundry other ne'ers-do-well, his constant pressure on licensees to toe the line, or the fact that the Queen's Arms, already with a grim reputation in the heart of one of Worcester's most notorious no-go areas, was little more than 100 paces from the police station-house. Now, in an article that had it been written today would surely have begged the headline 'what goes round, comes round', he'd had to call in his ex-colleagues to throw out a serial drunk and notorious kicker-off Charles Young of Birdport after he'd been refused any more drink and began smashing up what had already been a rough pub.

*PC33 George Langstone and new recruit this year, PC35 William Deakin who went on to serve until 1921, rising to Sergeant*

**PC** *(later Sergeant)* **George Langstone** (left) – *significantly one of those that had not signed the petition against his former chief* – was the constable summoned to put him out. Charles Young was fined 20s and 13s 6d costs or 14 days in gaol. The PC was not to be so fortunate in a violent affray next year...

In mid-April, **Arthur Edwin Sommers** made the headlines once again when the Queen's Arms' licence was temporarily transferred to George Henry Blackford, pending another up-coming appointment for the ex-police chief: this time it was with the Official Receiver. Less than a year after leaving the force with a not inconsiderable pension, he was already bankrupt and before the year was out would attempt suicide.

The first recorded incident involving a telephone call to the police (tel No9) occurred in April when a message was received at the station-house concerning a report of flames being seen rising above buildings in Angel Street adjoining the Five Ways Inn. **Tommy Wallace, Sergeants William James** and **Sam Grosvenor,** and **PCs 13 Thomas Love, No7 John Hazleton, No6 Nathan Harper** *(just two months with the force)*; **Frank Petty** *(who was to quit the following month)* and **No12 Thomas Jaynes** responded with the hose reel, but by the time they'd got there, the fire – in which a quantity of hay and straw was destroyed – was already out.

In May, several PCs complained that their new uniforms were not so comfortable nor so well made as their previous ones, prompting a flurry of correspondence between suppliers Dolans, the Trades Council and the police. Concerns were also voiced that the London firm's tender – consistently the lowest and thus the obligatory choice as contractor – was only successful because of the system of labour employed by the manufacturers sub-contracting to dozens of little 'sweat shops' in London's East End. Traditionally, local firms had competed for the police clothing contracts but had failed dismally – to the point that by 1898 none even bothered to send in estimates any more. In June, the *Journal's* 'Crowquill' penned a neat little article that sheds considerable light on the city of the time as well as taking the lid off the slightly sniffy attitudes of its editor and his professional principles. He wrote:

*'...Worcester is an attractive place. It is favoured largely by inhabitants of the Black Country who like its cleanness, the charm of its river, the fairness of its surroundings. They come in crowds and some of them singly. Within a few days there were two records of undesirable visits. Persons came here to spend money which had been dishonestly obtained. Two men were charged last Friday with robbing a man at Caerleon. They belonged to Tipton but did not return to that unlovely place to enjoy the fruits of crime. One journeyed to Worcester, bringing most of the plunder with him, but derived little pleasure from a full purse. There was speedy depletion. He fell among persons who took advantage of his criminal folly.*

- charge of manslaughter against Henry Walker, licensee of the Ewe and Lamb in the Butts for serving drink to a drunken person, a persistent female boozer named Bentley who'd died that same night (Dec 24th), is withdrawn

- 'Nobby' Guy, now 35, (see p366) described by Sgt Fred Tarrant as 'like a madman', falls off the wagon after several weeks' attempts at reclamation by the Salvation Army and is sentenced to six weeks' hard for an assault on PC4 George Turner

- Sgt Frederick William Peacock (later Inspector serving until February 1914) and PCs No8 William Hollis (later Sergeant serving up to 24th September 1920), No20 William Teale (later Sergeant serving up to 17th October 1919) and No27 Sidnam Cole are all seriously assaulted on the same weekend in February

- unnamed sergeant praised for saving life of a window cleaner who'd severed his radial artery in a fall through a window and walked from Bath Road en route to the Infirmary leaving a trail of blood before collapsing in High Street and given first aid

- PC1 John Hughes investigates William Morris who was so drunk in charge of a horse and trap he'd run into a German oompah band playing in Foregate Street and then narrowly missed running over a young girl

- lodging-house keeper Thomas Link of Newport Street logs his 60th court appearance mostly for d&d or drunk and incapable. Fined £1 with 2s 6d costs

- Tommy Byrne himself intervenes in a case of the Worcestershire Regiment's Quartermaster-Sergeant, 50-year old John Barnes found drunk and incapable in High Street. Concerned that the fall-out from an ensuing conviction would be out of proportion to the crime, he offered to withdraw the charge on payment of £1 to the police Superannuation Fund

- on April 14th., PC33 George Langstone charged ventriloquist Henry Wright with being drunk and incapable in the Tything. Fined 2s 6d including costs (all the newspapers failed – or more likely resisted – to mention gottles o' geer. BB)

- Alvina Williams drunk again, her 50th charge, found clinging to a wall in Angel Street on May 5th

- three deaths and eleven poisonings in the city put down to tainted pork pies

- PC6 Nathan Harper kicked 'in the abdomen' (probably nice-speak for genitals) when he is held by the arms and then savagely assaulted by 30-year old fireman David Evans of Watercourse Alley who said he held a grudge against the officer 'for the last time'. The PC is off work for several weeks and quits in December after just 18 months' service. Evans one month's hard

- spate of drownings in the Severn and canal mar the hottest summer for years

- PC26 John Penlington commended for talking (and physically restraining) drunken 18-year old Ephraim Baylis out of suicide by drowning

- body of two-week baby girl found in a bag dragged from the river by two lads near the Grandstand

- a black Saturday in August sees seven militiamen – one nicknamed 'The Brummagem Bruiser' – locked-up for various offences over the same weekend

- cab driver Frederick Lester (26) charged with manslaughter after his horse bolts 38 yards pinning William Henry Garforth against a building in Foregate Street, investigated by Sgt. Charles Thomas

- in November Tommy Wallace despatched to Gloucester to arrest newly-released prisoner Frederick King for the theft of a clock and some rings from the Bell in St. Johns

- on the same day at the end of the year Tommy Link is charged with d&d for the 61st time and one of his lodgers, Samuel 'Nobby' Guy makes his 22nd court appearance, this time for assaulting PCs 14 George Turner and No5 William Charles Fennel

- the same week, PC22 Francis Albert Gregory is savagely beaten up by William Kings in York Place and neighbours sign a petition for the 29-year old labourer's exclusion from the area

*He told the police that he somehow lost £27. He also lost his liberty and will not soon regain it. At West Bromwich a young woman was accused of stealing £9 from her grandfather. She also came to Worcester in company of a lover, and the money she brought soon went. It is to be hoped the fair name of Worcester will not be associated with many more cases of the kind. The city offers hospitality to all sorts of people and does not disdain the money even of Black Country trippers. But it does not want the patronage of purloiners'*

But by now, **Tommy Byrne** had put his less than auspicious start behind him and was beginning to make headway in official circles and garnering respect from his men and the city at large.

His first full-year report to the Brewster Sessions as Chief Constable was praised by the magistrates for being the clearest and most concise for many years, reflecting '...the highest credit upon the Chief Constable and the constables under him. It showed the Bench that charges of drunkenness and licensing offences were not brought without proper evidence to support them. With regard to the conduct of licensed houses he (*Ald Walter Holland*) was sorry to say there was a large increase in the number of prosecutions. The Chief Constable expressed his thanks for the kind expressions from the Bench. Such expressions would be a great encouragement to the officers to satisfactorily conduct themselves and bring cases before the court in a proper manner' wrote the *Journal*.

The year's public house black-list included the Great Western Hotel, the Ewe and Lamb and the Lamp Tavern.

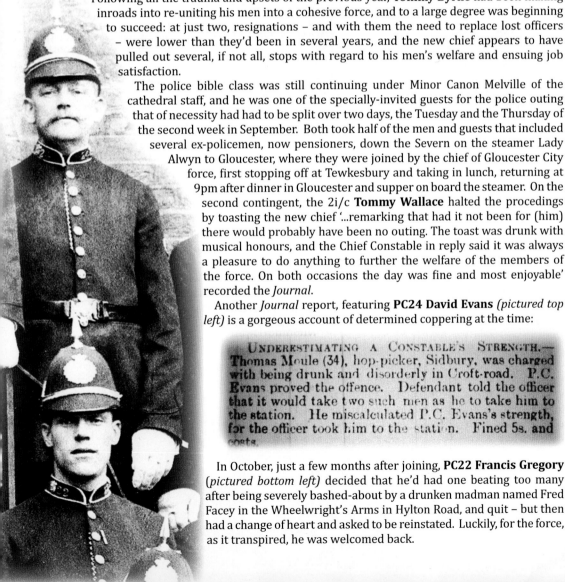

Following all the trauma and upsets of the previous year, **Tommy Byrne** had been making inroads into re-uniting his men into a cohesive force, and to a large degree was beginning to succeed: at just two, resignations – and with them the need to replace lost officers – were lower than they'd been in several years, and the new chief appears to have pulled out several, if not all, stops with regard to his men's welfare and ensuing job satisfaction.

The police bible class was still continuing under Minor Canon Melville of the cathedral staff, and he was one of the specially-invited guests for the police outing that of necessity had had to be split over two days, the Tuesday and the Thursday of the second week in September. Both took half of the men and guests that included several ex-policemen, now pensioners, down the Severn on the steamer Lady Alwyn to Gloucester, where they were joined by the chief of Gloucester City force, first stopping off at Tewkesbury and taking in lunch, returning at 9pm after dinner in Gloucester and supper on board the steamer. On the second contingent, the 2i/c **Tommy Wallace** halted the procedings by toasting the new chief '...remarking that had it not been for (him) there would probably have been no outing. The toast was drunk with musical honours, and the Chief Constable in reply said it was always a pleasure to do anything to further the welfare of the members of the force. On both occasions the day was fine and most enjoyable' recorded the *Journal*.

Another *Journal* report, featuring **PC24 David Evans** *(pictured top left)* is a gorgeous account of determined coppering at the time:

UNDERESTIMATING A CONSTABLE'S STRENGTH.— Thomas Moule (34), hop-picker, Sidbury, was charged with being drunk and disorderly in Croft-road. P.C. Evans proved the offence. Defendant told the officer that it would take two such men as he to take him to the station. He miscalculated P.C. Evans's strength, for the officer took him to the station. Fined 5s. and costs.

In October, just a few months after joining, **PC22 Francis Gregory** *(pictured bottom left)* decided that he'd had one beating too many after being severely bashed-about by a drunken madman named Fred Facey in the Wheelwright's Arms in Hylton Road, and quit – but then had a change of heart and asked to be reinstated. Luckily, for the force, as it transpired, he was welcomed back.

PC8
William
Hollis

PC20
William
Teale

A VIOLENT SCENE IN ALL HALLOWS.—James Wedgbury (42), labourer, Hylton-road, Walter Adams (52), labourer, no fixed address, and John Waterson (52), labourer, of the Crown Inn, Sidbury, were charged with being drunk and disorderly in All Hallows, on Friday night. Adams was also charged with assaulting P.C. Hollis, and Waterson with assaulting P.C. Langstone, in the execution of their duty. The case of Wedgbury was taken separately. P.C. Teale proved the case against him. Defendant resisted. He was fined 10s. and 4s. 6d. costs. P.C. Hollis and P.C. Langstone proved the case against the other defendants. It appeared that the men with Wedgbury were using obscene language, of which several people complained. They tried to get the men to go home quietly, but Waterson took off his coat to fight. P.C. Teale apprehended Wedgbury, P.C. Hollis apprehended Adams, and P.C. Langstone took Waterson. Adams was very violent and kicked and struck the constable. It took two constables and several civilians to take Adams to the station. He resisted violently and had to be carried. Waterson was also violent. He struck P.C. Langstone about the face and body, giving him a black eye and other injuries. The constable was for a short time unconscious, but Waterson was afterwards apprehended by P.S. Peacock. The defendants complained that the constables started the row by unnecessary interference. Adams was fined 10s. and 4s. costs for being drunk and disorderly. For the assault on the police he was sentenced to a month's hard labour. Waterson was similarly fined 10s. and 4s. costs for the first offence, and for the assault was sentenced to two months' hard labour. In both cases it was ordered that the imprisonment in default of payment of the fine should run concurrently with the other sentences.

On the same night that the Mayor, the Hon Percy Allsopp entertained 130 top-level guests including **Tommy Byrne** to a lavish banquet in the Guildhall – on the menu, Turbot et Sauce Homard, Lamproïses à la Matelote, Quenelles de Poulet aux Truffes, Salmis de Venaison, Lapin Sauté aux Champignons, Langue de Bœuf, Selle de Mouton à l'Anglaise and more – several of his men were getting a rare going-over in All Hallows when **PC8 William Hollis, PC33 George Langstone, PC23 William Teale and Sgt6 Fred Peacock** were all involved in a violent affray with a mob of labourers. The cutting (*above*) pulls few punches about the incident.

The *Journal*'s reporters could have been more selective in their choice of words towards the end of the year when the paper reported that: '*.. the Chief Constable said that in consequence of the conduct of such women (prostitutes) near the bridge, he had specially instructed plain clothes constables to watch*'.

The report followed an earlier account of 21-year old 'unfortunate' (polite-speak for prostitute) Elizabeth Reynolds and her client, 26-year old labourer Charles Page, behaving indecently in Severn Street. Because she had previous convictions, Reynolds was committed to fourteen days' hard labour and Page fined 10s 6d and costs.

**Gained:** *Francis Albert Gregory (who quit after a few months but had a change of heart), Albert Lemon*

**Lost:** *Francis Osborne, Nathan Harper, Frank Petty*

Sgt Fred
Peacock
ands
(below)
PC10
Joseph
Troughton

New year, same old routine: **PCs26 John Penlington** and **No8 William Hollis** were assaulted in the Pack Horse on New Year's Day, and City Coroner William Hulme's first week of the year involved eleven deaths requiring public enquiry. They included a suicide, a drowning, death from a fractured skull, another from fractured ribs, and a tragic number of deaths of infants: '...there has been one or two cases of overlying and one or two of burning through children being left alone with fires in their rooms. While one sympathises with the parents of these unfortunate children, one cannot but wonder that repeated warnings are ignored' noted the *Journal*.

The year's first Watch Committee addressed the issues of police Inspectors' salaries (*£100 7s 6d pa on appointment, rising to £118 12s 6d after nine years*) as well as the cost of insuring policemen on duty at fires, and whether or not to instruct the Chief Constable to clamp down hard on hairdressers remaining open on Sundays in defiance of the Sunday Observance Act: when the Corporation had previously tried to enforce similar action, the mayor's effigy had been burned in protest.

A curious situation arose with the visit of the Duke of York, later George V, for the laying of the foundation stone (*and inside it, a time capsule containing the coins and the newspapers of the day*) of the Victoria Institute on April 3rd. Due to the Shirehall and the statue of his mother Queen Victoria being sited within a small island of the County surrounded by the City, policing arrangements for the whole glittering day were entrusted to the County force under Colonel Carmichael.

Rarely visited by royals except for the passing-through of the Prince and Princess of Wales a decade earlier – the last time Worcester had been honoured by a royal guest had been 64 years earlier when the Queen, then still Princess, had visited the cathedral and Porcelain Works and created a near-riot when she lunched at the Hop Pole Hotel with her mother Adelaide – this time seemingly the whole of Worcester turned out to greet their future king.

Despite all the newspapers reporting the visit at length, amounting to hundreds of column inches, no mention is made of the role of the City Police in the day's proceedings. **Tommy Byrne** and his men must have been exceedingly miffed that the county force had stolen their thunder on their golden opportunity to put some of the grief of the previous few years behind them, to escape from the murk of everyday coppering, and to shine in the glitzy highlight of this, and many a previous, year. The only media coverage the force merited that week were the cases of George Price,

who'd been arrested by **Police Sergeant Fred Peacock** on a charge of stealing a macintosh at Ledbury and duly handed over by the attentive sergeant to Supt Phillips of the Ledbury police, and that of Fanny Godfrey (42) charged with being drunk in charge of a horse and cart in the Bath-road on April 6th: she '...was found by a policeman sitting almost asleep in the cart with the reins lying loosely on the horse's back. Fined 5s including costs'. The *Journal* hadn't even afforded the City's bobbies the honour of identifying the PC by name.

After the fireworks and non-stop action of previous years, 1894 was shaping-up as a hum-drum so-so year for Worcester City Police, the force seemingly plodding along, doing its bit and tackling whatever hassle had come its way. Much of the mid-year was spent by posses of constables actively responding to **Tommy Byrne**'s order of a heavy crack-down on the number of brothels in operation: in one case, **PC7 John Hazleton** admitted that he'd stood on a wall and looked into a room (*at 13 Court, Friar Street*) where what might today be termed 'a foursome' was under way with two women and two soldiers, resulting in 'Madame' Mary Greenway sentenced to a month's gaol.

As a result of the official police clamp-down on city-wide moral decline, a small army of children from several addresses complained-of as being in 'immoral surroundings', was taken into care by A. A. Maund on behalf of the Society for the Prevention of Cruelty to Children.

*PC7 John Hazleton got more than he bargained-for this year*

## Squaddie-related scuffles escalate

Despite Tommy Byrne's attempts at defusing the worsening situation with the military, few nights went by without some form of squaddie-initiated trouble.

This (*below, right*) is a typical mid-week morning's proceedings in the Guildhall. For all that, proof that **Tommy Byrne** was largely succeeding in his role as police chief was notably underlined in July when, on the second anniversary of his appointment, he put in for a pay rise without specifying a desired amount.

He'd been on £250 a year since his start '...and pointed out that with agreed allowances his predecessor's salary had been £285, and that when the Police Force Fire Brigade was formed, all the members except himself were granted additional pay'.

He was voted a 20% increase – taking his pay to £300 a year, plus £15 for fire duties – and significantly, the vote was unanimous '...cordial testimony being paid by several members to the efficiency of the force under the Chief Constable' (*Herald*). But when the matter came before the full council for ratification, yet again, several members railed against the expense and unwarranted generosity of the recommended amount, despite sometimes lavish praise for the way the 'new' chief, a shade over two years into the role, had conducted himself since his start...

**Tommy Byrne** '...has been with them (*the City police*)

ANOTHER DISORDERLY.—Joe Southall, a private in the Worcestershire Regiment from Norton, was charged with being drunk and disorderly in Camp hill road on Saturday, also with assaulting P.C. Pitt in the execution of his duty, and with doing wilful damage in a cell. P.C. Pitt said he was on duty in Camp hill road and saw defendant, who had hold of a girl. Defendant used bad language, and when the officer went up to him kicked the constable on the ankle. P.C. Teale corroborated, and P.S. Harley said that prisoner was very disorderly in the station cell and he put the damage to the seat at 2s. Prisoner, who is only 18, and alleged that the officers kicked him and put him across the table, was sentenced to two months' hard labour for the three offences, the Mayor commenting strongly on prisoner's conduct.

A BRAVE CONSTABLE: A BAD SOLDIER.—Frank Neal (22), private, Worcester Regiment, Norton Barracks, was charged with causing an annoyance by fighting in All Hallows on Saturday. P.C. Robinson was informed by a man, whose face was cut, that he had been knocked about by Militiamen who were fighting. The officer found defendant and others fighting with their doubled belts. With the assistance of a man named Wager, the officer got defendant, who offered some resistance, to the police-station. Defendant said he was "not a Militiaman, but belonged to the Line." There were Militiamen and civilians fighting together. A sergeant from Norton Barracks said that defendant bore a very bad character, having been convicted of many military offences. The Mayor remarked that the fact that the defendant was a Linesman rather aggravated his offence. Defendant was fined 10s, and costs, or 14 days' hard labour, and the Bench complimented P.C. Robinson upon his bravery in going into the affray, and also commended Wager for his conduct, awarding him 2s. 6d. for his assistance to the police, which it was the duty of every citizen to give upon occasions requiring it. The Chief Constable added his thanks for the assistance given to the police officer. Defendant, who said that the Militiamen had got him into that trouble, was sent down, being unable to pay the fine,

sufficiently long for them to have tested his capacity as regards their conduct; his masterly management of the fire brigade and his skill in marshalling processions has shown his qualifications for the office' stated one member; '...he could not help thinking that if the late Chief Constable was worth the [same] money, the present Chief Constable was worth even more. It is a farce to classify him with the late Chief but it was our fault if we paid (**Arthur Sommers)** a great deal more than he was worth' commented another. Approved – but only just: 17-13.

By way of comparison, the City Engineer's salary was £450, the Town Clerk's £700 but was soon to be raised to £900. At the same meeting, the Council agreed by a far greater majority to purchase Pitchcroft and land at the Moors – total area 73 acres, 4 roods, 24 poles – for £8,000.

There was also better news on the general disorder front and the drop in the number of drink-related cases drew praise for Tommy Byrne and his men by the new mayor, George Henry Williamson – brother of **Arthur Sommers'** friend and supporter, former Sherriff and Alderman William Blizard Williamson who was mayor 1883-4 and described as 'one of the most popular mayors for years' – who stated that '...the improvement was as much due to the education of the public as to the diligent efforts of the police to keep down offences of that character, and he thought the Magistrates had every cause to be satisfied with the progress in this direction, and with the conduct of the general citizens and the police'.

Even the ex-chief's outspoken old adversary Arthur Beauchamp, now heading Worcester Licensed Victuallers Association, paid tribute to the police role in the prosecution of just three licensed victuallers compared with 11 the previous year. Over the year, 153 men and 44 women had been proceeded against for drunkenness – 190 being convicted and 7 discharged. The previous year had seen 237 and the year before that, 225 – the same as in 1890. In the Worcester Division of the County, 126 persons had also been proceeded against for drunkenness, 94 men and 17 women – total 111 – being convicted.

By any stretch and despite sterling efforts by its police hard-liners, Worcester remained a hard-drinking town with a hard-drinking reputation.

The same week, Worcester Rovers FC (*9 points from 5 games*) moved up to second in the Birmingham and District Football League behind Aston Villa (*11pts*) but ahead on goal averages, of rivals West Bromwich Albion (*9pts*) and Wolverhampton Wanderers (*8pts*).

On November 5th., some much-needed high-profile PR for the force when almost the entire constabulary, the Watch Committee and the Mayor preceded a routine Police Court hearing with a presentation to '...a young man named George Penny, of Grimley, for gallantry in assisting a constable'.

He'd been the only one to respond when **PC1 John Hughes** who was coming off much the worse when called in to tackle a violent out-of-control drunk, and had ended up so badly injured that he hadn't been able to work since the fracas, precisely a month earlier on October 5th. The idea to publicly reward him for his actions and for the Mayor to 'do the honours' had been **Tommy Byrne**'s. Between them, the police had collected £2 17s 6d by way of a reward, made up to £5 5s by the mayor and Watch Committee, and further topped up to £10 by a personal donation from the mayor himself.

In addition, the have-a-go hero had been given a photograph in an oak frame showing the entire force with the inscription 'Presented to George Penny, by the Members of Worcester City Police Force, together with a sum of £10 as a token of their sympathy in the injury he sustained when assisting Constable Hughes with a prisoner; 5th November 1894'.

> During the presentation, the mayor... said that it was the bounden duty of every good citizen at all times, when called upon by any person in the service of Her Majesty, to go to his assistance, but unfortunately such gallantry was not always met with and it frequently occurred that a constable was left to struggle with a man in a drunken and violent condition until the constable was seriously injured. Penny, at great risk to himself, relieved the constable from a very serious position and in so doing had earned the thanks of the whole community. The Mayor then handed this sum [£10] and the photograph to Penny, remarking that he might in future look upon every member of the police force as a personal friend' (Herald).

At the end of the year, a spate of wanton cruelty to pigs that had been callously stabbed with forks was finally traced to two boys, George Potter (13) and Sidney Evans (11) both of Severn Street. In the last case of the last Police Court of the year they were each fined 2s 6d.

**Gained:** Charles Richard Pope (who was not to last the year), Thomas Mound, Albert Potter Bradley, William Deakin, Albert Hargreaves, John Wyatt
**Lost:** -

- police request military authorities to limit soldiers' passes to 11pm rather than midnight after another squaddies' free-for-all inside and outside the Albion

- on consecutive days in February, the force successfully tackles two serious blazes in Lowesmoor, one at Needhams Engineering Works and the other that threatened to destroy the 2nd Volunteer Battalion Worcestershire Regiment HQ

- Sgt Frederick Peacock investigates case of Dolday hawker George Clifford who sliced off his wife's nose in a violent 'domestic'. Six weeks' hard

- in July, PC33 George Langstone in company with bathing barge attendant Samuel Webb, carries the body of James Baker, foreman over female glovers at Dent Allcroft and Co, to the Grand Stand Hotel for inquest. He'd drowned himself in the Severn near the Pope Iron rather than face a pending sex scandal

- on August 31st PC28 John Hall discovers the decomposed body of an infant in an outhouse at the back of new houses being built in Shrubbery Avenue. Clothing it had been wrapped in was traced to servant at the Star Hotel, Alice Booton (21). Sentenced to one month's imprisonment without hard labour for concealment of birth

- sobs heard 'as he passed to the cells below (the Guildhall)' after Henry Brighton Cook is sentenced to six months' hard for a robbery at the Star Hotel, investigated by Tommy Wallace

- criticism over tenders for clothing with firms outside the city at a time of hardship for local journeymen tailors. Uproar at additional cost of 3d each for helmets and 3d a dozen more for gloves

- on December 28th PC17 Thomas Baynham (right) is temporarily blinded in an altercation with unwilling prisoner Alice Lloyd (25), arrested on d&d charges in Bank Streeet and fined 5s for drunkenness and 10s for assault

PC17
Thomas
Baynham

## 1895

January 14<sup>th</sup> saw the City rocked by the headline *'The Attempt to Murder Detective Wallace'* (*Herald*). Already monumentally grave, the charge took a distinctly darker turn when it was revealed that the alleged assassin, 49-year old Charles Young, was a former sergeant in the Worcestershire Constabulary and that his victim, already with 26 years' service and acting chief constable up to **Tommy Byrne's** appointment, was lying grievously injured in the Infirmary nursing four bullet holes and a head lacerated by a bullet that had been fired at a lateral angle and so had merely skimmed off his skull.

He was, in short, desperately lucky to be alive, and the prisoner fortunate not to be facing a murder charge and the ultimate penalty. *But it had been a close-run thing...*

### Tommy Wallace shot five times.... and survives

After being alerted to a wine and spirit merchant having stolen a pony and trap at Doncaster, **Tommy Wallace** had got wind of a man answering his description also, by coincidence, a wine and spirit merchant, also offering a pony and trap for sale in Worcester. Catching up with him in Lowesmoor, the 'tec and City police 2i/c asked him to accompany him to the station-house either to confirm or allay his suspicions, and when in the company of **Tommy Byrne** himself, the plausible con-man who also went by the alias of Charles Evans, offered to clear-up the misconception by showing them that *his* horse and trap were not the ones whose details had been circulated by the police at Doncaster. Better still, if the chief would permit

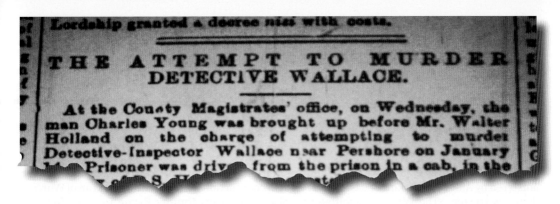

Lordship granted a decree nisi with costs.

# THE ATTEMPT TO MURDER DETECTIVE WALLACE.

At the County Magistrates' office, on Wednesday, the man Charles Young was brought up before Mr. Walter Holland on the charge of attempting to murder Detective-Inspector Wallace near Pershore on January ... Prisoner was driven from the prison in a cab, in the ...

his Detective Inspector to accompany him to (Drake's) Broughton, he would not only prove it, but would also pay the expenses.

With the chief's formal OK., Young, aka Evans, first hailed a hansom cab on the Cross to take them to Shrub Hill but when they got there, according to the *Herald*, the one o'clock train had already left:

> '... and prisoner asked the cabman (later revealed as John Gibbons) how much he would charge to drive to the cross-roads near Pershore Station. They drove to the crossroads. The cabman drove round the corner at the request of the prisoner who paid 8s for the fare, and told the cabman not to wait as he said he would drive the Inspector to the station in his pony and trap. They started to walk to Broughton'

If Tommy Wallace's subsequent account was true – and there's no reason to believe otherwise, although there were no witnesses – it was an incredible tale of heroism to the point of adventure comic stuff...

Young had led Wallace across several fields to a location called Holy Cross and then shot him in the back. While on the ground he then stood over him and again fired, hitting Wallace on the left temple, the bullet glancing off his skull. **Tommy Wallace** then said that he picked himself up, grabbed a large stick and went for Young, who fired another shot, this time into his upper arm and shoulder, and another, aimed at his head: '...the bullet struck the brim of the Inspector's hat but did not wound him' reported the *Herald*.

Then he fired again, hitting Wallace in the ribs. According to the report, the stricken detective still managed to keep on striking at Young with the stick, still backing from him until he managed to get close enough to hit the end of his pistol and deflect the last shot that Wallace suggested had been fired into the ground.

**Tommy Wallace** claimed it ended with Young up to his neck in an icy brook, before climbing out the other side and running away, and that his cries of 'Murder' had alerted three labourers in another field, John Long, Thomas Perry – who carried him to Pershore where he was attended by a doctor and then taken to Worcester Infirmary – and George Harley who tracked Young all the way back to Worcester where he was arrested, coincidentally, by **Sgt Henry Harley** in Edgar Street. Committed for trial at the Assizes.

When the Attempted Murder charge came to court a few weeks later under Mr. Justice Grantham, it emerged that the revolver was a small, self-acting American model that Young had acquired while in the States where he'd been imprisoned on several occasions after leaving Worcestershire Constabulary who come over as remarkably coy and reticent about revealing more of their mutual association. Young alleged the gun had either gone off of its own accord, or as the result of his being repeatedly hit with a stick by **Wallace** who he asked the court to believe had not been hurt anywhere near so badly as had been widely reported.

> 'In his summing-up, the Judge expressed his sympathy with the wounded officer, and said that Worcester people must feel proud that a member of their police force would have acted with the marvellous courage shown by the Inspector. They were all very glad that he was on the high-road to recovery. Was the attempt of the prisoner accidental? With regard to the first shot they could not say whether it was not accidental because Wallace had his back to the prisoner. But was the second shot which wounded the officer also an accident? Then Wallace saw the prisoner deliberately hold the pistol and aim it at his head and fire. Another accident? (Laughter). His Lordship said he thought all the witnesses in the case had acted with great discretion, and from the Chief Constables of the city and the county to the youngest lad, all deserved the greatest credit (Applause).

'The jury found the prisoner 'Guilty' after a brief consultation' (*Herald*).

Then a surprise: '...the Judge was proceeding to pass sentence when the prisoner asked that the Prison Surgeon might be sent for, as he thought he might explain that the injuries to his head would be calculated to cause mental disturbance at times. Mr G(eorge) Hyde was summoned, but it appeared Mr L. J. Wilding had been acting in his place during his illness. Mr Wilding, in answer to the prisoner, said that the injuries he had received had not had the slightest effect on the prisoner's brain'. It was never made clear what the injuries were or how he'd come by them. Sentence: 20 years imprisonment.

Not that he cared overmuch, but **Tommy Wallace**'s original guess was correct: the pony and trap that Young had put up for sale at Worcester, *had* been the same as that missing from Doncaster where he'd been known as Charles Evans.

The City Council immediately set up a fund for the future welfare of the incapacitated Inspector, administered by Alderman Firkins of 9 Foregate Street in conjunction with Mr Sutton Corkran of Worcester Old Bank as trustee. The Watch Committee was also pressed by **Tommy Byrne** to grant **Inspector Wallace** £30 as a reward for his conduct and compensation for the injuries he'd received – a request that had prompted calls for £50 as a more fitting gesture. But, just as in the past, official objections were raised about ratepayers' money being used in this way '...and the original resolution carried' drily noted the *Herald*.

At least, **Tommy Wallace** was on the mend. At the end of March, he wrote to the editor of the *Herald*:

> '...will you allow me the opportunity of expressing my thanks to the medical and nursing staffs of the Infirmary; and also to the public for the kind and sympathetic interest which has been shown towards me in my misfortune? I cannot be too grateful to Dr Crowe, Dr Bates and the assistant house surgeon of the Infirmary Mr Budden, for the pains and skill they displayed in extracting the bullets of my assailant, and the attention they afterwards bestowed during my illness. I am deeply indebted also to Sister Oakey, for the patient and watchful care with which I was tended throughout the long and painful weeks during which I was confined to the Infirmary, and for her special kindness in accompanying me when I gave my first evidence in the Board-room. And of her assistants, to whom I am also very grateful, I should like to mention Nurses Harrold, Greenlaw, Campbell and Gardner. My experience of the treatment of patients in the Infirmary leads me to express my deep sense of the blessing of such an institution to the city and county of Worcester.
> Yours truly, T. Wallace, Inspector City Police'.

In May, **PC17 Thomas Baynham** (*pic, previous page*) was severely censured by the magistrates for over-reacting after witnesses claimed he held down a drunk and violent labourer, 32-year old John Waterson, with one hand and struck him three times with his staff in the other. While on duty in Broad Street, he'd been greeted with the words 'Well, sleepy?' by Waterson who then tottered into the Leopard, followed by **Baynham** who ordered the landlady Mrs Willis not to serve him any more drink. When the PC turned to go, Waterson followed him out and hit him three times in the face. 14 days' gaol for d&d and a month for assault on the constable – although, noted the *Herald*: '...the Bench considered the PC should not have used his staff so freely'.

As W. S. Gilbert had written in 1879, 'a policeman's lot is not a happy one' (*for a delightful video of a more recent performance in New York, see **https://www.youtube.com/watch?v=OpVbBH9Ip8I***) and in some respects that sentiment was true of the city police this year. Ever watchful over his men's welfare, **Tommy Byrne** had responded quickly to their request for an additional day's leave a month. Up to now, theirs was a seven-days-a-week slog, the only respite being the annual seven days' leave – and even that was at the discretion of the Chief Constable. With typical sympathy for the policeman's 'lot', instead of making a decision, the Watch Committee referred the request to a special Police Sub-Committee.

Plus ça change #1.

The vacillations and tight-fistedness of the council must have been trying the patience of the entire force and a further incident some weeks later brought home just how petty and small-minded councillors in the Faithful City had been – *and still were...*

In attempting to halt a runaway horse and trap in St Swithin's Street, hero **PC1 John Hughes** had been knocked down and injured, **PC30 Richard Robinson** coming to the rescue and halting the horse without further damage before returning to assist his stricken colleague. **Tommy Byrne** was impressed, as was the rest of the city – all except the majority of the council who, requested by the chief to recognise the PCs' bravery with a gratuity of £1 to **Hughes** and £2 to **Robinson**, stated that the men were doing no more than their duty and that it was not their place to recognise it.

Despite an impassioned plea by the chief citing the Police Act that made provision for local authorities to recognise exceptional acts of bravery with suitable awards – and the readiness of authorities in most other towns to do so – they voted to contact the horse's owner, Mr Stiles to see if he would foot the bill instead.

As if to rub-in their clear snub to the force, at the same meeting a call was made to sell the Chief Constable's horse and trap, one councillor '...alleging that they were used for purposes other than those for which they were purchased. The Chief Constable, in the course of discussion, denied the imputations of improper usage, and said that he could bring nearly a dozen instances in which the trap had been out in the city making police enquiries. It had also been used in taking members of the Fire Brigade to

*PC01 John Hughes and PC30 Richard Robinson.*
*Their heroic actions divided the Council this year*

practice' (*Herald*). Then the inevitable: '...it was understood the matter would be discussed at the next meeting of the Streets Committee'. Plus ça change #2 and #3.

Despite some inevitable unrest among the men, the annual Inspection by Captain the Hon C.G. Legge, Her Majesty's Inspector of Constabulary for the Midland District proved a triumph despite the absence of a sergeant and two constables on duty and **Tommy Wallace** still on the sick-list – although he'd been recuperating at home, 6 East Street where lived with his wife Margaret and children Florence, William and Elizabeth. He'd returned to work by 9th July.

43 policemen of all ranks were paraded before the mayor, the Sherriff, Town Clerk Samuel Southall, two Aldermen, several members of the Council and the Inspector's retinue, and put through their paces in the police yard by Drill-instructor (*also PC16*) **Albert Smalley.** Capt Legge's only pessimistic note was the condition of the cells and the parade-room '...which he pointed out to members of the committee, was very scanty'.

With the force now numbering 47 – an up-to-par tally with the city's population of 46,766 – it had been noted that the present police accommodation had been provided thirty-four years earlier when the city's population was 12,000 fewer and the police force numbered 28. Now hungry eyes were being cast in the direction of the Dolphin Inn that butted-up to the police yard and the rear of the Guildhall. Its days were clearly numbered after 100 years' continuous existence as an inn and while its licensee Evelyn Helen Wells didn't yet know it, the next few months would be her last.

The City Council gave her notice to quit in February.

Being duffed-up was almost a rite-of-passage for Chief Constables of Worcester City Police (*see pages 56, 79-80, 86, 125, 149, 153, 158, 222 and 262*) and in June it was **Tommy Byrne's** turn after drunken plasterer 35-year old Frederick Bateman lashed out after the Chief had asked him to moderate his language during a heated 'domestic' with his wife outside the Infirmary.

## ASSAULT ON THE CHIEF CONSTABLE OF WORCESTER.

At the City Police-court, on Monday, before Messrs W. Winwood, W. Joseland, and Harry Day, Fredk. Bateman (35), plasterer, Surman's Buildings, the Moors, was charged with using obscene language in Castle street, and with assaulting the Chief Constable (Mr T. W. Byrne) whilst in the execution of his duty, on

Noted the *Herald*: '...the Chief Constable had a black bruise under his right eye'. He'd been punched twice, but had managed to hit back with two blows with his stick. Fourteen days' hard.

After a series of violent all-in scraps between the militia and the police, the autumn witnessed a welcome change when two

- in the same week that Tommy Wallace was shot, Lea & Perrins brought an action in the Chancery Court against a rival for marketing a similar product also called 'Worcestershire Sauce', and Nobby Guy had been up to his old tricks, seriously assaulting PCs George Turner (No4) and William Deakin (No35). 21 days' hard

- police investigate the suicide of 55-year old cab proprietor Thomas Stanley of Henwick Road. He'd sliced his own throat through business fears

- Tommy Byrne details PCs36 Albert Hargreaves and No23 George Aston (left) to keep a round-the-clock watch on a notorious brothel at Boar's Head Entry, Dolday, where male prostitutes and a 13-year old girl were also alleged to be working. 'Governess' Martha Wixey fined £2 and costs or 21 days' gaol

*PC23 George Aston*

- Sgt Sam Grosvenor spoils 22-year clean-sheet of noted City licensee George Seville, found drunk on his own premises, the Talbot in Sidbury after a steamer trip to Holt

- police investigate suicide of Asenath Pardoe, wife of the licensee of the New Pope Iron Inn, and murder of her baby Gertrude in the Severn near their home

- police follow-up a spate of accidents in the city after the new 'rule of the road' – that traffic should travel on the left side when meeting other traffic – becomes generally adopted, although not yet formally law

- Sgt Henry Harley, PC32 Alexander Millar and PC35 William Deakin (sloppy reporting by the Herald who referred to them as Miller and Deacon) assist in rescue of man drowning in the Severn and had refused to give his name. Suspected as having come from Droitwich, he was handed over to the County force and charged with attempted suicide

- the chief himself renders first aid to Frank Williams, proprietor of the Bell Hotel in Broad Street after he fell on the Cross and broke a leg

- the entire force keeps an eye on polling stations for corrupt practices as well as controlling a raucous mob at the victory celebration at another General Election. George Allsopp again returned with a 1,202 majority. Byrne praised for his handling of the proceedings.

- Sgt Samuel Grosvenor and PC26 John Penlington threatened by brewer George Hughes that he would 'pitch them into the river' when arrested for d&d in Bridge Street. Journal tersely notes 'he was carried to the Station-house'

- Tommy Byrne testifies that he 'had some doubts about the sanity' of Anna Maria Donisthorpe, who threw herself off the bridge in a suicide attempt after being divorced that very morning

- Nobby Guy clocks up 30th court appearance but claims his arm had been put out of joint by PC5 William Fennell during the arrest in which PC32 Alexander Millar had also been injured. 14 days' hard

- PC28 John Hall called into extricate drunken farmer Arthur Williams who'd tried to enter the Bush, St Johns, while still on his horse and cart. Fined 10s and 2s 6d costs

- at the end of a hectic picking season, the Journal notes 'cool winds have come and the moral atmosphere is better' following an unprecedented number of d&d and associated cases brought against itinerant 'casuals'

- Sgt Fred Tarrant and PC31 John Wyatt seriously roughed-up by brothers Henry and Arthur Weaver in Edgar Street in October

*Sgt Fred Tarrant in his 29th year with the force. He retired 1902 and died in 1934*

*PC6 Thomas Mound in his second year. He retired in 1931 and died in 1951*

militiamen, Harry Gibbons and John McCarthy, both privates stationed at Norton, came to the rescue of **Inspector Henry Joyner** who'd been coming off rather the worst after he'd been called on to turn violent drunk John Hobson out of the Talbot in Sidbury.   Pte. McCarthy had even given the 17-times convicted Hobson a glass of ale as a bribe to leave, but Hobson had drunk it and still refused to go.

When put out by **Joyner** and the two soldiers, he attacked all three and two of McCarthy's fingers were wrenched out of joint.  Fourteen days' hard for each of three offences – being drunk and refusing to quit, d&d in Sidbury, and assault on the two militiamen while assisting an officer in the execution of his duty; 42 days in all. The two soldiers received the thanks of the magistrates on the Bench.

**Gained:** *Charles Brotherton*
**Lost:** *Thomas Love*

At the end of the previous year, stalwart old-stager and chief architect of **Arthur Sommers'** downfall, **Sgt3 Charles Thomas** had announced his wish to retire after all-but 30 years: he'd joined on 6th February 1866 and retired on January 3rd this year on what might now be called an annuity of £57 10s.

Remarked the *Herald*, he: '...has soon found suitable light employment. He becomes the local Inspector of the Society for the Prevention of Cruelty to Animals, whose work deserves hearty support.  The sergeant has such kindly looks and manners, together with so much local knowledge, that it must be generally allowed there is a marked fitness for the appointment'.

By April, he had already successfully brought 2 cruelty cases to court, cautioned 22 individuals and had persuaded the owners of five injured horses to have them destroyed.  His salary had been raised by £10 and he was being asked to devote his whole time to the Society.  Whether his wisdom and experience was missed by the City police is not recorded, but it's all-but foregone that they were.

In its second edition of the year, the *Herald* reported on the Chief Constable's presentation to **Tommy Wallace** of 'a time-piece, two bronze ornaments, and a silver-mounted walking-stick, on his retirement from the City Police after serving 26½ years' (*mis-reported might be a more accurate description, referring to him throughout the article as W, or William*).

Aged 51, he'd joined on May 7th 1869.    In the same edition also appeared news of 36 hours of fighting in the Transvaal: it was the start of what was about to escalate into the Boer War.

The new mayor, 23-year old William, the 7th Earl Beauchamp, Viscount Elmley and Baron Beauchamp of Powyke later thought to be the model for Lord Marchmain in Evelyn Waugh's 'Brideshead Revisited', as portrayed by Sir Laurence Olivier in the BBC's much-praised 1981 series – chaired the year's first meeting of the Watch Committee at which it was unanimously agreed to promote **Sergeant Sam Grosvenor** to the rank of Inspector, just weeks ahead of completing 25 years with the force.

Following years of dodging any kind of decision on the state of police accommodation, the issue had reached such an impasse that by May a solution had become not only critical but also unavoidable... the station that had served for 35 years was now officially 'inadequate'.  The Chief Constable said so, HM Inspector of Police said so, most observers thought so, and now the Home Office was not only backing its Inspector but also adding that if enlargement and improvements were not carried out of the city's own accord, they would be under the instructions of the Home Office and with appropriate charges

*Sgt Charles Thomas resigned this year after 30 years (1866-96)*

*(Below) PC15 John Bishop*

– by implication, severe penalties – on the city and its infamously frugal fathers.

Nor would it mean a mere slap on the wrist: the implication was clear – put necessity above expediency or the Government grant would be withheld and the force's licence revoked. It was as stark as that.

Whether or not the phrase 'having kittens' was in vogue at the time isn't known, but it's probably a fair description of the way the City's mean-minded money-men must have felt. As like as not, hands were being desperately wrung when the chief's estimate of £2,030 14s for vitally necessary works was circulated in April – but at least it had been supported by the city's new nobleman mayor who '...moved that the original estimate, the revised estimate, the Inspector's letter and part of the Chief Constable's report should be printed and laid before the Council' even though he privately admitted that he considered Captain Legge's original letter to have been 'a fairly strong one for a Government official to write'.

But at least his was the foresight to carry the torch and to impress on the entire Corporation of Worcester that if action was not forthcoming **and now**, the future for Worcester City Police would be as good as nil. Visibly shaken and in no doubts about the consequences of shirking the issue yet again, the Watch Committee held an outraged and sulky debate on the pros and cons of the expense before duly voting on whether or not to recommend the full Council to approve the estimate and make a start on the work considered most critical. They voted in favour, but it was close: 6 for, 5 against.

In June, a most unusual sight on the city's streets – a negro, 63-year old Albert Lewis '...decked out in native costume' according to the *Chronicle*. He'd attracted so much attention that he was being followed by a crowd of up to 300 curious onlookers who jeered and threw stones at him. Police assistance arrived in the form of **PC06 Thomas Mound** who promptly decided that he was drunk – a view corroborated by **PC01 John Hughes** – and ran him in. Reported the *Chronicle*: '...that, he added in a tone of injured innocence, would be the last time he would ask the assistance of an English policeman. The Bench discharged him on condition that he left the town'.

The same day, noted nuisance Emily Taylor of Wellington Court Dolday was brought in by **Inspector Henry Joyner** for being 'as drunk as she could possibly be', swearing that '...it all arose out of the cruelty of her husband, who on every occasion knocked two of her teeth out'. Her 19th charge, it prompted one media wag to comment that she must have been born with 68 teeth.

The police outing this year (*on June 20th and 22nd*) again saw two detachments follow the same itinerary: journey 'by brakes' to Witley Court and Abberley Hall via Ombersley (*lunch in a meadow at Woodfield*) and Stourport, and dinner at the Hundred House followed by games, light refreshments and competitive tugs-of-war at the Red Lion Holt. That week had seen the highest temperatures ever recorded in the city till then – 89° in the shade.

*PC26 John Penlington*

Since his enrolment in September four years earlier, **PC26**, Staffordshire-born **John Penlington** now aged 23, had been regarded as a reliable and useful officer, if perhaps a stickler for doing things 'by the 'book', but he emerged in a heroic new light in an incident in July, as the *Chronicle* reported under the headline '***Constable as Bus Driver***', here reprinted in full:

'James Jones (34) 'bus driver, Bridge Inn, Bridge-street, was charged with being drunk in charge of two horses and a 'bus, on the Cross on August 13th. PC Penlington said that prisoner was driving the Hallow 'bus, and as he appeared drunk, witness asked him to get down but he refused, and witness then got on to the box and drove the 'bus to the Police Station. Defendant, who said it was his first day with the 'bus, was fined £1, including costs, or 14 days'.

**Gained:** Richard Gregory (who failed to last out the year), William Hollister Short, Alfred Tomlinson, Arthur Harry Guy

**Lost:** Tommy Wallace (after 27 years), Charles Thomas (after 30 years), Richard Robinson, Charles Hall

# Also this year: 1896

- Thomas Matthews caught shooting for fish in the Severn. Anglers were appalled, but that it was also out of season combined to blow the publicity surrounding the incident out of all proportion. Fined 1s and costs 8s

- the new craze of football becomes so popular that hours of police time are taken up in warning, and occasionally arresting, boys playing the game in the streets

- PC7 John Hazleton, now appointed Coroner's Officer, examines decomposed body of Eliza Brooks, dragged out of the Severn near the Grandstand having gone missing six weeks before, for identification

- in April, Tommy Byrne testifies at case of Beatrice Breeze, barmaid at the Hope and Anchor (now Vue Bar) who had given birth to a boy, put him in a box and left him to die

- violent police-hater John Hobson (see 1895) in court again for assaulting PC28 Joseph Williams in Lowesmoor

- PC25 George Phelps sent to tackle madman shoemaker George Green after a drunken window-smashing spree in which he'd put his fist through 48 panes of glass in Lich Street

- police raise fears over the 'enormous increase in cycling traffic, the number of women cyclists and the very dangerous pace the cyclists ride – making them not only a danger to foot passengers but also to themselves' (Worcester Chronicle)

- Det-Sergeant Fred Peacock highly commended by Bath Magistrates and by chief Tommy Byrne for his role in the arrest of two Frenchmen accused of a jewel robbery in Bath

- three officers, PCs 16 Albert Smalley, and No27 Sidnam Cole plus the chief himself (right) put out an extensive blaze in Severn Street so quickly and efficiently that it was all over by the time the Norwich Union brigade arrived

- Tommy Byrne's report to the Brewster Sessions reveals number of licensed houses in the city equates to 1:160 per head of population. Black-listed are Market Hall Vaults, Garibaldi Wylds Lane, Talbot Sidbury, Falcon Broad Street, Leopard Broad Street, Red Cow Birdport, Brewers Arms All Hallows, and Severn Trow, Quay Street

- police out in force to control crowds for the opening of the 173rd Music (later, Three Choirs) Festival

- and first performance of Edward Elgar's new oratorio, King Olaf [in the choir, tenor George Blandford, a personal friend of the composer and my great-great uncle. BB]

- PC28 John Hall called to examine body of a man found hanging from the handrail of the swingbridge at Diglis Locks, later found to be the city's Town Crier George Adams. Verdict: suicide whilst temporarily insane

- on October 1st the entire force including two mounted officers control massive crowds gathered for the opening of the Victoria Institute by the mayor and his sister Lady Mary Lygon, but not a formal guard of honour. That was provided by a 95-strong contingent from the Artillery Volunteers and Rifle Volunteers

- PC01 John Hughes has the unpleasant task of conveying 22-year old Henry Cox to the Infirmary (house surgeon rejoicing in the name Dr William Brodie-Brodie) after his head had been run over by the No7 tram at the Bridge Street end of the bridge. He died an hour later

- PC30 Richard Robinson resigns through ill-health after 11 years' service. He is refunded all the money he'd paid into the pension fund

- in November PC22 Francis Albert Gregory is slashed across the face by reins and a horse deliberately ridden at him by drunken farmer Harold Gossage

(right) PC27 **Sidnam Cole** and Chief **Tommy Byrne**. Both emerged as heroes with **PC16 Albert Smalley** following a fire in Severn Street this year

The Queen's Diamond Jubilee in June was going to be the event of the year, but until then, life went on as normal for the '*The Spike*' – the new street-name being bandied around with reference to Worcester City Police for evident and very visible reasons. The force was one of just three in the country to feature the distinctive spike crowning their helmets, first introduced at the end of **Arthur Sommers'** term as chief.

As preparations for the momentous royal milestone got under way, the advice 'don't joke with policemen' was offered by the *Worcestershire Advertiser* in the first week in January after **Sgt (*later Inspector*) John Bishop** and **PC21 Charles Lock** were told to put their heads in a watertrough in response to being invited to have a drink by Robert Alfred Tyler of 2 Rainbow Hill Terrace. He was summoned to court for d&d, but the case was dismissed, the Magistrates no doubt enjoying a suppressed titter of their own.

Journalists then, as now, got bored with writing the same story again and again so when it came to yet another 'policeman attacked by drunken yob' tale in March, the *Journal*'s unnamed reporter amused himself and his readers with the following account, worthy almost of a Booker Prize...

> *OUGHT TO BE SOMEWHERE ELSE. John Swain, 44, labourer, Rack-alley, ought to be engaged by the Turks or the Greeks, for there is no doubts that his fighting proclivities would be of material assistance to the belligerents. (He) is one of those who believe in the saying 'All come, all served'. He was in Broad-street, about 6.30 on Friday night and was testing his punching powers on the cranium of a woman. PC Turner* (pic page 359) *went to the latter's assistance, but he was attacked by the defendant. They fell to the ground, and in the general melee, Swain struck Turner a violent blow to the face. Assistance had to be obtained to take the defendant to the station. He was sent to Castle-street for 14 days.*

The tedium of walking the streets throughout the small hours was also highlighted by the *Journal* in another illuminating snippet about the coppers' lot (*cutting, below*) – as well as perhaps, something of a crueller side involving **PC3 Fred Hawker, Sgt Sam Grosvenor, PC24 David Evans** in an unguarded moment, and a badger (*it's thought possibly to be the one still preserved in the Museum*).

It was also the *Journal* that likened its reporters to the much put-upon police in the run-up to the Diamond Jubilee and its national holiday for rejoicing – Crowquill, as ever with his finger on the pulse, penning with perhaps not total sincerity that:

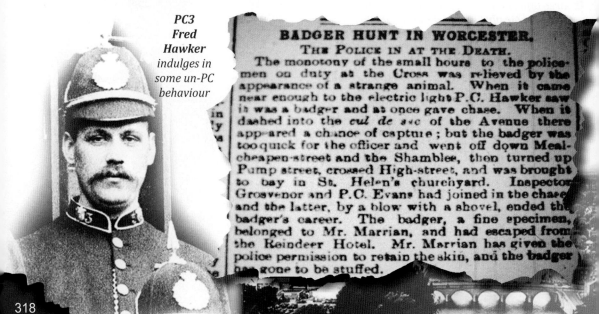

*PC3 Fred Hawker indulges in some un-PC behaviour*

**BADGER HUNT IN WORCESTER.**
THE POLICE IN AT THE DEATH.
The monotony of the small hours to the policemen on duty at the Cross was relieved by the appearance of a strange animal. When it came near enough to the electric light P.C. Hawker saw it was a badger and at once gave chase. When it dashed into the *cul de sac* of the Avenue there appeared a chance of capture; but the badger was too quick for the officer and went off down Mealcheapen-street and the Shambles, then turned up Pump street, crossed High-street, and was brought to bay in St. Helen's churchyard. Inspector Grosvenor and P.C. Evans had joined in the chase and the latter, by a blow with a shovel, ended the badger's career. The badger, a fine specimen, belonged to Mr. Marrian, and had escaped from the Reindeer Hotel. Mr. Marrian has given the police permission to retain the skin, and the badger has gone to be stuffed.

*'...roadmen, I see, are to have a holiday without losing the day's wages. I have not heard yet of arrangements for relieving the reporters. Like the police, I suppose, they must be on duty. They will celebrate the occasion by filling up their notebooks and producing columns of copy – which to them is always the great happiness of holiday-times'.*

In May a new record was set in the city – 138 court appearances resulting in 100 convictions, a remarkable tally clocked-up by 65-year old John Rowley, charged by **Det-Sergeant Fred Peacock** with being drunk and incapable in Newdix-court, High Street. It was his seventh appearance this year alone and by the end of the year it had been topped-up to 140 appearances and 102 convictions. *(Note: when I interviewed Ralph Gordon Banks, aka 'The Sherriff' on the occasion of his 96th conviction in 1985, he told me he wanted to make it the round 100 so's he'd get his telegram from the Queen! BB).*

A new official duty also fell on the police in mid-year – the capture and muzzling of stray dogs, under orders from the Board of Agriculture as the direct result of a rabies outbreak in the city. In consequence, several PCs gained the temporary title of 'catcher' and were issued with appropriate equipment: '...a cord loop at the end of a pole which may be drawn tight about the dog's neck, the advantage of the apparatus being that the dog cannot get away from the policeman, nor can it get too near. The only difficulty, probably, will be for the policeman to get near the dog' reported the *Journal*.

Stray dogs were kept in a pen at the Cattle Market for three days for reclaiming by their owners and released with appropriate charge – or alternatively, poisoned. On the first day alone they rounded-up four stray dogs, their owners each fined 2s; the daily tally continued at much the same pace for several weeks to come, and by the autumn, police were dealing with so many cases of unmuzzled dogs that magistrates upped the fine to 2s 6d and 5s for a second offence, but the prosecutions still showed no signs of letting-up. The temporary powers remained in place until the middle of the following year.

As Jubilee Day approached – *Tuesday, June 22* – **Tommy Byrne** gained some small comfort from the fact that, unlike the celebrations for the visit of the future George V for the laying of the Victoria Institute foundation stone three years earlier, this time the County police would be augmenting the City to the tune of 40 additional constables under his direction during the run of the rejoicings.

As if a dress rehearsal for the arrangements in crowd control for the next day's Jubilee, the police were out in full strength on June 21st when the streets were lined with people to hear the new mayor, Charles William Dyson Perrins, declare Pitchcroft now to be wholly the property of the citizens of Worcester and for their recreation. Celebrations included a full military parade and salute with a feu de joie involving 12 Artillery canons.

Though raucous and fervently ballyhooed by the entire city whose inhabitants turned out seemingly en masse the next day, the Jubilee celebrations went off almost without incident – the newspapers' virtual absence of reports on associated disorder or rowdyism standing mute tribute to **Tommy Byrne** and his men's control of the joyous and historic 60th anniversary event, the first in British history.

Only an unhappy band of boatmen, anticipating rich pickings from ferrying revellers from St Johns to the city and back created any appreciable hassle after they'd tried to break up a free 'Jubilee Bridge' consisting of '...canal boats with a footway of narrow planks' *(Journal)* that had appeared overnight linking Hylton Road with Pitchcroft. The bridge's success was such that calls were made for a permanent structure at much the same point, although it was to be the better part of a century before it became reality.

The now regular annual police outing – again in two detachments – took in lunch at the mayor's home Davenham in Malvern, a trek across British Camp and Eastnor Park ahead of dinner and rousing speeches at the Feathers in Ledbury, followed by team and individual sports including the 100 yards dash for a medal donated and presented by **Tommy Byrne**: the year's winner was newcomer **PC Alfred Tomlinson** who'd joined in March the previous year.

1897 had been shaping-up as a good year for the police: general public drunkenness was on a par with the previous twelve months, although the previous five years had shown marked decline, and reports of crime generally showed a welcome downwards trend. But if **Tommy Byrne** thought this was going to end up entirely blemish-free, he got a rude come-uppance in September when one of his newer constables, **PC31 Albert Lemon** *(pictured right)* who'd joined 9th

*PC31 Albert Lemon - perjury charge*

June 1893, was charged with perjury involving a case of obstruction and causing annoyance to passengers in the Shambles that he'd brought against fishmonger Elizabeth Thompson, wife of George. She claimed he'd been bullying and had targeted her having ignored others blocking the pathway: he denied it. He said she'd used bad language; she denied it. She said he'd threatened to have her locked up; he denied it. The case fell apart when it was revealed that George Thompson had already been prosecuted 32 times for obstruction, once for gambling and once for assaulting the police.

> *'The case was therefore dismissed, the magistrates expressing the opinion that it was a most heartless and cruel attempt to defame a man's character. There was no blame at all attaching to Lemon'* (Worcester Journal)

On consecutive days in September the same question arose: *did she fall or was she pushed*?

The first was when **Sgt (*formerly PC15*) John Bishop** and PCs **No2** also **John Bishop**, and No3 **Fred Hawker** were called in to the Yorkshire House (*now Imperial*) where the landlady, Emily Ellen Powell, was found in a pool of blood with her skull fractured having allegedly fallen from an upstairs bedroom window into the yard below. Husband Nathan Powell claimed she'd fallen after taking medicine.

The same question was asked the next day when PCs **29 Fred Cook** and **No14 Frank Steadman** took the body of Elizabeth Inight of 3, Hill Street, dragged out of the canal under Lowesmoor Bridge by a fitter at the nearby gas works only moments earlier, to the Guildhall for inquest where she was examined for tell-tale marks by Coroner's Officer **PC7 John Hazleton**. Witnesses stated that she'd led an immoral life after

## Also this year: 1897

- new year's courts abnormally hectic with a heavier-than-usual list of drunken and violent Christmas revellers

- controversial move to have all vehicles in the city lit with a lamp one hour after sunset and one hour before sunrise slung out at the Guildhall. Despite the set-back, it became a bye-law in October. Eleven offenders prosecuted on the first day

- police investigate when noted engineer John Cam, 71, slashes his own throat at Green Hill on February 1st. Verdict: suicide whilst temporarily insane

- language used by serial offender Nobby Guy during his 38th arrest considered so shocking that PC32 Alexander Millar prefers to write down 'a sample of the defendant's vocabulary' rather than repeat it in court. 14 days' gaol

- ambulance training extended to all members of the force in the wake of a spate of accidents, generally involving horses and traps

- PC24 David Evans disarms drunk and violent thug John Price in the Fish Inn after he'd attacked him with a poker and threatened to knock his head off. 14 days gaol

- George Munn of Broadheath ordered never to bring his 'frisky' pony into the city again after PC William Hollister Short summons him for furious driving in St Nicholas Street

- No24, PC David Evans is a busy bobby – even off duty. Walking home along Pitchcroft at 6.30 one May morning, he spots a body in the water and hails a passing boatman to help him

- recover it. It was later found to be Sidney G. Bourne, missing for six weeks

- the next week PC23 George Aston recovers the 'still warm' body of Selina Wiggin from the Severn at the Watergate near the cathedral. Despite applying artificial respiration for 40 minutes, she's pronounced dead

- PC24 David Evans (again) summons young newspaper vendor, Arthur Amett of Hare's Lane with causing annoyance by his shouting after a string of complaints: '...on being let off lightly – a fine of 2s 6d – the lad promised not to offend again' ran the Journal under the headline: 'A Stentorian Voice'.

- summer is marred by a rash of assaults on the police – almost all by drunk and pugilistic women: in one of the worst, PC (later Chief Inspector serving from 1894 to 1919) Albert Potter Bradley is seriously roughed–up in Quay Street by Margaret Jane Williams

- phenomenal bouts of drinking by hop-pickers are recorded in unusually crowded docks in the police court at the end of the season: in one, Thomas Billingham, arrested by recent recruit PC Charles Brotherton said he was paid 11s on the day of his arrest for d&d and now had 5½d., and John Henry charged by PC John Wyatt (top right - who was to die, still in service, at the end of the year) with being drunk and incapable in New Road had been paid 24s and when found by the constable, had nothing. It didn't stop the magistrates imposing a fine of 5s and 2s 6d costs, albeit 'with time to pay'

leaving her husband, and that a few days earlier she'd been in the company of a man whose wife had found them together and a claws-bared cat-fight had ensued. Inight's husband Henry was brought in for questioning about her death, but then suspicion fell on the wife of the man she'd been found with.

Coroner William Hulme stated that:

> '...it was possible that what had occurred might have upset her mind and caused her to take her own life (but) the evidence that she did so was very slight. However, unless the jury thought it necessary, he did not propose to call the other woman because he did not think it necessary to lay bare people's lives in that Court. The deceased might have fallen in or been pushed, and unless the jury were quite satisfied (as to which), they should return an open verdict'. Noted the Journal: 'The jury did not wish to hear the evidence of the woman who quarrelled with the deceased'.

**Gained:** Albert Bednall, Walter Repton, John Evan Febery, Charles Ernest Bailey
**Lost:** John Bishop (no 2), John Wyatt, Albert Smalley, Joseph Williams, Thomas Baynham

**Left:** two tragic Worcester City bobbies this year (1897). *Top,* **PC37 John Wyatt** who died on December 22nd and *(below)* **PC2 John Bishop** who quit on December 3rd this year, became a pub licensee in Walsall but was fatally injured in a scrap with a customer in October 1898 (*see page 323*)

## 1898

It was an unusually quiet start to the year, the newspapers seemingly more interested in the activities of the sports clubs that had sprung up over recent years – Worcestershire Cricket Club, Worcester Rowing Club, Worcester City and County Harriers, Worcester Coursing Club, Worcester Rugby Club, Worcestershire Quoiting League Association (*at which the City played at international level and fielded nine teams in the local league*) and the most prominent football clubs, Berwick Rangers and Worcester Rovers – than the everyday tale of front-line policing. Not only that, but the sudden and explosive rise in sporting pursuits had also spread on to the streets, the new craze of football taking the place of tip-cat as the means for depleting many a young man's excess energy.

By March, the issue of lads and men kicking balls about the streets had reached such a pitch that the police were ordered to crack down, a 'Crowquill' edit summing up the situation perfectly...

> 'The City Police are taking determined steps to put down the nuisance of football playing in the streets. Three days this week, gangs of youths were before the magistrates, and the ascending scale of the fines imposed, which, from half-a-crown on the first day, rose to seven shillings on the third [actually, 7s 6d], will perhaps be a warning to other lads that football is not an innocent amusement when played in public thoroughfares. The police are continually receiving complaints of property being damaged, horses frightened, and of pedestrians being struck by dirty balls or hustled and bustled about by street footballers who play without rules of "offside" or "outside". All this playing in the street must not be taken to indicate a need for more recreation grounds, because the nuisance chiefly occurs when the factory hands go to and return from dinner. The enthusiastic young men must be taught to get their digestive exercise in some other way, less troublesome to the rest of the public'.

Monday had seen Walter Hampton (15) of 10 Charles Street, Frederick Digger (19) of the Rovers Arms in Charles Street, William Roberts (16) of 3 St Stephens Terrace and Archibald Chance (16) of Charles Street all fined 2s 6d (Digger 5s as it was his third footballing offence) for playing in Charles Street and causing damage to property in the area. Tuesday had seen 5s fines imposed on Arthur Price (16) and Joseph Hemming (18) both of King Street, charged with causing an annoyance by playing football in Severn Street, and Wednesday saw Charles Quinney, Alfred Kite and Arthur Knight, all of Lion Row fined 7s 6d each for playing in Lowesmoor and Harry Greatbatch (15) Compton Road, and Robert Coombs of Hamilton House, Wylds Lane – both charged as 'younger boys' – fined 2s 6d and 5s respectively.

## Year kicks-off after an unusually quiet start

Even the *Journal* had remarked on the quietness of the year, observing that in the previous three months there had been neither an inquest nor a bankruptcy petition in the unusually placid city: '...one wonders if it was the joy of the Jubilee year that kept people from dying or committing suicide' ran an editorial.

Nor were the headlines much troubled with the likes of habitual offenders Nobby Guy, Tommy Link and Lizzie Dowling, while the colourful accounts of police beatings, battling women, immoral goings-on, assaults, hocusings, drunken rampages and inebriates found in all manner of curious situations and having to be carried off somewhere had just thinned-out; it's not until mid-summer that normal service Worcester-style appears to have been resumed.

Thus it was like a drop of water in the desert to come across three consecutive *Herald* snippets on the same day that restored lost faith and proved that no, the old City and its legions of ne'ers-do-well hadn't all died and gone to Hell:

● **PC14 Frank Steadman** had faced a tongue-lashing of coarse obscenities from Emma Burns of Dolday who was fined 5s and 9s costs

● **PC Walter Repton** who'd only been with the force for little over a year, had earned praise for prompt action in putting out a chimney fire in College Precincts, and

● **PC31 Lemon Albert Lemon** had come across Birmingham brass burnisher Harry Jones prostrate across the footpath and so hopelessly drunk that, finding a rail ticket sticking out of a pocket he personally carried him to Shrub Hill station to catch his train home.

*Pensioned this year after 28 years, Inspector Henry Joyner. He became grocer and off-licensee in Orchard Street.*
*Pps 347-8*

Even the *Herald* appeared to breathe a sigh of relief when in August it reported on Nobby Guy's 46th police court appearance 'after an unprecedented period of sobriety', concluding: '...of course, he went down'. Brought in by **PC26 John Penlington** on the usual d&d charge, he'd kicked-off in the station house where it took four officers to hold him down and handcuff him, and he later broke a seat and a window in his cell. 14 days for each offence.

Just two years earlier, another Guy had made his mark with the city police: this was **Arthur Harry Guy** who'd joined the force on 4th December 1896 aged 21 and was to continue as a PC for the next 27 years, retiring on 16th February 1923. The life-style of the two Guys couldn't have been less similar – one, born 1852 one of two boys to an unmarried mother and living in filthy conditions in Foundry Street and committed to a life of indolence, violence and petty misdemeanour; the other, born in 1875 in comparative luxury to a loving family father Henry, an importer of luxury goods and mother Harriet, the family home at 6 Church Terrace Malvern, committed by the nature of his career to suppressing crime and preserving law and order. On August 5th this year, he'd come in for a rare going-over after being called in to eject troublesome striker Charles Phillips from the Express in Lowesmoor. He'd been savagely kicked in the back and ribs and his tunic damaged to the tune of 13s. 28 days' hard.

Two weeks later, it was **PC8 William Hollis'** turn for more of the same – brutally set on by notorious serial offender and Dolday hard-case, labourer John Swain who'd punched and kicked him nearly senseless in Rack Alley before the ever-reliable **PC24 David Evans** plus a few local builders had weighed-in, managed to get his boots off and struggled all the way back to the station-house with Swain resisting every inch of the way. 14 days for being drunk and disorderly, and a month's hard for the assault.

It's barely surprising that **Tommy Byrne**'s annual report to the licensing committee showed that during the year 146 people had been proceeded against for drunkenness, 139 convicted and 7 discharged: the previous year had seen 194 proceeded against, 184 convicted and 10 discharged – a considerable decline. There were 280 licensed premises in the city.

A sad loss on October 21st when **Insp Henry Joyner** decided to call it a day after a shade over 28 years (*he'd been recruited on 7th October 1870*) and at the following Watch Committee, **Tommy Byrne** recommended **Sgt2 Francis Eli Brotherton**'s promotion in his place, and **PC23 George Aston**'s elevation to Sergeant. Both were to continue serving until well into the twentieth century. **PC Arthur Charles Budd**, recruited in January this year, was elevated from PC3rd Class to 2nd Class.

During the year, one PC was dismissed, **John Evan Febery** (*4th June 1897- 6th May 1898*) and another ordered to resign: **Arthur Charles Budd** (*14th January – 25th November 1898*).

As the year drew to a close, the cost of police uniforms was revealed as: Chief Constable's patrol jacket £2 15s and pair of trousers 1s 3d; inspectors' dress coats £2, great-coats £2 6d and trousers 17s 6d a pair; sergeants' and constables' tunics £1 3s 6d, great-coats £1 8s, day trousers 12s 6d, night trousers 13s 3d; silver chevrons and crowns 7s 6d, silver merit badges 2s 6d, first class stripes 1s 3d. The clothing contract had again been controversially awarded to Dolan's of Vauxhall in London as no city firms came even close in the reckoning. Two local firms had, however, managed to wrest some comfort from the annual tendering process – Butler and Kenward of High Street (Chief Constable's cap £1 11s 6d, inspectors' caps 14s, helmets 7s 9d, white Berlin gloves 8 1/2d., leather belts 3s and leather leggings 8s), and boot manufacturer Noke's (*Chief Constable's boots £1 1s a pair, sergeants' and constables' summer boots 14s 6d and winter boots 16s 6d*).

## New Mayor John Steward revives an ancient court custom

In November the new mayor, chemist John Alfred Steward who'd succeeded Alderman Albert Buck, took his place on the Magistrates' bench and instantly revived an ancient City custom of discharging without a hearing the first person summoned: the lucky man was shop assistant Arthur Hatfield of Hylton Road, summoned for riding a bicycle without a light in Sidbury on November 4th. Next man up, Tom Ineson of Penrith was not so fortunate, fined 5s 6d with 2s 6d costs for being 'topsicated' – as he admitted (also supported by **PC26 John Penlington**). Tuesday the following week proved to be a 'white gloves' day.

The talk in the city at the end of what had been a hum-drum year involved two not particularly savoury tales of ex-members of the City force: **PC2 John Bishop** who'd joined on 12th October 1884 (*just two weeks after another John Bishop, No15*) and quit on December 3rd 1897, and **PC12 Thomas Love** who'd been recruited on May 27th 1889 and walked away on 28th February 1895.

Immediately after leaving Worcester, **John Bishop** had taken over the licence of The Acorn Inn in Lower Rushall Street, Walsall. On October 25th this year he'd been hammered by George Ollerenshaw in a pub fight and died of his injuries some days later. 33-year old Ollerenshaw was later found guilty of manslaughter and sentenced to four months' imprisonment. It had been his 26th conviction.

Then on December 20th ex-**PC (*no13*) Tommy Love**, now licensee of the Royal Oak in York Place (*but not for much longer*) was once again on familiar territory and amongst ex-colleagues in the station-house: unfortunately for him, it was as prisoner having been found drunk and disorderly on the Cross and brought in by his old friend **PC04 George Turner**, after which he'd kicked-off and smashed two closets and two electric lamps at the station. It was later stated by **Sergeant William James** that '...he was like a raving madman and it was necessary to place two men with him until he was sober'. He'd earlier created a ruckus at the City Arms where he claimed the landlord owed him £60 and he'd gone there to 'get his rights'. Fined 5s and costs for the first offence and 10s and costs for the second, together with costs for the damage: £1 17s 6d in all or 21 days' hard.

- PC26 John Penlington, already with a reputation as a skilled horseman, rounds up three stray colts on the Cross

- Chief's wife, Mrs Hannah Byrne appointed to a committee to enquire into possibility of appointing a Missionary Officer to be attached to the Police Court

- PC24 David Evans awarded £1 gratuity for stopping a runaway horse, the property of Messrs Flay, grocers, in Broad Street

- the usual upturn in d&d, larceny, disorder and assault associated with the annual influx of hop-pickers proves well up to previous levels, plus a case of seven people setting about one picker, Joseph Buxton of Group Lane, in a revenge attack in Comer Road

- in September, police are called out en masse to quell a massive free-for-all at Foregate Street station following Bromyard Races. Brothers George and James Thompson of the Shambles and Friar Street respectively, are described as '...knocking people over like ninepins'

- on September 29th PC21 Charles Lock who was to die while still in service in 1908, takes on father and son George Ballinger Snr and Jnr – both described as 'a bad lot' by Tommy Byrne – in a set-to inside and outside the Falcon in Broad Street. Between them they had 22 (now 24) convictions

- in October, police called in to investigate death of an American hand named Russell, first assistant 'boss' canvas-man, employed for more than 30 years by showmen Barnum and Bailey. He'd twice been kicked by a horse on Pitchcroft as they arrived in the city for several days' performances, and was buried at Astwood Cemetery

- on the 29th., the Shambles congestion issue re-surfaces with up to 50 illegal hawkers' wagons blocking free passage. Tommy Byrne almost admits defeat

- on December 26th., PC Albert Bednall is set on by Dolday thug Charles Matthews, his wife and his dog who ripped his coat to shreds after he'd been sent in to quell a domestic disturbance. Albert Bednall was not to survive much longer...

Before Mr. W. H. Caldicott (in the chair) and Ald. W. Winwood.

Ex-P.C. in Trouble.—Thomas Love (29), publican, St. Mary's Terrace, Northfield street, was charged with being drunk and disorderly on the Cross on December 20th, and with doing wilful damage to the amount of 17s. to two closets and two electric lamps at the Police-station on the same date. Prisoner pleaded that the first charge was "too true." P.C. Turner said that at 12.20 he found prisoner drunk and kicking at the doors of the City Arms. He behaved in a disorderly manner, and went away, but on... accosted witness and P.C. Evans, to... disgusting language, and was... it was necessary to take him in... P.S. James stated that when... ought to the Police-station he... ll, in which he committed part... lleged. He was removed to... re he again committed similar... was like a "raving madman,"... essary to place two men with... s sober. Prisoner alleged that... City Arms to "get his rights,"... ted, £60 owing to him by the... d using the bad language. ...d that prisoner was... City Police Force. ...costs for the first ...the second offence, ...f the damage, £1 ...d labour.

It's to be assumed that he paid-up, as life on the inside for an ex-city policeman would have been a chastening experience (pic above).

Gained: Arthur Charles Budd (ordered to resign later this year), George William Drinkwater, George Barnet, Joseph Sparkes, Thomas Austin

Lost: Henry Joyner (after 28 years) John Evan Febery, Arthur Charles Budd

## 1899

Ever thankful for small mercies, a stroke of luck to begin the last year of an eventful century...

It had taken baker Thomas Brown three months to ride the bicycle he'd stolen at Carisbrooke on the Isle of Wight to Worcester, and he'd no sooner arrived than information received led him straight into the hands of Sgt02 (still not yet approved as Inspector) Francis Eli Brotherton. Handed over to the Newport (IoW) Police.

The same week, the court was operating at full tilt dealing with the usual spate of contrite (and not so contrite) Christmas revellers, and while on duty in All Hallows on the desperately cold night of January 2nd., PC22 Francis Albert Gregory threw all caution to the wind and took up a well-wisher's offer of a warming whisky or two in the Bridge Inn in Bridge Street. His action led to a court appearance for the landlord George Richard Jones and his barmaid Annie Cuff for serving a constable whilst on active duty, but **Tommy Byrne** thought that publicity surrounding the case would be sufficient for the ends of justice to be met.

The PC, who'd been five years with the force, was lucky not to have been sacked, but went on to a 14-year career with Worcester City Police, punctuated by a 2-year stint fighting in South Africa (1900-2).

January also saw unquestionably well-deserved praise heaped on the police when the previous year's net crime figures were released: 128 indictable offences committed, 75 proceeded against, 7 dismissed, 47 dealt with summarily, 18 committed to trial, and two otherwise disposed of.

Notably, there had been not a single case of what was termed 'very serious crime' – although despite the year's apparent tranquillity, the police court had still managed to deal with 930 non-indictable cases, with 642 people summoned. During this 'quiet' year, constables had also found 749 premises – 484 doors and 265 windows – insecure; 2,667 licenses had been issued for the removal of swine, and the Police Fire Brigade had attended 17 fires – five down in the previous year.

The Force was now 47 strong and despite the loss of **Henry Joyner** and the inevitable unpleasantness surrounding the **Budd** and **Febery** episodes, **Tommy Byrne** reported that the general conduct of the men had been very good.

The Mayor, John Steward also heaped praise on the way the force had been run, commenting: '...they might congratulate themselves upon that excellent report which showed great diligence upon the part of the Chief Constable and the men under him in suppressing crime. It was noticeable too that many of the offences were of a milder character than formerly'.

It was, noted old stager and unfailing **Byrne** supporter Alderman and ex-mayor Walter Holland, '...a splendid record of work done by the police force, and reflected great credit upon the city, seeing that little crime of a serious nature had been committed' (*Herald*).

At the same time, the city's Medical Officer of Health Dr Mabyn Read also reported on the reduction of births and deaths in the city over the same period.

The month also saw another of the force's great supporters and former mayor, Earl Beauchamp, now 27, take up the role of Governor and Commander-in-Chief of the Colony of New South Wales – it's thought in order to avoid a homosexual scandal that had also been covered-up by groundless counter-rumours alluding to his engagement to one or other of Queen Victoria's granddaughters. His leaving gift to the city was the gates to Pitchcroft, handing over the silver keys to mayor John Steward at the end of March. But within two years he was back at his family seat, Madresfield Court, model for Evelyn Waugh's Brideshead (see p315) his tenure as a Colonial Governor not having been hailed a success and with more than a whiff of the old scandal being bandied around as the main reason for his swift return (*and marriage in 1903*).

By March, **Tommy Byrne**'s performance as chief, the remarkable downturn in crime and the overall efficiency of the force as a whole had been universally welcomed and recognised – even by the City Council who, at the Watch Committee's recommendation, voted without dissent to increase the Chief Constable's salary by £50. John Steward was the first to back the proposal, stating that it was:

> '...eight years since Mr Byrne was appointed, and during that time his work has considerably increased. He is a most efficient officer, and has raised the standard of the police force considerably since his appointment. In addition to his ordinary duties, (he) has been of great service in organising processions. Only this morning the Sherriff had received a compliment from the Judge upon the freedom of the city from crime'

Inevitably – and perfectly justifiably given the high rents in the city as well as deductions for superannuation and medical attendance, but more particularly the fact that pay had remained static since December 1890 – it was swiftly followed by a request for an increase in his men's wages too. It was signed by every member of the force and handed over by the Chief. With a similar degree of inevitability, it was met with stunned silence and hedging tactics at the Guildhall – **Tommy Byrne** being first requested to go away in order to obtain statistics of pay and conditions in towns comparative to the city, before reporting back to undergo the usual round of shaking of heads, hand-wringing and feeble excuses.

In May, serial offender 60-year old Mary Ann Smith appeared in court on her 76th charge – behaving in a violent and indecent manner in the station-house after assaulting **PC27 Sidnam Cole** *(right)* after he'd picked her up for her usual 'trick' of calling into a public house, ordering her usual grog – beer with rum in it – and then, as the *Herald* put it: '...let(ing) the landlord whistle for his money'. Fined 40s or a month's gaol and intimation that the next time she appeared in court she would have to be sent to a home.

Just the day before Barnum and Bailey repeated their 'Best Show on Earth' spectacular on Pitchcroft (June 16th for one day only), another shooting case rocked the city...

### 'Excitement in court' after another shooting

Kate Hannah Jenkins of 2 Court, Hylton Road, had been shot at three times by her ex-lover William Sedgwick of Birmingham who had also fathered her 4-month old illegitimate child while she was in service to his publican parents at their pub, the Albion in Liverpool Street: one bullet had missed, but two had found their target as they'd walked along the riverbank opposite the Grandstand – one had hit her in the back, shattering two ribs, the other traversing 4 $\frac{1}{2}$ inches into her neck as she lay on the ground having fled in panic when he'd shown her the gun and said that three bullets were for her and three for him. He'd then kissed her and walked away.

Arrested by **PC01 John Hughes**, who'd found letters written by Sedgwick to his mother indicating his intended suicide after the planned murder, his trial to answer the

## SENSATIONAL LOVE AFFAIR IN WORCESTER.

### THREE SHOTS FROM A REVOLVER.

At the City Police-court this morning, before Ald. J. M'Illington and H. Urwick, William Sedgewick (22), brewer, Albion Tavern, 104, Liverpool street, Birmingham, was charged with attempting to murder Kate Jenkins, of 2 Court, Hylton road, with a revolver on June 15.

Prisoner, who is of comparatively short ature and of dark complexion, was respectably dressed, and appeared to be quite unconcerned. As the charge was read over a woman in the back of the Court, who had been standing, thrust a finger into each rear, and sank to a seat with a low cry.

The Chief Constable (Mr. T. W. Byrne) said that he proposed to ask for a remand, but before doing so he wished to detail the facts. Prisoner lived with his father and mother, wh kept a tavern in Birmingham, and the injure girl was formerly in their employ as a domest servant. She left some time ago, and about fo months ago gave birth to a child, of wh:ch s alleges prisoner to be the father. Yesterday prisoner ———— down from Birmingham, and in-

charge 'that he feloniously did shoot with a certain pistol, loaded with powder and divers leaden bullets, one Kate Hannah Jenkins with intent in so doing, then and thereby feloniously, and of his malice aforethought, to kill and murder the said Kate Hannah Jenkins' was postponed three times pending his victim's tenuous recovery.

During that time they'd written letters to each other, professing undying love and forgiveness. Sentence: 12 months' imprisonment, resulting in 'excitement in court which was immediately suppressed' recorded the *Herald*.

During his eight years with the force, **PC21 Charles Lock** who'd joined on 4th February 1891, had emerged as a useful slug-it-out constable, matching, and earning the respect of, many of the city's hard-cases when it came to a street brawl, and when at the end of June police-hater and vicious drunk John Waterson stripped on Pitchcroft, ready to fight and offering to take on the entire world, **Lock** was happy to oblige in the name of the Queen and the good name and reputation of the gentlemen of Worcester City Police.

As the *Herald* noted, with more than a hint of satisfaction: '...it took witness 20 minutes to overcome and handcuff him'. It was Waterson's 37th offence.

The same day, Nobby Guy – now in his mid-40s but showing no signs of slowing down – clocked up his 49th offence, but as he'd been sober since February this year, as stated by **Sgt Fred Tarrant**, his sentence was reduced to one day's gaol.

Another useful scrapper was **PC22 Francis Albert Gregory** (*pictured, right*) who'd earlier escaped the sack for drinking whisky on a cold January night. The *Herald*'s report of a set-to with another would-be world champion pugilist, drunk James Burton at South Quay, is a masterpiece of understatement – implying, although halting short of openly stating, that he took him on under his own terms, and then skipping the next ten minutes or so to conclude '...and Burton was handcuffed on the ground, but kicked and *bit till Gregory called for assistance. PC [Frederick John] Hawker went to the rescue...'* (Herald).

Whatever the actual facts of either case, both bobbies had got their man through what sounds like old-fashioned gentlemanly means at not inconsiderable risk to themselves yet without resorting to dirty tricks and unfair advantages even though the respective situations may well have justified them.

If nothing else, the last year of the old century had witnessed several police heroes emerging out of the blue ranks. Not that it was all work and no play...

At the annual police outing, **Insp. Francis Brotherton**'s 10-man tug o' war team out-pulled **Sgt Fred Tarrant**'s; **PC24 David Evans** won the 100 yards dash for men with more than eight years' service with **PC33 George Langstone** second and **PC 19 Charles Hall** third (*out of seven*); newcomer **PC Alfred Tomlinson** won the 120 yards race for men with less than eight years' service, **PC32 Alexander Millar** and **PC06 Thomas Mound** runner-up and third; **PC19 Charles Hall** threw a cricket ball 82 yards and 1 foot, **PC Alfred Tomlinson**, who also won the long jump contest, coming runner-up at 65 yards.

The same week, three (*of seven*) Foster brothers rattled-up 390 runs in the first innings for Worcestershire against Hampshire in this, the first year of the English County Championship: Henry 'Harry' Knollys (16); Wilfrid 'Bill' Lionel (140 and 172 not out in the second innings); and Reginald 'Tip' Erskine (134 and 101 not out second innings). These were maiden first-class centuries for Bill and Tip – the first pair of brothers to score two separate centuries each in the same first-class match, a feat since emulated by Ian and Greg Chappell in the 1974 Test, but remaining unique in English county cricket). Not surprisingly, the County was quickly dubbed 'Fostershire'.

On July 25th more police heroes emerged: at half past midnight, Merthyr madman Benjamin Williams had somehow got into Charlotte Gill's butcher's shop in Mealcheapen Street and was throwing scales, weights and knives through the smashed window and into the street. When **PC29 Fred Cook** was summoned and shone a light into the shop, it was met with a hurled knife and threats to murder. Then a stone bottle flew out of the window and smashed grocer Daniel Melia's window on the opposite side of the road. With police reinforcements called in and a hose turned on him, Williams climbed on to the roof and from there began throwing a barrage of bricks, slates and bottles into the street with the intention of maiming one or more of the people that had gathered to watch. Now brandishing a butcher's cleaver in one hand and a brick in the other and threatening to murder anyone that came close enough – *and that it wouldn't be the first time either* – **PC03 Fred Hawker** and (*again*) **PC22 Francis Albert Gregory** (*below*) followed him on to the roof. Gregory rushed him and disarmed him, later accompanying him to the station-house. The siege had lasted nearly four hours, and the final year of the century was shaping-up as one of unremitting action for the men of the City force.

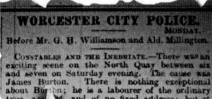

In September, **PC20 William Teale** told two determined slug-it-out scrappers to stop fighting in George Street, but later found them still hard at it in St Pauls Street. Both were charged with causing an annoyance and both sent down for seven days. One was 25-year old tinman Thomas Davis of Lowesmoor who'd met his come-uppance at the hands of the other, 20-year old hay trusser Frederick George Dancox (*erroneously printed as Dancocks*) of 2 Court, Foundry Alley. His name was to go down in posterity eighteen years later as a private in the 4th Battalion, Worcestershire Regiment for his action in capturing a German machine-gun nest in the Boesinghe sector, Belgium on 9 October 1917. His reward: the Victoria Cross, albeit awarded posthumously.

The last week of September saw **PC24 David Evans** add nimbleness of mind to his already evident nimbleness of limb. Patrolling his beat, he recognised an old face: this was Catherine Jordan who he'd arrested six and half years earlier (*March 18th 1893*) for creating a disturbance in the Farriers Arms, Quay Street with her live-in lover John Lyme who'd then both set about him and left him bleeding in the street before doing a runner. Despite summonses against them, no more was heard of either. Now he was to get his own back: though Lyme had since died in Wolverhampton, it must have been with some gleeful satisfaction that he arrested Jordan who at last copped for her 5s fine from six years earlier.

The Worcester Festival this year was a big one: it marked the first local performance of Edward Elgar's newest work, initially Symphonic (*later, Enigma*) Variations and thus attracted a massive crowd. No mystery or variation in the police's handling of the event though – high praise all round, with the Chief awarded 5gns for his extra duties, two inspectors and seven sergeants 14s each, and 37 constables 12s each.

As the Boer War escalated in far-off South Africa, Army Reservist **PC Albert Bednall** was called to the colours. Described as 'one of the smartest and best men in the force', he'd joined on 29th January 1897 and chief **Tommy Byrne** recommended that he be granted leave of absence with part of his 29s a week police salary paid to his family and his place kept open pending his return. It was to no avail: **Sergeant Albert Bednall** No2528 2nd Battalion Royal Scots Regiment attached to the South Africa Field Force contracted fever and died near Johannesburg on 17th February 1901, leaving a widow, Staffordshire-born Mary 32, and their son Gordon, 2. In April, the census shows them living at 15 Nelson Road, probably a police house, lodging or sharing with **PC Alfred Tomlinson** and his wife and 2-year old daughter (*at No 43 lived my maternal grandfather, Ernest Albert Harris, aged 6*).

The two constables had joined Worcester City Police within a few months of each other, and **Alfred Tomlinson** went on to serve up to 1921, retiring on May 20th that year.

At his outgoing speech in November, mayor John Steward made a special point of praising the police – something rarely done in recent years, even though few mayors had had cause for complaint, least of all since **Tommy Byrne**'s appointment. He concluded a rousing farewell with the words that he '...regarded the police force deserving of the highest praise. (*Hear, hear*). Only trivial complaints had been made against certain members of the force, and those were complaints that would not have been made against an ordinary civilian' he'd said.

The year – and the century – were drawing to a close, but 1899 still held a few jolts for the police force and its penny-pinching pay-masters: at the beginning of December, **Tommy Byrne** shook the Guildhall to its very foundations when he claimed that despite a 1:913 police:population ratio, the City force still remained undermanned to the tune of four constables, and this time put in strongly-worded request that the shortfall really should be made up – not least as the last increase had been six years earlier, and that the amount of property, not to mention people, that had to be protected had very visibly increased.

He added that the increase would provide the ratio of one officer per 841 of the population – but that even then, the city would have a lower police to population ratio than most other towns of similar size: '...the matter was referred to the Police Sub-Committee' dourly noted the *Herald*.

And then with distinct echoes of the Diglis swingbridge suicide three years earlier, **PC8 William Hollis** was called in to investigate a suicide by hanging – this time at 6, Skinner Street, St Johns: it was found to be another civic functionary, mace-bearer George Bould, found hanging from a beam in his outhouse. As in the case of Town Crier George Adams in 1896, the verdict was recorded 'suicide whilst temporarily insane'.

Maybe it was a taste of better things to come, but the last year of the old century was the first year not one single officer had left or put himself up for recruitment. It was a good start to the new century that promised much and was precisely the half-way point in the 134-year history of Worcester City Police.

*Gained: none  Lost: none*

## 'The Byrne years': continued in Vol 2 of 'The Spike'

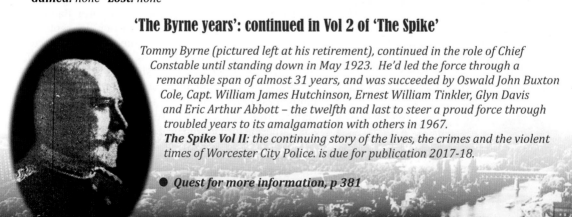

*Tommy Byrne (pictured left at his retirement), continued in the role of Chief Constable until standing down in May 1923. He'd led the force through a remarkable span of almost 31 years, and was succeeded by Oswald John Buxton Cole, Capt. William James Hutchinson, Ernest William Tinkler, Glyn Davis and Eric Arthur Abbott – the twelfth and last to steer a proud force through troubled years to its amalgamation with others in 1967.*

***The Spike Vol II**: the continuing story of the lives, the crimes and the violent times of Worcester City Police. is due for publication 2017-18.*

● *Quest for more information, p 381*

■ Harriet Whatmore, Worcester's first 'Woman in White' who attracts large crowds when she parades around town in her eccentric dress, is charged with assaulting PC24 David Evans and Fanny Cole, female searcher at the station and wife of PC27 Sidnam Cole

**TWO CAPTURES BY THE WORCESTER POLICE.**

A creditable capture was effected by P.C. Turner, of the Worcester City Police Force, on Monday evening. The officer was on duty on the Cross, about 7.30, when P.C. Poyner, of Droitwich, rode up on his bicycle and said that a dark grey worsted overcoat, with velvet collar, stolen from the Target Stores at Droitwich, P.C. Poyner went on to give information at the station in Copenhagen street. Meanwhile P.C. Turner met a man wearing an overcoat, answering to the description given, in the Foregate and at once arrested him, taking him to the station before P.C. Poyner had left. The prisoner turns out to be a tramp named John Ward, aged 21. Another capture was made by P.S. Bishop on Tuesday. While walking in All Hallows he met a man named John Badham, who is well-known to the police, and from a description received from Ledbury, arrested him on a charge of stealing rose briars.

■ The Herald tells the neat little tale of two captures on consecutive days (above): PC4 George Turner apprehends John Ward on suspicion of stealing a grey worsted coat from Target Stores in Droitwich, and Sgt (ex-PC15) John Bishop apprehends known offender John Badham in All Hallows, later found to have stolen rose briars from Ledbury

■ in February, the need for more men is highlighted after Tommy Byrne claims that the force is insufficient to patrol Pitchcroft, now included into the force's patrolling area, and puts in for four. The Guildhall silence was deafening

■ PC22 Francis Albert Gregory is hit, kicked, bitten and had his face spat in by out-of-control thug Charles Evans who'd locked his mother in her home and threatened to murder her. 14 days gaol

■ PC29 Fred Cook commandeers Grand Stand licensee Edward Skyrme's boat to reach the body of James Brown of Comer Gardens who'd drowned himself in the river in a fit of temporary madness

■ 10-year old John Greaves ordered to four strokes of the birch for stealing a cap, punishment witnessed by PC35 (later Sergeant) William Deakin

■ the same week, 11-year old newsboy Henry William Allen receives the same for stealing 13 dozen copies of the Worcester Daily Times

■ more squaddie outrages in April with several assaults on the police: in one, PC26 John Penlington has a packet of sausage meat thrown at him and his tunic smeared by Pte William Tilson of C Company 1st Worcestershires while being arrested on a d&d charge in Bath Road. Ordered to pay 12s 6d costs plus expense of cleaning the PC's tunic

■ on Friday June 16th, Barnum and Bailey's 'Best Show on Earth' is back in town for a one-day performance, this time concluding without the tragedy of the previous November's appearance, despite 800 in the retinue

■ the dangers of constables being accused of indecent assault when accompanying drunken women, either to the station house or home, is highlighted in July when Fanny Loveday accuses PC Joseph Sparkes, who'd only joined in November the previous year, of gross indecency. Case dismissed, Fanny Loveday fined 10s and 16s costs

■ on June 24th PC07 John Hazleton arrests 32-year old Silvanus Bozward of Blakefield Road for serious sexual assaults on two 8-year old girls, Alice Fulwell and Lily Davies. He'd afterwards given them 1d each

■ PC (later, Sgt) George William Drinkwater who was to go on to serve until 1925, identifies Royal Fusiliers' deserter John Tweedie in the York House, the Moors. Committed to prison to await escort

# 11:

# The good coppers...
# and the bad pennies

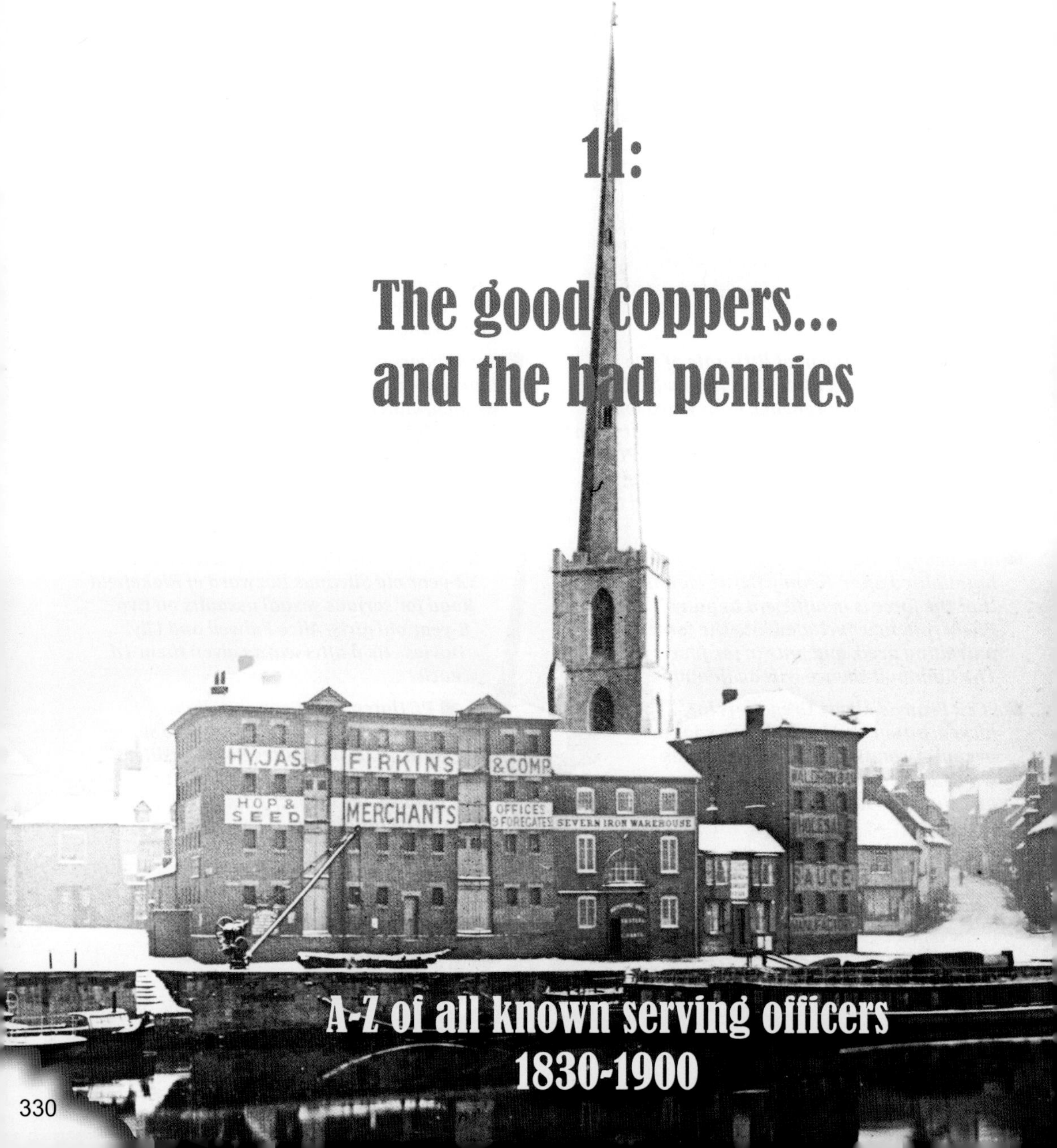

A-Z of all known serving officers
1830-1900

5.

# William Richardson

## OFFENCES.

| DATE. | OFFENCE. | PUNISHMENT. | REMARKS. |
|---|---|---|---|
| 1853 May 27 | Unnecessarily interfering with Mr Thomas Clearbury on his way home and assaulting and ill treating him at [...] [...] running while on duty | Severely censured and fined 5/- | The Constable's defence was that Mr Clearbury was drunk, that he was a character to [...] [...] that [...] Clearbury [...] a penalty [...] the Committee [...] satisfied that his object was [...] state but that he used unnecessary violence |
| 1855 March 2 | Using bad language to two Publicans when visiting their houses | Reprimanded | |
| 1857 October 9 | Allowing a prisoner charged with Rape to escape from his custody through neglect of due precaution | Cautioned to be more careful in future | |
| 1860 November 16 | Using abusive language to Sergeant Doughty while on [...] | Reprimanded | See Minutes Nov 16. 1860 |
| 1861 June 14 | Disobedience of orders of his Superintendent | Cautioned | See comments 14 June |
| Oct. 4 | Injudiciously making statements affecting the character of Mr [...] whilst he had not sufficient proof to support | Cautioned to be more circumspect in future | |
| 1862 March 10 | Conduct subversive of discipline and injurious to the police service by [...] the City without leave for 3 days | Censured [...] [...] conduct and cautioned to be more careful [...] [...] [...] and acting [...] the [...] of his duty | The Committee believing that he acted [...] [...] intentional [...] of discipline in disregard of his duty [...] had [...] [...] [...] [...] [...] as [...] kept so do |
| April 4 | Insubordination by using insulting language to his Superintendent | | [...] [...] [...] [...] [...] |

*Approbation Marks entries 1853-62 for ever-controversial PC, later Detective, William Richardson – a good copper and a bed penny – who, despite being an exceptional policeman/detective, appears to have fallen out with almost everybody he came into contact with. See p354*

*(Worcester CiCo/WAAS)*

Watchman  Mayor's Off  PC <1885  PC 1885<  Sergeant  Detective  Superintend't  Pubs books 2&3  Chief

# The good coppers... ...and the bad pennies

**Abraham, John**
24 May 1867 – (*not known*)
PC under Power

**Adams, Edwin**
23 Oct 1868 – 8 Oct 1874
PC under Power/Sommers. Died while serving

**Adams, George**
c1871
Not included in police records, but found in 1871 census listed as Police Officer so could be County, aged 21, lodging at 50 Moor Street with PC George Willis (25)

**Adams, Thomas**
24 Sep 1869 – 8 Oct 1869
PC under Power. Died while serving

**Andrews, Thomas (*above*)**
7 Feb 1882 – 31 Mar 1884
PC2 under Power and Sommers

**Andrews, William**
8 Apr 1868 – 7 May 1869
Short-lived PC under Power

**Andrews, William**
22 Feb 1886 – (*not known*)
PC under Sommers

**Archer, George**
30 May 1852 – 5 Jul 1869
Solid, dependable, former Supernumerary PC5 under Chipp and Power. Appointed Sergeant

1866. First on scene at murder of Elizabeth Hull, 195; assaulted by PC Preece No21, 219

**Archer, William**
13 Oct 1865 – 27 Aug 1867
PC4 under Power. Resigned

**Arkwell, William**
5 Dec 1858 – 13 Oct 1865
PC2 under Chipp and Power. Assaulted, 171; reprimanded for lateness, 178; investigates robbery 181. Resigned and became a farmer, living in Ombersley Road close to the New Inn

**Aston, George (*below*)**
25 Sep 1882 – 31 Dec 1908
No23 under Sommers. Born 1861, Pembridge, Herefordshire. In 1901 aged 40 lived at 4, Melbourne Street with his wife Ellen and daughter Elizabeth a bookbinder, 16. Commended for prompt action at a fire, 264; levity when he tackles a tricky customer, 264; tussles with squaddies, 277; attack outside the Bell St Johns leads to doubled police presence in the township [3]; Sommers' protest and signature 289; **photograph,** 314; promoted

Sergeant, 323. Retired on police pension and in 1911 lived at 54 Northfield Street. Died 1914.

**Aston, William**
20 Aug 1830 – 1 Feb 1836
Watchman and member of Original Force. Appointed, 55. Hero fire-fighter, 64; No2 under Douglas, 72

**Augustus, Charles**
21 Feb 1862 – ?? 1864
PC 3rd Class under Power. Assigned to plain-clothes duty, 191

**Austin, Thomas**
2 Dec 1898 – 3 Oct 1902

**Bailey, Charles Ernest**
24 Sep 1897 – 19 Jan 1922
Staffordshire-born, 1872, married to Lickey-born Emma and lived (1901) in Blakefield Road with daughter Elsie, aged one. 1911 living at 13 Sebright Avenue with his wife, two more daughters and a son. Died while serving

*Charles E. Bailey*

**Baldwin, George**
8 Mar 1872 – 22 Mar 1872
Joined and quit within 14 days, 216. Brother of...

**Baldwin, James**
22 Mar 1872 – 19 Apr 1872
Only slightly longer service record than his brother, George, 216 (*see also **Cooke, George and Oscar,** 238*)

**Ball, John**
c1830-1833
One of second draft of Watchmen. Appointed, 27

## Banner, Joseph
28 Apr 1848 – 20 Mar 1863
Prominent and active, served under Chipp and Power; promoted to Supernumerary Sergeant, 150; cautioned for drinking, 163 and 171; complaints, 167; appointed Sergeant, 167; assaulted 171; appointed Station Sergeant 182; s'annuated @ 11/6d a week.
*Extract from Approbation Marks book, right*

*Approbation marks book shows Sergeant Joe Banner as not entirely squeaky-clean*

## Bannister, George
10 May 1880 – 1 Sep 1882
Accused, with PC George Farley, of police brutality Xmas Eve 1881 [3]

## Barber, Henry
21 Dec 1877 – 28 Jun 1878

## Barker, James
11 Sep 1857 – 26 Oct 1866
No26 under Tommy Chipp. Takes on a prize-fighter, 162; investigates suicide, 163; crusade against erring pubs, 187; appointed Sergeant amid controversy, 188; reprimanded for neglect 194; assaulted 195; cautioned and asked to resign, 196; finally resigns, 202

## Barnes, Lewis
22 May 1868 – 26 Feb 1875
Served under Power. Born Little Hidcote, Glos, 1843; married Ellen from Strensham and in 1871 they were lodging with ex-PC Benjamin Holmes (39, then retired from the force but serving as a Mayor's Officer) at 13 Foregate Street, next door to the City Architect and Surveyor Henry Rowe. Took over as licensee of the Royal Oak in York Place, attempted suicide by slashing his throat (p234 and more [3]) Later took over Crowle House, 1879. 1881 living in Spring Gardens had been unemployed but listed as former milkman. Reprimanded for using undue force, 211; assaulted, 212; refused entry at the Alma, Diglis, [3]; commended for spotting and extinguishing fire at Swan with Two Necks (Nicks) 218; summons three in two days, 224;

quits, 226; attempts suicide, 234. Dies, aged 46, 1889, 235

## Barnet, George
9 Sep 1898 – 7 Dec 1906
Apprehends Army deserter who'd forged his Boer War embarkation papers, in the Virgin Tavern mid-1901 [3]

## Barrett, Thomas
28 Nov 1862 – 9 Jan 1863
Short-lived (7 weeks) PC under Power. Found drunk on duty Xmas Day, suspended then discharged

## Bartlett, Joseph
24 Apr 1874 – 9 Oct 1874

## Bateman, Thomas
18 Oct 1839 – 1854
Supernumerary, later served under Phillips and Chipp. Born St Johns 1807. Living Rainbow Hill 1851 with wife Jane (born All Saints ward) and daughters Mary Ann, Jane and Maria and grandson Alexander. Signature, 95; described as 'one of the elite',112; rumbles Lich St gambling den, 135; appointed Sergeant. Leads vice crack-down on Birdport and Lowesmoor brothels 135, 143; stabbed and forced to resign, 140; dies 150

## Baylis, Thomas
19 Jan 1836 – ?

## Bayliss, William
23 Mar 1860 – 20 Apr 1860
Served less than a month under Chipp

## Baynham, Thomas (below)
10 Jul 1885 – 29 Jan 1897
PC17 under Sommers, born Ross-on-Wye 1864. 1891 lodging in Britannia Road. Disarms would-be murderer and suicide, 286; Sommers' protest and signature 289; temporarily blinded, 310; censured for over-reaction, 312

## Beard, Frederick
29 Jan 1869 – 31 Dec 1869

## Beddoe, William
26 Sep 1856 – 5 Jun 1857
Supernumerary, promoted to 3rd class, assaulted, 157

## Bednall, Albert
29 Jan 1897 – 17 Feb 1901
Well thought-of PC under Byrne.

Has dog set on him in violent 'domestic', 324; called to the colours and dies of fever in South Africa, 327

**Bennell, Thomas Richard**
15 Nov 1880 – 10 Jun 1881
Served just seven months under Power

**Bennett, John**
17 Sep 1852 – 1 Sep 1854
Attempts return of coins swallowed by George Belcher, 145; gains reputation as pubs-buster, 147; hunch about 'Brummagem prigs' proves correct, 148

**Bennett, Richard**
6 Mar 1851 – 20 Mar 1851
Served just fourteen days under Chipp

**Berridge, William**
2 Feb 1855 – 7 Feb 1862
Respected, solid ex-Supernumerary with action-packed career under Chipp and Power. Born Notts, 1824 and married to Elizabeth. 1861 living at 17 Edgar Street with sons William and Francis and daughter Mary. Assaulted 153, 154, 157, 161, 163, 164; investigates child murder, 162; censured after visiting pubs and becoming abusive to his Sergeant, 166; spat with Det Richardson, 170; commended, 170; assaulted 171; awarded for bravery and censured for exceeding duty in the same week, 171; reprimanded for being asleep on duty 178; resigns and is appointed Streets Supt, 182; Approbation book (extract) 183

**Berrow, Thomas**
6 Jun 1856 – 18 Jul 1856
Served just six weeks under Chipp

**Berry, Richard**
15 Mar 1835 – 24 Feb 1860
Oxfordshire-born (1798) original Watchman, served under Douglas, Phillips and Chipp. Married to Weobley-born Sarah and living (1851) in Church Walk St Clements with daughter

dressmaker Louisa and cabinet maker son William; 10 years later aged 64 widowed and living with daughter Martha and employed as Sherriff's Bailliff . No7 under Douglas, 72; commended for bravery, 81; viewed as 'elite' 125

**Best, Benjamin**
29 Nov 1839 – 13 Oct 1841
Appointed, 96; **signature, 95**

**Bettington, Edward**
20 Feb 1863 – 15 Apr 1864
PC 2nd Class under Power. Quits after regular beatings by Blockhouse gangs and being found asleep while on duty, 191

**Bettington, Thomas**
11 Feb 1870 – (*not known*)

**Biddle, Edwin**
16 Aug 1886 – 2 Jan 1891

**Bills, Richard**
1833-36
Watchman and member of Original Force. Appointed, 55; No7 under Douglas, 72; dismissed 76

**Birt, Frederick William Smithsend**
23d Oct 1874 – 27 Aug 1875

**Bishop, John** (*above*)
29 Sep 1884 – 30 Dec 1910
PC15 under Sommers. Rescues PC Fred Cook from certain beating by squaddies, 282; Sommers' protest and signature 289; **photograph**, 315; regular confusion with namesake John Bishop (No2) who joined just two weeks later...

**Bishop, John** (*above*)
12 Oct 1884 – 3 Dec 1897
PC2 under Byrne. Investigates suspected murder of Yorkshire House (*now Imperial*) landlady, 320; **photograph, 321**; quit to become pub licensee in Walsall but fatally injured in fight with a customer, 321, 323

**Bliss, James**
2 Oct 1876 – 3 Nov 1876

**Blomely, Arthur**
12 Mar 1875 – 12 Sep 1877

**Booth, Thomas** (*above*)
7 Jul 1875 – 20 Jul 1888
Grimley-born (1849) ex-marine married to Irish-born wife Catherine and (1881) living in Cumberland Street with daughters Mary and Catherine and sons Jeremiah and William. PC6 under Matthew Power. violently assaulted, 234; witness when mother of ten is shot in the face, 246 and extended account, [3]

**Bouckley, George**
24 Jun 1864 – 19 Aug 1865
PC 2nd Class under Power. Dismissed

**Boulton, Robert**
9 Nov 1866 – 18 Jan 1867
Resigned after a matter of weeks

**Bourne, Charles**
23 Feb 1880 – 17 Jul 1880

**Bowen, John**
15 Oct 1847 – 2 Dec 1847

**Bowen, William**
4 Jul 1845 – ?
Appointed Constable of the Esplanade under Phillips and prevents major explosion, 126

**Bowkett (*not known*)**
1824
Parish-appointed Constable Appointed, 27

**Bowyear, Charles**
19 Jan 1836 -- ?

**Box, Walter (*above*)**
10 Jan 1879 – 6 Nov 1885
Pugilist-looking PC24 under Arthur Sommers. Wichenford-born 1857, married to Somerset-born Maria and living in Sansome Place (1881). Tangles with prostitute, 244; estimates speed, 250; savage assault, 260

**Boyd, John**
23 Aug 1861 – 18 Oct 1861
Dismissed for immoral conduct after seven weeks, 178

**Bradford, William**
1839 (?) – 3 Oct 1852
Signature, 95

**Bradley, Albert Potter (*above*)**
6 Jul 1894 – 9 Oct 1919
Born Stretton-on-Fosse, Warwickshire 1872, lodging at Bleathwood, 78 Woolhope Road profession Police Detective aged 29 (1901), three doors away from Inspector Frederick William Peacock. PC34 under Byrne later Inspector. 1911 appears to own the house and living there with Worcester-born Rose, son Charles Albert and daughter Nora Ellen. Died aged 80, 1st June 1952 living at Kenya, 2 Delamere Road Malvern and buried in Great Malvern. Probate granted to widow Rose, effects £1780 16s 7d.

**Brayley, William**
17 Jan 1868 – 27 Mar 1868

**Brewer, George**
23 Sep 1836 - ?
App'd 4th intake WCP No18, 79

**Bridges, John Barnet**
1 Jul 1870 – 26 Aug 1870
Dismissed for assault after seven weeks, 211

**Brimble, Frank**
18 Jul 1879 – 12 Mar 1880

**Broadfield, Thomas**
21 Feb 1862 – 21 Mar 1862

**Brookes (*not known*)**
1836
Constable of The Tything; assaulted, 66

**Brooks, William**
4 Apr 1850 – 24 Jul 1850
recruited in Tommy Chipp's frst intake, 141

**Brotherton, Charles**
1 Mar 1895 – 2 Apr 1920

**Brotherton, Francis Eli (*below*)**
16 Jan 1874 – 22 Jul 1905
Born Astwood Bank 1853 and (1881) living Palace Yard with wife Mary and sons Percival and Bertram; as Sergeant 1891 living in Melbourne Street; 1901 as Inspector aged 48 at 4, Wood Terrace and 1911 as 58-year old police pensioner at 18 Vine Street, still with Mary and 30-year old bachelor Bertram a school-master.  Selfless actions at a fire, 233; attacked in the station-house, 246; appointed Sergeant, 269; appointed Inspector, 323. Dies Feckenham 20th October 1931, aged 79

*Francis Eli Brotherton*

**Brown, John**
24 Aug 1860 – 5 Oct 1860

**Brown, Thomas**
3 Oct 1862 – 13 Apr 1866
No7 under Matthew Power. Assaulted, 195; charged with neglect 196; gains admirer, 198; dismissed for assault, 199

**Browning, Richard**
15 Oct 1880 – 1 Sep 1881

**Budd, Arthur Charles**
14 Jan 1898 – 25 Nov 1898
Ordered to resign after less than a year, 323

**Buckingham, William**
5 Sep 1862 – 3 Oct 1862

**Bullock, George**
20 Feb 1888 – 10 Apr 1888

**Bullock, Joseph**
9 Apr 1847 – 22 Sep 1850

**Bullock, Peter**
10 Sep 1858 – 14 Jan 1859

**Burden, Robert**
17 Dec 1847 – 28 Apr 1848

**Burch, Herbert**
12 Jul 1861 – 16 Nov 1861
Early Power recruit. Fined, charged with insubordination, discharged, 178.

**Burnham, ?**
20 Nov 1868 – 2 Jul 1869

**Burrow, Henry Alfred**
30 Nov 1849 – 7 Feb 1850

**Burrow, James**
23 Jul 1852 – not known

**Buswell, William** (*above*)
23 Oct 1883 – 27 Feb 1885
PC3 under Sommers

**Byng, Alfred E.**
27 Oct 1865 – 4 Feb 1867
PC 2nd Class under Power. Found drunk and twice found asleep while on duty. Ordered to resign

**Byrne, Thomas**
10 Jun 1892 - 1926
**The Byrne years, 294-329.**
Born 1861, lived Blackburn. Married to Hannah. 1901 census shows children Ellen, Henry, Thomas and Alice all living at the Police HQ in Copenhagen Street but no clue to the police chief or his wife. Selection, 298; character emerges after shaky start, 301; controversial recommendations for fire service, 302; steady progress, 308; comparison with Sommers, 309; assaulted, 313-14; renders first aid, 314; glowing appraisal, 324. *Photograph 295*

**Cadd, William**
3 Jun 1870 – 11 Dec 1871

**Carless, Charles**
27 Feb 1874 – 13 Mar 1874

**Carloss, William**
4 Apr 1861 – 2 Jun 1862
Fined, admonished, resigns, 178

**Carter, John**
7 Jun 1867 – 18 Jun 1869

**Caudle, Thomas** (*above*)
16 Feb 1883 – 27 Jun 1884

**Causier, George**
24 Sep 1877 – 8 Feb 1878

**Cecil, John**
16 Apr 1852 – 3 Sep 1852

**Chapman, Thomas**
5 Jun 1868 – (*not known*)

**Checkett, Robert**
15 Feb 1833 – 13 Nov 1835
One of the original Watchmen, included in second intake (of thirteen) to the original Police Force 1 Feb 1833, but dismissed on 13 Nov 1835 at the same

time as Richard Bills just weeks before the official formation of Worcester City Police. Appointed, 55; complaints, 68; No11 under Douglas, 72; heroic 'chace', 72; dismissed 76

**Chipp, Edward**
5 Jun 1857 – 26 Feb 1858
Stellar son of Thomas, born Worcester 1839. Recruited, 158; noticed within days, 160; disarms Gipsy Jack (*Joseph Moule*) in a set-to, 162; investigates child murder, 162; moves to Gloucestershire and appointed detective, 163

**Chipp, Thomas**
23 Sep 1836 – 10 Mar 1861
Born St Peters ward, Worcester, 1 May 1808. 1841 living 21, The Shambles with wife and children Lucy and Edward, thereafter the Station House, Queen Street where he died 10th March 1861, leaving his family –by now including three more children, William, Alfred and Ann – almost destitute. Appointed 4th intake of eight, September 1836 WCP No21. Appointed Sergeant c1839, 79; arrests, 89; tangles with eight navvies and is appointed Supernumerary Sergeant, 102; comes off worst against prizefighter Cornelius Bevan, 102; rises to prominence in murder case, 103-4; apprehends gunman, 105; investigates rape case, 105; criticised over cell death, 107; praise for gang-busting, 109; and a sovereign 112; roughed-up by navvies, 116; gets his own back, 123; accused of over-reaction, 129; charges against, 131. Appointed Superintendent and chief, 136. **The Chipp Years, 136-173.** Offered stolen goods by Birmingham thieves, 145; warns of 'unruly' Scots and Irish immigrants, 147; warns pawnshops not to pledge military uniforms; attacked by gang of militiamen, 153; accompanies coal dealer John Hodgetts to Liverpool in pursuit of his wife and family who had joined the Mormons, 156; seriously injured in a brawl, 158; awarded £40, 159; personally investigates murder case at the Hope&Anchor

(*now Vue Bar*), 165; dies suddenly, 172. Legacies, 177, 186-7

**Christian, William**
1 Feb 1833 – January 1836
Included in second intake (of thirteen) to the original Police Force 1 Feb 1833, but lasted just a month, his service terminated on 1 Mar that year.  Appointed, 55. Resigned, 55

**Clarke, Alexander**
16 Feb 1855 – 22 Jun 1855
Short-lived (16 weeks) constable, failed to complete six months

**Clarke, Isaac**
29 Nov 1861 – 7 Mar 1862
Pay docked and discharged, 179.

**Clarke, James**
19 Sep 1850 – 7 Mar 1862
Initially served as S'numerary, recruited in Tommy Chipp's first intake, 141

**Clements, Charles**
1 Jul 1859 – 12 Jul 1861
No3 under Tommy Chipp; described as 'young, but useful' by Chipp, 170; assaulted, 170, 172; neat work, 172; dismissed for attacking a prisoner, 177

**Clements, George**
21 Jul 1874 – 15 Jan 1875

**Clements, Henry**
22 Jan 1864 – 3 Mar 1865
2nd Class PC under Power. Discharged after being found drunk on duty

*Charles Clements, No3 under Tommy Chipp; described as 'young, but useful'. Dismissed for 'attacking a prisoner at the last Sessions', July 1861*

**Cole, James**
12 Feb 1875 – 21 Apr 1876

**Cole, Thomas**
11 Dec 1863 – 3 Jan 1868
Chequered career under Power including neglect of duty, being found asleep and insubordination. Foiled in bizarre case, 199

**Cole, Sidnam (*above*)**
9 Feb 1875 – 21 Jun 1906
Born Gretton 1856, 1861 living at his father's pub, 'The Ship Inn' Pershore High Street, 1871 living with his widowed father William at Flyford Flavell. Married Julia Fanny and living at 16 Brickfields Road ten years later.  Lived Grove Cottage, Knight Street with Julia Fanny and daughter Clara, then in police quarters at the rear of the Guildhall. No 27 under Sommers. Savage assaults, 260, 304 and in the Union, Union Street, [3]; turns rough against Salvationists, 260; promoted 1st Class, 274; discovers body in burned-out building, 277; role in Sommers' affair, 288; **photograph**, 317

Died Sandgate Villa, Fernhill Heath, 16th March 1911, aged 55. Probate effects £298 10s.

**Colley, John**
5 Jan 1866 – (*not known*)
Charges of neglect of duty and being found asleep on his beat

**Cook, John**
9 Apr 1847 – ?

**Cook, Charles**
6 Feb 1863 – 6 Mar 1863
Served just one calendar month under Power

**Cook, Frederick (*above*)**
11 Sep 1885 – 9 Mar 1900
PC29 under Sommers and Byrne. Attacked by Nobby Guy, 266; carries body of drowned boy through streets to his parents, 280; menaced by squaddies and rescued by PS15 John Bishop, 282; Sommers' protest and signature, 289; savage assault, 300; emerges with distinction from fire, 301; investigates suspected murder, 320; involvement in all-night stand-off in Mealcheapen Street, 326; recovers body of drowned suicide, 328

**Cooke, George Henry Reuben and Cooke, Oscar**
10 Jan 1879 – 20 Jan 1879
Brothers. Joined and left the same day after just 10 days, 238

**Coombs, William**
13 Jul 1849 – 2 Nov 1849
Short-lived, (4months) Supernumerary Constable

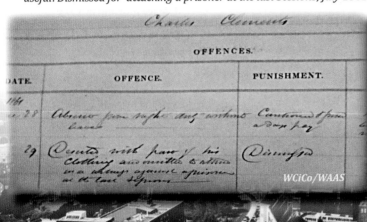

OFFENCES.

| DATE. | OFFENCE. | PUNISHMENT. |
|---|---|---|

WCiCo/WAAS

**Cooper, Howard**
10 Sep 1885 – 28 Jan 1886

**Cotton, Charles**
17 Jul 1857 – 18 Jun 1858

**Cowley, Wlliam**
23 Sep 1836 – 27 Mar 1838
Appointed in Douglas' 4th intake
(of eight). WCP No22, 79

**Crees, William Joseph**
17 Apr 1863 – 5 Aug 1864
No12 under Power.  Found drunk
and resigned

**Crockford, John**
11 Sep 1876 – 23 Nov 1876

**Croft, Thomas (*above*)**
28 Jun 1861 – 5 Jun 1891
Born 1838, Pirton. Labourer,
bricklayer and blacksmith before
marrying Phoebe Ann and later
joining the force in 1861. Ten
years later, as Sergeant, living
in the Blockhouse (no further
details) with children Emma,
Thomas, Albert and Herbert.
1881, still at the rank of Sergeant
aged 42, living in police quarters
in Copenhagen Street with an
addition to the family, Rose
aged 7. Still there ten years
later as Inspector.   No 23 under
Matthew Power. Appointed,
praise for raising fire alarm, 181;
rescued from baying mob, 187.
**Photograph 189.** Three charges
against, 201; finds drunken
cop Henry Naylor, dismissed
after just 4 hours' service, 207;
appointed Inspector, 258; charge
of misconduct, 271; praised for
tackling cruelty to animals and
vigilance at the Cattle Market,
283, 260 ; resigns age 53, 284

Retires 1891 and the following
year takes over as licensee of the
Old Greyhound in New Street.
Died there 18th April 1895,
probate effects £615

**Crowther, William**
9 Dec 1864 – 3 Feb 1865

**Cullis, John**
1 Jun 1860 – 6 Sep 1861
Spanned Chipp/Power change-
over. Praise for apprehending
two burglars; 181; reprimanded,
fined, dismissed, 178

**Cusack, Michael**
6 Mar 1861 – 11 Dec 1851.
Supernumerary humiliated by 'a
filthy act' but gets his own back
before quitting, 142-3

**Dallow, Richard**
1835 - (not known)
Serves under Douglas, 72;
seriously assaulted 74

**Dance, William**
4 Aug 1854 – 27 Oct 1854
Supernumerary, recruited,
assaulted and quits after 11
weeks, 150

**Dancy, ?**
20 Aug 1869 – 27 Aug 1869
Just 7 days' service under Power

**Danford, George**
17 Oct 1862 – 31 Oct 1862
Just 14 days' service under
Power

**Daniels, Thomas**
6 Jun 1845 – 2 Jan 1846
Short-lived, (6 months)
constable, initially served as
Supernumerary

**Darke, Leonard**
1823 - c1833
One of first Watchmen.
Appointed under 1823
Improvement Act, 27

**Darley, John**
10 Jun 1887 – 10 Dec 1887

**Davies, Edwin**
23 Feb 1872 – 25 Jul 1873
Found drinking while on duty,
215

**Davis, George**
18 Nov 1870 – 30 Jun 1871

**Davis, Henry**
31 Dec 1847 – 10 Mar 1848
lasted a shade over two months
from starting to quitting, later
refused to assist, 142

**Davis, Henry**
10 Jan 1862 – 24 Jan 1862
Appointed under Power - and
resigns after 14 days, 182

**Davis, James**
22 Dec 1843 – ?
Initially served as
Supernumerary.  Date/reasons
for leaving not recorded

**Davis, John**
30 Mar 1878 – 22 Apr 1881

**Davis, Thomas**
1823 - c1833
One of first Watchmen.
Appointed under 1823
Improvement Act, 27; gravely
assaulted, 31; *Herald* cutting, 41

**Deakin, William (*above*)**
6 Jul 1894 – 6 Oct 1921
Born 1873 Warwicks, married
to Mary Ann and in 1911
aged 38 and listed as 'Police
Sergeant', living at 22 Nash's
Passage with children Minnie,
Amy and William George. Died
Worcester 1930 aged 58.  PC35
under Byrne. **Photograph, 303;**
attacked by Nobby Guy, 314;
rescues suicide, 314; witness to
birching, 328

*William Deakin*

**Derry, Philip**
30 May 1850 – 20 Sep 1852
No22 recruited in Tommy Chipp's first intake, 141; assaulted 143

**Diver, Alexander**
5 Sep 1879 – 25 May 1881
Attacked by mob, 244; commended for busting gambling den, 246; severely assaulted, 246; and again in the Hare and Hounds, Sidbury, [3].

**'Dog'**
*(unknown)*
Terrier-type, possibly the first police dog, probably Tommy Croft's own. Disregarded photographer's request to 'stay quite still, please' on February 11th 1884

**Dolvere, Frederick**
5 Oct 1860 – 14 Jun 1861

**Dove, John**
7 Apr 1876 – 28 Jul 1876

**Dowdeswell, Edward Henry**
16 Aug 1867 – (*not known*)

**Douglas, James**
18 Jan 1833 – 6 Mar 1840
One of the first five of the original force [No4]. Appointed, 50; in court, 12-13; rises to prominence, 67; appointed Inspector, 69; **The Douglas years 70-96;** assaulted in affray, 80; investigates 10-year old 'Artful Dodger,' Michael Condlie and 12-year old prostitute Emily Evans, 83; opposes unruly public houses, 85; signature, (*below*); resigns, 94; final controversy, 95

**Doughty, John**
14 Feb 1845 – 26 Mar 1875
PC4 as resilient as his name suggests, his was a 30-year service, latterly promoted to Station Sergeant. Born 1810 St Albans ward, Worcester. As Sergeant (1861) lived 27 Sansome Street with wife Jane and children William, Mary Ann and Rhoda, and grandson Henry. Ten years later living in Station Yard, Copenhagen Street. Died 1876 aged 66. Recruited - and quickly assaulted, 124, 126. Catalogue of charges against, including drunkenness, 130, 141; investigates suicide, 143; severely assaulted after breaking up prize-fight, 143; appointed Sergeant, 146; more assaults, 154, 164; remarkable record, 156-7; censured, 167; spat with Det Richardson, 171; appointed Station Sergeant, 179; discovers suicide, 188; investigates

robbery at Pickford's, 195; assaulted in the station-house, 209; Approbation marks, 225; quits after 30 years, 226. Presentation at the Golden Lion, [3]

**Drew, James**
11 May 1855 – 29 Sep1865
No14. Attacked with glass, 159; investigates child murder, 162; assaulted twice, 164; reprimanded 169; appointed Sergeant; severely bitten 181; awarded 15/- for good conduct and devotion to duty, 189; shot in the face, 193-4

**Drew, William**
10 Jun 1881 – 8 Jul 1881

**Drinkwater, George William**
11 Feb 1898 – 18 Dec 1925
Identifies Royal Fusiliers deserter, 328

**Drinkwater, John**
11 Dec 1835 – Jul 1837
Final, and ill-fated, recruit to the Original Police Force, joining 11 Dec 1835 and transferred to Worcester City Police as one of the initial intake under James Douglas on 15 Jan 1836. Serves under Douglas, 72; resigns 85

**Dunk, Henry Griffiths**
11 Aug 1837 – 13 Jul1849
Born 1805, London. Retired from City police after 12 years and became a painter, living (1851) Little Park Street with wife Louisa, daughter Clarinda, son Albert and grandfather William Stinton, aged 74.

*Below: Sgt Herbert May Evans – overlooked for Chief's post aged 50 (next page). WCiCo/WAAS*

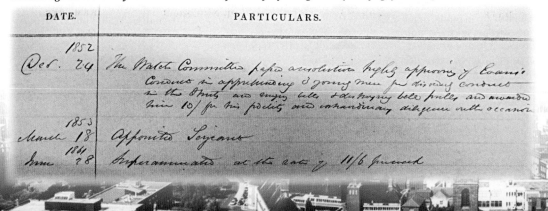

Involved in assault on Sgt Williams, 110; investigates fake half-crowns, 123

**Durant, Mark H. Harrison,**
14 Jun 1872 – 1 Nov 1872

**Dyer, William**
23 Sept 1836 – 1 Jun 1838
Appointed 4th intake WCP No20, 79; controversy on first day, 81-82, 87

**Eate, John**
3 Nov 1871 – 22 Mar 1872

**Edmonds, Richard**
21 Feb 1850 – 3 Sep 1852
No14, recruited from Birmingham and set on by gangs on his first night out, 139; assaulted again and finds body of murdered baby, 143

**Edwards, John**
12 Mar 1869 – 11 Aug 1870

**Edwards, Stephen**
17 Jun 1859 – 1 Jul 1859
Served 14 days

**Etheridge, John**
17 Sep 1852 – (*not known*)

**Evans, David** *(above)*
16 Oct 1885 – 21 Oct 1910
PC24 under Sommers. Investigates shooting, 272; roughed-up in public brawl, 272; investigates suicide of noted brewer, 276 and extended account, [3]; Sommers' protest and signature 289; **photograph** and cutting, 305; un-PC behaviour, 318; rewarded for halting runaway horse in Broad Street, 324; recognises an old adversary, 327; assaulted by Worcester's first 'Woman in White', Harriet Whatmore, 328

**Evans, George**
19 Mar 1871 – (*not known*)
Possibly one and the same as
**Evans, George**
12 Jan 1872 – 23 Feb 1872

**Evans, Henry**
15 Feb 1867 – 22 Nov 1867

**Evans, Herbert May**
1 Mar 1844 – 28 Jun 1861
Born September 1811, Stroud Glos. Solid, reliable but eventually disappointed after 17 years' sterling service. PC17 severely assaulted after breaking up prize-fight, 143; commended after apprehending three men, 145; appointed Sergeant, March 1853, 146; temporary chief following Chipp's death, 173; resigns in protest at being overlooked, 174. Superannuated at 11/6 a week and living (1871) at 10, Pheasant Street with wife Emma, daughters Emma and Harriet, son Henry, two granddaughters Eliza and Alice, taking in female lodgers. Still there aged 70, 1881 (renumbered No6), died the following year Q3.
*Approbation Marks log (previous page) makes no reference to reasons for leaving after 17 years' exemplary service*

**Evans, John**
19 Jan 1836 – 16 Feb 1836
Short-lived Supernumerary, one of four sworn-in four days after official formation of the force, lasted just 28 days

**Evans, Thomas**
28 Jul 1837 – 30 Oct 1840
Seriously assaulted, 91-3

**Ewins, George**
15 Nov 1871 – 21 Apr 1876

**Ewins, Alfred**
24 Jan 1873 – September 1873
No18 under Matthew Power. Permitted to resign after being found drinking while on duty, 222

**Fannon, Michael**
18 Jan 1833 – March 1833
One of first five of the original force and has the dubious

distinction of being the first member of Worcester City Police to be dismissed for drunkenness. He was not to be the last. Appointed, 50. Dismissed for drunkenness 12, 52

**Farley, George**
16 Dec 1876 –15 Jan 1883
Sees a man about a dog, 248; accused, with PC George Bannister, of police brutality Xmas Eve 1881, [3]

**Farley, James**
7 May 1869 – 20 Jun 1869

**Farr, Edwin**
8 Feb 1878 – 3 May 1878

**Febery, John Evan**
4 Jun 1897 – 6 May 1898
Dismissed after less than a year, 323

**Fennell, William Charles** *(above)*
8 Jul 1885 – 21 Jul 1911
Born Oadby, Northants 1864. 1901, aged 37 living at 88 Bransford Road with wife Mary Jane and seven children: William, Amanda, James, George, Beatrice, John and Charlotte. Ten years later and still PC, living at Elm Villas, 5 Happy Land West, St Johns and the family had grown to include two more children, Walter and Charlotte (ii). Died 26th June 1952 aged 87 at 18 Comer Road. Probate effects, £337 17s 9d. PC5 under Sommers. Grievous injuries in scrap and further assaults the next week, 268; severe assault in the Prince of Wales, Shrub Hill [3]; Sommers' protest and signature, 289; emerges with distinction from fire, 301; attacked by Nobby Guy, 314

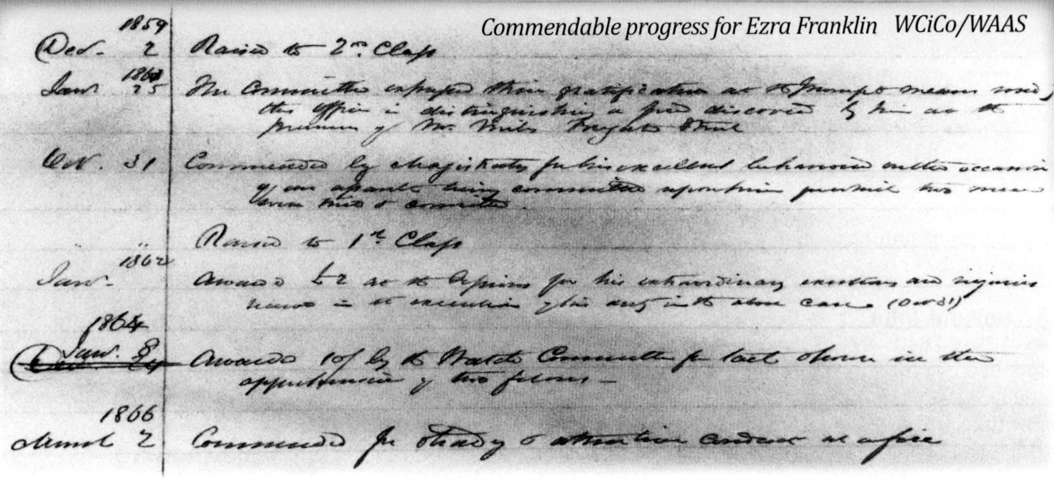

*(Handwritten ledger entries, partially legible)*

| 1859 | |
|---|---|
| Dec. 2 | Raised to 2nd Class |
| Jan. 25 1860 | The Committee expressed their gratification at the prompt manner [in] which the Officer in distinguishing a fire discovered by him as to the premises of Mr. Weals Frights Store |
| Oct. 31 | Commended by Magistrate for his excellent behaviour on the occasion of an assault being committed upon him [...] |
| Jan. 1862 | Raised to 1st Class |
| | Awarded £2 as the expenses for his extraordinary exertion and injuries [...] (O.W.S.) |
| Jan. 8 1864 | Awarded 10/ by the Watch Committee for [...] observed in the apprehension of two felons |
| 1866 | |
| March 2 | Commended for steady & attentive conduct at a fire |

---

**Fielders, James**
14 Aug 1857 – 31 Oct 1862
Useful if wayward PC under Chipp and Power. Assaulted, 171; fined, suspended, resigned, 178

**Firth, George**
12 Mar 1869 – 1 Jul 1870

**Fitzsimmons, John**
8 Oct 1869 – 7 May 1870

**Fitzsimmons, Samuel**
19 Jun 1868 – 11 Sep 1868

**Ford, Harvey William**
15 Jan 1875 – (*not known*)

**Foote, James**
11 Apr 1856 – 10 Oct 1856

**Footman, William**
5 Dec 1884 – 6 Mar 1885

**Fowkes, Richard**
9 Apr 1858 – 29 Sep 1865
No24 under Chipp and Power. Takes on hard-case Dowling, 165; assaulted, 170, 181; courageous conduct, 171; raised to 1st Class 179; fined for lack of zeal, 179; praise for raising fire alarm, 181; beaten-up by gipsies and unable to return to work. Resigns, 194

**Fox, Thomas**
1823 - c1826
One of first Watchmen. Appointed under 1823 Improvement Act, 27; arrests 34. Probably didn't last very long as his name fails to appear again after Jul 11 1826

**Foxhall, Walter**
31 Aug 1888 – 11 May 1889

**Franklin, Ezra**
12 Mar 1858 – 2 Dec 1880
Born Stonehouse, Gloucestershire 1829, joined aged 29, living (1861) at 14 Pheasant Street with wife Elizabeth and three daughters, Emma, Ann and May. Ten years on, living at 18 Lansdowne Street. Superannuated aged 52, (1881) moved to Bath. Died 1900, aged 68. Well-respected and dependable PC10 and 16 under Tommy Chipp, and Acting Sergeant. Assaulted, 164; takes on hard-case Dowling, 165; tackles two women, 170; distinguished conduct, 172; fined for neglect, 172; prompt action at a fire, 181; praised for excellent behaviour during assault, 181; more assaults, 187; investigates suspected murder, 187; commended for promptitude, 192. His Approbation marks record shows no transgressions and indicates exemplary service despite a record of being beaten-up in nearly every pub in St Johns

**Frankling, Jesse**
6 Mar 1851 – 20 Mar 1851
Remarkably short-lived (*14 days*) Supernumerary under Chipp

**Franks, William**
29 Jan 1869 – (*not known*)

**Fudger, George**
18 Feb 1842 – 16 Sep 1842

**Fudger, John**
7 Jul 1844 – 28 Jan 1850
Short-lived, (*7 months*) constable, initially served as Supernumerary. Roughed-up by navvies, 124; assists PC22 Grubb in personal theft issue, 128

**Futrill, William**
5 Jan 1866 – (*not known*)

**Gardner, John**
21 Feb 1862 – 28 Nov 1862

**Garland (*not known*)**
1824
Parish-appointed Constable, 27

**Geary, George Henry**
22 Jun 1883 – 31 Jan 1884

**Gibbons, Abraham**
7 Aug 1863 – 24 Dec 1863
PC 3rd Class under Power. Found in pub while on duty and dismissed after four months for neglect,192

**Gibbons, Daniel E**
3 Jun 1870 – 17 Jun 1870

**Gibbs, George**
12 Feb 1869 – 7 May 1869

**Glass, James**
20 Nov 1874 – 22 Oct 1875
Sued for false imprisonment, 228 and extended account, [3]; exceptional detective work in stolen leather incident, [3]; found on licensed premises and dismissed, 228 and extended account [3]

**Glover, John**
15 Sep 1876 – 14 Dec 1876
Assaulted and quit soon after, 231

**Glover, Richard James**
7 Dec 1888 – 4 Jul 1890
tussles with squaddies and quits not long afterwards, 277-8; rumbles 'most notorious man in Worcester', 279

**Golland, John**
10 Jan 1840 – 24 Jul 1840
Short-lived, (6 months) constable, initially served as Supernumerary. **Signature, 95**

**Goodwin, Fredrick**
9 Nov 1876 – 18 Jan 1878
violently assaulted, 234

**Goodwin, John**
10 Jan 1862 – 9 Jan 1863

**Goodwin, Thomas**
9 Apr 1870 – 19 Jan 1872
Found drinking while on duty, 215

**Goodyear, George**
17 Sep 1877 – 10 Jun 1878

**Goodyear, Thomas**
5 Mar 1852 – 19 Mar 1852

**Gough, John Martin William**
25 Jan 1901 – 5 Aug 1904

**Green, James**
24 Jul 1840 – ?

**Green, Thomas**
11 May 1866 – (*not known*)
Short-lived, dismissed after being found drunk

**Greenall, Alfred**
20 May 1859 – 17 Jun 1859

**Greenhill, William**
30 Dec 1870 – 26 Jan 1872

**Gregory, Francis Albert** (*above*)
9 Jun 1893 – 30 Aug 1907
PC22 under Byrne. Beating leads to residents' petition to banish his attacker, 304; quits after another beating, then re-applies, 305; horse-whipped, 317; caught drinking while on duty, 324; emerges scrapper of renown, 326; involvement in all-night stand-off in Mealcheapen Street, 326; another nasty assault, 328

**Gregory, Richard**
3 Jan 1896 – 4 Dec 1896

**Griffiths, Jabez**
6 Feb 1863 – 20 Feb 1863

**Griffiths, James**
26 Mar 1847 – 31 Dec 1847
Short-lived, (9 months) constable, initially served as Supernumerary

**Griffiths, John**
15 Jan 1835 – 10 Jan 1840
No8 under Douglas, 72; assaulted and reprimanded, 68

**Grosvenor, Samuel** (*right 1884 and far right 1892*)
24 Mar 1871 – 22 Mar 1901
Originally engine-driver, Ombersley-born PC, later Inspector, with model 30-year career. Assaulted on St Johns beat, 224; all-night vigil nabs 60 illegal drinkers, 237; **photograph**, and involvement with Tommy Wallace in violent affray with squaddies, 239 and extended account [3] emerges 'hero', 244; investigates

*Samuel Grosvenor*

suicide, 251; leads clamp-down on brothels, 264; Sommers' protest and signature, 289; emerges with distinction from fire, 301; appointed Inspector, 315; un-PC behaviour, 318. 1881, aged 29 with wife, Hallow-born Mary Jane. Retires 1901, age 48 living at 30 Northfield Street. 1911 living at Stannage, Vernon Park Road. Died 11 January 1932. Probate effects £1301 0s 8d.

**Grubb, Albert**
20 Jan 1882 – 31 Aug 1882

**Grubb, Edward**
4 Aug 1843 – 4 Mar 1853
Born Ludlow, 1809. Married to Mary, also Shropshire. 1851 living in Police headquarters at 2, Queen Street. Recruited No 22 under Phillips, 112; rises to prominence tackling navvies, 118; warned of excessive use of violence 119, 129, 131; apprehends Worcester highway robber in Cheltenham, 122; face-to-face with 'Chilly' Chillingworth 123; wades into navvies, 123; comical description, 125; accused of theft, 129; gets his come-uppance, 140; investigates concealment of birth, 145; quits and joins Hereford Police as Superintendent, 147; near fatal accident, 149

**Grubb, George**
28 Oct 1881 – 16 Dec 1881
Short-serving (*39 days*) PC under Power

**Gummery, Ezekiel**
25 Aug 1848 – 20 Sep 1852
Initially served as Supernumerary Constable

**Guise, George**
15 Apr 1864 – 17 Oct 1864
Short-lived PC 3rd Class under Power. Assaulted, 195. Discharged after being found 'associating with suspicious characters'

**Guy, Arthur Harry**
4 Dec 1896 – 16 Feb 1923
Comparison with namesake 'Nobby' (Samuel), 322

**Hale, George**
1824
Constable of St Nicholas. Appointed 27; assaulted, 32

**Hale, William**
20 Aug 1830 – 17 Feb 1844
One of second draft of Watchmen. Appointed 27, 55, 102; No5 under Douglas, 72; tragic drowning 73; frustrated in murder case, 74; assaulted in affray, 80; No1 under Phillips; assaulted by Supernumerary Phelps, 108; praise for gang-busting, 109; rescues navvie later found dead; resigns to become City Bellman 119; dies, 167

**Halford, Richard**
20 Jun 1856 – 18 Jul 1856
Short-lived (*28 days*) Supernumerary, one of eleven recruited in the troubled year 1856 and one of the three that failed to complete the first year

**Hall, Charles (*above, right*)**
17 Mar 1883 – ?
No18 under Sommers, 19 under Byrne. Savagely assaulted, 260; Sommers' protest and signature, 289; **photograph 299**; throws cricket ball 82 yards and 1 foot, 326

**Hall, Frederick**
15 Feb 1867 – 24 May 1867
Appointed, found drunk while on duty, fined 2/6d allowed a month to resign. But again found drunk and dismissed, 203

**Hall, John (*above*)**
14 Mar 1888 – 14 Mar 1913
From Rock, born 1869 and 19 when recruited. In 1891 living at 23 Bedwardine Road (at 24 lived PC Thomas Langstone) with wife Emma and son Ernest John. PC19 under Byrne. involvement in Oakey's sacking, 294-298; savage assault, 300; tackles persistent drunk James Wedgbury at the Kings Head St Johns ([3]); finds decomposed baby's body, 310; cuts down body of suicide George Adams, Worcester Town Crier, 316

*(Below)* a typical arrest by solid Watchman and member of the original force, Joseph Hall, 26th December 1838 (WCiCo/WAAS)

**Hall, Joseph**
15 Mar 1833 – ? May 1849
Watchman and member of Original Force. Appointed, 55. Assaulted 56-59, 81, 88, 107; No10 under Douglas and Phillips, 77 and 79; cracks charity scam, 111; more praise when he attempts rescue of would-be suicide in the river, 121. Dies after contracting disease following another river rescue, 134. Details of a typical arrest (*foot of page*)

**Hall, Thomas**
21 Mar 1862 – (*not known*)

**Hall, William**
28 Oct 1853 – (*not known*)
Supernumerary constable, date/reason for leaving not recorded

**Hamshire, William**
24 Jul 1840 – 5 Sep 1850
Involved in assault on Sgt Williams, 110.; disfigured after being shot in the face, reward offered, 111

**Handley, John**
6 Mar 1863 – (*not known*)

**Harden, James**
1 Jul 1870 – 16 Jun 1871

**Harding, Edward**
28 Oct 1833 – 22 Nov 1835
Serves under Douglas, 72; tracks burglars, 74; dismissed, 76

**Harding, Henry**
23 Nov 1866 – 6 Mar 1888
Accused of being drunk after heavily tackling revellers in the Bell, St Johns, 201; assaulted, 205; commended for spotting and extinguishing fire at Swan with Two Necks (Nicks). 218; **photograph, 236, 269**; twice fined for drunkenness, 236; promoted to Sergeant, 264; commended, 264; investigates shocking child cruelty, 266

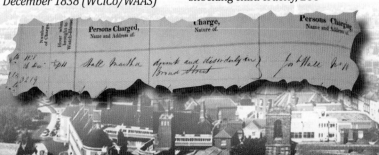

| Number of Charge | Hour when brought to Watch-House | Persons Charged, Name and Address of. | Charge, Nature of. | Persons Charging, Name and Address of. |
|---|---|---|---|---|
| | | Hall Martha | drunk and disorderly etc Broad Street | Jos Hall No 10 |

**Hardwick** (*not known*) **1823**
One of second draft of Watchmen. Appointed, 27; Constable of St Johns

**Hardwick, Christopher**
9 Mar 1885 – 25 Sep 1885

**Hardy, Frederick**
25 Jul 1850 – (*not known*)
recruited in Tommy Chipp's first intake, 141

**Hargreaves, Albert** *(above)*
3 Aug 1894 – 9 Feb 1903
Rochdale-born (1868) PC36 under Byrne, later promoted to Sergeant, living (1901) St Oswald's Cottage, St Oswald's Road with wife Gertrude (née Hargreaves, 25). Transferred as Inspector to Middlesbrough, 1903

**Harley, Henry**
15 Sep 1877 – 2 Oct 1903
Born 1859, Pershore, recruited at 18. By 1891, aged 31 living at 23, Derby Road married to Emily with three children, Winifred, William and May. 1901 living Woolhope Road with another daughter Mary. Retired on police pension 1903, later (1911) living in Edgar Tower as Gate Porter aged 52. PC16 under Sommers, PS5 under Byrne. Attack outside the Bell St Johns leads to doubled police presence in the township ([3]); attacked in the station-house, 246; solves robbery, 250; promoted 1st Class, 274; again assaulted, 277; and in the Lord Nelson, [3]; Sommers' protest and signature 289; appointed Sergeant, 301; **photograph, 301**; role in Insp Wallace murder attempt, 311

**Harmer, Joseph**
22 Jun 1866 – 22 Jan 1869

**Harper, Nathan**
( ? - Dec 1893)
Quits after savage assault by confessed police-hater, 304

**Harris, Edward**
19 Jun 1891 – 15 Jul 1892
PC26 under Sommers. Sommers' protest and signature 289; charged with causing actual bodily harm and sacked after affray in the Green Dragon Newport Street, 299-300, and extended account [3]

**Harris, Sydney**
17 Apr 1877 – 31 Aug 1877

**Harris, Thomas**
30 Jun 1876 –22 Jan 1877

**Harris, William Henry**
19 Mar 1878 – 25 Jul 1878

**Harrison, Alfred**
26 May 1865 – 14 Jul 1870
PC 2nd Class, under Power, commended for tackling a prisoner. Summons music-seller William Henry Elgar for obstruction in High Street, 198

**Harrison, Joseph**
13 Jan 1840 – 21 Aug 1840

**Harper, Nathan**
24 Feb 1892 – 8 Dec 1893
PC6 under Sommers; Sommers' protest and signature, 289

**Harper, Richard**
22 May 1885 – 16 Jul 1885

*A solid 26-year career with Worcester City Police: Henry Harley (left) as PC16 under Sommers and (above) as Sergeant 05 under Byrne. He was later Gate Porter at Edgar Tower*

**Harvey, Francis**
9 Dec 1864 – 29 Jan 1875
Well respected, twice commended (forbearance and detective work) PC 1st Class under Power; assaulted, 202; investigates 'smashing' gang, 212; disarms attempted murderer, 215; apprehends naval deserters, 218

**Hathaway, Frederick**
23 Jan 1879 – 10 Jul 1879

**Hawker, Frederick John** *(above)*
3 Jun 1887 – 20 Jun 1913
PC3 under Sommers; Sommers' protest and signature, 289; **photograph**, 318; un-PC behaviour, 318; investigates suspected murder of Yorkshire House (*now Imperial*) landlady, 320; involvement in all-night stand-off in Mealcheapen St, 326

**Hawker, William**
28 Jan 1859 – (1859)
Recruited, almost immediately
beaten-up and resigns, 166

**Hawker, James**
24 Feb 1860 – 20 Apr 1860

**Hawker, Thomas**
4 Apr 1850 – (not known)
recruited in Tommy Chipp's first
intake, 141

**Haycox, Richard**
9 Oct 1846 – 8 Oct 1847
Quit a day short of a calendar
year after being assaulted, 125

**Haynes, George**
2 Feb 1855 – (not known)

**Haynes, George**
28 Nov 1884 – 26 Jan 1885

**Hayward, Tom**
23 Feb 1900 – 17 Mar 1900

**Hazleton, John Henry**
*(above)*
15 Sep 1881 – 30 Jan 1903
Walsall-born (1860), married
Maria Fenn and lived in her
father's house in Moor Street
1891. 1901 living at 14, St.
George's Lane with Maria (32)
and children John Henry and
Geraldine May. PC26 under
Sommers. PC7 under Byrne.
Solves robbery, 250; roughed-up
in public brawl, 272; Sommers'
protest and signature, 289; gets
more than he bargained for, **and
photograph**, 308; appointed
Coroner's Officer, 317; arrests
Sylvanus Bozward for sexual
assault of two 8-year old girls,
328. Died Stoke on Trent, March
1926 aged 66

**Heapy, William**
20 Jul 1880 – 8 Dec 1882
A violent arrest, 246; accused
of using unnecessary force,
[3]; estimates cabbie driving at
'furious' speed of 13mph in St
Nicholas Street, [3]

**Heming, William**
13 Jun 1873 – 31 Oct 1873
Resigns, 223

**Hemming, Edwin**
27 May 1881 – 20 Jan 1882

**Heritage, Ernest Albert**
8 Dec 1882 – 16 Feb 1883

**Herrington, George**
20 Jul 1880 – 11 Oct 1880

**Hickman, Thomas**
13 Dec 1872 – 14 May 1873
Beaten-up and quits the next day,
223

**Hill, Charles**
18 Oct 1861 – 25 Dec 1861

**Hill, George**
26 Jan 1872 – 1 Sep 1889
PC 14 under Matthew Power,
**photograph, 222**; praised by
Council, 225; ordered to keep
special watch on Prince of Wales
pub in Newport Street [3];
assaulted by Annie Kelley, 248;
dies while still serving, 279

**Hill, Henry**
25 Mar 1870 – 3 Jun 1870

**Hill, James**
27 Jan 1860 – 5 Feb 1863
No22 under Tommy Chipp.
Assaulted 170, 171, 172, 188;
accused of drunken assault, 171;
censured and resigns, 188

**Hill, Richard**
1786
First known of the Watchmen (St
Nicholas). Assaulted, 18

**Hill, Thomas**
1823 - c1833
One of first Watchmen. Appointed
under 1823 Improvement Act,
27; arrests, 34

**Hill, William**
12 Sep 1856 – 21 Oct 1864
Assaulted, 164; severely bitten,
181

**Hill, William**
17 Mar 1858 – 21 May 1859

**Hinett, Albert Edward**
1 Nov 1889 – 25 Nov 1889

**Hitch, William**
26 Jan 1872 – 12 Mar 1874
Threatened with drowning, 223

**Hobbs, William**
25 Apr 1884 – 5 Aug 1887
Injuries sustained in tangle with
drunken Ann Hodgkins, 264

**Hodges, Edward**
19 Jan 1866 – 6 Dec 1867
Censured for gossiping on his
beat, later charged with using
undue force in apprehending a
prisoner

**Hollis, William**
17 Sep 1889 – 24 Sep 1920
Joined aged 19, born Barnt
Green. 1911 living at 68 Malvern
Road with wife Eliza Ann (born
Broadheath) and daughter Elsie
Rose. PC8 under Sommers.
Sommers' protest and signature,
289; savagely assaulted, 304, 306,
307, 322; **photograph, 306**;
cuts down body of suicide George
Adams, Town Crier, 327. Died 4th
June 1938 aged 68, at home, 16
Cypress Street. Probate effects
£212 3s 1d.

*William Hollis*

## Holmes, Benjamin
18 Dec 1853 – 4 Nov 1870
6' 7" stalwart with a reputation for wading-in to any situation and counted extremely fortunate to have survived a mob attack in 1855. Born Cumberland 1833. Rapid progress after recruitment, Aged 28 in 1861, already Detective and married to Worcester-born dressmaker Lucy with two children, Thomas and Edith and living at 3, Queen Street. Later living at 13 Foregate Street with Lewis Barnes and his sister Ellen as housekeeper. Further progress 146, 157; murderous assault, 151-2; Approbation Book, 157; assaulted, 171, 195; appointed Station Sergeant, 176; courageous conduct, 183; investigates baby's murder, 198; disarms gunman, 201; resigns to become Sergeant-at-Mace, 209; trouble with corpse mix-up, 246; appointed Sword-bearer and Billet-Master, 278 appointed Coroner's Officer, 285; dies 9th January 1892, 285. Probate effects £111 11s 6d

## Holtham, William
21 Feb 1850 – 16 May 1850
recruited in Tommy Chipp's first intake, 141

## Holyfield, Thomas
10 Jun 1864 – 24 Nov 1865
PC3rd Class under Power, dismissed after charges of drunkenness and absence from beat

## Hood, Frederick John
24 Mar 1848 – (not known)

## Hooper, George (above)
20 Oct 1884 – 18 Nov 1910
Born Whitbourne 1863, recruited aged 21. PC9 under Byrne. Tackles a notorious hard-man, 280. Police pensioner from 1910, the following year aged 48 living at 5, St Stephen's Street with Worcester-born wife Mary Jane and children aged between 22 and 3, Edward George, Albert, Leonard, Florence Emma, Margaret, Percy, Mabel and Ethel

*George Hooper*

## Hooper, Andrew
19 Mar 1852 – 10 Oct 1856
Chipp's No20 bettered in a public scrap with Sgt3 George Williams, 147; assaulted 150 and 154

## Hopley, Stephen
22 May 1885 – 19 Jun 1885

## House, Thomas
29 Sep 1890 – 31 Oct 1891

## Howard, Robert
13 Nov 1835 – 10 Jan 1840
A late addition to the Original Police Force, joining 13 Nov 1835, just two months later being included in the initial intake to Worcester City Police under James Douglas on 15 Jan 1836. He served to 10 Jan 1840. Serves under Douglas, 72

## Howse, William
14 Jul 1871 – 11 Aug 1871

## Howell, William
20 Nov 1891 – 22 Jan 1892

## Hughes, Eli Emanuel
8 Aug 1850 – 12 Dec 1850
Short-lived, (4 months) constable, initially served as Supernumerary. Recruited in Tommy Chipp's first intake, 141

## Hughes, John (right)
2 Sep 1884 – 30 Apr 1906
PC1 under Byrne. Investigates tragic suicide, 264; attacked by Nobby Guy, 266; disarms would-be murderer and suicide, 278; comes off worst in squaddie attack, 309; knocked down by horse, 312-13; on scene at horrific rta, 316; involvement in shooting case, 325

## Hughes, Richard
1841 – 24 May 1844
PC18 under Phillips. Disbelieved in court and clash with Mayor's Sergeant-at-Mace Harper, 102; assaulted, 102 and 109; investigates 'dud' sixpences 112

## Hughes, William Henry
12 Mar 1886 – 3 Sep 1886

## Humphreys, George
19 Nov 1858 – 3 Dec 1858

## Hunting, John
10 Jun 1853 – 20 Oct 1861
Supernumerary but puts up such a fight in a vicious assault, he's recruited to the full force, 146-7; escapes murderous assault and another, 153; commended, 159 and 160; takes on two troublesome cads, 162; investigates extreme child cruelty, 162; more assaults 163, 164; resigns after spate of injuries, 178; dies, 178

## Hunt, Charles
22 May 1868 – (not known)

## Hunt, Matthew
18 Oct 1872 – 5 Sep 1873

## Hyett, George
4 Jun 1875 – 28 Jan 1876

## Hyslop, William
3 Sep 1841 – 20 Jan 1843
Originally Supernumerary. No 11 under Phillips, gravely assaulted weeks after joining and again at Christmas the same year, 109

*PC1 John Hughes*

**Incell, Charles**
5 Oct 1860 – 26 Jul 1861
Appointed under Chipp, WCP
No23, later 25, 79; resigns 178

**Innell, (or Incell) Henry**
15 Sep 1865 – 30 Dec 1865
PC 3rd Class under Power
resigned (*no reasons given*) after
three months

**Inight, John**
29 Aug 1856 – September
1856
Supernumerary, breaks knee in a
streetfight and quits, 162

**Insell, Frederick**
8 Sep 1875 – 9 Sep 1877

**Jackman, John**
6 Mar 1840 – January 1850
**signature, 95**; accused of
excessive use of stave, 130

**James, John**
12 Apr 1867 – (not known)

**James, William**
5 Nov 1869 –13 Nov 1903
Born 1846 or 8 Bishop's Frome,
later lived in Credenhill, Hereford.
Joined Worcester City Police aged
21 and by 1881 living at 3, Russell
Terrace (off Tybridge Street), still
a constable with wife Hannah
and children Annie, Frederick,
Herbert and Alice. Ten years on
and appointed Sergeant, living
at Glyndon Villa, Happy Land
North with further additions,
Bertha, Sarah, John and Freda.
No13 under Matthew Power
and Arthur Sommers, Sergeant
4 under Byrne. Rumbles illicit
drinking den by discovering
'password', 212; talks would-be
suicide out of committing the

act, 218; rescues two children
thrown out of upstairs window,
218, fined, 222; assault charge,
237; severely assaulted, 246;
investigates shocking child
cruelty, 266; estimates cabbie's
speed in Broad Street at 15mph,
[3]; promoted Sergeant, 273;
discovers boys' bodies in fire, 278

**Jauncey, Ernest George**
9 Feb 1900 – 9 Feb 1926

**Jauncey, William**
5 May 1900 – 17 Jun 1926

*Thomas Jaynes*

**Jaynes, Thomas (*above*)**
13 Oct 1890 – 17 Oct 1919
Born Bredon, 1865, joined
aged 25. In 1901 living at
Rose Cottage, 3 Crown Street
with Guarlford-born wife Rosa
Hannah, son Arthur, daughter
Gladys and a niece, Alice Willis,
later added to by another
daughter, Winifred Violet. The
couple had lost three other
children. Died 5th January 1939.
Probate effects £371 14s 6d.
PC12 under Sommers; Sommers'
protest and signature, 289

*(Below) William James PC13
under Power and Sommers and
as Sergeant 04 under Byrne*

**Johnson, John**
7 May 1847 - 9 Feb 1849
No18 under Phillips. Assaulted
129

**Jolley, Thomas**
1823 - c1833
One of first Watchmen. Appointed
under 1823 Improvement Act,
27; assaulted 29

**Jones, George**
21 Oct 1836 – 24 Jan 1840
Reprimanded by the Mayor for
drunkenness, 88; sacked, 96

**Jones, George**
6 Jun 1845 – 16 Jul 1847

**Jones, Richard**
29 Oct 1852 – 1864
Served under Chipp. Dismissed

**Jones, Henry**
14 May 1880 – 1 Oct 1880

**Jones, Thomas**
27 Dec 1839 – 21 Jul 1843
Signature, 95

**Jones, Thomas**
23 Oct 1874 – 6 Nov 1874

**Jones, William**
15 Feb 1833 – 16 Oct 1835
Watchman and member of
Original Force. Appointed,
55; served under Douglas, 72;
dismissed 76

**Jordan, William**
20 Apr 1848 – (*not known*)

**Joyner, Henry**
7 Oct 1870 – 21 Oct 1898
Joined City force aged around
20 from Churchill, Oxfordshire.
In lodgings with the Hainsworth
family in Chestnut Street in
1871 but within ten years and
by now Sergeant, married to
Annie from Powick where they
lived for a while before moving
to 12 Pitmaston Road with son
and daughter Albert and Maud.
After retirement (1898, aged
48) became 'grocer, shopkeeper,
ale and porter store' owner at
Thornelow House (sic) Orchard
Street, later moved to Brighton
Villas, Colwall. 28 years' service,

**Kinnersley, John**
17 Mar 1865 – (*not known*)
Short-lived PC 3rd Class under Power

**Knott, John**
18 May 1860 – 1 Jun 1860
Twice severely beaten in a matter of weeks and quits, 153

**Lake, Daniel**
16 Apr 1876 – 17 Aug 1876

**Lamb, George**
31 Aug 1866 – 7 Mar 1867
Nabs three publicans for illegal activities in one week, 200; commended for arrest of pickpocket gang, 201; appointed Detective and beaten-up by 'Nobby' Hardwick, 202. Resigns

Died 13th August 1934. PC33 under Byrne. Severely beaten, kicked and bitten, 285 (twice); tackles several disturbances at the Bear, Hylton Road ([3]); accused of drunkenness in comical tale, 285; **photograph, 303**; savage assault, 306; recovers suicide, 310

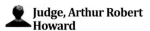

serving under Power, Sommers and Byrne, rising to Inspector and Byrne's 2 i/c. Cuts down hanged suicide at station-house, 237; brutality charge, 239; **photograph, 242;** investigates baby's body found in suitcase at Foregate Street Station, 275 and extended account, [3]; appointed Inspector 283; discovers suicide in Watery Lane, 283; savage assault, 300; attacked by Nobby Guy, 304; retires, 322. Later off-licensee

**Judge, Arthur Robert Howard**
20 Jan 1879 – 8 Sep 1879
quits after one too many goings-over, 239

**Keith, William**
18 Mar 1864 – 7 Mar 1867
No22 under Power. Assaulted, 195; convicted of perjury and allowed to resign, 200

**Kennard, Edward**
7 Oct 1839 – 18 Feb 1842
No22 under Phillips; signature, 95; living in Trinity, 103; charged with assault, 106-7

**Lane, William Henry**
11 May 1883 – 23 Apr 1884.
(*Above*) Short-lived PC who joined in May of the worst year for manpower turnover, 1883, and failed to survive the whole year, spanning the Power/ Sommers change-over

**Langstone, George William**
(*above right*)
1 Jun 1886 – 20 Oct 1911
Fladbury-born (1864) recruited aged 22. Married to Worcester-born Ann, children Albert Henry and Sarah Kate. In 1891 living at 24 Bedwardine Road (at 23 lived PC John Hall); 1901, aged 37 living at 39 McIntyre Road plus two more children: Maud and William. With another son, Arthur Edward born 1907, and promotion to Sergeant aged 50, the family moved to police house in Nash's Passage.

**Layton, Henry**
26 Nov 1886 – 22 Jun 1888

**Leary, John**
18 Jan 1833 – ? Feb 1833
One of first five of the original force. Appointed, 50. In court, 12-13

**Lemon, Albert** (*above*)
9 Jun 1893 – 21 Feb1913
Teignmouth-born (1870) recruited aged 23. In 1901 married to Mary Ann and living at 4, Cecil Terrace, St George's Walk. PC31 under Byrne. Died Upton-on-Severn September 1927 aged 57. Perjury charge, 319; finds drunk in street, discovers rail ticket and carries him to Shrub Hill Station, 322

**Leek, Henry John**
23 Mar 1900 – 30 Nov 1900

 **Lewis, Ernest John**
30 Nov 1900 – 27 Feb 1913

 **Lewis, John**
20 Oct 1871 – 2 Jan 1872

 **Littler, William**
5 Aug 1881 – 16 Sep 1881

**Lloyd, Charles**
4 Dec 1846 – 3 Dec 1847

 **Lock, Charles**
4 Feb 1891 – 8 Oct 1908
Hard-man copper with a reputation as a fighter. PC21 under Sommers. Sommers' protest and signature 289; assault charge, 300; **photograph, 300**; takes on notorious father and son, 324; emerges scrapper of renown, 326; takes out hard-case James Gunnell of Broadheath in a bloody set-to at the Kings Head, St Johns ([3])

**Locke, George**
13 Oct 1890 – Jan 1892
Quits after severe going-over by Band brothers, 284

**Love, Thomas (above)**
27 May 1889 – 28 Feb 1895
PC19 under Sommers, PC13 under Byrne, later licensee Royal Oak, York Place. Carries body of drowned boy through streets to his parents, 280; Sommers' protest and signature, 289; emerges with distinction from fire, 301; resigns, later found drunk and kicks off in the Station-house, 323-4

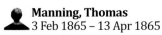 **Lucas, George**
19 Apr 1875 – 25 Sep 1876
With PC Matthew Henry Parsons, criticised in court after being sent as a spy to trap colourful St George's Tavern licensee George Cullis for serving out of proscribed hours, [3]

 **Mann, Joseph Herbert**
2 Feb 1855 – 6 Sep 1872
Initially Supernumerary, promoted to constable

**Manning, Thomas**
3 Feb 1865 – 13 Apr 1865

**Marelli, John**
24 Jan 1840 – ?

**Martin, Charles**
26 Mar 1858 – 25 Feb 1859
No25 under Tommy Chipp, 164; dismissed for drinking while on duty, 166

**Martin, George**
27 Aug 1847 – (10 Jul 1863)
Extra and Constable for College Precincts, funded by Dean and Chapter

**Martin, Jeremiah**
!st Feb 1833 – 15 Mar 1835
Watchman and member of Original Force. Appointed, 55; served under Douglas, 72; dismissed, 76

**Mason, James**
1823 - c1833
One of first Watchmen. Appointed under 1823 Improvement Act and Constable of All Saints, 27

**Mason, John**
4 Feb 1836 - (not known)
Recruited in third intake (Feb 4 1836). Date/reasons for leaving not recorded

**Mason, Joseph**
16 Jan 1874 – 14 Jan 1876
Left to become School Board Officer

**Matthews, Arthur**
6 Apr 1900 – 16 Nov 1900

 **Matthews, Charles**
17 Oct 1862 – 9 Jan 1863

 **Matthews, James**
19 Jan 1891 – 13 Feb 1891

**Mayfield, Joseph**
1 Feb 1833 – 4 Feb 1836
Watchman and member of Original Force. Appointed, 55; served under Douglas, 72; assaulted in affray, 80. Service with the city ended after just a few weeks as he was promoted to Inspector at Kidderminster 4 Feb 1836

**Meredith, Thomas B**
14 Aug 1857 – 4 Apr 1861
Recruited under Chipp. Special responsibility for monitoring prostitutes on the bridge. Thought to have originated infamous 'Street Walkers List'. Assaulted, 171

**Merrick, Eli**
5 May 1848 – 24 Aug 1849 (broken 30 Jun 1849 to 13 Jul 1849)

**Meakins, John**
9 Nov 1975 – 14 Jul 1876

**Miles, Charles**
14 Aug 1876 – 8 Sep 1876

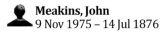 **Millar, Alexander Addison (above)**
21 Sep 1891 – 17 Feb 1922
Scots-born (Aberfeldy Perthshire, 30th January 1869) married to Louisa (born Hanley Castle) and living at 25 Nash's Passage at the same time as George Langstone. Died 17th December 1951 aged 82 at 58 Ombersley

Road. Probate effects £408 18s 6d. PC32 under Sommers and Sergeant under Byrne. Hassles with crowds in Cornmarket, 285; Sommers' protest and signature, 289; rescues suicide, 314; attacked by Nobby Guy, 314

*Alexander Millar*

**Millard, Albert**
15 Sep 1865 – 29 Sep 1865

**Millichap, George**
27 Apr 1866 –17 Aug 1866

**Millward, George**
19 Jun 1868 – 7 May 1869

**Mitchell, James William**
29 Nov 1839 – 2 Aug 1844
Signature, 95; severe going-over in the Blockhouse, 111; private life exposed 119

**Morgan, Amos**
9 Dec 1864 – 3 Mar 1865
Injured in heated 'domestic', 198; twice found drunk on duty and dismissed

**Morgan, David**
2 Apr 1863 – 10 Nov 1865
No 15 under Power. Assaulted, 195; resigned when accused of irregularities over oil

**Morris, James**
17 Oct 1862 – 20 Mar 1863
Recruited under Power, found drunk three times and dismissed

**Morris, John**
4 Jun 1869 – 8 Oct 1869

**Morris, John Spencer**
26 Jan 1872 – 2 May 1873

**Morris, William**
22 Jul 1864 – 3 Mar 1865
Rumbles illicit drinking den, 196, but twice found drunk on duty and later resigned

**Moseley, Henry**
29 Mar 1867 – (*1870*)
Reprimanded for using unnecessary violence, 204; resigns after gross assault in St Johns, 212

**Moule, Frederick**
26 Aug 1859 – 9 Sep 1859

**Moule, George**
15 Jun 1860 – 3 Oct 1861 and 17 Aug 1866 – ??
Censured for trespass, 177; cautioned for unnecessary violence, 178; assaulted 181; guilty of lying and dismissed Oct 3 1860, 178 and 187; re-applies and re-joins 17 Aug 1866

**Moule, Thomas**
17 Sep 1852 – 26 Nov 1852

**Mound, Thomas (*above*)**
22 Jun 1894 – 1 Nov 1931
Born Ludlow 1874, recruited aged 20. PC6 later Sergeant under Byrne, living (1911) Netherton Villa, The Butts, with Mary Elizabeth Smith Mound (born Bewdley 1874) and children Gladys Edith, Thomas George Harvey, Ernest and Trevor Osmond. **Photograph,** 314; apprehends drunken negro, 316. 37 years service, Chief Inspector, Acting Chief Constable

*Thomas Mound*

**'Mrs Smith'**
1876
The only female in this section. Real name unknown and ID protected as she's revealed as a 2s-a-day spy working for Matthew Power to trap unwary landlords selling beer out of hours, 230 and extended account [3]

**Murt, Michael**
6 Dec 1867 – (not known)

**Naylor, Henry**
8 May 1868 – one day only
Force's shortest service - 4 hours. Dismissed after visiting every public house in his beat on day 1. Instantly dismissed for being drunk and gaoled for 7 days, 207

**Neville, Charles**
7 Sep 1900 – 6 Sep 1901

**New, Samuel William**
2 Jul 1869 – 5 Nov 1869

**Newell, John**
2 Feb 1855 – 23 Dec 1855
Quit after ten months following severe beating by boatmen, 153

**Newman, Charles**
8 Oct 1868 – 12 Mar 1869

**Newman, George Frederick**
2 Jun 1881 – 23 Dec 1881

**Nichols, John**
1824
Parish-appointed Constable, 27

**Norman, Joseph**
23 Sep1836 - ?

**Nott, George**
1 Feb 1833 – 9 Mar1860
Watchman and member of Original Force. Appointed, 55; No17 under Douglas, 72; assaulted, 109

**Nottingham, Amos**
i) 18 Oct 1872 – 22 Mar 1878
ii) 23 Dec 1881 – 8 Dec 1882
Investigates coin counterfeiting ring, 223; investigates suspected murder, 228; drags river in search of suicide, 248

**Oakey, Edwin**
17 Jun 1870 – 3 Jun 1892
One of the few from the force born locally (Grimley, 1845), joined aged 25. Married Deborah (also born Grimley, 1849). Living (1881) Middle Road St Johns with children Lizzie, Edith, Thomas, Annie, Arthur and George. Ten

*(Left) Possibly Worcester City Police's worst 'bad penny' up to the Sommers affair in 1892: **Henry Naylor** lasted just four hours as a bobby on the beat, 8th May 1868 (p 207)*

years later at 37 Blakefield Road. Found drinking while on duty, 215; ordered to supervise parents' flogging of their erring son, 223; investigates suspected murder, 228; cuts down hanged suicide at station-house, 237; refused admission at the Railway Bell, [3]; fails attempt to avert suicide, 250; assaulted, 259, 276; raises eyebrows in court, 285 (more extensively covered in [3]); alleged theft incident leads to sacking, 294-298, after which he became a greengrocer operating on his own account from his home 49 (later renumbered 51) Boughton Street. Died 1927

*Edwin Oakey*

*Sgt Edwin Oakey (above), callously sacked in a moment of panic after being found guilty of stealing cider, ending a 22-year career. See account pps 294-8*

**Oldbury, Albert**
24 Apr 1885 – 7 Feb 1886

**Onions, William Thomas**
27 Feb 1885 – 29 Apr 1885

**Onslow, Emanuel**
15 Jan 1833 – 4 May 1838
On the wrong side of the fence, 34; assigned to St Johns, 61; No15 (later No19) under Douglas, 72; makes the headlines, 73; tracks burglars, 74; seriously assaulted. 74; more arrests 75, 81; appointed Sergeant, 78; assists Douglas in affray, 80; cracks robbery at Three Tuns, 82; more detective work, 86

**Orchard, Joseph**
1824-?
Parish-appointed Constable and high-profile Mayor's Officer. Appointed, 27; assaulted, 32; arrests 35, 38, 42, 63; censured, 40; rises to prominence, 66

**Osborne, Francis**
23 Sep 1892 – 3 Sep 1893

**Osborne, Herbert**
7 Aug 1863 – 31 Aug 1883
Another of just a few locally recruited, born Crowle, 1842. Joined aged 21, and in 1871, aged 29, lodging at 48 Moor Street South. Next door at 50 lived two more contemporaries also lodging, George Willis (25) and George Adams (21). Aged 39 in 1881 living at 23 Moor Street with wife Eliza (42) and neice aged 3. Long service (20 years) despite shaky track record including asleep on duty, want of energy, and drunkenness, reprimanded, fined and reduced in rank. Assaulted days after joining, 191; fined for being drunk on duty, 192; tackles four at the Wheatsheaf London Road, 193; commended, 194; assaulted by prostitute Sarah Hartwright, 202; investigates arson, 207; investigates messy suicide, 212; fined, 222; again assaulted, 231; charges against, 236; incapacitated and forced to retire, 258. Died Upton-on Severn 1888, aged 47. ***Approbation marks book, next page***

**Owen, Joseph**
14 Jul 1871 – 3 Oct 1873
Drags bodies of mother and child from canal after murder/suicide, 223

**Packwood, Luke**
15 Mar 1835 – 1 Mar 1844
Originally a Supernumerary and late addition to the Original Police Force, joining 15 March 1835 alongside Joseph Hall and Richard Berry, and transferred to Worcester City Police as one of the initial intake under James Douglas on 15 Jan 1836. Assaulted 68, twice more within a few weeks, 105, against 'Chilly' Chillingworth 110, 111; No17 under Douglas, 72; comes in for praise, 79 and 111; arrests, 89

**Page, Charles**
22 Nov 1867 – 22 May 1868

**Pagett, Samuel**
8 Aug 1873 – (1879)
Spirited defence, 238

**Pardoe, Walter**
31 Jul 1885 – 6 Jan 1888

**Parry, Walter**
28 Mar 1884 – 29 Aug 1890
Two violent altercations in second week, 264; discovers body in burned-out building, 277; charge of drinking while on duty, 278; assaulted by squaddies in Bath Road and quits the next day, 280

**Parsons, Matthew Henry**
11 Sep 1876 – 28 Sep 1876
With PC George Lucas, criticised in court after being sent as a spy to trap colourful St George's Tavern licensee George Cullis for serving out of proscribed hours and lasted just 17 days [3]

**Partington, Charles**
25 Jan 1850 – (*not known*)
former Supernumerary, recruited in Tommy Chipp's first intake, 141

**Payter, Richard**
6 Feb 1863 – 27 Jul 1863
Unreliable, short-lived PC under Power. Charged with drunkenness in April, insubordination in July and dismissed

62  *Herbert Osborne*

## OFFENCES.

| DATE. | OFFENCE. | PUNISHMENT. | REMARKS. |
|---|---|---|---|
| 1863 Aug. 21 | Asleep in the College Precincts while on duty early in the morning of the 12th | Severely reprimanded | |
| Dec 24 | Being under the influence of drink while on duty on the night of the 12th December | Fined 5/- | and told that for the next offence he would be discharged |
| 1864 Feb. 5 | Asleep upon his beat on Clandown to 25. ult | Fined 5/ and severely reprimanded | |
| Sept | Asleep on a door step while on night duty | Fined 1/ by Supt | approved / Comr |
| Nov 11 | Drunk while on duty on Sunday night | Reduced to 3rd Class — Severely Censured and told that next offence he will be discharged | |
| 1865 Sept 29 | Want of energy in keeping back a crowd at a Fire | Fined 1/ by Supt | approved by Comr |
| Oct 13 | Asleep on his beat on the morning of 29. September | Severely reprimanded | |

**Peacock, Frederick William (*above*)**
16 Jan 1888 – 13 Feb 1914 Northampton-born (1863), married to Ann from the Isle of Ely and living Farmers House (?) Woolhope Road 1901 with sons George Robert Frederick and Sidney Arthur. Four doors away lived PS Fred Tarrant. PS6 under Byrne. Sent to Birmingham to arrest fraudulent horse-dealers, 278; appointed Sergeant.

Savagely assaulted, 304 and 306; investigates 'domestic' involving wife with her nose sliced off, 310; commended after arrest of two French robbers in Bath, 316; arrests John Rowley (his 138th), 319. Later promoted to Inspector, living (1911) 2 College Precincts with wife Ann Emma, children Sidney Arthur, Ann Elizabeth, Raymond George and mother in law Ann Clark aged 89. Died Worcester, March 1939, aged 76

**Pearson, Jeremiah**
26 Jan 1872 – (*not known*)

**Penlington, John (*below left*)**
9 Sep 1892 – 17 Jan 1919 Staffordshire-born (1873) recruited aged 19, PC26 under Byrne. 1901 living at 'Dresden', Diglis Lane aged 28 with wife Annie and son John. Possibly widowed the same year as by 1911 he has a new wife, Emily married 1902 and is living at 7 Blakefield Road with son John (2) and further additions Mabel (3) and Percy (1). Appointed Detective-Sergeant. Sommers' protest and signature, 289; commended for talking would-be suicide out of committing the act, 304; assaulted, 307; **photograph**, 316; emerges hero after halting Hallow omnibus, 316; and again after rounding up three stray colts on the Cross, 324. Died

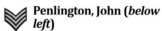

March 1959 Avonside Hospital Evesham aged 88, married to Dorothy Violet and living at 15 Cyril Road. Worcester

*John Pearlington.*

**Penn (*not known*)**
1824
Parish-appointed Constable
Appointed, 27

**Perry, Thomas**
11 May 1855 – 1864
Served under Chipp and Power. Dismissed

**Petty, Frank**
12 Feb 1886 – 25 May 1893
PC31 under Sommers. Gravely injured in Station-house fracas, 278; nabs a drink-driver, 284; Sommers' protest and signature 289; subject of unlawful harbouring charge against King William IV Vaults licensee [3]

**Phelps, George (*above*)**
29 Jul 1892 – 10 Apr 1914
No25 under Byrne

**Phillips, John**
15 Jan 1836 - 4 Jul 1849
One of the first intake (of 15) constables sworn in under the Municipal Corporations Act 1835. No4 and later Sergeant under Douglas, 72; assaulted, 86; signature, 95; appointed Superintendent and third Chief of Worcester City Police 1st March 1840; **Phillips years, 98-135;** shows himself kind-hearted, 100-1; investigates poisoning of family of nine, 103; solutions to navvie issues, 116; crack-down on aggressive prostitutes on the bridge, 123; dies, 134-6

**Phillips, George**
17 Dec 1847 – 14 Jan 1848
Sharing his chief's surname but few of his qualities. Sacked (and fined) after three weeks for drunken brawl with fellow officer, 127

**Phillips, John**
2 Jul 1858 – (not known)

**Phillips, Joseph**
15 Aug 1856 – 16 Jul 1858
Appointed Markets Constable, 163

**Phillips, William**
12 Apr 1833 – 8 Feb 1839
Watchman and member of Original Force. Appointed, 55; serves under Douglas, 72

**Phillips, William**
5 Aug 1864 – 6 Jan 1882
PC later Sergeant under Power. Given the runaround by false murder confession, 215; appointed detective and cracks-down on prostitutes, 236; investigates theft of valuable books stolen from WH Elgar, 240

**Phipps, James**
8 Apr 1868 – (not known)

**Phipps, William**
1 Aug 1856 – 26 Sep 1856

**Pitt, Francis John (*above*)**
25 Sep 1885 – 17 Nov 1911
PC11 under Sommers and Byrne; Sommers' protest and signature, 289

**Pitt, John**
17 Sep 1852 – 24 Jul 1853

**Poole, George**
17 Dec 1847 – (*not known*)

No20 under Phillips. Discovers body in Swan Pool, 128; assaulted outside Unicorn and quits, 135

**Poole, Henry**
4 May 1849 – 16 Nov 1849

**Pope, Charles Richard**
5 Jan 1894 – 31 May 1894

**Pountney, Charles**
31 Aug 1866 – 26 Apr 1867
Ever controversial under Power. Found asleep on duty, took time off for illness due to excessive drinking, failing to make his point on Blockhouse Bridge (*denied*); arrests drunk, later found to be teetotal campaigner, 201; charged with assault, 202; other charges against, tenders resignation, refused and sacked, 203

**Powell, George**
2 Aug 1844 – 21 Sep 1849
Assaulted by navvies, 125, 128; settles heated 'domestic', 132

**Power, Matthew**
1 Jun 1861 – 6 Feb 1884
Born Waterford, Ireland, 1826. Chief, **The Power years, 174-252;** former Irish Revenue Police (*as was his elder brother Thomas who followed him to Worcester*). 1871 listed as Head Constable and living at the Station-house, Copenhagen Street with wife Mary Evans Power, daughters Georgina and Ophelia. Selection and career, 174-6; introduces white gloves, 177; beset with early problems, 175-7; clashes with authority; heads call for police to be armed, 204-5; defends 'French spy system'; under fire for 'police manufactured crimes', 214; personal vendetta against Oddfellows Arms, Carden Street; praised by Mayor Richard Evans Barnett, 217; assaulted, 222; supports reduced drinking hours, 224; spat with *Herald*, 225; as chief of Fire Brigade, 226; Secretary of SPCA, 226; sued for false imprisonment, 228; methods criticised, 229; quits as head of fire service, but retracts, 233; pride in dress, 241; clocks-

up 20 years as chief, 245; accused of planting spies, 248; objects to licence of Grosvenor Arms on moral grounds ([3]); proves exceptional police chief, 248; dies aged 58 (6th Feb 1884), 252-3; full turn-out for funeral, 254. Personal estate (probate date 6 March 1884) valued at £1,731 10s 1d

**Preece, William Charles**
28 Nov 1862 – 7 Oct 1890
Wayward, and occasionally insubordinate but promising PC21 under Matthew Power. Promoted to sergeant; emerges with distinction after 'Providence Street Riots'. 198; **photograph, 219;** reprimanded for being found asleep while on duty, 219; suspended, sacked and then reinstated for assaulting PC George Archer No5, 219; severely bashed-about in Stationhouse, 250; major fracas in the Freemasons Arms Carden Street, [3] with PC Henry Willis; calls for curb on prostitutes viewing city as location for easy pickings, [3]; promoted Det-Sgt and investigates alleged murder of Golden Hart licensee Henry Powell, 274-5 and extended account [3]

**Presdee, Stephen**
17 Oct 1873 – 17 Jul 1874

**Presdee, William**
17 Oct 1850 – 20 Feb 1852
recruited in Tommy Chipp's first intake, 141

**Preston, Richard**
25 Sep 1873 – 17 Oct 1873
Resigns after three weeks, 223

**Price, John**
27 Dec 1839 – ?
Signature, 95

**Price, William James**
9 Oct 1891 – 20 Nov 1891

**Pritchard, Albert**
2 Feb 1883 – 22 Jun 1883

**Pritchard, William**
11 Sep 1877 – 21 Dec 1877

**Pugh, John**
2 Apr 1872 – 5 Jul 1889
No8 under Matthew Power. Arrests deserter, 205; **photograph, 222;** murder attempt, 244; severe assault in the Woolpack [3]; refused admission at the Railway Bell [3]

**Pullen, Joseph**
23 Oct 1878 – 31 Dec 1878

**Pursell, George**
2 Jan 1846 – ?

**Quinn, James**
31 Oct 1861 – 5 Jun 1868

**Quinney, James** (*above*)
8 Jan 1883 – 16 Oct 1884
PC9 under Matthew Power. Assaulted, 231; accused of collusion with counterfeiters [3]

**Quinney, Thomas**
9 Jul 1876 – 6 Apr 1877

**Rawlings, William**
4 May 1849 – (*not known*)

**Reeve, ??**
19 Aug 1864 – (*not known*)
Extra Constable, and Relieving Officer for Vagrants

**Reeves, William**
29 Nov 1861 – 27 Dec 1861

**Repton, Walter**
12 Mar 1897 –18 May 1923
Commended for action at a fire in College Precincts, 322

**Richard, John**
19 Jan 1866 – 16 Feb 1866

**Richards, ?**
9 Aug 1861 – 23 Aug 1861
Appointed, reprimanded for drunkenness and losing his hat, fined and dismissed, 178

**Richards, John**
8 Oct 1869 – (1872)
Roughed-up by a mob of around 40, 216

**Richardson, George**
11 Aug 1837 – 3 Sep 1841

**Richardson, George**
12 Mar 1875 – 26 Jul 1875

**Richardson, James**
3 Aug 1881 – 23 Feb 1888
PC18

**Richardson, William**
10 Dec 1852 – 3 Oct 1862
Consistently controversial, generally unpopular and insubordinate, but essentially effective and successful detective (*appointed Aug 1st 1856*) and scourge of the criminal classes. Appointed, 145; rapid progress, 146; censured, 146; falls to Noah Dayus, 150; charges against, 156; appointed Detective, 158; assaulted, 164; commended, 167; a good year, 169; spat with Bill Berridge, 170; spat with John Doughty, 171; marks of Approbation (extract), 171; distinguished conduct, 172; more praise, 181; exceeds bounds of duty, 182-3; admonished and resigns, 186; appointed Supt at Stratford-upon-Avon, 186. ***Approbation marks entry, p 331***

**Roberts, George**
29 Sep 1876 – 7 Sep 1877

**Roberts, Thomas**
13 Aug 1858 – 19 Nov 1858

**Roberts, William**
16 Sep 1887 – 23 Oct 1890
Discovers children's bodies in fire, 278

**Robins, George**
20 May 1859 – 10 Oct 1860

**Robinson, Richard** (*above*)
11 Sep 1885 – 15 Oct 1896
PC30 under Sommers. Investigates murder/manslaughter, 285; severely hammered, 285; Sommers' protest and signature, 289; rescues PC1 John Hughes, but sparks controversy, 313; **photograph**, 313; resigns through ill-health, 317

**Rogers, Henry (*above*)**
21 May 1883 – 18 Nov 1884
PC5 under Sommers. Disarms Irish would-be assassin, 260

**Roseblade, Thomas William**
24 Dec 1885 – 28 May 1886

**Ross, John Alfred**
17 Jul 1857 – 11 Nov 1857
Short-lived (12 weeks) constable

**Rudniski, Francis**
17 Oct 1862 – 4 Sep 1863
Witnesses attempted murder incident at Shrub Hill Station, 188; gravely assaulted, 191

---

Later licensee of the Canon in Carden Street where he earned a reputation for being as hard as his customers (*see Bob Backenforth's Worcester Pubs Then and Now, vols i and ii p293*)

 **Ruff, John**
26 Feb 1875 – 7 May 1875

 **Sanday, Jesse**
2 Sep 1853 – 24 Nov 1854

**Sanders, Benjamin**
17 Jul 1857 – 26 Mar 1858
One of three constables recruited on the same day (17 Jul 1857 – see also Cotton, Charles and Ross, John Alfred) none of which completed a year's service

**Sanders, George**
16 Sep 1842- 16 Oct 1851
PC 12 assaulted, 143

**Sanders, John**
10 Oct 1856 – 18 Aug 1860
PC12 under Chipp and Power. Assaulted, 170; ordered to resign, but re-instated; halts racing horses in Lowesmoor, 172; appointed Sergeant. Drowned in the Severn, 195

**Sanders, William**
15 Oct 1830 – 15 Jan 1847
Watchman later inducted into the Original Police Force in the second intake (Oct 1833) under Henry Sharpe and later PC6 under James Douglas, later promoted to Sergeant Appointed, 55; No6 under Douglas, 72; appointed Sergeant and 2i/c under Phillips, 100; threatened with a gun 105; praise for gang-busting, 109; tackles navvies, 116; investigates suicide at the Raven, 119; apprehends Worcester highway robber in Cheltenham, 122; leg broken in Guildhall tussle, 123

**Saunders, Timothy**
1824
Parish-appointed Constable. Appointed, 27

**Sedgeley, George**
3 Mar 1854 – 2 Apr 1863
Hammered in a vicious

---

Merryvale free-for-all, 153; attacked with boiling water, 159; youth he captures described as 'juvenile delinquent', 162; complaints, 167; resigns, 188

**Sharpe, Henry**
18 Jan 1833 – 24 Apr 1835.
First Inspector of the original Police Force, **49-68**. Ex-Sergeant, Metropolitan Police. Appointed, 50. In court, 12-13; demands increase in numbers, 55; gravely injured in fracas, 56; dies, 69. *The Sharpe years, 48-69*

**Sheen, Frederick Samuel**
11 Nov 1882 – 8 Dec 1882
Rumbled as a spy; reports men betting in the Rising Sun, and quits after 83 days, 248

**Sherwood, Thomas**
24 Dec 1879 – 9 Jan 1880
Christmas 1879 and the New Year appear to have proved too much: he served just 16 days over the festive period

**Short, Edwin**
7 Jun 1844 – 9 Oct 1846

**Shipley, Samuel**
30 May 1862 – 3 Oct 1862
Dismissed for leaving the city without permission, 187

**Short, William Hollister**
17 Jan 1896 – 17 Jan 1930
Served precisely 34 years
Promoted to Inspector
*(More in Vol II of 'The Spike')*

**Silvester, John**
23 Sep1836 – 10 Jan 1840
Appointed 4th intake WCP No19, 79; assaulted, 82; arrests, 89

**Slinn, John**
11 Sep 1885 – 13 May 1887
Assault under Edgar Tower, 268; further assaults, 268; accused of rough handling, admits to being drunk, quits and joins the Army

**Smalley, Albert** (*above*)
23 Dec 1892 – 16 Jul 1897
PC16 and Drill-Master under Byrne, 313

**Smith, Albert**
10 Apr 1885 – 23 Jul 1886

**Smith, Arthur**
30 May 1873 – 3 Oct 1873
Resigns, 222

**Smith, Charles**
20 Sep 1861 – 29 Mar 1866
No 4 and 13 under Matthew Power with chequered history including asleep while on duty and absenteeism. Savage assault, 184; charged with neglect, 196; allowed to resign after more charges, 199

**Smith, Charles**
31 Oct 1879 – 11 Jun 1880
Sacked and then attacks PC Arthur Smith, 264

**Smith, George**
11 Mar 1859 – 7 Apr 1859

**Smith, Henry**
4 Feb 1852 – (not known)

**Smith, Richard**
4 Jun 1869 – 18 Oct 1872

**Smith, William**
16 Jun 1876 – 3 Nov 1879
Twice assaulted by squaddies in the same week, 231; attempts to bribe, 232 and extended account, [3]; assaulted 234, and in the Leopard, [3]

**Soles, Thomas**
12 Aug 1870 – 5 May 1871

**Sommers, Arthur Edwin**
15 Feb 1874 – 10 Jun 1892
Chief Constable February 1884 - June 1892. Confiscates obscene postcards, 224; makes his mark, 227; **photograph, 228;** rises to prominence, 228; prompt action at a disastrous fire, 233 and extended account, [3]; all-night vigil nabs 60 illegal drinkers, 237; rapid promotion, 247; embarrassing conflict with Tolley, 248; vendettas against Sow and Pigs, Dolday and Coventry Arms Friar Street (*now Cardinals Hat*) [3]; appointed chief, 255; **The Sommers years, 254-293;** courtroom clashes, 259; 'dark' character emerging and doubts about sobriety, 262-3; accused of spy-techniques after PC Sheen is rumbled at the Farmer's Arms, The Pinch ([3]); ordered to wear uniform in court, 266; falls out of favour with Mayor and others, 268; creates a storm when he calls the Angel Inn (St Johns) 'no better than a brothel' ([3]); role in controversial perjury charge against licensee of the King's Head, St Johns ([3]); takes control of case involving Militia Sgt-Major and a 6-year old girl, 272; TUC complaint, 273; clashes with prison surgeon George Hyde, 277; takes on 'the King of England', [3]; shows compassionate side, 281; integrity tested, 281; protests after shocking scenes in the station house, 287-293; resigns and subsequent issues, 291-3; bankrupt and attempts suicide, 303. Died September 1916

**Sparkes, Joseph**
19 Nov 1898 – 14 Mar 1924
Accused of gross indecency, 328

**Spencer, John**
26 Jul 1861 – 9 Jan 1863
Fined, reprimanded, censured, 178; courageous conduct, 183; stabbed in fracas, 187; quits after three serious assaults, 189

**Spilsbury (*not known*)**
1835- (*not known*)
Constable of St Johns, 61; beer-house action, 67

**Spilsbury, George**
30 Jan 1874 – (not known)

**Stallard, Charles**
14 Apr 1875 – 4 Jun 1875

**Stanton, George**

**Stanton, John**
3 Dec 1869 – 24 Feb 1871

**Stanton, John**
3 Oct 1873 – 27 Jan 1874

*Arthur Edwin Sommers. Centre of Worcester City Police's most inglorious episode of the Victorian years*

**Stanton, William**
14 Nov 1879 – 21 Nov 1884
PC26

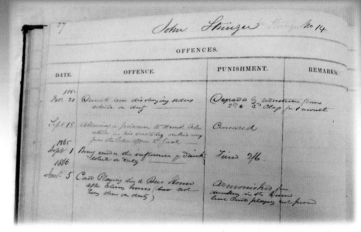

*John Stringer's Approbation marks entry shows his wayward nature (WCiCo/WAAS*

**Steadman, Frank (*above*)**
4 Dec 1891 – 6 Dec 1920
Warminster (Wilts)-born (1869)
recruited at 22. Married to Annie,
born Leigh Sinton and living
(1901) at Imber Villa, Wylds
Lane. PC14 under Sommers and
Byrne, appointed Sergeant and
living (1911) 34 Fort Royal Hill
with Annie, son Hubert Frank and
three lodgers. Sommers' protest
and signature, 289; investigates
suspected murder, 320. Died 22
January 1962 aged 93 at Shrub
Hill Hospital, home 7 Vernon
Park Road. Probate to newsagent
son, Hubert Frank Hill Steadman,
effects £1,972 10s

*Frank Steadman*

**Stone, Alonzo**
27 Apr 1888 – 4 Jan 1889

**Stoneley, George**
10 Oct 1834 – 12 May 1843
Commended, 67; complaints,
68; No16 under Douglas, 72;
heroic 'chace', 72; takes on three
and wins, 81; loses prisoner,
101; assaulted, 102; apprehends
gunman threatening to shoot
Sgt Sanders, 105; promoted
Sergeant

**Stringer, John**
28 Jun 1861 – 25 Feb 1870
PC14, appointed, raised to 2nd
class, downgraded to 3rd class;
tangles with 'Gipsy Moule', 181;
censured, 187; commended for
sturdy action at a fire, 198

**Tallis, William**
9 Apr 1874 – 14 Jan 1876

**Tandy, John Winwood**
27 Jul 1860 – 10 Aug 1860

**Taplin, Arthur**
26 Feb 1876 – 25 Mar 1876

**Tarrant, Frederick (*above*)**
5 Jan 1876 – 7 Feb 1902
Super-reliable PC (no12) joined
aged 19 in Jan 1876 later
Sergeant with 27-year career
under Power, Sommers and
Byrne. Born Birlingham 1857,
married to childhood sweetheart
Maria born a year later. Aged
25 in 1881 he's living in Lower
Chestnut Street and (1891) living
at Fernville, Woolhope Road, with
sons Frederick Arthur and Ernest
Francis and daughters Ellen
Maria, Maud Beatrice and Elsie
Winifred. Still at the same address
1901 and retires the

following year. Roughed-up by
mob, 240; **photograph, 242**;
two distressing cases, 243;
intervenes in violent domestics
at the Grosvenor, St Johns after
wife kicks the door down, and
attempted murder at the Anchor
Diglis (both [3]); involved in
regular violent shindies at the
Apple Tree, Tybridge Street ([3]);
investigates animal cruelty, 246;
disarms would be murderer,
246; severely assaulted, 246, 28
and in Cumberland Street [3];
discovers boys' bodies in fire, 278;
Sommers' protest and signature
289; assaulted, 314. Pensioned
in February 1902, he became a
verger, living at 12 Bolston Road.
Died 28 August 1934 and left
effects (£502) to Elsie Winifred.
Maria Tarrant died at the same
address 24th January 1937

*Frederick Tarrant*

**Taylor, David**
5 Apr 1884 – 14 Aug 1884
PC15 under Sommers. Dismissed
and gaoled for assault and
absconding, 261

**Taylor, John**
1828 - (*not known*)
Tything Parish Constable.
Investigates murder, 41

**Taylor, William**
13 May 1875 – 25 Aug 1876

 **Teale, William (*above*)**
13 Oct 1890 – 17 Oct 1919
Stoulton-born (1869) recruited aged 21, PC20 under Sommers; Sommers' protest and signature 289; savagely assaulted, 304 and 306; **photograph, 306**; arrests Fred Dancox, 326. Married to Florence Maria and (1911) living at Rose Villa, 15 Greehhill London Road, with their daughter Florence Beatrice with two lodgers/boarders. Died 20 January 1938 at South Bank Nursing Home. Probate granted to Florence Beatrice (£892 11s)

*William. Teale*

**Thomas, Charles (*above*)**
6 Feb 1866 – 3 Jan 1896
Hallow-born (1842) married to Kempsey-born Ann, 1881 and still PC, living Northfield Street with daughters Annie, Alice, Ada (5,4,2). Long-service, dependable and reliable with no known transgressions.

Investigates murder attempt at Swan with Two Necks (Nicks), 231; attacked in the station-house, 246; **photograph, 247;** appointed Station Sergeant and averts suicide in the cells, 249; as leading fire fighter (photograph), 226; instrumental and chief complainant in Arthur Sommers' assault affair, 286-292; letters to Town Clerk, 286, 289; signature, 289; elevated to Court Officer; retires after 30 years, 315; appointed Inspector SPCA (Society Against Cruelty to Animals), 315. 1901 aged 59, living with Annie, Alice Gertude and son William Charles (9) at Glendale, 42 Woolhope Road with PC Charles Lock (age 35) as neighbour at Grosvenor Villa. Widowed by 1911 (aged 69) and living with Alice and William. Died December 1917, aged 75

**Thomas, Joseph**
19 May 1848 – 30 May 1852

**Thomas, Joseph**
24 Aug 1849 – 30 May 1852

**Thompson, Frederick**
10 May 1867 – 27 Mar 1868

**Thompson, John**
27 Mar 1868 – 8 Apr 1868
Served just 12 days

**Thompson, Richard**
20 Feb 1863 – 3 Aug 1863
Served under Power. Resigned after six months, no reasons given

**Thorne, Frederick William**
6 Dec 1867 – 24 Sep 1873
Sergeant under Matthew Power. Placed under gipsy curse, 214; dies two years later, 222

**Tilt, Thomas**
1824
Parish-appointed Constable and high-profile Mayor's Officer. Appointed, 27; cracks jewellery theft, 74

**Tolley, Matthew**
13 May 1878 – 8 Dec 1882

**Tolley, Thomas**
21 Nov 1862 – 17 Apr 1887
Born Droitwich 1841, recruited aged 22, married to Sabina (also Droitwich). 1871 aged 30 living at 25 Toll Houses St Johns with wife and sons Thomas Henry and Charles. Later Detective-Sergeant. Charged with assaulting passenger at Shrub Hill Station, 191; fined for leaving his beat, 199; interrupts rape, 201; **photograph, 206;** role in controversial perjury charge against licensee of the King's Head, St Johns ([3]); commended for forbearance and good temper under provocation, 206; commended after fire, 244; accused of using undue force, 246; embarrassing conflict with Sommers, 248; accused of being sneaky and underhand carrying out Sommers' orders at the Crown, Friar Street, [3]; called to messy suicide on the railway, finds it's his close neighbour and friend, 260; dies while serving aged 46, 269. Possibly separated from Sabina as his address is given as 4 Melbourne Street (probably a police house), Sabina's 1 Cheltenham Villas Lansdowne Street. Personal estate £84 11s.

*Thomas Tolley, commended for forbearance and good temper under provocation, 206*

**Tomkins, George**
6 Sep 1861 – 20 Sep 1861
Appointed, fined, dismissed after 14 days, 178

**Tomlinson, Alfred**
12 Mar 1896 – 20 May 1921
Excels in police sports outing, 319

**Trickey, Frederick Francis**
7 Mar 1862 – 28 Nov 1862
Quits after eight months following serious assault, 187

**Troughton, Joseph William (*above*)**
23 Dec 1881 – 27 Jun 1906
Born 1863 Leigh, Worcs. PC10 under Sommers and Byrne. Assaulted, 248; investigates staggering cutlery theft, 250; **photograph, 282**; recovers body of drowned boy from under Chambers Bridge, Perdiswell, 282; severely hammered, 285. 1891 living 13 Astwood Road with wife Annie and daughters Annie Elizabeth and Emily Sarah, ten years later with a son, Joseph. Dies mid-1906, aged 42

**Trueman, Thomas**
28 May 1866 –
6 Dec 1867
Chequered 18-month career, twice found drunk while on duty and twice found asleep

**Turner, George (*above*)**
2 Aug 1889 – 28 Feb 1922
Born 1867 Bredicot, married Mary Ann from Defford, one son, John Russell. PC4 under Sommers. Severely assaulted, 285; intervenes in violent 'domestic', 286; **photograph, 301**; emerges with distinction from fire, 301; falls foul of Nobby Guy, 304 and 314; betters violent wife-beater, 318. 1911, living police Station Yard, Copenhagen Street. Among the longest-serving officers spanning 32½ years. Died Martley, June 1947 aged 80

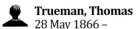

**Twigg, Samuel**
15 Oct 1852 – 1 May 1853

**Tyler, William**
8 Jan 1883 – 2 Mar 1883

**Underwood, James William**
28 Jun 1878 – 18 Oct 1878

**Underwood, William**
1 May 1863 – 10 Jul 1885
Ombersley-born (1842) married Ann, children Alice, William and Annie. Living (1881) 18 Park Street St Peters, then Police Sergeant. Detective under Matthew Power. Investigates arson at the Saracens Head, 215; investigates baby murder at the Wheelwright's Arms, 216-

7; **photograph, 217**; arrests boatman in Stourport, 218; investigates child murders, 223, 236; Investigates murder attempt at Swan with Two Necks (Nicks), 231; recovers revolver associated with attempted murder case, [3]; recovers body of drowned 7-year old, 234; sent to South Africa and returns empty-handed, 247; severely assaulted in the Eagle Vaults, [3]; disarms would-be murderer, 248; assaulted, 260; retires as Det Police Sergeant 1885 and becomes a gardener. Dies six years later, 12 November 1891, 284. Probate granted to Ann Underwood and Arthur Edwin Sommers (Jan 1892). Effects £52 2s.

**Vaughan, Charles**
9 Dec 1853 – 7 Nov 1870
Born in the City – a rarity – 1824. High profile PC later Sergeant under Chipp and Power. Recruited, 146; assaulted x2, 149; commended, promoted 149-50; again assaulted 153, 171, 181, 188; **Approbation Book, 155**; censured for trespass, 177 and 196; sent to Warwick to arrest murder suspect, 181; investigates baby murder, 191; gravely assaulted 191; investigates severed hand, 196; appointed Sergeant, 196; sent to Pontypool to arrest suspected murderer; commended for sturdy action at a fire, 198; leads bust on Horn and Trumpet that reveals 22 prostitutes working from there, 205. 1861 aged 34, living King William Street with wife Eliza (also born Worcester) daughter Sarah (10 months) and mother in law Ann Trueman, 70. 1871 listed as shopkeeper at 14 King William Street with several family additions. Died 6th September 1873 aged 49 and buried St Paul's parish. Probate effects under £20

Appointed 9. December 1850

## MARKS OF APPROBATION.

| DATE. | PARTICULARS. |
|---|---|
| 1854 May 12 | Awarded a gratuity of £2 for extraordinary diligence and exertion used by him in apprehending a man named Lloyd, a notorious character, on which occasion he was severely beaten by Lloyd and two other men — he also received a commendable recommendation from the Magistrates on the occasion |
| 1854 Oct. 13 | Raised to 2nd Class |
| 1856 Sept 12 | Raised to 1st Class |
| 1862 Feb 21 | Commended for his skill & tact and promptness in discovering several robberies lately |
| July 11 | Commended by the County Magistrates for his perseverance in apprehending a man for stealing Guns and awarded 10/- by the Committee |
| 1864 Sept 2 | Appointed a Sergeant |
| 1856 March 7 | Commended for ready and attentive conduct at a fire |

*(Above) Charles Vaughan's Approbation Marks entry (extract)*

**Vaughan, George**
9 Oct 1846 – 26 Mar 1847

**Vaughan, Thomas**
16 Apr 1876 – 21 Oct 1878

**Vick, John**
14 Dec 1849 – (*not known*)

**Vine, Alfred**
18 Oct 1861 – April 1862
Quits after six months following severe going-over by boatmen, 187

**Wadley, George**
17 Oct 1850 – 23 Jan 1851
recruited in Tommy Chipp's first intake, 141

**Waldron, Jabez**
22 May 1868 – 28 Dec 1879
violently assaulted, 234; neighbour troubles, 234; recovers body from canal at George Street, [3]; permitted to resign in distressing circumstances, 241

**Wall, Edward**
8 Jul 1876 – 9 Sep 1881
prompt action at a disastrous fire, 233; violently assaulted, 234 and in the Half Moon, Diglis, [3]; quits to become licensee in Grimley, 248

**Wall, George**
18 Nov 1870 – 29 Jan 1875
Censured for failing to intervene in cat-fight, 223

**Wall, John**
26 Sep 1856 – 13 Apr 1865
Discovers suicide, 169; appointed Sergeant

**Wallace, Thomas**
7 May 1869 – 17 Jan 1896
Born 1842, Cookley, recruited aged 27. Married to Shropshire-born Margaret and living (1881) in Northfield Street with daughters Florence, Edith and Lizzie, son William and four boarders. Ten years later, now Inspector (1891) at 6, East Street, later re-numbered 7. 1901 widowed and retired age 56
**Photograph, 211;** violent affray with squaddies, 238; charged with brutality, 243; commended after fire, 244; attacked, 245, 259, 260 and [3]; leads clamp-down on brothels, 264; sent to Liverpool to arrest wife-stealer and robber, 264; recovers body of drowned lock-keeper, 268; praise for 'clever arrest', 276 and

extended account, [3]; more praise for exceptional work, 278; apprehends meat thieves [3]; appointed Inspector and assaulted, 282; violent affray in the Boar's Head [3]; appointed temporary chief following Sommers' resignation, 294; investigates horse-fixing ring, 300; tracks burglar to Gloucester, 304; murder attempt, 310-312; retires, 315. Died 29 September 1910 aged 65. Effects £135

**Walker, George**
9 Mar 1877 – 13 Sep 1877

**Walker, John**
21 Jun 1867 – 15 May 1868
Left to become Assistant Relieving Officer, Worcester Union (Workhouse)

**Walker, William**
19 Mar 1852 – *not known*

**Walton, Edward**
13 Jan 1840 – 24 Jul 1840
Short-lived, (6 months) constable, initially served as Supernumerary Signature, 95

**Wanklin, John**
15 Apr 1864 –13 May 1864

**Wargent, Albert Henry**
5 Jun 1876 – 23 Apr 1880

**Wargent, George**
14 Jul 1876 – 9 Feb 1877

**Warren, Alfred**
26 Feb 1875 – 2 Jul 1875

*Tommy Wallace (far left, in 1884 under Sommers aged 42) and left as Inspector under Byrne in 1894. The archetypal hero British bobby, he survived a determined murder attempt to face his attacker in court despite having been shot several times.*
**Pages 310-17**

**Watkins, John**
12 Jun 1863 – 27 Nov 1863
Short-lived PC 3rd Class under Power. Resigned when faced with charges of immoral conduct

**Watkins, Thomas**
1823 - c1830
One of first Watchmen (St Helens). Appointed under 1823 Improvement Act, 27; assaulted 29, 32, 33; arrests, 35, 38; death, 32, 42. Makes an arrest, July 1826 when he brings in Charlotte Ann Griffiths for disorderly conduct (*see below*)

**Watson (Walton?), James**
11 Dec 1876 – 3 May 1878

**Weaver, Joseph**
3 May 1872 – 4 Oct 1872

**Weston, Alfred**
13 Oct 1854 – 8 Dec 1854

**Westwood, Samuel**
17 Mar 1865 – 31 Aug 1866
Charged with neglect, resigned in consequence of ill-health

**Wheeler, James**
20 Jan 1843 – 1 Oct 1852

**White, Charles**
4 May 1860 – 13 Jul 1860

**White, Edward**
26 May 1854 – (*not known*)

**White, William**
16 Aug 1878 – 23 Oct 1880

**Whitehouse, John**
6 Feb 1863 – Nov 1866
No 23 under Matthew Power. Investigates double murder, 194; assaulted, 195; investigated for repeated absenteeism, 196; arrests Benjamin Dalton in New York, appointed Sergeant 11th May 1866 and dies of cholera six months later, 199

**Wilcox, Walter Hawkins**
16 Feb 1883 – 13 Apr 1883

**Wild, William**
14 Jun 1878 – 3 Nov 1879

**Wilde, William**
23 Mar 1860 – 5th April 1860
No7 under Chipp. Recruited, found drunk, commits assault, absconds and sacked in the space of two weeks, 171

*The first entry in a new Book of the Watch, dated July 11th 1826. Watchman Thomas Watkins apprehends Charlotte Ann Griffiths, charged with being disorderly conduct in the streets*

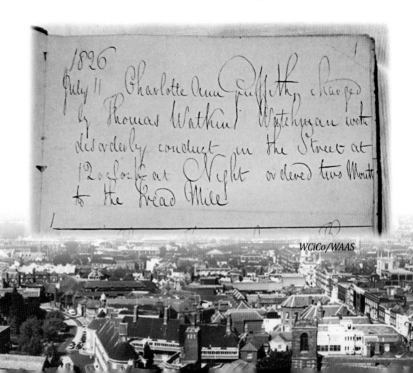

WCiCo/WAAS

WCiCo/WAAS

REPORT of Charges coming under the cognizance of the P

to the 2⁴ day of          183

| Number of Charges | Hour when brought to Watch-House. | Persons Charged, Name and Address of. | Charge, Nature of. | Persons Char Name and Address |
|---|---|---|---|---|
| 2⁺ Dec⁺ | 2 OClock | Robert Featherstone | Charged with violently | |
| | " | John Rathbone | Assaulting Williams | |
| | " | William Rathbone | No 3 Police Constable | Williams |
| | | Robert Smith | Do as to endanger his | No 3 |
| | | John Bradley | Life | |
| | | Thomas Bradley + | | |
| 4079 | | William Mann | | |

**Williams, Abraham**
7 Oct 1870 – 30 Dec 1870

**Williams, George**
18 Jan 1833 – 9 Apr 1858
PC2 and one of first five of the original force, later No3. Appointed, 50. In court 12-13; assaulted 56-59, 110; No3 under Douglas, 72; appointed Sergeant 76; arrests 89; savage attack, 91-3 *(actual Charge Book entry above refers)*; assaulted by hard-case Dowling, 135; betters upstart No20 Andrew Hooper in public street brawl, 147; commended after talking neighbour out of suicide, 147; dies, 163

**Williams, James**
7 Oct 1859 – 30 Jan 1860

**Williams, John**
1823 - c1833
One of first Watchmen. Appointed under 1823 Improvement Act, 27; assaulted 29; arrests, 34

**Williams, Joseph** *(below)*
24 Feb 1888 – 21 May 1897
PC28 under Sommers. Assaulted by leader of 'White Horse Gang', 282; assaulted, 285; Sommers' protest and signature, 289; assaulted by known police-hater, 316

**Williams, Thomas**
23 Jan 1863 – 11 Sep 1868
Occasionally insubordinate PC (no28) under Power. Awarded gratuity for detective work,

196; commended for arrest of pickpocket gang, 201

**Willis, Henry**
8 Apr 1868 – 6 Dec 1875
Found drinking while on duty, 215; refused entry to Crown, Friar Street, [3]; given the run-around at the Bakers Arms (later Liverpool Vaults), [3]; called to major incident in the Freemasons Arms Carden Street, with PC William Preece, [3]; cracks down on prostitutes at the Malt Shovel, [3]

**Willis, James**
15 Jan 1875 – 29 Jan 1875

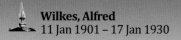

*(Below) 4th March
1839 must have
been a rough old
night in the Station-
house – the blood
stain over the entry
of William Onions,
found by No2 James
Workman fighting
in Diglis Street
remains a silent
witness*

*(WCiCo/WAAS)*

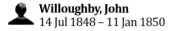

# 12:

# The rogues and bad 'uns of a lawless city

While it'd be impossible – not to say exceedingly tedious – to list every petty felon, fighter, drunk, thief, badtime bedtime-time gal, minor outlaw and general nuisance hauled up before the courts and subsequently made infamous in the columns of the 'sheets', the following section lists a small army of persistent offenders, included here exclusively by dint of being regulars in one or other of the Guildhall court-rooms, most with several convictions and some with considerably more.

Every single one would have been known by name and face to the hard-pressed coppers on the beat and their names entered in the charge book so regularly that the desk sergeants – *and, come to that, the newspaper reporters* – might have done well to have got stencils cut.

No doubt Queen Victoria knew nothing of life here in the Faithful City – and if she did, it's unlikely she'd have approved: 'we are not amused' is a phrase she might well have used in the same breath as 'Worcester and its folks'.

## The Hard Men

**Archibald M'Quillan** a private in the 80th Foot, billeted in the Boar's Head Newport Street. Hits, kicks and bites PC John Hunting in a vicious brawl, 153

**Augustus Williams.** Gives police chief Tommy Chipp a severe battering in Silver Street, 158

**George Ballinger** (*father and son of the same name*). Described as 'a bad lot' by chief Tommy Byrne after another violent set-to, this time in the Falcon, Broad Street. 24th convictions, 324

**Band brothers, William and Sidney,** hard-cases whose territory was Newport Street, 285

**'Brummagem Bruiser'** *real name Ernie Stubbs,* Private in the 29th Regiment, a regular handful until banned from coming into Worcester on Saturday nights and weeknights after 9pm, 304. See also *Squaddies*

**Charles 'Punch' Freeman** celebrated hard-man of Dolday [2]

**Collins brothers, Thomas, Jesse and Aaron** of the Blockhouse, waged war against everybody, but especially the Irish, 198

**Cornelius 'Neely' Bevan,** noted pugilist and prize-fighter. Lays flat Tommy Chipp and by-stander Jeremiah Fudger, p102; killed in Pitch-croft prize-fight by John Cuff, 110

**Dayus family: Noah (Snr), Noah (Jnr), William, Aaron, Enoch, John**
**Noah Dayus**, father and son of the same name coal dealers of the Blockhouse, regularly cropping-up in the annals of infamy, and their reputation as hard-drinking, hard fighting thugs is set in stone, although not all bad. In 1884, Noah Snr. rescues drowning boy from the canal. Snr. Hammers William Richardson, 150; **Noah Dayus junior** takes on all-comers in Lowesmoor, 170

**Aaron Dayus** beats up Luke Packwood in Lowesmoor, 112; **William Dayus**, charged with attempted murder of his wife, 205
Also... Black sheep **Enoch Dayus (see p375)** and **John Dayus (p375)**

**Edward Lloyd, alias 'The Herefordshire Pet'** Hammers patrolman John Pidduck, 52

**Edward Sellis,** noted police-hater but meets his match in PC3 George Williams, 119

**Frederick 'Nobby' Hardwick,** Birdport hardman and prize fighter whose regular visits to the station house were only accomplished with the combined efforts of four policemen. Said to have a pathological hatred of Detective Lamb who he assaulted on every possible occasion with kicks and a flurry of punches and before witnesses in court, threatened to kill him even if he had to wait twenty years [2]

**George 'Cloggy' Smith**, hard-case around the city centre pubs with a reputation as a fearful kicker using his weapons of choice, heavy-duty wooden clogs [2]

**George and Henry Edwards,** noted police-haters, 102

**George Lampitt**, described by the mayor as 'the most ruffianly blackguard [he had] ever met with' after a savage assault on two officers, Tommy Wallace and Edwin Oakey, 259

**'Gipsy Moule'** (also **'Gipsy Jack'**, *real name Joseph Moule)* known around the St Johns pubs as a rough-and-ready character, often seen with Elizabeth Brown who would steal items from drinkers' bags or baskets and if caught or threatened, would call him up to settle the affair with a heavy fist. Bettered by chief's son Edward Chipp, 162; tussles with PC14 Stringer, 181

**Henry and James Guise,** brothers and notorious hassle-mongers in the Newport Street area, 260

**James Bryant,** acquitted despite heavily hammering an unnamed PC on the day of Victoria's accession. Full account, 83

**James Smith,** prize-fighter who takes on four bobbies armed with a poker after they'd been called in to quell a 'domestic', 145

**John Attwood, 'Three-Finger Jack',** gangleader, housebreaker, robber and hardman operating out of the Horse and Jockey Pump Street, brought to book by Chipp, Sanders and Hale, 109

**John Hobson** 'violent as a madman' labourer who takes four PCs and two civilians to subdue after one, of many, violent incidents, 285

**John Phelps,** another notorious police-hater, 102

**John Hobson** of Newport Street, whose determined antipathy for policemen regularly resulted in court appearances [2]

**John Staples** sentenced with Butcher Tom, p11; assault on Watchman Hale, 31

**John Swain** notorious boozer and brawler of Rack Alley described by Chief Tommy Byrne after a vicious assault on PC8 William Hollis as 'so disgraceful (he) had to keep a constable on special duty in Dolday in order to prevent him from creating a serious disturbance', 323

**John Waterson,** thief, all-round thug and noted police hater with 40 convictions, mostly for assaults on the police. In 1899, PC21 Charles Lock took him on in a scrap and bettered him after 20 minutes, 326. Two weeks later, tussles with PC Walter Repton in Sidbury but complains of being charged with assault as only one blow had been struck on either side. 'You can't call that a fight' he moaned

**Robert Tyler** who'd already laid a militiaman flat in a free-for-all in Merryvale, batters PC George Sedgeley, 153

**Reuben Hathaway** a notorious brawler who lived in New Street, noted for a livid facial scar, the result of being glassed by a prostitute named Broughton in a drunken brawl at the Painter's Arms. Gaoled in manslaughter case, 110

**Samuel ('Nobby') Guy**
Celebrated hard-case and former soldier claiming active service in India.. Born Blockhouse Worcester, 1852, 322; regularly in court for drunkenness and violence and not above noisy outbursts in court and foul-mouthing his captors with threats of violence when he came out, a habit not tending to promote leniency. Regular sentences of three months' hard handed down but he still came back

for more, his usual excuses being that he'd twice suffered from sunstroke in India and retaliation for being tormented by boys. Regular Saturday ritual saw him stripped to his trousers offering to fight 'the best man in Worcester' and the 'sheets' contain dozens of reports about violent conduct and taking four or five officers to get him to the cell which he then regularly smashed-up. Picture and cutting p266, comparison with namesake PC Arthur Harry Guy, p322-3; six weeks hard, 304; 22nd court appearance, 304; 30th court appearance, 314; language shocks court, 320; 46th appearance, 322. Described himself as labourer although not above begging in the street, and throughout his life lived at low lodging houses including Norman's in Dolday and Tommy Link's in Little Newport Street

**Squaddies:** too numerous to mention individually and a constant thorn in the side of the police force, causing disorder and discontent wherever they went. Most were handed over to the military for treatment under courts martial, but some were just too dangerous to be let loose and were dealt with in the civil courts – typically, James Murphy, sentenced to 2 months' hard in the civil court after a paticularly nasty assault in the Station-house, 280. The cause of many a PC's absence through injury, 282, 306-8

**Thomas 'Butcher Tom' Evans,** born Worcester 1822 or 3 and with a growing reputation as a bruiser and hard-case before being convicted of receiving and sentenced to 7 years' transportation to the Colonies, 6-13; arrest (*and report*) 52-3; transported and return, 378-381

**Thomas Link,** infamous lodging house keeper almost on a par with Samuel 'Nobby' Guy, who resided at his equally notorious lodging house, for arrests for violence and similar. Threatens to destroy his wife and children by cutting off their heads then attacks PC James Workman and another policeman sent in to apprehend him, 153; 56 residents including 11 men in a single room, found on his premises in a 'bust', 240; makes 50th court appearance and beats-up PC Edwin Oakey, 276; 60th and 61st court appearances, 304; later hands over lodging house to his son Frank, but still regularly assaults lodgers and all-comers

**Thomas Mott** hard-case boatman gaoled for beating up PC Luke Packwood in the Black Horse, Lowesmoor, 105

**Thomas Soley** leader of the 'White Horse Gang', ordered to 21 days hard for assault on PC28 Joseph Williams 282

**Tiney Watkins** and his gang (2-i/c **Walter Mowbray**). Thugs who controlled most of the organised crime and protection in Worcester, the gang waging a five-year campaign of terror in the city before being broken and brought to book by Detective William Richardson [2]

**William Cotterill,** puts PC John Fudger out of action for several weeks, 124

**Willliam Chesterton,** gangleader and thug. Beats-up Emanuel Onslow, p74; gets come-up-pance, 75-6; beats-up no10 Joe Hall, 81

**William Dowling,** notorious thug with a constant string of sentences for assault and general thuggery. Hammers George Williams but escapes, 135; takes on Fowkes and Franklin, 165

**William and John Bryan** ringleaders and chief-protagonists in the fracas that resulted in the grave assault and eventual death of police chief Henry Sharpe, 56-59

**William Phillips**, beats-up police chief James Douglas in the Falcon, 80

**William Vaughan,** noted thug and police-hater, 128

**William 'Chilly' Chillingworth,** notorious boat-man and hard-case, involved almost weekly in some violent assault or another often several policemen at a time and regularly serving one or two months' hard. Hammers PC Luke Packwood, 110; meets his match in Edward 'Grubber' Grubb, 123

**William Hancocks,** another Dolday labourer with a passionate hatred of the police whose behaviour regularly earned him 2-month spells of 'hard' [2]

**William Hancocks** of the 3rd Battn Worcestershire Regiment. Takes on four policemen. The following week militiamen are banned from coming into Worcester on Saturday nights, 300

**William Hardman,** aptly-named gang-leader of St Johns. Beats up (*again*) Ezra Franklin, 187

**William 'Tinker' White,** another celebrated fighter of Dolday, described as '...the most notorious and most frequent visitor of our Police

Courts', the mere sight of a police uniform usually being enough to spark instant unrestrained violence. Hammers Charles Vaughan, 149

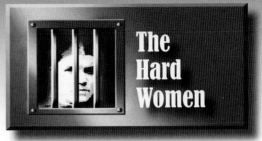

# The Hard Women

**Alice Lloyd,** who temporarily blinded Thomas Baynham with her fingernails while resisting arrest, 310

**Ann Gomer,** takes on two policemen, Sanders and Ward, in the Mug House in St Johns, after she'd already flattened the landlord, William Stalworth, 161

**Ann Jenkins and Ann Band,** battling women who savagely attacked PC 16 Ezra Franklin, 169-70

**Buffalo Bet** – battling vixen who proved more than a match for many a man who she left bloodied and prostrate on the ground – usually for no other reason than that he was in the wrong place at the wrong time [2]

**Caroline Ford** another 'Pugilistic Female' (*Herald*) of 13 Court, Dolday [2]

**Caroline Newman**, takes on Ezra Franklin in the Station-house, p164

**Charlotte Wheeler** described as 'a drunken virago' and police-hater regularly sent to gaol for two weeks when she smashed up her cell and sent back for another two weeks [2]

**Charlotte Wheeler** regularly in the Police court for creating disturbances and then taunting magistrates with comments like 'I'll do it like a brick' when sentenced to yet another month's hard

**Eliza Cox**. Attacks PC James Drew with a shard of glass after she'd smashed a window while resisting arrest,159

**Emily Brighton,** pugilistic female of Dolday who, it was said, 'would fight anybody or anything' [2]

**Florence Edwards** of the Moors. Drunk and fighting mad whose record of at least 25 d&d

and riotous convictions took up two pages of the police record book [2]

**Jane Young** described as having been '...in prison many times, a notorious character', 34-5

**Julia Briscoe** takes on John Doughty who calls her 'the strongest woman I ever met with', 164

**Marion Price** female brawler who lays flat PC Walter Parry in the Farmers Arms, Bridge Place. Takes three to get her to the Station-house, 264

**Mary Ann Darke** noted as 'a very old offender', 34-5; cutting, 40

**Sarah Birt** much given to knocking out other women with a single punch when drunk, at least 25 convictions [2]

**Sarah Loveland,** glasses William Walker in the Red Cow after accusing him of drinking her beer, 102

**Selina Hodges** described as 'a great, stalwart red-headed woman' regularly in court for getting drunk and committing various act of violence [2]

The Goodtime Bedtime girls

**Ann Thomas** regularly being sent to down for the usual two-week stint for following her calling [2]

**Annie Yeates** notorious Farrier Street brothel 'Madame' [2]

**Bess France** – real name Elizabeth Francis – who plied her trade in Newport Street and was not above assaulting her clients, often inflicting grievous injuries with her heavy-duty navvies' boots [2]

**Bewdley Sal,** *real name Harriet Rogers*, a nimble-fingered prostitute whose beat was Bank Street and was said to be able to sense where an unsuspecting punter kept his cash or purse and could spirit it away in seconds before making a bolt [2]

**Brummagem Ria.** Real name Maria Hands, 'a very vulgar-looking prostitute' according to the *Herald*, who worked out of the Barracks in Watercourse Alley [2]

**Catherine Riley.** Persistent prostitute with a string of convictions [2]

**Charlotte Moses**, hardened prostitute at 13. Four years on, the *Herald* commented 'although she is very young in years she is already very old in vice' [2]

**Cockney Poll *(real name Mary Williams)*** prostitute working the Lich Street area, particularly around the Mitre, found guilty of attempt to murder and highway robbery (with Phoebe Hughes and Charles Smith) [2]

**Eliza Barnacle** another habitual drunk regularly sent down for fourteen days' hard for her usual offence of getting drunk and using obscene language [2]

**Eliza Lewis** whose drunken antics were considered so shocking that when she appeared in court in 1870 to answer charges of yet another drunken outburst, several publicans all lined up to testify against her [2]

**Elizabeth Barlow** notorious brothel keeper of Grope Lane [2]

**Elizabeth Loveland** who lived in Bull Entry and was reputed to have talons instead of hands – an adornment that the police regularly came to experience, often appearing in court with deeply gouged faces [2]

**Eliza Morris** another noted Barracks inmate [2]

**Elizabeth Smith** described by the *Herald* in 1850 as '...aged 17, a prostitute for several years and literally tumbling to pieces from the effects of disease and dissipation' [2]

**Elizabeth Wall,** of Quay Street, prostitute and thief. A tale of her cunning, netting £138 (nearly £60,000 today) from unsuspecting farmer John Owen, 229

**Elizabeth Wheeler.** Persistent prostitute with a string of offences [2]

**Elvina *(sometimes Alvina)* Baker** a disorderly prostitute much given to smashing windows and creating a ruckus in order to get a bed for the night [2]

**Emma (*sometimes Elizabeth*) Lemm** persistent offender described as 'a wretched girl whose sins against decency and sobriety are legion' [2]

**Emily Evans,** seasoned prostitute aged 12. Gaoled the same week as Victoria's accession, 83

**Emma Gardner and Fanny Stockall** two more of the 'frail sisterhood' (*Herald-speak for prostitutes*) whose method of attracting customers was by singing on street corners and thus luring unsuspecting men [2]

**'Flighty' –** *real name Ellen Hopkins.* Persistent prostitute with a string of offences [2]

**'Flying Dutchman' –** *real name Anna Jordan –* notorious for preying on drunken boatmen and spending the night with them before making a flit after rifling their pockets and making off with their possessions [2]

**'Gipsy Charlotte'** the most notorious of at least twenty-two known prostitutes working at the Horn and Trumpet in Angel Street [2]

**Harriet Jackson** who had a habit of attacking men who spurned her advances with a fearful set of fingernails [2]

**Jemima Perks.** Persistent prostitute with a string of convictions [2]

**Jesse Folkes** '...whose name is so exceedingly familiar to the readers of police reports' (*Herald*). Arch-enemy of Elizabeth Loveridge, aka 'Ledbury Bess'. These two hated each other with a vengeance and every time they met, had to be pulled apart. The scene was generally left strewn with torn clothes and clumps of hair.

**Julia Briscoe** – described as 'a specimen of the 'out-and-outer class who alternates between gaols, union-houses, police stations and common lodgings' and who, it was said, would attack any man and come off best. Described in court as '...a tigress, the strongest woman I ever met' by PC4 John Doughty [2]

**Julia Holder** Preferred beat Rack Alley, notorious and regularly interrupted, and convicted for daylight liaisons against a wall [2]

**Ledbury Bess,** *real name Elizabeth Loveridge* , who with Jesse Folkes was regarded as the worst of their 'wretched and degraded class' [2]

**'Little' Hall** – real name Louisa, a prostitute aged 11 in 1844 when she was brought up to answer a charge of prostitution and of stealing a flat iron. The *Herald* described her as '...the poor creature had scarcely a rag upon her, starvation was written very legibly in her face, along with that most horrid disfigurer of young lineaments, a precocious acquaintance with the vices of mature age' [2]

**Maria Cooke.** Persistent prostitute with a string of offences [2]

**Martha Wixey,** 'Governess' of a notorious brothel in Boars Head Entry, Newport Street that also offered male prostitutes. Busted by PC George Aston and others, 314

**Mary Ann Bush.** Another persistent prostitute with a string of convictions [2]

**Mary Ann Poole, Mary Ann Davis and Jane Caton** '...three dirty young women, belonging to a vile class' (*Herald*) whose pitch ('haunting' is how the *Herald* describes it) was the bridge where they were regularly found guilty of using obscene language and shamelessly attacking others who'd invaded their patch.

**Mary Greenway,** 'Madame' of a notorious brothel off Friar Street, busted by PC John Hazleton, 308

**Mary Morgan** who had yet another 14-day sentence for drunkenness, disorderly conduct and for being a common prostitute halved on her promise of leaving town on her release [2]

**Mary Wright.** Persistent prostitute with a string of offences [2]

**Meg Merrilees –** *alias Elizabeth Batter –* a fighting virago with a pathological dislike of police officers. PC John Doughty tells Magistrates that when he got her to the station, he '...might have wrung his shirt, so perspiring and so exhausted was he from the battery he had suffered', 154

**'Ophelia' Hamlet,** described as 'as miserable a collection of human integuments and filling-up as is to be seen in our day, walking the earth as an ugly old woman' (*Herald* –1847) [2]

**Phoebe Gardiner.** Persistent prostitute with a string of offences [2]

**Rebecca Roden.** Persistent prostitute with a string of offences [2]

**Rose Pritchard** who regarded Dolday as her personal territory [2]

**Sal Wall** who worked at brothel in Friars Alley Her trick was to 'accidentally' cause a tear in a man's coat and then invite him back to her abode to have it stitched. Once there the unfortunate victim was surrounded by several of her friends and minders and robbed of his cash and valuables [2]

**Sarah Tovey.** Persistent prostitute with a string of offences [2]

**Susan Adams,** resident of the Barracks in Watercourse Alley who, having been found in possession of a purse belonging to labourer William Cole, told the court that Cole had endeavoured to take improper liberties with her and that his purse must've got from his pocket to her handkerchief in the "scrimmage what was quite promiskuss, like" [2]

**Susan Denson.** Persistent prostitute with a string of offences [2]

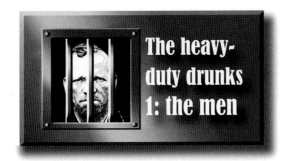

The heavy-duty drunks 1: the men

**'Blind Robert' (Robert Wormington)** – known for prodigious bouts of drinking. Died, aged 29, at the Glo'ster Arms at Christmas 1847, 126

**Charles Askew,** stonemason, regularly up for d&d who, when his name was called, would draw out the statutory 5s fine, throw it down and walk away without another word being uttered on either side [2]

**George Curtis** Leather parer of Birdport, viewed as a regular handful and a violent drunk with 23 convictions

**James 'Jemmy' Gomersky,** labourer, described as 'a rale Irisher with great sandy whiskers and a pyramidal face'. 106 convictions, mostly d&d, last court appearance Christmas 1886 aged 96, sentenced to 42 days' hard. Died at the beginning of 1897 aged 108. Detailed profile in *'Worcester Pubs Then and Now' Vol2, p 484-5.* In court again, 172; threatens revenge, 208

**John Rowley,** 138 court appearances resulting in 100 convictions, 319. By the end of 1897 it had been topped-up to 140 appearances and 102 convictions

**Sandbed Sandy,** a persistent, but generally gentle and amusing drunk brought up before the Bench so many times that all the local reporters formed an attachment for him [2]

**'Shanter' Evans,** habitual drunk and a regular on the treadwheel at the City Gaol following yet another (actual number uncounted) sentence to seven day's hard [2]

**'Watercress Jemmy'** – real name **James Edwards.** Persistent drunk with a string of offences [2]

**Walter Vippon *(occasionally Vipon and Vipond*)** shoemaker of Blackfriars and his lover, later wife, Mary Ann Parton of Dolday, habitual drunks 'inspired by Bacchus' for whom few weeks went by without a night in the station house followed by a spell in the City nick. Mary stabs Walter, 195

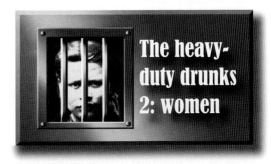

The heavy-duty drunks 2: women

**Alvina Williams** of Bowling Green Terrace whose decline into drink and depravity can be mapped from the scores of newspaper reports. At least 56 convictions, 301, 304

**Ann Hurst** with the dubious distinction of appearing on the first page of the new Charge Book for being drunk and disorderly in Broad Street, July 27th 1838. Picture, 88

**Catherine Egan**, an appalling drunk with a shocking track record. Graphic and amusing account of tussle with Grubb, 124

**Elizabeth Gough** of Dolday, persistent drunk with a string of offences [2]

**Elizabeth Loveland,** described by the *Herald* as 'with nothing very lovely about her' and 'familiar to frequenters of our police office' regularly summoned for d&d, 112

**Esther Greenwood** drunk in the habit of singing obscene ballads in the Cornmarket and selling printed copies. Arrested, 169

**Elizabeth Martha Davis**, persistent drunk with a habit of standing in the Cornmarket and stripping off her clothes attracting crowds of hundreds [2]

**Emily Taylor** Incurable drunk with more than 35 convictions [2]

**Emma Wall,** persistent nuisance, offender and police-baiter, 208

**Ellen Lowell** Persistent drunk with a string of convictions [2]

**Emily Taylor** of Quay Street with dozens of appearances for drunkenness and riotous conduct, but formed an attachment for two local beat bobbies, **PC27 Sidnam Cole** and **No33 George Langstone**

**Florence Higgins** of Rack Alley, another persistent drunk with 27 convictions for drunk and riotous also given to stripping off her clothes in front of shocked policemen and anybody else when arrested [2]

**'Great Western' aka Mary Lilley** who, with her husband Thomas were notorious for their numerous court appearances. Found dead, 124

**Hannah Dilley**, drunk frequenting all of the Newport Street pubs, averaging four convictions a year for bad behaviour/riotous actions/bad language and generally misbehaving, throughout the 1880s-90s

**Jane Harris,** drunk who on her 16th court appearance pleaded 'Please Sir, give me another chance' to which Mayor Walter Holland responded "We will. 10 days to consider it". It came with hard labour [2]

**Jane O'Brien** notorious regular at the Copenhagen Street nick whose annual 7-day drunk and riotous conviction could be timed with accuracy: the same day that pea-picking ended [2]

**Jane Powell** a regular inmate at the police station-house – where several times she attempted suicide while still drunk [2]

**Lizzie Whitehouse** Incurable drunk with a string of offences, much given to resisting arrest by lying down in the streets and having to be transported to the station-house strapped to a cart [2]

**Maria Ricketts** Incurable drunk with a string of offences

**Mary Ann Smith**, appeared at least 75 times for rooking pub landlords by ordering a pint of grog (beer and rum), drinking it 'and letting the landlord whistle for his money' (*Herald*), 325

**Mary Bromwich** of Blackfriars, sentenced for being drunk and disorderly so many times that no-one, not even several police chiefs, knew how many. Yet more appearances, 165, 191

**Mary Brown** sets about unnamed PC13 in the Swan, Lowesmoor, 153

**Mary Coldrick** said to have been 'a miserable creature of the most surpassing ugliness' who seems to have spent her days alternating between spells in the workhouse and periods of shocking drunkenness and sleeping in the gutters [2]

**'Noisy Mary'** – **Mary Morris,** prostitute and habitual drunk who'd been sentenced for the same misdemeanour of getting drunk and disturbing the streets at least thirty times [2]

**Phoebe Harber** of Bromwich Lane Incurable drunk with a string of convictions [2]

**Polly Hoban** battling virago. Attacks three policemen in the Station-house and then attempts to hang herself in the police cells, p246

**'Sabrina' aka Jane Severn** another regular member of the 'd&d Brigade' which the *Herald* regularly headlined its reports of typical Monday morning court sessions [2]

**Susan Connop** persistent offender and called 'the greatest blackguard in town' by Tommy Chipp in 1859 after another episode of '...drunk and disorderly, and using most disgusting language' [2]

# HORRIBLE MURDER IN THIS CITY,

## AND ATTEMPTED SUICIDE OF THE MURDERER.

Early on Wednesday morning last, this city was thrown into a state of painful excitement in consequence of its becoming known that a murder had been committed in the course of the previous night, in Pheasant-street, Lowesmoor, and that the murderer had made a desperate attempt at suicide. The unfortunate victim, Joseph Hooper, was a child of about six years of age, living with his parents Joseph and Sarah Hooper, who keep a huckster's shop at the end of Pheasant-street, near to St. Martin's school; ... Jabez Hooper, a single man, ... me of perpetrating this horrible ...

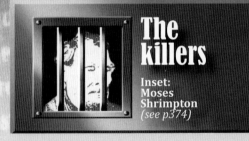

## The killers

Inset:
Moses
Shrimpton
*(see p374)*

**Alice Booton,** servant at the Star Hotel, murders her child and disposes of its body, 310

**Alice Packwood** who smashed her baby's skull than claimed it was an accident after falling on ice, 240

**Beatrice Breeze,** barmaid at the Hope and Anchor *(now Vue Bar)* who had given birth to a boy, put him in a box and left him to die, 317

**Betsy Ann Willis,** charged with wilful murder of her baby, poisoned with acid and left in a canvas bag at Shrub Hill Station, 250

**Charles Goodman,** licensee of the Hope & Anchor *(now Vue Bar)* sentenced for manslaughter of Edward Hill outside the front door, 86

**Charles Young** *(alias Evans)* ex-Worcestershire Constabulary PC sentenced to 20 years for the attempted murder of Insp. Tommy Wallace, 310-12

**'Clayton',** killed butcher Thomas Houton in the Shambles with a single punch, 102

**Eliza Ross,** already known to the police and lived in a low tenement off Lowesmoor, first gave her baby prussic acid and then swallowed the remainder of the bottle. *Herald* headline, 251

**Elizabeth Banks (17)** and her aunt **Leah (19),** conspired in the death of Elizabeth's new-born daughter at the Wheelwright's Arms, 216-7

found dead in the Shades in Mealcheapen Street, poisoned with arsenic, 105

**Robert Pulley,** executed Worcester gaol for the murder of Mary Ann Staight, 134

**Robert Lilley,** hung at the County Gaol for the murder of Jonathan Wall, 64

**Samuel and Joseph Boswell** executed at the County Gaol for the murder of Frederick Stevens, the Duc d'Aumale's gamekeeper, 280

**Sarah Poulteney,** murders her baby and flings the body in a dung-heap, 145

**Sarah Rallings,** murders her baby by suffocation, 221

**Thomas Wheeley,** poisons his wife Mary with fatal dose administered in a glass of ale drawn at the New Inn, Claines, 85

**Thomas Whiteley,** 67 year old tailor accused of murdering his 13-year old lover's baby, 40-2

**William Jenkins, Wiliam Lampitt,** both suspected of murdering flighty maid Caroline Williams but both acquitted, 128

**William Lessemore and Thomas Dyson,** boatmen charged with murdering one of their own, 81

**William Lightband,** executed Worcester Gaol for murder, 83

**William Salmons,** suspected of the murder of his wife Jane, 127

**William Sedgwick,** charged with attempted murder of Kate Hannah Jenkins of 5 Court Hylton Road after shooting her twice on the towpath opposite the Grandstand. Two more shots had missed, 325

**William Thomas,** accused of murdering his lover Lucy Tredwell, found in the canal at Blockhouse bridge with her head caved in, 159

**Ellen Vaughan** 'cannibal' of Dolday, much given to biting her victims – in one instance, PC John Davies in 1881 en route to the Station-house after being found d&d. He quit a few days later

# Deviants and perverts

**Enoch Dayus** of Pheasant Street, father of 18 children and persistent paedophile with a penchant for young girls. Charged with two counts of indecency on consecutive days. They were his fourth and fifth charges in as many years, 300. Related to...

**John Dayus** also charged with sexually assaulting a 9-year old, Martha Billington in Newtown Road, but released after he said he'd only picked her up after some friends had tipped her out of a wheelbarrow

**George Bond,** serial flasher of Rainbow Hill Parade.

**Henry Willis,** landlord of the Black Lion in Dent Street, charged with indecent assault on a 9-year old, Fanny Hall, 300

**Henry Allen** charged with criminal assault and indecent assault on 11-year old Edith Phœbe Davis, 300

**Henry Sheen** paedophile with a reputation for preying on young girls in the Flagge Meadow area

**James Cullis,** a sweep and serial 'flasher' regularly up before the justices charged with persistent indecent exposure, a sentence that carried a sentence of two months' imprisonment in the City Bridewell, 85

**Silvanus Bozward** of Blakefield Road. Assaults two 8-year old girls, Alice Fulwell and Lily Davies, afterwards giving them 1d each, 329

**Thomas Turner,** hung at Worcester gaol for the rape of a child, Louisa Blissett, 43

**William Prince,** 'inhuman wretch' and vampire, given to biting his victims, 181

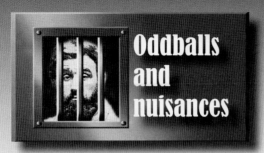

# Oddballs and nuisances

**The Aborigine.** One time circus-show freak much given to committing petty offences with the intention (failed) of being transported back to Australia and home [2]

**'Argus'** *(possibly Hargist)* Fagin-like character who kept a cider shop and rowdy-house in King-street, frequented by youngsters of both sexes with the reputation of being little more than a youthful brothel and vice den, 86

**Billy Barnett** the blind fiddler who proved so popular at his craft he was able to buy a number of cheap tenements in Merryvale that he ran as lodging houses –and earned a reputation for extortion, often with menaces [2]

**Clara Collins,** 26-year old bigamist, 258

**Emma Blackburn,** thief and eccentric police-hater persistently inventing wildly-imagined and implausible complaints against innocent officers

**Fisher** George – well-known fruit and fish hawker George Saunders who dealt in stolen produce which he sold from a basket around the city's pubs [2]

**Foxhound (***name unknown***)** dog with a penchant for attacking policemen reported in the Herald under the headline *'A Dog That Dislikes Policemen',* 277

**George Green**, phantom window smasher of Lich Street. A lunatic, normally locked up in his mother's home for his own good, but when he escaped, his was a penchant for smashing his fist through every window in the street, on one occasion destroying nearly 50 before he was stopped, 317

**Harriet Whatmore,** Worcester's first *'Woman in White'* who attracted large crowds when she paraded around town in her eccentric dress. Charged with assaulting **PC24 David Evans** and Fanny Cole, female searcher at the station and wife of **PC27 Sidnam Cole**, 329

**James Hayward,** transported to Australia for 7 years for a catalogue of misdemeanours, 120

**John Tussell,** navvie bettered by **Sgt William Sanders,** 116

**Mormons.** Descend on Worcester, 155; Tommy Chipp pursues to Liverpool, 156

**Mary Brown,** usually found begging in and around the Tything pubs, singled out, jostled and jeered in the City for having a flock of half-caste children (*her husband was said to have been a black man living in Birmingham*) '...and that she had two or three more specimens of the interesting type of children at home'

**Martin Smith,** associate of **Thomas *'Butcher Tom'* Evans**, transported to Australia for seven years. Full accounts 6-13; 53, 378-381

**Mary Ann Loosemore** of York Place, mad woman much given to wandering about, taken to the Workhouse unable to account for herself before being re-claimed by her mother after a week's search

**Maria Cox** old beggar seen around town for many years under a placard 'struck blind by lightning'

**Marshalls** – battling family of the Blockhouse forever in-fighting and causing disturbances, although actually two families – milkman William a widower with his own family who married widow Sarah who also had an existing family. They all lived together in unpeaceable disharmony, the women generally proving to be the more violent and disreputable [2]

**Mary Wood** who earned her living singing in many of the Worcester pubs but when she couldn't raise the price of a lodging house for the night, would break a window so as to get a night's board and breakfast at the station house [2]

**Michael Condlie** ingenious juvenile super thief aged 10 likened to the Artful Dodger. Hauled into court by chief Douglas, 83

**Megrary, Gerby and Evans,** navvies, sorted out in a free-for-all in the Plough by **Chipp, Grubb and Workman,** 124

**Negroes:** very few and far between in Victorian Worcester but the cause of so much public and media curiosity that trouble was never far behind: two – Albert Lewis and Nellie Johnson – were also both persistent drunks, Johnson even attacking **PC08 William Hollis** in court and had to be forcibly removed by two other officers, 316. Also, 112

**Nizziata Gizzo** Odd-ball Italian immigrant noted for hawking birds snared from the hedgerows and regularly charged with obstruction. She was eventually ordered to leave the city (1885)

**'Nottingham' (Henry Copley)** navvie with a dreadful track record who regularly spent nights in the station house after wreaking havoc and mayhem in one of several public houses, also said to have had the most prodigious appetite 105

**Samuel Davis:** a catalogue of charges, 104

**Jerry (*Geraldo*) Moiland** another Italian immigrant, unable to speak a word of English – not even 'fine' which was regularly applied in consequence of creating an obstruction with his barrel organ

**John Hunt** 14-year old gin drinker, petty criminal and seasoned house-thief, transported to Australia after police crack-down on illicit gaming, 110

**John Rowley**, *alias Thomas Cowley* arrested by PC24 David Evans for his 139th court d&d appearance in 1897. On several occasions his liberty had lasted just a few hours after being released before re-offending

**Grubb, aka William Montague,** talented violinist of Queen Street, regularly found playing on street corners for pennies with a harpist of similar ability

**James 'Ratty' Phillips** – notorious house-breaker, cat-burglar and rat-catcher extraordinaire of Watercourse Alley who only escaped a lengthy sentence of six months' hard labour by agreeing to emigrate to the colonies at his own expense [2]

**Philip Boucher,** police hater who 'committed a filty act' in PC Michael Cusack's hat, 142, and come-uppance 144

**'Pilgrim' (of Love)** real name Joseph Harris said to have been spurned by a lover and spent his days getting drunk, howling in the streets and banging on doors, looking for his lost love [2]

**Robert Osbaldeston,** son of 'The Lunatic Doctor'. fires two pistols inside the Crown Hotel, 64

**Robert Pulley.** Last man to be publicly hanged on the roof the County Gaol in March 1849. Crimes and *(possibly)* post-execution cast of his head, 134

**'Tea-leaves Charlotte'** notorious fleecer of young girls, she made a living from fortune-telling by reading tea leaves [2]

**Thomas 'Piggy' Nash** Colourful pig farmer and slaughterer operating out of the yard of the Queen Caroline in Quay Street, regularly in court for misdemeanours with more than 30 convictions for petty thievery, threats to kill and cruelty to his pigs, with an interesting sideline as a bawdy-house and brothel-keeper. After his wife Fanny left him for another man, he picked up with a succession of live-in lovers, all of whom gave up on him after a succession of beatings-up for which he would serve the statutory 21 days hard before directing his attentions to the next 'victim'

**Tommy' White** – also known as 'The Acrobat of The Butts' much given to staging amazing displays at the drop of a hat, causing crowds to gather and creating obstructions [2]

**'Wedgie' (Samuel Wedgbury)** pugilistic navvie, later found drowned in the Severn, 105

**William Perkins,** pickpocket, allegedly aged 5 ordered to serve 5 years in a reformatory, but this may be questionable, 165-6

**Worcester Alice Grey** aka **Mary Everton** a plausible, if habitual thief, sentenced time and again for obtaining goods under false pretences [2]

# 13:

# What happened to Butcher Tom?

If Butcher Tom and Martin Smith and the other Worcester lads sentenced to transportation that day – Saturday March 2nd that year of our Lord 1833 – thought they were going to be playing sailors during a bracing sea cruise followed by a life of idleness, hunting kangaroos and lazing in a sun-kiss'd paradise chasing natives  on the other side of the world, they were in for the shock of their lives.

*In fact, it's probably fair to say that nothing could have prepared them for what was about to befall them.* **Nothing.**

Still chained, they'd have been taken from the Guildhall cells and trundled back to the Friar Street bridewell to await the next cart to Woolwich.  Chances are that it left the following morning. Ahead of the still-chained convicts lay a rough ride 130 miles south-eastward, every bump in the road keenly felt.  If the weather was kind, they'd be there in two days, aching but at least dry.  If it was not – and it was not as 1833 was one of the coldest March months ever recorded – they'd arrive wet, stinking, hungry and stiff, four or even five days later.

Awaiting them was the formidable prison hulk Discovery which was to be the new home of all five and was to remain so for months to come. According to a contemporary newspaper report, the month before Butcher Tom and Martin Smith's convictions, the convict hulks were home to 3,899 prisoners – almost all destined for Australia, although 1833 was also to see 400 shipped to Bermuda.

*Discovery* had once been a proud full-rigged 10-gun sloop almost 100 ft long. She'd been built at Rotherhithe, very close to where she was now beached, by Randall, Grey and Brent, launched in November 1789 and purchased for the Navy in 1790. After nine years' illustrious service captained by George Vancouver on voyages of exploration in the Pacific, she was first converted into a bomb vessel seeing war action under Commander John Conn at the Battle of Copenhagen 1801, and then 'hulked' – stripped of every element save its shell and floors, barely five feet apart – and beached, first at Sheerness before being towed to her final destination, Woolwich.

Butcher Tom and Martin Smith weren't to know it, but they were to be among the last of a long string of villainous occupants as she was broken up the following year, 1834.

If they thought life in Worcester Gaol was bad, they were in for a serious shock. The life of a convict on board a convict ship awaiting transportation was about as bad as it could get: they were double-ironed at the waist and ankles, hygiene was nil, disease spread like wildfire and

there was no separation between the sick and the still – *but probably not for long* – healthy. Gaol fever, typhus and cholera saw off hundreds, while dysentery, with all its stinking after-effects, was the price everyone paid just for being there.

Whatever their state of health, convicts lay on the bare floor and even the prison authorities were prepared for mortality rates among convicts awaiting transportation to be one in three. Overcrowding was gross and whoever you had the misfortune of being chained to and standing/sleeping/pissing next to – and bear in mind, these were all convicted felons including lunatics, murderers, thieves, rapists, gang members and the desperate scum and low-life of a lawless Britain – was your neighbour until fate lent a hand and you were on your journey to the Colonies and the misery began all over again.

The life of degradation and hopelessness was compounded by those appointed to control the hulks' festering population – although the word 'sentenced' could almost apply as much to the officers and their men as to their charges. The clothes and scant provisions allowed by the authorities rarely reached the convicts and the often sadistic officers had a tendency to amuse themselves with regular floggings of the miserable creatures in their not-so tender mercies.

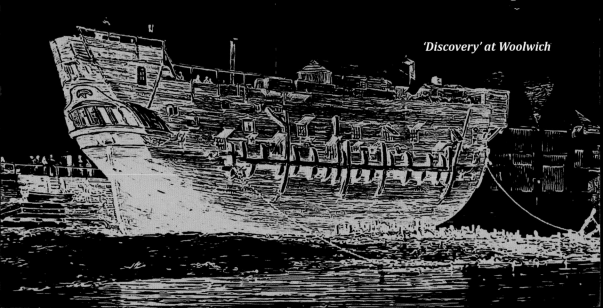

*'Discovery' at Woolwich*

What little food was allowed to the prisoners was meagre and generally mouldy, drinking water was drawn direct from the Thames and escape was impossible as the hulk was sunk deep into mud that sucked down and swallowed whole many a prisoner who'd broken free and thought he'd got away.

It was said that the smell of the Discovery and her 300 inmates could be detected more than half a mile away and the hulks became known as 'the infernal academies' on account of the grounding in crime given the convicted felons by their more hardened companion inmates.

It's unlikely that the Worcester lads sentenced that day saw much of each other after being slung into the Discovery, given a dousing in cold water and issued the rough prison clothes that was about the only act of kindness and humanity they could expect until their arrival in the New World.

For Martin Smith, that date was August 19th and his destination New South Wales. He was transferred to the vessel 'Lloyds' with 200 fellow convicts including other Worcester men Henry Collins, David Guest, James Phillips, 50-year old nail maker Sampson Taylor convicted of highway robbery and, one of 72 others under a sentence of transport for life, 14-year old William Price.

They arrived on December 18th 1833.

### Transported with 376 others on the 'Fairlie' to New South Wales

By then, Butcher Tom was also on his way to the same destination. He'd been transferred to the 756-ton 'Fairlie' on October 14th (**Source**: *Australian Convict Transportation Registers – Fleets and Ships 1791-1896*) after more than five months aboard the prison hulk. On the same ship under Master Henry Ager, was Benjamin Berry and John Staples who'd also been sentenced to seven years' transportation by Sergeant Ludlow who it's unlikely had spared even a moment's thought to the Worcester ne'ers-do-well he'd condemned almost six months earlier, or the years they'd been forced to erase from their young lives as a result.

Also on board was Michael Peake, convicted for lifetime transportation at the County Assizes held on the same day as Tom Evans' and Martin Smith's trial, alongside Henry Jones, 14-year old William Gregory and eight more Worcester men all convicted on 1st July: James Pardoe (life); Benjamin Hayes and John Brookes (14 years); and William Featherstone, William Vaughan and Charles Whateley all sentenced to life as transported convicts on July 18th.

'Life' usually meant a term of hard labour lasting fourteen years after which the convict could apply for his ticket-of-leave which might, or might not, be granted entirely at the whim of the Colony Master and dependent solely on the applicant's track record of docility and subordination. Just one misdemeanour could, at worst, **double** the original sentence, with no appeal mechanism open to the convicts. 'Hard' when applied to the term 'labour' was barely the word: 'brutal' might be a better word.

376 men embarked that day on a voyage that lasted 111 days. Also on board were 4 women, 12 children and 3 female servants. Average sentence was 10 years with 164 sentenced to life. 372 survived, and when they arrived at their destination, virtually every man-jack was ordered to the hardest of hard labour building roads, felling trees, digging ditches and other public works.

A list of all those on board the Fairlie is available here:

*http://www.convictrecords.com.au/ships/fairlie/1833*

Order was kept by a military guard made up of 29 rank and file men of the 17th, 21st, 39th and 50th regiments including soldiers Thomas Burgen, Joseph Crowden, Michael Murphy, Patrick Conlon and Michael Scanlan. **The Fairlie** – built in 1811 and one of fourteen convict ships arriving in New South Wales in 1834 – arrived in Port Jackson on 15 February.

According to a diary kept by the **Fairlie**'s Surgeon Superintendent Alick Osborne:

*'...the prisoners were mustered on board on 24th February 1834 by the Colonial Secretary - 367 men mustered; sick on shore 3; committed for trial 2; died at sea 4 (Francis Long and Francis Scaling + two others). Twenty six of the prisoners were under the age of 16. Two - William Adams and Edward Johnson were only 13 years old'.*

Of the 372 male convicts who'd arrived on the **Fairlie**, 319 were assigned to private service; 3 in hospital; 9 found unfit for assignment; 24 were placed in an iron gang; 4 sent to Norfolk Island; 3 sent to Port Macquarie (specials); 8 sent to Carter's Barracks; and 2 committed to gaol for trial.

It's interesting to note that several generations on, 87 families in Newcastle and Lake Macquarrie in the Hunter Valley region 120 miles north of Sydney can trace their backgrounds to convicts who'd arrived on the *Fairlie* at the same time as Thomas Evans, alias Butcher Tom.

By chance, a *Herald* report from 1834 reveals something of the life the one-time cock o' Worcester, convicted for receiving a miserable haul of a few pairs of shoes and clogs had now been reduced to:

*'...punishment is rendered as severe as any punishment on earth may be supposed to admit. Shut up at night within a wretched hovel on a rock in the ocean, as soon as the prisoners are called from their rest in the morning, they are fed with a dish of porridge, composed of flour and water with a little salt. They then embark in boats and row seven miles to the wood-cutting stations, where they continue to work until their return at night; they are then supplied with the only substantial meal they receive in 24 hours. Their labour consists in cutting up the trees growing near the coast in heavy logs, which they carry on their shoulders, or slide to the water's edge and form into rafts. During the greater part of this duty, the convict has to work up to his middle in water and even in the woods, from the moist and swampy nature of the country, his employment is of the most disagreeable and harassing kind'.*

Labour continued from sunrise to sunset six days a week, with an interval of one hour for dinner. The Australian hardwoods also turned work into heavy labour '...that the English-made tools break like glass before the strokes of the workman, the thermometer usually ranging in the middle of the day from 80° to 100°'.

Neglect of work, insolence or insubordination resulted in flogging, while others were forced to construct public roads, chained together in 'iron gangs': small wonder suicide was common.

That looks like an option Butcher Tom rejected – though no doubt would have considered – and while his life in Australia went unrecorded, there is evidence that he served his time, obtained his ticket of leave and came back to Worcester where he continued his life of crime – *and this is where we came in...*

On 30th Dec 1844 he was convicted of larceny at Worcester Assizes and sentenced to 14 days. He was aged 30. He is believed to have died, in Worcester during the first quarter of 1879 unloved and unmourned.

A thorough bad 'un.

# The Spike - Vol II
## Request for information

*The Spike - Vol II* is in course of production and is due for publication soon.

Continuing the account of the sometimes shocking lives, crimes and violent times of Worcester City Police during the years 1900 up to the force's final demise in 1967, more surprises are in store under chief officers every inch as colourful and controversial as their (*generally*) illustrious 19th century forerunners:

● **Thomas Byrne,** who continued in office up to May 1923: 31 years in all

● **Oswald John Buxton Cole**, to January 1929 (*a period that included the notorious triple murder at the Garibaldi in Wylds Lane committed by a serving police officer, Herbert Burrows, subsequently hanged at Gloucester*)

● **Capt. William James Hutchinson** to 1st November 1931

● **Ernest William Tinkler,** 24 years that included the troublesome war years that saw the city take on the character of pitched battlefield between rival squaddies and then the GIs

● Controversy under **Glyn Davis** (*1st February 1955 to 1st October 1958*). And finally,

● **Eric Arthur Abbott**, the twelfth and last to steer a proud force through sometimes troubled years.

Photographs, diary extracts, memorabilia and any other relevant information of all serving officers are requested for possible inclusion.

**Please feel free to e-mail:**
**bob@the-whole-picture-publishing-company.co.uk**

*All messsages will be responded-to.*

# The Spike - Volume II and suggested

As outlined on the previous page, The Spike - Vol II is in course of production. It is due for publication 2017-18.

Most of the content of this book is the result of countless hours of painstaking research trawling through the newspapers archived at the Hive – mostly the *Worcester Herald* and *Worcester Journal*, but also the *Worcester Daily Times, the Advertiser* and the *Chronicle*.

As an ex-newspaper man, this proved to be no chore: every minute proved a joy, while my admiration for the journalists and editors of the day increased as every visit revealed yet more priceless gems that coloured my affection for my home town, The Faithful City, Worcester...

I didn't set out to write a book about Worcester City Police, it just happened.

It began while researching information about the City's rich heritage of pubs for the two volumes of '*Bob Backenforth's Worcester Pubs Then and Now*' published to date, and I count myself fortunate that control of the pubs and beer-houses of the day was in the hands of the police and the magistrates, and that mixed-in with the reports of licensing affairs was the day-to-day business of Worcester's boys in blue.

It took no time at all for amazing tales of heroism, blood-and-guts and devotion beyond the call of duty to emerge... and this, so far, is the result.

I would add that there's more – *lots more* – to come.

In the meantime, here's an introduction to further reading on the colourful and often shocking story of the police force and the daily dose of dire dangers they faced on the streets of the *Civitas in Beero et Pubbi Fidelis* – the city faithful to its beer and its pubs.

## E-mail: bob@the-whole-picture-publishing-company.co.uk

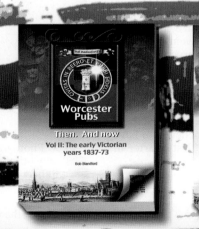

Bob Backenforth's Worcester Pubs Then and Now - Vol 1. Published 2013. 484pps

Bob Backenforth's Worcester Pubs Then and Now - Vol 2. Published 2015. 518 pps

Bob Backenforth's Worcester Pubs Then and Now - Vol 3. Publication pending

# further reading on local policing

**Bob Backenforth's Worcester Pubs Then and Now Volumes I, II and III** *(Vol III pending publication).* In-depth tales of Worcester's never-ending love affair with its rich heritage of pubs, beer-houses and drinking establishments, containing hundreds of photographs previously unseen and continuing the tale of the biggest single thorn in the side of Worcester City Police.

Just as the history of Worcester and its pubs are one and the same, so is the history of Worcester's pubs and its police.

The two cannot be divorced and the books give further colourful insight into the force's never-ending battle against the drunks and the unremitting violence they were capable of.

Vol I and II are both local best-sellers.

*Volume I* lists and details 656 Worcester pubs from around 1500; *Volume II* covers the years 1837-1873 and Vol III 1873-1901.

Signed and personalised copies are available direct from The Whole Picture Publishing Company, price £17.99

Vol III is written and presently, *(October 2016)* undergoing production for publication pegged for the near future.

**From Fruit Trees to Furnaces**, written by former Worcestershire Constabulary Inspector, Bob Pooler and telling the tale of Worcestershire Constabulary from 1839 to the date of publication *(2009)*.

Virtually sold out, a limited few copies are still available from the author at *Blacksmith Publishing, The Paddock, Lower Moor, Pershore, WR10 2PA,* or local libraries. Bob is also curator of West Mercia police archive material now privately stored in the south of the County.

**A History of Worcester City Police, 1833-1967** written by Inspector Colin Glover and published to mark the amalgamation with other forces to form West Mercia in 1967.

Written by a still *(then)* serving officer, its focus is on procedures and corporate issues rather than the personalities. Now out of print, this *(below)* is my original copy (not in the best nick) but if you're lucky, others may be available from specialist antique booksellers and online.

The reference section at the Hive also has a copy *(not for lending)*

*'The Spike' Vol II*
*Due for publication*
*2017-18*

*From Fruit Trees to Furnaces,*
*Bob Pooler.*
*Published 2002. 168pps*

*A History of Worcester City*
*Police. Insp Colin Glover*
*Published 1967. 168 pps*

# Special thanks

...are due to the following, without whose assistance, advice, guidance, input and generous goodwill, this book would be a pale shadow of what it has become:

**Bob and Matt Pooler** whose research into the identification of officers and putting faces to names is a major piece of forensic sleuthing that added a whole new dimension to this work. Their contribution in this respect cannot be overstated and their support and friendship is genuinely valued.

**Malcolm Price** for allowing me to photograph helmets and other original Worcester City police insignia, and to draw freely from other sources from his lovingly-gathered and impressive private collection of international police memorabilia.

**Peter Oleksy and Mark Harding** of the Guildhall staff, for whom no request proved too troublesome or onerous, and **Julian Pugh**, Worcester City Council Democratic Services Administrator for valued assistance with the legals.

**Staff at the Hive** for patient toleration of repeated requests to delve even further than what might be considered normal bounds of duty – and in most instances to return, smiling and triumphant, having succeeded, and particularly **Lisa Snook RMARA**, User Services Manager, Worcs Archive and Archaeology Service for support, advice and sorting out the copyright minefields

**The Haynes brothers**, *Clive and Malcolm*, whose photographs from the CFoW (*Changing Face of Worcester*) provide a major backdrop to anything associated with Worcester and whose input into the two existing Worcester pubs books, and this one, cannot be overstressed

And to **you**, for sharing my passion for all things Worcester. Until the next time...

**Bob Blandford, Worcester, 2016**

*Police pic: late September 1894*
*Background pic: Friday, July 22nd 2016*